Dealing With
# COMPLEXITY in
## DEVELOPMENT
## EVALUATION

My appreciation to Frans Leeuw and Mita Marra for co-teaching with me a series of IPDET workshops on evaluating complex development programs which greatly strengthened my thinking about complexity. Thanks also to the participants in my workshops at IPDET, FAO, AEA, UNICEF, UNDP, and the University of Bologna Centre for International Development whose shared experiences helped ensure the approaches presented in this book were grounded in the realities of real-world evaluation.

To Elizabeth for patience, support, and encouragement throughout the production of the book, and to Marcus, Josh, Alex, and Noah—the next generation who will pickup from where we left an increasingly complex world—Michael

To Erna—Jos

To Dominique, my parents, and Professor David Lindauer for their invaluable contributions to my own "voyage of discovery"—Estelle

# Dealing With
# COMPLEXITY in
# DEVELOPMENT
# EVALUATION

*A Practical Approach*

## Michael Bamberger

Independent Consultant,
Former World Bank
Senior Sociologist

## Jos Vaessen

Maastricht University

## Estelle Raimondo

George Washington
University

**Editors**

Los Angeles | London | New Delhi
Singapore | Washington DC

**SAGE** was founded in 1965 by Sara Miller McCune to support the dissemination of usable knowledge by publishing innovative and high-quality research and teaching content. Today, we publish more than 850 journals, including those of more than 300 learned societies, more than 800 new books per year, and a growing range of library products including archives, data, case studies, reports, and video. SAGE remains majority-owned by our founder, and after Sara's lifetime will become owned by a charitable trust that secures our continued independence.

Los Angeles | London | New Delhi | Singapore | Washington DC

# Praise for *Dealing With Complexity in Development Evaluation*

*"This volume provides useful guidance to development evaluation specialists to deal with their increasingly complex contexts and tasks."*

—Mark Ginsburg, Senior Technical Advisor, Global Education Department at FHI 360

*"This book is impressive in its breadth and depth of coverage of a topic increasingly on the minds of evaluation practitioners. It provides much needed practical guidance and valuable conceptual insights in an area that's often discussed but rarely well understood. The book will appeal to a wide range of experienced evaluation professionals, emerging evaluators, and students of evaluation."*

—Penny Hawkins, Head of Evaluation, Department for International Development (U.K.)

*"This is the first book that seeks to operationalize a complexity perspective into mainstream development evaluation, focusing on the specificities of this broad based sector, encompassing multiple objectives, institutions, contexts, constituencies, and beneficiaries. The main conclusions can speak then to larger audiences of evaluators, program designers, managers, and researchers throughout the world, making a very useful contribution to evaluation culture and practice."*

—Mita Marra, Assistant Professor,
University of Salerno and President of the Italian Evaluation Society

*"The book shows, through a meticulous review of academic studies and some specific cases of real evaluations, that complex development interventions can be evaluated effectively and some of the techniques that make this possible."*

—John Mathiason, Managing Director, Associates for International Management
Services and an Adjunct Professor at the Cornell Institute of Public Affairs, Cornell University

*"This is an extremely useful book when managing and carrying out evaluations of the increasingly complex nature of international development. It should be required reading for everyone involved in assessing results of development cooperation."*

—Per Øyvind Bastøe, Director, Evaluation Department,
Norwegian Agency for Development Cooperation

*This is the "nuts and bolts" book that evaluation practitioners have been waiting for. Authored by highly experienced evaluators and grounded in real life examples from all parts of the world, it illuminates the core ideas of complexity theory, makes sense of abstruse systems concepts, and guides the reader through the contemporary maze of program theory, mixed methods, and web-based information technologies. A lucid and comprehensive treatment of the evaluation state of the art, it is a must-have text for emerging evaluators, advanced evaluators, and evaluation managers operating in uncertain, turbulent, and conflict ridden environments."*

—Robert Picciotto, Visiting Professor, Department of Political Economy, King's College
and Former Director–General of the Independent Evaluation Group of the World Bank

*"This is one of the most important books ever published in the field of development evaluation. Dealing with complex systems is a premier challenge for evaluators working in real life situations. As a practitioner in the field I cannot emphasize the value of this book enough. The authors tackle the issue of complexity and its critical significance from both theoretical and practical points of view. They offer concrete ways in which evaluators and organizations can deal effectively with complexity. The editors, each one of them an eminent authority in the field, have put together a group of authors who bring a wealth of knowledge and experience to the table. Highly recommended to evaluation commissioners and practitioners, as well as those with an interest in the scientific aspects of evaluation approaches and methodologies."*

—Juha Uitto, Director, Independent Evaluation Office, Global Environment Facility

Los Angeles | London | New Delhi
Singapore | Washington DC

FOR INFORMATION:

SAGE Publications, Inc.
2455 Teller Road
Thousand Oaks, California 91320
E-mail: order@sagepub.com

SAGE Publications Ltd.
1 Oliver's Yard
55 City Road
London EC1Y 1SP
United Kingdom

SAGE Publications India Pvt. Ltd.
B 1/I 1 Mohan Cooperative Industrial Area
Mathura Road, New Delhi 110 044
India

SAGE Publications Asia-Pacific Pte. Ltd.
3 Church Street
#10-04 Samsung Hub
Singapore 049483

Printed in the United States of America

ISBN 978-1-4833-4424-9

This book is printed on acid-free paper.

Acquisitions Editor:   Helen Salmon
Editorial Assistant:   Anna Villarruel
Production Editor:   Libby Larson
Copy Editor:   Sarah J. Duffy
Typesetter:   C&M Digitals (P) Ltd.
Proofreader:   Annie Lubinsky
Indexer:   Jean Casalegno
Cover Designer:   Candice Harman
Marketing Manager:   Nicole Elliott

15 16 17 18 19 10 9 8 7 6 5 4 3 2 1

# Brief Contents

# Detailed Contents

# List of Figures

# List of Tables

# List of Boxes

# Foreword

Ray C. Rist

The evaluation community is experiencing increased pressure to "clean up its act." There is growing dissatisfaction among clients, donors, and stakeholders that the evaluation community is taking the easy path, the less rigorous and methodologically demanding way as it undertakes its studies. This indictment comes from such organizations as the Center for Global Development and its no-holds-barred 2006 challenge to evaluation: *When Will We Ever Learn?* This book makes explicit the organization's concerns that evaluators were content to take the path of least resistance—work with modest evaluation designs that did not demand much skill and effort (e.g., desktop reviews, a few interviews), were not difficult to execute (maybe a focus group or two), and where little to nothing was learned (except to document an output or two).

There are a set of evaluators that are taking this critique to heart and trying to push the evaluation community to intellectually and methodologically respond. This present book is one wonderful example. I can think of evaluators now on three continents that are systematically trying to push evaluation into systems and complexity thinking. Essentially, to notch up and strengthen the approach of evaluation to its conceptualizations, to the understanding of its problems, of the context in which change is going to happen (or not), and how one can come to determine cause, evaluators are turning to systems thinking and the intricacies of complexity analysis.

The chief rationale for the upswing in popularity of complexity thinking and the systems approach to thinking through evaluation conditions and challenges is that the evaluation community had failed to acknowledge that all was not as simple as it might at first glance appear. The evaluation community kept sending the signal that interviews, surveys, and desk reviews were enough to learn how a program worked, what consequences it might have, and whether it was to be replicated. Development in particular was not too complicated, just hard work. And so long as the evaluation community kept behaving in a way that signaled it thought issues were not especially complicated, that answers were rather readily to be had, and that present methods were sufficient, then all was well.

One of the things that is so interesting in reading through the chapters of this book is that one quickly comes to the sense that these authors are trying to push back the fog, to create space for new thinking, new perspectives, and new definitions. Indeed, they call it a "voyage of discovery." The voyage is so new and in such uncharted waters that there is still no definition for the term *complexity*. Here is the core concept of the entire book, and there is not yet a definition. It is like the authors are saying we believe that this concept is important, that it can help redefine evaluation thinking, but we are still not exactly sure what it is or how we should constrain it.

This is when you genuinely get the sense of intellectual ferment, of new thinking breaking down old categories, but not at all sure what to put in its place. I commend this book for one key reason—it is exciting. Recognize that when you open the book, you are also going on a voyage of discovery. No one is exactly sure where they are headed, what new intellectual categories or frameworks will be discovered, or where they will end up. But we and they are surely on a voyage. And might I add a short postscript: When is the last time you read that an evaluation book was exciting?

Some of the intellectual work here is really first-rate. The thinking is clear, the rationale is clear, and parts of the voyage are entirely understandable. The practical frameworks offered on how to deal with complexity are helpful. Yet there are a number of those in the book, which can leave the reader with the impression that dealing with complexity may not always be that practical as suggested by the book's title. This paradox—dealing with complexity in a practical manner—is not something that can be resolved overnight. I am sure that this book will inspire debates to come. For the moment, the practical guidance offered is both constructive and provocative.

To the reader, might I suggest: Come take the voyage. It is interesting and you will learn from the authors' effort to make the discipline stronger. We are not doing so well; we are lax in our methods, and we are doing hundreds of evaluation studies every year that are of no consequence. We need stronger and more focused questions, as we need stronger and more focused methods to answer these questions. Thinking clearly should not be a chore. It should be a wonderful opportunity so we can all grow!

# Preface

*Readers' Guide*

The book is targeted to a number of different audiences who are concerned in various ways with the need for dealing with complexity in development evaluation. These include the following:

- Students who have taken only introductory courses of program evaluation but who recognize that even basic program evaluations often involve elements of complexity
- Advanced students and researchers who are familiar with the established evaluation methodologies and perhaps with the complexity literature
- University faculty who are looking for a text that can be used as an introduction to complexity in evaluation or who seek to delve into particular dimensions of complexity with a more advanced text
- Evaluation practitioners working in the field of development evaluation and seeking practical guidance for dealing with complexity
- People who manage evaluations and who commission or use evaluations (policymakers, planners, advocacy organizations, and program managers)

All chapters include an abstract and a practical applications section that will help readers decide which of these chapters they might wish to explore. All readers are encouraged to review one or more of the case studies in Part V to understand how complexity-responsive evaluation approaches are actually applied in the field.

That said, for the purpose of this guide we divide readers into three main groups, with the following suggestions:

Group 1: *Less experienced evaluators.* Six of the chapters can provide an overview of the approach (the Introduction plus Chapters 1, 2, 3, 7, and 13). In addition, the book is designed to provide an introductory review of the main evaluation methodologies so that less experienced evaluators can use these chapters as an introductory or refresher course. The review chapters are Chapter 4 (overview of the main evaluation methodologies), Chapters 5 and 6 (review of theory-based evaluation), and Chapter 8 (review of mixed methods evaluations).

Group 2: *More advanced evaluators.* Most chapters contain introductory as well as more advanced material, and the guide highlights some of the more advanced topics covered in each chapter.

Group 3: *Evaluation managers.* Evaluation managers vary in terms of their experience with evaluation methodologies, so they should follow the guide for groups 1 and 2 as appropriate. However, Chapter 3 is written specifically for evaluation managers, showing the critical role that managers play at all stages of the design of an evaluation. It is also recommended that all evaluation managers read the Introduction and Chapters 1, 2, and 7 to understand the complexity-responsive evaluation approach proposed in the book.

| Readers' Guide | | | |
|---|---|---|---|
| | **Less experienced evaluators**<br><br>May also review the abstract and practical applications sections of more advanced chapters | **More advanced evaluators**<br><br>Chapters with more advanced material are identified but advanced readers will find all chapters include new material | **Evaluation managers** |
| Introduction | ✓ | | ✓ |
| **Part I. Dealing With Complexity in Development Evaluation: A Framework** | | | |
| Ch. 1. Complexity in Development Evaluation: The Framework of the Book | ✓ | | ✓ |
| Ch. 2. Toward More Complexity-Responsive Evaluations: Overview and Challenges | ✓ | Includes an overview of approaches stemming from complexity science and their application to evaluation | ✓ |
| Ch. 3. Management of Complexity-Responsive Evaluations | ✓ | | Written specifically for evaluation managers |
| **Part II. Dealing With Complexity in Development Evaluation: Methodological Approaches** | | | |
| Ch. 4. Impact Evaluation Approaches and Complexity | Slightly more advanced but can be used as an overview of impact evaluation methodology | Review of the main qualitative, quantitative, and mixed methods evaluation approaches and strengths and challenges when applied to complexity | |

| Readers' Guide | | | |
|---|---|---|---|
| Ch. 5. Understanding What Is Being Evaluated: Theory-Based Evaluation (TBE) | Slightly more advanced but can be used as an overview of theory-based evaluation principles | Comprehensive review of seven theory-based evaluation approaches and their application to complexity | |
| Ch. 6. Five Practical Evaluation Problems to Which TBE Can Contribute | Slightly more advanced but provides practical illustrations of the different ways that theory-based evaluation is used in practice | Detailed discussion of how theory-based evaluation can be applied to five common evaluation problems | |
| Ch. 7. Dealing With Complexity by Unpacking and Reassembling Elements of a Complex Program | ✓ | Presents a key practical approach for dealing with complexity in large or multidimensional programs | Slightly more advanced but should be reviewed as it presents a key practical approach for dealing with complexity in large or multidimensional programs |
| Ch. 8. The Importance of a Mixed Methods Approach for Evaluating Complexity | Useful refresher review of mixed methods, which are essential for complexity-responsive evaluation | | |
| **Part III. Emerging Data and Innovative Techniques to Deal With Complexity in Development Evaluation** | | | |
| Ch. 9. Complexity in Review and Synthesis Studies | More advanced but not too technical; synthesis reviews are widely used, so worth a quick review | Comprehensive review of the strengths and challenges of systematic reviews for addressing complexity | |
| Ch. 10. Emergent Technologies and Creative Use of Multiple Sources of Information | | Comprehensive review of current approaches to data management, warehousing, etc. | |
| Ch. 11. Applying Emergent Technologies to Complex Program Evaluation From the INGO Perspective | Slightly more advanced but not too technical; useful introduction to mobile phones and other new technologiesthat are essential for data collection in the context of complexity-responsive evaluations | Comprehensive review of how new information technologies are being used in the field (NGOs are at the forefront) and specific applications to the evaluation of complexity | |

*(Continued)*

(Continued)

| Readers' Guide | | | |
|---|---|---|---|
| Ch. 12. The Evaluation of Complex Development Interventions in the Age of Big Data | | Review of the challenges and opportunities for using big data in the evaluation of complexity and the implications for rethinking current approaches to evaluation | |
| **Part IV. Dealing With Complexity in Development Evaluation: The Institutional Challenges** | | | |
| Ch 13. Dealing With Institutional Complexity: Implications for Evaluation Design, Process, and Use | ✓ | Comprehensive review of the institutional dimensions of complexity, which are frequently ignored | More advanced but managers will probably find useful the discussion of institutional issues that evaluations face |
| Ch 14. Gender Equality in Development Evaluation: The Intersection of Complexities | Slightly more advanced | Analysis of how all of the dimensions of complexity discussed in the book apply to gender evaluation; many of the issues also apply to rights-based, empowerment, and emancipation evaluations | |
| **Part V. Complexity of Evaluation in Practice: Case Studies** | | | |
| Ch 15. A Case Study in Complexity: Evaluating a Long-Term Effort to Prevent Gender-Based Violence in El Salvador | All readers are encouraged to read at least one case study in an area in which they are interested to better understand how complexity issues are addressed in evaluations in the field. | Advanced readers may wish to select one or more cases in areas of interest. The cases are important as illustrations of the real-world challenges of addressing complexity in the field. | Managers are encouraged to review at least one case study in an area in which they are interested to understand how complexity-focused evaluations are implemented in the field. |
| Ch 16. Microcredit and Women's Empowerment: Complexity in Systematic Review | | | |

| Readers' Guide | | | |
|---|:---:|:---:|:---:|
| Ch 17. Evaluation of Coordination Against Trafficking in Persons: A Case Study of a Complexity-Responsive Evaluation | | | |
| Ch 18. Complexity From the Perspectives of Philanthropic Foundations and Their Evaluation | | | |
| Ch 19. Evaluating General Budget Support | | | |
| Ch 20. Dealing With Complexity in a Realist Synthesis: Community Accountability and Empowerment Initiatives | | | |
| Glossary | ✓ | ✓ | ✓ |

# Acknowledgments

This book project started in the minds of Michael Bamberger and Frans Leeuw and while Frans did not end up taking part in the editorial team, his influence on the book's trajectory has remained significant throughout the project. We are particularly thankful to the chapters and foreword authors. Their contribution went beyond their respective chapters and shaped our thinking about complexity. They worked with us tirelessly through the several rounds of edits and comments. We are most grateful to the following reviewers whose honest and constructive feedback helped us tremendously in sharpening our arguments and frameworks: Mark Ginsburg, Global Education Department, FHI 360; Gillette H. Hall, Georgetown University; John Mathiason, Cornell Institute of Public Affairs; and Donna M. Mertens, Gallaudet University. We also thank the entire SAGE team, especially Helen Salmon, Anna Villarruel, Libby Larson, and Nicole Elliott for their continuous assistance and encouragement, and for turning our manuscript into a polished publication. Our thanks also extend to our talented copy-editor, Sarah Duffy whose attention to details and fast turnaround made a valuable contribution at a critical time. Finally, we thank Heather Britt, Patricia Rogers, Aaron Zazueta and Juha Uitto for helping us make this book come to life by participating in a presentation panel at the American Evaluation Association annual meeting in Chicago.

# Introduction

Estelle Raimondo, Michael Bamberger, and Jos Vaessen

## 1. Starting "A Voyage of Discovery"

In his astute observations of development projects, Albert O. Hirschman had already noticed in the 1960s that some projects have what he called "system-quality." He observed that a "system-like" project tended to be made up of many interdependent parts that needed to be fitted together and well adjusted to each other for the project as a whole to achieve its intended results (such as the multitude of segments of a 500-mile road construction). These projects could also be particularly exposed to the instability of the sociopolitical systems in which they were embedded (such as running nationwide interventions in ethnically divided and conflict-ridden countries). Hirschman (2014) considered these projects a source of much uncertainty and he claimed that the observations and evaluations of such projects "invariably imply voyages of discovery" (p. 42).

Today, evaluators are increasingly likely to have to embark on "voyages of discovery." While part of the complexity of development programs is not new, but rather an intrinsic feature of the development process, relatively new trends have emerged that make the development landscape look more and more like a complex system. New actors, such as foundations, private companies, development agencies and banks from emerging countries, have joined existing ones (bilateral and multi-lateral aid donors and nongovernmental organizations [NGOs]) in an increasingly intricate web of partnerships. Development objectives have become more ambitious (e.g., to create shared prosperity while sustaining the environment and enhancing the quality of people's lives). They are also more difficult to measure. In most countries that are recipients of international development assistance, aid has become less important in comparison to other financial flows and processes such as international trade, foreign direct investments, remittances, and domestic fiscal systems. The boundaries of development programs are increasingly elusive, as they often cross national borders and are defined at a higher level of intervention, via broad budget support schemes, country-level policy initiatives, sector-wide strategies, or transnational public-private partnerships. Defining and assessing success against this complex backdrop is further complicated by the number and diversity of stakeholders, with divergent expectations and interests, engaged in particular development interventions.

At the same time, the demand for rigorous evidence of "what works" in development practice has become more pressing. Evaluation has become one of the main accepted mechanisms to tell success apart from failure, to foster learning from past experience, and to hold development organizations accountable to stakeholders for delivering on their mandate. Yet there is a growing sense of awareness in the evaluation community that established evaluation methods are unable to fully capture the complexity of development processes and therefore inhibit the ability of evaluations to achieve these purposes.

In this book, we welcome Hirschman's invitation to start a voyage of discovery into the complexity of development interventions and their context. More specifically, this book seeks to address the evaluative challenges that one encounters during such a voyage: How can we deal with complexity in development evaluation while operating under real-world constraints and at the same time needing to respond to the pressing demand for rigorous evidence? How can we make sense of a complex development world when well-established evaluation designs are often inadequate for the task at hand?

As indicated by the subtitle of the book, we aim to present a practical perspective on complexity that offers realistic and useful guidance to policymakers, managers, and evaluation practitioners on how to address complexity within the real-world constraints within which they operate. While it may seem paradoxical to some to include the words *complexity* and *practical* in the same sentence, this book shows that the two can, and indeed, should be reconciled. Evaluation is applied policy-oriented research under (often) less than ideal political, time, budget, and data constraints, which calls for practical (feasible and useful) solutions to address complexity challenges. As the book will show, sometimes complexity calls for innovative conceptual and methodological solutions. In other cases, the claim that an intervention is complex may be overestimated. Sometimes, an intervention that is initially diagnosed as too complex to evaluate can be usefully broken down into evaluable parts without losing touch with the interrelations between the different parts as well as the complex contextual factors that shape the intervention and its influence on processes of change.

# 2. What We Mean by Complexity

As expected in such a voyage of discovery, there can be some confusion about what the voyage is really about. The extensive literature on complexity and evaluation presents a variety of conceptual frameworks for thinking about complexity. However, they seem to converge toward five main sources of complexity: the nature of the program (what does the intervention look like), the context within which the program is embedded, the interactions among the different stakeholders and agencies involved in the program, the nature of processes of change and causality (how does the program effect change in society and how can we capture this change), and the nature of the evaluation process (how to deal with divergent stakeholder interests and incentives, data availability, resources, etc.). These five aspects taken together determine the complexity challenge that evaluators have to deal with. Given that these dimensions are closely interlinked, it is likely that a given evaluation will have to deal with several of them concomitantly:

- One of the most fascinating, but also difficult, parts of the voyage of discovery is getting a clear understanding of the context in which the program operates: How do the historical, economic, political, sociocultural, administrative, eco-logical, and legal contextual factors influence the course of an intervention? While some aspects of this context (e.g., norms, beliefs) are slow to change, others can be very dynamic and evolve quickly. All of these contextual factors are highly interconnected, and it is challenging to define the right boundaries of the "system" to be taken into account in the evaluation.

- The extent to which each of these contextual features matters for the evalua-tion depends to a large extent on the second dimension: What is the interven-tion about? What is it trying to achieve, and how? Understanding the nature of the intervention, making sense of its design, delineating its size and scope, as well as the different levels at which it operates and how these levels are nested into each other, are fundamental pieces of the puzzle.

- A third piece of the puzzle takes us away from the more technical part of the program toward the human part. A program is essentially a social system made up of a variety of actors. Part of the voyage of discovery is thus to under-stand the diverse and sometimes divergent narratives and assumptions of the main actors regarding the program. Implementing agencies, donors, politi-cians, beneficiaries, and evaluators often do not see eye to eye on issues such as the program's objectives and their relative importance, the worth of particu-lar activities, the allocation of resources, and so on. Making sense of these dissonant stories is thus part and parcel of solving the complexity challenge.

- The fourth complexity dimension is what sets the evaluative voyage of dis-covery apart from other voyages: grasping causality and change. In particular, causality in the light of dynamic and interlinked processes of change in which interventions are embedded. To continue the metaphor of the voyage of dis-covery, the path toward the achievement of program objectives is not linear, but rather uncertain and subject to a multitude of causal factors; in fact, there may be many paths to get to the same destination. Some of these paths will take the travelers through multiple loops, there might be setbacks along the way, and the final destination may look very different from what the travelers imagined it would be.

- Taken together, these four dimensions influence the extent to which the voy-age of discovery will be easy or challenging. In other, less metaphorical words, apart from challenges in delimitation, sense-making, and causal analysis, in reality, complexity-responsive evaluations are conducted within the con-straints and opportunity space determined by such factors as the purpose of the evaluation, the timeframe, the available resources and expertise, and so on.

All in all, one of the main messages of this book is that in today's development landscape, most programs and their contexts exhibit some complexity traits. Evaluations thus need to be *complexity-responsive*. However, these evaluations are not necessarily (technically or humanly) complex. In this book we propose a number of practical ways to design and implement complexity-responsive evaluations that can be undertaken in the real world of time, budget, data, and political constraints.

# 3. A Pragmatic, Practitioner-Oriented Approach to Complexity

The fact that there is no standard recipe for dealing with complexity in evaluation can lead some development agencies to believe that it is not possible to deal with complexity in ways that are methodologically rigorous, and they might decide to ignore complexity aspects altogether. However, the central message of this book is that there are a number of approaches that can produce operationally useful and methodologically sound complexity-responsive evaluations. *Practical* for us means, among other things, being curious and eclectic, that is, dealing with complex aspects of the evaluation process, the institutional context, and the program in ways that make sense and are feasible without advocating for a particular set of methods or concepts. A creative, resourceful, and flexible attitude is required from evaluators to come up with adequate evaluation designs; the various chapters of this book demonstrate in great depth and breadth what this may entail. The following are a number of useful guiding ideas for agencies commissioning complexity-responsive evaluations and for evaluators that are tasked with designing and implementing them:

- It is important to be familiar with the basic concepts of complexity and to be able to understand in what ways and the extent to which a program is (or is not) complex. While most programs have some complex aspects, not everything in a program or its context is fundamentally complex. Agencies can be tempted to claim that their programs are all-around complex as this makes the program seem more important (some cynics would say this is also an excuse to avoid having to expose programs to rigorous evaluation). Evaluators may also claim complexity as a way to justify a larger and more expensive evaluation. So before commissioning an evaluation it is important to understand the nature and degree of complexity and what this means for evaluation design and implementation in practice.
- Even when an evaluation is facing multiple complexity challenges (e.g., in terms of the nature of the intervention, the lack/availability of data), it is often valid to use an established evaluation approach to focus on the key issues of importance to policymakers and managers at a given point in time. For example, when a new program is being launched, the main concern may be a *proof of concept* evaluation to assess whether the program concept makes sense and is likely to work in a given context. Once it has been established that the program concept works, particular complexity dimensions may

become more salient, especially when evaluating the effectiveness of the full-fledged program operating on a larger scale or in more diverse geographical areas. It is often possible to "unpack" complex programs into separate elements, each of which can be evaluated separately. If individual components are found to work, the challenge will be to reassemble the different program components to assess how effectively the whole program operates. However, it is critical that this unpacking-reassembling process be informed by a careful mapping of the various complexity dimensions. Our message here (and also with regard to the previous bullet point) is not that complexity should be ignored, but rather that a complexity perspective can be introduced in a phased approach.

- No single evaluation method is able to fully address all dimensions of complexity. Consequently, it is almost always necessary to use a mixed methods design that combines the strengths of a number of so-called quantitative and qualitative methods. Moreover, while no established evaluation approach is fully equipped on its own to deal with complexity, existing established approaches can be the building blocks for evaluation designs tackling complexity. In many cases, these designs may need to be enhanced with more novel approaches for data collection and analysis.

- In this respect, much can be learned from complexity science and systems thinking. The challenge for complexity-responsive evaluations is thus to find practical ways to operationalize the ideas, tools, and techniques emanating from complexity science and apply them to real-world evaluations. Some evaluators have made substantial progress in using these tools to make sense of key properties of complex social phenomena using concepts such as boundaries, to look at how programs change over time (emergence), interactions among (networks of) actors, tensions arising within systems and these are resolved, as well as the important role of history and customs in determining how organizations and systems adapt to or resist change.

In the spirit of pragmatism, each chapter in this book has a concluding section with practical applications for policymakers, planners, evaluation managers, and other commissioners and users of evaluations, many of whom are not specialists on complexity or even necessarily on program evaluation. The message that we want to convey is that there are almost always ways to obtain useful and methodologically credible assessments of complex interventions embedded in complex contexts, even within the real-world constraints of budget, time, data, and institutional pressures.

# 4. Overview of the Book

The book is divided into five parts. Part I sets out the conceptual and methodological framework of the book. Part II describes key recurrent methodological challenges when dealing with complexity in development evaluation and offers a range of solutions to address the various complexity dimensions. Part III is dedicated to exploring how emergent technologies and innovative data sources can be leveraged to strengthen the evaluation design. The last two parts focus on the practical dimensions of complexity. Part IV focuses on the institutional context of development evaluation, which can add to the complexity of evaluation in practice and the complexity dimensions of gender-focused evaluation. Finally, Part V presents six in-depth cases of how evaluators have dealt with various complexity dimensions.

- **Chapter 1** first addresses the question of why a complexity perspective is important in development evaluation. It describes the move toward more complex development interventions. At the same time, the growing demand for evaluative evidence among donors and other stakeholders has increased the pressure on the evaluation community to produce credible evidence of these interventions. We then present our framework for dealing with complexity in development evaluation. The framework revolves around five main dimensions of complexity: embeddedness and the nature of the system, the nature of the intervention, institutions and stakeholders, and causality and change. We show how these four dimensions in turn influence the fifth dimension, which is the evaluation process: how to design, implement, and use complexity-responsive evaluations.
- **Chapter 2** reviews the strengths and weaknesses of current approaches to the evaluation of complex interventions. We begin by presenting four common scenarios in development evaluation and discuss their weaknesses when dealing with complexity issues. We then review a number of approaches that are more closely aligned with complexity science and systems thinking. We conclude with a number of ideas about how to bridge the existing gap between the two, toward more complexity-responsive evaluation designs. These ideas are further explored in subsequent chapters.
- **Chapter 3** presents a succinct step-by-step approach to the evaluation of complex programs. It is conceived as a practical guide for program managers who may not be evaluation experts and a road map for evaluators and evaluation managers who engage in a complexity-responsive evaluation process.
- **Chapter 4** reviews the most widely used impact evaluation approaches, including experimental, statistical, theory-based, case-based, and participatory approaches, as well as review and synthesis studies. The relative strengths and limitations of these established approaches in the context of complexity are then assessed. Each approach is assessed on several dimensions: the potential to attribute a particular change to an intervention, the potential to explain why a particular change took place, the potential to make sense of multiple causal pathways with multiple (un)intended effects, and the potential to capture highly uncertain, nonlinear, and emergent change processes.
- **Chapter 5** discusses how to understand what is being evaluated. It begins by explaining the principles of theory-based evaluation (TBE). Subsequently, several approaches to TBE are described: realist evaluation, theories of

change, contribution analysis, the policy-scientific approach, the strategic assessment approach, the elicitation approach, and approaches stemming from behavioral economics. The chapter then offers a useful warning against tendencies toward "complexification," making programs and evaluation appear more complex than they really are or need to be. It ends by flagging some pitfalls that should be avoided when doing TBE.

- **Chapter 6** is a direct segue from the previous chapter and describes five practical evaluation problems to which TBE can contribute: (1) defining and operationalizing key performance indicators, (2) defining the counterfactual when it is not possible to use an experimental or quasi-experimental design, (3) when an experimental or quasi-experimental design has been conducted but does not provide a satisfactory explanation, (4) conducting a prospective evaluation at the program design stage to assess how effective a program is likely to be, and (5) assessing during implementation how effective a program is likely to be. The chapter concludes with an explicit discussion of how TBE can contribute to the evaluation of complex interventions.

- **Chapter 7** presents ways to unpack complex programs into separate parts that are easier to evaluate and approaches to reassemble these parts into a big picture. The chapter lays out five main levels: (1) mapping the various complexity dimensions, (2) the choice of a unit of analysis, (3) the choice of a methodological approach for unpacking the intervention, (4) options for reassembling the various parts into a whole that assesses how the full program actually operates in the field, and (5) going back to a systems perspective. A variety of methodological options are proposed for each level. The chapter concludes with a discussion of the limitations of this approach and how to address them.

- **Chapter 8** discusses the importance of a mixed methods approach for the evaluation of complexity. It is argued that complexity inherently requires a mixed methods approach as no single method is able to fully address all of the dimensions of complexity. The benefits of mixed methods are discussed and contrasted with single method approaches in terms of their adequacy for delineating the program, describing complex causal pathways, examining the context-specific embeddedness of interventions, and analyzing behavioral complexity. The elements of a fully integrated mixed methods approach are then described, and their applications for the evaluation of complexity are discussed.

- **Chapter 9** discusses review and synthesis studies. With the increasing number of (impact) evaluations that are conducted worldwide across sectors, more and more evaluators are becoming "synthesizers" of existing evidence. Review and synthesis studies fill the demand gap of providing synthetic rigorous evidence on what works (and under what circumstances) based on existing primary studies to support strategic decision making. The chapter discusses the main types of review and synthesis approaches, distinguishing between systematic and nonsystematic reviews. Finally, a number of challenges from a complexity perspective are elucidated.

- **Chapter 10** introduces the contribution of emergent technologies and the use of multiple sources of information in the evaluation of complexity. Challenges that evaluators often face with regard to, for instance, the absence of baseline data or the need to integrate multiple and highly diverse data sources can be solved by using emergent technologies. The processes for data collection, integration, and analysis are described in detail. These are applied to the rapidly evolving field of big data.

- **Chapter 11** presents an in-depth analysis of the experience of NGOs in applying emergent technologies to their monitoring and evaluation systems. Widely used technologies are mobile phones, GPS and GIS, social media, web-based databases, audio and interactive voice response, and digital video and cameras. The main ways in which these technologies are used for monitoring and evaluation are discussed, including data collection, ICT for development, surveillance and reporting systems, information dissemination, smartphone-based systems for patient tracking, crowdsourcing reporting systems, public dialogue, and mobile banking. The chapter also discusses what complexity means for NGOs' evaluation, and identifies some promising new directions.

- **Chapter 12** begins by defining *big data*, tracing its rapid expansion and discussing how big data challenges the traditional vision of evaluation. The chapter explores the argument that the dramatic increase in the range of data that can be collected and the speed with which they can be processed will have implications for the practice of evaluation: from being largely reflective and retrospective, there will be a push toward real-time assessment of how interventions are affecting outcomes. The chapter also explicitly discusses how to infer causality from big data. It ends with institutional considerations and lays out possible scenarios of what lies ahead in the integration of big data into evaluation practice.

- **Chapter 13** starts by mapping out the complex institutional context surrounding the practice of development evaluation, including policy and organizational contexts. It is argued that the evaluation system can itself be a source of complexity for evaluation practice. Two major sources of institutional complexity are likely to impact the evaluation process: the engagement of multiple stakeholders and the political constraints inherent to the very notion of development intervention. The chapter discusses the implications of institutional complexity for the use of evaluation for learning and accountability. It ends by exploring a number of avenues for making well-established results-based management systems more complexity-responsive.

- **Chapter 14** lays out the multiple dimensions of complexity inherent to the assessment of the differential impacts of development processes on women and men. The chapter begins with a discussion of complexity from a gender equality perspective. The main argument is that because all development projects are laden with gender dimensions, complexity-responsive evaluations should also be gender-responsive. It then lays out various methodological developments in gender-responsive evaluations. The chapter discusses the institutional and operational challenges that such evaluations face and proposes avenues to overcome these challenges. It concludes with practical applications, some of which are illustrated in the following chapter.

- **Chapter 15** explores the evaluation of a complex program by a coalition of actors coordinated by Oxfam America to combat gender-based violence in El Salvador. The case provides an example of putting into practice a *rights-based* philosophy in NGOs and the corresponding move toward complexity. The case is an illustration of the adoption of new approaches to evaluation stemming from the rights-based movement, including innovations in policy advocacy evaluation, network evaluation, and campaign evaluation.

- **Chapter 16** presents a systematic review of the effects of microcredit on women's control over household spending (i.e., a proxy of women's empowerment). Three dimensions of complexity are addressed: the conceptualization and measurement of the construct of women's empowerment, the choice of a methodological approach to review and synthesis, and the nature of the evidence base. The methodological procedures for searching and selecting primary studies, reviewing the evidence base on microcredit interventions' impacts, and the use of meta-analysis are described, as are the mechanisms through which microcredit might affect women's control over household spending.

- **Chapter 17** reports on an evaluation of the effectiveness of international coordination of programs to combat human trafficking. In addition to the complexity of the coordination mechanisms, the evaluation process itself can be considered complex as it attempted to cover all international programs and did not target any particular project or program. Another dimension of (institutional) complexity was that the evaluation was commissioned by the Swedish Ministry for Development Cooperation, while the programs under evaluation were managed by other agencies that had not been involved in the decision to conduct the evaluation. After describing the complex nature of trafficking, the chapter discusses the evaluation process and some of the main findings. A number of lessons for managing complexity are drawn from the evaluation experience, including the exploration of opportunities for simple designs.

- **Chapter 18** tackles the challenges of evaluating the growing contribution of philanthropic institutions in development. Complexity is discussed from the perspective of the multiple divergent actors in the field and the different approaches to evaluation and learning. It is concluded that while some major foundations have relatively sophisticated evaluation and learning systems in place, for the sector as a whole the approaches to evaluation are still at a relatively early stage of development.

- **Chapter 19** delves into the complexities of evaluating general budget support, the importance of which has been high in recent years in the context of the new aid paradigm and the achievement of poverty reduction goals. After discussing the special challenges of evaluating budget support, the chapter reviews current practice. The evaluation methodology for addressing complexity is illustrated through seven country case studies, which were selected to ensure heterogeneity in terms of the size of budget support and ratings on the worldwide governance index.

- **Chapter 20** applies a realist synthesis to the evaluation of community accountability and empowerment initiatives. It begins with an overview of the review in terms of its scope, methodology, and findings. It then analyzes the review in terms of Pawson's (2013) VICTORE framework (see also Chapter 5) to demonstrate the complexity of the review topic, how complexity was reflected in the findings, and how the methodology of realist synthesis was helpful to manage and deal with complexity. It then discusses how the findings from a realist synthesis can assist in dealing with the complexities of policy and program management in the real world.

# References

Hirschman, A. O. (2014). *Development projects observed.* Washington, DC: Brookings Institution Press.

Pawson, R. (2013). *The science of evaluation: A realist manifesto.* Thousand Oaks, CA: Sage.

# PART I

## Dealing With Complexity in Development Evaluation: A Framework

# CHAPTER 1

# Complexity in Development Evaluation

*The Framework of the Book*

Michael Bamberger,
Jos Vaessen, and Estelle Raimondo

*There is a growing awareness that complexity matters in development programs and development evaluation. In this chapter we present our framework for dealing with complexity in development evaluation. We address the question: What do we mean by complexity? An important message is that dealing with complexity in development evaluation does not necessarily require that evaluators learn to apply unfamiliar and highly technical designs. While some evaluations will draw on concepts from complexity science that may be unfamiliar to many evaluators, most of the complexity-responsive approaches we describe are based on the application of established quantitative, qualitative, and mixed methods tools and techniques, but applied within a complexity-responsive framework. What is required is for evaluators and evaluation managers to have a good understanding of the various complexity dimensions that may impact an intervention. We present a framework to make sense of these dimensions. In Section 1 we take the example of a program to combat gender-based violence in El Salvador to illustrate the five dimensions we use to define complexity. In Section 2 we discuss a number of recent trends that underline the need for a complexity focus in international development. In Section 3 we present a number of conceptual frameworks to make sense of complexity as it relates to the practice of evaluation. In Section 4 we pull everything together and present a practical framework for addressing complexity in evaluation. The chapter ends with a discussion of practical applications for policymakers, managers, and evaluators.*

# 1. Experiencing Complexity: Evaluating a Program to Combat Gender-Based Violence in El Salvador

We begin with a real-world example to illustrate what complexity means in practice. Chapter 15 describes a 10- to 15-year program to combat the serious problem of gender-based violence (GBV) in El Salvador (see Box 1.1). This case illustrates the five dimensions of complexity that constitute the framework of this book. GBV is caused or condoned by social attitudes and practices concerning the appropriate behavior of men and women in the home, the community, the workplace, and the wider society and the stresses caused by changes in the economic, social, or political situation of women and men. In the El Salvador case, GBV is caused and perpetuated by historical, political, legal, economic, and sociocultural factors that operate at national, community, and household levels. All of these factors are interconnected, so an intervention addressing one area is affected by multiple other factors. Complexity researchers use terms such as *embeddedness, interconnectedness*, and *path dependence*[1] to describe these relations.

---

**BOX 1.1 A COMPLEX PROGRAM TO COMBAT GENDER-BASED VIOLENCE IN EL SALVADOR**

The case describes a 10- to 15-year ongoing program funded by Oxfam USA to combat gender-based violence (GBV) in El Salvador. GBV has very serious consequences at the national, municipal, community, and household levels and has multiple causes relating to the high levels of violence following the civil war, the growth of gangs, and other historical, economic, legal, and sociocultural factors. The political, legal, and judiciary systems have not proven effective in addressing GBV, and there has been only limited action at the municipal level. Moreover, the level of public awareness has been rather low, particularly due to the much greater attention the mass media has given to high levels of general violence resulting from the uneasy peace settlements after the civil war. The Oxfam program that began in 2005 sought to build a broad-based alliance involving political, national, and municipal women's and community organizations. The program combines alliance building, awareness-raising through training and the mass media, and demonstration action programs in seven municipalities. The combined effect of these actions was intended to increase women's self-confidence in their ability to confront and reduce GBV; create effective local alliances between communities, schools, health services, the police, and local government; promote new proactive policies by local government and the judiciary; promote new legislation; and promote broad-based national and regional coverage of GBV in the mass media.

A second source of complexity resides in the nature of the intervention and stems from the fact that it is implemented by many national and municipal government agencies, the police, nongovernmental organizations (NGOs), women's organizations, and community groups; it has many different components and continues to evolve and change over time. Its implementation in seven largely autonomous municipalities adds to the diversity in delivery mechanisms and processes. There are also different government and civil society funding sources. Finally, all of these various components interact and affect each other in multiple ways that are difficult to capture. A third source of complexity relates to the fact that all of the participating agencies have their own governance structures, data collection systems, understandings of what the program entails, and what they hope it will achieve. Some agencies have traditionally worked well together, some have very little experience of coordination with other partners, and there are some recurrent areas of tension (e.g., between police and communities, between some government agencies and some local organizations). In addition, there are other groups interested in or affected by the program. The interaction among all of these stakeholder groups, and more generally the institutional environment, can have an important influence on program priorities, areas of resistance, and how the program operates.

A fourth dimension concerns the causal relations between program inputs and intended outcomes. In El Salvador multiple factors might contribute to a reduction in GBV, including new legislation, improved police training, improved relations

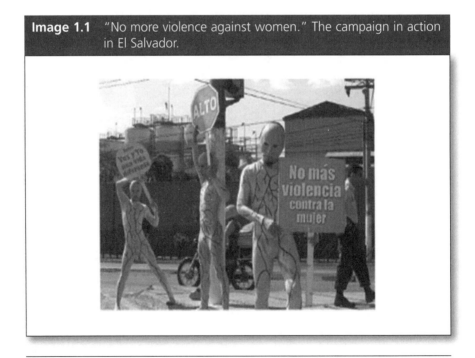

**Image 1.1**   "No more violence against women." The campaign in action in El Salvador.

SOURCE: Oxfam (2007). Program Strategy Paper for the Program to Prevent Gender Based Violence in El Salvador.

between police and local communities, more effective community awareness and prevention programs, and mass media campaigns encouraging women to be more proactive in preventing GBV. All of these interventions and policy changes interact with local economic, political, and sociocultural factors. Furthermore, different combinations of factors operate in different municipalities, and the same factors have different outcomes in different municipalities. Also, the causal relations may best be described as nonlinear, as an intervention in one area may produce feedback loops that change the very conditions in which the intervention operates. For example, when women gain more control over their lives, by advancing in the labor market or by taking direct action to confront GBV, initial successes may lead to negative reactions from men (or even some women) who feel that women have gone too far. Consequently, initial progress might be followed by increased domestic or public opposition so that some progress is lost (blowback). Results vary over time and across thematic and geographical areas, with slow but steady advances in some areas but negative results in others (e.g., legislation or public policies that limit women's freedom). Evaluating progress over the lifespan of a 10- to 15-year program in which processes of change are diffuse and difficult to track can be very challenging.

In addition to these four sources of complexity stemming from the intervention, its environment, and its processes of change, other factors can influence the degree of complexity of the evaluation process. In this particular case, critical data on, for example, how the police services respond to GBV or how municipal government policies are implemented on the ground is very limited, and it is also difficult to combine and compare data across different agencies. Moreover, the complex and dynamic nature of the political system has a bearing on the choices evaluators make about design and implementation. There are different constraints posed by the evaluation process itself (e.g., the purpose of the evaluation, expectations of stakeholders, time and budget constraints). Box 1.2 articulates the four dimensions of complexity laid out above as well as how these dimensions affect the level of complexity of the evaluation.

---

## BOX 1.2 DEFINING COMPLEXITY OF THE INTERVENTION AND THE EVALUATION

*Complexity of an intervention* (see Box 1.1 and Table 1.2) is determined by the intersections among four dimensions: (1) contextual factors and the nature of the system within which the program is embedded, (2) the characteristics of the intervention, (3) the institutions and stakeholders and how they interact, and (4) the nature of causality and the processes of change.

In addition *the complexity of the evaluation* is also determined by (a) the purpose of the evaluation, (b) the choice of evaluation design, (c) budget and time constraints, and (d) the value orientation of both stakeholders and evaluators and the methodological preferences of the client(s) and other key stakeholders.

In short, the level of complexity of an evaluation is the result of complexity issues relating to the intervention and its wider context and a number of aspects specific to the evaluation process itself.

When discussing evaluation issues, throughout the book we refer to the distinction between *established evaluation approaches* that are used to evaluate interventions with a relatively low level of complexity (i.e., simple projects) and *complexity-responsive evaluation* approaches that are appropriate for the evaluation of complex interventions. The distinction is explained in Box 1.3.

---

**BOX 1.3 ESTABLISHED EVALUATION APPROACHES AND COMPLEXITY-RESPONSIVE EVALUATION**

Throughout the book we refer to *established evaluation approaches* as the quantitative, qualitative, and mixed methods approaches and methods that are widely used in development evaluation (summarized in Chapter 4 and covered in most evaluation textbooks). *Complexity-responsive evaluation* addresses complexity issues by building on established evaluation approaches (and approaches that are commonly used in complexity science; see Chapter 2) and relying on a number of steps that are discussed in subsequent chapters (see Chapters 3 and 7).

---

# 2. The Growing Need for a Complexity Perspective in Evaluation

## 2.1 The Move Toward "Complex" Development Interventions

Over the past decade there has been a move toward more complex development interventions on the part of international development agencies, governments, and many NGOs. In 2000 most international development agencies adopted the Millennium Development Declaration,[2] which defined development objectives in terms of eight broad goals (Millennium Development Goals; MDGs) encompassing the main areas of development and which proposed a broad framework for assessing the overall contribution to development of the large numbers of projects and programs being supported by different development agencies.

The MDG initiative was also driven by increasing demands from parliaments, public opinion, civil society, and academia to address the question: Does aid work? These concerns were reflected in the 2002 Monterrey Consensus on Financing for Development, which sought to distribute more money to the world's poorest people while at the same time increasing the efficiency and effectiveness with which aid is managed. The Monterrey Consensus also had important implications for both the focus of development evaluation (assessing the broader impacts of aid rather than the impacts of individual projects) and how evaluations should be managed (greater participation of the recipient country in the management of evaluations and greater cooperation among donor agencies in the conduct of evaluations)

(Morra Imas & Rist, 2009, p. 76). The focus on broader, national development objectives was further formalized in the 2005 Paris Declaration on Aid Effectiveness. As a result of these and subsequent agreements (such as the 2008 Accra Accords[3]), development has evolved toward a more comprehensive agenda, increasingly addressing country policy reforms, capacity building, and global concerns (Morra Imas & Rist, 2009, pp. 77–78).

Similar trends can be observed in industrialized countries where complex policy initiatives are not restricted to addressing "big challenges" but also focus on more routine initiatives such as school achievement, urban planning, and public health (Forss, Marra, & Schwartz, 2011). National governments are also increasingly involved in regional and global cooperation, working within transboundary legal, fiscal, economic, immigration, and health protocols. These trends significantly increase the complexity of policy and program planning and evaluation. There are also increasing numbers of international organizations involved in the formulation, regulation, and management of these transboundary initiatives.

Many large NGOs also recognize the need for broader and more complex interventions to achieve development goals. For example, the outcome of programs to promote gender equality, social justice, or conflict reduction are affected by a wide range of sociocultural, economic, political, legal, administrative, and often ecological factors, all of which interact in complex and unpredictable ways. There is increasing recognition that established evaluation designs are not equipped to assess the interactions among all of these dimensions, and many of the forward-looking NGOs are beginning to consider the need for complexity-responsive evaluations.

Finally, the post-2015 development agenda emphasizes the need for a global shared responsibility in addressing the world's problems based on a common agenda for sustainable development (encapsulated by the Sustainable Development Goals). This will only increase the need for the evaluation community to address highly complex and international policy initiatives and to take its place as an instrument of learning and accountability.

## 2.2 New Developments in Data Collection and Analysis

The rapid digitalization of society and the increasing use of new technologies change how people inform themselves about the world around them and how they act. These new sources of information provide new opportunities for more extensive and rigorous analysis of complexity, but also give rise to new challenges as organizations struggle to establish systems to manage the new sources of data (see Chapters 10, 11, and 12).

In addition, new streams of data have become available on a variety of phenomena related to human behavior, including social media and market data, which can help evaluators and policymakers better understand human behavior and how individuals and groups are affected by policy interventions. The rapid evolution of systems for the management and warehousing of multiple sources of data (see Chapter 10), the rapidly increasing use of smartphones and handheld data collection and analysis technologies (see Chapter 11), and the real-time availability of big data are starting to affect how evaluations are designed and conducted. Some specialists argue that the move toward digitalization and big data will significantly change how both monitoring and evaluation are conducted (see Chapter 12).

There is also a marked increase in the number of evaluations, policy analyses, and policy-oriented academic studies. The number of academic journals continues to grow, and studies are now widely available on the Internet. With the increasing numbers of studies, analyses, and evaluations, the practice of synthesizing evaluative knowledge has gained in importance (see Chapter 9 and Popay, 2006). Review and synthesis approaches now include such methods as narrative review, meta-ethnography, realist synthesis, and systematic review (see, e.g., Popay, 2006). At the same time, the growing number of meta-studies such as systematic reviews has provided new impetus to so-called repositories of knowledge or second-order evidence-producing organizations (Hansen & Rieper, 2010). Examples of such organizations are the Cochrane Collaboration, the Campbell Collaboration, and, particularly relevant for development, the International Initiative for Impact Evaluation (also known as 3ie).

## 2.3 The Demand for Results-Based Evidence

The increased demand for measurable and credible results, combined with recognition that the evidence base on the effects of development interventions has been rather weak (Evaluation Gap Working Group, 2006), has led many agencies to adopt results-based management (RBM) systems (Kusek & Rist, 2004; Morra Imas & Rist, 2009). These systems are based on intervention logics that provide the basis for the definition and measurement of a set of numerical indicators of program outputs and outcomes with defined milestones by which numerical targets should be achieved. Most international development agencies now use some variant of RBM. Yet the challenge of addressing attribution in RBM systems remains quite daunting, especially when taking into account the many types and levels of interventions for which conventional quantitative counterfactual methods do not work.

The increased recognition that development processes are complex brings new challenges for the institutional and organizational processes underlying RBM. As Patton (2011), among others, makes explicit, tensions can emerge between a somewhat rigid and linear planning and reporting model and a need for managerial and institutional flexibility that complex interventions and contexts demand. Reynolds (2015) argues that RBM systems are designed to provide evidence of the achievement of narrowly defined results that capture only the intended objectives of the agency commissioning the evaluation. Furthermore, he argues that this narrow and inflexible approach, which he calls the "iron triangle of evaluation," is unable to adapt to the broad context within which complex programs operate and address the needs of different stakeholders. A number of reforms to make RBM more complexity-responsive have been introduced in various contexts. In Chapter 13, we present some of these options.

# 3. What Does Complexity Mean in Development Evaluation?

In this section we discuss a number of conceptual perspectives on complexity that have inspired the development of the conceptual framework of this book, which is presented next.

## 3.1 The Complexity Science and Systems Perspectives

Systems theory and complexity science represent a variety of approaches to thinking about complexity. There is no common intellectual foundation of thinking about complexity, and many definitions of complexity have been proposed by scholars. Until very recently, evaluators have made only limited use of complexity science, but this is likely to change as there are many potentially important applications. As usefully categorized by Morin (2008), two main strands of complexity theory can be identified in the literature: restricted complexity and general complexity. Box 1.4 summarizes the key elements of the two approaches and explains how in this book we incorporate elements of both approaches.

---

### BOX 1.4 RESTRICTED AND GENERAL COMPLEXITY

Two main types of complexity have been conceptualized in the social sciences: restricted and general. These quite fundamentally different definitions and corresponding worldviews have implications for the type of evaluation approach that can and should be applied:

- *Restricted complexity* refers to a perspective whereby complexity only stems from human interactions. It does not grant any causal power to context and structures, and it is based on a conception of human agency as following a set of patterns and rules. According to this perspective complexity is amenable to mathematical treatment, through, for example, agent-based modeling and nonlinear equations. It can also accommodate modes of inquiry such as quantitative counterfactual evaluation.
- By contrast, the *general complexity* perspective is imbued with the spirit of holism and relies heavily on the concept of multilevel emergence. Complex systems are not just the product of interactions between people but have properties of their own that have to be addressed in and of themselves. One of the implications of this perspective is that variable-based methods are inherently constrained to detect empirical regularities and, instead, careful mapping and comparison of complex and context-dependent causation are required to make sense of complexity in a given geographic and temporal setting. What is needed is an account of how transformation happens by capturing the interactions between various elements (individuals, organizations, institutions, localities) and their respective causal effects on the whole system, making sense of people's agency beyond narrow behavioral rules, and exposing underlying mechanisms.

*(Continued)*

---

(Continued)

In this book we do not make an explicit choice between the two. Both views and their methodological and practical implications have merit in different evaluation contexts. Our conceptual framework—which defines complexity as the interaction of multiple dimensions, including embeddedness, and the nature of the system and institutions—is very much in line with a general complexity perspective. Some of the methodological approaches that we put forth (e.g., realist evaluations, qualitative comparative analysis, case-based methods of unpacking and reassembling) are also compatible with this view of the world. On the other hand, we also suggest that some tools from complexity sciences (e.g., systems mapping, modeling) or variable-based methodologies (e.g., regressions, [quasi-]experimental designs) can also be valuable in dealing with complexity in development evaluation. The latter are implicitly aligned to a restricted complexity perspective.

SOURCES: Adapted from Byrne (2013), Byrne & Callaghan (2014), Morin (2008).

A number of authors have started translating some of the complexity concepts into an international development language. Ramalingam, Jones, Toussaint, and Young (2008) usefully distinguish between the following three dimensions.[4]

*Complexity and systems:*

- Systems are interconnected and interdependent.
- Systems are full of feedback loops.
- Emergence: The dynamics of the system are unpredictable.

*Complexity and change:*

- Change is nonlinear.
- Change is path-dependent but there are also possible system shocks; systems are in continuous flux with quasi-chaotic features.

*Complexity and agency:*

- Adaptive agents continuously react to the system and each other, which can sometimes lead to patterns of regularity.
- Self-organization can be an emergent property, which may last for a time.
- A result of interconnectedness is co-evolution of actors and parts of the system.
- The move toward participatory planning and evaluation increases the number of agents (NGOs, community organizations, advocacy groups, etc.), which increases the complexity of the evaluand.

While readers may find many of these concepts intuitively clear, Ramalingam et al. (2008) provide a detailed discussion of these aspects. In this book we take a somewhat broader complexity perspective than the now common systems theory or complexity science approaches (Patton, 2011; Ramalingam et al., 2008; Williams & Hummelbrunner, 2011; Wolf-Branigin, 2013). We recognize that complexity is first and foremost the property of a system, but there are a number of dimensions underlying the day-to-day practice of evaluation in the development context that we consider eminently complex and yet do not fit well in a systems theory approach.

## 3.2 Distinguishing Between Simple and Complex Interventions

A well-known distinction is the one between simple, complicated, and complex problems (Glouberman & Zimmermann, 2002):

- Simple problems (like following a recipe) might require a certain level of expertise, but they can be mastered and carry a high probability of success in future attempts to replicate the recipe.
- Complicated problems (like sending a rocket to the moon) require coordination and specialized expertise, but outcomes can be predicted with a fairly large certainty.
- Complex problems (like bringing up a child) can have some features of complicated problems, but they are also characterized by interdependency and nonlinearity. Complex systems carry elements of ambiguity and uncertainty as they have the capacity to adapt to changing conditions.

This simple, complicated, complex heuristic framework has been recurrently applied in the evaluation literature (e.g., Bamberger, Rugh, & Mabry, 2012; Patton, 2011; Rogers, 2008) and has been helpful in assessing the degree of complexity of different types of interventions. However, the limited practical applicability due to a significant degree of overlap (and potential confusion) between complicated and complex interventions has also been highlighted in the literature (Patton 2015; Rogers, 2011). Moreover, the use of the terms *simple projects, complicated programs,* and *complex interventions* may also suggest a strong association between the nature (and complexity) of the intervention itself and the nature (and complexity) of processes of change induced by the intervention. This is not necessarily the case. Simple projects can result in causal processes of change that can be considered complex (for a discussion of complexity in processes of change, see Chapter 4). Similarly, large scale, multi-actor, multilevel (e.g., international, national), multi-site (e.g., covering different countries) interventions may affect the behavior of institutions and individuals in ways that are relatively easy to capture.

In this book we use a somewhat different heuristic framework for assessing the degree of complexity, which enables decision makers, managers, and evaluators to assess the level of complexity of a program and its context on the dimensions of complexity discussed in Section 4 of this chapter.

## 3.3 Pawson's Complexity Framework

Pawson (2013, p. 29) argues that from a realist evaluation perspective, complexity in the social world is ubiquitous. One of the key assumptions of realist evaluation is that programs are complex interventions introduced into complex social systems (Pawson, 2013; Pawson & Tilley, 1997). For instance, apparently simple interventions can be very intricate, the same intervention can provoke change in a myriad of ways, and each intervention is located "within a dynamic policy and social system surrounding it and within a dynamic cognitive and behavioral system that underpins it" (Pawson, 2013, p. 30). However, Pawson cautions against the risk of aspiring for the holy grail of holistic evaluation and recommends prioritizing the inquiry of seven sources of complexity in relation to policy interventions and their effects (see Table 5.1 in Chapter 5 for the VICTORE checklist).[5] Mapping the various dimensions of complexity according to a checklist such as this one allows the evaluator to delineate the contours of the system and make better informed decisions about empirical data collection and analysis.

We will refer to realist evaluation throughout the book both because it is one of the relatively few evaluation frameworks specifically designed to address complexity and because of its emphasis on the complex behavioral mechanisms (many of which were not intended or anticipated) through which change occurs. The approach also emphasizes the unpredictable nature of these behavioral changes and the fact that these mechanisms can operate quite differently in different program contexts.

# 4. Toward a Practical Framework for Addressing Complexity in Evaluation

## 4.1 The Complexity Framework of This Book: Five Dimensions of Complexity

Pawson and Tilley (1997) describe policy interventions as open systems within open systems. It is often not (immediately) apparent where an intervention begins or ends. Programs also first and foremost exist in the mind of the stakeholders involved in their design and implementation. Is the intervention, such as a training program in agricultural land use techniques, simply the aggregate of the inputs, activities, outputs, and different stakeholders involved? Or are there important linkages with, for example, the previous knowledge of the trainers accumulated during past training programs, the social structures in farmer communities, the implementing organization's microcredit component that in the past provided loans to part of the participating farmers, and so on? To what extent are contextual factors like religious beliefs, the availability of non-farm employment opportunities, or cultural differences between program staff and farmers important factors influencing the implementation and potential effectiveness of the program? How far does the influence of the training program in land use techniques go? Does it affect the knowledge levels and behavioral attitudes of farmers? Does it influence land use behavior, yields of crops, and subsequently market volumes and prices of crops? Do farmers and trainers learn from the experience and share this knowledge elsewhere?

The example of the intervention to combat gender-based violence in El Salvador at the beginning of this chapter highlights two key challenges that each evaluation should address: defining *boundaries* for the evaluation and *sense-making of diverse perspectives*. Boundaries refer to two related aspects: the scope of the intended program coverage and impacts as well as the purpose and scope of the evaluation. For example, is the evaluation intended to assess the overall program effects or only to focus on a particular component or a particular geographic region? Does the evaluation focus only on direct project effects, or does it also consider indirect (secondary) effects?

Sense-making is the process by which people give meaning and value to experience. Complexity-responsive evaluation stresses the importance of understanding the perspectives that different groups use to make sense of the nature and purpose of a program and its results. Evaluators and evaluation stakeholders (e.g., donors, decision makers) need to ask themselves: What is a useful way to delimit the boundaries of an intervention and the boundaries of the evaluation? How is it embedded in and connected to different (historically determined and contemporary) societal processes? How can one make sense of the intervention and the processes of change that may be influenced by it?

While these questions are a good starting point for thinking about complexity, they represent only a first step toward a more comprehensive set of questions around complexity and evaluation. In this book we distinguish between five dimensions of complexity, all interrelated: the nature of the intervention, institutions and stakeholders, causality and change, embeddedness and the nature of the system, and finally the evaluation process itself. We discuss each of these dimensions below (see Figure 1.1).

### Dimension 1: The Nature of the Intervention

In the past, evaluations tended to be primarily project-oriented. While this is still an important level at which a lot of evaluative inquiry is taking place, at the same time evaluation is increasingly focusing on higher levels of intervention: sector-wide programs, country programs, multi-country thematic strategies, etc. The defining feature of such interventions is that they involve multiple activities at different levels (e.g., local, national) with different stakeholder groups. In turn, processes of change are likely to be difficult to map as the confluence of different combinations of activities at different levels in divergent social and institutional contexts can lead to a very broad and varied spectrum of change.

---

**BOX 1.5 QUESTIONS TO BE ADDRESSED CONCERNING DIMENSION 1**

With regard to this dimension one can ask the following questions:

- What is the purpose of the intervention? To what extent have the multiple activities at different levels been clearly defined and logically linked to assumptions about processes of change contributing to the achievement of the intervention's purpose?
- What is the scope and size of the intervention? What can be said about the number and diversity in activities, actors, locations, etc.?
- To what extent does the intervention include a comprehensive monitoring framework used to periodically collect data? What sources of data are available to capture the intervention processes and activities?

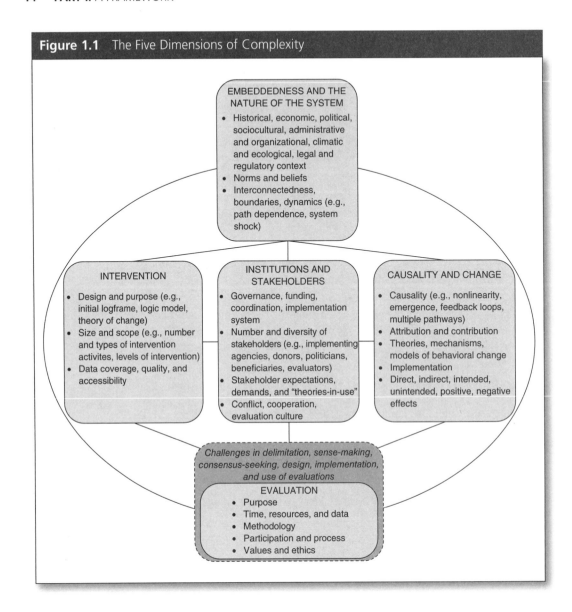

**Figure 1.1**    The Five Dimensions of Complexity

A number of variables can be helpful in characterizing the complexity of interventions:

- *Scale and geographic spread:* In general, programs with larger target populations or populations that are geographically dispersed tend to be more complex.
- *Diversity of the target population:* The more diverse the intervention's population, the more complex it is. Programs that serve a range of different ethnic or cultural groups or clients with different social, psychological, economic, and substance abuse problems tend to be more complex. Programs that seek to address the many different types of homeless populations is an example.
- *Number and diversity of program components:* The more different the components and the greater the diversity, the more complex the program. In general,

a program that provides a wide range of similar services (e.g., a primary health care program) is less complex than a program whose services are more diverse (e.g., a program that provides job placement, education, substance abuse counseling, child care, and housing services to the homeless).

- *Organizational complexity:* Programs that involve a number of different funding agencies, a implementing agencies, and oversight agencies tend to be more complex than a large, multicomponent program managed by a single agency.
- *Range, clarity and logical coherence of program objectives and theory of change (design):* The broader the range of program objectives, the greater the complexity. Complexity is also affected by any lack of clarity in the definition of objectives, the overall theory of change, or the program design and implementation strategy.

## Dimension 2: Institutions and Stakeholders

The social and institutional structure of an intervention poses one of the most challenging features of an evaluation. Interventions are human constructions and each aspect of planning, funding, design, coordination, implementation, reporting, and evaluation is subject to negotiations and interactions among different stakeholders. Complexity is thus affected by how the program is governed and coordinated; the number and diversity of stakeholders; the number and diversity of funding sources; stakeholder expectations, their theories of how the program will operate (theories of change), and the level of consensus among them; and the level of conflict or cooperation among agencies. The extent to which stakeholders consider a program complex will also be important for the evaluation.

Within the context of an evaluation, it is essential to carefully map the institutional system of an intervention (i.e., the stakeholders involved in processes of governance, coordination, management, implementation, etc.). Moreover, apart from the formal institutional context, there are many informal channels through which stakeholders interact and negotiate on particular aspects of an intervention.

---

**BOX 1.6 QUESTIONS TO BE ADDRESSED CONCERNING DIMENSION 2**

With regard to this dimension, one can ask the following questions:

- What are the types and number of stakeholders associated with a particular intervention (e.g., donors, decision makers, managers, beneficiaries)?
- What are the characteristics of the systems of governance, coordination, implementation, and so on that bring these stakeholders together?
- What are the main assumptions and expectations of different stakeholder groups regarding how an intervention works or should work? To what extent do stakeholders differ in terms of these expectations and assumptions?
- To what extent can different stakeholder arenas surrounding an intervention be characterized as cultures of conflict, cooperation, learning, and so on?

*Dimension 3: Causality and Change*

Causal change processes are often nonlinear and characterized by emergence[6] and feedback loops.[7] Moreover, intervention outputs can affect multiple causal pathways. For example, conditional cash transfers to poor households can lead to higher school enrolment rates and have motivational effects on students. The more complex the intervention, the more likely that a complex array of causal pathways is (in)directly influenced by the intervention. Different sense-making and measurement techniques should be considered by evaluators when trying to capture and analyze complex processes of change.

---

**BOX 1.7 QUESTIONS TO BE ADDRESSED CONCERNING DIMENSION 3**

With regard to this dimension, one can ask the following questions:

- In a particular intervention context, what are the defining characteristics of causal change processes?
- How do these characteristics affect the prospects for meaningfully analyzing the attribution of change to particular intervention outputs? To what extent should evaluations employ a contribution perspective (i.e., to study the confluence of causal factors influencing a particular process of change)?
- What theories, mechanisms, or models of behavioral change can be meaningfully employed to better understand and analyze processes of change?
- To what extent are implementation processes across an intervention homogeneous? Are there any implementation failures? How does this affect the analysis of causal change?
- What is the full range of changes influenced by an intervention? What are the direct, indirect, positive, negative, intended, and unintended effects of an intervention?

---

It is useful to distinguish between the following parameters for delineating the effects of an intervention (Leeuw & Vaessen, 2009):

- *The level of effects:* Institutional level versus beneficiary level. Some development interventions focus on the institutional level (e.g., the quality of governance, national policies, or legislation) and through these changes affect the well-being of communities and individuals (beneficiary-level change). Other interventions (e.g., vaccination programs, conditional cash transfer programs, rural roads) can directly affect the beneficiary level.
- *The timing of effects:* Short-term versus long-term. Some effects (e.g., changes in attitudes and capacities of individuals) can occur in the short term, while others (e.g., changes in the species diversity in a particular ecosystem) can take many years to become manifest.

- *The nature of causality and direct and indirect effects:* Causal processes between interventions and (expected) change can be relatively straightforward and direct or can be long and diffuse, with many other factors influencing potential changes further down the causal chain. The following are characteristics commonly associated with processes of change from a complexity perspective (see, e.g., Ramalingam et al., 2008): nonlinearity, irreversibility, feedback loops, emergence, path dependence, multiple causes explaining a single outcome, the same outcome being achieved through different combinations of causes, the same set of causes producing different outcomes in different settings, and nonproportionality—the notion that small interventions can result in large effects (the "tipping point") or large interventions can produce very small effects (inertia).

From an evaluation perspective, a key task is making sense of the complexity in processes of change that may be influenced by a development intervention. Sometimes this involves striking a difficult balance between empirical reality (the potential direct and indirect effect to which an intervention may contribute) and stakeholder priorities (see Leeuw & Vaessen, 2009). Again, the reconstruction of the theory of change is a good way to start. By reconstructing the causal assumptions connecting different components of an intervention to processes of change, one can start to build a picture of the nature and level of effects of an intervention. From the point of view of the policymaker and program manager, it is important to distinguish between processes they can control or influence and those they cannot. Finally, the inherent diversity in the nature of change processes at different levels (individual, institution, community, ecosystem, etc.), evaluation designs should encompass multiple methods of data collection and analysis.

## Dimension 4: Embeddedness and the Nature of the System

Development interventions, the communities and regions in which they are implemented, the groups in society that are (in)directly affected by them, and the stakeholders involved in funding and implementing the interventions do not exist in a vacuum. They exist in contexts with particular economic, political, and social characteristics; they are affected by the divergent norms, beliefs, and opinions of different stakeholder groups. To illustrate, two projects on sexual and reproductive health, which on paper look quite the same in terms of budget, activities, content, and so on and are implemented in different regions, can turn out to be completely different interventions in terms of the way they are perceived and acted on by target groups and health workers. For example, the local gender norms regarding a woman's right to make decisions about her health-seeking behavior, the involvement of husbands in health consultation processes, the prevalence of extramarital relationships, and the use of birth control measures are but a few factors that define the context of such a project.

**BOX 1.8 QUESTIONS TO BE ADDRESSED CONCERNING DIMENSION 4**

With regard to this dimension, one can ask the following questions:

- What are the key historical, economic, political, sociocultural, administrative and organizational, climatic and ecological, legal and regulatory contextual factors that have a bearing on a particular intervention?
- What are the prevailing norms and beliefs of key stakeholder groups or specific actors that may have a bearing on the intervention?
- What are the boundaries of the intervention system? More specifically, what is the sphere of influence of an intervention? At what levels (local, regional, national, international) can one expect the process of change to occur?

*Dimension 5: The Evaluation Process*

The interplay between the complexity of the intervention, the institutional context, the (potential) processes of change influenced by an intervention, and the way these three dimensions are embedded in broader economic, social, cultural, and political systems affects the opportunity space for evaluators (and other evaluation stakeholders[8]). What creative solutions can evaluators (and other evaluation stakeholders) employ to improve their understanding and delimitation of intervention contexts and the design, implementation, and use of evaluations?

**BOX 1.9 QUESTIONS TO BE ADDRESSED CONCERNING DIMENSION 5**

With regard to this dimension, one can ask the following questions:

- What is the purpose of the evaluation? To what extent should complexity be addressed to fulfill the expectations of evaluation stakeholders?
- What are the time, data, and resource constraints that affect the design and implementation of the evaluation? To what extent can complexity challenges be addressed given these constraints?
- What combination of methods can be used to adequately address pertinent complexity challenges? What (innovative) methods can be used to adequately address the challenges of attribution and contribution in evaluation?
- What mechanisms are used to involve stakeholders in the process? What are the costs and benefits of participatory evaluation processes in a specific evaluation context?
- What are the explicit and implicit values of evaluators determining the characteristics of the evaluation? To what extent do they coincide with or diverge from the values of other stakeholders? What are the ethical obligations of evaluators and other stakeholders in a particular evaluation context?

Table 1.1 presents examples of six programs (four included in this book) to illustrate the first four dimensions of complexity. The fifth dimension—how the specific constraints and opportunities of the evaluation context together with an assessment of the first four dimensions may result in a complexity-responsive evaluation design and implementation—is a recurrent aspect that is discussed in most chapters of the book.

**Table 1.1** Examples of Evaluations That Address Different Dimensions of Complexity

| Evaluation | Source | Examples of different dimensions of complexity |
|---|---|---|
| 1. A 10-year program to combat gender-based violence in El Salvador | Discussed above and in Chapter 15 | *Embeddedness and the nature of the system:* Gender-based violence is caused and perpetuated by the high levels of violence following civil war, the growth of gangs, and historical, cultural, and legal factors. |
| 2. Coordination of international programs to combat human trafficking | Chapter 17 | *Institutions and stakeholders:* There were multiple problems relating to difficulties of coordination among many different agencies, with different agendas and operating procedures and often working with limited resources. |
| 3. General budget support to seven developing countries | Chapter 19 | *Causality and change:* There is no generally accepted theory of change to track the complex processes of change with multiple and different sets of factors in each country. Additional challenges for causal analysis include contagion of effects from other programs, definition of boundaries, and diverging country contexts. |
| 4. A systematic review of microcredit programs and women's empowerment | Chapter 16 | *Causality and change:* Change and resistance to change are affected by multiple cultural, political, historical, institutional, and economic factors, making it very difficult to isolate the effect of a particular intervention (microcredit). Also, change takes place over a long period of time and often cannot be captured within the evaluation time horizon. |
| 5. A multi-year, multi-agency program to make Ontario tobacco free | Schwartz & Garcia (2011) | *Complexity in the intervention:* The program included 12 prevention areas, each managed by a number of different agencies. Many of these were new and technically challenging, and often available documentation was limited. |
| 6. Evaluating complex strategic development interventions: the challenge of child labor | Perrin & Wichmand (2011) | *Complexity in the intervention:* Fourteen activities to combat child labor are identified, and many programs include several of these activities, each with a different implementation process of affecting child labor over different time horizons and at different levels, many of which are interlinked. |

SOURCE: All of these examples come from either this book (chapter number is given) or Forss et al. (2011).

## 4.2 A Checklist for Assessing the Level of Complexity of a Program or Intervention

In the previous section we identified four dimensions of complexity relating to an intervention and its context. Each of the four dimensions includes a number of categories. *Complexity* is a relative term, and a program and its context may be characterized as having a high degree of complexity on some categories but a low degree on others. The checklist presented in Table 1.2 describes for each category what would be considered a low level and what would be considered a high level of complexity. These low and high levels are derived from the framework discussed earlier. A program and its context can be rated on an ordinal scale from 1 (*low*) to 5 (*high*) for each category. It is also possible to use a summary rating for each dimension.

**Table 1.2**  Checklist for Assessing Levels of Complexity

| | | Level of Complexity | | | | | | |
| --- | --- | --- | --- | --- | --- | --- | --- | --- |
| | **Low** | ← | | | | → | | **High** |
| | | **Complexity rating** | | | | | | |
| | | **1** | **2** | **3** | **4** | **5** | | |
| **Dimension 1: The nature of the intervention** | | | | | | | | |
| 1. Objectives | Few and relatively clearly defined | | | | | | | Multiple, broad, and often not clearly defined |
| 2. Size | Affecting small population | | | | | | | Affecting large population |
| 3. Stability of program design | Relatively stable | | | | | | | Emergent design |
| 4. Implementation procedures | Clearly defined in project design | | | | | | | Often not clearly defined and changing |
| 5. Services or components | Relatively few | | | | | | | Large number |
| 6. Technical complexity | Low | | | | | | | High |
| 7. Social complexity | Low | | | | | | | High |
| 8. Duration | Clear start and end dates | | | | | | | No clear end date and sometimes no clear start date |
| 9. Testing of program design | Well tested and used many times | | | | | | | Relatively new and untested |

| | | Level of Complexity | | | | | | |
|---|---|---|---|---|---|---|---|---|
| | | **Low** | ← | | → | | | **High** |
| | | | **Complexity rating** | | | | | |
| | | | **1** | **2** | **3** | **4** | **5** | |
| **Dimension 2: Institutions and stakeholders** | | | | | | | | |
| 10. Budget | Use of funds clearly defined | | | | | | | General budget support with no clear definition of services to be funded |
| 11. Funding and implementing agencies | Relatively few | | | | | | | Large number |
| 12. Stakeholders | Relatively few and with similar interests | | | | | | | Many and diverse |
| **Dimension 3: Causality and change** | | | | | | | | |
| 13. Causal pathways | Single causal pathway | | | | | | | Multiple causal pathways (nonlinear, interconnected, recursive feedback loops) |
| 14. Certainty on outcomes | Relatively high degree of certainty | | | | | | | Low degree of certainty |
| 15. Agreement and clarity on appropriate actions to address problems | High level of agreement and clarity | | | | | | | Low level of agreement and clarity |
| **Dimension 4: Embeddedness and the nature of the system** | | | | | | | | |
| 16. Clarity on contextual factors that influence implementation and change | Contextual factors known and knowledge on their potential influence available | | | | | | | Contextual factors and their potential influence on implementation and change largely unknown |
| 17. Processes of behavioral change | Simple processes that are well understood | | | | | | | Multiple mechanisms to promote complex behavioral change |

The checklist requires field testing and refinement and can of course be adapted to the requirements of a particular program that is being evaluated. However, the practical value of this framework is that it provides guidance to an agency in deciding whether a program and its context should be considered as having a high, medium, or low level of complexity for the purpose of deciding which evaluation design to use. Further discussion of these issues is introduced in subsequent chapters, especially Chapters 3 and 7, which provide more detailed guidance on how to deal with complexity issues. In general, the lower the level of complexity, the more feasible it is to use established evaluation designs; the higher the level of complexity, the greater the need to develop a complexity-responsive evaluation design.

A point of clarification is in order when assessing the level of complexity. Some scholars may argue that all programs and the way they are embedded in multilayered societal processes, structures, belief systems, and so on are complex. We do not fundamentally contest this point of view. For us, and for the purposes of evaluation, the key question is: How complex are a program and its context given the purposes and (potential) uses of the evaluation? This is a rather different question; it is about how much of the underlying complexity surrounding programs should be taken on board to produce credible evaluation findings and recommendations that serve their purpose and use. In sum, assessing complexity is about taking into account the operationally relevant level of complexity of different characteristics of interventions and their contexts (see Figure 1.1.) while at the same time keeping in mind the question of how complexity-informed the evaluation should be, given its purpose and use.

# 5. Practical Applications

The following are some practical guidelines for agencies commissioning and managing evaluations of programs and interventions that may have complex elements.

- It is important to be familiar with the basic concepts of complexity. Not all programs are equally complex, but there is sometimes a tendency for agencies or evaluators to believe that their programs are very complex. So before commissioning an evaluation, it is important to understand to what extent and in what ways a program and its context are complex and how important the dimensions of complexity are in practical terms. While a theorist can always show that a program has many dimensions of complexity, these may not be important from an operational or policy perspective.
- Our message is not that complexity can be ignored, but rather that it can be introduced in a phased approach. For example, in the first phase of an evaluation, careful judgment is required to decide to what extent different dimensions of complexity should be addressed given stakeholder priorities and resources. On the basis of discussions between evaluators and stakeholders about the needs for further information for program improvement

or roll-out (e.g., scaling up, replication), and gaps in knowledge about the effectiveness of the program in particular settings, a more elaborate complexity-responsive evaluation can be designed in phase 2.

- Table 1.2 presents a checklist for assessing the level of complexity of a program and its context on the different dimensions of complexity. The checklist can be used to determine the extent to which and in what ways the program and its context should be considered complex from an evaluation perspective. Box 1.10 presents an overview of the main frameworks of guidance on complexity-responsive evaluation that are discussed in this book.

---

**BOX 1.10 GUIDANCE ON THE DESIGN OF COMPLEXITY-RESPONSIVE EVALUATIONS**

In several chapters we provide guidance on complexity-responsive evaluation. The reader may wish to consult the following three main frames of reference:

- Table 1.2 in this chapter provides an initial complexity checklist that helps decision makers and evaluators assess the extent and nature of complexity of a program and its context.
- Chapter 3 presents a step-by-step approach to managing a complexity-responsive evaluation process (see Figure 3.1 for a summary).
- Chapter 7 discusses a five-level approach to unpacking complex programs into evaluable parts and reassembling them into an overall evaluative perspective (see Figure 7.1 for a summary).

---

# References

Bamberger, M., Rugh, J., & Mabry, L. (2012). *RealWorld Evaluation: Working under budget, time, data, and political constraints* (2nd ed.). Thousand Oaks, CA: Sage.

Byrne, D. (2013). Evaluating complex social interventions in a complex world. *Evaluation, 19*, 217–228.

Byrne, D., & Callaghan, G. (2014). *Complexity theory and the social sciences: The state of the art*. Milton Park, UK: Routledge.

Evaluation Gap Working Group. (2006). *When will we ever learn? Improving lives through impact evaluation*. Washington, DC: Center for Global Development.

Forss, K., Marra, M., & Schwartz, R. (Eds.). (2011). *Evaluating the complex: Attribution, contribution and beyond*. New Brunswick, NJ: Transaction.

Glouberman, S., & Zimmerman, B. (2002). Complicated and complex systems: What would successful reform of Medicare look like? (Discussion Paper No. 8). Retrieved from http://c.ymcdn.com/sites/www.plexusinstitute.org/resource/collection/6528ED29-9907-4BC7-8D00-8DC907679FED/ComplicatedAndComplexSystems-ZimmermanReport_Medicare_reform.pdf

Hansen, H. F., & Rieper, O. (2010). Institutionalization of second-order evidence-producing organizations. In O. Rieper, F. L. Leeuw, & T. Ling (Eds.), *The evidence book: Concepts, generation, and use of evidence.* New Brunswick, NJ: Transaction.

Kusek, J., & Rist, R. (2004). *Ten steps to a results-based monitoring and evaluation system.* Washington, DC: World Bank.

Leeuw, F. L., & Vaessen, J. (2009). *Impact evaluations and development: NONIE guidance on impact evaluation.* Washington, DC: Network of Networks on Impact Evaluation.

Morin, E. (2008). *On complexity.* Cresskill, NJ: Hampton Press.

Morra Imas, L. G., & Rist, R. C. (2009). *The road to results: Designing and conducting effective development evaluations.* Washington, DC: World Bank.

North, D. C. (1990). *Institutions, institutional change and economic performance.* Cambridge, UK: Cambridge University Press.

Patton, M. Q. (2011). *Developmental evaluation: Applying complexity concepts to enhance innovation and use.* New York, NY: Guilford Press.

Patton, M. Q. (2015). Book review: Evaluating the complex: Attribution, contribution and beyond. *American Journal of Evaluation.* Advance online publication. doi:10.1177/1098214015569758

Pawson, R. (2013). *The science of evaluation: A realist manifesto.* Thousand Oaks, CA: Sage.

Pawson, R., & Tilley, N. (1997). *Realistic evaluation.* Thousand Oaks, CA: Sage.

Perrin, B., & Wichmand, P. (2011). Evaluating complex strategic development interventions: The challenge of child labor. In K. Forss, M. Marra, & R. Schwartz (Eds.), *Evaluating the complex: Attribution, contribution and beyond* (pp. 243–282). New Brunswick, NJ: Transaction.

Popay, J. (2006). *Moving beyond effectiveness: Methodological issues in the synthesis of diverse sources of evidence.* London, UK: National Institute for Health and Clinical Excellence.

Ramalingam, B., Jones, H., Toussaint, R., & Young, J. (2008). *Exploring the science of complexity: Ideas and implications for development of humanitarian efforts* (Working Paper 285). London, UK: Overseas Development Institute.

Reynolds, M. (2015). (Breaking) the iron triangle of evaluation. *IDS Bulletin, 46,* 71–86.

Rogers, P. J. (2008). Using Programme theory to evaluate complicated and complex aspects of interventions. *Evaluation, 14*(1), 29–48.

Rogers, P. J. (2011). Implications of Complicated and complex characteristics for key tasks in evaluation. In K. Forss, M. Marra, & R. Schwartz (Eds.), *Evaluating the complex: Attribution, contribution and beyond* (pp. 33–53). New Brunswick, NJ: Transaction.

Schwartz, R., & Garcia, J. (2011). Intervention path contribution analysis (IPCA) for complex strategy evaluation: Evaluating the smoke-free Ontario strategy. In K. Forss, M. Marra, & R. Schwartz (Eds.), *Evaluating the complex: Attribution, contribution and beyond* (pp. 187–208). New Brunswick, NJ: Transaction.

Williams, B., & Hummelbrunner, R. (2011). *Systems concepts in action: A practitioner's toolkit.* Stanford, CA: Stanford University Press.

Wolf-Branigin, M. (2013). *Using complexity theory for research and program evaluation.* Oxford, UK: Oxford University Press.

# Notes

1. Change has a certain starting point, and the nature of that starting point (e.g., the different characteristics of institutions, rules, norms, and beliefs) determines the change process. The term *changes at the margin* is sometimes used to indicate that change is often not abrupt but gradually arises from deviations in a number of issues at the same time (for a discussion of this issue, see North, 1990).

2. http://www.unorg/millenniumgoals.

3. http://www.unctad.org/en/docs//tdxii_accra_accord_en.pdf.

4. For reasons of space and simplicity, some of the terms are explained slightly differently than in the original text, also taking into account the literature on institutional change in the field of institutional economics (e.g., North, 1990).

5. The seven dimensions of the VICTORE framework are volitions, implementation, context, time, outcomes, rivalry, and emergence (Pawson, 2013, ch. 5).

6. Emergence can be defined as a situation in which collective phenomena (e.g., mass migration, climate change) are the outcomes of interactions between individual elements of a system that are seemingly chaotic or random.

7. Something causes something else to happen, which in turn reinforces the initial causal factor. Feedback loops can be circular or more complex.

8. For example, donors, decision makers, program managers, beneficiaries.

# CHAPTER 2

# Toward More Complexity-Responsive Evaluations: Overview and Challenges

Estelle Raimondo, Jos Vaessen, Michael Bamberger

*Dealing with complexity in development evaluation requires more than a good understanding of the various complexity dimensions that characterize an intervention and its context. It requires a set of methodological approaches that can address particular aspects of complexity in the evaluation design and implementation. A key question raised in this chapter is thus: How can established evaluation approaches be adapted to take account of complexity issues while operating within the real-world conditions of data, budget, and time constraints? We start by presenting a few scenarios under which development evaluations are typically conducted and discuss some of the challenges encountered in established evaluation approaches from the perspective of complexity. In the remainder of the chapter we explore several strategies for developing complexity-responsive evaluations. One of these strategies relies on approaches stemming from complexity science; another consists of strengthening established evaluation approaches to take better account of complexity.*

In Chapter 1 we pointed out that complexity is a multifaceted construct with no single agreed-upon definition. This diversity of views on the nature of complexity translates into a range of possibilities for developing methodological approaches that are well suited to a complexity perspective. The idea that there is still no widely accepted methodological road map to deal with complexity poses a challenge and can be difficult to communicate to decision makers and managers. At the same time, the absence of such a road map opens the door to renewed creativity. For instance, in this chapter we will see that some methods stemming from complexity science can usefully contribute to making sense of certain complexity dimensions, such as nonlinear causal processes or systems relationships. Yet these techniques have their own limitations and might be less helpful for dealing with other complexity dimensions, such as complex institutional processes or conflicting stakeholder relations. Moreover, the choice of evaluation design must often balance the need for methodological soundness and real-world challenges of time, resources, and data constraints while ensuring the use of evaluation findings.

To arrive at a complexity-responsive evaluation approach, a key question is thus: How can established evaluation methods be adapted to take account of complexity issues? We do not propose a major overhaul of the field of development evaluation to tackle complexity. Instead our approach is premised on the twin ideas that complex interventions do not always warrant complex evaluation designs and it is possible to strengthen established evaluation designs and techniques to make them complexity-responsive. In this chapter and the remainder of the book, we argue that all development evaluations should be complexity-responsive by meeting three minimum requirements: (1) demonstrate awareness of the larger system in which the intervention and its evaluation are embedded; (2) understand how the various dimensions of complexity will affect the design, implementation, and use of the evaluation; and (3) explicitly address and deal with some of the complexity dimensions in the evaluation design, process, and ultimately findings. While all evaluations should strive to be complexity-responsive, this need not necessarily be technically, institutionally, or financially demanding. Consequently, we refrain from using the term *complex evaluations*.

The next chapter goes one step further by discussing in more detail how evaluations can be designed to include complexity issues in a systematic and stepwise manner, taking due account of the demands and restrictions of a particular evaluation setting. Subsequent chapters discuss in detail a number of methodological approaches—some already known and used in development evaluation, others less known—that are well-equipped to address one or more of the complexity dimensions discussed in Chapter 1.

# 1. Common Scenarios in Development Evaluation

Development evaluation encompasses a broad field of practices in very divergent circumstances (e.g., in terms of stakeholders, nature of the evaluand, target group, etc.). At the risk of oversimplification we distinguish between five common evaluation scenarios. For lack of a better term, and because a unifying heuristic is sometimes necessary, in what follows we use the term *established evaluation approaches*, which share the following common features:

- They are well known within existing evaluation systems and build on existing evaluation capacities in development organizations.
- They are composed of well-known data collection and analysis methods.
- They offer the flexibility to be adjusted to real-world constraints regarding data availability, budget, and time restrictions and political challenges.
- They intend to provide information that is readily usable by program managers and decision makers.

The majority of development evaluations conducted to date fit into one or more of the following evaluation scenarios. These five scenarios do not provide a comprehensive picture of all development evaluations, and they sometimes overlap. But they paint in broad brush strokes some typical situations for development evaluation managers and practitioners.

Some of these scenarios have more latitude than others for developing and implementing an evaluation design that is amenable to dealing with complexity, but it is possible to address complexity within each scenario. The main issue is often to arbitrate between scope and depth.

- *Rapid evaluations:* These are conducted within a limited number of working days. While some of them may be well funded and deploy many evaluators concurrently in various places (most are conducted with limited resources), the rapidity of the exercise often means limited depth. Most commonly, these are retrospective evaluations typically relying on reviews of secondary data combined with key informant interviews and often short field visits to conduct case studies in a number of program locations through focus groups, in-depth interviews, or rapid surveys. Usually there are no systematic baseline data to draw on.
- *Large-scale, long-term evaluations:* These multi-year programs (e.g., programs to combat smoking, homelessness, or child labor) may include substantial funding and time for an evaluation. Many of these evaluations involve a number of stages to adapt the evaluation design as the program evolves and often to contribute to refining the program design and implementation strategy (formative evaluation). Typically, the evaluation involves ongoing consultations with stakeholders, and a significant amount of time is spent on developing and refining the program theory. These evaluations typically use multiple sources of evidence collected through a wide range of data collection methods.
- *Experimental manipulation and/or reliance on primary data collection:* In recent years there has been growing interest in the use of experimental (randomized controlled trials) and quasi-experimental designs to assess more systematically the effects of program interventions. There is a continuing debate about the feasibility and appropriateness of experimental approaches to program evaluation. However, it is generally agreed that experimental designs work best when complex interventions can be unpacked so that experimentation can be applied to a single component (see Chapter 7), but it is probably not possible to use these approaches in isolation to assess the overall impact of a complex, multi-component intervention (Vaessen, 2011). Other evaluation designs also rely heavily on primary data collection. These include ethnographic studies as well as quasi-experiments and statistical analysis based on survey data.
- *Systematic reviews[1]:* These synthesize the findings of existing evaluations (that meet certain standards of relevance and rigor) so as to provide an overall assessment of the theory of change or the impacts of an intervention (e.g., microcredit) on one or more outcomes (e.g., the creation of small enterprises, women's economic empowerment). While systematic reviews have great potential as a tool for addressing complexity in evaluation, they are best suited to assess the relationships between specific inputs

and specific outcomes, rather than to assess the combined effects of multiple inputs (including the interactions among inputs) on multiple outcomes.

- *Participatory evaluations:* Stakeholder participation is a potentially important aspect of any type of evaluation. Over time, a set of evaluation approaches was developed that puts participation at the center of evaluative inquiry. Participation in evaluation can serve multiple purposes. First, it can improve the quality and depth of data collection. Second, participatory models are often used to enhance the relevance, ownership, and use of evaluations by stakeholders. Finally, participatory evaluations can also support transformative processes such as stakeholder empowerment and control over the program that is the subject of the evaluation (see, e.g., King, Cousins, & Whitmore, 2007). While potentially offering a number of distinct advantages, participatory models of evaluation are sometimes also criticized for their costliness or susceptibility to bias.[2]

Table 2.1 provides more background information on the five evaluation scenarios.

| **Table 2.1**  Five Common Scenarios for Development Evaluation | | |
|---|---|---|
| **Scenario** | **Common features** | **Examples** |
| 1. Rapid evaluation | • Short time frame for conducting the evaluation and limited resources<br>• Usually retrospective<br>• Limited access to baseline data<br>• Relies heavily on secondary data and key informant interviews<br>• May include case studies on a few countries or program sites<br>• Makes use of rating scales (e.g., OECD-DAC) | • SIDA evaluation of its HIV/AIDS programs<br>• UNICEF evaluation of its HIV/AIDS programs; UNESCO evaluation of its HIV/AIDS program<br>• IEG Project Performance Assessment Reports. |
| 2. Large-scale, long-term evaluation | • Design evolves and changes as program evolves and is better understood<br>• Often has formative function to help refine the definition of program objectives and implementation<br>• High level of stakeholder involvement<br>• Investment of time in developing program theory model<br>• Multiple streams and sources of data | • Poverty impact of European support to Tanzania (Toulemonde, Carpenter, & Raffier, 2011)<br>• Multi-agency response to homelessness in Australia (Wilkins, 2011)<br>• Swiss smoking prevention program (Spinatsch, 2011)<br>• Smoke-free Ontario strategy (Schwartz & Garcia, 2011)<br>• Child labor prevention (Perrin & Wichmand, 2011)<br>• Evaluating the effectiveness of weather-indexed crop insurance in Ethiopia (Bamberger, 2015) |

*(Continued)*

| **Table 2.1** (Continued) | | |
|---|---|---|
| **Scenario** | **Common features** | **Examples** |
| 3. Experimental manipulation | • Randomized controlled trials when subjects can be randomly assigned to treatment and control groups<br>• Quasi-experimental designs when randomization is not possible but when treatment and comparison groups can be statistically matched<br>• Works better for assessing effects of single treatments on individual outcomes but not to assess influence of multiple inputs on multiple outcomes<br>• Design is often combined with other (qualitative) methods | • Deworming in Kenya (Miguel & Kramer, 2004)<br>• Education in India (Banerjee, Cole, Duflo & Linden, 2007)<br>• Monitoring corruption in Indonesia (Olken, 2007)<br>• Returns to capital and access to finance in Mexico (McKenzie & Woodruff, 2008)<br>• Microcredit in the Philippines (Karlan & Zinman, 2007)<br>• Indian Panchayat Reform Program (Bamberger et al., 2010) |
| 4. Systematic review | • Review of all evaluations that meet acceptable standards of rigor and relevance<br>• Current methodologies focus on assessing effects of specific interventions on specific outcomes<br>• Difficult to apply to assessing effects of multiple inputs on multiple outcomes<br>• Can be combined with theory-based approaches to review and synthesis | • Effects of conditional cash transfers on child nutrition in Latin America (Leroy, Ruel, & Verhofstadt, 2009)<br>• Effects of microcredit, micro-savings, and micro-leasing on promoting access of poor people and especially women to economic opportunities (Stewart el al., 2012) |
| 5. Participatory evaluation | • Often used in evaluations with a formative purpose<br>• Often used in community-based programs<br>• Can be costly to implement in evaluations of multi-site, multi-actor interventions | • Supporting indigenous governance in Colombia (Estrella & Gaventa, 1998)<br>• Various examples (Chambers, 2007)<br>• Use of empowerment evaluation to build the capacity of Aymara women artisans in Puno, Peru (Sastre-Merino, Vidueira, Diasz-Puente, & Fernandez-Mora, 2014) |

# 2. Limitations and Challenges Encountered in Established Evaluation Approaches From the Perspective of Complexity

As argued by Mowles (2014), many evaluations that claim to be sensitive to complexity issues are in fact paying lip service to it. In other words, there is often a disconnect between the theoretical discussion of complexity and the approaches that are actually used to address complexity in evaluation (Forss & Schwartz, 2011; Funnell & Rogers, 2011; Patton, 2011; Rogers, 2011). What follows are some examples of common pitfalls encountered in established evaluation approaches from the perspective of dealing with complexity. Broadly, they fit into two categories: overlooking and oversimplifying some dimensions of complexity.

## 2.1 Overlooking Complexity

- Most development evaluations do not address the issues discussed in the literature on the nature of complexity.
- Most program theory models (see Chapters 5 and 6) do not adequately address complexity and are developed and presented in similar ways for simple and complex interventions.
- Methodologies for identifying unanticipated outcomes are not incorporated into most evaluation designs.
- Differences between target populations and institutional contexts across interventions pose particular challenges for the generalizability of evaluation findings; these challenges are often disregarded in established evaluations (Pritchett & Sandefur, 2013).

## 2.2 Oversimplifying Complexity

- Many established evaluation approaches are intrinsically reductionist; they harvest particular variables from a complex context and end up decontextualizing the intervention while focusing on the effect of a controlled variation in one part (i.e., an intervention) on specific outcomes. Yet as highlighted by Byrne and Callaghan (2014, p. 173), the presence of emergence implies that such reductionist approaches are missing a vital part of the processes of change and effects of an intervention.[3] In Chapter 7 we discuss the circumstances under which such deconstructions are feasible.
- The power dynamics, the conflicting perceptions, and the changing nature of interactions among many different stakeholders and actors are rarely addressed in evaluations and the focus tends to be on the influence of a small number of stakeholders, each examined individually.
- Most designs do not adequately address the problem of assessing changes that take place over long periods of time. Woolcock (2013), among others, argues that the important piece of information that evaluation should bring to the program manager is not an estimate of impact at a given point in time but rather an accurate picture of the likely impact trajectory over time. While most established evaluation approaches implicitly assume that the impact trajectory is linear, in reality most development interventions have an impact trajectory that either follows a J-curve (things get worse before improving) or has a tipping point (i.e., the idea that things do not change until they dramatically do). Moreover, development interventions seeking to be transformational at the level of norms and culture (e.g., interventions seeking to change gender relations) are subject to particularly long causal pathways of change.

The challenges presented above are illustrative of the limitations of established evaluation approaches from the perspective of complexity. Under certain circumstances, methodologies emerging from complexity sciences can be usefully leveraged to address some of the complexity dimensions of our framework. Below we introduce some of these approaches and discuss their respective strengths and limitations.

# 3. Methodological Approaches Stemming From a Complexity Science Perspective

*Complexity science* is an umbrella term encompassing a vast and eclectic field of academic inquiry with roots in various philosophical branches and disciplines as well as many ramifications in the social sciences. In the field of complexity science a number of well-defined methods for studying complexity have been developed, ranging from network analysis to soft systems methodologies. Most of these approaches share the objective of modeling multi-component systems that organize spontaneously. In recent years, many social science disciplines have attempted to adapt some of these methods of inquiry to the study of the social world. The work of the Santa Fe Institute of Science for a Complex World, for example, is particularly praiseworthy in its endeavor to provide insights into the complexity of human behavior, institutions, and social systems.

## 3.1 Succinct Overview of Complexity Science Approaches

As usefully summarized by Williams (2015), the development of the field of complexity science can be characterized by three main waves. The first wave, dating back to the 1960s, was mostly concerned with dynamic interrelationships and has inspired methods such as systems dynamics and complex adaptive systems modeling. The second wave, starting in the 1970s, paid closer attention to the issue of multiple perspectives, recognizing that there were often many ways of understanding each relationship in a given system. This wave inspired the soft systems methods. The third and most recent wave emphasizes the importance of delineating boundaries to otherwise limitless systems; it gave rise to critical systems thinking (Williams, 2015, p. 9). Given the variety of models and techniques that are associated with complexity science, our goal here is not to be exhaustive but rather to present a sample of approaches that have some degree of compatibility with evaluation and the potential to help address some of the complexity dimensions covered in this book's framework (laid out in Chapter 1). Additionally, we attempt to represent the diversity within complexity science. Table 2.3, later in the chapter, summarizes these approaches. Below we discuss various methodological approaches, organized by complexity dimension (see Chapter 1).[4]

*a. Dimension 1: Nature of the Intervention:*
*Dealing With Complex Theories of Change*

- **Systems Mapping**

*Systems mapping* is an umbrella term to describe a range of methods aimed at providing a visual representation of a system. Systems mapping helps identify the various parts of a system as well as the links between these parts that are likely to change. In a subsequent step, the evaluator attempts to find measurement methods to check whether the anticipated system changes have actually occurred. Systems maps are closely related to theories of change (TOC), but they differ from the majority of TOC and logic models by doing away with the assumption of successionist causal relationships[5] between inputs, outputs, and outcomes. Systems mapping can be done via a participatory process. For instance, CARE International recently engaged in an overall assessment of its internal systems for collecting, brokering, and transferring information and used systems mapping to document and monitor its envisaged systems change. Three maps were produced by a consulting firm: a baseline map, an intervention map, and a conclusion map. Figure 2.1 displays the intervention map. The advantage of such a map is that several dimensions of a theory of change can be represented at the same time, and complex connections at several levels of intervention can be illustrated. For example, the map in Figure 2.1 displays the CARE USA level along with the Regional level and the Country level, and the arrows show how these different levels interact in top-down, bottom-up, and sideways directions. External actors with an influence on the strategy can also be integrated in the systems, in this example, the Media/Public as well as U.S. government policymakers.

### b. Dimension 2: Institutions and Stakeholders: Dealing With a Large Number and Diversity of Stakeholders

- **Social Network Analysis**

Social network analysis (SNA) is particularly useful for modeling complex stakeholder relationships and describing how information flows and decisions are made, including through the dynamic use of feedback. SNA studies the connections within systems and acknowledges that social units are interdependent and have multiple layers of relationships by relying on concepts stemming from graph theory and matrix operations (Wolf-Branigin, 2013, pp. 64–65). Drew, Aggleton, Chalmers, and Wood (2011) report on their experience with using SNA to evaluate a particularly complex intervention in the framework of the Global Dialogue on Sexual Health and Well-Being. At the core of this large program lies a network of individuals, the Sexual Policy Watch, based in Rio de Janeiro and composed of key informants who are connected to various organizations. The evaluators thus resorted to SNA to identify (1) the organizations that each key informant was involved in, (2) the geographical and thematic focus of their work, and (3) their links to up to 10 other key informants working in the field of sexual health. The mapping process was produced iteratively with various informants, entered into a database, and analyzed through tables of attributes. The process helped to visualize the various circles of influence and to get a sense of the magnitude of the outreach of the program.

### c. Dimension 3: Causality and Change: Dealing With Various (Nested) Levels of Effects

- **Agent-Based Modeling**

Various agent-based modeling (ABM) techniques have been developed to accommodate for multiple levels of reality (e.g., the macro-level of the external environment of the system, the meso-level of an organization, the micro-level of

**Figure 2.1** Example of a Systems Map

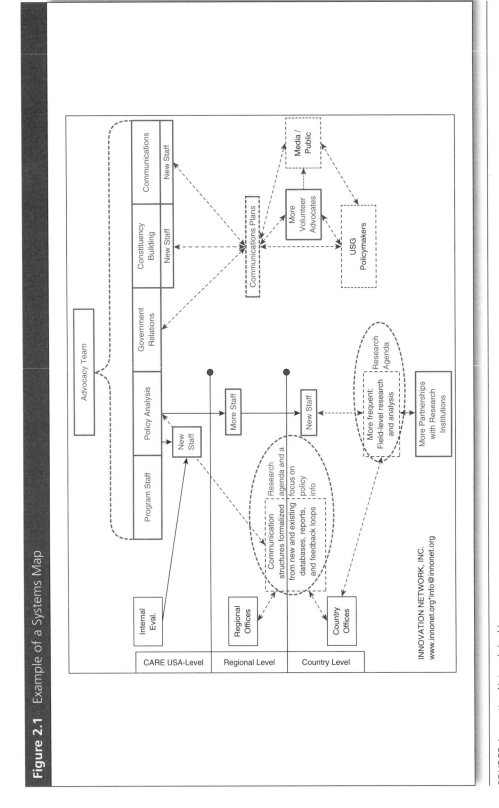

SOURCE: Innovation Network (n.d.).

individual behavioral characteristics; Byrne & Callaghan, 2014). ABM consists of computationally simulating the interactions, preferences, and characteristics of individual agents to assess their effect on entire systems. While ABM has not yet been widely applied as an evaluation tool, it has proven useful to analyze program implementation in which actors go through repeated interactions with the liberty to pick their strategy (Hermans, Cunningham, & Slinger, 2014). ABM offers a formal approach that forces evaluators to simplify the description of social interactions down to their most basic features. For example, ABM has been used to assess the effectiveness of a greenbelt at the border between a rural and urban area as a way to delay the urbanization beyond a particular fringe and to preserve environmental diversity outside the city (Brown, Page, Riolo, & Rand, 2004). A model was developed with simple assumptions about the trade-off between the greenbelt placement, its effect on the development rate beyond the belt, and how these factors interact with agents' heterogeneous characteristics and preferences as well as their varied but imperfect level of information.

## d. Dimension 4: Embeddedness and the Nature of the System: Dealing With Interconnectedness and Dynamic Boundaries

- **System Dynamics**

System dynamics (SD) is an approach for capturing the dynamic behavior of (social) systems. It borrows from engineering and management and relies on the analysis of relationships between stock and flow variables that are quantified. A simulation model is then crafted by assembling all the elements to express the various relations as mathematical equations.

Applied to evaluation, SD can be particularly useful when attempting to capture how complex systems are affected by development interventions and affect these interventions in return. SD can help improve our understanding of dynamic interrelationship along the theory of change (Befani, Ramalingam, & Stern, 2015). For instance, Williams and Hummelbrunner (2011) describe the use of SD in the evaluation of a microloan project targeting sex workers in a broader HIV/AIDS prevention program in a mining area of West Africa. SD was used to explain why the popularity of the microloan schemes would swing dramatically among the target population of sex workers depending on a range of factors (Williams & Hummelbrunner, 2011, p. 49). Three stocks were identified: the popularity of the program, the number of loans, and the financial liability of the funding company. The only flow of the scheme was the rate of new loans issuance. The evaluators proceeded with several simulations that they compared to real-life patterns. A number of lessons were learned, notably that the system will improve with time even if nothing is done; improving the performance of the funder seems more effective than improving the communication with beneficiaries.

## e. Dimension 4: Embeddedness and the Nature of the System: Dealing With Embedded Norms and Beliefs

- **Critical Systems Heuristics**

Critical systems heuristics (CSH) is premised on the idea that the decision of what lies within the boundary of a system determines the focus of attention, while the rest is put aside. This decision is principally an ethical decision involving value judgments. Being reflexive about where one draws the line is the core of critical systems approaches (Hummelbrunner, 2011). The definition of a critical system revolves around four main categories: motivation, control, expertise, and legitimacy. Table 2.2 summarizes the example of the CSH application described by Williams and Hummelbrunner (2011). It is based on the abovementioned intervention aimed at reducing the incidence of HIV in African mining communities where there is a large population of sex workers. As described by the authors, the intervention had three main goals: (1) ensure that sex workers know about sexually transmitted infections

| **Table 2.2**  Example of Critical Systems Heuristic Application | |
|---|---|
| Motivation (value basis) | There is a range of embedded assumptions about the appropriateness of sex work as a commercial activity, the appropriateness of condom use, and so on that might have been patronizing to the beneficiaries. |
| Purpose of the system | Health education and economic empowerment |
| Beneficiaries of the system's purpose | Commercial and occasional sex workers in mining towns |
| Indicators of success | • Less reliance on commercial sex for income<br>• Target group access to health facilities<br>• Consistent use of condoms<br>• Increased awareness of modes of HIV transmissions among sex workers |
| Control (power basis) | While peer educators and health workers were key actors in the intervention, they had little power over the resources they needed, leading, for example, to shortages of condoms and little uptake of distributed drugs because the health workers were instructed to sell the drugs and not provide them for free, as the donors' assumption was that patients would use them better if they had to pay for them. |
| Expertise or knowledge (knowledge basis) | There was a clear expert bias in both the design and implementation. This limited beneficiaries' involvement from the beginning and left stringent assumptions unchecked:<br><br>• that sex workers had no knowledge of STI and HIV transmissions, when in fact they did; beneficiaries considered the educational material irrelevant<br>• that sex workers were better positioned to distribute condoms in the community when it turned out that the men (clients) were better positioned to make the distribution |
| Legitimacy | Certain boundary decisions were taken too narrowly and uncritically. For instance, the focus was on street-based commercial sex workers, leaving out occasional sex workers and sex workers based in hotels. The normative worldview of the program was reflective of the funder's take on the legitimacy or lack thereof of sex work. |

SOURCE: Adapted from Williams & Hummelbrunner (2011, pp. 310–315).

(STIs), HIV/AIDS, and reproductive health services through a peer education project, (2) offer alternative sources of income through a microcredit scheme, and (3) provide access to reproductive health services. However, while the project's theory of change sounded quite plausible, the empirical reality proved otherwise. CSH was used to make sense of what went wrong and to better understand whether the lack of success was mostly due to implementation, or design failure as a result of boundary definition issues.

## 3.2 Applicability of Complexity Science Approaches in Development Evaluation

Some of the approaches presented above have started to make their way into the methodological repertoire of development evaluators. Systems mapping, for instance, is now routinely used by evaluators faced with complex interventions in lieu of a more traditional theory of change. For instance, the Global Environmental Facility (GEF) has developed a general theory of change for its role and intended impact on the environment that leverages several concepts of systems thinking as presented in Figure 2.2. The map features, among other things, the display of feedback loops. In the area of GEF contribution, the knowledge and information, implementation strategies, and institutional capacity are meant to build on each other in a positive reinforcement loop. Likewise, the larger transformational process can be understood as a causal loop whereby behavioral changes are encouraged by and feed into successes, mainstreaming environmental issues and replicating successful interventions. Finally, the arrow that gets wider and wider illustrates that change is often nonproportional when a positive feedback loop is activated.

Methods narrowly associated with a complexity science perspective are particularly instrumental in pushing evaluators to focus on the nature of relationships and interdependences within systems, to lay out and explain the multidirectional linkages between a given intervention and its outcomes, whether intended or not. Some of these tools are also proving to be useful in dealing with the fact that some interventions are embedded (nested) in broader policy frameworks. One of the main challenges faced by evaluators dealing with complexity is to understand how different components interact the way they do and why some interactions lead to positive change, while others lead to stasis or negative (unintended) change. Tools inspired by systems thinking can help answer these questions. Table 2.3 summarizes the comparative advantages of these various complexity science approaches in dealing with particular dimensions of complexity and how they can usefully be applied to evaluation.

However, while these and other complexity science approaches are quite promising for the field of development evaluation, they are not silver bullets, and as with any other methods, there are notable limitations:

- One of the main issues with some of the systems approaches described above is that they often result in a high level of abstraction, primarily relying on imagined properties of agents and imagined rules describing their behavior that are only loosely connected with real data (Byrne & Callaghan, 2014).

**Figure 2.2** The Outcome to Impact Pathway of the Global Environmental Facility

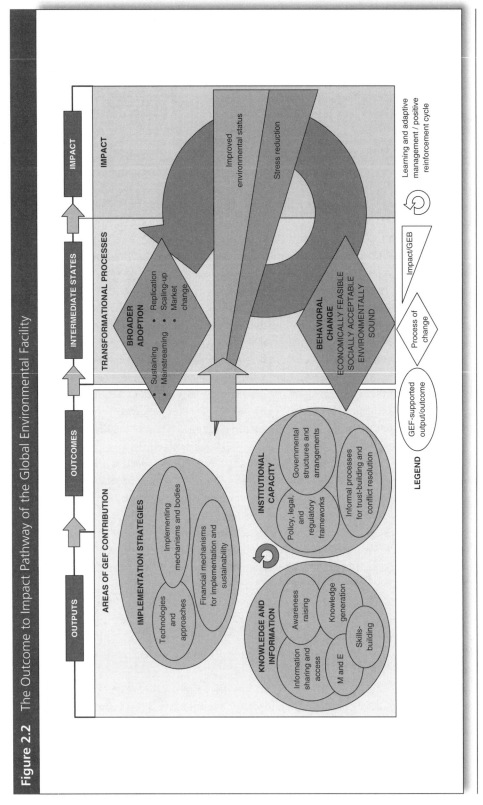

SOURCE: GEF Independent Evaluation Office (2013).

| **Table 2.3** Possible Uses of Complexity Science Approaches in Evaluation | | |
|---|---|---|
| **Methods** | **Dimensions of complexity** | **Use in evaluation** |
| System dynamics | Dealing with interconnectedness and dynamic interrelationships | • Map the program context<br>• Test assumptions underlying a particular causal chain within a theory of change<br>• Assess the change in the state of a system based on different hypotheses about the dynamics of an intervention |
| Critical systems heuristics | Dealing with embedded norms, beliefs and values | • Elicit particular motivations, values, and perspectives held by a range of program stakeholders<br>• Assess how these different values and perspectives can lead to possible design failures |
| Systems mapping | Dealing with complex theories of change | • Map the various complexity dimensions of an intervention and its context<br>• As the basis for pre and post comparison (comparing a systems map at the end of an intervention to a systems map prior to the start of an intervention) |
| Social network analysis | Dealing with a large number of stakeholders and their relationships | • Identify the multiple layers of relationships among various stakeholders<br>• Explore the structures that form or are formed by networks<br>• Assess how different patterns of networks illustrate differential levels of capacity, communication, resource movement, etc. |
| Agent-based modeling | Dealing with complex causal processes | • Model various levels of reality (e.g., macro level of society, meso-level of an organization, micro-level of a program)<br>• Anticipate the outcome of a situation based on the simulation of interactions, preferences, and characteristics of individual agents |

- While complexity science approaches are useful for diagnostic or planning studies and simulations can be used to reconstruct scenarios that can be used as counterfactuals, these techniques need to be combined with more established evaluation techniques in order to address the evaluation questions of what works in what context.
- The statistically based techniques often rely on a narrow definition of complexity and emergence as resulting from interactions among micro-level entities that follow certain rules. Consequently, these techniques are largely unable to deal with social forces that shape the context of the agents' actions (Byrne, 2013; Byrne & Ragin, 2009). Other systems methods such as systemic questioning, critical

systems heuristics, or soft systems methodology are better able to deal with the embeddedness of norms and values (Williams & Hummelbrunner, 2011).

- Many of the methods introduced above are often still the object of experimentation and need refinement. They are not yet ripe for practical applications in real-world evaluation settings.

- Some of the approaches also require a high level of proficiency in quantitative and computational techniques that many real-world evaluators do not possess. Moreover, the types of results that these approaches produce are not easily translatable in a language that decision makers and program managers can readily put to use.

- Most methods require a large amount of data, which are not available (or are too costly to acquire) in many real-world development evaluation settings.[6]

Given the above, one way forward is to promote the use of complexity science approaches and adapt them to development evaluation real-world conditions. For some methods (e.g., social network analysis) this is certainly feasible, yet in other cases (e.g., agent-based modeling) the applicability gap may currently be too wide. A different way forward is to start out from established development evaluation methods and discuss how they might be adapted to include some of the features of the approaches discussed above. A first step toward more complexity-responsive evaluations is discussed below.

# 4. Bridging the Gap: Principles for Addressing Complexity Issues in Established Evaluation Approaches

The overarching methodological approach of this book is based on the basic premise, raised in Chapter 1, that all interventions are inherently complex but the nature of complexity and the need for addressing complexity in particular ways (from an evaluation perspective) can widely differ. The practical and methodological implications are as follows: Evaluators always have to keep in mind that some elements of the evaluand, the context, and the processes of change induced by the intervention are complex and may require particular solutions that differ from business as usual (i.e., established approaches) and require a specific (methodological) reflection and response. This book presents a number of alternative and complementary methodological approaches to address different dimensions of complexity. The methodological approaches discussed in subsequent chapters can be defined as complexity-responsive and are based on one or more of the following strategies:

- Systems thinking strategies (some of which were presented in Section 3) to map out the complexity dimensions of an intervention and its context and to assess changes in the dynamics of the system

- Strategies that consist of strengthening established evaluations by expanding their scope and/or introducing novel data collection and analysis methods to better capture various complexity dimensions

- Unpacking and reassembling strategies that consist of breaking down systems into identifiable parts and reassembling them to better understand change in the big picture
- Holistic strategies that consist of seeking a comprehensive understanding of all the complexity dimensions of a particular intervention and its context

As illustrated in Figure 2.3, a complexity-responsive evaluation often builds on several of these strategies. For instance, in Chapter 7 we argue that a complexity-responsive evaluation that opts for unpacking interventions into various parts needs to build on a holistic view of the intervention and its context, both ex ante (when identifying the most relevant unit of analysis) and ex post (when assessing how much of the state of the system has been covered by the evaluation design).

Apart from being grounded in the four aforementioned approaches, complexity-responsive evaluations follow one or more of the following principles.

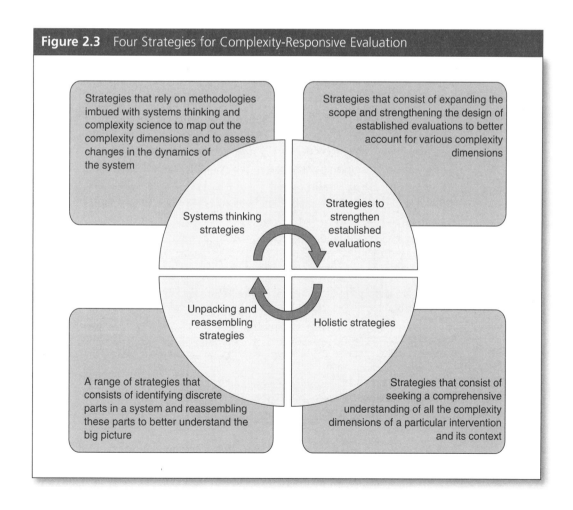

**Figure 2.3**   Four Strategies for Complexity-Responsive Evaluation

Strategies that rely on methodologies imbued with systems thinking and complexity science to map out the complexity dimensions and to assess changes in the dynamics of the system

Strategies that consist of expanding the scope and strengthening the design of established evaluations to better account for various complexity dimensions

Systems thinking strategies

Strategies to strengthen established evaluations

Unpacking and reassembling strategies

Holistic strategies

A range of strategies that consists of identifying discrete parts in a system and reassembling these parts to better understand the big picture

Strategies that consist of seeking a comprehensive understanding of all the complexity dimensions of a particular intervention and its context

## 4.1 Clarifying the Relevant Aspects of the Systems

Mapping the system is an essential aspect of an evaluation dealing with complexity. Looking at the complexity framework presented in Chapter 1, there are at least three major categories of systemic elements that should be articulated in a systems map: the nature of the intervention (e.g., the nature, level, and number of activities); the different stakeholders of the intervention and their interests/demands; the political, economic, cultural, and other factors that shape how individuals and institutions (inter)act, anticipate, and reflect about the intervention. All of these aspects are interrelated. Complex interventions tend to have more components and consequently more interactions among components and are thus exposed to a wider range of contextual factors. An articulation of the organizational structures and the relationships among different agencies and actors is thus warranted. Many evaluations also model power relations and pathways through which different partners can influence how the program is formulated and implemented, and how it achieves outcomes.

## 4.2 Relying on Theory-Based Principles (see Chapters 4, 5, and 6)

Interventions are theories and evaluations are the test. This well-known proverb points at the heart of evaluative inquiry, the reconstruction of causal assumptions that underlie an intervention. These assumptions can be based on stakeholder expectations, existing documentation, empirical data collection and analysis, or a combination thereof. Theory-based evaluation refers to those evaluations that in some way rely on such sets of assumptions (i.e., the theory of change or the intervention theory) as guiding principles of the evaluation exercise. To avoid bias (e.g., pro-intervention bias, confirmation bias of entrenched beliefs about effectiveness), theories should be perceived as "living" abstractions of reality—with new evidence coming in, theories can be further refined.

Theory-based evaluation approaches that focus on multiple causal pathways are particularly well suited to model the implementation design and the mechanisms through which outcomes are expected to be achieved. Part of the task of mapping complexity also includes a detailed explanation of how the program design is intended to achieve program objectives. In this regard, a fully specified theory of change can also profitably make use of a systems map as mentioned above. The many ways in which theory can be used in evaluation are discussed in subsequent chapters of the book.

## 4.3 Unpacking Complex Interventions Into Evaluable Parts (see Chapter 7)

Complex programs usually have many different components that are also implemented in different locations or through different partner agencies. This poses a key challenge in evaluation design. An evaluator can try to simplify or standardize the design by unpacking the program so as to focus on key elements. As we further explain in Chapter 7, a key issue concerns the unit of analysis for deconstruction. Sometimes it makes sense to deconstruct a program into groups of similar activities (e.g., activities relating to the provision of monetary incentives versus activities relating to the transfer of knowledge). Another example is deconstruction into levels of intervention (e.g., local versus national versus international), all of which may exist within a complex intervention.

The other side of the coin of unpacking is reassembling, trying to make sense of the whole by combining information about its parts. Reassembling also refers to making sense of a particular part of a complex intervention (e.g., how does program coordination work in an interagency context? What are the effects of capacity development activities for primary school teachers?) across different intervention contexts. In other words, reassembling can relate to making sense of the complexity of different intervention components at the level of the overall intervention, or it can relate to looking at particular parts across interventions and saying something about how these parts work, for whom, and under what conditions.

## 4.4 Using a Mixed Methods Approach (see Chapter 8)

Given the many different kinds of intervention strategies, components, actors, and geographical or organizational locations, most complexity-responsive evaluations draw on multiple evidence streams and sources of data. In some cases there is a clearly defined mixed methods strategy in which quantitative and qualitative methods are integrated in a systematic way,[7] but in many cases the approach is more opportunistic, with evaluators drawing on whatever sources of primary and secondary data are available. Given a lack of standardized solutions for dealing with complexity, evaluators can use creative and flexible designs that evolve as the evaluation progresses. For instance, it is not uncommon to have multi-stage evaluations, often with emergent designs that are adapted to changes in how the program actually operates on the ground. This contrasts with many of the established quantitative approaches that tend to have a relatively inflexible design (e.g., with a pretest-posttest comparison group design). Additionally, one particular approach to evaluation is intently developmental and allows the program to evolve as the evaluation is ongoing, rather than requiring the program design to be frozen. The developmental evaluation approach relies on tight information loops that feed back into the program implementation process (Patton, 2011).

## 4.5 Dealing With Attribution (see Chapters 4, 5, and 6)

Attribution refers to the question of whether and the extent to which changes are due to an intervention, controlling for other factors. It is often used in tandem with the concept of contribution. The latter emphasizes the confluence of multiple factors influencing a particular change (with one of these factors being the intervention). Experimental and quasi-experimental methods are often favored to address the attribution issue. These methods rely on the principle of a counterfactual (i.e., what would have happened if the intervention had not taken place). For example, through the principle of randomization one can approximate this counterfactual by generating equivalent groups (equivalent on all observable and unobservable variables) but for the intervention (which is specifically assigned to a group). Any changes over time, given this equivalence, can be attributed to the intervention. While this is a powerful principle, it has a number of shortcomings as well. Apart from challenges in applicability, counterfactual designs are not (specifically) equipped to address the emergent nature of complex programs (i.e., both program design and intended outcomes often change in response to contextual, organizational, and political factors); to analyze multiple, nonlinear, and recursive causal pathways; and to identify unintended outcomes. In the case of complex interventions, quantitative counterfactual methods are applied after unpacking an intervention into smaller parts (see discussion above). Alternative methods are more appropriate to address one or more of the challenges described above. Examples are causal chain analysis (using, for example, process tracing) or quantitative comparative analysis (see Chapter 4).

## 4.6 Making Use of Innovative Data Collection Techniques and Sources of Data (see Chapters 10, 11, and 12)

Evaluation design and the validity of its findings can be strengthened by making optimal use of innovative techniques of data collection and sources of data, such as data on mobile phone use, geographic information systems, and biometric data. The increasing availability of very large data sets ("big data") is creating more opportunities for using new mathematical and statistical approaches to data mining and data analytics in complex program evaluation (UN Global Pulse, 2012).

# 5. Practical Applications

- Established evaluation approaches have several limitations with regard to addressing complexity issues. In practice, this often results in overlooking and/or oversimplifying essential complexity issues that one may wish to address in evaluations because of their bearing on intervention processes and outcomes. To deal with this issue, this chapter has discussed two options:
  - Using methods from complexity science to address particular complexity dimensions (see Chapter 1). The comparative advantages and limitations of these methods are discussed in this chapter.
  - Applying a number of principles to strengthen established evaluation approaches: clarifying elements of the system; relying on theory-based principles (see Chapters 5 and 6), unpacking complex interventions into evaluable parts (see Chapter 7), using a mixed methods approach (see Chapter 8), dealing with attribution (see Chapter 4), and using innovative techniques and sources of data (see Chapters 10, 11, and 12).

# References

Bamberger, M. (2015). *Measuring resilience: Lessons from the design and implementation of monitoring and evaluation methodologies of the Horn of Africa Risk Transfer for Adaptation (HARITA)/R4 Rural Resilience Initiative: A case study.* Boston: Oxfam USA.

Bamberger, M., Rao, V., & Woolcock, M. (2010). Using mixed methods in monitoring and evaluation: Experiences from international development. In A. Tashakkori & C. Teddie (Eds.), *Sage handbook of mixed methods in social and behavioral research* (2nd ed., pp. 613–641). Thousand Oaks, CA: Sage.

Banerjee, A., Cole, S., Duflo, E., & Linden, L. (2007). Remedying education: Evidence from two randomized experiments in India. *Quarterly Journal of Economics, 122,* 1235–1264.

Barron, P., Diprose, P., & Woolcock, M. (2011). *Contesting development: Participatory projects and local conflict dynamics in Indonesia.* New Haven, CT: Yale University Press.

Befani, B., Ramalingam, B., & Stern, E. (2015). Introduction: Towards systemic approaches to evaluation and impact. *IDS Bulletin, 46*(1), 1–6.

Brown, D. G., Page, S. E., Riolo, R., & Rand, W. (2004). Agent-based and analytical modeling to evaluate the effectiveness of greenbelts. *Environmental Modelling & Software, 19,* 1097–1109.

Byrne, D. (2013). Evaluating complex social interventions in a complex world. *Evaluation, 19,* 217–228.

Byrne, D., & Callaghan, G. (2014). *Complexity theory and the social sciences: The state of the art.* Milton Park, UK: Routledge.

Byrne, D. & Ragin, C. (2009). *The Sage handbook of case-based methods.* Thousand Oaks, CA: Sage.

Chambers, R. (2007). *Who counts? The quiet revolution of participation and numbers* (Working Paper 296). Brighton, UK: Institute of Development Studies. Retrieved from https://www.ids.ac.uk/files/Wp296.pdf

Drew, R., Aggleton, P., Chalmers, H., & Wood, K. (2011). Using social network analysis to evaluate a complex policy network. *Evaluation, 17,* 383–394.

Estrella, M., & Gaventa, J. (1998). *Who counts reality? Participatory monitoring and evaluation: A literature review* (IDS Working Paper No. 70). Brighton, UK: IDS.

Forss, K., & Schwartz, R. (2011). Introduction. In K. Forss, M. Marra, & R. Schwartz (Eds.), *Evaluating the complex: Attribution, contribution and beyond* (pp. 1–32). New Brunswick, NJ: Transaction.

Funnell, S. C., & Rogers, P. J. (2011). *Purposeful program theory.* San Francisco, CA: Jossey-Bass.

GEF Independent Evaluation Office. (2013). *Fifth overall performance study: Impact of the GEF OPS5* (Technical Document #2). Retrieved from http://www.thegef.org/gef/sites/thegef.org/files/EO/TD2_Impact%20of%20the%20GEF.pdf

Hermans, L., Cunningham, S., & Slinger, J. (2014). The usefulness of game theory as a method for policy evaluation. *Evaluation, 20,* 10–15.

Hummelbrunner, R. (2011). Systems thinking and evaluation. *Evaluation, 17,* 395–403.

Innovation Network. (n.d.). *System mapping: A case example.* Retrieved from http://www.innonet.org/client_docs/File/advocacy/CARE_systems_map.pdf

Karlan, D., & Zinman, J. (2007). *Expanding credit access: Using randomized supply decisions to estimate the impacts* (Working Paper 108). Washington, DC: Center for Global Development.

King, J., Cousins, B., & Whitmore, E. (2007). Making sense of participatory evaluation: Framing participatory evaluation. *New Directions for Evaluation, 114,* 83–105.

Leroy, J. L., Ruel, M., & Verhofstadt, E. (2011). The impact of conditional cash transfer programmes on child nutrition: A review of evidence using a programme theory framework. *Journal of Development Effectiveness, 1*(2), 103–129.

McKenzie, D., & Woodruff, C. (2008). Experimental evidence on returns to capital and access to finance in Mexico. *World Bank Economic Review, 22,* 457–482.

Miguel, E., & Kramer, M. (2004). Worms: Identifying impacts on education and health in the presence of treatment externalities. *Econometrica, 72*(1), 159–217.

Mowles, C. (2014). Complex, but not quite complex enough: The turn to the complexity sciences in evaluation scholarship. *Evaluation, 20,* 160–175.

Olken, B. (2007). Monitoring corruption: Evidence from a field experiment in Indonesia. *Journal of Political Economy, 115,* 200–249.

Patton, M. Q. (2011). *Developmental evaluation: Applying complexity concepts to enhance innovation and use.* New York, NY: Guilford Press.

Perrin, B., & Wichmand, P. (2011). Evaluating complex strategic development interventions: The challenge of child labor. In K. Forss, M. Marra, & R. Schwartz (Eds.), *Evaluating the complex: Attribution, contribution and beyond* (pp. 243–282). New Brunswick, NJ: Transaction.

Pritchett, L., & Sandefur, J. (2013). *Context matters for size: Why external validity claims and development practice don't mix* (Working Paper 336). Washington, DC: Center for Global Development.

Rao, V., & Ibanez, A. M. (2003). *The social impact of social funds in Jamaica: A mixed methods analysis of participation, targeting and collective action in community-driven development* (Policy Research Working Paper 2970). Washington, DC: World Bank.

Rogers, P. J. (2011). Implications of Complicated and complex characteristics for key tasks in evaluation. In K. Forss, M. Marra, & R. Schwartz (Eds.), *Evaluating the complex: Attribution, contribution and beyond* (pp. 33–52). New Brunswick, NJ: Transaction.

Sastre-Merino, S., Vidueira, P., Diasz-Puente, J., & Fernandez-Mora, J. (2014). Capacity building through empowerment evaluation: An Aymara women artisans organization in Puno, Peru. In D. Fetterman, S. Kaftarian, & A. Wandersman (Eds.), *Empowerment evaluation* (2nd ed., pp. 76–85). Thousand Oaks, CA: Sage.

Schwartz, R., & Garcia, J. (2011). Intervention Path Contribution Analysis (IPCA) for complex strategy evaluation: Evaluating the smoke-free Ontario strategy. In K. Forss, M. Marra, & R. Schwartz (Eds.). *Evaluating the complex: Attribution, contribution and beyond* (pp. 187–208). New Brunswick, NJ: Transaction.

Spinatsch, M. (2011). Evaluating a complex policy in a complex context: The elusive success of the Swiss Smoking Prevention Policy. In K. Forss, M. Marra, & R. Schwartz (Eds.), *Evaluating the complex: Attribution, contribution and beyond* (pp. 170–206). New Brunswick, NJ: Transaction.

Stewart, R., van Rooyen, C., Korth, M., Chereni, A., Rebelo Da Silva, N., & de Wet, T. (2012). *Do micro-credit, micro-savings and micro-leasing serve as effective financial inclusion interventions enabling poor people, and especially women, to engage in meaningful economic opportunities in low- and middle-income countries? A systematic review of the evidence.* London, UK: EPPI-Centre.

Toulemonde, J., Carpenter, D., & Raffier, L. (2011). Coping with the evaluability barrier: Poverty impact of European support at country level. In K. Forss, M. Marra, & R. Schwartz (Eds.), *Evaluating the complex: Attribution, contribution and beyond.* New Brunswick, NJ: Transaction.

UN Global Pulse. (2012). Big data for development: Challenges and opportunities. Retrieved from http://unglobalpulse.org/projects/BigDataforDevelopment

Vaessen, J. (2011). Challenges in impact evaluation of development interventions: Randomized experiments and complexity. In K. Forss, M. Marra, & R. Schwartz (Eds.), *Evaluating the complex: Attribution, contribution and beyond* (pp. 283–314). New Brunswick, NJ: Transaction.

Wilkins, P. (2011). Monitoring and evaluation of a multi-agency response to homelessness: An Australian case study. In K. Forss, M. Marra, & R. Schwartz (Eds.), *Evaluating the complex: Attribution, contribution and beyond.* New Brunswick, NJ: Transaction.

Williams, B. (2015). Prosaic or profound? The adoption of systems ideas by impact evaluation. *IDS Bulletin, 46*(1), 7–16.

Williams, B., & Hummelbrunner, R. (2011). *Systems concepts in action: A practitioner's toolkit.* Stanford, CA: Stanford University Press.

Wolf-Branigin, M. (2013). *Using complexity theory for research and program evaluation.* Oxford, UK: Oxford University Press.

Woolcock, M. (2013). Using case studies to explore the external validity of "complex" development interventions. *Evaluation, 19,* 229–248.

# Notes

1. A systematic review is actually part of a broader group of review and synthesis approaches. See Chapter 9 for a discussion.

2. Examples of potential biases are elite capture of participatory processes and groupthink. The latter refers to a situation in which a desire for consensus or harmony within the group may actually crowd out viable and critical ideas.

3. In complex systems we are no longer dealing with a single cause-and-effect relationship, but rather with multiple interacting causes. Emergence denotes the idea that programs change the conditions that make them work. Consequently, what really matters is the interaction among various elements that causes the state of a system at any given time in its trajectory, rather than a particular single effect on a single outcome.

4. There is no clear-cut one-on-one relationship between complexity dimension and methodological approach. We are merely pointing out in which area of complexity particular methodological approaches are likely to have a comparative advantage.

5. The idea that a change in variable x causes a rather direct change in variable y.

6. While this is true for some of the established evaluation techniques (e.g., quasi-experimental and other econometric approaches), many of the complexity science approaches are particularly demanding in terms of data.

7. For examples of evaluation designs in which the mixed methods approach is fully integrated from the start of the evaluation, see Barron, Diprose, and Woolcock (2011); Rao and Ibanez (2003); and Bamberger, Rao, and Woolcock (2010).

# CHAPTER 3

# Management of Complexity-Responsive Evaluations

Michael Bamberger

*This chapter emphasizes the critical role that the evaluation manager must play at all stages of the design, implementation, and dissemination of a complexity-responsive evaluation. An important contribution of the manager is to ensure that the evaluation addresses the key questions of concern to all stakeholders. The manager must also ensure the evaluation design is based on a thorough understanding of the different dimensions of complexity and that it takes into account real-world budget, time, and data constraints.*

*This chapter discusses seven steps in the management of a complexity-responsive evaluation. Figure 3.1 shows how these steps are linked to the stages in the design of the evaluation and indicates the chapters of the book that discuss the different stages of the evaluation methodology.*

Throughout most of the book we discuss issues relating to the design of complexity-responsive evaluations and the selection of appropriate methodologies, tools, and techniques. The purpose of this chapter is to stress the important role of the evaluation manager at all stages of the evaluation. While the evaluation team (whether internal or external) grapples with the many methodological challenges relating to complexity-responsive evaluations, it is the responsibility of the evaluation manager to ensure that the evaluation addresses the key questions of concern to the different stakeholders; that the questions can be addressed within the decision makers' time frame, which is different and usually shorter than that of the evaluators; and that the questions can be addressed within the real-world budget, time, data, and political constraints within which the evaluation will be conducted. It is also essential to ensure that the evaluation is based on a full understanding of all four dimensions of complexity, that it does not ignore important complexity issues but also that it does not exaggerate the real level of complexity.

Figure 3.1 identifies seven steps in the management of a complexity-responsive evaluation and shows that each step provides feedback on the design of the evaluation. In the following sections we describe how each step in the evaluation management process helps strengthen the evaluation design. In this chapter we do not discuss the stages of the evaluation design, as they are discussed in other chapters, but the design steps are included in the figure to illustrate the links with the different stages of the evaluation management process.

# 1. Managing the Evaluation

Throughout the planning and design of a complexity-responsive evaluation, a number of management actions must be taken to ensure that the evaluation focuses on the key questions of interest to stakeholders; the evaluation design is compatible

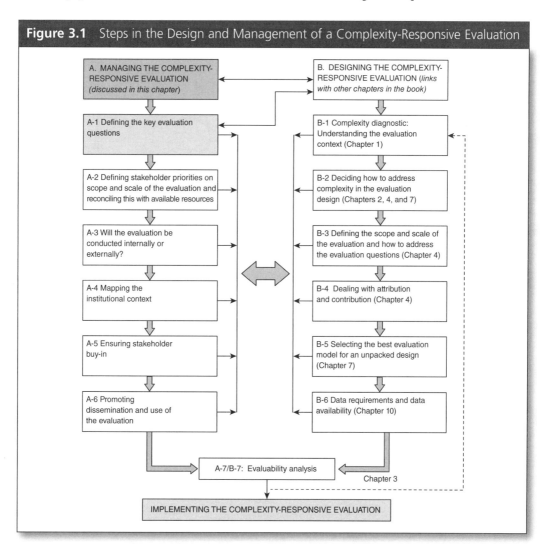

**Figure 3.1**  Steps in the Design and Management of a Complexity-Responsive Evaluation

with real-world budget, time, data, and political constraints and with the most important dimensions of complexity; the evaluation is efficiently managed; and the findings are disseminated and used in a timely manner. In this section we identify some of the key steps and actions that the evaluation manager must take.

## STEP A-1  1.1 Clarifying the Key Questions to Be Addressed in the Evaluation

One of the evaluation manager's main responsibilities is to help identify the key questions that the evaluation must address and then to help the evaluation team select the best evaluation design to answer these questions. We included a direct arrow in Figure 3.1 from Box A-1 to the evaluation design column to emphasize the importance of defining and responding to the key evaluation questions. Stern et al. (2012) identify four key impact evaluation questions. We have adapted these questions, and added a fifth question, to focus specifically on the evaluation of complex programs:

1. To what extent has the intervention contributed to the achievement of a specific impact or set of impacts? Is it possible to directly attribute these impacts to the intervention?

2. Did the intervention make a difference? Were all the effects intended or were some effects unintended (e.g., spillover and emergent effects)?

3. How has the intervention made a difference? Which components of the program made the greatest difference? Who was affected positively? Were any groups (either in the target population or more broadly) affected negatively?

4. Will the intervention work elsewhere? What configuration of factors was necessary for the impacts to occur, and what are the circumstances in which these configurations may occur in other contexts? What factors in the system or in the broader context within which the program operates contributed to or constrained the achievement of impacts, and how likely are these to occur in other areas where the program may be replicated?[1]

5. Will the evaluation include a value dimension? In addition to the above four questions, it is also important to clarify whether the client requires, explicitly or in many cases implicitly, that the evaluation incorporate a certain value orientation such as equity, empowerment, or human rights.[2]

In order to contribute to successful evaluation design, the following kinds of questions must be addressed:

---

**BOX 3.1 EXAMPLES OF QUESTIONS TO ADDRESS AT STEP A-1**

Question 1:  Which of the five evaluation questions must the evaluation address? What are the special challenges in addressing these questions?

Question 2:  Will the evaluation include a value dimension? If so, how will this affect the design of the evaluation?

| STEP A-2 | ## 1.2 Defining Stakeholder Priorities on the Scope and Scale of the Evaluation and Reconciling These With Available Resources |
|---|---|

Complex programs frequently have multiple components, cover many different populations or groups often scattered across wide geographical areas, and operate on different levels (e.g., national, regional, local, household or individual). Consequently, many evaluations of complex programs do not try to cover all components, regions, and levels, and an important task for the evaluation manager is to determine the key information needs of different stakeholders and consequently the key issues that the evaluation must address. There are a number of ways that the scope of the evaluation can be limited:

- Horizontally: only covering certain geographic regions
- Vertically: only focusing on, for example, the national, regional, or local level
- Historically: only studying a limited period of time (e.g., the past 4 years)

Complexity often increases the costs of data collection and analysis. It is the responsibility of the evaluation manager to estimate the additional time, budget, and professional resources that may be required and to ensure that the evaluation design is compatible with the available budget and professional resources available to the evaluation unit. Planning, design, and data collection and analysis may all take longer than expected. For example, more time may be required for exploratory field studies and for review of secondary data. Also, more extensive consultations may be required with different stakeholder groups.

It is useful to prepare a detailed timeline and budget for the different phases of the evaluation and to identify at each stage the additional time and resource requirements to address the different dimensions of complexity. The evaluation manager should also consider whether there are any ways to reduce the costs of data collection and analysis by, for example, using some of the new data collection and analysis technologies for mobile phones and other handheld devices (see Chapter 11).

---

### BOX 3.2 EXAMPLES OF QUESTIONS TO ADDRESS AT STEP A-2

Question 3:  Do stakeholders require an overall evaluation of the program, or are there particular aspects that are most important?

Question 4:  Does the evaluation need to cover all geographic areas where the program is operating, or is it sufficient to select a few representative areas?

Question 5:  Which are the most important levels: international, national, regional, local, or household/individual?

Question 6:  How far should the evaluation look into the history of the program?

*(Continued)*

(Continued)

Question 7:   Have all of the additional cost and resource requirements (result-
              ing from addressing complexity issues in evaluation) been identi-
              fied for each stage of the evaluation?

Question 8:   Are there any ways to reduce costs of data collection and analysis
              (e.g., using new data collection and analysis technologies, relying
              on existing data)?

**STEP A-3**    ## 1.3 Deciding Whether to Conduct the Evaluation Internally or Externally

Whether the evaluation is conducted by an agency's evaluation office or externally using national or international consultants can influence the choice of evaluation design as well as the quality and utilization of the findings. Given the higher
level of technical expertise required and the novelty of a complexity-responsive
orientation, many agencies may require more external support than might be the
case for other types of evaluations. Many of the issues discussed in this chapter are
addressed differently depending on whether the evaluation is conducted internally
or externally.

**BOX 3.3 EXAMPLE OF QUESTIONS TO
ADDRESS AT STEP A-3**

Question 9:   If the agency normally conducts evaluations internally, does it have
              the capacity to conduct a complexity-responsive evaluation? What
              kind of external support might be required?

**STEP A-4**    ## 1.4 Mapping the Institutional Context

Evaluations are conducted in an institutional, organizational, and political context, all of which affect how the evaluation is planned, implemented, and used (see
Chapter 13). Data must be collected from many different agencies, each of which has
a particular way of collecting and managing data. This may make it relatively easy to
collect certain kinds of information and more difficult to collect other kinds. A
complexity-responsive evaluation often requires new kinds of information to be collected or collected in a different way. There may be some information that agencies
have difficulty collecting or that they do not wish to collect. Any new information
collection is an additional burden for already busy staff, so part of the resistance may
be related to the inconvenience, time demands, or costs. In other cases agencies may
feel the information is too sensitive or they do not see the purpose. So however rigorous the evaluation methodology, the success of an evaluation depends to a considerable extent on how effectively data can be collected from agencies that may have a
low capacity or low motivation to collect or share the required information.

One area that can often present management challenges concerns the introduction of equity, rights-based, or empowerment-focused dimensions into the evaluation. Staff with different professional backgrounds may have different perspectives on the need to incorporate value orientations. For example, there is often initial resistance from many staff to the incorporation of a gender focus in program design or evaluation.

All of the above challenges are multiplied for complexity-responsive evaluations (see chapter 14). So evaluation managers often find it useful to prepare a simple systems map (see Chapter 2) or a matrix identifying the kinds of information required, which agencies it will come from, how it will be collected, and how overall data management will be coordinated.

---

**BOX 3.4 EXAMPLES OF QUESTIONS TO ADDRESS AT STEP A-4**

Question 10: What institutional and organizational factors are likely to prove most challenging for the management of the evaluation? How can they be addressed? Hint: It might be useful to prepare a systems map or a matrix to identify the potential issues and challenges.

Question 11: Which kinds of information will be most difficult to collect? What are the reasons for this, and what actions can be taken?

Question 12: Will the evaluation address any issues relating to equity, gender, human rights, or empowerment? Are there areas with which program staff are already familiar? If not, which areas are new? Are staff and stakeholders likely to accept the introduction of these issues, or is there likely to be some resistance? What measures are proposed to gain understanding and acceptance of these issues?

---

## STEP A-5   1.5 Ensuring Stakeholder Buy-In

Active stakeholder participation in evaluation design, implementation, analysis, dissemination, and use are particularly critical for complexity-responsive evaluations for a number of reasons. First, complexity makes it more difficult to ensure that evaluators are asking the right questions, so stakeholder inputs help ensure the evaluation has the correct focus. Second, multiple and nonlinear causal pathways make it difficult to track the progress of the program and to assess its contributions to observed outcomes. Stakeholder perceptions are helpful as they tend to focus more directly on actual outcomes and those that are considered valuable. Third, stakeholders help understand the program's contribution to equity, human rights, and empowerment. Finally, behavioral change, which is an important mechanism for achieving outcomes, is difficult to observe directly, so inputs from stakeholders provide important insights.

In addition to the widely used individual and group meetings with stakeholders, a number of participatory techniques can be particularly effective for involving vulnerable groups who normally remain voiceless (see, e.g., Mikkelsen, 2005; see also Chapter 4).[3]

---

**BOX 3.5 EXAMPLES OF QUESTIONS
TO ADDRESS AT STEP A-5**

Question 13:    Who are the key stakeholders and what are their priorities and concerns?

Questions 14:    Have the evaluators identified the most vulnerable and poorest groups, and have these groups been consulted? Have their interests been incorporated into the evaluation design?

---

### STEP A-6    1.6 Promoting Evaluation Utilization

One of the major challenges for evaluation offices is the underutilization of evaluation findings.[4] The problem does not relate just to poor-quality evaluations, as many well-designed evaluations are also underutilized. The following reasons for underutilization apply to all evaluations, but they are particularly problematic for complexity-responsive evaluations:

a. *Bad timing*: The results are presented after decisions have already been made about the future trajectory of the program, or, less commonly, the report is presented too early, before decision makers or the public have begun to focus on an issue (e.g., before there is awareness about a humanitarian crisis or concern about a particular aspect of global warming). Timing is even more challenging for complexity-responsive evaluations as complex programs have many different stakeholders and components, so different parts of the evaluation may be completed over a period of many years, which makes it is even more difficult to coordinate the best timing for each component and stakeholder group.

b. *Lack of flexibility and responsiveness to the information needs of key stakeholders*: Evaluations are often conducted according to the administrative needs of the funding agencies and frequently do not have the flexibility to respond to the priorities of different stakeholders. This is particularly problematic for complex interventions, both because of the large number of stakeholders with different information needs and because the focus of the program and its different components often change significantly over time.

c. *Wrong questions and irrelevant findings*: Complex interventions tend to have a larger and more diverse set of stakeholders, so it is more difficult to ensure the evaluation addresses the needs of all stakeholders. Relevance becomes even more challenging for evaluations that are committed to issues of equity and social justice as new methodologies are required to understand and respond to the needs of vulnerable groups. There is always a danger that an evaluation will mainly focus on the interests of a few influential stakeholders or sometimes the academic interests of the evaluators rather than the interests of the intended target groups.

d. *Narrow focus on program impact:* Many evaluations focus only on the estimation of program impacts, whereas the more immediate concerns of stakeholders may be to learn how effectively the program is being implemented and whether services are reaching the right groups. In other cases policymakers and donors may need information on high-level issues such as policy coherence.

e. *Difficulties of attributing causality for complex programs*: For clients who are used to evaluations that are not complexity-responsive and where there are clear statements about the effects of the program on specific outcome variables (often with tables indicating the statistical significance of the findings), a report of a complexity-responsive evaluation may seem disappointing. The report often indicates that the program is one of many contributing factors and that it is difficult to assess the precise contribution of a particular donor's support. For agencies that are competing for budgets or that need to convince the legislature or the public that their taxes are being well spent, it may be difficult to present these more nuanced findings. This may contribute to lower utilization of the evaluation by some agencies.

f. *Expensive complexity-responsive evaluations that make heavy demands on the time of overworked staff*: These concerns become even more problematic for evaluations whose immediate benefits may be less clear.

g. *Lack of local expertise to conduct, review, and use evaluations*: In countries or agencies where a culture of evaluation is not well developed, managers and decision makers may have difficulty understanding and utilizing the findings of even simple evaluations. Consequently, it becomes even more difficult to use complexity-responsive evaluations whose methodology may be even more difficult to understand and whose findings and recommendations are more nuanced.

The evaluation manager has a major role in promoting utilization. The following eight actions, adapted from Bamberger, Rugh, and Mabry (2012, ch. 8), provide a framework for promoting utilization of the evaluation findings:

1. Ensure the evaluation is based on a full understanding of clients' and other stakeholders' information needs, the nature of the program, and the context within which it will be implemented (Steps A-1 to A-3).

2. Use a formative evaluation strategy designed to help improve program implementation and to assess outcomes.

3. Maintain constant communication with the client and other stakeholders throughout the evaluation. In addition to providing feedback on actions to improve program implementation, this also ensures that clients are aware of findings that are emerging on different components of the program. A useful guideline for evaluators is "no surprises"; in other words, the client and key stakeholders should be aware of likely findings, particularly any controversial issues, before they are published in a report.

4. Establish an active evaluation capacity development program for all organizations involved in the program.

5. Use "carrots" (positive incentives), "sticks" (negative sanctions such as reducing budgets), and "sermons" (e.g., indications of support for the evaluation from high-level and prestigious persons; see Bemelmans-Videc & Rist, 1998; Mackay, 2007).

6. Develop strategies to overcome political and bureaucratic challenges to the evaluation. Some actions can include mapping the institutional context (Step A-4) to identify and address potential areas of conflict, redesigning management systems to focus on results, creating incentives for higher program performance, and agreeing on performance indicators at all levels of the program.

7. Develop effective strategies for communicating the evaluation findings. This involves an understanding of what stakeholders want to know, how different groups like to receive information (e.g., reports, workshops, videos, informal briefings), the technical level at which the information should be presented, and when the information is needed. Different kinds of presentations may be required for different audiences: some more focused on evaluation methodology and others on policy and operational implications. A completely different kind of presentation may be required for community groups or other populations who were the intended beneficiaries of the program.

8. Develop a follow-up action plan. Many organizations now develop a management action plan that assigns responsibility for implementing every recommendation included in the evaluation report and for monitoring progress on the implementation of the agreed actions.

---

**BOX 3.6 EXAMPLES OF QUESTIONS
TO ADDRESS AT STEP A-6**

Question 15: Have potential factors that could reduce evaluation utilization been identified, and are there plans to address these potential problems?

Question 16: Is there a strategy to ensure effective dissemination and utilization of the evaluation, and is the plan being implemented? Does it take into account the eight recommendations presented above?

---

### STEP A-7   1.7 Evaluability Analysis

The final step before the evaluation begins is to assess the feasibility and appropriateness of the proposed evaluation design—the evaluability analysis.[5] This must be conducted by independent evaluation specialists not involved in designing the evaluation. Consequently, the evaluation manager is usually involved in the coordination of the evaluability analysis. The assessment involves a review of the proposed evaluation design to assess the following:

- Is the methodology sound? Does the evaluation design adequately address the complexity issues that are deemed important in the context of the evaluation?
- If an unpacking design is proposed (see Chapter 7), does it adequately address the different dimensions of complexity? When some dimensions of complexity are not addressed, have the consequences of these exclusions been carefully assessed and are the reasons convincing?
- Does unpacking programs into components introduce any sources of bias, and if so are they adequately recognized and, where possible, addressed?
- Is the evaluation designed to provide the key information required by stakeholders, and is it realistic to expect the evaluation to produce this information? Can the information be produced within the required time frame to contribute to key decisions?
- Is the evaluation based on a coherent and specific logic model that captures the different dimensions of complexity?
- Will critical data and other sources of information be available?
- Will the evaluation have access to key informants?
- Can the evaluation be implemented within the time and budget constraints?
- Can it be implemented within the existing organizational, institutional, and political context?
- Does it use a participatory methodology that will actively involve all stakeholders, including the most vulnerable and socially marginalized groups?
- Is the value orientation of the evaluation clearly defined (i.e., does it have equity, human rights, or empowerment/emancipation objectives) and clearly incorporated into the evaluation design?
- Is the evaluation likely to produce sufficiently important findings to justify the major investment of resources and time?

If methodological issues arise during the evaluability analysis, it may be necessary to review and possibly revise the proposed methodology (hence the feedback loop in Figure 3.1 that returns from the evaluability analysis box to Step B-1 and the start of the evaluation design process).

# 2. Practical Applications

There are two central messages that readers should take away from this chapter. First, evaluation managers, and often program managers, must play an active role in the planning, design, and implementation of an evaluation. Second, it is essential for the evaluation team to have a full understanding of how the four dimensions of complexity (see Chapter 1) affect the program and how they will affect the evaluation.

With respect to the role of the evaluation manager, the following are some of the areas in which she or he must play an active role:

- Ensure that the evaluation is asking the right questions (and that the interests of all stakeholders are addressed). While the evaluation may primarily focus on the estimation of impacts, many stakeholders are also interested in the efficiency of the program, coherence with other policies and programs, and the value orientation of the evaluation.

- Ensure that the evaluation follows the principles of a complexity-responsive design. It must be informed by a full understanding of the different complexity dimensions, and these factors must be kept in mind throughout the evaluation (including when deciding whether it is appropriate to unpack a complex program; see Chapter 7). Also, it is essential, once the different elements of the evaluation have been conducted, that there is a strategy for reassembling the findings of these elements to understand the overall effectiveness and impact of the program within the complex setting in which it operates.
- Ensure that evaluators from different professional backgrounds can work well together. Complexity-responsive evaluations often require bringing new areas of professional expertise into the evaluation team.
- Ensure that the evaluation uses the appropriate combination of methods and tools. Many evaluators have a preference for a particular methodological approach (e.g., randomized controlled trials, qualitative/participatory methods), and it is important to work with the team to review and assess a range of methods before finalizing the design.
- Finally, the manager has a key role to play in ensuring that the findings and lessons from the evaluation are utilized.

# References

Bamberger, M., Rugh, J., & Mabry, L. (2012). *RealWorld Evaluation: Working under budget, time, data, and political constraints.* Thousand Oaks, CA: Sage.

Bemelmans-Videc, M. L., & Rist, R. C. (Eds.). (1998). *Carrots, sticks and sermons: Policy instruments and their evaluation.* New Brunswick, NJ: Transaction.

Mackay, K. (2007). *How to build M&E systems to support better government.* Washington, DC: World Bank.

McNulty, J. (2012). Symbolic uses of evaluation in the international aid sector: Arguments for critical reflection. *Evidence & Policy, 8,* 495–509.

Mikkelsen, B. (2005). *Methods for development work and research.* Thousand Oaks, CA: Sage.

Stern, E., Stame, N., Mayne, J., Forss, K., Davies, R., & Befani, B. (2012). *Broadening the range of designs and methods for impact evaluation* (Working Paper No. 38). London, UK: Department of International Development.

Wholey, J. (1979). *Evaluation: Promise and performance.* Washington, DC: Urban Institute.

Wholey, J., Hatry, H., & Newcomer, K. (Eds.). (2010). *Handbook of practical program evaluation.* San Francisco, CA: Jossey-Bass.

# Notes

1. In order to address some of these broader questions, a systems-oriented research approach may be required that complements but goes beyond a specific program-oriented evaluation. For example, a research approach might be helpful to understand the confluence of factors that contribute to changes in outcome indicators.

2. Such an orientation may affect the choice of evaluation methods (e.g., in some cases requiring a qualitative design). An equity focus, for example, will require that the evaluation also address questions relating to who benefits from and who is excluded (intentionally or unintentionally) from the program.

3. The nature and level of participation of different stakeholder groups can vary given the nature of the intervention (e.g., general budget support vs. community-based natural resource management programs).

4. See Bamberger, Rugh, and Mabry (2012), Chapter 8. Wholey, Hatry, and Newcomer (2010) also discuss political and bureaucratic challenges affecting the use of evaluations in the United States (see Chapter 27, Exhibit 27.1). See also McNulty (2012) on symbolic use of development evaluation.

5. There is an extensive literature on evaluability analysis (see, e.g., Wholey, 1979). The discussion in this chapter emphasizes some (but not all) of the elements that are often associated with this process.

# PART II

Dealing With Complexity in Development Evaluation: Methodological Approaches

# CHAPTER 4

# Impact Evaluation Approaches and Complexity

Jos Vaessen, Estelle Raimondo, and Michael Bamberger

> *In Chapter 1 we introduced the book's conceptual framework for complexity. One of the key dimensions of the framework concerns the nature of causal change. In (development) evaluation, the field of evaluation approaches that specifically deals with causal change is impact evaluation. Impact evaluation looks at the changes in society and the extent to which they are attributable to an intervention, also taking into account other factors. In practice, a number of questions relate to the broader question of impact. In turn, divergent methodological designs are available that are equipped to deal with one or more of these questions. This chapter presents the most prevalent impact evaluation approaches used in development evaluation practice. Subsequently, the strengths and limitations of these approaches are discussed in terms of how they address a number of key complexity issues. The discussion is illustrated with a case study.*

## 1. Key Questions Addressed in Development Impact Evaluations

One of the main purposes of impact evaluation[1] is to assess the extent to which changes in society that the program was designed to influence can be attributed to the program. Addressing this question requires a method of causal inference that seeks to connect causes with effects (outcomes, impacts). In recent years, there has been an extensive debate in international development on this issue (see Cohen & Easterly, 2009). While advocates of certain approaches, particularly randomized controlled trials (RCTs), continue to argue that a certain method or set of methods is the best (the "gold standard"), it is now generally acknowledged that there are a number of different approaches to assess causality. Donaldson, Christie, and Mark (2009), in *What Counts as Credible Evidence in Applied Research and Evaluation Practice?* present a range of approaches that are widely used and considered credible by different disciplines and audiences. Several authors argue that evaluators continue to be narrowly focused on the merits and/or limitations of experimental designs as the appropriate standard for evidence-based evaluation and related debates on quantitative versus qualitative approaches. As a consequence very little serious attention has been given to a wide range of potentially useful research approaches that are used in other branches of the social and physical sciences. Scriven (2009) presents a number of alternative ways to think about causality, while Greene (2009) argues that what some researchers consider as "proof" of causal relations should more modestly be considered as "inklings." Rieper, Leeuw, and Ling (2010) also argue that while there is broad acceptance of the general movement toward evidence-based policy, disciplines differ as to what is considered appropriate evidence. White and Phillips (2012) discuss a range of qualitative methods that are particularly pertinent in the case of evaluating the impact of small "$n$" interventions, that is, those with small target groups for which statistical analysis is not feasible (e.g., the impact of capacity development initiatives on the quality of policy formulation in educational planning units of ministries of education).

Stern et al. (2012, pp. 36–37) identify four impact-related questions of interest to policymakers:

- To what extent can a specific (net) impact be attributed to the intervention?
- Did the intervention make a difference?
- How has the intervention made a difference?
- Will the intervention work elsewhere?

Each of these questions usually requires a different evaluation design, and a design that works well to address one question may not be appropriate for a different question. It is important to ensure that the evaluation design is driven by the questions being asked (issues driven) and not by the researcher's preference for a particular methodology (methods driven). In addition to the evaluation questions guiding the evaluation design, the characteristics of the intervention are another important factor that should inform the design (Stern et al., 2012).

# 2. Established Evaluation Approaches in the Context of Impact Evaluation

## 2.1 Overview

There is an extensive literature available on different methods for impact evaluation in the context of international development (see, e.g., Gertler, Martinez, Premand, Rawlings, & Vermeersch, 2011; Khandker, Koolwal, & Samad, 2009; Leeuw & Vaessen, 2009; Stern et al., 2012). Table 4.1 provides an overview of the main approaches to impact evaluation based on a recent study commissioned by the

| Table 4.1 Main Approaches to Impact Evaluation | | |
|---|---|---|
| **Design approach** | **Specific variants** | **Basis for causal inference** |
| Experimental | RCTs, quasi-experiments, natural experiments | Counterfactuals, the copresence of cause and effects |
| Statistical | Statistical modeling, longitudinal studies, econometrics | Correlation between cause and effect or between variables, influence of (usually) isolatable multiple causes on a single effect, control for confounders |
| Theory-based | *Causal process designs*: Theory of change, process tracing, contribution analysis, impact pathways<br><br>*Causal mechanism designs*: Realist evaluation, congruence analysis | Identification/confirmation of causal processes or chains<br><br>Supporting factors and mechanisms at work in context |
| Case-based | *Interpretative:* Naturalistic, grounded theory, ethnography<br><br>*Structured*: Configuration, process tracing, congruence analysis, QCA, within-case analysis, simulations and network analysis | Comparison across and within cases of combinations of causal factors<br><br>Analytic generalization based on theory |
| Participatory | *Normative designs*: Participatory or democratic evaluation, empowerment evaluation<br><br>*Agency designs*: Learning by doing, policy dialogue, collaborative action research | Validation by participants that their actions and experienced effects are caused by the program<br><br>Adoption, customization and commitment to a goal |
| Review and synthesis | Meta-analysis, narrative synthesis, realist synthesis | Accumulation and aggregation within a number of perspectives (statistical, theory-based, ethnographic, etc.) |

SOURCE: Adapted from Stern et al. (2012).

Department for International Development. Needless to say, underlying each of these types of approaches is a multitude of specific data collection and analysis techniques such as surveys, focus groups, participant observation, and so on, which will not be discussed here (see, e.g., De Leeuw, Hox, & Dillman, 2008; Mikkelsen, 2005).

In the remainder of this section we discuss each of these approaches. For each category of approaches, we provide some examples of particular methods. For a more comprehensive discussion of these methods, see, for example, Stern et al. (2012) for an overview, Khandker et al. (2009) and Gertler et al. (2011) on quantitative impact evaluation approaches, Funnell and Rogers (2011) on theory-based evaluation approaches, Byrne and Ragin (2009) on case-based evaluation approaches, Cousins and Whitmore (1998) on participatory evaluation approaches, and Popay (2006) on review and synthesis approaches. Further references on prevalent methods under each of the approaches can be found in the discussion below.

Given the pivotal role of theory-based evaluation in the context of complexity-responsive evaluation, this book includes two chapters on the topic (Chapters 5 and 6). In addition, Chapter 9 is devoted to different approaches to review and synthesis. Consequently, the discussion on this topic in this chapter will be limited, referring the reader to Chapter 9.

## 2.2 Experimental, Quasi-experimental, and Non-experimental Quantitative Approaches

In this section we discuss quantitative impact evaluation approaches (rows 1 and 2 in Table 4.1). Experimental and quasi-experimental approaches are based on the principle of counterfactual analysis. In various ways they try compare what has happened during the intervention with what would have happened without the intervention. Non-experimental approaches try to capture the effect of an intervention with the help of statistical controls. For example, with the help of multiple regression analysis one can estimate the effect of an intervention variable (which can be dichotomous or continuous) on a dependent variable controlling for all other relevant variables in the regression equation (statistical controls). Because many quasi-experimental techniques also use statistical modeling, we do not discuss non-experimental quantitative approaches separately.

### a. Experimental Approaches

For the purpose of defining the evaluation design, the basic causal question can be reformulated as "What would have happened without the intervention?" The conventional way to address this question is to compare the observed world with a theoretical world where the program intervention did not occur. This process is sometimes called a *thought experiment* as it is not possible to observe this theoretical world directly. The established evaluation approach is defining the counterfactual through an *experimental* or *quasi-experimental* design. The experimental approach randomly assigns subjects to the treatment and control groups. If the experiment is well designed, this eliminates (controls for) all factors other than the experimental treatment, and if a statistically significant difference is found between the two groups after the treatment has been administered, this provides initial evidence that the program treatment has contributed to the observed effects. Ideally, the experiment should be repeated several times to determine if the results are robust when replicated in a similar setting or under different conditions. However, in the real world, due to budget and time pressures, decisions about program effectiveness are often based on a single test.

The two most common variations of randomized evaluation designs are (1) the "intention to treat," which compares outcomes for all subjects in the treatment group, some of whom may not participate in the program, with those assigned to the control group; and (2) "treatment on the treated," which compares subjects who actually received the treatment with those who did not (Khandker et al., 2009).

The design is generally considered to be the strongest quantitative evaluation design with respect to attribution in situations to which it can be applied. As Woolcock (2013) points out, development programs with low causal density (few causal pathways) are well suited to RCTs. In this type of intervention, one can expect that the impact can be isolated and studied in conjunction with experimentation on slight variations of the intervention (e.g., different grant sizes for small and medium enterprise investment). For this type of intervention, repeated RCTs can bring us closer to a proof of concept. When the design is properly implemented and the sample is sufficiently large, statistically robust and unbiased estimates of the magnitude of outcomes that can be attributed to the intervention are obtained. The achievement of unbiased estimates is the major benefit of this design as almost every other design is subject to potential selection bias, which affects the validity of the attribution analysis. The rapidly growing body of RCTs means that precise evaluation design protocols now exist for many sectors. It is also possible for most sectors to conduct systematic reviews (see Chapter 9) of significant numbers of studies that have been conducted. The growing interest in RCTs has also challenged evaluators using other designs to assess the potential methodological weaknesses of their approaches and to pay greater attention to evaluation design and threats to validity (see Cook & Campbell, 1979).

RCTs also have a number of general limitations (see, e.g., Cook & Campbell, 1979; Bamberger & White, 2007). First of all, the counterfactual answers only *setting-specific questions* (e.g., Did it work here, for this particular group?) and cannot generalize to other settings (low external validity). Second, the design analyzes only linkages between intervention outputs (causes) and outcomes (effects) and does not examine processes (what happens between intervention outputs and outcomes). It does not explain how the outcomes are achieved or how and why the assumed causes contributed to the outcomes. Third, there are serious constraints to applicability. RCTs work better for certain kinds of interventions and in some kinds of project settings than for others. There are also many constraints on when randomization can be applied. Fourth, the interpretation of findings is complicated by *early preemption* (things that happened before the effects) and *late preemption* (things that happened after the effects). Finally, it is important to note that experimental designs conducted under field conditions are much less methodologically rigorous than laboratory experiments.[2]

## b. Quasi-experimental Approaches

Quasi-experimental designs (QEDs) are used when randomization is not possible but when a comparison group can be identified. Sample selection takes place either after subjects have made the decision whether to participate in the program or when an administrative agency has made the decision to provide services to certain subjects or communities and not to others. In either case there is the possibility of systematic differences between the two groups (selection bias), which may significantly affect program outcomes. QEDs match the two groups as closely as possible, using either statistical matching techniques such as propensity score matching or judgmental matching with the comparison group selected using the advice of experts, community leaders, or similar groups and using whatever kinds of secondary data are available.

In strong QEDs the treatment and comparison groups are statistically matched (e.g., through propensity score matching). These designs are statistically weaker than RCTs as there is likely to be a selection bias due either to self-selection or to the selection procedures adopted by the implementing agency. There are a wide range of QEDs that vary in terms of their statistical strength and consequently in the adequacy of the counterfactual for causal attribution (analysis). Examples are regression discontinuity, propensity score matching, difference-in-difference regression, pipeline design, and judgmental matching. In general, quasi-experimental approaches can be characterized by two features: the modality of defining the group comparisons and the number of data points over time. Regarding the latter, the higher the number of data points in time (e.g., annual measurements of household savings and expenditures), the higher the likelihood that one can capture effects over time.

A QED has the advantage that it is more flexible to adapt to the program design as the project and comparison groups are normally chosen after project participants have been selected. This means the evaluation design does not impose constraints on how participants are selected in the way that an RCT does, making the design more acceptable to program managers. The design also has more flexibility to adjust to changes in program design. This is an important practical advantage because the strict program design requirements for using RCTs means that they can probably be applied in perhaps only 1%–2% of projects; the greater flexibility of QEDs means that they can be applied in many more program evaluations (see Bamberger & White, 2007). Quasi-experimental and non-experimental statistical approaches are also useful for looking at larger and more complex interventions (e.g., budget support, sector budget support).[3]

Designs such as the pipeline design are particularly useful for evaluating interventions that are designed to cover the whole target population, meaning there is no comparison group. These designs can be applied in creative ways to take advantage, for example, of planned phased implementation of programs with national coverage or of programs that encounter unanticipated delays in some areas. In both cases the regions or areas where there are planned or unanticipated delays can be used as the comparison groups.

Most of the limitations of RCTs also apply to QEDs. In addition, the issue of selection bias is a major challenge as changes that are assumed to be due to the program intervention may in fact be partially or mainly due to special attributes of the project group.

## 2.3 Theory-Based Approaches

Theory-based evaluation is discussed extensively in Chapters 5 and 6. The core of theory-based evaluation is the so-called intervention theory, or theory of change, a set of causal assumptions that explain how an intervention works (or is intended to work) and contributes to processes of change in society. These causal assumptions have to be made explicit, refined, and tested using a variety of methods and sources of information. The main approaches and principles of theory-based evaluation explained in Chapters 5 and 6 also apply to impact evaluation. Here, we focus explicitly on theory-based evaluation in relation to the evaluation of impact.

Broadly, one can discern two different approaches to theory-based impact evaluation:

- *The intervention theory (or theory of change) as the overarching framework of the evaluation.* Typically, evaluators reconstruct the intervention theory (or even multiple rival theories). Subsequently, the theory is empirically tested, matching the appropriate methods to particular assumptions of the theory. Theory-based evaluation is not method-specific; any appropriate method (and ideally multiple methods) may be applied to test a particular assumption. For example, assumptions regarding the outreach and accessibility of mobile sexual and reproductive health clinic programs can be studied using information on routes, communities visited, registry data of patients, and visits to (a purposive/random sample of) communities to interview patient and non-patient households. The effect of health services on health indicators could, for example, be studied in a more tightly controlled experimental (RCT) setting.
- *The intervention theory (or theory of change) as a tool for refining and testing the causal logic underlying an intervention eventually resulting in a causal impact narrative.* Realist evaluation fits into this category (e.g., Pawson & Tilley, 1997). Contribution analysis (Mayne, 2001) is another example. The main difference with the previous approach is that the refinement of the theory is the focus of the evaluation and also often the output of the evaluation (a refined theory). The emphasis is on explanation through an iterative process of revising the theory and collecting new empirical evidence. Another variant is process tracing (see below). Here, the emphasis is on systematically assessing each causal step in the theory using four tests. Finally, qualitative comparative analysis (QCA; which is discussed later as a separate approach to impact evaluation) is about identifying causal packages, sets of independent and dependent variables, which recur across settings. Understanding that processes of change are about the confluence of a number of factors (including the intervention) influencing a number of causal pathways is at the heart of this method. QCA can help to identify theories around these patterns of association.

To elaborate on the first bullet point above, as argued by Cook (2000), the choice between quantitative counterfactual analysis and theory-based evaluation is a clearly false one as the two complement each other in many ways:

- The intervention theory will help indicate which of the intervention components are amenable to quantitative counterfactual analysis through, for example, (quasi)experimental evaluation and how this part of the analysis relates to other elements of the theory.
- The intervention theory approach will help identify key determinants of impact variables to be taken into account in a quantitative impact evaluation.
- The intervention theory approach can provide a basis for analyzing how an intervention affects particular individuals or groups in different ways. Although quantitative impact evaluation methods typically result in quantitative measures of average net effects of an intervention, an intervention theory can help to support the analysis of distribution of costs and benefits.
- The intervention theory can help strengthen the interpretation of findings generated by quantitative impact evaluation techniques.

## 2.4 Case-Based Approaches

Our discussion of case-based approaches is purposely limited to two relatively novel approaches. The reason for this is threefold. First, the number and diversity of methods under this approach is high. It would take up a lot of space to adequately capture this diversity. Second, most approaches are well described in the literature (see, e.g., Byrne & Ragin, 2009). Finally, we have noted that there has been increased interest in the evaluation community to apply approaches that we discuss below: process tracing and qualitative comparative analysis.

### a. Process Tracing

Process tracing (PT) is a method of inquiry premised on the idea that a theory can be tested based on the evidence in a case against new factors or new evidence in the same case. This method shares some similarities with detective work and relies heavily on Bayesian logic, particularly with regard to the requirement of constantly updating prior knowledge based on new evidence. It is also closely related to theory-based evaluation and in fact can be considered an application of it (see Chapters 5 and 6). In PT causal inference about the relations between an intervention and an outcome is thought to be mediated by a causal mechanism with several components, each of which is a necessary part of a complete causal mechanism that in itself may be sufficient for the effect to occur but might not be necessary (since the effect might be reached through other causal mechanisms).

PT is essentially about analyzing trajectories of change and causation. It relies on careful description as well as examination of diagnostic evidence of a causal mechanism. In practical terms, an evaluator using PT describes and articulates with great detail the causal chain mediating the relationships between the intervention and the outcome. In PT, the quality of the causal inference depends on how fine-grained the descriptions of the micro-mechanisms joined in the causal chain are (Befani, 2012).

The basic logic underlying process tracing is that tracing the processes that may have led to an outcome helps narrow the list of potential causes. By doing so, it seeks to eliminate a large number of alternative explanations for an effect, more than most other methods that eliminate single causes one by one. Rather than operating with single variables, process tracing methods eliminate rival causal chains (George & Bennett, 2005). PT enables evaluators to assess transparently and in a systematic manner the confidence that can be placed in the causal mechanism underlying the theory of change of an intervention. In particular, its application enables evaluators to confirm or disconfirm a hypothesis about why an intervention does or does not work in a particular context (based on Bennett & Elman, 2006; Collier, 2011).

To test causal relationships, PT relies on four empirical tests to determine whether a particular condition is necessary and/or sufficient to affirm causal inference. Table 4.2 reproduces Collier's (2011) presentation of the four tests. These tests share the objective of progressively eliminating rival hypotheses, but they differ in their capacity to do so. Further discussion of different variants of process tracing can be found in Beach and Pedersen (2013).

**Table 4.2** Four Tests Used in Process Tracing to Assess Causal Inference

| | | Sufficient for Affirming Causal Inference | |
|---|---|---|---|
| | | No | Yes |
| **Necessary for Affirming Causal Inference** | No | 1. Straw in the Wind | 3. Smoking Gun |
| | | a. Passing: Affirms relevance of the hypothesis, but does not confirm it | a. Passing: Confirms hypothesis |
| | | b. Failing: Hypothesis is not eliminated, but is slightly weakened | b. Failing: Hypothesis is not eliminated but is somewhat weakened |
| | | c. Implications for rival hypotheses: Passing: *slightly* weakens them Failing: *slightly* strengthens them | c. Implications for rival hypotheses: Passing: *substantially* weakens them Failing: *somewhat* strengthens them |
| | Yes | 2. Hoop | 3. Doubly Decisive |
| | | a. Passing: Affirms relevance of hypothesis but does not confirm it | a. Passing: Confirms hypothesis and eliminates others |
| | | b. Failing: Eliminates hypothesis | b. Failing: Eliminates hypothesis |
| | | c. Implications for rival hypotheses: Passing: *somewhat* weakens them Failing: *somewhat* strengthens them | c. Implications for rival hypotheses: Passing: eliminates them Failing: *substantially* strengthens them |

SOURCE: Adapted from Collier (2011, p. 825).

## b. Qualitative Comparative Analysis

Qualitative comparative analysis (QCA) refers to a family of methods that seeks to identify causal packages. It focuses on a limited number of empirical cases, for which configurations of effects (outcomes, impacts) and conditions for effects are captured in a *truth table*. In this table, each configuration of conditions or factors is represented by a series of zeros and ones that translates into the absence or presence of a given condition.

QCA sees cases as complex systems and does not attempt to decompose the causal configurations into variables with equal causal power (Byrne & Ragin, 2009). To start with, QCA is an approach that considers cases in their entirety rather than simply harvesting variables across a large number of cases, as is done in variable-based approaches. It also takes for granted that it is a combination of causal conditions that eventually generates an outcome, not simply one particular cause. In development processes, there are a number of *ground-preparing causes* that are necessary elements of development success, but are not sufficient by themselves (Befani, 2013). For example, three conditions without a fourth may not lead to any meaningful change, but the presence of the four factors together might allow a program to go from poor performance to excellent results, in a nonlinear causal pattern (Befani, 2012). QCA is also grounded in an embedded contextual view of reality: Depending on the context, a given set of conditions may very well lead to different outcomes. Finally, QCA relies on the idea that multiple causal chains coexist and lead to the same effects (equifinality) and considers as relevant all the potential causal paths that can lead to a given outcome. The result of QCA is the identification of a number of causal paths that are sufficient to produce a given outcome.

As a family, QCA encompasses three main types of techniques, each relying on a different set-theory. Crisp-set QCA (csQCA) applies Boolean logic to the various conditions by dichotomizing each condition into absence or presence (0 or 1). Multi-value QCA (mvQCA) allows for multiple category conditions. Finally, fuzzy-set QCA (fsQCA) enables the researcher to assign a degree of membership to each condition rather than a dichotomized membership (Ragin, 2000). Box 4.1 illustrates a simple application of QCA to the assessment of the effectiveness of an irrigation assistance project in Nepal (Lam & Ostrom, 2010).

---

### BOX 4.1 APPLICATION OF QCA

Lam and Ostrom (2010) evaluated the impact of an innovative irrigation assistance project that was undertaken in 19 irrigation systems in Nepal starting around 1985. This project had various innovative components, including provision of technical and financial assistance, partial funding for physical infrastructure, extensive involvement of farmers in the decision-making process, and farmer-to-farmer training. For the evaluation, data were collected in three time periods (at the start of the program in 1985, in 1991, and in 1999). The availability of structured information over time allowed the evaluators to look at how the irrigation effectiveness

*(Continued)*

(Continued)

had changed over the years using statistical analysis. This analysis revealed fluctuating patterns across systems and time periods. The authors identified three main sources of complexity that needed to be addressed: (1) the effect of a particular factor is contingent and combinatorial (it is the articulation of several factors that produce the outcome), (2) the effects are not linear, and (3) the complex dynamics of institutional change needed to be captured.

The authors therefore used QCA to identify a set of causal conditions, amid the diversity of experiences, conducive to sustained intervention effects. Through an in-depth literature review and interviews with the farmers, they identified five key conditions (continual assistance on infrastructure improvement, existence of formal rules for irrigation operation, provisions of fines, consistent leadership, and collective action among farmers for system maintenance) that could explain why high performance was sustained in some systems but not in others. All conditions were dichotomized as being either present or absent from the system. One of the outcome variables was the availability of water during the winter. The truth table below summarizes the 11 unique configurations of factors for the 15 systems for which water supply measurements were available.

| Five causal conditions | | | | | Number of systems | |
|---|---|---|---|---|---|---|
| Assistance (A) | Rules (R) | Fines (F) | Leadership (L) | Collective action (C) | Sustained performance | Not sustained performance |
| Absent | Present | Absent | Present | Present | 1 | 1 |
| Absent | Present | Present | Present | Present | 2 | 0 |
| Present | Present | Absent | Present | Present | 2 | 0 |
| Present | Present | Present | Present | Present | 2 | 0 |
| Absent | Absent | Absent | Absent | Present | 1 | 0 |
| Absent | Present | Absent | Absent | Present | 1 | 0 |
| Absent | Absent | Present | Present | Present | 0 | 1 |
| Present | Absent | Absent | Absent | Absent | 0 | 1 |
| Present | Present | Present | Absent | Absent | 1 | 0 |
| Present | Present | Absent | Absent | Present | 1 | 0 |
| Present | Present | Present | Absent | Present | 1 | 0 |

The fsQCA software was used to operate the Boolean minimization and come up with a parsimonious solution that related the sustained performance of irrigation as measured by the availability of water in winter and the various causal conditions. By going back and forth between the cases and the truth table, the authors identified the following equation: W = AR (+IF) + CLRF + Calf.[4]

Three groups of explanatory configurations emerged. Here we present only one of them. The first configuration showed that ongoing infrastructure investment can enable sustained performance only if farmers have developed rules (AR go together). These combined factors are a necessary but not sufficient part of success. They should be present in a context where either collective action takes place or fines are imposed in a context of weak leadership.

SOURCE: Adapted from Lam & Ostrom (2010).

## 2.5 Participatory Approaches

Participatory evaluation designs involve a wide range of stakeholders in the design, implementation, interpretation, and use of the evaluation. Participatory approaches may be used for methodological reasons, to strengthen data quality and validity, or for ideological reasons (Cousins & Whitmore, 1998). Participatory approaches are often used in many mixed methods designs to triangulate among different sources of data to increase reliability and validity of the data. In contrast, the ideological dimension of participatory approaches is central to empowerment, feminist, or equity-oriented evaluation as part of a process of political and social empowerment.

A potential downside is the risk that participatory processes may be monopolized by politically or socially more powerful groups. With the increasing use of mobile phones and other new information technology, there is also the risk of selection bias as people who have access to mobiles and other devices are likely to be the wealthier and better educated groups. There may also be a gender bias as, in some contexts, women may have less access to mobile phones or more generally are not in a position to speak freely.

There are many participatory approaches to evaluation (see Kumar, 2002). Examples of participatory techniques in the context of impact evaluation include the following:

- *Outcome mapping:* This focuses on outcomes as behavioral change (Earl, Carden, & Smutylo, 2001). It recognizes that external partners do not directly produce outcomes, but rather they work with boundary partners (local agencies) that directly produce the changes. As most programs involve multiple boundary partners, each with its own interests and priorities, programs are likely to produce a wide range of outcomes, not all of which were planned or even necessarily desired by the external agencies. Outcome mapping involves three stages: intentional design (designing the program in a participatory way in collaboration with boundary partners), outcome and performance monitoring, and evaluation planning.

- *Outcome harvesting:* This approach, which builds on outcome mapping, "enables evaluators, grant makers and managers to identify, formulate, verify and make sense of outcomes" (Wilson-Grau & Britt, 2012, p. 1). Information is gleaned from reports, personal interviews, and other sources to document how a given program has contributed to outcomes. Outcomes can be positive or negative, intended or unintended, but the connection to the intervention must be verifiable. Wilson-Grau and Britt (2012, Box 1) draw the analogy with forensic science as a wide range of techniques is used to "sleuth the answers" by generating evidence-based answers to the following questions:

  - What happened?
  - Who did it (or contributed to it)?
  - How do we know this? Is there corroborating evidence?
  - Why is this important? What do we do with what we found out?

- *Most significant change:* "The process involves the collection of significant change (SC) stories emanating from the field level, and the systematic selection of the most significant of these stories by panels of designated stakeholders or staff. The designated staff and stakeholders are initially involved by 'searching' for project impact. Once changes have been captured, various people sit down together, read the stories aloud and have regular and often in-depth discussions about the value of these reported changes. When the technique is implemented successfully, whole teams of people begin to focus their attention on program impact" (Davies & Dart, 2005, p. 8).

## 2.6 Review and Synthesis Approaches

Review and synthesis approaches involve the practice of identifying and selecting existing evaluation studies, reviewing and extracting information, and aggregating and synthesizing information into an overall perspective on what works (for whom and under what circumstances). Over the last decade, with the increasing availability of impact evaluation studies, there has been a marked increase in the application of review and synthesis studies in the context of international development cooperation. Chapter 9 discusses some of the prevalent approaches in review and synthesis, while Chapters 16 and 20 present examples on microcredit interventions and community accountability and empowerment initiatives, respectively.

# 3. Strengths and Limitations of Established Impact Evaluation Approaches in the Context of Complexity

In this section we discuss some of the comparative advantages and limitations of different methodological approaches in terms of addressing complexity. A few qualifying remarks are in order:

- In Chapter 1 we distinguished between a general complexity and restricted complexity perspective. Our discussion of complexity in relation to established impact evaluation approaches is mainly framed within the latter.
- Below we distinguish between several aspects of complexity in the light of causal change. While we try to discuss these aspects separately for each of the six impact evaluation approaches, it should be noted that in reality they are closely related. For example, the occurrence of multiple causal pathways, multiple (un)intended effects, emergence, and other aspects of the nature of causal change (e.g., uncertainty) are all closely linked to each other.

The core of the impact evaluation debate in the context of complexity revolves around the discussion of the nature of causal change and how it relates to development interventions, one of the dimensions of the book's conceptual framework.

In order to assess the strengths and limitations of the impact evaluation approaches discussed in this chapter with respect to this dimension, we focus on the following issues:

- *Attribution:* This refers to the extent to which a particular change can be attributed to an intervention, taking into account other variables. Here are a couple of important impact evaluation questions: Has the intervention led to change? To what extent has it made a difference?
- *Explanation:* Development interventions aim to change the behavior of individuals and organizations. At the same time, the likelihood and nature of change is dependent on the behavior of a multitude of actors affected by underlying contextual conditions. Here are a couple of important impact evaluation questions: How do interventions work? How are they affecting the behavior of different actors?
- *Multiple causal pathways:* An intervention (especially if the intervention encompasses multiple activities at different levels) can trigger multiple causal pathways of change. This idea is more in line with the concept of contribution, that is, a confluence of factors affecting a particular change or multiple changes. In the latter case one can speak of causal packages.
- *Nature of causal change:* Causal change is often path dependent yet at the same time can be highly uncertain, nonlinear (abrupt, gradual, or both, over time), and emergent (see below).
- *Emergence:* The principle of emergence is also an element of the nature of causal change yet deserves particular attention. A development intervention has only imperfect control over the possible achievement of its objectives, especially because the program changes the conditions that made the program work in the first place. Consequently, the most successful programs and organizations are those that adapt to this emergent change. Emergence is also closely linked to the concepts of uncertainty and dynamics in both implementation (interventions change over time, they are not stable) and changes in society.
- *Scope of effects:* Interventions may affect multiple processes of change at different levels, resulting in a number of intended and unintended outcomes. The extent to which the evaluation is able to capture all effects is important here.

Our succinct discussion of how the main impact evaluation approaches deal with complex causal change is presented in Table 4.3.

It is very clear that the different methodological approaches have comparative advantages in dealing with particular aspects of causal change. In practice it is therefore important to adopt a mixed methods approach. Chapter 8 explains the different principles and variations of mixed methods evaluation within the framework of complexity. In Box 4.2 we illustrate various aspects of complexity in causal change in relation to method choice using an example of an evaluation on the topic of payments for environmental services in Latin America.

**Table 4.3**    Strengths and Weaknesses of Established Impact Evaluation Methods With Regard to Complexity in Causal Change

| Methodological approach | How is causal change addressed? |
|---|---|
| Experimental | *Attribution:* Very strong on determining the effect of an intervention on a limited number of effect (outcome and impact) variables. In Chapter 7 we discuss the principle of unpacking complex interventions into evaluable parts. Within this framework experimental and quasi-experimental designs can be compatible with complexity-responsive evaluation.[5] |
| | *Explanation:* RCTs are not designed to explain why certain changes occur as they control for (but do not measure or theorize on) all other observable and non-observable characteristics that may influence the causal change process. In quasi-experimental designs, to the extent that confounding factors are measured and included in the (regression) model, some aspects of causal exchange may be explained. Due to the variable-based approach there are also serious challenges in terms of construct validity. |
| | *Multiple causal pathways:* Limited options for dealing with multiple causal pathways, for example, through randomized experiments incorporating multiple treatments. |
| | *Nature of causal change:* The important factor here is the number of data points, the availability of data over time. Posttest-only or pretest-posttest designs are inherently limited in terms of dealing with nonlinearity. Multiple data points (longitudinal designs) can show the patterns of change (a limited number of variables) over time. |
| | *Emergence:* Effect (outcome and impact) variables remain constant over time. Moreover, posttest-only or pretest-posttest designs are inherently limited in terms of dealing with dynamics over time. In case there are changes in the intervention over time and/or how the intervention influences change processes, this cannot be captured by quantitative methods for two reasons. First, quantitative methods are not designed to detect such changes. Second, the definition and selection of variables for which data are collected over time are determined before the first data point (e.g., ex ante baseline survey) and remains constant over time. |
| | *Scope of effects (unintended effects):* Focus on a limited number of effect variables. Very reductionist in focus. No attention to unintended effects. |
| Statistical | *Attribution:* Strong on determining the effect of an intervention on a limited number of effect (outcome and impact) variables. |
| | *Explanation:* In multivariate designs, to the extent that confounding factors are measured and included in the (regression) model, some aspects of causal change may be explained. Due to the variable-based approach there are also serious challenges in terms of construct validity. |
| | *Multiple causal pathways:* Limited options for dealing with multiple causal pathways. |

| Methodological approach | How is causal change addressed? |
|---|---|
|  | *Nature of causal change:* See *experimental*. Longitudinal designs can deal with nonlinearity to some extent. |
|  | *Emergence:* See *experimental*. |
|  | *Scope of effects (unintended effects):* Focus on a limited number of effect variables and the relationships with a number of independent and confounding variables. Reductionist in focus. No attention to unintended effects. |
| Theory-based | *Attribution:* Strong on making explicit the causal assumptions that could explain how interventions are expected to lead to change. The quality of the theory is highly dependent on the resources and specific methods for the reconstruction and refinement of the assumptions. The quality of attribution analysis is highly dependent on the underlying methods for testing particular causal assumptions and the corresponding data (see Chapter 7 on unpacking). The potential for a good macro-perspective on causal change (i.e., explaining the different steps in causal change processes, theorizing on causal change) is high, but not necessarily with respect to specific causal linkages between intervention outputs and outcomes. |
|  | *Explanation:* See *attribution*. The strength lies in explaining causal change processes, but this is highly dependent on the quality of underlying data and methods for looking at particular causal assumptions. |
|  | *Multiple causal pathways:* Can clarify multiple causal pathways between different intervention components and different processes of change. The same disclaimer as above applies. |
|  | *Nature of causal change:* Theorizes on the nature of causal change (taking into account existing knowledge from multiple sources), which then may be used to guide data collection and analysis to empirically capture this. Data collection over time or access to long-term data is important. |
|  | *Emergence:* Theories of change should be periodically updated and revised to reflect changes in the dynamic and complex reality of a development intervention. To the extent that this is done, theory-based approaches can address emergence. If they are not periodically revised, it is likely that a discrepancy between the dynamic reality and the theory will arise, making the theory less and less useful as an abstraction of reality and a framework for complexity-responsive evaluation. |
|  | *Scope of effects (unintended effects):* Once a theory of change has been reconstructed, it can cause bias in terms of how evaluators view the intervention and its context. Such bias may draw attention away from the complexity of causal change in practice. For the same reasons, unintended effects may go undetected. Multiple theories of change and/or multiple iterations to adapt the theory on the basis of new data and insights are important. |

*(Continued)*

| **Table 4.3** (Continued) | |
|---|---|
| **Methodological approach** | **How is causal change addressed?** |
| Case-based | *Attribution:* Different principles for dealing with attribution are available in this set of approaches. Process tracing is potentially very strong on attribution. Rich description of complex causal change processes, part of many qualitative case-based methods, can also strengthen attribution claims in specific situations. Generalization of findings to the overall target population may be challenging. |
| | *Explanation:* Case-based methods should ideally be theory-driven and in this sense are closely aligned to theory-based evaluation (some case-based methods are often classified as part of the theory-based evaluation tradition). A general constraint in most case-based methods is the quality of the (initial) theory of causal change. A theory-based framework may be helpful in reconstructing realistic initial theories of change that guide further data collection and analysis. |
| | *Multiple causal pathways:* This is the core of QCA, the identification of multiple causal packages. Measurement issues and model specification are potentially important constraints. Other qualitative case-based methods are strong on identifying multiple causal pathways through in-depth analysis of the case and its embeddedness in the wider context. |
| | *Nature of causal change:* Qualitative case-based methods are strong on the in-depth analysis of the case and its embeddedness in the wider context. Data collection over time or access to long-term data is important. |
| | *Emergence:* Same as above. Process tracing and QCA are not particularly strong on this point. Using particular underlying methods and data (i.e., that provide evidence on respectively the causal assumptions and the variables for process tracing and QCA) that are sensitive to emergence to some extent can be helpful. |
| | *Scope of effects (unintended effects):* Some methods that rely heavily on rich description and in-depth context-specific data collection are more likely to capture the full range of potential effects of an intervention at a particular level (e.g., household, community). Often, this information cannot be generalized beyond the case. In multilevel, multisite interventions, depending on the unit of analysis (i.e., the case), this may be an important limitation. |
| Participatory | *Attribution:* Taking on board different stakeholder perspectives can significantly increase the evaluator's understanding of the nature, diversity, and extent of changes brought about by an intervention. Rich descriptive information may be helpful in understanding complex processes of change and attribution. Generalizability of the findings may be an important constraint. Biases such as groupthink, knowledge limitations, and cognitive bias need to be taken into consideration. |

| Methodological approach | How is causal change addressed? |
|---|---|
| | *Explanation:* Perspectives from different stakeholders can generate a unique multi-angle perspective of an intervention. |
| | *Multiple causal pathways:* Same as above. |
| | *Nature of causal change:* Same as above. Data collection over time or access to long-term data is important. |
| | *Emergence:* Participatory methods can be particularly strong on detecting emergence in terms of evolving patterns of implementation and change. This potential becomes stronger with higher degrees of participation and involvement of stakeholders in data collection and analysis over time. This is especially true for implementation but not necessarily for processes of change. These may occur at levels of analysis (e.g., regional employment effects, climate change, biodiversity, inequality) that may not be directly perceived by stakeholders. |
| | *Scope of effects (unintended effects):* Some changes induced by an intervention may affect (or be of importance to) only one particular stakeholder group. Involving a broad range of stakeholders enhances the likelihood of generating a comprehensive perspective on the effects of interventions. Effects at higher levels (the detection of which requires other data and methods) may go undetected by stakeholders. |
| Review and synthesis | *Attribution:* The extent to which effects can be attributed to an intervention, and the extent to which intervention change processes can be explained, is largely reliant on the type of review and synthesis approach (i.e., systematic review may be strong on the first; realist synthesis may be strong on the second) and the underlying evidence base. Systematic review (using meta-analysis) is very strong on attribution for a very limited set of effect (outcome and impact) variables. |
| | *Explanation:* Systematic review using meta-analysis is usually very weak on explanation. By contrast, realist synthesis focuses on how interventions work and affect the realities of different stakeholders. |
| | *Multiple causal pathways, nature of causal change, emergence, scope of effects:* By and large, for systematic review many of the same strengths and limitations of experimental and statistical approaches apply. By contrast, narrative reviews and realist syntheses are more similar to case-based approaches and their strengths and limitations. In general, the option of triangulating evidence from multiple studies enables the evaluator to strengthen the validity of claims on these criteria as well as attribution and explanation. |

NOTE: Methodological approaches are often implemented in combination. For example, theory-based evaluation constitutes the framework for many of the other approaches. In any case, all the assessments refer to the specific methodological approach, not taking into account that some of the shortcomings in practice are compensated for through complementarity of methods in mixed methods designs.

## BOX 4.2 ILLUSTRATING THE COMPLEXITY OF EVALUATING CAUSAL CHANGE: THE REGIONAL INTEGRATED SILVOPASTORAL APPROACHES TO ECOSYSTEM MANAGEMENT PROJECT

The Regional Integrated Silvopastoral Approaches to Ecosystem Management Project (RISEMP) was implemented in the period 2002–2008. It was a GEF-World Bank project, designed as an innovative pilot initiative, which would promote silvopastoral practices through technical assistance and payments for environmental services (generated by these practices). The project was implemented in three countries: Nicaragua, Costa Rica, and Colombia.

At the level of the three pilot sites, the project focused on three main areas of work: improvements of silvopastoral land use systems, improved management of farms, and restoration of rural landscapes. The funding model was innovative. Improvements in land use (LU) were expected to generate environmental services, particularly improved biodiversity (e.g., agrobiodiversity and regional biodiversity through improved connections of habitats and improved ecosystems between protected areas and the private farms in between protected areas [i.e., the corridor function]) and carbon sequestration (e.g., in the soil and the vegetation). Farmers were paid for the environmental services (biodiversity, carbon sequestration) generated by improvements in LU. Detailed studies analyzing the relationships between different LUs and environmental services resulted in indices that provided the basis for payments for environmental services to land users. Findings were recorded in academic and policy-oriented publications. The principle of payments for environmental services also closely related to the idea that eventually the beneficiaries of environmental services (e.g., tourists, the general public) would compensate the land users for generating them. This idea of market creation was not tested in this project (i.e., the project represented the beneficiaries of environmental services).

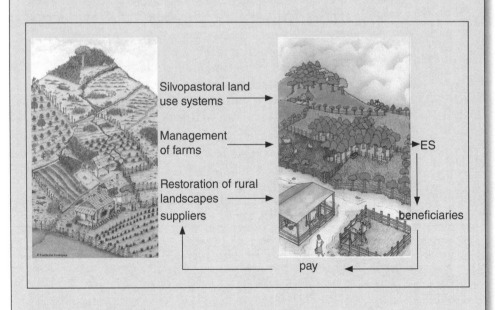

In 2009 the GEF Evaluation Office commissioned an assessment of the project's monitoring and evaluation framework and its potential for assessing the project's effects. One of the main reasons for this was that the project was based on a randomized experiment that was expected to generate rigorous evidence on the project's outcomes and impacts. More specifically, both payments for environmental services and technical assistance were randomly allocated to farmers. Through the principle of randomization and group comparison, it was expected that changes in LU (and subsequent changes in environmental services as well as economic effects) could be attributed to different project incentives, controlling for all other (observable and non-observable) factors (Vaessen & Van Hecken, 2009).

In light of the substantial external pressure on the GEF to build in randomized experiments in the design and monitoring and evaluation (M&E) frameworks of GEF projects, the assessment was intended to provide an objective view on the strengths and weaknesses of randomized experiments in the context of GEF projects. Below we discuss some elements of complexity with respect to the intervention and its context and how they could be addressed.

### Attribution

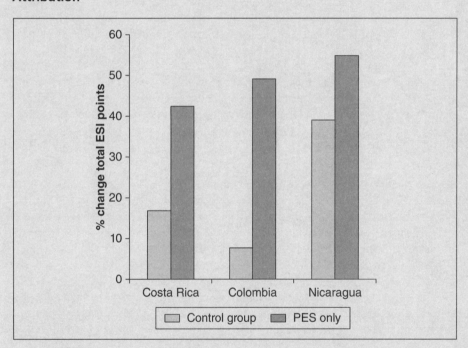

SOURCE: Vaessen & Van Hecken (2009).

NOTE: ESI refers to environmental services index, which captures the relationship between land use systems and environmental services generated.

The assessment of the project's randomization model and corresponding measurements of LU, environmental services, and other factors concluded that, to some extent, the project was able to generate rigorous evidence on the effects of different incentives (see Vaessen & Van Hecken, 2009, for a discussion on the threats to validity of findings

*(Continued)*

(Continued)

on attribution). The figure above shows the differences in changes in the environmental service index over time between (randomly determined) groups of farmers receiving payments for environmental services and control groups.

## Explanation

A base theory of change was developed (see next page) that makes explicit the relationships between project incentives and the conditions under which particular types of farmers were expected to change their LUs and eventually generate environmental and economic benefits. This theory was developed by the evaluators. Several surveys and semistructured interviews were undertaken which in principle would allow the evaluators to analyze the question: What types of farmers, and under what circumstances, will undertake particular LU changes?

## Multiple Causal Pathways

Through field observation and interviews with stakeholders at different levels, the evaluators identified three main levels at which the project was expected to contribute to change: farm, regional, international. The implicit theory of change of the project, which was made more explicit by the evaluators, was limited to effects at the farm/household level. There were no implicit (or explicit) theories of change for changes at the regional level or the international level. However, there were intended effects at the regional and international levels. In addition, the evaluators identified a number of unintended effects. These could not be captured through the project's M&E framework (see discussion below).

## Nature of Causal Change

The project's framework for data collection and analysis as well as its randomization model were well equipped to address direct effects (e.g., LU) and indirect effects (e.g., environmental services). However, in general environmental change is difficult to capture. The project's multiyear monitoring of LUs, the studies on ecosystems, and biodiversity was very detailed and able to unravel a lot of the complexity regarding the nonlinear relationships between, for example, LU and species abundance. However, the corridor biodiversity function of LU in agricultural landscapes in between protected (biodiversity-rich) areas was very difficult to capture. At what point and in what ways will biodiversity at the regional level benefit from improved ecosystems in farms? Given the nonlinear and emergent nature of these processes, the analysis would have required very long monitoring over time and detailed studies beyond the project area level.

## Emergence

Apart from the emergent nature of environmental effects (especially regarding biodiversity), there were a number of other aspects that can be characterized as emergent. For example, the relationships between changes in LU, increases in production levels of certain crops and livestock products, evolutions in prices (inputs and products), and availability of labor affect household incomes and potentially local and regional economic growth. These interactions are complex and difficult to capture (e.g., through system mapping and modeling). Another interesting aspect was that despite the rigid restrictions on implementation (for the randomized experiment to work, implementation should be homogeneous across farmers and over time), there were changes in implementation over time. For example,

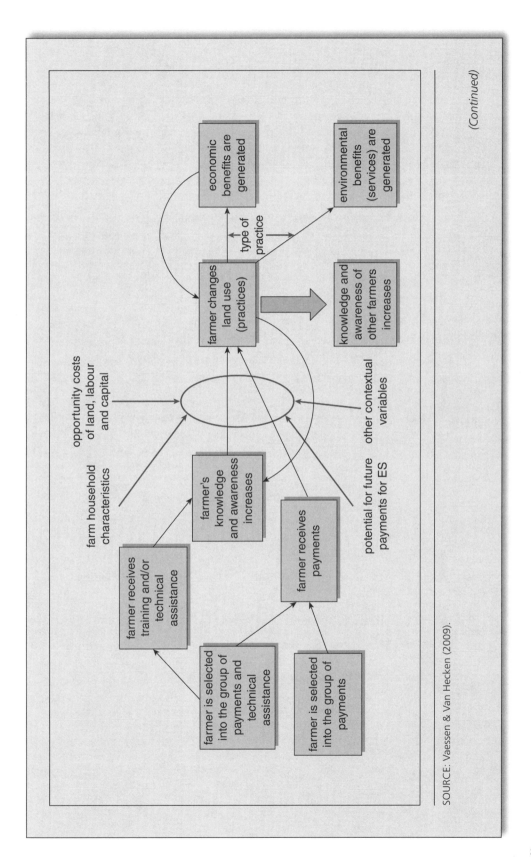

SOURCE: Vaessen & Van Hecken (2009).

(Continued)

there were differences (between countries but also within project areas) and changes over time in payment levels and in the modalities of technical assistance delivery (e.g., working through farmer groups vs. working with individual farmers). Apart from affecting the validity of the experimental findings, these changes also affected change processes in ways that were more difficult to trace and understand in comparison to homogenous implementation across farmers over time.

## Scope of Effects

The assessment exercise identified the (likely) existence of a number of unintended effects, yet there were no data or data collection exercises planned to evaluate these in more detail. The effects not covered by the project's M&E framework can be summarized by the following causal assumptions. Please note that for each assumption there were empirical indications that these effects were in fact occurring.

Farm/household-level effects:

1. IF farmers are selected for the control group or the group without technical assistance THEN they may still learn from other farmers and implement LU practices. (unintended)

2. IF farmers are selected for the control group THEN they may change LU practices based on expectations about future payments and/or motivated by competition. (unintended)

3. IF farmers from different treatment groups (e.g., technical assistance vs. control) change their LU practices THEN it is likely that there are differences in quality in application. (intended)

Regional effects and effects outside the project area:

4. IF LU practices are implemented THEN land prices may rise; IF land prices increase THEN farmers may sell their land. (unintended)

5. IF LU practices are profitable THEN employment opportunities for external labor may increase. (intended)

6. IF farmers own land outside the project region THEN environmentally destructive LU may be displaced. (unintended)

National and international effects

7. IF innovative knowledge about the relationship between LU and environmental services or other topics is generated and published THEN this may contribute to replication of (parts of) the project elsewhere. (intended)

8. IF project staff and GEF or World Bank staff disseminate knowledge about the project THEN this may contribute to replication of (parts of) the project elsewhere. (intended)

It should be noted that a much wider range of methods would have to be applied to look into these different assumptions about possible effects. For example:

- Assumption 3: field observation and interviews with farmers
- Assumption 5: surveys and system modeling
- Assumption 7: bibliometric analysis and interviews based on a purposive sample of (inter)national stakeholders

# 4. Practical Applications

- There are considerable limitations in using established quantitative impact evaluation approaches in the context of complexity-responsive evaluations. However, unpacking complexity is often possible and the effects of particular intervention activities may be addressed by these approaches (see Chapter 7). Other methods are needed to shed light on, for example, context-specific implementation and change processes embedded in different systems of norms, beliefs, and values as well as interactions between different intervention processes and different stakeholder groups.

- Impact evaluations usually rely on combinations of methodological approaches. Very often, a theory of change (or multiple theories of change) constitutes the basis for framing the evaluation design and the choice of methods to look at particular causal assumptions (see Chapter 8).

- Different impact evaluation approaches each have their comparative advantages in terms of helping to address particular aspects of complexity in causal change.

- Evaluators should be open to the possible occurrence of unintended effects. The nature of complexity (e.g., emergence, unintended effects) generally makes it more difficult to plan for data collection processes over time. Next to the measurement of key variables over time, there should be space for exploratory qualitative research at different points in time during an intervention.

- A lot of the methodological debates on complexity are about how and with which tools to look at the empirical reality surrounding development interventions. Insufficient attention is given to data collection over time. Increasing the number of data points in time improves the likelihood of detecting patterns of change in key variables that are influenced by an intervention.

# References

Bamberger, M., & White, H. (2007). Using strong evaluation designs in developing countries: Experience and challenges. *Journal of Multidisciplinary Evaluation, 4*(8), 58–73.

Beach, D., & Pedersen, R. (2013). *Process-tracing methods: Foundations and guidelines.* Ann Arbor: University of Michigan Press.

Befani, B. (2012). Models of causality and causal inference. In E. Stern, N. Stame, J. Mayne, K. Forss, R. Davies, & B. Befani (Eds.), *Broadening the range of designs and methods for impact evaluation* (Working Paper No. 38, pp. 103–126). London, UK: Department of International Development.

Befani, B. (2013). Between complexity and generalization: Addressing evaluation challenges with QCA. *Evaluation, 19,* 269–283.

Bennett, A., & Elman, C. (2006). Qualitative research: Recent developments in case study methods. *Annual Review of Political Science, 9,* 455–476.

Byrne, D., & Ragin, C. (Eds.). (2009). *Sage handbook of case-based methods.* Thousand Oaks, CA: Sage.

Cohen, J., & Easterly, W. (Eds.). (2009). *What works in development? Thinking big and thinking small.* Washington, DC: Brookings Institution Press.

Collier, D. (2011). Understanding process-tracing. *Political Science and Politics, 44,* 823–830.

Cook, T. D. (2000). The false choice between theory-based evaluation and experimentation. In P. J. Rogers, T. A. Hacsi, A. Petrosino, & T. A. Huebner (Eds.), *Program theory in evaluation: Challenges and opportunities* (pp. 27–34). San Francisco, CA: Jossey-Bass.

Cook, T. D., & Campbell, D. T. (1979). *Quasi-experimentation: Design and analysis for field settings.* Chicago, IL: Rand McNally.

Cousins, J. B., & Whitmore, E. (1998). Framing participatory evaluation. In E. Whitmore (Ed.), *Understanding and practicing participatory evaluation* (pp. 5–23). San Francisco, CA: Jossey-Bass.

Davies, R., & Dart, J. (2005). *The "most significant change" technique: A guide to its use.* Retrieved from http://www.mande.co.uk/docs/MSCGuide.htm

De Leeuw, E. D., Hox, J. J., & Dillman, D. A. (Eds.). (2008). *International handbook of survey methodology.* New York, NY: Lawrence Erlbaum.

Donaldson, S. I., Christie, C. A., & Mark, M. M. (Eds.). (2009). *What counts as credible evidence in applied research and evaluation practice?* Thousand Oaks, CA: Sage.

Earl, S., Carden, F., & Smutylo, T. (2001). *Outcome mapping: Building learning and reflection into development programs.* Ottawa, Ontario, Canada: International Development Research Center.

Elbers, C., Gunning, J. W., & De Hoop, K. (2008). Assessing sector-wide programs with statistical impact evaluation: A methodological proposal. *World Development, 37,* 513–520.

Funnell, S., & Rogers, P. (2011). *Purposeful program theory.* San Francisco, CA: Jossey-Bass.

George, A. L., & Bennett, A. (2005). *Case studies and theory development in the social sciences.* Cambridge, MA: MIT Press.

Gertler, P. J., Martinez, S., Premand, P., Rawlings, L. B., & Vermeersch, C. M. J. (2011). *Impact evaluation in practice.* Washington, DC: World Bank.

Greene, J. C. (2009). Evidence as "proof" and evidence as "inkling." In S. I. Donaldson, C. A. Christie, & M. M. Mark (Eds.), *What counts as credible evidence in applied research and evaluation practice?* (pp. 153–167). Thousand Oaks, CA: Sage.

Khandker, S. R., Koolwal, G. B., & Samad, H. (2009). *Handbook on quantitative methods of program evaluation.* Washington, DC: World Bank.

Kumar, S. (2002). *Methods for community participation: A complete guide for practitioners.* London, UK: ITDG.

Lam, W. F., & Ostrom, E. (2010). Analyzing the dynamic complexity of development interventions: Lessons from an irrigation experiment in Nepal. *Policy Science, 43,* 1–25.

Leeuw, F. L., & Vaessen, J. (2009). *Impact evaluations and Development: NONIE guidance on impact evaluation.* Washington, DC: Network of Networks on Impact Evaluation.

Mayne, J. (2001). Addressing attribution through contribution analysis: Using performance measures sensibly. *Canadian Journal of Program Evaluation, 16*(1), 1–24.

Mikkelsen, B. (2005). *Methods for development work and research.* Thousand Oaks, CA: Sage.

OECD-DAC. (2002). *Glossary of key terms in evaluation and results based management.* Paris, France: Author.

Pawson, R., & Tilley, N. (1997). *Realistic evaluation.* Thousand Oaks, CA: Sage.

Popay, J. (2006). *Moving beyond effectiveness: Methodological issues in the synthesis of diverse source of evidence.* London, UK: National Institute for Health and Clinical Excellence.

Ragin, C. (2000). *Fuzzy-set social science.* Chicago, IL: University of Chicago Press.

Rieper, O., Leeuw, F. L., & Ling, T. (2010). *The evidence book: Concepts, generation and use.* New Brunswick, NJ: Transaction.

Scriven, M. (2009). Demythologizing causation and evidence. In S. I. Donaldson, C. A. Christie, & M. M. Mark (Eds.), *What counts as credible evidence in applied research and evaluation practice?* (pp. 134–152). Thousand Oaks, CA: Sage.

Stern, E., Stame, N., Mayne, J., Forss, K., Davies, R., & Befani, B. (2012). *Broadening the range of designs and methods for impact evaluation* (Working Paper No. 38). London, UK: Department of International Development.

Vaessen, J., & Van Hecken, G. (2009). *Assessing the potential for experimental evaluation of intervention effects: The case of the Regional Integrated Silvopastoral Approaches to Ecosystem Management Project (RISEMP)* (Impact Evaluation Information Document No. 15). Washington, DC: GEF Evaluation Office.

White, H. (2010). A contribution to current debates in impact evaluation. *Evaluation, 16,* 153–164.

White, H., & Phillips, D. (2012). *Addressing attribution of cause and effect in small impact evaluations: Towards an integrated framework* (Working Paper 15). New Delhi, India: International Initiative for Impact Evaluation.

Wilson-Grau, R., & Britt, H. (2012). *Outcome harvesting.* Cairo, Egypt: Ford Foundation. Retrieved from http://usaidlearninglab.org/sites/default/files/resource/files/Outome%20 Harvesting%20Brief%20FINAL%202012-05-2-1.pdf

Woolcock, M. (2013). Using case studies to explore the external validity of "complex" development interventions. *Evaluation, 19,* 229–248.

# Notes

1. The OECD-DAC (2002) defines impacts as "positive and negative, primary and secondary long-term effects produced by a development intervention, directly or indirectly, intended or unintended" (p. 24). However, when we look at the body of research under the banner of impact evaluation, a substantial part of it is not on long-term results nor on indirect and unintended results. In fact, a lot of impact evaluation is about analyzing the attribution of short-term outcomes to a particular intervention. For a wider discussion on the different interpretations of impact evaluation and the term impact, see White (2010).

2. Different kinds of unintended behavioral effects may affect the experiment that have nothing to do with the intervention (see Vaessen & Van Hecken, 2009, for an example).

3. See, for example, Elbers, Gunning, and De Hoop (2008).

4. Note that in Boolean algebra capital letters signal the PRESENCE of a condition and noncapital letters signal the absence of a condition. Addition is equivalent to OR, and multiplication means conjunction of causal factors.

5. Quantitative counterfactual designs are compatible with a restricted complexity perspective (see Chapter 1 for a succinct discussion) but have been criticized by scholars whose ontology and epistemology is situated within the general complexity perspective.

# CHAPTER 5

# Understanding What Is Being Evaluated

## *Theory-Based Evaluation (TBE)*

Frans L. Leeuw[1]

> *Programs are theory incarnate.*
>
> Ray Pawson

> *Theory-based evaluations help to get at the why and how of program success or failure.*
>
> Carol H. Weiss

> *The theory we accept shapes our policy decisions.*
>
> Ethan Zuckerman

Theory-based evaluation (TBE) is widely used as the framework for the design and interpretation of evaluations of complex development programs. It has the flexibility to address the multiple dimensions of complexity and to overcome the limitations of most established evaluation designs for addressing complex causality and the processes of interaction between a complex program, the multiple stakeholders with which it interacts, and the system and context in which it is embedded. This chapter describes the tools and techniques of TBE and discusses how these can be used to deal with complexity in evaluation.

Section 1 defines the main characteristics of TBE and Section 2 describes seven approaches. Section 3 discusses the concept of complexification, the fact that programs are often assumed to be more complex than they really are. Section 4 discusses how TBE can contribute to the evaluation of complex development programs, and the final section identifies some of the pitfalls to be avoided when using TBE.

hapter 1 highlighted several characteristics of complexity in evaluation. One of the consequences of complexity is that evaluation models used to evaluate "simple" projects are usually not adequate to model the different dimensions of complexity. Consequently, the evaluation of complex programs tends to draw heavily on program theory (Box 5.1 lists examples of different TBE approaches used in other chapters). The complex nature of program designs and the processes through which outcomes may be achieved means that many evaluations spend more time developing and refining program theory than in the case of simple projects or activities. This chapter discusses particular dimensions of complexity that TBE can help elucidate.

Theory-based evaluations may have started with the work of the German-English sociologist Karl Mannheim, who in 1934 coined the concept of *principia media*, that is, time and space restricted assumptions about what makes planning effective (Mannheim, 1951). A different approach is found in the work of cognitive psychologists who during the 1950s and 1960s started to unpack "lay theories of behavior" (people using them were often called "lay psychologists"). Here the focus was on unpacking the beliefs and causes lay persons attribute to their own behavior and to that of others. The Popperian tradition of critical rationalism, which seeks to make theories more testable, also influenced the development of TBE. This idea can also be applied to assumptions underlying policies and programs. Finally, during the 1960s policy scientists and evaluators started to think in terms of models, theories, and assumptions underlying policies and programs.

Over the last 40 years a number of publications (e.g., Chen & Rossi, 1980; Donaldson, 2007; Funnel & Rogers, 2011; Leeuw, 1991; Pawson & Tilley, 1997; Suchman, 1967; Weiss, 1995) have contributed to the development of what can be called a theory-oriented evaluation tradition, mostly known by names such as *theory-based evaluation, theory-driven evaluation*, or *program theory evaluation*. We use the terms *theory-based evaluation* and *program theory evaluation* interchangeably.

---

### BOX 5.1 DISCUSSION OF TBE IN OTHER CHAPTERS

This chapter explains that there are many different approaches to TBE. We list here other chapters that illustrate some of these different applications.

Chapter 4    TBE is presented as one of the established impact evaluation approaches.

Chapter 7    TBE is presented as one of the approaches used in the unpacking strategy for evaluating complex interventions.

Chapter 15    A theory of change provides the framework for the evaluation of a 10-year program to combat gender-based violence in El Salvador.

Chapter 16    A realist evaluation approach is used as part of the systematic review of the impacts of microcredit on women's empowerment.

Chapter 20    A realist synthesis approach is used in the systematic review of accountability and community empowerment initiatives.

# 1. Defining Theory-Based Evaluation

TBE focuses on the assumptions (theories) of policymakers, program officers, and/or stakeholders about programs and interventions. It models the stages through which a project/program is implemented to achieve its objectives while also identifying the key assumptions on which the model is based and providing a framework for identifying key issues the evaluation should address.

When the focus is on the implementation processes, TBE looks into the assumptions underlying these processes (referred to as the *operational logic*). TBE can also help provide an alternative counterfactual when conventional comparison group designs cannot be used. When assessing public sector programs and interventions, TBE focuses on the "tools of government" like sticks (regulation, penalties), carrots (incentives), sermons (information diffusion through mass media and social media), and pillories (naming and shaming, reputation-oriented tools). TBE is closely related to the realist evaluation approach.

TBE is not a one-size-fits-all approach, and different routes can be followed. Some reconstruct the theory underlying a program being implemented; others focus on an ex-post assessment of the assumptions underlying a completed intervention that has already been evaluated but whose findings require further explanation. Sometimes the program theory is tested by using insights from knowledge repositories like 3ie's Evidence Library, Eppi's Evidence Library, or the Campbell Collaboration repository, and sometimes the program theory is confronted with an "anti-theory" (a rival hypothesis) that articulates why the opposite of what the policymakers expect may happen. TBE is widely used with mixed methods and with many qualitative as well as experimental and quasi-experimental designs.

## 1.1 Characteristics of TBE

TBE has several characteristics:

- It focuses on assumptions called the *program theory* that are defined with sufficient precision to be testable.
- Central elements of these theories are mechanisms and their links with context and outcomes. Mechanisms are the "cogs and wheels that have brought the relationship [between policies and outcomes] into existence" (Elster, 1989, p. 3; 2007, p. 36).
- TBE has two vital components. Conceptually, it explicates a program theory, and empirically, it investigates how programs cause intended or observed outcomes (Coryn, Noakes, Westine, & Schröter, 2010, p. 5).
- Testing the assumptions can be done on the basis of existing studies and/or new empirical (quantitative and qualitative) data.
- Program theory can be used to guide planning, design, and execution of the evaluation and as a platform for debate.
- Ideally, TBE also describes the context in which a program operates and if and how contextual factors can affect program operation.

TBE can describe interactions among multiple actors and across multiple components. It can also describe complex processes of behavioral change and the operation of the mechanisms through which the program or intervention is expected to produce its intended outcomes. It can also break down a multicomponent program into its constituent elements, making it easier to evaluate and to describe the linkages and interactions among the individual components.

## 1.2 An Example of TBE:
## A Comparative Evaluation of Social Funds

Social fund agencies channel resources to small projects ranging from infrastructure and social services to training and microenterprise development that have been identified by communities and other public and private groups and presented to the social fund for financing (Carvalho & White, 2004). Social funds most typically finance social infrastructure (schools and clinics), though the menu of projects can also include roads, bridges, water supply and sanitation, and credit schemes. The trend is toward requiring that (sub)project proposals be made by the beneficiary community, not by governments. Carvalho and White (2004) call that the *community-based model.*

One of the issues addressed in this chapter is "whose theory is studied and evaluated, as there may be competing views about how a program works":

> That is certainly the case for social funds. For example, some believe that the social funds' invitation of subproject proposals from community groups results in the selection of projects which mainly benefit the local elite (a phenomenon known as "elite capture"), or that rather than building government capacity in planning and implementing small-scale infrastructure projects, social funds might undermine such capacity by taking both resources and functions from government agencies. (Carvalho & White, 2004, p. 144)

Given this diversity of views, Carvalho and White identify both a theory derived from the writings of the supporters of social funds and an anti-theory based on the views of critics. Figure 5.1 shows the community-based model of social funds.

Carvalho and White (2004) focus on the issues of subproject sustainability and institutional development impact. They show the processes at work, especially at the community level, and test the assumptions underlying social fund subproject sustainability and institutional development impact.

# 2. Approaches to TBE

Theory-based evaluation is an approach in which attention is paid to theories (i.e., collections of assumptions and hypotheses that are empirically testable) of policymakers, program managers, or other stakeholders that are logically linked together. An essential element of these theories is the mechanisms that make the

**Figure 5.1** Theory of Social Funds: Community-Based Model

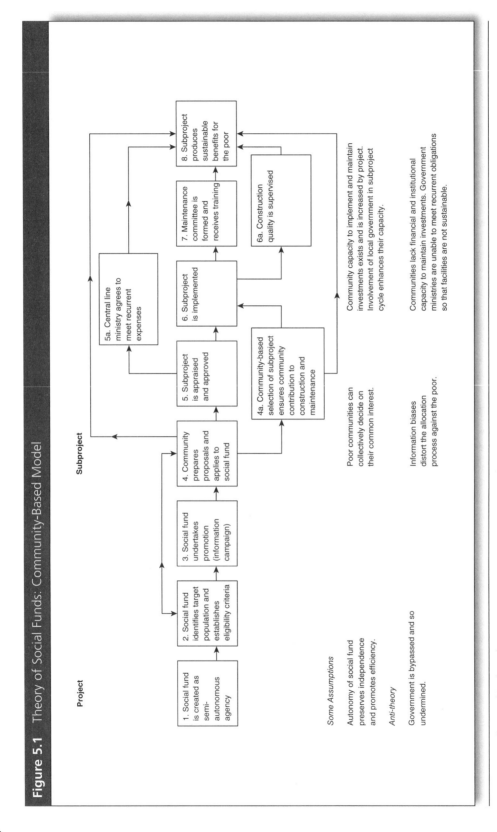

**Project**

**Subproject**

1. Social fund is created as semi-autonomous agency

2. Social fund identifies target population and establishes eligibility criteria

3. Social fund undertakes promotion (information campaign)

4. Community prepares proposals and applies to social fund

4a. Community-based selection of subproject ensures community contribution to construction and maintenance

5. Subproject is appraised and approved

5a. Central line ministry agrees to meet recurrent expenses

6. Subproject is implemented

6a. Construction quality is supervised

7. Maintenance committee is formed and receives training

8. Subproject produces sustainable benefits for the poor

*Some Assumptions*

Autonomy of social fund preserves independence and promotes efficiency.

*Anti-theory*

Government is bypassed and so undermined.

Poor communities can collectively decide on their common interest.

Information biases distort the allocation process against the poor.

Community capacity to implement and maintain investments exists and is increased by project. Involvement of local government in subproject cycle enhances their capacity.

Communities lack financial and institutional capacity to maintain investments. Government ministries are unable to meet recurrent obligations so that facilities are not sustainable.

SOURCE: Carvalho & White (2004).

interventions work. Mechanisms are not the input-output-results chain, the logic model, or statistical equations. They concern beliefs, desires, cognitions, and other decision-making processes that influence behavioral choices and actions, and they explore the mechanisms policymakers believe make the policy effective and compare these with research-based evidence.

Theories can be tested on the basis of existing or new data, both quantitative (experimental and non-experimental) and qualitative. TBE does not favor any particular research method, and the choice of methods depends on the evaluation design that is appropriate to answer the evaluation questions. Theories underlying a policy or program are often not directly visible or knowable to evaluators and are often not explicitly expressed in official documents. Evaluators have to search for these theories and reconstruct them in a testable way.

This chapter presents seven approaches on how to do this (see Box 5.2). The list is not exhaustive and is largely based on Leeuw (2003) and the chapter on theory-driven evaluations in the *Evalsed Sourcebook: Methods and Techniques* (regional and urban policies).[2]

---

### BOX 5.2 SEVEN APPROACHES TO TBE DISCUSSED IN THIS CHAPTER

1. Realist evaluation
2. Theory of change approach
3. Contribution analysis
4. Policy scientific approach
5. Strategic assessment approach
6. Elicitation approach
7. Behavioral economics

---

## 2.1 Realist Evaluation

The term *realist evaluation* was coined by Ray Pawson and Nick Tilley (1997). The approach stresses the importance of the context, mechanism, and outcomes configurations basic to policies and programs (see Chapters 16 and 20 for illustrations).

Making and sustaining different choices requires a change in stakeholders' reasoning (e.g., values, beliefs, attitudes, or the logic they apply to a particular situation) and the resources (e.g., information, skills, material resources, financial support) available to them. This combination of reasoning and resources is what enables the program to work and is known as a program *mechanism*. The program works in different ways for different people and can trigger different change mechanisms for different stakeholders.

The contexts in which the program operates make a difference to the results. Program contexts include features such as social, economic, and political structures;

organizational context; program stakeholders; program staffing; geographical and historical context; and so on. Some contextual factors may either enable or prevent particular mechanisms to be triggered. There is always an interaction between context and mechanism, and that interaction is what creates the program's results:

$$context + mechanism = outcome$$

Because programs often work differently in different contexts and through different change mechanisms, they cannot simply be replicated from one context to another and automatically achieve the same results. Knowledge about what works for whom, in what contexts, and how is, however, portable. Therefore, one of the tasks of evaluation is to learn about contexts in which particular programs do and do not work and what mechanisms are triggered by what programs in what contexts.

A realist approach assumes that programs are *theories incarnate*. Whenever a program is implemented, it is testing a theory about what might cause change, even though that theory may not be explicit. One of the tasks of a realist evaluation is to make the theories within a program explicit by searching for statements (assumptions, practice hypothesis) about how, and for whom, programs might work.

Pawson and Sridharan (2010) present the following methodological steps for a realist reconstruction and analysis of assumptions underlying policy programs. Although program theories sometimes are easily spotted, these theories are best elicited from their procreators and this may involve either

- reading and closely analyzing program documentation, guidance, regulations, and other factors related to how the program will achieve its ends and/or
- interviews with program architects, managers, or practitioners on how their intervention will generate the desired change.

Program theories normally flow quite readily from these interviews, though some related difficulties should be noted. The first, at the political level, is a tendency to ambiguity in policy discourse. The second, at the program practice level, occurs when the core theory is either seemingly so obvious or buried tacitly in the minds of the program makers that it can fail to surface in the interview. In these situations, persuasion is sometimes needed to encourage practitioners to spell out how their actions influence participants' choices (Pawson & Tilley, 1997). Pawson's (2013) VICTORE model (see Table 5.1) is useful, particularly when complex programs have to be evaluated.

Having found a means to elicit the program theories at work, the next step is to codify or map them. An array of techniques is available for this task, known variously as, for example, concept mapping, logic modelling, system mapping, problem and solution trees, scenario building, and configuration mapping. All try to articulate the process through which the program achieves its ends, usually in diagrammatic form. These maps may identify the various causes of the problem, the administrative steps to take, the unfolding sequence of program activities and inputs, the successive shifts in dispositions of participants, the progressive targeting of program recipients, and the sequence of intervention outputs and results.

| **Table 5.1** | Pawson's VICTORE Complexity Checklist |
|---|---|
| Volition | Most social interventions rely on participants' behavioral change to reach their expected outcomes. The agency of subjects is volatile and unpredictable, and the pathway of participants' choice is never uniform. "The choice architecture is multi-dimensional" (p. 35). |
| Implementation | Implementation inconsistency is also ubiquitous, especially when the intervention chain is lengthy (in terms of the number of personnel and institutional steps required for completion). What is delivered is composed of micro-processes embedded in other processes. |
| Context | Contextual layers are intertwined and in motion. The realist approach identifies four key elements of context that directly affect the intervention (the four i's): individuals, interpersonal relations, institutional setting, and infrastructure. |
| Time | Interventions' history and timing are additional sources of complexity. History also explains the conventional administrative arrangements and practices that an agency will seek to use in order to implement the new intervention. Often these may not be appropriate and will limit the ability to effectively implement the new intervention. This also helps predict and explain path dependency. |
| Outcome | Each link in the causal chain is essentially plural. Moreover, the interpretation of outcome is often contested, especially when compared across settings. |
| Rivalry | Given that interventions are always delivered in a context of multiple existing programs, the interaction and rivalry between interventions create a dynamics of their own. "In this policy-saturated world, it is increasingly difficult to see where one program starts and another one ends" (p. 22). |
| Emergence | Given that interventions often seek to change people's interpretation of their place in the world, they can lead to change, no change, or unintended change. The intervention has only imperfect control over outcomes, especially because the program changes the conditions that made the program work in the first place. Therefore, the most successful programs and organizations are those that adapt to this emergent change. "Components in a system will often combine to produce novel components, thus continually changing the composition of the system under investigation" (p. 45). |

SOURCE: Adapted from Pawson (2013, Box 3.1).

After eliciting, mapping, and selecting program theories, the next step is to formalize them. They need to be transformed into hypotheses suitable for empirical testing. Program theories originate as insights, brain waves, bright ideas, and informed guesses that evaluation research must translate into testable propositions.

Testing the reconstructed theory is the next step. Data collection and analysis using qualitative and quantitative methods are used to understand, test, and refine program theories. Realist evaluators speak of "interrogating the program theories," which they refer to as theory refinement. The objective is not to accept or reject program theories but to improve them.

## 2.2 Theory of Change Approach

Carol Weiss (1995) popularized the term *theory of change* (TOC). She hypothesized that a key reason complex policies or programs are so difficult to evaluate is that the assumptions that inspire and guide them are poorly articulated. Stakeholders of complex initiatives are often unclear about how the change process will unfold and therefore pay little attention to the early and midterm changes required to achieve longer term goals. Weiss defined TOC as a way to describe the assumptions that explain both the mini-steps that lead to the long-term goal and the connections between policy or program activities and results that occur at each step. Her work challenges designers of complex initiatives, such as development aid programs, to be specific about the TOC guiding their work and suggests that doing so would improve their policies and strengthen their ability to claim credit for outcomes that were predicted in their theory.

The following steps elicit the TOC underlying a planned program. A precondition is that the evaluator work collaboratively with a wide range of stakeholders.

*Step 1:* The focus is on a longer term vision usually relating to a timescale longer than the program timeframe. For example, a smoking cessation program might have a long-term vision of eradicating inequalities in smoking prevalence by 2020.

*Step 2:* Having agreed on the program's ultimate aim, stakeholders are encouraged to articulate the necessary results required by the end of the program to achieve these goals. They might, for instance, anticipate a decrease in the gap between the most and least deprived areas.

*Steps 3:* At this stage those involved with the program consider the most appropriate activities or interventions to bring about the required change. Different strategies of engagement might be used to target pregnant women, middle-aged men, and adolescents, for example.

*Step 4:* Finally, stakeholders consider the resources that can realistically be brought to bear on the planned interventions, including staff and organizational capacity, the existence of supportive networks and facilities, and financial capability.

Following a collective and iterative process, the resulting program theory must be plausible, doable, and testable. It needs to be articulated in such a way that it can be open to evaluation; this is only possible if there is a high degree of specificity concerning the desired outcomes. Only then can the TOC be interrogated to ensure that the underlying logic is acceptable to stakeholders. The evaluator then takes the program map generated through this process and, using appropriate data collection techniques, monitors and analyzes how the program unfolds and integrates the findings.

## 2.3 Contribution Analysis

Many evaluations assume the program can take credit for all of the observed results. However, reporting on results and proving attribution are two different things. Attribution, the process of drawing causal links between observed changes and specific interventions, is often very difficult and expensive to establish. However, demonstrating a program's contribution to a result is crucial if the value of the program is to be demonstrated and to enable decisions to be made about its future direction (Mayne, 2001, 2012).

Rather than trying to causally link a program to desired outcomes, contribution analysis seeks to provide plausible evidence that can reduce uncertainty regarding the difference a program is making to observed outcomes (Mayne, 2001, 2012). The following seven methodological steps constitute a contribution analysis.

*Step 1: Set out the cause-effect issue to be addressed.*

✓ Would the expected intervention make a difference to the problem?
✓ What aspects of the intervention or the context would lead to a contribution being made?
✓ What would be credible evidence that the intervention made a noticeable contribution?
✓ Is the expected contribution plausible given the nature of the intervention? If not, the value of further analysis needs to be reassessed.

*Step 2: Develop the TOC.*

Contribution analysis needs straightforward, not overly detailed results chains, especially at the outset. Refinements to further explore some aspects of the theory of change can be added later.

*Step 3: Critically review the resulting contribution story.*

✓ Assess the logic of the links and test the plausibility of the assumptions in the TOC: Are there any significant gaps in the theory? Can they be filled by refining the TOC? If not, is it worth continuing?
✓ Identify where evidence is needed to strengthen the contribution story: Which links have little evidence? Which external factors are not well understood?
✓ Determine how much the theory of change is contested: Is it widely agreed on? Are specific aspects contested? Are there rival TOCs at play?

*Step 4: Gather existing evidence on the TOC.*

Before gathering new data, it is useful and cost-effective to look at existing data and information about the TOC. The purpose is to provide empirical evidence for the contribution story: on activities implemented, observed results, underlying assumptions and relevant external factors. At this point a TOC for the intervention has been developed and the available evidence supporting the TOC collected; the TOC has to some extent been tested.

*Step 5: Reassess the contribution story and challenges to it.*

The theory of change can be critically assessed in light of the existing evidence:

✓ Which links in the theory of change are strong (strong logic, good evidence supporting the assumptions, low risk, and wide acceptance), and which are weak?
✓ How credible is the story overall? Does the pattern of outcomes and links between them validate the contribution chain?

✓ Do stakeholders agree with the contribution story developed?

✓ Is it likely that any external factors have had a noteworthy influence on the results observed?

✓ What are the main weaknesses in the story? Where would additional data or information be useful?

*Step 6: Seek out additional empirical evidence.*

This is where the primary data gathering begins, informed by the previous steps where the need for additional evidence was identified.

✓ Evidence is gathered to strengthen the contribution story, using appropriate data gathering techniques, such as surveys and administrative data. There may be evidence on results, on the validity of the assumptions and risks in the theory of change, and on significant external factors.

✓ There may be chances to use quantitative techniques (experimental and non-experimental designs) involving comparison groups that could be used to explore elements of the TOC.

✓ From a theory-based perspective, several frequently used data gathering techniques can be strengthened, including key informant interviews, focus groups and workshops, and case studies.

*Step 7: Revise and strengthen the contribution story.*

The newly collected empirical evidence should be used to build a more credible contribution story with strengthened conclusions on the causal links in the TOC. Contribution analysis works best as an iterative process, and the analysis may return to Step 5 to reassess strengths and weaknesses of the contribution story and decide if further analysis is useful or possible.

## 2.4 Policy Scientific Approach

The policy scientific approach focuses on document analysis, argumentation analysis, and testing (Leeuw, 2003).

*Step 1: Identify behavioral mechanisms expected to solve the problem.*

Documents and interview transcripts can elicit statements about the goals of the policy or program under review and why it is believed to be important. These statements point to mechanisms considered to be the "engines" driving the policies or programs and believed to make them effective.

*Step 2: Statements that have the following form are especially relevant for detecting these mechanisms:*

● "It is evident that *x* will work."

● "In our opinion, the best way to go about this problem is to . . ."

● "The only way to solve this problem is to . . ."

● "Our institution's *x* years of experience tells us that . . ."

*Step 3: Compile a survey of these statements and link the mechanisms with the goals of the program or policy under review.*

*Step 4: Reformulate these statements in conditional "if-then" or similar proposition structures (e.g., "The more x, the less y.").*

*Step 5: Search for "warrants" identifying missing links in or between different propositions through argumentation analysis.*

A central concept of argumentation analysis is the warrant—the *because* part of an argument. It says that B follows from A because of a (generally) accepted principle. For example, "The organization's performance will not improve next year" follows from "The performance of this organization has not improved over the last 5 years" because of the principle "Past performance is the best predictor of future performance." The *because* part of such an argument is often not made explicit and must be inferred by the analysis. The focus when searching for warrants is on mechanisms: social, behavioral, cognitive, and institutional. (See Chapter 10, section 4.3, for a fuller discussion of argumentation mapping.)

*Step 6: Reformulate these warrants in terms of conditional "if-then" (or similar) propositions and draw a chart of the (mostly causal) links.*

*Step 7: Evaluate the validity of the propositions by looking into the logical consistency of the set of propositions and the consistency of their empirical content with the state of the art within the social/behavioral/economic sciences on these mechanisms.*

Evaluating the reconstructed program theory can be done in different ways. One is to confront (or juxtapose) different theories (like Carvalho & White, 2004, did with regard to social funds). Another approach is to test the program theory by making use of primary or secondary data, both qualitative and quantitative. A third possibility is to organize an iterative process of continuous refinement using stakeholder feedback and multiple data collection techniques and sources (in the realist tradition). A fourth is to use already published reviews and synthesis studies (see Chapter 9). These studies can play a pivotal role in marshaling existing evidence to deepen the power and validity of TBE, to contribute to future knowledge building, and to meet the information needs of stakeholders. Visualization or mapping software can help in this task.

## 2.5 Strategic Assessment Approach

The strategic assessment approach has four stages (Leeuw, 2003; Mason & Mitrof, 1981).

*Stage 1: Group formation*

A cross-section of individuals with an interest in the relevant policy or program is selected. They are divided into groups, taking care to maximize convergence of viewpoints within groups and to maximize divergence of perspectives between groups.

*Stage 2: Assumption surfacing*

Groups separately unearth the most significant assumptions that underpin their preferred policies or programs using two main techniques. First, *stakeholder analysis* is used to identify the key individuals or groups on whom the success or failure of their preferred strategy would depend. Second, *assumption rating* involves searching for statements about symptoms of the problem that have to be solved through a policy or program and assessing how important this assumption is in terms of its influence on the success or failure of the strategy and how certain we are that the assumption is justified. Each group then is able to identify a number of key assumptions on which the success of its strategy rests.

*Stage 3: Dialectical debate*

Groups come together to make the best case for their preferred strategy while identifying its key assumptions. Informative questions are followed by an open debate focusing on which assumptions are different between groups, which are rated differently, and which of the other groups' assumptions each group finds most troubling. Groups should develop a full understanding of each other's preferred strategies and their key assumptions.

*Stage 4: Synthesis*

Assumptions are negotiated, and modifications to key assumptions are made. Agreed assumptions are noted and form the basis for consensus around a new strategy. If no synthesis can be achieved, points of disagreement are noted and the question of what research might be done to resolve these differences is discussed.

## 2.6 Elicitation Approach

The mental models or cognitive maps of people in organizations implementing policies and programs (i.e., their theories) are important for understanding the anticipated impact of their policies or programs, organizational cognitions, and the relationships between these cognitions and organizational performance. Most stakeholders have cognitions (i.e., theories) about the organization and its environment, the organizational strategies, their chances of success, the role power plays, their own roles, and the relationships with the outside world, and these maps partly determine their behavior. Parts of these maps or theories are implicit and are tacit knowledge, both on an individual level and on a collective level. By articulating these mental models, it is possible to compare them with evidence from scientific organization studies and to help organizations to become "learners."

The following are examples of techniques for reconstructing, eliciting, and assessing these mental or cognitive maps:

- Maintain a record of strategic intentions, through studying documentation designed to direct behavior (e.g., protocols, board memos, contractual arrangements).

- Engage in decision making in action; an anthropological observer approach. Watch decision makers, and listen to stories.
- Work with managers on strategic breakdown situations. Become immersed in the thinking and the social process of *strategic firefighting*.
- Use trigger questions in interview situations so that *theories in use* can be detected. Follow interviews with feedback to individuals and to the team. The elicitation cycle is built on responses to designed trigger questions. The process uses five techniques:
  - ○ Create an open-ended atmosphere in the interview.
  - ○ Create a playful atmosphere in which it is easier to deviate from the formal phraseology and the official script.
  - ○ Set the interviewees up against themselves.
  - ○ Create dialectical tension by asking the interviewees to adopt unusual roles.
  - ○ Listen very carefully for internal inconsistencies in what is being said.
- Apply data/content analysis or other text analysis programs to the interview reports and documents.
- Confront the results of these content analysis activities with relevant (social) scientific research.

## 2.7 Behavioral Economics

Behavioral economics studies the effects of psychological, social, cognitive, and emotional factors on the decision-making processes of individuals and institutions. This approach is related to realist evaluation and the policy scientific approach discussed earlier. Drawing on insights from robust research in psychology, (social) neurosciences, sociology, and microeconomics, it challenges the widely held assumption that individuals and institutions act rationally by seeking to maximize their utility. Authors such as Kahneman (2011) and Thaler and Sunstein (2009) describe a large body of psychological research identifying the mechanisms that influence how individuals make decisions and showing how these insights can contribute to policymaking in many different fields. Two main mechanisms are discussed in the literature on individual choice behavior:

- *Heuristics:* People simplify decision making through rules of thumb rather than relying on strict logic. Kahneman (2011) identifies two systems governing decision making. System 2 involves deep mental activity such as difficult mathematical computations or careful analysis of different aspects of a problem. This requires considerable time and effort, and the brain uses System 2 sparingly. In contrast, the much more widely used System 1 draws on well-tested rules of thumb to simplify the time and effort required to make judgments. Examples of these simplifying heuristics include making judgments based on small numbers, using anchors to provide reference points for assessing a likely answer for an unfamiliar situation, using easily available data, and being influenced by emotional cues (e.g., preferring warm rather than cold, judging tall people more favorably than shorter people, feeling positive toward people who smile).

- *Framing:* In the social sciences framing comprises a set of concepts and theoretical perspectives on how individuals, groups, and societies organize, perceive, and communicate about reality (Druckman, 2001). In economics, studies of the framing effect have focused on how well rational choice models explain how humans and organizations actually make decisions. There is a large body of research on how the framing of a question or communication can influence decisions and what these influences tell us about decision-making behavior. For example, the U.K. Cabinet Office created the Behavioral Insights Team (BIT),[3] commonly known as the "Nudge Unit" (after the popular book by Thaler and Sunstein). The BIT conducted a number of large-scale randomized control trials in which the wording of government communications to the public was randomly changed. The findings of the research showed that how a choice is framed (presented) strongly affects the choice that results. For example, repayment of back taxes was significantly increased when the communication included information on the percentage of households in the local neighborhood who had begun to repay their back taxes. Other forms of social influence were also investigated. For example, counselors in government employment agencies negotiated, with randomly selected job seekers, personal contracts whereby the client agreed to make a certain number of contacts with potential employers during the following week. This approach increased job placement rates compared to clients receiving traditional services (i.e., information on job vacancies but with no special encouragement to pursue these contacts). Similarly, requiring people to opt out of a desired program (e.g., for organ donors) produced much higher rates of the desired behavior than requiring people to opt in. This is called the *line of least resistance.*

The concepts and lessons from behavioral economics can make important contributions to the understanding of the behavioral processes underlying the operation of the different kinds of macro and micro mechanisms through which programs seek to achieve their objectives (e.g., the "naming and shaming" programs designed to control sexual predators). These involve a number of communication strategies and forms of social control that draw on mechanisms similar to those used in behavioral economics.

# 3. Complexification

"Life is not simple, but many of the logic models used in programme theory evaluation are" (Rogers, 2008, p. 29). This is a serious point. One of the aspects of simplicity in program logics is that unintended side effects of policies are not taken into account. One of these side effects is the phenomenon referred to as *(intended) complexification* in public and private organizations and policymaking. Natsios (2010) describes mechanisms through which development aid in the United States has become extremely complicated and multilayered with regulation and oversight requirements that create a world of auditors, compliance officers, and evaluators to check, recheck, and meta-check as one of the causes (see also National Council of Nonprofits, 2010; Wiig & Holm-Hansen, 2014, p. 3).

Claiming things are complex instead of simple pays off: Those who work on simple, straightforward problems often have a lower status in organizations with fewer perks[4] than those who work on so-called complex problems. What Wilson (1991) called the role of special interest groups is another factor. There are a number of institutional settings in which the influence of these groups markedly increased over time and contributed to complicating and delaying management processes. Public choice economists link this to rent-seeking (Henderson, 2008). With regard to complexity claims, a similar process can take place: Those involved in and with complex programs try to obtain benefits for themselves (e.g., more money for evaluations of complex compared to simple programs)[5] by focusing on complexity.

It is wise for an evaluator to be as critical as possible about claims that policies, programs, and problems are complex. Accepting the received wisdom that what looks or is claimed to be complex is indeed complex is not commendable. Instead, taking notice of mechanisms that can create the impression or perception of complexity, simply because stakeholders benefit from it, needs to be on the agenda for evaluators.

Theory-based evaluation can help clarify how complex programs really work by analyzing underlying assumptions of programs that claim to be complex. Pawson's (2013) VICTORE approach (see Table 5.1) is one of the devices to do so; Coleman's (1990) model in which three types of mechanisms (situational, action-formation, and transformational) are presented is also useful. Analytical sociology (Hedstrom & Bearman, 2011) helps to test claims about complex social structures, cultures, and other configurations by focusing on human agency (Homans, 1964; i.e., look into behavioral aspects of what is believed to be complex). Most recently, behavioral economics, including cognitive studies, has been contributing to our understanding of these issues (see Section 2.7).

The evaluation of complex programs should also take into account the existence of demi-regularities. "*Demi-regularity*, originating from Lawson (1997), suggests that human choice or agency manifests itself in a semi-predictable manner—*semi* because variations in reoccurring, predictable patterns of behavior can be attributed to differences in the contextual dimension from one setting to another" (Jagosh et al., 2011, p. 7). Dieleman, Wong, and Marchal (2012, p. 27) define a demi-regularity as "a semi-predictable pattern or pathway of program functioning; i.e., certain people tend to behave in certain ways under certain situations." Shepperd et al., (2009) give an example from evaluations of complex health interventions (CHIs), arguing that the demi-regular patterns of interactions between the components that make up CHIs with similar goals can be explained by middle-range theory. For any similar group of CHIs (e.g., smoking cessation interventions), the myriad of contexts influencing behavior to generate outcomes are the "'raw materials' from which demi-regularities can be identified" (Shepperd et al., 2009, p. 5).

For the unpacking of complexity claims, this idea is crucial. What at first glance appears to be complex may actually resemble other so-called complex situations (i.e., a demi-regularity), in which a few behavioral mechanisms operate in a more or less similar way though in different contexts. Karlsson (2011) studied the openness and closeness of social systems, which is related to the complexity of systems, and concluded that "people can not only open closed systems, they can also close open systems" meaning that through their choices and behavior people can work toward closing and thereby de-complexifying their world. Karlsson adds that "the circumstance that people can *partly close open systems is an overlooked phenomenon in critical realism*" (p. 152). "In fact, if all social systems were always open in the sense of exhibiting no regularities social life would not be possible. It is hard to imagine social life entirely without regularities" (p. 161).

Notwithstanding the above, the methodological individualistic approach in no way neglects evidence that when emergent outcomes are at stake, threshold effects and tipping points play a role, and when there is nonlinearity and recursive causality, complexity is likely to be present.

# 4. The Contributions of TBE to the Evaluation of Complex Interventions

## 4.1 A Framework for Modeling the Evaluation of Complex Programs

A TBE approach provides a sound framework for modeling the evaluation of complex programs. While TBE has the flexibility to model multi-component programs with multiple actors and multiple causal pathways, it is necessary to adapt the conventional TBE model to capture the different dimensions of complexity. Figure 5.2 illustrates the elements of an expanded complexity-responsive TBE model.

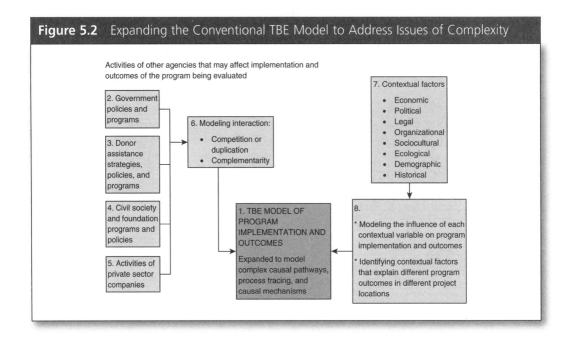

**Figure 5.2** Expanding the Conventional TBE Model to Address Issues of Complexity

- Box 1 in Figure 5.2 is the conventional TBE model of program implementation and outcomes. For complexity analysis this usually requires a more detailed articulation of causal pathways, causal mechanisms, and process tracing.
- Boxes 2–5 identify activities of four kinds of agencies that may potentially influence implementation and outcomes of the program being evaluated. The agencies and activities are government policies and programs; donor assistance strategies, policies, and programs; civil society and foundation programs; and activities of private sector companies. The latter can include effects of regular company economic activities as well as special social development initiatives they may organize.[6]
- Box 6 includes the analytical tools required to model how the activities identified in boxes 2–5 affect implementation and outcomes of the program being evaluated. Some of the activities may represent *competition* by offering similar programs that may draw potential beneficiaries away from the program being evaluated or by competing for funds or resources. Other activities may *complement* the programs, for example, by providing additional resources or offering complementary services. An example of the latter would be a program that strengthens public transport, thus making it easier for students to attend the schools that are part of an education program being evaluated.
- Box 7 identifies the different contextual factors that can affect implementation and outcomes.
- Box 8 includes the analytical tools for assessing the overall influence of each contextual variable. Importantly, this also examines the contextual factors that contribute to different responses of communities or groups to the program.

## 4.2 Examples From Practice

A first example is when (global and/or policy) networks are part of an intervention or when an intervention itself is a network operation. An example of such an operation is when persons and groups are building coalitions between stakeholders to realize a certain goal. Then assumptions about social capital within networks are part of the intervention theory, indicating how social capital works for whom, for how long, when social capital may turn into "sour capital," where and when structural holes in networks appear, and how new networks emerge out of existing networks or become less important and even disappear. Honeycutt and Strong (2012) applied social network analysis to studying early collaboration on advocacy activities in advocacy coalitions in the context of health insurance coverage. Another study applying social network analysis emphasizes the need to understand social relationships using tools other than simple frameworks of direct causality from inputs to outputs to outcomes. "The network evaluator is often faced with a 'messy' situation in which activities and results are unpredictable and hard to make sense of" (Drew, Aggleton, Chalmers, & Wood, 2011, p. 384). Reconstructing the underlying network (social capital) assumptions is of great importance to understand the processes to be described and evaluated.

With collaboration, public policy networks, and coalitions (like the ones that were built when the Kyoto Protocol or the Paris Declaration was developed and agreed upon), knowing about theories on social capital and its many forms and processes is relevant for evaluators in practice.

A third example concerns the Robert Wood Johnson Foundation (RWJF) Urban Health Initiative, a 10-year effort to improve health and safety outcomes in distressed cities in the United States (Weitzman, Mijanovich, Silver, & Brecher, 2009). The broader focus was on efforts to change public systems and policies and falls under the umbrella of comprehensive community initiatives (CCIs). Rather than directly funding new, improved, or expanded services, CCIs focus on the review and revision of programs and policies, strengthening of community institutions, and redirection of public and philanthropic dollars as the means to improve outcomes for families and children.

The evaluation sought to address the challenges posed in evaluating a long-term, citywide, comprehensive initiative by combining a quasi-experimental design, including a group of comparison cities, with a theory of change approach. While comparison cities were not studied in as much depth, efforts were made to understand their local landscape in regard to youth problems and their solutions. A nationwide theory of change was articulated in combination with more regional/ local theories. The national theory of change embraced a political theory in which a multi-sector, data-driven planning process, engaging both the civic elite and the public at large and emphasizing a close reading of the literature on best practice models, would lead to a shared understanding of the problems facing youth and a common vision regarding the strategies to ameliorate them. It was then "de-nationalized" by the staff of the RWJF in such a way that more precise predictions suggested what this national strategy would and would not do. "The theory of change, developed by the evaluation team through an iterative process with senior staff from RWJF . . . , was used to define the initial set of intended impacts" (Weitzman et al., 2009, p. 498).

# 5. Some Pitfalls When Doing TBE

Evaluators must be aware of a number of potential pitfalls when doing TBE, which can lead to significant error costs (i.e., the costs of making mistakes[7]).

## 5.1 Avoid Sloppy Reconstructions and Tests of Underlying Program Theories

Tilley (1999) identified several bad practices that contribute to the production of error costs. Sloppy reconstructions and tests of underlying program theories is one; neglecting contextual differences when comparing results from evaluations (in different time periods) is another. Misinterpreting what caused a program not to work (by confusing implementation problems, measurement problems and difficulties with the program theory) is another (Tilley, 1999). Error costs include programs that could have been effective sometimes being terminated or considered not ready for implementation, because of a faulty theory reconstruction; increased inefficiency; resources being wasted in developing the program; and conducting an evaluation of a poorly designed program. There is also the opportunity cost resulting from the fact that the underlying social problem to be remedied by the program continues to exist. Related to this is what Funnel and Rogers (2011) call the *"No Actual Theory"-trap:* An evaluator refers to program theories that are in fact not theories at all; instead, "they simply display boxes of activities and boxes of outcomes without demonstrating logical and defensible relationships between them and the various items listed in the boxes" (p. 42).

## 5.2 Address the Problem of Concatenation of Mechanisms

Hedstrom (2005) argued that "it is often necessary [when doing a TBE] to consider several mechanisms simultaneously in order to make sense of a specific social phenomenon," adding that "these mechanisms may interact with another in a complex way" (p. 56). Often the TBE addresses only a limited set of mechanisms.

## 5.3 Prevent "Designed Blindness"

Practitioners and evaluators can become so intensively focused on the program theory that they start to frame every program activity in terms of this theory (Friedman, 2001) and start to believe that the program theory is inherently valid and good. This point is related to the psychological mechanism of tunnel vision. The error cost is that the possibility for a serious test of the theory is very small.

## 5.4 Prevent the "Polishing Up" or Quasi-enrichment of the Policy Theory

This happens when policymakers ask evaluators to refine or enrich assumptions about policies that are grounded on rather thin assumptions. The error costs are twofold: First, it resembles impression management (the "rich" program theory forms the fundament of an intervention that is largely a "show policy"); second, it can set in motion a process of imitation in organizations, which will create future failures and faulty processes.

## 5.5 Avoid the Pitfall of Not Using the Program Theory for Evaluation

Funnel and Rogers (2011, pp. 50–51) refer to this trap. It boils down to the discrepancy between developing or reconstructing the program theory on the one hand but doing the (empirical) evaluation without paying attention to this theory. It can be labeled a case of wasted words.

# *Notes

1. This chapter is based on a report the author wrote for the DG for Regional Policy, European Commission's Evalsed program, and on other articles by the author. Thanks to Michael Bamberger and anonymous reviewers for comments and suggestions.

2. http://ec.europa.eu/regional_policy/sources/docgener/evaluation/guide/evaluation_sourcebook.pdf.

3. The behavioral insights team recently became independent of the UK government. See http://www.behaviouralinsights.co.uk.

4. Abbott (1981, 322-23). Divacultura says, "Even simple information is transformed into something terrifying through ambiguous and complicated language," and quotes Tom Peters: "Beware of complexifiers and complicators. Truly 'smart people' simplify things." http://divacultura.blogspot.nl/2012/04/complexification-is-killer.html.

5. Henderson (2008) gives as examples steel producers seeking restrictions on imports of steel, and licensed electricians and doctors often lobby to keep regulations in place that restrict competition from unlicensed electricians or doctors. "Licensed complexity evaluators" could do the same to their more "simple colleagues."

6. Examples of special corporate initiatives are the collaborative program that Coca Cola Corporation is implementing with UN Women to increase the number of small women entrepreneurs as distributors of Coca Cola products and the corporate social responsibility initiatives that many large international corporations now organize.

7. See Leeuw (2010) in the Zeitschrift fur Evaluation on costs and benefits of evaluations.

*The references for chapter 5 have been combined with those in chapter 6 and appear on p. 123.

# CHAPTER 6

# Five Practical Evaluation Problems to Which TBE Can Contribute

Frans L. Leeuw

*Sections 1–5 of this chapter illustrate how theory-based evaluation (TBE) can contribute to addressing five common evaluation problems: helping define and operationalize performance indicators; defining an alternative counterfactual when a statistical counterfactual is not possible; when the findings of an impact evaluation are not clearly explained, assessing at the program design stage how effective a program is likely to be; and assessing during implementation how effective a program is likely to be. Section 6 concludes with practical applications.*

## 1. Problem 1: What can TBE contribute to define and operationalize key performance indicators for program, policy, and other interventions?

There are at least three sets of theories explaining the relationship between TBE and key performance indicators (KPIs). The first theory argues that KPIs promote mechanisms that drive workers and management to work in line with the goals set by the organization, making it possible to compare the performance of divisions, departments, and outside organizations. A second theory argues that while some indicators may contribute to learning, others may stimulate "cooking the data," bureaucratization, red tape, dramaturgical compliance, and the performance paradox (van Thiel & Leeuw, 2002). More recently, Pollit (2013) identified a set of competing theories of performance management "that dilute or distort the simple, instrumental rationality of 'hit your target and get rewarded'" (p. 351).

We do not address these two sets of theory here. Instead we discuss what program/intervention theory can contribute to developing and implementing effective KPIs. Bickman (1996) suggested that a logical starting point for developing the most appropriate KPIs was to create a model or program theory. Birleson, Brann, and Smith (2001) did that in a paper on clinical and community care in child and adolescent mental health services (CAMHS) in hospitals. They articulated the program theory of different services by addressing program operations, proximal outcomes and final outcomes, and relationships between them. They showed that without an articulated program theory, KPIs were likely to be less relevant, overly inclusive, or poorly linked with the program operations they purport to measure. Birleson et al. recommend that "the KPIs chosen for CAMHS should be consistent with the program theory outlined" (p. 15). (See also Hakkert, Gitelman, & Vis, 2007, for a similar approach to road safety in Europe.)

Lindgren (2001) shows how problematic the use of indicators can be *if there is discrepancy between the program theory and the performance indicators available.* The study shows how thin the ice is for performance measurement when indicators are developed and used without taking notice of the (richness of the) program theory. The case concerns popular adult education in Sweden and how those activities are monitored by indicators.

Four activities are central to link TBE with key performance indicators:

- (re)constructing the theory underlying the program/intervention and developing indicators covering the richness of the underlying theory
- understanding that indicators can trigger behavioral responses, leading to a performance paradox. Organizations good in measuring performance indicators are not necessarily the most effective organizations. Smith (1995) calls this *measurement fixation.* An example of such a trigger mechanism is when policymakers and managers emphasize compliance with protocols and procedures that can often lead to the production of data largely or only to satisfy the principals' need for sound protocols and procedures.
- understanding how these mechanisms can contribute to an *unintended performance paradox;* van Thiel and Leeuw (2002) also point to the problem that there are mechanisms leading to an *intended performance paradox.* These are "cognitive sabotage" of performance measurements and audits, including "cooking" the data, "creaming" (focusing on the "best" cases), and myopia (only information on short-term objectives is presented, while more information is available).
- preventing the performance paradox. Meyer and Gupta (1994) recommend that organizations adopt a *paradoxical model of performance assessment* with multiple, uncorrelated, and varying but comparable performance indicators. They also recommend the use of targets and comparisons over time, between organizations and/or different units within the same organization.

## 2. Problem 2: What can TBE contribute to defining the counterfactual when it is not possible to use statistical (experimental and quasi-experimental) evaluation designs?

### 2.1 Counterfactual History

This approach addresses "what if" questions known as counterfactuals. It explores history and historical incidents by extrapolating a timeline in which certain key historical events did not happen or had an outcome that was different from what did in fact occur. Fogel (1964) addressed the question of where the United States would have been (in terms of its GDP) had there been no railroad construction boom in the 19th century. Examining transportation costs, Fogel compared the actual 1890 economy to a hypothetical 1890 economy in which transportation infrastructure was limited to wagons, canals, and rivers. Fogel found that the impact of railroads was small—about 7% of 1890 GDP—and as a substitute technology, the more extensive canal system, would have been able to achieve a comparable economic growth.

Fogel's work is linked to the *nomothetic theory-testing approach*. The argument is that whenever there is a well-defined and corroborated general theory (e.g., about the relationship between money supply and inflation), with well-defined antecedent conditions (e.g., the Russian economy in January 1992), specific counterfactuals can be deduced (e.g., if the Russian Central Bank had adopted monetary policy X, then *ceteris paribus*, inflation would have taken value V; Tetlock & Belkin, 1996).

Another approach is *ideographic counterfactuals*. In-depth case studies of the key players in a given historical situation, their beliefs and motives, and the political-economic and cultural constraints under which they worked provide historical predictions. After Fogel's, other counterfactual historical studies were published, including work combining experimental psychology and history. Methodological rules of thumb are available to undertake this work and to judge its quality (Tetlock & Belkin, 1996). Tetlock and Belkin (1996) also collect data from hundreds of experts who predict the counterfactual future/past. By analyzing their answers, patterns, and (ultimately, when time progresses) the validity of their statements, these researchers are trying to unpack what worked in predicting the future (and vice versa: the past).

For evaluators, a similar approach is possible. If, for example, the impact of a grant to companies to stimulate innovation or a new system of knowledge brokers for small and medium enterprises has to be assessed and statistical evaluation designs are not feasible, evaluators can be asked to develop a counterfactual for the situation had there been no grants or knowledge brokers available.

### 2.2 Hypothetical Question Methodology

The counterfactual question can be answered by employing a *hypothetical question methodology*, known from policy acceptance studies and marketing research. Respondents are confronted with information on policy measures that do not exist (in the world of the respondents). Sometimes by adopting the social psychological theory of reasoned behavior, sometimes through other approaches, respondents' decision-making processes are followed and registered by asking them if and to what extent their behavior would have been changed if policy intervention Y had (not) been implemented.

An example is the sequence of studies of (existing and nonexisting) family and population policies in the Netherlands by Rozendal, Moors, and Leeuw (1985) based on Thompson and Appelbaum's (1974) evaluation of the impact of population policy interventions in the United States. More recently, economics and psychology have developed more advanced approaches under the heading of *contingent valuation* studies, also known as the stated preference method, and willingness-to-pay studies. MacMillan (2004) presented an overview.[1]

# 3. Problem 3: What can TBE contribute at the program design stage in assessing how effective the proposed programs, policies, or other interventions are likely to be?

Assessing the potential effectiveness of a new intervention requires analysis of the theory underlying the intervention, which in turn requires *opening up the black box of the intervention.*

Consider the case of "naming and shaming" interventions.[2] Over the last decade, policymakers, legislators, the police, and regulators have been increasingly active in implementing a range of naming and shaming programs, for example, dissemination of information via websites and newspapers about organizations that do not comply with rules and regulations (e.g., car manufacturing safety standards), professors that do not teach (or teach badly), politicians and bureaucrats filling their own pockets with public money, or released sex offenders. It is believed that naming and shaming of noncompliant and/or deviant behavior will lead to behavior changes in the desired direction. What does the opening up of the black box look like in a specific case, such as reducing reoffending by sex offenders (see Pawson, 2002)?

The model identifies two examples of situational mechanisms, which can affect how released sex offender naming and shaming policies work. *Agenda setting* describes the processes by which widespread and extensive media coverage can influence public opinion about how to respond to the issue of released sex offenders living in the community. In a context of strong social pressure to do something about the problem, policymakers and law enforcement officials typically decide to invest in sex offender registration and information management systems. It is assumed that these activities will then lead to a diffusion process, whereby residents will receive accurate and timely information about registered sex offenders who reside in their neighborhood.

*Diffusion* describes how information about registered sex offenders spreads through particular communication channels over time among the members of a social system. In practice, the dissemination of information can occur in a variety

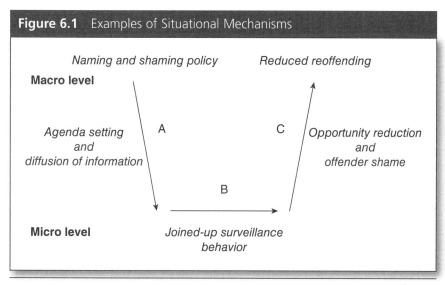

**Figure 6.1** Examples of Situational Mechanisms

*Source:* Astbury and Leeuw (2010).

of ways: through the Internet as well as interpersonal communication channels such as police-community consultative groups and informal meetings of concerned local citizens. However, this is not enough to make naming and shaming work. The next link in the chain involves individual actors responding appropriately to information once it is received. According to the basic intervention theory, police officers, members of the community, heads of schools and teachers, sports mentors, and others will accept information about registered sex offenders, assume that it is valid, and act on it. Acting implies increased joined-up surveillance behavior, which also implies that the framing of what constitutes suspicious behavior is more or less similar among different stakeholders in different contexts. It also implies that the results of surveillance activities are fed back into information management systems.

*Transformational mechanisms* aggregate the individual joint (surveillance) actions to a level that is believed to make a difference for the behavioral choices of registered sex offenders. Aggregated surveillance increases the (perceived) likelihood of being caught, leading to the possible activation of an opportunity reduction mechanism. It also has the potential to trigger a shame-inducing mechanism among potential reoffenders. Finally, the joining up of the different mechanisms, so the theory goes, will lead to a reduction in reoffending.

## 3.1 Two Case Studies

### a. Case 1: School Feeding Programs

The Cochrane review of school feeding programs for disadvantaged children included trials from five continents and spanned eight decades (Greenhalgh, Kristjansson, & Robinson, 2007). Although the authors found that the programs had significant positive effects on growth and cognitive performance, simply knowing that feeding programs work is not enough for policymakers to decide on the type of intervention to implement. Greenhalgh et al. (2007) analyzed the 18 studies included in their review using the methods of a realist review.

> Realist review exposes and articulates the mechanisms by which the primary studies assumed the interventions to work (either explicitly or implicitly); gathers evidence from primary sources about the process of implementing the intervention; and evaluates that evidence to judge the integrity with which each theory was actually tested and (where relevant) adjudicates between different theories. (p. 858)

Systematic reviews rarely give detailed information on the context, mechanisms, and outcomes of interventions and the theories that underpin them. This realist review describes the theory and processes in 18 trials of school feeding programs. The findings are summarized in Boxes 6.1 and 6.2. The first lists probably positive factors; the second highlights factors that probably reduce the efficacy of school feeding programs.

---

### BOX 6.1 PROCESS FACTORS THAT SEEM TO ENHANCE THE EFFICACY OF SCHOOL FEEDING PROGRAMS

**Strong process evidence across many trials**

- The target group had clear nutritional deficiency (usually inadequate energy intake), and the trial is oriented to correcting this rather than to short-term hunger relief.
- Well-organized schools formed part of an efficient distribution chain for the supplement.
- The intervention was developed with local teams rather than designed by distant experts.
- The supplement was piloted to exclude intolerance and confirm palatability and acceptability.
- Measures were in place to ensure that the food supplement was consumed (e.g., close supervision of eating).
- In disaffected young people, attention was paid to social aspects of the meal.

**Limited process evidence from one or a few trials**

- Local ingredients and cooking methods were used.
- In extreme poverty, the intervention was designed so that attending school was more economically viable than keeping children at home.
- The intervention sought to induce a change in home diet by educating or inspiring children.

**Possible factors that might be tested in future studies**

- Better nutrition and health literacy in this generation reduces an intergenerational cycle of poverty.

---

SOURCE: Greenhalgh, T. Kristjansson, E. and Robinson (2007

**BOX 6.2 PROCESS FACTORS THAT SEEM TO REDUCE THE EFFICACY OF SCHOOL FEEDING PROGRAMS**

- Participants were not aware of, signed up to, or trained to take account of the research dimension of the trial.
- The study design involved role conflict or ethical difficulties for staff (e.g., requirements to serve nutritious meals to some but not all undernourished children).
- Insufficient measures were in place to reduce confounding (e.g., controlling for benevolent attention).
- There was an adverse prevailing policy climate (e.g., policy conflicts with trial protocol, prompt rebranding of mainstream activity to gain research funding).
- There were measurement issues.

SOURCE: Greenhalgh, T. Kristjansson, E. and Robinson (2007) .

*b. Case 2: Fear-Arousal Communication and Behavior Change*

This case deals with the fight against cocaine swallowing by persons traveling between the Dutch Antilles and the Netherlands. Young (deprived) men were paid by organized crime to travel between the Antilles and Amsterdam and to swallow small balls filled with cocaine and deliver the drugs in Holland. The Dutch government significantly reduced this drug trafficking through an almost 100% control of passengers arriving to Amsterdam from certain regions. However, the policy was expensive, which made officials start to think about an alternative. Could a public information campaign using leaflets, mass media, and local media to present *fear-arousal information* about the medical dangers of the internal concealment method and the likelihood of arrest be an effective (and less expensive) intervention to reduce trafficking? Kruisbergen (2005) evaluated this policy idea. He synthesized results from evaluations of the impact of fear-arousal health education programs in general (about smoking, dangerous drinking, etc.) and compared the mechanisms and contexts found in these studies with the existing information regarding the Dutch Antilles and about social and behavioral characteristics of cocaine swallowers. There was a huge discrepancy between contexts and mechanisms of successful fear-arousal communication health campaigns and the specific characteristics of cocaine swallowers and their contexts. Crucial conditions that made fear-arousal communication successful did not exist in the case of cocaine-swallowing behavior. Kruisbergen's conclusion was that the likelihood of preventing illegal "immigration" of cocaine to the Netherlands through a public awareness campaign would be small to very small. In other words, the plausibility of the theory that fear-arousal communication would reduce drug trafficking using the internal concealment method was very limited.

## 3.2 Prospective Evaluation Synthesis

The U.S. General Accounting Office (GAO, 1995) developed an approach called *prospective evaluation synthesis* (PES), combining (1) a textual analysis of a proposed program, designed to clarify the implied goals of that program and what is assumed produces results; (2) a review and synthesis of evaluation studies from similar programs; and (3) summary judgments of likely success, given a future context that is not too different from the past. The focus of PES is on how evaluation studies cast light on the potential for success of the proposed programs, as opposed to reaching conclusions about the actual performance of existing programs. PES applies evaluation methodology to assess the potential consequences either of an individual proposal or of alternative and competing policy proposals. It combines the construction of underlying models of proposed programs or actions for evaluability assessment with the systematic application of existing knowledge as developed in the evaluation synthesis methodology.

An example of the GAO approach is the ex ante evaluation of two different proposals for a law aimed at reducing unwanted teen pregnancies in the United States during the late 1980s. The GAO analyzed the conceptual and operational assumptions underlying both proposals concerning action formation and situational mechanisms, while the analysis of assumptions regarding the operations were linked to transformational mechanisms. The conceptual analysis helps focus the operational analyses and answer the question: Logically, should the proposal work? The operational analyses address the question: Practically, could the proposal work? The analyses of empirical evidence can answer the question: Have activities conceptually and operationally similar to the proposal worked in the past? Finally, PES takes into account ways in which the past is and is not likely to be similar to plausible future conditions.

More recently (but without referring to PES), two developments related to the PES work were presented in the literature. The first, a project called MINDSPACE (Dolan, Hallsworth, Halpern, King, & Vlaev, 2010), was developed at the request of the UK government by the UK Institute for Government. This approach is strongly related to behavioral economics, which we mentioned earlier (see Chapter 5). The idea is that as policy is always focused on changing minds and behavior, robust information from behavioral theory and research should be used to guide policymakers in their (ex ante) decision making. MINDSPACE focuses on exploring how behavior change theory can help meet current policy challenges, such as reducing crime, tackling obesity, and ensuring environmental sustainability.

MINDSPACE is a "simple mnemonic which can be used as a quick checklist when making policy" (Dolan et al., 2010, p. 8). The core idea is to use information on nine mechanisms when trying to predict how and if policies will work (see Table 6.1).

While MINDSPACE was developed to help assess likely outcomes of proposed policy and program interventions (prospective evaluation), the approach can also be used to help assess the likely effectiveness of ongoing  programs or policies (see discussion of problem 4 below) and to propose ways to improve implementation. For example, the concept of Messenger can be used to assess the extent to which program information is communicated through, or has the support of, established opinion leaders. In contrast, the Defaults concept is similar to the extensive behavioral economics literature on thinking automatically

| **Table 6.1**  Nine Central Mechanisms Underlying Policy Interventions | |
| --- | --- |
| Messenger | We are heavily influenced by who communicates information. |
| Incentives | Our responses to incentives are shaped by predictable mental shortcuts such as strongly avoiding losses. |
| Norms | We are strongly influenced by what others do. |
| Defaults | We "go with the flow" of preset options. |
| Salience | Our attention is drawn to what is novel and seems relevant to us. |
| Priming | Our acts are often influenced by subconscious cues. |
| Affect | Our emotional associations can powerfully shape our actions. |
| Commitments | We seek to be consistent with our public promises and reciprocate acts. |
| Ego | We act in ways that make us feel better about ourselves. |

SOURCE: Dolan et al. (2010).

and thinking with mental models (World Bank, 2015, Chs. 1 and 3), which challenges the conventional economics assumption that people make decisions based on economic rationality. A third example, the Ego concept, can be helpful in areas such as obesity, where many experts criticize current communication strategies that make overweight people feel bad about themselves, producing a negative body image, which creates resistance to accepting the health messages that are being communicated.

## 3.3 Mechanism Experiments

Another recent development, *mechanism experiments* (Ludwig, Kling, & Mullainathan, 2011, p. 5), highlights the importance of understanding mechanisms when developing and evaluating policy programs ex ante. New empirical research is carried out to ascertain to what extent (assumed) mechanisms are able to steer behavior. A mechanism experiment does not test a policy; it directly tests the causal mechanism that underlies the policy. The argument is that after opening up the black box of proposed future policies, policymakers and evaluators should use that information to design mechanism experiments:

If we believe we know something about the mechanisms through which the policy might operate, why limit ourselves to using this information only after a policy evaluation has been designed and carried out. Why not use this information to help inform the design of the experiment that is being run? Why not design experiments that are explicitly focused on isolating the effects of candidate mechanisms? (Ludwig et al., 2011, p. 9)

Mechanism experiments are simpler to undertake than policy experiments, but their contribution to making policies effective is potentially quite large. The argument is that when such an evaluation

> failed to find the causal mechanism operative . . . would we [then] even need to run a policy evaluation? . . . Running the far cheaper mechanism experiment first serves as a valuable screen. Conversely, if the mechanism experiment found strong effects, we might now run a policy evaluation to calibrate magnitudes. (Ludwig et al., 2011, p. 19)

Keizer et al. (2008, p. 1681) undertook a mechanism experiment to test the "broken window theory" of crime prevention:

> Imagine that the neighborhood you are living in is covered with graffiti, litter, and unreturned shopping carts. Would this reality cause you to litter more, trespass, or even steal? A thesis known as the broken windows theory suggests that signs of disorderly and petty criminal behavior trigger more disorderly and petty criminal behavior, thus causing the behavior to spread. This may cause neighborhoods to decay and the quality of life of its inhabitants to deteriorate. For a city government, this may be a vital policy issue. But does disorder really spread in neighborhoods? So far there has not been strong empirical support, and it is not clear what constitutes disorder and what may make it spread. We generated hypotheses about the spread of disorder and tested them in six field experiments. We found that, when people observe that others violated a certain social norm or legitimate rule, they are more likely to violate other norms or rules, which causes disorder to spread.

In a rather different field, Leeuw and Leeuw (2012) present an analysis of 14 studies of interventions suggested in the literature to prevent and/or reduce digital piracy and in particular look at the working of the mechanisms implied by hypothetical interventions.

# 4. Problem 4: What can TBE contribute to find out—during implementation—how plausible the effectiveness of a program, policy, or intervention probably will be?[3]

## 4.1 Route 1: Generalizing From Implementation Research

Synthesis studies on implementation failures and factors affecting outcomes have been published in, among others, the following domains: health (Carrol et al., 2007; Greenhalgh et al., 2007); energy (efficiency; Harmelink, Nilsson, & Harmsen, 2008); and crime and justice (Lipsey, 2009; Nas, van Ooyen-Houben, & Wieman, 2011). These and other studies focus on *implementation fidelity* (the degree to which an intervention or program is delivered as intended). Nas et al. (2011) studied 20 recent Dutch evaluations of behavior modification interventions and sanctions focusing on crime prevention and reduction. Table 6.2 lists the main implementation factors and failures that were found. The study identified four sets of factors that reduce program effectiveness. First, guidance documents either do not exist or are not clear. Second, implementers and participating organizations continue to follow their own ideas and approaches and do not accept the proposed program approaches. Third, either the human resources are insufficient to implement the program or there are insufficient potential participants. Finally, programs did not adequately address the complexities and challenges of interagency coordination and cooperation. While this is an example of a synthesis study covering a very specific kind of intervention, many of the findings have much wider application. For example, many of the case studies included in *Evaluating the Complex* (Forss, Marra, & Schwartz, 2011) identify similar kinds of interagency coordination problems. So these kinds of synthesis studies can provide a valuable tool for the planning and evaluation of a wider range of interventions.

In their study on evaluating energy efficiency policy instruments in the European Union, Harmelink et al. (2008) identified 20 instruments contributing to success or failure. Although the projects were of different types and targeted different sectors, the authors were able to make some general observations based on the recurrence of certain observations made independently in the different case studies.

**Table 6.2**    Implementation Failures Reported in 20 Evaluations of Interventions Focusing on Preventing/Reducing Crime in the Netherlands

| Implementation failure | Number of process evaluations reporting the failure |
|---|---|
| No guidance document on how to implement the intervention | 15/20 |
| Guidance document is unclear | 10/20 |
| Implementers follow their own ideas | 5/10 |
| Lack of acceptance of the intervention by implementers and the organizations | 10/20 |
| **Human resources problems** | |
| Not enough personnel to deliver the intervention | 10/20 |
| Quality of personnel | 9/20 |
| Personnel lacking experience to deliver | 3/10 |
| Not enough participants to work with the intervention | 9/20 |
| Problems dealing with interorganizational collaboration between organizations active in the security and justice chain | 7/20 |

SOURCE: Nas et al. (2011, p. 17).

This kind of empirical evidence of implementation failures and causes increases the validity of the assumption that the new intervention will be able to make a difference. The more there is reason to believe that implementation failures are likely to occur, the smaller the chance that the intervention will make a difference.

## 4.2 Route 2: Doing RIPI Evaluations

Evaluation time and political time are different. When practitioners and policymakers cannot wait several years to say something about the probable likelihood of success of policies being implemented, RIPI evaluations can help. Kautto and Similä (2005) are the founding fathers of this approach, which stands for *recently introduced policy instruments.* In their approach a central role is given to the intervention theory. One case study assesses the transposition of the European Union's Directive 96/61 on Integrated Pollution Prevention and Control into the Finnish legal system. At the core of the reform was the integration of five permits (air pollution, water pollution, waste management, protection of health, and neighborhood relations) into one environmental permit. To avoid waiting several years to assess the impacts, Kautto and Similä started a process evaluation soon after the announcement of the new directive. They unpacked the intervention theory (Why will a reduction from five permits to one be effective in terms of environmental protection?) and collected data on outputs that were already available. Information on outcomes, of course, was not yet available. Because more than 600 permits (i.e., outputs) had been granted during the first 2 years of implementation, it was possible to assess whether the (policy) assumptions about the characteristics of the outputs were correct. Kautto and Similä state:

> This enabled us to say something important about the effectiveness despite the fact that the (final) outcomes had not yet occurred. The evaluation itself may have an impact on the implementation and as a result, or for other reasons, the authorities may place greater emphasis on gaps and priorities in the future. In this context, the intervention theory was not used to predict the future, but to guide the evaluation. (p. 64)

# 5. Problem 5: What can TBE contribute when the findings of an impact evaluation are not clearly explained?

Evaluators applying experimental or quasi-experimental designs often do not pay attention to the social and behavioral mechanisms underlying the interventions they assess. The interventions, Pawson and Tilley (1997, p. 50) claim, are seen almost as black boxes, whereas to understand why things work (assuming that they do work), one needs to know which social and behavioral mechanisms are active and in which contexts.

## 5.1 What can be done to remedy the lack of explanations?

The first answer is to open up the program black box and search for mechanisms that explain the findings: What mechanisms are believed to make the intervention work? How plausible is it that these mechanisms do the job? To detect these mechanisms, one has to search in documents, interviews, transcripts, and speeches (of policymakers, civil servants, etc.) for statements that address why it is believed (or hoped) that the new policy will make a difference.

It is crucial to be clear that mechanisms are not the input-throughput-output-outcome variables, nor are they the dimensions usually addressed in logical frameworks, logic models, or statistical equations. Mechanisms operate at a deeper level: "We must go below the 'domain of empirical,' surface level descriptions of constant conjunctions and statistical correlations to identify the underlying mechanisms that account for regularities in the joint-occurrence of events" (Astbury & Leeuw, 2010, p. 368).

By opening up the black box of interventions and policies, the evaluator can understand why it is assumed that intervention or policy X is believed to make a difference. The evaluator searches for mechanisms that are believed to make things happen in the context of the policy intervention to be developed (Pawson & Tilley, 1997).

In recent years, there have been attempts to group mechanisms into common categories. For example, building on Coleman's (1986, 1990) macro-micro-macro model of social action, Hedström and Swedberg (1995) suggest that there are three interrelated types of mechanisms:

- *Situational mechanisms* operate at the macro-to-micro level. These show how specific social situations or events shape the beliefs, desires, and opportunities of individual actors. A belief formation mechanism such as the self-fulfilling prophecy is a good example of a situational mechanism. This mechanism has been shown to affect the way teachers interact with disadvantaged children in the classroom. Another is the community opportunity structure that characterizes a village or city; the more opportunities for, say, crime or employment, the larger the chance that crimes will be carried out or jobs will be found.
- *Action formation mechanisms* operate at the micro-to-micro level. These examine how individual choices and actions are influenced by specific combinations of desires, beliefs, and opportunities. Festinger's (1957) theory of cognitive dissonance illustrates different types of action formation mechanisms used by individuals to reduce psychological distress that often arises when a person holds two contradictory ideas simultaneously. Smokers, for example, often use techniques of rationalization to avoid quitting despite strong evidence that smoking reduces life expectancy (e.g., lung cancer only happens to heavy smokers).
- *Transformational mechanisms* operate at the micro-to-macro level and show how a number of individuals, through their actions and interactions, generate

macro-level outcomes. An example is cascading, by which people influence one another so much that people ignore their private knowledge and rely instead on the publicly stated judgments of others. The bandwagon phenomenon—the tendency to do (or believe) things because many other people do (or believe)—is related to this, as are groupthink, the common knowledge effect, and herd behavior (Elster, 2007).

Although there are not yet repositories on these mechanisms, several scholars have provided useful summaries of the research literature on mechanisms. Elster (1989, 2007), for example, draws on insights from neuropsychology, economics, and political science to identify and discuss some 20 mechanisms that underlie a range of social phenomena.

The second answer is to combine (quasi-)experimental (i.e., counterfactual) impact evaluations and realist evaluations. Van der Knaap, Leeuw, Bogaerts, and Nijssen (2008) describe an approach combining the Campbell Collaboration standards with the realist notion of addressing contexts-mechanisms-outcomes (CMO) that underlie interventions to prevent or reduce violence in the public and semi-public domains. To merge Campbell standards and the realist evaluation approach, the realist approach was applied after finishing the Campbell-style systematic review. This idea of combining schools of thought (statistical impact designs and realist [CMO] evaluations) is winning ground.[4]

Chapter 16 presents an example that deals with the role of microcredit in relation to the empowerment of women in household decision making (see also Vaessen et al., 2014), which also combined the Campbell Collaboration approach with searching for evidence regarding the role mechanisms play in this empowerment process. Jagosh et al. (2011) applied this approach when assessing the outcomes of participatory research and synthesizing the literature for a realist review.

# 6. Practical Applications

TBE has a number of important advantages compared to conventional quantitative approaches for the evaluation of complex development interventions:

- TBE articulates the processes and mechanisms through which a program is intended to achieve its objectives. Often the underlying program model has never been made explicit, and there may be different understandings by different agencies or between implementers and evaluators. Articulating the model in a step-by-step fashion can help ensure that there is agreement on the objectives of the program and how these objectives are to be achieved.
- TBE models have the flexibility to describe how multicomponent programs are intended to operate.
- TBE can incorporate the contextual factors that affect implementation and outcomes in different program locations.
- At the same time TBE draws attention to the possible existence of demi-regularities, it can reduce complexity.

- TBE can be presented using simple graphical techniques that make them easy to understand by nonspecialists, including, when necessary, community leaders and local officials.
- TBE has the flexibility to be combined with a wide range of other approaches to (impact) evaluation. It can provide the framework on which other models can be built.
- TBE can help identify the key issues and critical assumptions that must be tested in the evaluation.
- It is possible to develop two or more models based on different assumptions as to how the program is expected to work. One or more of these can be rival hypotheses put forward by critics of the program explaining why they believe it will not achieve its objectives. Designing the evaluation to test both the program and the rival hypotheses greatly strengthens the methodological rigor of the evaluation.
- There are seven approaches to TBE (see Chapter 5) that can help evaluators and practitioners detect and articulate (reconstruct) the assumptions underlying interventions and programs in ways that can be replicated by others. These approaches have their own limitations, which means that they cannot be used as a cookbook. The approaches function as guidance on how to do the work.

# References (for Chapters 5 and 6)

Abbott, A. (1981). Status and status strain in the professions. *American Journal of Sociology, 86,* 819–835.

Astbury, B., & Leeuw, F. L. (2010). Unpacking black boxes: Mechanisms and theory⊠building in evaluation. *American Journal of Evaluation, 31,* 363–381.

Bickman, L. (1996). A continuum of care: More is not always better. *American Psychologist, 51,* 689–701.

Birleson, P., Brann, P., & Smith, A. (2001). Using program theory to develop key performance indicators for child and adolescent mental health services. *Australian Health Review, 24*(1), 10–21.

Carrol, C., Patterson, M., Wood, S., Booth, A., Rick, J., & Balain, S. (2007). A conceptual framework for implementation fidelity. *Implementation Science, 2*(1), 40.

Carvalho, S., & White, H. (2004). Theory-based evaluation: The case of social funds. *American Journal of Evaluation, 25,* 141–160.

Chen, H. T., & Rossi, P. H. (1980). The multi-goal, theory-driven approach to evaluation: A model linking basic and applied social science. *Social Forces, 59,* 106–122.

Coleman J. S. (1986). Social theory, social research, and a theory of action. *American Journal of Sociology, 91,* 1309–1335.

Coleman, J. (1990). *Foundations of social theory.* Boston, MA: Belknap Press.

Coryn, C. L. S., Noakes, L. A., Westine, C. D., & Schröter, D. C. (2010). A systematic review of theory-driven evaluation practice from 1990 to 2009. *American Journal of Evaluation, 32,* 1–28.

Dieleman, M., Wong, G., & Marchal, B. (2012, October–November). *An introduction to realist research.* Presentation at the Second Global Symposium on Health Systems Research, Beijing, China.

Dolan, P., Hallsworth, M., Halpern, D., King, D., & Vlaev, I. (2010). *Mindspace: Influencing behavior through public policy.* London, UK: Cabinet Office and Institute for Government.

Donaldson, S. I. (2007). *Program theory-driven evaluation science.* New York, NY: Psychology Press.

Drew, R., Aggleton, P., Chalmers, H., & Wood, K. (2011). Using social network analysis to evaluate a complex policy network. *Evaluation, 17,* 383–394.

Elster, J. (1989). *Nuts and bolts for the social sciences.* Cambridge, UKL Cambridge University Press.

Elster, J. (2007). *Explaining social behaviour: More nuts and bolts for the social sciences.* Cambridge, UK: Cambridge University Press.

Festinger, L. (1957). *A theory of cognitive dissonance.* Stanford, CA: Stanford University Press.

Fogel, R. (1964). *Railroads and American economic growth: Essays in econometric history.* Baltimore, MD: John Hopkins University Press.

Forss, K., Marra, M., & Schwartz, R. (Eds.). (2011). *Evaluating the complex: Attribution, contribution and beyond.* New Brunswick, NJ: Transaction.

Friedman, V. (2001). Designed blindness: An Action science perspective on program theory evaluation. *American Journal of Evaluation, 22,* 161–181.

Funnell, S., & Rogers, P. (2011). *Purposeful program theory: Effective use of theories of change and logic models.* San Francisco, CA: Jossey-Bass.

Greenhalgh, T., Kristjansson, E., & Robinson, V. (2007). Realist review to understand the efficacy of school feeding programmes. *BMJ, 335,* 858–861.

Hakkert, A. S., Gitelman, V., & Vis, M. A. (Eds.). (2007). *Road safety performance indicators: Theory.* Deliverable D3.6 of the EU FP6 project SafetyNet.

Harmelink, M., Nilsson, L., & Harmsen, R. (2008). Theory-based policy evaluation of 20 energy efficiency instruments. *Energy Efficiency, 1,* 131–148.

Hedstrom, P. (2005). *Dissecting the social: On the principles of analytical sociology.* Cambridge, UK Cambridge University Press.

Hedstrom, P., & Bearman, P. (2011). *The Oxford handbook of analytical sociology.* Oxford, UK: Oxford University Press.

Hedström, P., & Swedberg, R. (Eds.). (1998). Social mechanisms. An analytical approach to social theory. Cambridge, UK: Cambridge University Press.

Henderson, D. R. (2008). Rent seeking. *The Concise Encyclopedia of Economics.* Retrieved from http://www.econlib.org/library/Enc/RentSeeking.htm

Homans, G. C. (1964). Bringing men back in. *American Sociological Review, 29,* 809–814.

Honeycutt, T., & Strong, D. A. (2012). Using social network analysis to predict early collaboration within health advocacy coalitions. *American Journal of Evaluation, 33,* 221–239.

Jagosh, J., Pluye, P., Macaulay, A. C., Salsberg, J., Henderson, J., Sirett, E., . . . Green, L. W. (2011). Assessing the outcomes of participatory research: Protocol for identifying, selecting, appraising and synthesizing the literature for realist review. *Implementation Science, 6,* 24–31.

Kahneman, D. (2011). *Thinking, fast and slow.* New York, NY: Farrar, Strauss & Giroux.

Karlsson, J. (2011). People can not only open closed systems, they can also close open systems. *Journal of Critical Realism, 10*(2), 145–162.

Kautto, P., & Similä, J. (2005). Recently introduced policy instruments and intervention theories. *Evaluation, 11,* 55–68.

Keizer, K., Lindenberg, S., & Steg, L. (2008). The spreading of disorder. *Science, 322,* 1681–1686.

Kruisbergen, E. W. (2005). Voorlichting: doen of laten? Theorie van afschrikwekkende voorlichtingscampagnes toegepast op de casus van bolletjesslikkers [Educational campaigns: To do or not to do? Theory of deterring educational campaigns applied to the case of drug couriers]. *Beleidswetenschap, 19*(3).

Lawson, T. (1997). *Economics and reality.* London, UK: Routledge.

Leeuw, F. L. (1991). Policy theories, knowledge utilization, and evaluation. *Knowledge and Policy, 4,* 73–92.

Leeuw, F. L. (2003). Reconstructing program theories: Methods available and problems to be solved. *American Journal of Evaluation, 24,* 5–20.

Leeuw, F. L. (2012). Linking theory-based evaluation and contribution analysis: Three problems and a few solutions. *Evaluation, 18,* 348–363.

Leeuw, F., & Leeuw, B. (2012). Cyber society and digital policies: Challenges to evaluation? *Evaluation, 18,* 111–127.

Lindgren, L. (2001). The non-profit sector meets the performance-management movement: A programme-theory approach. *Evaluation, 7,* 285–303.

Lipsey, M. (2009). The primary factors that characterize effective interventions with juvenile offenders: A meta-analytic overview. *Victims and Offenders, 4,* 124–147.

Ludwig, J., Kling, J. R., & Mullainathan, S. (2011). Mechanism experiments and policy evaluations. *Journal of Economic Perspectives, 25*(3), 17–38.

MacMillan, D. (2004). *Actual and hypothetical willingness to pay for environmental outputs: Why are they different?* Aberdeen, Scotland: University of Aberdeen.

Mannheim, K. (1951). *Man and society in an age of reconstruction.* The Hague, Netherlands: Martinus Nijhoff.

Mason, I., & Mitroff, I. (1981). *Challenging strategic planning assumptions.* New York, NY: Wiley.

Mayne, J. (2001). Addressing attribution through contribution analysis: Using performance measures sensibly. *Canadian Journal of Program Evaluation, 16*(1), 1–24.

Mayne, J. (2012). Contribution analysis: Coming of age? *Evaluation, 18,* 270–280.

Meyer, M., & Gupta, V. (1994). The performance paradox. *Research in Organizational Behavior, 6,* 309–369.

Nas, C., van Ooyen-Houben, M. M. J., & Wieman, J. (2011). *Interventies in uitvoering: Wat er mis kan gaan bij de uitvoering van justitiële (gedrags) interventies en hoe dat komt* [Interventions under implementation: What can go wrong with judicial (behavioral) interventions and why]. The Hague, Netherlands: WODC Memorandum.

National Council of Nonprofits. (2010). *Costs, complexification, and crisis: Government's human services contracting "system" hurts everyone.* Washington, DC: Author.

Natsios, A. (2010). *The clash of the counter-bureaucracy and development.* Washington, DC: Center for Global Development.

Pawson, R. (2002). *Does Megan's Law work? A theory-driven systematic review* (Working Paper 8). London, UK: Queen Mary University of London, ESRC UK Centre for Evidence Based Policy and Practice.

Pawson, R. (2013). *The science of evaluation.* London, UK: Sage.

Pawson, R., & Sridharan, S. (2010). Theory-driven evaluation of public health programmes. In A. Killoran & M. Kelly (Eds.), *Evidence-based public health: Effectiveness and efficiency* (pp. 42–62). Oxford, UK: Oxford University Press.

Pawson, R., & Tilley, N. (1997). *Realistic evaluation.* London, UK: Sage.

Pollit, C. (2013). The logics of performance management. *Evaluation, 19,* 346–363.

Rogers, P. J. (2008). Using programme theory to evaluate complicated and complex aspects of interventions. *Evaluation, 14,* 29–48.

Rozendal, P., Moors, H., & Leeuw, F. (1985). *Het bevolkingsvraagstuk in de jaren 80: Opvattingen over overheidsbeleid* [The population issue in the 1980s: Views on government policy]. The Hague, Netherlands: Nidi.

Shepperd, S., Lewin, S., Straus, S., Clarke, M., Eccles, M. P., Fitzpatrick, R., . . . Sheikh, A. (2009). Can we systematically review studies that evaluate complex interventions? *PLoS Medicine, 6*(8), e1000086.

Smith, P. (1995). On the unintended consequences of publishing performance data in the public sector. *International Journal of Public Administration, 8,* 277–310.

Suchman, E. (1967). *Evaluative research.* New York, NY: Russell Sage Foundation.

Tetlock, P. E., & Belkin, A. (1996). Counterfactual thought experiments in world politics: Logical, methodological, and psychological perspectives. In P. E. Tetlock & A. Belkin (Eds.), *Counterfactual thought experiments in world politics: Logical, methodological and psychological perspectives* (pp. 3–38). Princeton, NJ: Princeton University Press.

Thaler, R. H., & Sunstein, C. R. (2009). *Nudge: Improving decisions about health, wealth, and happiness.* New York, NY: Penguin Books.

Tilley, N. (1999). Evaluation and evidence-(mis)led policy. *Evaluation Journal of Australasia, 11,* 48–63.

Thompson, V. D., & Appelbaum, M. (1974). *Population policy acceptance: Psychological determinants.* Chapel Hill, NC: Carolina Population Center.

U.S. General Accounting Office. (1995). *Prospective evaluations methods.* Washington, DC: Author.

Vaessen, J., Rivas, A., Duvendack, M., Palmer Jones, R., Leeuw, F. L., van Gils, G., . . . Waddington, H. (2014). *The effects of microcredit on women's control over household spending in developing countries.* Oslo, Norway: Campbell Systematic Reviews.

Van der Knaap, L. M., Leeuw, F. L., Bogaerts, S., & Nijssen, L. T. J. (2008). Combining Campbell standards and the realist evaluation approach: The best of two worlds. *American Journal of Evaluation, 29,* 48–57.

van Thiel, S., & Leeuw, F. L. (2002). The performance paradox in the public sector. *Public Productivity and Management Review, 25,* 267–281.

Weiss, C. H. (1995). Nothing as practical as good theory: Exploring theory-based evaluation for comprehensive community initiatives for children and families. In J. Connell, A. Kubisch, L. B. Schorr, & C. H. Weiss (Eds.), *New approaches to evaluating community initiatives: Volume 1, concepts, methods, and contexts* (pp. 65–92). New York, NY: Aspen Institute.

Weitzman, B., Mijanovich, T., Silver, D., & Brecher, C. (2009). Finding the impact in a messy intervention: Using an integrated design to evaluate a comprehensive citywide health initiative. *American Journal of Evaluation, 30,* 495–514.

Wiig, H., & Holm-Hansen, J. (2014). *Unintended effects in evaluations of Norwegian aid: A desk study* (Report 2/2014). Oslo, Norway: NORAD.

Wilson, J. Q. (1991, June). The government gap. *The New Republic.*

World Bank. (2015). *Mind, society and behavior: World development report 2015.* Washington, DC: Author.

Zuckerman, E. (2010, February 22). Internet freedom: Beyond circumvention. *My Heart's in Accra.* Retrieved from http://www.ethanzuckerman.com/blog/2010/02/22/internet-freedom-beyond-circumvention

# Notes

1. http://www.ecosystemvaluation.org/contingent_valuation.htm; http://www.scotland.gov.uk/Resource/Doc/1037/0003474.pdf.

2. Largely based on Astbury and Leeuw (2010).

3. Largely based on Leeuw (2012).

4. See the approach followed by 3ie in their requests for proposals; see the Netherlands Institute of Justice Research (wodc.nl) as well as several other research organizations.

# CHAPTER 7

# Dealing With Complexity by Unpacking and Reassembling Elements of a Complex Program

Michael Bamberger, Estelle Raimondo, and Jos Vaessen

An important insight from complexity science concerns the need to pay particular attention to the interrelations between programs and the contexts in which they are embedded, and between the different elements of the program itself. These dimensions call into question the applicability of many widely used evaluation designs that are based on the assumption that different components of a program can be evaluated separately, ignoring the interconnectedness of the different parts and the complex interplay with contextual factors. At the same time it is impossible to capture simultaneously all of the complexity dimensions, so critical choices must be made in terms of boundaries and units of analysis. In this chapter we propose a practical middle-ground approach that breaks down complex programs into separate components that can more easily be evaluated. Once individual components have been evaluated—using a combination of evaluation tools and methods—the findings are subsequently "reassembled." This approach recognizes that the whole is greater than the sum of the parts and that the process of reassembling must capture interactions among the different elements of the system. A final look at the big picture should inform how much of the system has been covered by the evaluation and how much is left unexplained.

Policymakers, managers, and evaluators must navigate a course between the practical need to capture and understand program performance and the necessity to gain some insights into how complexity dynamics can affect the validity of evaluation findings.

"Unpacking" is common practice in evaluation where, for various reasons (e.g., policy priorities, resource constraints), evaluators make abstractions of program realities that (implicitly or explicitly) favor particular levels of analysis or program components. The process of reconciling the pragmatic analytical perspective of the evaluator, and more specifically the principle of unpacking, with insights from complexity science is not self-evident. In some instances, the parts of a system might be so tightly connected that separating them will not be appropriate or even feasible. Yet, even in such cases, evaluators need to make choices about relevant boundaries, units of analysis, variables, and factors of interest, which, as we will show, requires a certain type of unpacking.

We propose a five-level process of unpacking and reassembling an intervention. By this we mean, respectively, the deconstruction of an intervention into meaningful units of analysis that can constitute the foci of an evaluation and the synthetic exercise of putting the pieces back together. The five levels are as follows: (1) conducting an initial diagnostic study to map the complexity dimensions, (2) selecting a unit of analysis, (3) identifying an approach to unpacking, (4) reassembling the various elements into a whole picture, and (5) taking a systems perspective.

For each of these levels of analysis, evaluators can choose from a range of strategies. This chapter is organized along these five levels, and each option is succinctly described in Figure 7.1.

# 1. Level 1: Conducting a Diagnostic Study to Map the Complexity Dimensions

Some of the techniques discussed in Chapters 1 and 2 can be used to understand how the program interacts with different components of the system within which it is embedded (e.g., systems mapping) and how it rates on the four dimensions of complexity. The checklist presented in Table 1.2 (Chapter 1) can be used for this purpose.

# 2. Level 2: Choosing a Unit of Analysis for Unpacking Complex Interventions Into Evaluable Components

One of the four dimensions of complexity concerns the nature of the intervention. When an intervention is large, made up of diverse types of activities and multiple levels of intervention, spanning a wide geographical scope, it can be challenging to capture this in its entirety. It is often necessary to break down this large intervention into smaller pieces that are more amenable to analysis. The selection of the unit of analysis is thus critical. Here we present four options: implementations components, phases, and themes; program theories; cases; and variables.

| **Figure 7.1** | Summary of the Unpacking-Reassembling Approach |
|---|---|
| **Level 1** | **Mapping the complexity dimensions** |
| | • Assessing the level of complexity of each dimension (Chapter 1 checklist) <br> • Assessing the level of connectedness between the various parts of the intervention |
| **Level 2** | **Selecting a unit of analysis** |
| | • Implementation components, phases, and themes <br> • Program theories <br> • Cases <br> • Variables |
| **Level 3** | **Unpacking the system into various parts** |
| | • Operational approaches <br> • Theory reconstruction approaches <br> • Rich description <br> • Variable-based approaches |
| **Level 4** | **Reassembling the parts into a whole** |
| | • Systems modeling: *Linking* <br> • Portfolio analysis: *Overviewing* <br> • Review and synthesis: *Aggregating and synthesizing* <br> • Comparative case study approaches: *Comparing* <br> • Descriptive and inferential statistics: *Linking and aggregating* <br> • Rating scales: *Valuing* |
| **Level 5** | **Going back to the big picture** |
| | • Accounting for the possibility of emergent, spillover, and displacement effects <br> • Accounting for coordination issues <br> • Accounting for policy coherence (internal, historical, horizontal, and vertical) |

## 2.1 Implementation Components, Phases, and Themes

The conception and implementation of complex programs is often administratively translated into various components, implementation phases, often nested under larger programmatic themes. It might thus make sense for an agency to focus an evaluation around units of analysis that are administratively defined, especially for accountability purposes.

---

**BOX 7.1 COMPONENTS OF A HYPOTHETICAL MINISTRY OF TRANSPORT SUPPORT PROGRAM TO STRENGTHEN DECENTRALIZED PLANNING AND MANAGEMENT**

This hypothetical program (see Figure 7.2) includes the following main components:

- provision of computers and financial planning and management software
- reorganization and training support for financial planning and management systems
- decentralized planning of rural transport infrastructure with participation of local communities
- communication strategies to inform districts and local communities about the program
- micro-grants to local communities for transport infrastructure

---

- *Implementation components:* Large interventions are often articulated into components that may operate at various geographical levels or target various populations. Box 7.1 lists the components of a hypothetical support program to a ministry of transport to strengthen decentralized program planning and management. A useful way to categorize program components is the idea of policy instruments, which constitute the basis for public intervention anywhere. A well-known classification is "carrots, sticks and sermons" (Bemelmans-Videc & Rist, 1998), which respectively refer to economic incentives (e.g., tax reduction, subsidies), regulations (e.g., laws, protocols), and indications of support from high-profile figures (e.g., senior government officials, opinion leaders, international agencies) supported by information (e.g., education, technical assistance).
- *Implementation phases:* Interventions follow an administrative process made up of a sequence of phases, such as design, planning, implementation, and reporting. For some evaluations, it makes sense to select these phases as primary units of analysis.
- *Programmatic themes:* Interventions are generally designed to feed into an organization's overarching objectives, which themselves highlight various facets of the organization's core missions. For example, in the past decade, many multilateral agencies as well as NGOs and foundations have subscribed to the overarching goals of, for example, advancing poverty reduction and gender equality in their core activities.

## 2.2 Program Theories

Chapters 5 and 6 lay out the principles of theory-based evaluation (TBE) and how this approach can be used to better understand complex evaluands and their contexts. TBE is a family of approaches that seek to explicate and test policymakers', managers', and other stakeholders' assumptions (or theories) about how a program intends to bring about a desired change. The following are some of the ways in which TBE can be used to unpack complex structures.

- *Levels and scope:* A program can be broken down into micro (e.g., household, community, school), meso (e.g., district, province), and macro (e.g., national, international) levels. Each level can be examined individually (e.g., impacts of the small grants program in Figure 7.2 on community transport infrastructure), and then the linkages between levels can be assessed.
- *Causal pathways:* TBE describes a program in terms of stages of implementation. For example, the Smoke-Free Ontario strategy (Schwartz & Garcia, 2011) identified eight causal pathways expected to contribute to a social climate that would reduce smoking initiation and use among young adults.[1] Each causal pathway was evaluated independently, and it was found that only three had a measurable effect on the two outcomes.[2]
- *Contextual factors:* TBEs can also identify the economic, political, organizational, sociocultural, ecological, psychological, and historical dimensions that can affect implementation and outcomes. Each of these dimensions can then be evaluated individually. For example, it may be found that where the local economy is growing, farmers may be more able and willing to purchase crop insurance, or parents to pay for their children to go to secondary school.
- *Mechanisms:* Mechanisms are the nuts and bolts (Elster, 2007) that identify the psychological and sociological processes through which behavioral change takes place. Mechanisms are described in Chapter 6.

## 2.3 Cases

Some evaluations take a case, with all of its internal complexities, as the unit of analysis (Bevan, 2009; Byrne & Ragin, 2009). A case can be as small as an individual or household, or as large as an organization, community, agency, or even country. Chapter 19 presents an evaluation of a complex budget support strategy in which seven country case studies were compared. *Casing* (defining the case to be studied) is a critical step in the evaluation process, and evaluators should always seek to define/construct the case that is most appropriate for their study.

## 2.4 Variables

Evaluations using a quantitative approach tend to focus on variables as their main units of analysis. These variables are often categorized into three groups. First, there are outcome or dependent variables that the evaluation seeks to explain, such as student enrollment, productivity per hectare, or birth rate. Second, independent or explanatory variables (often program inputs) are those that are meant to account for the variation in the outcome variables. Third, confounding variables (e.g., age, sex, farm size) are controlled for through design-based controls (randomization of the intervention or treatment) or statistical controls (e.g., difference-in-difference regression). Particular input or outcome variables could be taken as the unit of analysis.

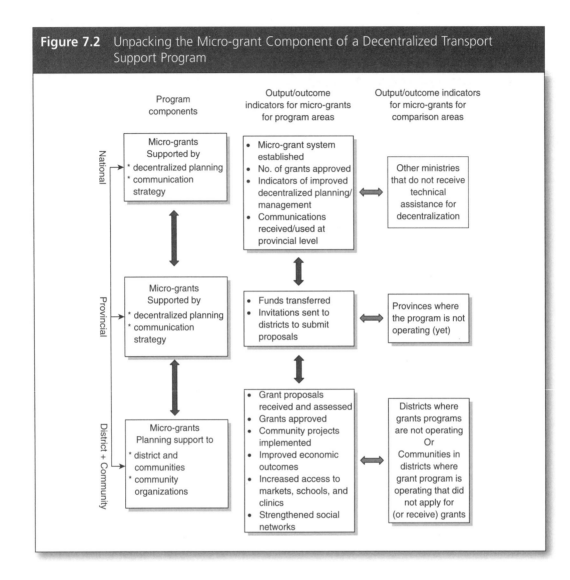

**Figure 7.2** Unpacking the Micro-grant Component of a Decentralized Transport Support Program

# 3. Level 3: Choosing an Approach to Unpacking

The selection of an approach to unpacking unfolds from the choice of unit of analysis described in the previous section. For each unpacking approach there are a number of methodological options. In this section we review four main approaches to unpacking.

## 3.1 Operational Unpacking of Portfolios of Complex Interventions

When the primary units of analysis are the various operational (administrative) components, phases, or themes of programmatic portfolios, unpacking consists of identifying each of these components and how they relate to each other. An advantage of this unpacking strategy is that it is frequently possible to identify a comparison group based on organizations or regions either that are not included in the program or where there will be a delay (planned or unintended) in starting to receive services. Figure 7.2 illustrates how the micro-grants component of the larger intervention introduced in Box 7.1 could be isolated and evaluated. At each level the figure describes a possible comparison group.

## 3.2 Variable-Based Approaches to Unpacking

When the primary units of analysis are a set of dependent, independent, and control variables, unpacking boils down to identifying proxy measures to capture the constructs of interest and devising tools to collect data systematically across individuals, communities, regions, and so on. In practice, many data sets are available on various issues such as demography, income, and health.

## 3.3 Theory Reconstruction Approaches

Theory-based evaluation can be applied at different levels, ranging from the micro to the macro. Regarding the former, this refers to intervention theories of activities or projects, which are discussed in Chapters 5 and 6. At the macro level, one should think about the complex interventions such as (multi-)country programs, thematic strategies, international conventions, and so on. Box 7.2 shows how the basic intervention theory of a complex intervention, the 1972 convention on the protection of cultural and natural heritage, can be further unpacked into more specific (micro-level) intervention theories.

---

**BOX 7.2 UNPACKING THE IMPACT OF A COMPLEX INTERVENTION: MULTI-SITE IMPACT EVALUATION AND NESTED THEORIES OF CHANGE**

In the framework of the 1972 convention on the protection of cultural and natural heritage, UNESCO and its implementing partners intervene at different levels (international, national, program) to promote and implement the principles of the convention with different stakeholders and target groups across the world. The complexity of evaluating the convention stems from the multiplicity and variety of activities and stakeholder configurations in specific contexts at each level of intervention. A first step in the evaluation process is thus to develop the overall framework of expected causal linkages connecting activities and outputs to expected processes of change, as shown in the figure below. Subsequently, each level can be further unpacked into more specific nested theories of change as guidance for causal analysis.

*(Continued)*

(Continued)

To illustrate:

- At the international level UNESCO promotes the ratification of the convention and facilitates the collaboration between member states to agree on shared principles.
- At the national level UNESCO helps raise awareness of decision makers (e.g., parliamentarians, senior civil servants) on how the convention relates to national policy initiatives and encourages inclusion in national strategies and plans.
- At the policy and program implementation level UNESCO helps member states design interventions in alignment with the convention's objectives, strengthens institutional capacities in government agencies, and supports the preservation and sustainable use of natural and cultural heritage.
- At the level of individual heritage sites, UNESCO assists member states in assessing threats to preservation and in contributing to the protection of world heritage.

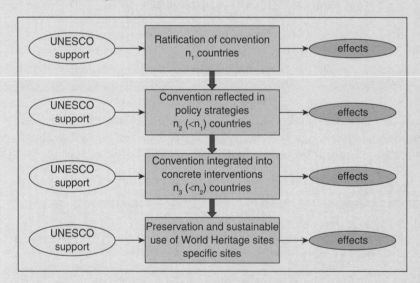

In order to assess the overall relevance and impact of UNESCO's work within this framework, one can synthesize information across contexts according to the logic of the different theories of change at different levels. Subsequently, by reassembling all of the theories and corresponding empirical data back into the overall theory of change, one can develop the overall perspective, the big picture. The advantage of this approach clearly lies in its potential to make sense of a complex multi-site, multi-level intervention. Drawbacks are the time and resources needed to agree on and use the different theories of change as a basis for rigorous data collection.

SOURCE: Authors; see also UNESCO (2013).

A number of other methods can be used to identify, trace, and unpack the various elements of a theory of change (e.g., process analysis, process tracing, results chains).[3]

## 3.4 Rich Description

While variable-based approaches reduce social phenomena (e.g., participation in a development program) to a set of measurable variables, other approaches rely on rich description to make sense of the phenomenon. Ethnographic researchers unpack programs by viewing them through multiple perspectives (e.g., participants, program staff, nonparticipants, partner organizations) and through various angles (changes at individual, household, community level, both expected and unanticipated). For example, Chapter 17 presents an evaluation of coordination against trafficking in persons. The focus of the evaluation is on the mechanisms of coordination among different multilateral and bilateral agencies, resulting in a rich description of the coordination mechanisms by consulting with many stakeholders through interviews and surveys at various levels of the systems.

Rich descriptions often rely on participatory data collection and analysis processes. For example, Chapter 15 uses participatory mapping in an evaluation of a long-term effort to prevent gender-based violence in El Salvador. The various stakeholders of the coalition supporting the program mapped expected outcomes through major milestones over a period of 10 years, which was the basis for identifying relevant evaluation indicators of success.

# 4. Level 4: Choosing an Approach to Reassembling the Various Parts Into a Big Picture

Once evaluators have developed a better understanding of how individual units of analysis "work," the challenge is to reassemble these individual assessments into an overall assessment of the program. Reassembling the various elements does not mean that the final big picture will be identical to the original one. Instead, in the process of unpacking and reassembling, the evaluation will have identified the changes that took place at a higher level of the system. This task is particularly challenging in complex interventions due to emergence, dynamic relationships, issues of coordination, and possible spillover or counteracting effects. For instance, when the main unit of analysis is a program component, it is quite possible that many of the individual components are found to have achieved their objectives, yet the overall program may not have achieved its broader goals. This may be because of problems of coordination among different components or because of weaknesses in the overall program logic. For example, the five program components outlined in Box 7.1 may not be sufficient to strengthen decentralized planning and management in the ministry of transport. On the other hand, the whole might be more than the sum of its parts, especially if there are positive emergent or spillover effects from the interaction of the various components. Other challenges for reassembling and assessing overall change include the following:

- There is frequently an absence of a well-defined intervention theory capable of explaining how the different contextual factors, mechanisms, and intended outcomes fit together and how various configurations are expected to complement each other to achieve overall program objectives.

- It is often difficult to understand the influence of contextual factors that may have different effects across project locations or on different components and to assess the interactions among different contextual factors.
- There is often a lack of a common metric for combining different kinds of elements: Outcomes are often measured in different ways, systematically comparing cases is often challenging due to the lack of a common set of dimensions, and synthesizing different theories of change is rendered more difficult due to the absence of a unique perspective on intended changes.

In this section we present six ways of reassembling evaluated parts of an intervention into an overall perspective. These approaches rely on different combinations of analytical principles (e.g., linking, aggregating, comparing, synthesizing, overviewing, valuing).

## 4.1 Systems Modeling

One of the greatest challenges for both unpacking and reassembling is to understand the dynamics of the networks or systems within which the program operates. In order to reassemble the intervention, evaluators need to determine how closely or loosely each component is linked to other components and how the linkages operate. With systems modeling, reassembling essentially consists of applying the principle of *linking* components together. A first group of methods—systems dynamics, structural equation models, and hierarchical models—builds on conventional regression techniques but relaxes some stringent assumptions such as the independence between variables. A second group encompasses visual models of systems and networks and uses qualitative principles to make sense of the linkages between each component. In this category we find, among other techniques, social network analysis, Venn diagrams, causal loop diagrams, and soft systems methodologies[4] (see Chapter 2).

## 4.2 Descriptive and Inferential Statistical Analysis

While some of the systems approaches can provide an aggregate measure of the effect of an intervention on an outcome of interest, most of them do not. Their comparative advantage lies in assessing the strength of the relationships between the various components. Bivariate and multivariate (descriptive and inferential) statistical techniques, by looking at associations between variables, also adhere to the principle of *linking*. However, the latter also relate to another way of reassembling, which could be described as *aggregation*. Both descriptive and inferential statistical methods have been used to assess overall effects. Examples are meta-analysis (see Chapter 16), cluster analysis (Uprichard, 2009), and regressions with nonlinear functional forms or with interaction terms.

## 4.3 Comparative Case Study Approaches

Often evaluators are tasked not only with answering the question of whether an intervention reached a particular outcome, but also with understanding why this particular effect took place. Consequently, reassembling various cases sometimes means *comparing* them to understand the conditions that enabled the intervention's success.

A wide range of comparative case study designs are available, ranging from non-systematic to very systematic (Byrne & Ragin, 2009; Carden, 2009; Yin, 2013). For example, in Chapter 15 an in-depth comparison of the impact of municipal action to reduce the incidence of gender-based violence in two regions of El Salvador was justified by the clients' desire to better understand how the work at the national level articulated with local level politics and activities. These two cases were selected because they contrasted in terms of their municipal government political affiliation and because one province was rural and the other urban.

Other case-based methods use mathematic logic when comparing the various case attributes and are often referred to as qualitative comparative analysis (QCA). This approach examines the association between different combinations (configurations) of attributes and the presence (or absence) of outcomes. QCA identifies three types of conditions:

- What attributes are found in all instances where the outcome is present? (necessary conditions)
- Is the outcome always present when particular attributes or combinations of attributes are present? (sufficient conditions)
- Are there combinations of factors that are jointly sufficient?

Box 7.3 describes how QCA essentially integrates unpacking and reassembling in a single approach. Chapter 4 includes a detailed discussion of QCA and illustrates its application by describing the evaluation of an irrigation assistance project in Nepal.

---

### BOX 7.3 UNPACKING AND REASSEMBLING USING QUALITATIVE COMPARATIVE ANALYSIS

QCA integrates unpacking and reassembling in one approach, differentiating between three levels:

*Level 1: Choosing a unit of analysis*—In QCA the main unit of analysis is a case.

*Level 2: Unpacking the intervention into different components*—In QCA each case is unpacked in a configuration of factors that the evaluator believes to be critical for the program outcome(s) to be achieved. For each case, the evaluator records whether a condition was present or absent from the case. Level 2 culminates in the presentation of a truth table (see Chapter 4 for an example).

*Level 3: Reassembling the explanation*—In QCA the last step consists of identifying causal packages through a systematic comparison of cases that applies the following heuristic: If two cases share a similar outcome but differ on one particular condition, then this particular condition is not necessary for the outcome to take place and is eliminated from this particular configuration of enabling factors (Raab & Suppert, 2014).

## 4.4 Portfolio Analysis

Portfolio analysis develops a set of simple matrices that can be used to describe and assess each performance area and provide an overview of the performance at the level of the entire portfolio. Portfolio analysis can be used in two main ways:

- To organize basic information on all project activities in programs for which little systematic information exists.
- To rate performance on a set of key dimensions for programs that cover a large number of countries or regions, each of which includes a number of standard activities. An example is the World Bank evaluation of how well its gender policies were being implemented in approximately 100 countries. The evaluation began by rating major activities and classifying countries according to how well they were performing on gender indicators. Based on this rating, a sample of countries was selected for more in-depth analysis (see Figure 7.3). Portfolio analysis has a number of advantages for complexity-responsive evaluations; it is a simple way to organize information from multiple interventions. The ratings maximize information from diverse sources and quantitative and qualitative information can be combined.

## 4.5 Review and Synthesis Approaches

Chapter 9 distinguishes between two main types of reviews leveraging a distinct reassembling principle: aggregative and configurative. On the one hand, meta-analysis and other types of systematic reviews seek an *aggregate* measure of effect sizes by combining similar types of data across homogenous studies. Chapter 16 provides a step-by-step illustration of this type of reassembling, which is generally applied when the main units of analysis are (1) a particular outcome variable (e.g., women's control over household expenditures) and (2) a particular treatment variable (e.g., participation in a microcredit program). On the other hand, configurative reviews are used when the main unit of analysis is a program theory and applies the principle of *synthesizing* evidence to refine the theory underlying a complex intervention and to engage in explanation building (Pawson, 2006). Once the various pieces of evidence have been gathered from primary studies, they are absorbed and reassembled into a richer and evolving model of how the intervention works, for whom, and under what circumstances. Pawson (2006) identifies a number of analytical principles that can be used to reassemble the various pieces of evidence:

- *Juxtaposing*: when one study provides information on the process and another on the outcome
- *Reconciling and adjudicating*: when two studies provide contradictory judgment on the effectiveness of an intervention
- *Consolidating*: when the various pieces of evidence provide information on multiple facets of an intervention
- *Situating*: when the various pieces of evidence provide information on the contextual characteristics that make an intervention successful in a particular environment and less successful in another

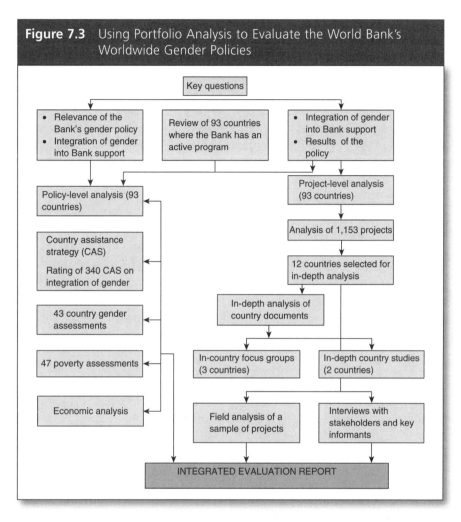

**Figure 7.3**   Using Portfolio Analysis to Evaluate the World Bank's Worldwide Gender Policies

In their application of realist synthesis to community accountability and empowerment initiatives (described in Chapter 20), Westhorp, Walker, and Rogers describe the challenges of relating program mechanisms to diverse categories of interventions. The design of programs influences the type of mechanisms that can be fired, and a given mechanism can also be triggered in multiple categories of programs.

## 4.6 Rating Scales

Other approaches to reassembling rely on the principle of *valuing* a particular intervention while taking into account its various components. A relatively simple and rapid approach is to develop a set of rating scales that assess different dimensions of a program. Often these are based on the OECD-DAC (2010) criteria: relevance, effectiveness, efficiency, impact, and sustainability.[5] In practice, there is a lot of flexibility in developing appropriate (semantic) scales to assess interventions on the different criteria. Rating is used in evaluations of single interventions but also in the analysis of portfolios of interventions.[6] The rating itself can be conducted by one or more evaluators. At the level of portfolios, to avoid inconsistencies in ratings across interventions, some type of validation of ratings is essential (e.g., using an approach whereby two or more reviewers independently rate an intervention, calculating inter-rater reliability scores).

In addition to the efficiency and relatively low cost of using a rating approach, the advantage for complexity-responsive evaluation is the flexibility to adapt rating criteria and semantic scales to the complexity of a specific intervention and its context.

# 5. Level 5: Going Back to the Big Picture: Limitations, Gaps, and Delimitations

After the process of unpacking and reassembling, the evaluator again looks at the intervention and its context from a holistic perspective. This involves reflecting on what aspects of the system have been left out of the inquiry and what dimensions have been only partly covered. It also means taking stock of what the evaluation is in a position to say about the whole system. As already pointed out by Hirschman (2014), an important source of uncertainty in a development project lies in "the extent to which many interdependent components have to be fitted together and adjusted to each other for the project . . . to yield the output for which it was designed" (p. 40). A number of key questions must be asked to assess the extent to which a complexity-responsive evaluation following an unpacking strategy has been successful at fitting the various systems elements into a big picture. For example:

- *To what extent did the evaluation account for the possibility of emergent, spillover, or displacement effects?*

Determining the extent to which the various elements of an intervention change the context in which it operates and how these changes affect the other elements of the intervention (whether these elements are other subprojects, or program mechanisms, or variables of interest) is paramount to understand the system quality of an intervention. For instance, in Chapter 4, we described the example of a project on payments for environmental services, which resulted in a number of displacement effects.

- *To what extent did the evaluation take due account of coordination issues?*

The need for coordinating and fitting various parts of an intervention into a whole is a challenge both on the operational side and during the evaluation, and the effectiveness of individual projects/components is often reduced due to coordination problems. For interventions that do not have clearly defined objectives, coordination can be more difficult to observe from an evaluation standpoint, but if it does not take place, multiple individually successful parts may not fit into a successful whole. Chapter 17 presents a discussion of the coordination mechanisms among various agencies working toward reducing human trafficking.

- *To what extent did the evaluation take due account of policy coherence?*

Another important task at this level of analysis is to determine the extent to which a particular intervention coherently fits within the larger policy framework. There are four important dimensions of policy coherence that warrant attention:

- *Internal policy coherence* corresponds to whether various stakeholders share a common understanding of an intervention's purpose and its theory of change, and how these fit with their own interests and objectives. In Chapter 13, we elaborate on this theme and propose a framework for eliciting stakeholder values and assumptions regarding a program.
- *Horizontal policy coherence* has to do with how different programs operating at the same level fit together. Are their objectives aligned? Are their modi operandi compatible? Horizontal coherence can become particularly challenging if there is little coordination among donors and/or implementing organizations.
- *Vertical policy coherence* assesses the extent to which a given program is aligned with a broader and higher-level policy framework. For instance, over the past 15 years, development programs were assumed to contribute to one or more of the Millennium Development Goals.
- *Historical policy coherence* refers to the consistency between interventions over time in a particular region or policy field or with respect to a particular target population. For instance, the Ministry of Foreign Affairs of the Netherlands conducted a review of Dutch support to basic education between 2000 and 2009, synthesizing lessons from underlying empirical evaluation studies conducted within the framework of the overall evaluation of Dutch support to basic education. Among other things, the review sought to assess the historical consistency over a decade of support in order to account for investments made by the Ministry of Foreign Affairs and learn from past experiences (IOB, 2011).

# 6. Practical Applications

- Almost all complexity-responsive evaluations rely on a strategy that consists of unpacking complex programs into evaluable parts. Unpacking permits the use of established (quantitative, qualitative, and mixed methods) evaluation designs. Essentially this process operates at five levels of analysis:
  - Level 1: Mapping the complexity dimensions. The complexity checklist (Chapter 1) can then be used to assess complexity levels and to determine the degree of complexity responsiveness that is warranted in the evaluation.

- ○ Level 2: Deciding on the appropriate unit of analysis to unpack the program into evaluable parts.
- ○ Level 3: Selecting the appropriate evaluation design (or designs) for evaluating the different parts.
- ○ Level 4: Reassembling the findings of the individual parts to assess the overall effectiveness of the whole intervention system. This step is critical because it is possible that even if most of the components achieve their objectives, the overall program may not achieve its overarching goals.
- ○ Level 5: While unpacking and reassembling a complex intervention are valuable approaches to make complexity more manageable, it is critical not to lose sight of the bigger picture by
  - ▪ assessing the intervention in the light of emergent designs, spillover, and displacement effects;
  - ▪ addressing coordination issues and the influence of different perspectives and objectives of stakeholder groups on program coherence and effectiveness;
  - ▪ addressing policy coherence issues.
- A final word of caution is in order. It may be tempting to skip Levels 4 and 5 and to base the evaluation findings on the findings of Level 3. This may result in a significant bias and overestimation or underestimation of the overall program impact, as it is likely that systemic factors that can significantly reduce or enhance overall impacts would be ignored.

# References

Bemelmans-Videc, M. L., & Rist, R. C. (Eds.). (1998). *Carrots, sticks and sermons: Policy instruments and their evaluation.* New Brunswick, NJ: Transaction.

Bevan, P. (2009). Working with cases in development contexts: Some insights from an outlier. In D. Byrne & C. Ragin (Eds.), *Sage handbook of case-based methods* (pp. 467–493). Thousand Oaks, CA: Sage.

Byrne, D., & Ragin, C. (Eds.). (2009). *Sage handbook of case-based methods.* Thousand Oaks, CA: Sage.

Carden, F. (2009). Using comparative data: A systems approach to a multiple case study. In D. Byrne & C. Ragin (Eds.), *Sage handbook of case-based methods* (pp. 331–344). Thousand Oaks, CA: Sage.

Elster, J. (2007). *Explaining social behavior: More nuts and bolts for the social sciences.* Cambridge, UK: Cambridge University Press.

Hirschman, A. (2014). *Development projects observed.* Washington, DC: Brookings Institution.

IOB. (2011). *Education matters: Policy review of the Dutch contribution to basic education 1999–2009.* Retrieved from http://www.iob-evaluatie.nl/node/194

OECD-DAC. (2010). *Glossary of key terms in evaluation and results based management.* Paris, France: OECD.

Pawson, R. (2006). *Evidence-based policy: A realist perspective.* Thousand Oaks, CA: Sage.

Raab, M., & Suppert, W. (2014). *Review of evaluation approaches and methods for interventions related to violence against women and girls.* Retrieved from http://r4d.dfid.gov.uk/pdf/outputs/misc_gov/61259-Raab_Stuppert_Report_VAWG_Evaluations_Review_DFID_20140626.pdf

Schwartz, R., & Garcia, J. (2011). Intervention path contribution analysis (IPCA) for complex strategy evaluation: Evaluating the Smoke-Free Ontario strategy. In K. Forss, M. Marra, & R. Schwartz (Eds.), *Evaluating the complex: Attribution, contribution and beyond* (pp. 187–208). New Brunswick, NJ: Transaction.

UNESCO. (2013). *Draft structure of the theory of change of the World Heritage Convention.* Unpublished working document, Internal Oversight Service, UNESCO.

Uprichard, E. (2009). Introducing cluster analysis: What can it teach us about the case? In D. Byrne & C. Ragin (Eds.), *Sage handbook of case-based methods* (pp. 132–147). Thousand Oaks, CA: Sage.

Westhorp, G., Walker, B., & Rogers, P. (2012). *Under what circumstances does enhancing community accountability and empowerment improve education outcomes, particularly for the poor? A realist synthesis.* London: University of London, Institute of Education, Social Science Research Unit, EPPI-Centre.

Williams, B., & Hummelbrunner, R. (2011). *Systems concepts in action: A practitioner's toolkit.* Stanford, CA: Stanford University Press.

Yin, R. (2013). *Case study research: Design and methods.* Thousand Oaks, CA: Sage.

# Notes

1. These included youth action alliances, high school grants, youth access to tobacco restrictions, taxes, smoking cessation, and various media campaigns.

2. Youth action alliances, high school grants, and the "leave the pack behind" media campaign.

3. These and other theory-based methods are presented in Chapters 4, 5, and 6.

4. Williams and Hummelbrunner (2011) provide a practitioner's toolkit that describes many of these approaches in detail. Chapter 2 presents some examples of systems approaches.

5. Other criteria are used in practice as well (e.g., policy coherence, value for money).

6. Either by validating and aggregating existing project-specific ratings or by applying a new rating approach to all projects (informed by desk study and possibly other sources of information).

# CHAPTER 8

# The Importance of a Mixed Methods Approach for Evaluating Complexity

Michael Bamberger

*As interventions become larger and more complex, it becomes increasingly difficult to find any single evaluation method that can assess all of the different dimensions of program processes and outcomes. Consequently, the evaluation of most complex interventions requires the use of a mixed methods design that has the flexibility to model and measure the complex processes of causal change. This chapter presents a rationale for the use of mixed methods to evaluate complex interventions and an overview of the different strategies and methods.*

*Following the introduction, Section 2 presents the reasons for using mixed methods and Section 3 details the benefits of mixed methods. Section 4 describes the integrated mixed methods approach, and Section 5 shows how mixed methods approaches help evaluate complex interventions. The final section discusses practical applications.*

## 1. Dealing With Complexity Inherently Requires a Combination of Methods

Complex programs involve many different processes and require the combination of multiple analytical frameworks and data collection methods. Consequently, as no single evaluation method can capture all of the dimensions of complexity, almost all complexity-responsive evaluations rely heavily on mixed methods (MM) approaches. Box 8.1 offers a working definition of mixed methods, quantitative, and qualitative approaches and designs. It stresses that the distinction between quantitative and qualitative evaluation methods is a simplification of the research process. It is possible to conduct quantitative analysis on data that were collected using qualitative methods and to conduct qualitative analysis on data collected through, for example, sample surveys. In fact, most evaluations use at least some combination of qualitative and quantitative methods during data collection and data analysis.[1]

All four dimensions of complexity discussed in earlier chapters present methodological challenges that cannot be resolved though reliance on any single evaluation method. Consequently, complexity-responsive evaluations require the use of multiple methods that are able to capture the multiple dimensions of the interventions and systems being studied and that have the flexibility to adapt to changes in project design and implementation as well as the program context. Also, complexity-responsive evaluation requires the capturing of multiple perspectives and multiple voices (Mertens & Hesse-Biber, 2013). Many authors also argue that the experiences and opinions of the communities that programs are intended to benefit (particularly the poorest and most vulnerable) should be privileged in the MM evaluation design (Chambers, 1997, 2010). There are still very few tried and tested designs for complexity-responsive evaluation, and consequently most MM designs adopt a pragmatic approach in which new evaluation designs are developed for each particular study rather than drawing on a range of established designs, as can be done for evaluations of "simple" programs. For example, all of the complex evaluation case studies presented in *Evaluating the Complex* (Forss, Marra, & Schwartz, 2011) use this pragmatic approach, creatively developing new evaluation designs to suit the specific characteristics of each evaluation, and none claim to be replicating an established evaluation design.

---

## BOX 8.1 DEFINING TERMS: QUANTITATIVE, QUALITATIVE, AND MIXED METHODS

*It is important to recognize that the distinction between quantitative and qualitative evaluation methods is a simplification of the research process. It is possible to conduct quantitative analysis on data that were collected using qualitative methods and to conduct qualitative analysis on data collected through, for example, sample surveys. It is also possible to convert quantitative data into qualitative variables and vice versa.*

**Mixed methods (MM) designs:** Evaluation designs that combine quantitative and qualitative approaches in one or more stages of an evaluation. A fully integrated MM design incorporates quantitative and qualitative approaches in all stages of the evaluation, but in practice most MM designs combine approaches only in a few stages of the evaluation—most commonly in data collection. A key instrument for MM evaluation is triangulation, which compares data collected through different research methods, using different interviewers (e.g., male and female, different races and ethnicities), in different locations and at different times. MM approaches also emphasize the importance of articulating

*(Continued)*

(Continued)

the perspectives of different groups, ensuring that vulnerable groups are heard and understanding the views of different stakeholder groups. Some theorists also see MM as a tool for social action to promote social justice, equity, or emancipation. Recently MM researchers have also focused on the integration of different social science paradigms such as development economics, sociology, political science, ethnography, and demography into the evaluation design.

**Quantitative (QUANT) approaches and methods:** Mainly working with numerical data and quantitative analysis. QUANT researchers work in the postpositivist research paradigm, which holds that the world consists of "social facts" that are objective and are not influenced by the observer. The use of statistical methods for sample selection and data analysis provides breadth and permits generalizations to the total study population.

**Qualitative (QUAL) approaches and methods:** Mainly working with narrative data and qualitative analysis. This approach provides depth, documentation of lived experience, and multiple perspectives. It is able to reach and to give voice to vulnerable and difficult-to-reach groups. Qualitative researchers mainly work in the constructivist research paradigm, which holds that all observations are socially constructed and that different people (researchers and the people they study) observe and interpret the world differently.

SOURCES: The definitions are adapted from Teddlie & Tashakkori (2009, ch. 2). The discussion of multiple perspectives and values is adapted from Mertens & Hesse-Biber (2013).

Until recently the focus of most MM research was the integration of QUANT and QUAL approaches. While this distinction is still central to the literature, it is becoming recognized that often the most important challenge is the integration of the approaches of different social science disciplines, particularly development economics and other social science disciplines. Often both disciplines employ QUANT and QUAL methods and the difference in approach is more fundamental, being based on different research paradigms and the related ontological and epistemological assumptions (Bevan, 2009; Bowman & Sweetman, 2014; Greene, 2007; Teddlie & Tashakkori, 2009).

Another important feature of MM is the incorporation of different lenses to provide different perspectives on a problem or on the interpretation of data and findings. Triangulation, which is a central element of MM, provides a systematic way to obtain different perspectives that can be compared to provide points of convergence and divergence. Capturing different voices, particularly the voices of vulnerable groups, has always been a central focus of feminist and empowerment evaluation, but triangulation can also be used to compare the perspectives of economists, sociologists, political scientists, and other social science disciplines. While QUANT-oriented evaluators often use triangulation to determine the "best" estimate when there are inconsistencies among different sources of data, complexity-responsive evaluation often adopts the multiple lens approach as it is usually not possible (or appropriate) to identify a single best interpretation of complex situations.

## 2. The Reasons for Using a Mixed Methods Approach in Complexity-Responsive Evaluation

MM offer benefits for all evaluations, including value diversity; triangulation; development of the research design; generating new insights (Greene, 2005, pp. 255–256); eclectic methodological pluralism; improvisation and innovation adaptive iteration; plural perspectives; being open, alter, and inquisitive; and defining optimal ignorance (Chambers, 1997, 2010). In addition to these general benefits, MM offer some important advantages for complexity-responsive evaluations:

- *Delineating the evaluand.* Complex interventions are frequently difficult to describe as different funding and implementing agencies provide different packages of services, often nonstandard or not clearly documented. Implementing strategies may involve mechanisms that are difficult to monitor. These often involve both QUANT and QUAL dimensions that cannot be fully captured by a single method (SM) approach. The scientific realist approach is well suited to describe the characteristics and operation of complex evaluands.
- *Describing complex causal pathways and outcomes/impacts.* Multiple causal pathways that are often nonlinear, nonproportional, and involve feedback loops cannot be adequately described with SM approaches. A well-articulated theory of change can outline the main causal pathways, and case studies can provide detailed descriptions of how causal pathways operate for different individual cases. Also, many outcomes are multidimensional, often combining both QUANT and QUAL dimensions so that different methods are required to provide a fully articulated description.
- *Understanding the context-specific embeddedness of the intervention.* The design, implementation, and outcomes of complex programs are affected by a wide range of contextual factors that also interact, making the analysis of their effects even more difficult to trace. A combination of many different methods is required to describe each factor and to assess its effects. Case studies, where the project is the unit of analysis, are one of the useful MM approaches.
- *Understanding behavioral complexity.* The mechanisms through which programs are intended to achieve their outcomes are complex and difficult to evaluate. Many evaluation designs do not even address these mechanisms, and SM approaches are able to provide only a superficial analysis. A more complete analysis requires combining a range of methods, including QUANT techniques such as sociometric analysis, analysis of social networks, and attitude surveys, and QUAL methods such as participant·observation, content analysis of videos, focus groups, and in-depth interviews.

# 3. Illustrating the Benefits of a Mixed Methods Approach

Let us illustrate the benefits of MM for evaluating a hypothetical rural health centers program on the health of women and children.[2] At the end of the section, we cite several studies demonstrating the benefits of the mixed methods approach in different contexts.

The evaluation was conducted by the National Statistics Institute (NSI), which specializes in quantitative survey research. The NSI was aware from previous surveys that poor and less educated women are reluctant to speak freely about their experiences with the health services, and there were concerns about accessibility of the health services to poor and vulnerable sectors of the population, complaints about sexual harassment in some clinics, and poorer service for low-status women. To address these concerns, the NSI invited a research center specializing in gender research with a qualitative methods focus to collaborate in the next round of the evaluation. Figure 8.1 describes the MM evaluation design developed between the NSI and the research center.

The evaluation began with an in-depth ethnographic study in which researchers lived for several weeks in villages broadly representative of the various regional and ethnic groups to understand different cultural traditions and beliefs relating to health, to observe the operation of the health centers, and to identify issues to be explored in the QUANT survey. This was followed by a nationally representative household survey, similar to previous NSI evaluations of rural health programs.

A statistical analysis of the survey was conducted to estimate proportions of women using the health centers and their satisfaction with the services provided. The analysis also developed a typology of villages and households in terms to their response to the health centers. This was used to select a statistically representative sample of villages for more in-depth QUAL studies of attitudes, beliefs, and socio-economic, cultural, and other contextual factors affecting the use of the health centers and to obtain more reliable estimates of actual use of the centers and the behavior of health center staff.

The selection of a statistically representative sample of communities and households for in-depth studies was essential because QUAL studies tend to unearth problems (e.g., sexual harassment or lack of respect by program staff for ethnic minorities or poorer women) that are not detected in the QUANT surveys. In the past the Ministry of Health had dismissed these negative findings by claiming that the selection of communities was intentionally biased to include villages where there were problems with the services.

Triangulation can be used in many different ways (see Table 8.2). In the present example, triangulation compared the findings from the QUANT surveys and the QUAL data collection. Where inconsistencies were found (e.g., a higher proportion of reported problems with health center operation in the QUAL studies), the QUANT and QUAL research teams met to discuss the reasons for the differences. Where the reasons were not clear, researchers returned to the field to determine which estimates were the most credible. The evaluation report integrated the QUANT and QUAL findings, often using QUAL data to explain and illustrate the QUANT findings.

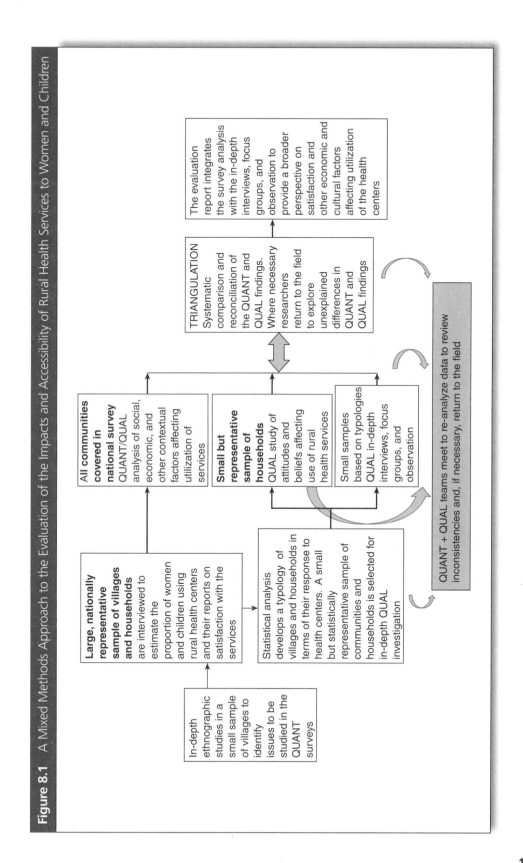

**Figure 8.1** A Mixed Methods Approach to the Evaluation of the Impacts and Accessibility of Rural Health Services to Women and Children

In-depth ethnographic studies in a small sample of villages to identify issues to be studied in the QUANT surveys

**Large, nationally representative sample of villages and households** are interviewed to estimate the proportion of women and children using rural health centers and their reports on satisfaction with the services

Statistical analysis develops a typology of villages and households in terms of their response to health centers. A small but statistically representative sample of communities and households is selected for in-depth QUAL investigation

**All communities covered in national survey** QUANT/QUAL analysis of social, economic, and other contextual factors affecting utilization of services

**Small but representative sample of households** QUAL study of attitudes and beliefs affecting use of rural health services

Small samples based on typologies QUAL in-depth interviews, focus groups, and observation

TRIANGULATION Systematic comparison and reconciliation of the QUANT and QUAL findings. Where necessary researchers return to the field to explore unexplained differences in QUANT and QUAL findings

The evaluation report integrates the survey analysis with the in-depth interviews, focus groups, and observation to provide a broader perspective on satisfaction and other economic and cultural factors affecting utilization of the health centers

QUANT + QUAL teams meet to re-analyze data to review inconsistencies and, if necessary, return to the field

Using the typology discussed in the next section, this study is classified as a sequential QUAL-QUANT-QUAL balanced design that gives equal weight to QUANT and QUAL methods.

Table 8.1 presents examples of the value-added that mixed methods designs can bring to many different kinds of evaluation. In *Example 1* (evaluation of a program to prevent gender-based violence in El Salvador), MM provided a deeper understanding of processes of behavioral change that are difficult to capture through quantitative surveys. Triangulation was used to strengthen weak and incomplete numerical data on, for example, police reports on gender-based violence and to assess the effectiveness of advocacy campaigns.

In *Example 2* (evaluation of a program to strengthen household well-being through promoting women's savings groups), ethnographic studies that dug deep found that while the QUANT survey found that women did not extend their circle of contacts through the program, women strengthened their social capital by increasing the frequency of interactions in their existing groups.

In *Example 3* (evaluation of a program to strengthen resilience of small farmers in drought-affected areas of Ethiopia), a mixed methods design was able to compensate for the relatively small sample for the QUANT survey (which did not permit statistical comparisons among the five villages, but only aggregate analysis for all five villages) through the use of focus groups that permitted some exploratory comparisons among communities.

In *Example 4* (evaluation of a federal housing subsidy program), it was originally planned to only conduct parallel QUANT and QUAL studies. The reanalysis of the original results found that there were major differences in outcomes between programs for rural populations (which were largely White with smaller, better off, and more integrated families and where the program worked well) and urban populations (which were largely Black, poorer, and less stable and where the program did not work well).

# 4. The Integrated Mixed Methods Approach

In practice many evaluations incorporate MM into only one stage of the evaluation (e.g., using rapid QUAL studies to help design a QUANT survey, using case studies to illustrate some of the points in the QUANT data analysis). However, as we show in this section, a fully integrated MM design requires using both QUANT and QUAL methods or frameworks at every stage of the evaluation (Bamberger, 2012; Morgan, 2014; Teddlie & Tashakkori, 2009).

## 4.1 Four Dimensions for Classifying Mixed Methods Evaluation Designs

*a. Dimension 1: Sequential and Parallel Designs*

- *Sequential Designs*

In sequential designs QUANT and QUAL methods are used one after the other. Figure 8.2 is an example of a sequential design used to assess interhousehold transfers as a survival strategy of poor families. The evaluation began with an

**Table 8.1** Examples of Mixed Methods Evaluation and the Value-Added They Bring

| Study | Mixed methods design | Value-added of the mixed methods design |
|---|---|---|
| 1. Evaluating a program to prevent gender-based violence (GBV) in El Salvador (Chapter 15 of this book) | • National secondary data used to obtain numerical data on GBV<br>• Two in-depth case studies on the impacts of municipal actions<br>• Advocacy evaluation of the coalition's tactics and their influence on change<br>• Direct observation of program implementation strategies<br>• Type of design: parallel/multilevel | • There was deeper understanding of processes that are difficult to capture through surveys.<br>• Triangulation was used to strengthen weak and incomplete statistical data from police records.<br>• Innovative methodologies assessed the effectiveness of advocacy campaigns. |
| 2. Evaluating Savings for Change Mali, promoting women's savings groups to strengthen household welfare (Bureau of Applied Research in Anthropology, 2013) | • Randomized control trial (RCT) covered 6,000 women in project and control groups focused on changes in social capital (talking to village chief, attending meetings, and voting)<br>• In-depth ethnographic studies of household and social dynamics<br>• Type of design: sequential/single level | • RCT found women had not formed new relationships and there were no significant increases in social capital.<br>• However, ethnographic studies found that while new contacts did not increase, contacts with existing social networks were strengthened and this strengthened social cohesion.<br>• Ethnographic studies also found that older women (the majority of savings group members) preferred to diversify risk and to invest in small animals rather than banking systems. |
| 3. Evaluating a program to strengthen the resilience of farmers in Ethiopia in drought-affected areas (Bamberger, in press) | • A pretest-posttest comparison group design studied the effects of a weather-indexed group insurance program on farmers in five villages<br>• Focus groups with male and female farmers who purchased crop insurance<br>• Type of design: sequential/single level | • Due to the relatively small survey sample size (400 households), it was not possible to conduct statistical comparisons between villages but only to test effects for all villages. The focus groups were able to obtain comparative data between villages but only with small samples.<br>• Focus groups were able to dig deeper and to identify new trends since the survey instrument was developed. |

*(Continued)*

**Table 8.1** (Continued)

| Study | Mixed methods design | Value-added of the mixed methods design |
|-------|---------------------|------------------------------------------|
| 4. Evaluating a U.S. federal housing subsidy program (Trend, 1979, cited in Teddlie & Tashakkori, 2009) | • The QUANT study combined data on housing quality and household characteristics. Forms were used to follow the progress of participating families and to interview families at predetermined intervals.<br>• The QUAL component generated 8 case studies on different housing projects using field observation, interviews and documents.<br>• The mixed methods component was only introduced at the end and involved integrating the QUANT and QUAL studies to reconcile significant differences in the findings.<br>• Type of design:<br>   ○ QUANT and QUAL designs: parallel/single level<br>   ○ Mixed methods: sequential/multilevel | • The QUANT component was an outcome-based evaluation that addressed the questions: Did the program work? Did it achieve its objectives? This found that the program had achieved its objective in terms of the number of low-income families placed in housing.<br>• The QUAL study was a process evaluation that assessed how the program actually operated on the ground. This found serious problems and poor-quality implementation. There was great hostility to the implementing agency as there was significant pressure to place families due to pressure to achieve quotas without concern to help families find suitable housing. Many staff resigned before the end of the program.<br>• The mixed methods component was introduced only after the inconsistencies were found between the QUANT and QUAL studies. Reanalysis of the data found major differences between outcomes for housing programs in rural areas (where most families were White, smaller, somewhat better off, and easier to place at a lower cost) and programs in urban areas (where most families were Black, larger, poorer, and more difficult to place). |

ethnographic (QUAL) study to understand the characteristics of the communities, followed by a QUANT household survey and econometric analysis of the findings. See Table 8.1, Examples 2, 3, and 4 for other examples of sequential designs.

- *Parallel Designs*

In parallel designs, the QUANT and QUAL approaches are used at the same time. An example of a parallel design is one in which QUANT and QUAL data are collected simultaneously, using triangulation to compare information on outcomes, impacts, and other key indicators from different independent sources. Another example is when QUAL methods are used to conduct a contextual analysis of a project site at the same time that a QUANT sample survey of households or individuals is being carried out. Parallel designs permit a very rich but more complicated analysis in which the interactions between the setting (context) and the project implementation process are analyzed. See Table 8.1, Example 1 for another example of parallel designs.

## b. Dimension 2: Designs in Which One Method Is Dominant Versus Designs in Which QUANT and QUAL Are Balanced

Most evaluators have been trained in either a QUANT or a QUAL tradition, and consequently one or the other approach is dominant in many MM evaluations.[3] MM designs are used differently and have different purposes by evaluators with QUANT and QUAL professional backgrounds.

Figure 8.2 describes a sequential design with a dominant QUANT approach. This is a study of interhousehold transfers of money and goods as a survival strategy among poor urban households in Cartagena, Colombia (Wansbrough, Jones, & Kappaz, 2000). These interhousehold transfers were difficult to identify and measure, so an anthropologist lived in the community for a month to study the patterns of transfers and to help design the questionnaire for the QUANT survey, which was then administered to several hundred households. The data were analyzed using QUANT econometric methods.

Figure 8.3 illustrates a QUANT-QUAL-TRIANGULATION design with a balanced QUANT and QUAL approach. It describes the evaluation of a village savings program in Mali designed to strengthen women's social capital through helping women increase the number of people with whom they were in contact. While the RCT did not detect any significant increase in the number of people with whom the women were in contact, the in-depth ethnographic study found that women increased the number of interactions with people with whom they were already in contact—a different definition of social capital. Triangulation was used to understand the reasons for the different findings and concluded that the ethnographic study was able to dig deeper and to discover patterns of interaction not captured by the RCT.

## c. Dimension 3: Single- and Multilevel Mixed Methods Designs

MM is also a powerful tool for the evaluation of service delivery systems (e.g., district education departments, a national program to strengthen municipal governments) that require description and analysis of linkages between different levels. Figure 8.4 illustrates a hypothetical multilevel MM design to evaluate the

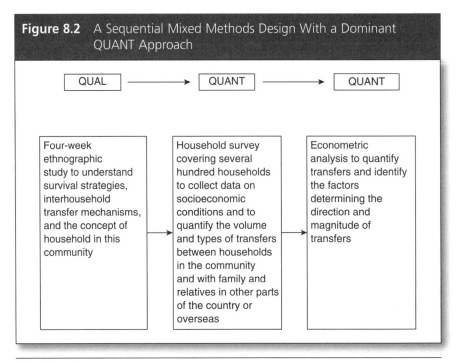

**Figure 8.2**    A Sequential Mixed Methods Design With a Dominant QUANT Approach

SOURCE: Adapted from Wansbrough, Jones, & Kappaz (2000).

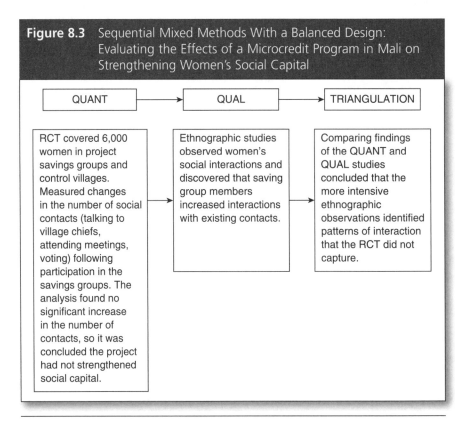

**Figure 8.3**    Sequential Mixed Methods With a Balanced Design: Evaluating the Effects of a Microcredit Program in Mali on Strengthening Women's Social Capital

SOURCE: Adapted from Bureau of Applied Research in Anthropology (2013).

social and economic effects of a microcredit program on women entrepreneurs and to strengthen women's economic and social empowerment—something that is difficult to capture with purely QUANT surveys.[4] The program was assessed at different levels: the district office of the village bank, the individual village bank, the individual solidarity lending groups (usually around eight members), the individual borrowers, and the household of the borrowers. In addition to the analysis at each separate level, the effectiveness of the program was also determined by the interaction among the different levels. Figure 8.4 shows the types of QUAL and QUANT data collection methods used at each level.

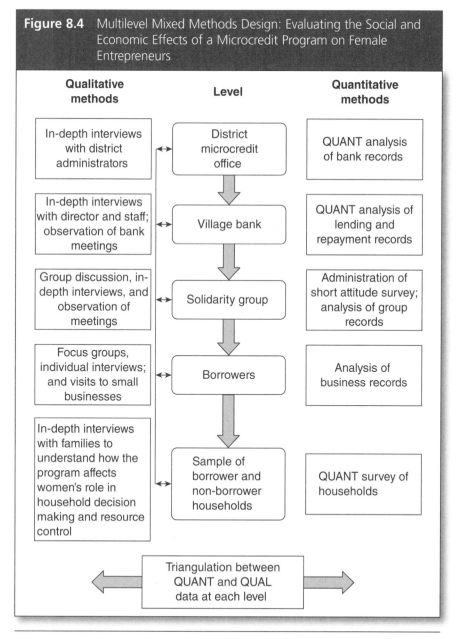

**Figure 8.4**  Multilevel Mixed Methods Design: Evaluating the Social and Economic Effects of a Microcredit Program on Female Entrepreneurs

Also at each level there is a process of triangulation between the QUANT and QUAL data to check for consistency and to explain inconsistencies. An important element of the multilevel design is the analysis of linkages and interactions between and among the different levels. For example:

- The researchers may attend meetings between the district office and the village bank, or between the village bank and individual solidarity groups, to observe the relationships between the levels, the kinds of issues discussed, and how problems are resolved.
- The researchers compare the perspectives of individual borrowers, the solidarity group, and the village bank on how loans are approved and managed and the support provided.
- The researchers compare the perspectives of different household members, the borrowers, and the village bank on the social and economic effects of the program.

### d. Dimension 4: Stages of the Evaluation Cycle at Which Mixed Methods Are Used

Probably most MM designs combine QUANT and QUAL methods in only one or a few stages of the evaluation—most frequently data collection or data analysis. However, a fully integrated MM approach combines QUANT and QUAL approaches at all stages of an evaluation. The stages at which mixed methods can be used are described below and then illustrated with respect to a complexity-responsive evaluation in Section 5:

- *Formulation of hypotheses.* Many QUANT evaluations derive hypotheses *deductively* from existing theories or literature reviews, while QUAL evaluations frequently develop hypotheses *inductively* as the study evolves. MM combine both approaches. For example, QUANT hypotheses may be developed deductively from a review of the literature, which are then explored and refined through QUAL approaches such as interviews or observation.
- *Sampling.* QUAL evaluations normally use a relatively small number of subjects selected purposively (theoretical sampling) to ensure that all important groups are covered. In contrast, QUANT evaluations normally use a relatively large, randomly selected sample permitting generalizability to larger populations. MM sampling uses the same sampling frame to generate a large QUANT survey sample and to select a small but representative sample for in-depth QUANT analysis. *Ensuring QUAL samples are reasonably representative of the total sample population is one of the most important contributions of MM designs.*
- *Data collection and recording methods* (see Table 8.2). Whereas QUANT evaluations collect standardized, numerical data, QUAL evaluations often use less structured data collection methods that provide greater flexibility and that seek to understand the complexities of a situation (see Chapter 4). MM

data collection builds on the strengths of QUANT data while digging deeper, capturing sensitive data, and studying processes and behavioral change.

- *Triangulation*. MM designs triangulate data from QUANT and QUAL estimates to: enhance the reliability and validity of estimates of key indicators by comparing information from different sources; deepen the understanding of the meaning of statistical relationships identified in the quantitative analysis; and ensure that the perspectives of all key stakeholders, with particular emphasis on poor and vulnerable groups, are captured and compared. While triangulation is most frequently used to reconcile differences among estimates and to find the "best" estimate of a key indicator, another tradition uses triangulation to identify divergence and to highlight different perspectives and values. The divergence approach is a key element of feminist evaluation, which gives voice to the weak or powerless and recognizes that different voices, values, perspectives can have equal value. The divergence approach is particularly valuable for understanding complex phenomena where complex adaptive systems may tend toward diversity (Williams, 2015).

- *Data analysis* (see Table 8.2). QUAL evaluators use a wide range of data analysis methods to identify broad patterns and relations and to obtain a holistic overview of the complex interactions between a project and the setting in which it is embedded. The purpose of QUANT analysis, on the other hand, is to describe the statistical characteristics of the key variables, to determine the statistical significance of differences between project and comparison groups, and to identify factors contributing to the magnitude and direction of change. MM data analysis uses QUAL analysis to help understand the meaning that different subjects or groups give to the statistical associations found in the QUANT analysis and to provide cases and examples to illuminate the findings. On the other hand, QUANT analysis can be used to assess how well the cases included in the QUAL studies represent the total population of interest and which if any sectors have not been covered.

# 5. Using Mixed Methods to Evaluate Complex Interventions

The following are some of the contributions that MM can make to complexity-responsive evaluations.

## 5.1 Scoping the Evaluation

Before selecting the evaluation design, it is important to understand the context in which the evaluation will be conducted. This involves the following:

- *Delineating the evaluand and the complex causal pathways through which outcomes and impacts are expected to be achieved*. This often involves an MM diagnostic study that can capture the multiple dimensions of the program context and causal pathways.

**Table 8.2**   Examples of Mixed Methods Data Analysis

| Approach | Description | Example |
|---|---|---|
| Parallel mixed methods data analysis | This involves two separate analysis processes: QUANT data are analyzed using conventional QUANT methods such as frequency tables, cross-tables, and regression analysis, while a separate analysis of QUAL data is conducted using QUAL methods such as content analysis. The findings of the two sets of analysis are then compared. | In the World Bank 2003 Poverty Assessment in Guatemala, separate teams were responsible for collecting QUAL and QUANT data. QUAL analysis was conducted on five pairs of villages representing the main ethnic groups. QUANT data from the same set of villages was analyzed separately, and the two sets of data were integrated only in the final stage of the analysis. The combination of the two independent analyses provided a broader political and historical context for understanding the program operation impacts (Teddlie & Tashakkori, 2009, Box 11.5). |
| Conversion mixed methods data analysis | QUAL data are converted into QUANT indicators ("quantitizing") using rating, scoring, and scaling so that QUANT analysis techniques can be used.<br><br>QUANT data are converted to QUAL indicators ("qualitizing") so that QUAL analysis procedures can be used. | Data on the political, economic, social, environmental, legal, and administrative context in which a project operates are often presented in a narrative, qualitative form. The indicators can be "quantitized" (Teddlie & Tashakkori's, 2009, term) by conversion to dummy variables. For example: "the economy is growing" = 1, "the economy is not growing" = 0. These dummy variables can then be incorporated into the regression analysis. |
| Sequential mixed methods data analysis | QUAL data analysis is followed by QUANT analysis.<br><br>QUANT data analysis is followed by QUAL analysis.<br><br>Iterative MM designs: The analysis includes sequential QUANT and QUAL steps. | In Figure 8.2 the study of survival strategies begins with a QUAL analysis of narrative reports on the patterns of interhousehold transfers providing support for vulnerable households. The QUAL analysis helps in the design of the QUANT survey of interhousehold transfers, which is then analyzed using econometric techniques. |
| Multilevel mixed methods data analysis | QUANT and QUAL analysis techniques are used at different levels of a multilevel evaluation design. | Figure 8.4 illustrates a multilevel MM analysis to evaluate the socioeconomic impacts of a women's microcredit program. Both QUANT and QUAL analyses were conducted sequentially at different levels. The design permitted analysis of the interlinkages between the different levels.[5] |

SOURCE: Adapted from Teddlie & Tashakkori (2009, ch. 11). Most of the examples were developed by the present author.

- *Contextual analysis.* This involves a diagnostic study that examines the contextual factors that influence how the program is formulated, designed, managed, and evaluated. Some of the contextual factors will be defined using QUANT indicators (e.g., migration, other demographic changes), some will use QUAL (e.g., assessing which political groups support and oppose the program), and some will combine both (e.g., the effects of climate change).
- *Defining key evaluation questions.* The more complex the questions the evaluation must address, the greater the need for an MM design.

## 5.2 Selecting the Appropriate Mixed Methods Design

In addition to the usual range of issues affecting choice of the appropriate evaluation design (e.g., key evaluation questions, data availability, affordable sample size), additional issues affect the choice of the MM design in general and specifically for the evaluation of complex programs:

- It is essential to identify the multiple perspectives of different stakeholders because the multiple dimensions of complexity, in particular the complexity of causal pathways, mean that there are many different ways to interpret how program outcomes are achieved.
- MM also stresses the importance of clearly defining the value orientation of the stakeholders and the evaluation team. While value orientations and research paradigms are often not addressed in QUANT evaluation designs, they are considered essential for MM designs and significantly affect the choice of methodology.
- For many complex programs it is not possible to use a statistical counterfactual. Consequently, alternative models must be identified for assessing the extent to which the program and its different components have contributed to intended (and unintended) outcomes (see Chapter 4).
- The absence of critical data, or the poor quality of available data, is a frequent challenge in complex programs. In addition, the many constructs required to capture complex processes and outcomes requires the combination of QUANT and QUAL indicators. This is an area where MM data collection approaches are essential.
- Complexity often requires the use of MM sampling strategies that combine probability (QUANT) and purposive (QUAL) sample designs.
- Finally, it is necessary to decide whether the MM design will operate only on a single level or whether it will be multilevel.

## 5.3 Choice of Methods

MM designs can draw on the whole range of data collection and analysis techniques. Two or more techniques will be combined depending on the specific needs of the evaluation. MM has a distinct approach to each of the evaluation designs described in Chapter 4. For example, the MM approach to RCT is sometimes called

"RCT+" as it compensates for weaknesses in established RCT designs by incorporating analysis of the implementation process and processes of change induced by the program (the black box), through analysis of contextual factors, by combining QUANT and QUAL outcome indicators and by using triangulation to strengthen the validity of the measurements.

## 5.4 Using Mixed Methods to Assess Complex Processes of Behavioral Change

The process of program implementation is often less straightforward than it first appears due to processes of behavioral change in target populations and between them and program staff. MM are well suited to incorporate the behavioral approaches described in Chapter 5. MM can draw on multidisciplinary research literature to help understand these decision-making processes (Kahneman, 2011; World Bank, 2015).

Realist evaluation, which makes extensive use of MM, shows that how individuals and groups respond to a program and how they communicate their experiences to friends, neighbors, and coworkers can influence how programs operate, often in quite subtle way. These dynamics call for a combination of data collection and analysis tools to understand (see Chapters 5, 9, 16, and 20).

## 5.5 Using Mixed Methods to Assess Vulnerability and Access to Services

A challenge for many development interventions is to identify any sectors of the target population that are excluded, intentionally or unintentionally, from access to program benefits. Excluded groups tend to be the most vulnerable are often not easy to detect. The following are some of the ways that MM designs can assess vulnerability:

- A rapid diagnostic study conducted at the start of the evaluation can describe social stratification and identify the marginal and vulnerable groups that might be excluded from access to project benefits. Initial QUAL analysis can be combined with a rapid QUANT survey to estimate the magnitude and distribution of vulnerable groups.
- Program monitoring can be broadened to provide more detailed information on the characteristics of the social groups that do have access to project services.
- The Bottleneck Analysis Framework developed by UNICEF (see Chapter 14) can provide for a more rigorous analysis of the factors determining which sectors do and do not have access to the project benefits (Bamberger & Segone, 2011).
- A number of QUAL techniques are available to observe whether any groups are excluded during project implementation (e.g., participant observation; panel studies where individuals, households, or communities are visited periodically throughout the project; focus groups and participatory appraisal).

# 6. Practical Applications

- In contrast to the evaluation of simple projects and programs, when evaluating complex interventions there is never a single explanation of the multiple factors that contributed to intended (and unintended) outcomes that can be stated with a high degree of statistical confidence. Complexity-responsive evaluation requires the combination of a number of different evaluation approaches. No single evaluation design is able to adequately capture all of the different dimensions of a complex intervention.

- A key element of a MM approach is that it recognizes that there are multiple perspectives on the objectives of the program, the explanation of what changes have occurred and what were the causes, and importantly the value that is attached to these changes by different groups.

- In contrast to top-down approaches in which evaluations are largely designed to ask whether the objectives of the funding and implementing agency have been achieved, a MM approach offers the possibility of understanding a program in a much broader context. In fact, many advocates of MM view evaluation as a process of achieving broader social objectives such as social justice, gender equality, and emancipation.

- The practical application for managers and evaluators is to clarify with clients whether mixed methods are seen as a tool to strengthen evaluations that only ask the question "Has the program achieved the intended objectives of the clients who commissioned the evaluation?" or whether mixed methods are seen as a tool for promoting broader social and political objectives.

- Understanding complexity requires the combination of QUANT and QUAL methods. Many complex programs are designed to benefit very large numbers of people, so it is necessary to use methods that can estimate the numbers of people who benefit as well as the numbers that do not. At the same time it is necessary to use QUAL methods that help understand the complex processes through which programs are implemented as well as the processes of behavioral change.

- At this point in time evaluators have not yet developed a standard toolkit of methods for evaluating complexity, and consequently evaluators have to adopt a pragmatic, flexible approach that creatively combines different QUANT and QUAL methods as seems appropriate for a particular program.

# References

Bamberger, M. (2012). Introduction to mixed methods in impact evaluation. *Impact Evaluation Notes,* 3. Washington, D.C. : Interaction.

Bamberger, M. (in press). *Measuring resilience: Lessons learned from the design and implementation of monitoring and evaluation methodologies of the R4 Rural Resilience Initiative, a partnership between Oxfam America and the World Food Program.* Boston, MA: Oxfam America and the Rockefeller Foundation.

Bamberger, M., & Segone, M. (2011). *How to design and manage equity-focused evaluations.* New York, NY: UNICEF. Retrieved from http://mymande.org/sites/default/files/EWP5_Equity_focused_evaluations.pdf

Bevan, P. (2009). Working with cases in development contexts: Insights from an outlier. In D. Byrne & C. Ragin (Eds.), *The Sage handbook of case-based methods* (pp. 467–493). Thousand Oaks, CA: Sage.

Bowman, K., & Sweetman, C. (2014). Introduction to gender: Monitoring, evaluation and learning. *Gender and Development, 22,* 201–212.

Bureau of Applied Research in Anthropology. (2013). *Final impact evaluation of the Savings for Change Program in Mali (2009–2012).* Tucson: University of Arizona and Innovations for Poverty Action.

Chambers, R. (1997). *Whose reality counts? Putting the last first.* Rugby, UK: Practical Action.

Chambers, R. (2010). *Paradigms, poverty and adaptive pluralism* (IDS Working paper 344). Sussex, UK: Institute of Development Studies.

Forss, K., Marra, M., & Schwartz, R. (Eds.). (2011). *Evaluating the complex: Attribution, contribution and beyond.* New Brunswick, NJ: Transaction.

Greene, J. (2007). *Mixed methods in social enquiry.* San Francisco, CA: John Wiley & Sons.

Kahneman, D. (2011). *Thinking, fast and slow.* New York, NY: Farrar, Straus and Giroux.

Mertens, D. M., & Hesse-Biber, S. (2013). Mixed methods and credibility of evidence in evaluation. *New Directions for Evaluation, 138,* 5–13.

Morgan, D. (2014). *Integrating qualitative and quantitative methods: A pragmatic approach.* Thousand Oaks, CA: Sage.

Teddlie, C., & Tashakkori, A. (2009). *Foundations of mixed-methods research.* Thousand Oaks, CA: Sage.

Trend, M. G. (1979). On the reconciliation of qualitative and quantitative analysis: A case study. In T. D. Cook & C. S. Reichardt (Eds.), *Qualitative and quantitative methods in program evaluation* (pp. 68–85). Thousand Oaks, CA: Sage.

Wansbrough, G., Jones, D., & Kappaz, C. (2000). Studying interhousehold transfers and survival strategies of the poor in Cartagena, Colombia. In M. Bamberger (Ed.), *Integrating qualitative and quantitative research in development projects* (pp. 69–84). Washington, DC: World Bank.

Williams, B. (2015). Prosaic or profound? The adoption of systems ideas by impact evaluation. *IDS Bulletin, 46,* 7–16.

World Bank. (2015). *Mind, society and behavior: World development report.* Washington, DC: Author.

# Notes

1. For example, at the level of measurement you have qualitative (nominal, ordinal scale) and quantitative (interval and ratio scale) data. One level higher, qualitative methods such as semi-structured interviews can be used to collect both qualitative and quantitative data. The same goes for quantitative methods such as surveys, which can be used to collect both qualitative and quantitative data.

2. This is adapted from a study conducted as part of a national gender strategy planning with which the author was involved in North Africa. Some of the details have been changed for the purpose of illustrating how mixed methods designs are used.

3. A new generation of evaluators trained in mixed methods as an integrated evaluation approach is emerging and some studies are starting to appear with a more balanced approach without a dominant orientation, but these are still in a minority. *The Journal of Mixed Methods Research* is a good source for examples of balanced designs.

4. The example is a synthesis of approaches compiled from experiences with evaluation designs used to assess many different microcredit programs.

5. For example, the analysis of district-level records can identify schools with above- and below-average attendance and performance scores. This can be used to select above- and below-average schools to be included in the sample. In-depth interviews with teachers could be used to select a sample of students with particular characteristics for focus groups.

# PART III

Emerging Data and Innovative Techniques to Deal With Complexity in Development Evaluation

# CHAPTER 9

# Complexity in Review and Synthesis Studies

Jos Vaessen

*Review and synthesis studies address the questions of whether and how interventions work across settings. In principle these studies are confronted with the same challenges as the primary studies they rely on. In addition, there are a number of specific challenges to review and synthesis work. In this chapter I first discuss some of the most frequently used review and synthesis approaches in the context of international development. The purpose is not to be exhaustive but to present some of the diversity in purpose and approach to review and synthesis. Subsequently, I discuss a number of challenges in review and synthesis studies from a complexity perspective. In the discussion, the focus is mainly on systematic review (and comparisons with other approaches) given the increasing popularity of this approach in the international development community.*

O ver the last decade or so there has been a marked rise in the application of review and synthesis approaches to better capture and understand the impact of development interventions. As the international community became more focused on impact, as evidenced by the endorsement of the Millennium Development Goals and their corresponding targets, and pressed by the weak evidence base on impact (e.g., Center for Global Development, 2006), funding and work on the impact of development interventions markedly increased. With more studies on impact available, the practice of review and synthesis became more and more popular among donors and academics.

Review and synthesis approaches include such methods as narrative review, meta-ethnography, realist synthesis, and systematic review (see, e.g., Popay, 2006). The growing number of review and synthesis studies, particularly systematic review studies, has provided new impetus to so-called repositories of knowledge or second-order evidence-producing organizations (Hansen & Rieper, 2009). Examples of such organizations are the Cochrane Collaboration, the Campbell Collaboration, the Evidence for Policy and Practice Information and Coordinating Centre, and, particularly relevant for development, the International Initiative for Impact Evaluation. The idea of such repositories is to promote high-quality review and synthesis research, provide peer review and quality assurance, and develop synthetic evidence on the effectiveness and impact of policy interventions, open to policymakers, funders, and other stakeholders.

There are good reasons for promoting review and synthesis studies, from both a methodological and a policy use perspective. Regarding the former, it is well known that many rigorous impact evaluation studies optimize the internal validity of findings. For example, experimental and quasi-experimental approaches are set up to control for as much external heterogeneity as possible, thereby isolating the effect of the intervention on particular variables of change. For example, by design, variation in observable and non-observable variables is controlled for in a randomized controlled trial. Through the principle of randomization, equivalent groups are generated that differ only in terms of the type of intervention they are exposed to or part of. In such a design, it is very difficult to extrapolate findings from particular study contexts to other settings. Group averages are compared, and even though subgroup analysis is sometimes possible, this type of counterfactual analysis generally does not reveal how interventions work and how they may affect types of beneficiaries in different ways. Review and synthesis approaches bridge the boundaries of different study contexts by taking together evidence from across different settings. This is done in different ways depending on the methodology and the type of evidence used in the study.

From a policy use perspective, there are at least two major advantages of review and synthesis approaches in comparison to "regular" impact-oriented evaluations. First of all, the broad scope of the review and synthesis study. Policymakers more often than not are interested in the effectiveness of a particular intervention across countries or regions rather than a specific intervention in one setting. Second, decision-making cycles have their own dynamics. Unfortunately, in many development intervention contexts, despite the fact that there may be clearly defined project cycles, it is often the case that evaluation findings are available only after decisions have already been made. This is particularly likely in the case of impact evaluations. While some impact evaluation designs are integrated into project designs and tied to decisions on future resource allocations, in probably most cases, impact evaluations are implemented months or even years after a project has been closed. This mismatch between intervention cycles and policy cycles (see, e.g., Pawson, 2002) has created a need for existing evidence about impact to become available to decision makers at strategic decision moments.

For the development evaluation practitioner community, the implication of the above is that there is more demand for synthetic analysis, and more evaluation professionals are becoming synthesizers of existing evidence. Review and synthesis studies are not a silver bullet. Overall, they offer the potential to determine if a particular type of intervention has been effective and may even uncover patterns of regularity of what works across interventions and settings. On the other hand there is a greater distance between the reviewer and the empirical reality. The reviewer does not have firsthand knowledge of the underlying studies that are analyzed and is dependent on the evidence presented in primary studies. Consequently, by necessity the growth in review and synthesis studies should go hand in hand with a global research agenda to improve the coverage and quality of primary research on the impact of development interventions.

# 1. Prevalent Review and Synthesis Approaches

In recent years methodological innovations have led to a growth in different review and synthesis approaches (see, e.g., Popay, 2006). These may differ in terms of:

- the main review question that is addressed by the review (e.g., the effect of intervention $x$ vs. the main factors that explain effect $y$),
- the unit of analysis (e.g., the effect a particular intervention vs. a theory of change regarding a particular intervention),
- whether or not the study is based on a clear protocol with a priori procedures and decision criteria that guide the review (e.g., systematic vs. nonsystematic reviews),
- the type of evidence included in the review (e.g., qualitative and/or quantitative evidence; methodological design applied in the primary study),
- particular methods used for extracting and synthesizing information (e.g., narrative synthesis vs. quantitative meta-analysis).

In this chapter I look only at review and synthesis approaches that focus on effects (outcome/impact). Does intervention $x$ work, under which circumstances, for whom? This is certainly the prevalent question in review and synthesis approaches but not the only one. Gough, Thomas, and Oliver (2012) classify review and synthesis approaches into two main groups: aggregative and configurative. Aggregative reviews tend to use predefined methods, combining similar forms of data from homogeneous studies. Configurative reviews tend to be more exploratory, and there is more flexibility in the review and synthesis process. Review questions associated with aggregative reviews include the following: What is the effect of the intervention? How effective is an intervention relative to its cost? Here are a few examples of review questions associated with configurative reviews: What theories can be generated from the literature? How is a particular issue conceptualized and analyzed across different research traditions? Gough et al. also identify questions that are associated with review approaches that are both aggregative and configurative, for example, the question of what works and why under what circumstances and for whom, a question that is at the core of realist synthesis (Pawson, 2006).

Another dimension that is useful for classifying review and synthesis work is the unit of analysis. Without being exhaustive, one can discern quite significant differences here with implications for the nature of the review and synthesis exercise. The most common unit of analysis is the type of intervention (e.g., a particular vaccine administered to patients, a subsidy on fertilizers for smallholder farmers, capacity development workshops to micro entrepreneurs, microcredit targeting poor women). The narrow scope of the review permits an in-depth analysis of effectiveness across contexts, including, in the right conditions of data availability and quality of primary studies, the use of statistical data and meta-analysis to arrive at pooled estimates of effectiveness. The second example described in Box 9.1 (Waddington, Snilstveit, White, & Fewtrell, 2009) is about a systematic review of particular types of interventions. A second unit of analysis could be the field of policy intervention (e.g., rural infrastructure, biodiversity conversation). The first example in Box 9.1 (Mansuri & Rao, 2013) concerns the review of a field of intervention: participatory development. Another example is a study commissioned by the Operations and Policy Evaluation Department of the Dutch Ministry of Foreign Affairs on the topic of food security, which was a narrative review of the literature on the main types of interventions in this policy field. Moreover, the study builds on existing gaps in the literature, focusing on those policy areas (in the field of food security) where no review has yet been conducted. The study focuses on four broad categories of interventions: increasing production, developing value chains, reforming market regulations, and improving land tenure security (IOB, 2011). A third unit of analysis could be a heterogeneous portfolio of interventions. An example is the Global Environment Facility (GEF) Evaluation Office's Review of Outcome to Impact. This approach, building on a generic theory of change, rates project evaluations on the degree to which intermediate conditions have been achieved in order to subsequently arrive at an assessment of likelihood of impact. The approach then allows for aggregating ratings across very different types of interventions (GEF, 2009). Finally, the unit of analysis can be the theory of change. Realist synthesis is a theory-based approach to review and synthesis (see Chapter 20 for an example). An evaluator employing a realist synthesis approach typically gathers evidence to clarify and refine the explanatory mechanism of change. Any evidence that may shed light on how behavioral change is triggered by a particular type of intervention under certain conditions can be part of the puzzle to make sense of causal change processes (Pawson, 2006).

The most prevalent review and synthesis approach is the family of systematic review approaches. In contrast to what may be labeled as nonsystematic review studies, systematic reviews are based on a clear protocol. The protocol sets out the different steps of the review: the review purpose and question(s), the search strategy for evidence, the inclusion criteria for considering a primary study to be included in the review (e.g., characteristics of the study, relevance, quality), and the methodology for data extraction and synthesis. Systematic reviews strive for comprehensiveness and absence of bias in the identification and inclusion of evidence (within the boundaries of the scope). By doing so, they increase the breadth of (traditional) literature review while retaining a clear focus. At the same time, they clearly distinguish between original empirical data and preconceived knowledge. Finally, through the principle of transparency in all steps of the review process, they are open to close scrutiny (by peers) and amenable to replication or updating in the future (see, e.g., Mallet, Hagen-Zanker, Slater, & Duvendack, 2012).

The following are common elements of a systematic review protocol (Higgins & Green, 2011):

- Clearly defined research question with information on the target population, the intervention, the outcome, and (sometimes) the comparison condition[1]
- Search strategy with information on
  - definition of keywords and search strings (including Boolean operators, etc.)
  - identification of data sources: academic and non-academic databases, journals and books not covered by these databases, websites of institutions relating to the intervention under review
  - keyword searches and hand searches (including backward citation searching and forward citation searching of already identified studies)
- Inclusion/exclusion criteria: criteria for identifying relevant studies of sufficient quality[2]
- Templates and/or methods for extracting qualitative and/or quantitative data from selected studies
- Method(s) for synthesizing data toward an overall perspective

Apart from the protocol, which opens up systematic reviews to external scrutiny, other mechanisms for quality assurance are use of commonly accepted methodologies and guidelines for searching, selecting, and synthesizing evidence; independent coding and data extraction by different reviewers in the team; and external peer review at different stages in the review process.

Nonsystematic reviews include a broad range of review approaches that do not follow a systematic protocol for review. Examples are narrative review and realist synthesis (see Box 9.1 for an illustration; for an example of a realist synthesis, see Chapter 20).

## BOX 9.1 AN ILLUSTRATION OF ONE NONSYSTEMATIC AND ONE SYSTEMATIC REVIEW STUDY

### Nonsystematic Review—Mansuri and Rao (2013): Localizing Development: Does Participation Work?

*Purpose and scope:* This review constitutes one of the most comprehensive synthetic analyses on participatory development. The purpose of the review was to assess the impact of large-scale, policy-driven efforts to induce participation. The review covered a broad array of research questions (many more than one would encounter in a systematic review, for example), which are organized under three main questions: How important is (elite) capture? Does participation improve development outcomes? Does participation strengthen civil society?

*Methodology:* The review developed a conceptual framework on inducing participation, which among other things focuses on the nature of civil society failures (next to market and government failures). This framework served as a guide for drawing broad lessons on the literature. The study reviewed almost 500 studies on participatory development and decentralization. The review relied mostly on primary studies that had some type of rigorous (quantitative) counterfactual analysis, primarily econometric analyses. In addition, (qualitative) case studies were used to enrich the synthetic analysis. Also, primary studies published in peer-reviewed journals or written by scholars with a strong track record were favored. This criterion was not applied in a strict manner as other evidence was allowed to fill gaps in the evidence base to cover dimensions of interest to the study. Findings were presented through an analytical narrative.

*Conclusions:* The review generated a broad range of findings under the three categories of questions (with subquestions). For example, it found evidence that the poor tend to benefit less from participatory processes than the better off. In addition, as most participatory processes are driven by incentives from the intervention, when the latter are withdrawn, participatory mechanisms (e.g., networks) often dissolve. In its discussion of the findings, the review highlights the role of a responsive state and the importance of context in determining the effectiveness of participatory interventions.

## Systematic Review—Waddington et al. (2009): Water, Sanitation and Hygiene Interventions to Combat Childhood Diarrhoea in Developing Countries

*Purpose and scope:* The purpose of the review was to assess the effects of water, sanitation, and hygiene interventions on the reduction of childhood diarrhea. The study was a systematic review based on a protocol for searching for, selecting, and analyzing and synthesizing information from primary studies.

*Search process:* Primary studies were searched using academic and other online databases, searching books and journals not covered by these databases, contacting key researchers, and identifying new studies through scrutiny of reference lists of identified studies. From over 19,000 titles, the full text of 168 studies was analyzed, and finally 65 studies were selected for analysis.

*Inclusion:* Only studies employing experimental and quasi-experimental methods were included in the analysis.

*Synthesis:* The methodological quality of studies was assessed and studies were categorized as low or high quality, using several criteria such as the comparability of treatment groups and the clarity of defining diarrheal diseases. Subsequently, qualitative information on how the intervention works (relating this intervention to predefined intervention theories) and quantitative data on, for example, effect sizes and confidence intervals were extracted. By pooling effects sizes of different studies for different groups of water and sanitation interventions, the study developed a picture of the overall effectiveness of different intervention types. Furthermore a theory-based analysis of quantitative and qualitative evidence was conducted to try to explain differences in effectiveness.

*Conclusions (examples):* Among other things the study identified important gaps in the literature and the need for more research on interaction effects in case of combined water and hygiene/sanitation interventions. The study also called into question the assumed effectiveness of water quality interventions, especially the sustainability of effects of this type of intervention. Source: Mansuri and Rao (2013) .

SOURCE: Mansuri and Rao (2013) .

The type of evidence included in a review and synthesis study constitutes another key defining characteristic. Systematic reviews in the tradition of the Cochrane and Campbell Collaborations adhere to a clear hierarchy of evidence that is based on the extent to which a particular methodological design is equipped with generating findings with a high level of internal validity. Randomized assignment of the intervention with multiple data points in time is considered the highest standard of evidence. Figure 9.1 provides an overview of different quantitative methodological designs that are used to address the attribution problem[3] through statistical design and/or controls. The hierarchy (based on the extent to which a particular design is expected to be able to generate unbiased estimates of the net effects of an intervention) is implied in the figure moving from the top downward.

Systematic reviews relying primarily on quantitative evidence derived from (quasi-)experimental primary studies are prevalent in particular policy fields such as public health and education mostly in developed countries and are increasingly implemented in the context of international development interventions. There are multiple reasons that affect the applicability and utility of this type of review (see next section). Reviews based on qualitative evidence are often focused on a different

**Figure 9.1    Classification of Different (Quasi-)Experimental Approaches**

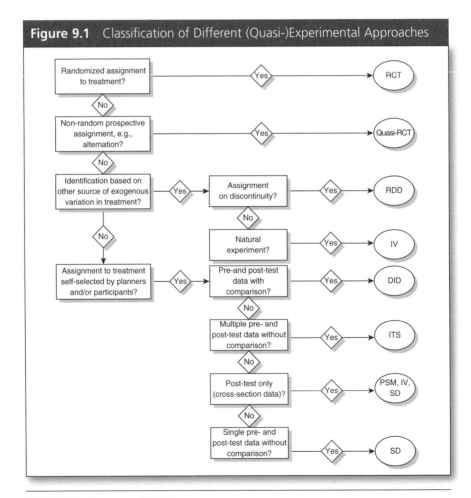

SOURCE: Waddington et al. (2012).

issue such as developing a better conceptual and theoretical understanding of a particular type of intervention (e.g., on the basis of different in-depth case studies). More recently, systematic reviews building on qualitative evidence have become more popular. The combination of quantitative and qualitative evidence, possibly with divergent methods applied within the same review and synthesis study, has been advocated by several authors in the field (see, e.g., Van der Knaap, Leeuw, Bogaerts, & Nijssen, 2008; see also Chapter 16). One of the main reasons for doing so has been the potential to combine statistical analysis with a more in-depth and qualitative understanding of how interventions work.

The approach to synthesis is closely related to the purpose of the review, the type of evidence included, and the way data is being extracted, analyzed, or interpreted. Narrative reviews have been characterized as employing a *configurational* approach to causality (see Pawson, 2002). From a selection of studies, outcome patterns are recorded and at the same time an inventory is made of (possible) independent variables (contextual conditions, characteristics of the target group and the intervention) that are assumed to be associated with outcomes. Subsequently, these patterns become the basis for a narrative (Pawson, 2002). Alternatively, this type of approach can also constitute the basis for qualitative comparative analysis, a mathematical technique based on fuzzy sets theory, which can help identify patterns of regularity among independent and dependent variables, so-called causal packages (see Chapter 4). A second approach is theory-based synthesis (e.g., realist synthesis), which works quite differently. The causal theory of change constitutes the framework for making sense of and synthesizing the data extracted from primary studies. This can work in different ways. One way is a kind of iterative approach in which the initial theory is continuously, through multiple iterations, further refined on the basis of different sources of data (pertaining to different causal assumptions in the theory). The outcome is a refined explanatory theory of the effectiveness of a particular type of intervention. A different, more summative approach is to make a rigid distinction between theory reconstruction and theory testing (i.e., "formal" empirical tests of predefined causal assumptions; see Chapter 4). A third example of a synthesis method frequently applied in review and synthesis studies, is meta-analysis, which concerns the extraction and pooling of effect sizes[4] from primary studies based on (quasi-)experimental designs in the context of a systematic review (see Lipsey & Wilson, 2001; see Chapter 16 for an illustration).

# 2. Dealing With Complexity in Review and Synthesis Exercises

A key contested issue in debates on complexity concerns the question of whether (or the extent to which) one can study the causal relationship between an intervention and a particular change in isolation from its context. This issue also relates to the distinction between a restricted or a general complexity perspective (Morin, 2008; see also Chapter 1). Within the framework of the former, one can look at causal processes in isolation, focusing on a particular intervention and a possible effect variable while controlling for other variables. From a general complexity perspective, such an approach is rendered meaningless due to the complex interconnectedness between system variables. One can understand processes of change only through a broad lens that captures the interactions between multiple factors.

As discussed in Chapter 4, the way in which review and synthesis approaches can address complexity issues depends on the review question(s) and approach as well as the type of evidence that is considered in the study. From a review and synthesis perspective, one could claim that evidence of the net effects of an intervention (controlling for all other factors) across contexts is useful information. However, given the potentially high level of complexity of factors influencing particular processes of change, it is also essential to understand how these processes work.

Continuing with the example of payments for environmental services (PES) discussed in Chapter 4, one of the figures in Box 4.2 shows the estimated net effects of a PES project in three pilot areas in three countries. The net effect estimations are based on a scheme of random designation of farmers to either a PES group or a control group.[5] Notwithstanding some threats to internal validity that affected the methodological design in practice, the estimates of the net effects can be considered "reasonable."[6] If the three sites were in fact three different independent studies, instead of three pilot sites, then our example would be similar to a review and synthesis case. The principle remains the same. From the figure one can deduce the mean difference in the Environmental Services Index (ESI)[7] between the PES group and the control group for the three sites. This information is useful; it shows not only that PES has been effective in different settings, but also that it has been effective overall.

At the same time there are clear limitations to these findings and to the principle of conducting a quantitative synthesis based on (quasi-)experimental data that should be noted. These limitations concern aspects such as the applicability of (quasi-)experimental evaluations and by implication meta-analysis in international development, the comprehensiveness of information in primary studies and the extent to which these studies report on the entire intervention process and the full range of (potential) effects over time, the definition and construct validity of variables representing a particular complex construct, and the extent to which heterogeneity can be addressed in review and synthesis:

- *The applicability of quantitative impact evaluation studies and consequently systematic review with meta-analysis.* Conducting (quasi-)experimental studies in developing countries' contexts can be costly and difficult. Moreover, they are applicable to particular types of interventions only (i.e., clearly delineated simple interventions targeting clearly delineated target groups). For multiple reasons only a small minority of development interventions can be subject to this type of quantitative impact evaluation, which in turn constitute the basis for quantitative synthesis (see, e.g., Bamberger & White, 2007).

- *Distinguishing implementation from theory failure.* In a review and synthesis context, primary studies do not always provide information on implementation. One cannot simply assume that implementation was without problems across the selected studies, and one has to be able to access evidence that permits verifying output delivery. If one does not find a difference between a treatment group and a control group, for example, and one does not have consistent information on output delivery, in many cases one would not be able to differentiate between implementation failure (the lack of change in a particular outcome is due to outputs not being delivered) or theory failure (the intervention outputs are not the right way to influence particular outcome variables).[8]

• *Capturing the full range of effects of a particular intervention across settings.* Environmental change is by nature unpredictable, nonlinear, and emergent. Consider again the example of the PES evaluation introduced in Chapter 4. Despite the fact that the ESI was based on thorough site-specific research, it did not capture the full extent of environmental effects of land use both in terms of scope and over time. Review and synthesis approaches that look only at quantitative data are inevitably missing out on the full extent of changes (partly) induced by an intervention. In this particular example, apart from the way environmental change is captured, there are also clear limitations in time and scope. Starting with the latter, the monitoring and evaluation system of the project looked only at change in farms of participating farmers in the project area. Land use behavior of the same farmers outside of the project area was not taken into account. In practice there were instances when farmers simply displaced environmentally unsustainable land use to land areas beyond the scrutiny of the project monitoring system. Time is of course also an important factor. Some land use changes are more sustainable than others, and the timing of data collection is a crucial component. Review and synthesis studies are bound by the limited data points incorporated in the primary studies. This crucial limitation again points at the need to combine measurement with understanding the pathways of change (see Woolcock, 2009). Without a good analysis on how change is brought about, one should be very careful with estimates of net effects of interventions on particular variables.

• *The evidence paradox.* Primary studies that rate highly in terms of internal validity of findings (see Figure 9.1) are unfortunately very often not especially informative about other dimensions of the effectiveness story: information on implementation processes and output delivery, on the nature of causal processes of change, or on the divergent characteristics within the target group and how they relate to change, and so on (Mallet et al., 2012).

• *The definition of independent and dependent variables across studies.* Review and synthesis studies may look at diverse outcomes. In order to identify patterns of regularity among interventions and their effects, there has to be some degree of similarity across primary studies. Chapter 16 describes how challenging this can be for the case of empowerment of women in relation to microcredit. Even though the complex construct of empowerment is deconstructed into different dimensions and there is a focus on women's control over household spending, the latter dimension is captured quite differently across studies. In other words, there are potentially serious threats to the construct validity of findings. On the independent variable side, it is important to realize that interventions never work in isolation. In the case of randomized designs, by design the intervention is (at least in the implementation phase) disconnected from other interventions. In practice, most development interventions often constitute packages of activities. For example, in the case of microcredit one can find combinations between microcredit, microsavings, microinsurance, training, group building, and awareness raising on social issues and other factors. A review and synthesis study may look at the microcredit component only, but the primary study may not have provided enough information on how microcredit is connected to other interventions. As a consequence, the review and synthesis study may not be able to use particular primary studies that are insufficiently clear on the nature of the intervention.

- *The differential effect of development interventions.* Let us consider the PES example again. The data shown in Box 4.2 (in Chapter 4) reflects group averages. Usually, averages and standard errors are provided in primary studies based on (quasi-)experimental designs. In reality, these averages may represent quite divergent subgroups of different types of individuals or institutions. Interventions affect individuals and institutions in different ways; the way payments affect the opportunity structure and perception of farmer A can be quite different from farmer B. In this particular study, subgroup analysis would reveal different types of farmers. One would find associations between characteristics of farm households and land use behavior patterns. In order to be able to conduct subgroup analyses, one would need to have (quantitative and qualitative) data on these dimensions from (preferably) the same studies that provide data on average net effects.

From the above one can deduce that the analysis of intervention effects in any given context is challenging. If one moves from the single study to the review and synthesis level, the challenges are compounded by the fact that most studies are likely to lack bits and pieces of key information relating to causal change processes, making it difficult to adequately capture or understand processes of change induced by development interventions.

What are possible methodological options to address some of the abovementioned challenges? Snilstveit (2012) recommends moving from "bare bone reviews" (i.e., systematic reviews that focus on the identification, extraction, and synthesis of quantitative effect size information) to a broader review and synthesis approach that contains reconstruction and refinement of one or more theories of change as well as a broader range of evidence, qualitative and quantitative, on implementation and change processes relating to the intervention. In addition, she argues that the systematic review protocol, and the transparency and openness to scrutiny that it brings to the study, should be maintained.

Let me illustrate these and other points. To begin with, one could make better use of the evidence to be found in primary studies with a high internal validity of findings. Van der Knaap et al. (2008) advocate for a review and synthesis approach that employs a "Campbellian" approach to systematic review[9] but at the same time looks at the underlying mechanisms of change, which is the bread and butter of realist synthesis. The rationale for combining the Campbellian and the realist tradition can be summarized as follows. First of all, the authors argue that realist synthesis is subject to bias as it does not separate high-quality studies from low-quality ones. To put it bluntly, there is no explicit method that separates evidence from, for example, peer-reviewed journal articles from newspaper articles or opinion surveys. By contrast, the rigorous methodological assessment of primary studies as employed in the Campbellian tradition constitutes a transparent and systematic way to separate high-quality studies (from the perspective of attribution or internal validity of findings) from low-quality ones. Second, Van der Knaap et al. argue that traditional systematic reviews in the Campbellian tradition use only a limited part of the information available in the primary studies (i.e., information on methodological design and quality, and quantitative data on effects sizes). With this information one can respond to the question of "does it work" but not "how does it work" and "under what circumstances." Review and synthesis studies should focus on the latter two questions by opening the black box of the intervention and uncovering the causal logic underlying change processes induced by interventions. To achieve this, Van der Knaap et al. propose a method for reconstructing the underlying theory change from the available information in primary studies, using argumentational analysis.

Much can be said for the approach advocated by Van der Knaap et al. (2008). However, given the existence of the evidence paradox (see above), quantitative studies that are strong on attribution often do not contain much information that helps uncover the underlying theory of change of the intervention. Another way to strengthen the potential of review and synthesis studies to develop an overall understanding of how causal change works is to include more (qualitative) studies in the review. This generates at least two methodological puzzles. First, by expanding the evidence base to include (more) qualitative studies, the issue of methodological quality assessment becomes more complicated. While there are widely accepted and clear criteria for methodological quality when it comes to quantitative evidence, especially with respect to the internal validity of findings (see, e.g., Cook & Campbell, 1979), this is not the case for qualitative research. In any case, it would be quite difficult to employ the same criteria for qualitative and quantitative evidence (Mallet et al., 2012; Thomas et al., 2004). Second, when should the reviewer stop the search for new evidence? In the case of quantitative evidence in the context of a systematic review, the "rules" for comprehensive searches and subsequent selection of evidence are quite clear. In fact, the transparency of the process and the argumentation underlying the exclusion and inclusion of primary studies is one of the strengths of systematic review (see Chapter 16).

In the case of qualitative evidence or nonsystematic review, it is less clear. If one abandons the principle of hierarchy of evidence or if one aims to cover a particular field of (qualitative) research relevant to the review, how far should one go? How does one justify the results of a particular search and selection process as a basis for claiming to generate credible (and even unbiased) findings across interventions of a particular type? One particularly interesting angle is the principle of the so-called theoretical saturation point. The idea is that one starts out from a reasonably realistic theory of change and subjects it to empirical testing. The theory could be a micro theory on a particular mechanism of change or a broader theory with multiple causal pathways (see Chapters 5 and 6 for examples). Through an iterative process of collecting more and more empirical evidence and using the evidence to confirm/reject/refine causal assumptions, at some point the reviewer arrives at the stage where no new evidence is found that adds value to the iterative theory-building process. This is when the theoretical saturation point has been reached. Assuming that the reviewer (or the review team) is experienced, has a good overview on where potential evidence can be found, and has cast a wide enough net to find evidence, the principle of the theoretical saturation point is quite defensible as a research strategy.

Another option to strengthen a review and synthesis study's explanatory power and its potential to provide useful policy-relevant information is the following. From a policy use perspective it makes sense to use multiple units of analysis (multiple interventions) in a review and synthesis approach. Much of the foregoing discussion concerns reviews that focus on a specific type of intervention as a unit of analysis. What if one would conduct a review of the effects of different interventions on one type of outcome? To illustrate, one can review the evidence base on the effects of PES on conservation and sustainable use of agrobiodiversity, for example. By complementing this exercise with a review of other interventions that may affect the conservation and sustainable use of agrobiodiversity, one could potentially answer a complementary policy question: What would be the most (cost-)effective intervention,[10] or what combination of interventions would be the most (cost-)effective in terms of achieving conservation and sustainable use of agrobiodiversity? By adding a second review (even if not as elaborate as the first one), one enhances the policy relevance of the findings of both reviews (see Waddington et al., 2012, for a succinct discussion on this).

Finally, it is important to keep in mind that review and synthesis work is time-consuming and costly. One could argue that more financial resources need to be made available to fund this type of work. Given the public good nature of the knowledge produced through review and synthesis studies, many institutions do not have as strong an incentive to invest in this type of study as one would hope for. In addition, review and synthesis studies—not only systematic reviews but also other variants such as realist synthesis—require specialized expertise. Finally, review and synthesis studies rely on (quasi-)unlimited access to existing primary studies on a particular type of intervention. Access to academic databases, which is an essential element of this, is often restricted in developing countries. Addressing the capacity development and data access issues in developing countries are important elements in the promotion of evidence-based policymaking through review and synthesis.

# 3. Practical Applications

- It is useful to distinguish studies of high quality (in terms of being able to attribute change to a particular intervention) from those of low quality. However, reviews should not be restricted to high-quality studies only, given the existence of the evidence paradox. Both qualitative and quantitative evidence is needed to develop a comprehensive picture of the effects induced by an intervention and how the underlying causal processes work.
- A protocol for review and synthesis increases the transparency of the study, and consequently the prospects for close scrutiny and replicability. It can also be seen as a living document, which can be continually updated to strengthen the rigor and comprehensiveness of the review and synthesis study. It is also helpful for replication (i.e., validation) and follow-up work.
- Review and synthesis studies, especially systematic reviews, can be expensive and time-consuming. If planned well ahead of time and with the purpose of feeding into strategic decision moments (e.g., decision making on the allocation of financial resources to strategic priorities), they can be very valuable.

- Review and synthesis studies are a cost-effective way to generate credible evidence on the extent to which and how particular interventions contribute to change across different settings. To further promote the approach, one should invest more in capacity development and the accessibility (e.g., open access) of academic and non-academic primary studies on effectiveness and impact.

# References

Bamberger, M., & White, H. (2007). Using strong evaluation designs in developing countries: Experience and challenges. *Journal of Multidisciplinary Evaluation, 4*(8), 58–73.

Center for Global Development. (2006). *When will we ever learn? Improving lives through impact evaluation.* Washington, DC: Author.

Cook, T. D., & Campbell, D. T. (1979). *Quasi-experimentation: Design and analysis for field settings.* Chicago, IL: Rand McNally.

Global Environment Facility. (2009). *The ROtI handbook: Towards enhancing the impacts of environmental projects.* Washington, DC: Author.

Gough, D., Thomas, J., & Oliver, S. (2012). Clarifying differences between review designs and methods. *Systematic Reviews, 1*(28), 1–9.

Hansen, H. F., & Rieper, O. (2009). Institutionalization of second-order evidence-producing organizations. In O. Rieper, F. L. Leeuw, & T. Ling (Eds.), *The evidence book: Concepts, generation and use of evidence* (pp. 27–49). New Brunswick, NJ: Transaction.

Higgins, J. P. T., & Green, S. (Eds.). (2011). *Cochrane handbook for systematic reviews of interventions* (Version 5.1.0). Retrieved from http://www.cochrane-handbook.org

IOB. (2011). *Improving food security: A systematic review of the impact of interventions in agricultural production, value chains, market regulation, and land security.* The Hague, Netherlands: Ministry of Foreign Affairs, Operations and Policy Evaluation Department.

Lipsey, M. W., & Wilson, D. B. (2001). *Practical meta-analysis.* Thousand Oaks, CA: Sage Publications.

Mallett, R., Hagen-Zanker, J., Slater, R., & Duvendack, M. (2012). The benefits and challenges of using systematic reviews in international development research. *Journal of Development Effectiveness, 4,* 445–455.

Mansuri, G., & Rao, V. (2013). *Localizing development: Does participation work?* Washington, DC: World Bank.

Morin, E. (2008). *On complexity.* Cresskill, NJ: Hampton Press.

Pawson, R. (2002). Evidence-based policy: In search of a method. *Evaluation, 8,* 157–181.

Pawson, R. (2006). *Evidence-based policy: A realist perspective.* London, UK: Sage.

Popay, J. (2006). *Moving beyond effectiveness: Methodological issues in the synthesis of diverse source of evidence.* London, UK: National Institute for Health and Clinical Excellence.

Snilstveit, B. (2012). Systematic reviews: From "bare bones" reviews to policy relevance. *Journal of Development Effectiveness, 4,* 388–408.

Suchman, E. A. (1967). *Evaluative research: Principles and practice in public service and social action programs.* New York, NY: Russell Sage Foundation.

Thomas, J., Harden, A., Oakley, A., Oliver, S., Sutcliffe, K., Rees, R., . . . Kavanagh, J. (2004). Integrating qualitative research with trials in systematic reviews. *British Medical Journal, 328,* 1010–1012.

Vaessen, J., & Van Hecken, G. (2009). *Assessing the potential for experimental evaluation of intervention effects: The case of the Regional Integrated Silvopastoral Approaches to Ecosystem Management Project (RISEMP)* (Impact Evaluation Information Document No. 15). Washington, DC: GEF Evaluation Office.

Van der Knaap, L. M., Leeuw, F. L., Bogaerts, S., & Nijssen, L. T. J. (2008). Combining Campbell standards and the realistic evaluation approach: The best of two worlds? *American Journal of Evaluation, 29*(1), 48–57.

Waddington, H., Snilstveit, B., White, H., & Fewtrell, L. (2009). *Water, sanitation and hygiene interventions to combat childhood diarrhoea in developing countries* (Synthetic Review 001). New Delhi, India: International Initiative for Impact Evaluation.

Waddington, H., White, H., Snilstveit, B., Garcia Hombrados, J. G., Vojtkova, M., Davies, P., . . . Tugwell, P. (2012). How to do a good systematic review of effects in international development: A tool kit. *Journal of Development Effectiveness, 4,* 359–387.

Woolcock, M. (2009). Toward a plurality of methods in project evaluation: A contextualized approach to understanding impact trajectories and efficacy. *Journal of Development Effectiveness, 1,* 1–14.

# Notes

1. For example, the effects of conditional cash transfer programs to poor households on primary school enrolment rates in developing countries (in comparison to control group conditions of poor households without such support).

2. Often supported by an elaborate risk of bias assessment of selected studies (looking at methodological design and quality).

3. The extent to which a change in a particular outcome variable of interest can be attributed to an intervention controlling for all other factors (i.e., the net effect on an intervention).

4. For example, mean standardized differences between a treatment group and a control group.

5. In reality, the scheme was somewhat more elaborate, but for the purposes of argument I limit the discussion to these two groups.

6. Especially in the case of Nicaragua, there were significant threats to validity: problems with random assignment to groups and unintended behavioral effects especially in the control group (see Vaessen & Van Hecken, 2009).

7. An index based on elaborate field research that captures the biodiversity and carbon sequestration value of a particular land use.

8. See Suchman (1967), who introduced these two concepts.

9. A term sometimes used to refer to systematic reviews produced within the framework of peer review and quality assurance of the Campbell Collaboration. Although the Campbell Collaboration in principle advocates a mixed methods approach, in practice it adheres to the principle of a hierarchy of evidence, with the core of the review and synthesis work focusing on meta-analysis of high internal validity (quasi-)experimental primary studies.

10. Payments for environmental services, environmental education, awareness-raising campaigns on the importance of agrobiodiversity, farm inspections, land use laws and enforcement, and so on.

# CHAPTER 10

# Emergent Technologies and Creative Use of Multiple Sources of Information

Susan van den Braak, Sunil Choenni, and Michael Bamberger

*In this chapter, we explain how data from various sources can be used for development evaluation and their particular importance in the evaluation of complex development programs. We begin with a review of the importance of databases for development evaluation. We then present a number of techniques that can be used to reconstruct baseline data when these were not collected as part of the evaluation design. Subsequently, we explain how data from multiple sources can be collected and integrated using a data warehouse or a dataspace approach. The integration of databases is important for the evaluation of programs in which the context appears to be critical. While a single database generally provides a single view of context, combining different databases offers a more comprehensive view, and therefore a better understanding of the program context may be obtained. Finally, various techniques for analyzing such integrated data are described. These methods can be used on either quantitative (data mining, big data) or qualitative data (argument mapping).*

## 1. The Relevance of Databases for the Evaluation of Complex Development Programs

Today, we distinguish user-generated data (e.g., from social media or websites), machine-generated data (e.g., tracking data, sensor data, application logs), and registry data (e.g., data that governmental organizations need for their operational tasks). These data are often stored in database systems that are essentially organized collections of the data that model reality to a certain extent. Typically, they are used to input, store, retrieve, and manage large quantities of information. A database system consists of a database management system and a set of databases. A database management system provides an interface between users and one or more databases; it allows users to access the data in it. Moreover, it supports users in querying, adding, modifying, or deleting data. Finally, administration tasks can be performed, such as monitoring users and performance, and enforcing data integrity and security. In contrast to individual (organized) datasets such as spreadsheets, database systems are optimized for rapid search and retrieval. The data in these systems can be accessed quickly, easily, at any time, and by multiple users simultaneously. While a database management system is usually a commercial off-the-shelf product, this is not the case for a database. A database should be designed to meet the information needs and intended usage of its users. This is a time-consuming task that is done on several levels by database experts.

A database system has several advantages over other data solutions. Two major advantages are the so-called program-data independency and conceptual-physical independency (Elmasri & Navathe, 2004). The first advantage refers to the fact that no knowledge is required about how data are physically organized in a system in order to query data. A user specifies which data are needed and does not need to specify how the data should be retrieved from the system. The second advantage refers to the fact that there is no need to adapt a conceptual database schema if the physical organization of the data is changed. A conceptual schema provides an overview of the data and the relationships between these data that are stored in a database. For reasons of performance, the physical organization of data is tuned to the expected workload on a database system. However, in the course of time, the (expected) workload on a database system may change significantly, which may result in a badly performing system. To solve or prevent this problem, the data in the system need to be reorganized.

For the evaluation of (complex) programs, a database system may be a useful tool since data for subgroups, such as predefined populations, geographical regions, and predefined sectors, can easily be retrieved and presented to the user. Furthermore, the data in a database are consistent in the sense that data items are not in contradiction with each other and the semantics of data items are clearly described. The truthfulness and quality of the data are dependent on how the data are collected. For example, questionnaires filled in by respondents give rise to more subjectivity and noise compared to data collected by sensors. Suppose one wants to know the three locations that are most frequently visited by a certain individual. This can be answered by keeping track of the locations that are visited by means of an embedded GPS system in an embedded device and selecting the three most frequented locations. The question can also be enclosed in a questionnaire. The latter has the disadvantage that someone may have the perception that he or she visits some locations quite often while in reality this might not be the case. Furthermore, someone may give socially acceptable answers or deliberately mention other locations than those that are frequently visited.

As discussed in Chapter 1, program evaluations are focusing more and more on sector-wide programs and thematic strategies at country or even multi-countries level. Moreover, various institutions and groups of stakeholders are involved in these programs. Also in the light of complex causal change, a broad set of dimensions might be directly or indirectly influenced by complex programs. Therefore, the evaluation of (complex) programs requires a comprehensive view of a phenomenon or an intervention from different perspectives. To obtain a (more) comprehensive view, a wide range of databases is needed. These databases should also be linked and integrated. This entails a number of challenges. Since these databases are collected for different purposes and by different institutes, data are organized, formatted, and stored in different ways and on different types of systems. Furthermore, the quality of the data may differ. The search for suitable features that can be used to link different databases to each other might not be trivial as well. Once an integrated set of data has been obtained, these data have to be analyzed in an effective and efficient way. In the remainder of this chapter, we provide a more detailed overview of these issues and how to address them.

We note that although, compared to a single database, the integration of multiple databases provides a more comprehensive view of a phenomenon in society, this view remains a model of a real-world phenomenon. Therefore, the restrictions that hold for models should be taken into account when interpreting such a view.

# 2. Reconstructing Baseline Data[1]

Baseline data represent the conditions before the start of the program and can be compared with observed or estimated program outcomes or impacts at the time of project completion. However, many evaluations do not begin until a program has been operating for some time, either because the evaluation was commissioned late in the project cycle or because there were delays in the launch of the evaluation. Both scenarios mean that there are no baseline reference data against which to compare the outcomes. Even if baseline data are available, one needs to realize that these data represent the real world as it was at the time that the data were collected. In general, it may take a long time between the implementation of an intervention and the moment that the intervention is ready for evaluation. In the meantime there might be occurrences in a society that influence the intervention. Consequently, the differences between the data collected during the evaluation and the baseline data may not fully be caused by the intervention. To capture this shortcoming, research designs introduce control groups. However, it is not always possible to find or define control groups, especially in the cases of complicated programs and complex development interventions.

In order to exploit the collected baseline data in an effective way, these data may be combined with other datasets, for example, data that pertain to occurrences that took place between the start of the collection of the baseline data[2] and the start of the evaluation of an intervention. This combination may lead to a better understanding and assessment of the impact of the intervention. Suppose that a set of interventions X is introduced to increase the Dutch language skills of children at primary school and that during the baseline data collection the language skills of these children are rated as C. If between the start of the baseline data collection and the start of the evaluation of X, a significant number of children with poor Dutch language skills immigrated to the Netherlands, then it may make sense to revise the rating obtained during the baseline data collection. Relevant data about the immigrated children may be used to do so.

Data that pertain to occurrences between the start of the collection of baseline data and the start of the evaluation of an intervention may also be used to simulate, to a certain extent, the real world during the collection of the baseline data as if these occurrences would have taken place. In this case, the data are used to simulate in some sense counterfactuals. For example, data about the immigrated children can be combined with baseline data collected for assessment purposes to simulate the ratings at primary schools including the immigrated children.

However, during the research design of intervention evaluations, it is hard to predict the (relevant) occurrences that will take place during the implementation of an intervention, and therefore data collection for these occurrences often is not planned. Consequently, no data are collected about these occurrences for evaluation purposes. Luckily, in the digitalized world of today, large streams of both quantitative and qualitative data become available rapidly. These data may be exploited for evaluation purposes. In the following sections we present some of the approaches that can be used to reconstruct or recreate baseline data.

## 2.1 Using Administrative Data Collected by the Project

Many projects collect monitoring and other kinds of administrative data that could be used to estimate baseline conditions for the project population. Examples include socioeconomic data included in the application forms of people or communities applying to the project, planning and feasibility studies, and project monitoring reports. Sometimes information on people not accepted for the project can be used to construct a comparison group of nonparticipants. It is always important to assess the quality of the project data and to identify possible sources of bias.

In the following example, we illustrate how administrative data in the context of a criminal justice system may be used for evaluation purposes. In a criminal justice system different stages are distinguished: investigation, prosecution, trial, and execution. Let us assume that we want to gain insight into the functioning of this criminal justice system. The elapsed time of a case is an important indicator. For several reasons, long elapsed times are undesired (Netten, van den Braak, Choenni, & Leertouwer, 2014). The elapsed time may conceptually be defined as the time at which a case exits the criminal justice system minus the time at which it enters the system.

Organizations involved in the criminal justice system carry out certain tasks and store data about their core tasks in their own database systems. Consequently, the

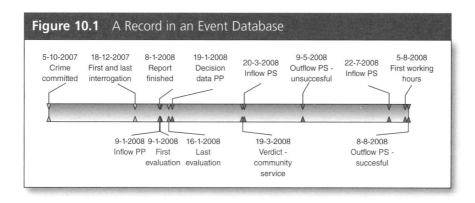

**Figure 10.1**   A Record in an Event Database

data required to compute elapsed times are scattered over different database systems. To compute the elapsed time, all relevant databases have to be linked. The date values can then be extracted and transformed into an "event database." A record in this event database is a timeline for a case (see Figure 10.1). In Section 3, we will discuss the basics to obtain such an event database. Using this event database, the time elapsed between several activities can be computed easily. For example, for the case depicted in Figure 10.1, the elapsed time between the date that the crime was committed and the decision of the public prosecutor is 106 days ((19-01-2008) – (5-10-2007)). Such an event database can be a useful tool for evaluation purposes, for instance, when a new intervention is introduced that is supposed to decrease elapsed times. The average elapsed time for cases before and after the implementation of the intervention can easily be computed and compared.

## 2.2 Using Secondary Data

Censuses or surveys conducted around the time the project began can provide information required on the baseline conditions of the project group. Many countries conduct periodic income and expenditure surveys that include extensive social and economic data on households as well as information on access to services. When surveys are conducted at least once a year, it is possible to find a survey conducted close to the time of the project launch, thus providing a potentially good baseline. However, when using surveys that cover the whole population, the sample of project households is often too small to be statistically representative. It is always important to assess whether the data satisfy the requirements of the evaluation. Does the survey cover the required time period? Does it include the required information and cover the right people? Does the information accurately cover both men and women?

Documentary data may also be available from sources such as government statistics agencies, planning departments, universities, health centers, schools, commercial banks and credit programs, accreditation agencies, professional and licensing agencies, the courts, and the mass media. Demographic data on births, deaths, and marriages may also be available from records maintained by government, community, or religious institutions.

## 2.3 Conducting Retrospective Surveys (Recall)

Recall techniques are widely used in areas such as poverty analysis as well as demographic and income and expenditure surveys. Although it is difficult to use recall to obtain precise numerical data such as income, incidences of diarrhea, or farm prices, it can be used to obtain estimates of major changes in the welfare conditions of the household. For example, families can usually recall which children attended school outside the community before the village school was opened, how children traveled to school, and how much the travel time and cost were. Families can also often provide reliable information on access to health facilities, for example, where they previously obtained water and how much it cost. However, families might be reluctant to admit that their children had not been attending school or that they had been using traditional medicine. They might also underestimate how much they spent on water to convince planners that they are too poor to pay the water charges proposed in a new project.

The Living Standards Measurement Survey program conducted assessments on the use of recall for estimating consumption in developing countries (Deaton & Grosh, 2000). A major challenge in using recall is that estimates are very sensitive to changes in the research design methods, particularly the method used for data collection, the period over which estimates are obtained, and how the questions are formulated (Gibson, 2006).

Another potentially useful approach uses calendars and time diaries to help respondents reconstruct past events. These methods, often referred to as Life Course Research, encourage respondents to incorporate temporal changes as clues in reporting events such as their parental status, childhood experiences, schooling, marriages, relationships, wealth, work, stressors, health conditions, and how they spent their time during the past day (Belli, Stafford, & Alwin, 2009). Alwin (2009) shows how statistical models such as the Latent Markov Model can assess the reliability of event data (e.g., whether a person was or was not married or was or was not working at a particular point in time).

## 2.4 Using Key Informants

Key informants such as community leaders, doctors, teachers, local government agencies, nongovernmental organizations, and religious leaders may be able to provide useful reference data on baseline conditions. When selecting informants, it is important to recognize that people have their own perspective and often their own axe to grind. This may affect the quality of the data, since people may have different incentives, which affect the extent to which they are being truthful as respondents. Furthermore, the sensitivity of topics may force people to give (socially acceptable) answers that are not in agreement with reality. Consequently, the researcher should select people with different sources of information (e.g., people who know prostitutes in their family setting or community, as commercial associates or clients) as well as different perspectives (e.g., the police, neighborhood associations trying to force the prostitutes out of the community, religious leaders). It is also important not to assume that all informants should be in positions of authority. The perspective of a child, neighbor, or friend is just as important.

## 2.5 Using Participatory Evaluation Methods

A broad range of participatory research and evaluation techniques has become widely used in developing countries. Participatory research methods—which have a number of different names, including participatory rural appraisal and participatory learning and action—are based on the principle of empowering the community to conduct its own analysis of its needs and priorities and to translate these into a plan of action. All these approaches work through community groups rather than individuals and rely heavily on mapping and other graphical techniques, partly to work through group processes and partly because a high proportion of people in many rural communities are illiterate. These approaches have developed a wide range of techniques for reconstructing the history of the community and the identification of critical events in the life of the community. Techniques include seasonal calendars, time trends, historical profiles, critical incidents, and causal analysis (Kumar, 2002; Theis & Grady, 1991).

# 3. Data Collection and Integration[3]

As complex interventions relate to various different aspects of society and have multiple stakeholders, an insight into their effects can be gained only by relating and integrating data from different sources in a coherent matter. This is the case, for example, in the domain of public safety. Public safety relates to various social phenomena, including crime, annoyance, and youth issues. In order to gain insight into the effect of a new policy on the safety of a certain region, safety-related data from various sources need to be gathered and combined. This can, for instance, be information from registry systems of organizations in the justice system (e.g., the police, the courts), survey data on experienced crimes and annoyance by civilians, and press coverage of safety-related subjects. From these sources, measurable (quantitative) variables can be derived, such as the number of registered crimes, the perceived amount of litter in a neighborhood, and the number of school dropouts. A combination of these variables can be used to measure how safe a certain region was and is now and how the policy affected this. Thus, data from database systems may be of value to determine how complex interventions affect society. In fact, for evidence-based evaluation they are of crucial importance.

In this section, we discuss the issues that should be addressed when combining data from different databases. Then we discuss two architectures, data warehouses and data spaces, that facilitates data integration.

Data can be integrated on two levels: individual or aggregate. Integrating data on an individual level involves data reconciliation, that is, the identification of data in different sources that refer to the same entity. In the next section we show how this can be done by using data warehouses. In some cases, only statistical, aggregate data are available. As a result, data integration cannot be based on unique identifiers. For this task, a dataspace approach was developed. Both approaches are outlined in the following subsections. When data from multiple sources are collected and integrated, one has to take into account that redundancy, semantic changes, and dependencies in the data may occur.

First, data redundancy occurs when a certain field, or attribute, is repeated in multiple tables or databases. Inconsistencies arise when different values for the same attribute appear. To avoid this problem, redundancy in a database system should generally be avoided by design. When integrating redundant data, inconsistencies have to be identified and resolved. This can be done by choosing one of the values and dismissing the other. To do this in an effective and systematic way, a set of rules or criteria needs to be defined. These rules might be based on widely accepted heuristics. For example, when several addresses are found for the same person, the most recent address should be taken as value in the integrated database. The reason behind this is that research has pointed out that there is a higher chance that the most recent address is the correct address. Also, specific domain knowledge might be exploited to define the set of heuristics. Suppose that a source X is more reliable for an attribute A than source Y; then the value of X is taken as the value for attribute A.

Second, semantic changes arise when the meaning of an attribute changes over time, for example, because of new rules or regulations. Consider, for instance, municipal reorganizations. Due to this, cities are expanded and names are changed. In older databases these names are not always updated, and the meaning of the old names may become unknown over time. Additionally, when cities are expanded but retain their old name, the meaning of the name is changed. It is important to record semantic changes. Otherwise, data may be combined improperly or wrong conclusions may be drawn based on them.

Third, quantitative, qualitative, semantic, and structural dependencies may exist within and between data sources. This is the case whenever certain attributes or values are strongly related. In the justice domain, an example of a quantitative dependency relates to the date on which a crime is committed. In practice, this date is usually equal to the date that the crime is reported to the police. Another example is that the number of cases that are sent from the police to the prosecution always has to be greater than or equal to the number of cases that the prosecution receives.

Qualitative dependencies can also exist in databases. For instance, it is generally assumed that the value of a certain attribute does not change dramatically in a few years. Therefore, it is recommended to compare the value of an attribute in a certain year to its value in preceding years in order to detect large deviations. For example, the number of registered crimes changes gradually in a stable society, since a number of parameters, such as police forces and economic developments, influence crime. If these parameters show only small fluctuations over the years, it is not expected that the number of registered crimes will change dramatically in successive years.

Semantic dependencies have to do with the meaning of the attributes stored in databases and the relations between them. It is important to know and record these relations. For example, different organizations in the justice domain store data about the same entities, but often label or classify these data differently. For example, in case of a robbery, the police may classify it as a violent crime, while the prosecution classifies it as a crime against property. Thus, counting the number of robberies from the police database yields a different number than counting them from the prosecution database.

Finally, structural dependencies entail that the value of an attribute is determined, without any doubt or uncertainty, by the value of another set of attributes. For example, the age of a person is determined by his or her date of birth.

All these types of dependencies have to be taken into account, and preserved as much as possible, when data from different sources are combined. Contemporary database management systems provide database designers with facilities to manage the different types of dependencies.

## 3.1 Data Warehouses

In a data warehouse (Kimball & Ross, 2002), data from different sources (not necessarily databases) that refer to a single entity are transformed and loaded. Thus, a data warehouse is a central repository of data collected from multiple sources. These data are stored and structured in a way that facilitates querying and reporting. It provides a uniform data model for all data regardless of their source. Generally, a data warehouse consists of three layers for storage, integration, and access (see Figure 10.2). The storage layer contains the original data sources. In the integration layer, raw data from these sources are extracted, cleaned, transformed, and loaded into a data warehouse. As a result, the data warehouse now contains data coming from different databases that are combined and ordered. This layer also holds information about the data in the data warehouse. This information is stored in a "meta-database." This meta-database contains information about the

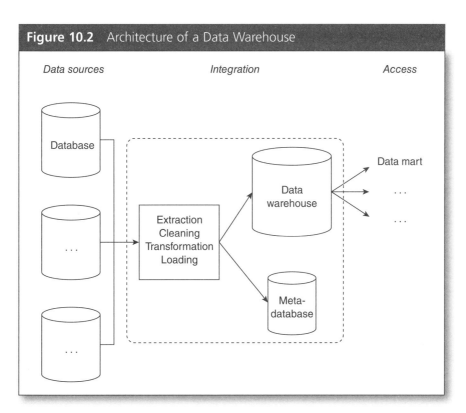

**Figure 10.2**   Architecture of a Data Warehouse

sources and adaptations of the data. Finally, the access layer provides data from the data warehouse to end users through data marts. A data mart is a selection of the data in a data warehouse with a certain purpose.

The event database described in Section 2 can be regarded as a data warehouse. This data warehouse consists of timelines of cases. Suppose that an intervention is implemented to decrease the elapsed time of a certain type of case, for example, robberies. A data mart can be built for robberies, which contains only the relevant timelines that pertain to robberies.

Besides integrating data from multiple sources into a single database so that these data can be queried easily and rapidly (using only a single query), data warehouses provide several advantages: They allow one to maintain data history, improve data quality, and prevent inconsistencies. This is because the database analyst has to design and maintain a uniform data model.

The key step in developing a data warehouse is data reconciliation (Choenni, van Dijk, & Leeuw, 2010). This step involves identifying how data sources are related and identifying which data refer to the same entity. Usually, this is done using unique (primary) keys. See, for example, Figure 10.3, which shows that when a company has two databases, one with client information and one with order information, both can be combined using the unique client ID.

**Figure 10.3**   Snapshots of Three Relations With Same Primary Key

| Client ID | Name | Street | Zip code |
|---|---|---|---|
| AB123 | Sophie Jones | 251 First Street | 51853 |
| AC221 | Harry Smith | 34 Pine Avenue | 35733 |
| BE321 | Emma Williams | 1009 Main Street | 92646 |

| Client ID | Order ID | Product ID | Order total |
|---|---|---|---|
| AB123 | 123-ABC-3 | 7223446 | 45,95 |
| AC221 | 412-ADB-4 | 8923458 | 30,90 |
| AB123 | 523-BAD-2 | 2436912 | 21,95 |

| Client ID | Name | Address | Order ID | Product ID | Order total |
|---|---|---|---|---|---|
| AB123 | Sophie Jones | 251 First Street 51853 | 123-ABC-3 | 7223446 | 45,95 |
| AC221 | Harry Smith | 34 Pine Avenue 35733 | 412-ADB-4 | 8923458 | 30,90 |
| AB123 | Sophie Jones | 251 First Street 51853 | 523-BAD-2 | 2436912 | 21,95 |

However, in some situations such identifiers are not available, for instance, due to privacy-related restrictions. In such cases other overlapping information in the to-be-combined databases has to be exploited. This can be either information about the database schemata or information that is extracted from the database content. To be able to use this information, domain knowledge from experts is needed. To establish whether two records from different database systems denote the same object, the following general rule of thumb can be applied (Choenni & Meijer, 2011): The larger the number of common attributes with the same values for two records from two different systems, the higher the chance that the records relate to the same object in reality. Note that this rule of thumb requires that the selectivity factors of the common attributes are small (Choenni, Blanken, & Chang, 1993).

## 3.2 Dataspaces

In a dataspace approach, also three layers are distinguished (see Figure 10.4): dataspace, space manager, and interface. The dataspace layer contains a set of (cleaned) databases that may be related. The relations that exist between these databases are stored in a relationship manager in the space manager layer. This layer maintains data quality (the plausibility and consistency of the data) by providing rules to which the data must adhere. For this purpose, the relationship manager may contain rules.

These rules make it possible to assess the quality and reliability of the data and to warn users when there are problems. Moreover, they can be used to complete datasets that are incomplete. Such a rule may work as follows. Suppose that we have two different sources: one source records the birth date of individuals, while the other records the age of the same individuals. If for some of the individuals the ages are missing in the latter source, the birth dates in the former source may be used to derive the ages.

Besides providing a relationship manager, the space manager serves as a communicator between the database and the user interface. This is done by the query scheduler. Based on the questions of the users at the interface level, this scheduler decides which databases to query in order to answer each question. Once the answer is retrieved from the databases, it is displayed to the user through the interface.

While database management systems provide an extensive set of tools to manage data in a database, tools to manage data between different databases are lacking. Yet there is a practical need for such tools. Because database design primarily focuses on serving the information needs of a select group of users, it is not a common practice to establish relationships between different databases. A database is considered an independent and autonomous unit in which relationships with other databases are neglected and therefore not specified. With respect to exactly this property, a data warehouse or dataspace system differs from a database system. A data warehouse aims to create a uniform view of the data extracted from a collection of databases. Kalidien, Choenni, and Meijer (2010) argue that developing a data warehouse is a costly effort and that the development of a dataspace system not only is cheaper but may be also more effective for heterogeneous data management,

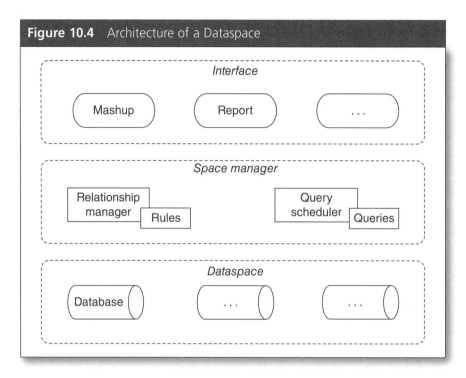

**Figure 10.4**   Architecture of a Dataspace

for example, in the field of justice. This is due to the fact that there is no need for data reconciliation using unique identifiers. In a dataspace, related sources are linked using rules based on domain knowledge.

# 4. Data Analysis

For evaluation purposes, to benefit from the data stored in a data warehouse or a dataspace, they need to be analyzed, as this may lead to the discovery of new information or conclusions. Statistics (e.g., correlations, scatter plots, general linear models) may be considered as a standard tool for data analysis. However, nowadays the amount of data collected and stored has grown exponentially. Therefore, automated and more advanced techniques have been developed. In many fields, data mining (Tan, Steinbach, & Kumar, 2005) has proven to have an added value over statistics in analyzing large amounts of data (Choenni, Bakker, Blok, & de Laat, 2005). This technique can be used to reveal useful knowledge that is hidden in a large amount of data. Recently, the constantly increasing amount of data available has given rise to a new field of study: big data. Finally, when quantitative data are not available, qualitative data may be used for evaluation purposes. One technique for analyzing qualitative data is argument mapping.

## 4.1 Data Mining[4]

Data mining is the process of searching for statistical relations, or patterns, in large datasets. It is often used to gain a different perspective on the data and to extract useful information from them. Conventional data analysis tools are inadequate to extract this knowledge, while manually extracting this knowledge is a time-consuming and tedious process at best. Therefore, there is a practical need to (partially) automate this process. Data mining contributes to fulfilling this need by combining techniques from different fields, such as database technology, machine learning, statistics, and artificial intelligence. Commonly used methods include rule learning (searching for relationships in the data), clustering (discovering groups in the data that are similar), and classification (generalizing known structures to new data). Thus, data mining is able to reveal useful knowledge that is hidden in a large amount of data.

Data mining algorithms induce models from large databases, which contain observations from the real world. The goal is to provide an insight in a phenomenon of interest that is part of the real world. This insight may help in understanding the phenomenon and predicting the outcome of similar phenomena. Statistical techniques also induce models, but there are some major differences between statistics and data mining.

First, statistical techniques require that a model or hypothesis is given beforehand. The data are used to test the model in order to accept or reject it. Data mining algorithms work the other way around: They use the data to come up with (useful) models for a user. Although the number of models that can be induced from a set of data is enormous and grows exponentially with the size of a database, data mining algorithms are currently able to handle this complexity due to the arithmetic power of contemporary computers.

Second, data mining algorithms typically use a combination of different databases with noisy or contradictory data. Additionally, decisive attributes essential for the mining process may be missing simply because the databases used are set up and maintained for other reasons than data mining. This complicates the induction of models. In statistics, on the other hand, data are collected for the purpose of testing hypotheses, and therefore the focus is on the collection of relevant and useful data. Missing or noisy data are usually not a big problem, and all data needed are stored in a single database.

An example of an application of data mining that clearly shows the difference with statistics is Walmart that combined the data from its point-of-sale systems with its loyalty card system. In this way a data warehouse can be set up in which information about the items bought by each customer on different days at a Walmart site are stored. Today it is a common practice to scan and store the items that are bought by customers in a supermarket in a data warehouse. By mining the data of Walmart, a remarkable result was found: a connection between diapers and beer. It appeared that most young American males who bought diapers also bought six-packs of beer. This correlation between diapers and beer was rather unexpected, and statistical researchers have never formulated a hypothesis regarding such a correlation. Consequently, the correlation could never be found with statistical tools. Data mining tools are able to find such a correlation since they exploit the computing power of machines and search for all possible correlations. Therefore, unexpected results are floating up to the surface.

Applications of data mining technology can be found in a wide variety of fields. For example, airline companies analyze historical reservation data to get a better profile of their customers. In the field of marketing, data mining is used to decide which customers to send an advertisement to, while insurance companies use data mining algorithms to discriminate between "good" and "bad" clients.

However, in some fields the straightforward application of data mining techniques may be risky. As has been pointed out in the literature (Hand, 1998), data mining results need to be evaluated by experts to determine whether they hold in the real world. The main reason for this is that data mining is based on induction, so the results may be true given the data, but not in the real world. For example, assume that all swans in a given databases are white, then it may be induced from the database that all swans are white. However, it is very well possible that only features of white swans are stored in the databases and that the very small group of black swans is neglected. As a result, the induced knowledge with regard to swans does not hold in the real world. So although data mining algorithms induce models from a large set of observations from real life, this does not necessarily mean that these models are correct. Therefore, it is of vital importance to evaluate the validity of data mining results. In social sciences, evaluation is even more important because, as opposed to findings in exact sciences, findings in social sciences are changing in the course of time. For instance, Newton's laws of motion were true decades ago and still hold today, while, for instance, the age-crime distribution in crime science is changing over time and might be different for different populations in different countries. While in exact sciences it is aimed to produce theories that are based on "solid" proofs, which are not open to discussions, in social sciences middle range theories are subject to refinement or refutation based on new empirical insights.

Another reason to be cautious with data mining results in social sciences is the fact that, since data collection is a time-consuming and difficult process, often legacy databases are used for data mining. Such databases contain large amounts of data that were collected and stored in the past, sometimes decades ago. As a result, these databases mostly reflect the situation in the past, so mining these databases results in knowledge about the past. Evaluation of such data mining results is important for three reasons. First, it has to be determined whether this knowledge corresponds with the real world of the past. Second, it has to be determined whether the knowledge still holds in the real world of today. Third, it has to be determined whether it is useful to apply the obtained knowledge (e.g., in developing new policies).

Finally, since data mining tools are developed to find patterns based on any correlation in data, they can find patterns that use personal characteristics of groups of individuals. This may lead to discrimination and stigmatization of these groups. For instance, assume that data mining algorithms are employed on a database of sex offenders that is enriched with demographic and economic data. A likely data mining result would be that unemployed white men are responsible for 80% of the sex offenses. There are two problems with such a statement. First, it could lead to stigmatization as the relation to the total population of unemployed white men is not made clear. Second, using it to discover new (unknown) sex offenders leads to discrimination because suddenly all unemployed white men are suspects, while only a small number of them are actual sex offenders.

## 4.2 Big Data[5]

In order to take advantage of the explosive growth of data, there has been increasing interest in research and development in the field of big data. This field is concerned with datasets that are large, complex, and difficult to process using standard tools. Therefore, technologies are explored that allow for the processing of large amounts of complex data in a timely matter before the data lose their value and without putting restrictions on the type of data.

The field of big data may have an enormous impact on social research, especially on behavioral sciences. In social sciences, a well-known method to collect data is questionnaires that ask a series of questions of respondents. It is, however, a tough task to determine whether or not a respondent gives a socially accepted, and not honest, answer. By equipping a respondent with sensors, many questions do not need to be asked, as they may be answered by processing the information of a sensor. For example, one may ask a respondent which shops she visited in the last 10 days, but this question may also be answered by tracking her mobile phone. Another example is wanting to know how a respondent is feeling right now. This question may be answered by measuring a number of bodily functions, for example, blood pressure, heart rate, or perspiration level.

Using sensors has two major advantages over using questionnaires. First, the chance that a respondent gives socially accepted answers is minimized. Second, it shortens questionnaires, while respondents may be unburdened from some sensitive questions that are involved in a questionnaire. This may increase the number of respondents.

In the field of social research, up-to-date information is considered an important parameter for decision making. Due to big data, decision makers may be able to obtain a more accurate and complete picture of a situation. Additionally, developments in the field of big data may make it possible for smart devices to sense the environment and to communicate with users and other devices in it. These capabilities make smart devices useful tools for understanding the complexity of an environment or situation and to respond to it. For example, one may equip a mobile phone with a sensor that keeps track of the environment; whenever the environment changes significantly, the phone may send a warning to the owner of the phone. An overview of applications can be found in Stembert, Conradie, Mulder, and Choenni (2013) and Choenni, Shoae Bargh, Roepan, and Meijer (in press).

## 4.3 Argument Mapping

When evaluating the impact of new policies or reconstructing theories behind programs or policies, one of the most important, yet difficult, tasks is to make hidden assumptions or premises explicit. To do so, policymakers or advisers may benefit from concepts taken from the field of argument diagramming (or argument visualization). It is this field that aims to visualize and reveal the structure of an argument by representing its premises and conclusions as well as the possible sources of doubt. However, argument diagramming may not only be used to analyze and evaluate arguments in discourse, it can also be used to make assumptions underlying programs or policies explicit. Thus, argument diagrams function as (external) representations of the structure of the underlying assumptions. In this way, the evaluation process is made transparent, transferable, and verifiable. Moreover, this method not only allows a person to express his or her support for certain assumptions, but also encourages the person to comment on or make objections to other assumptions. Moreover, when it is used in collaboration it may have even more apparent advantages, as a collective memory of assumptions is created and all group members are made aware of the assumptions that are believed by the group. Thus, argument diagramming can be used for recording discussions.

In essence, an argument diagram is a visual representation of the elements of an argument, often in the form of a tree. Typically, such a tree is made up of two basic components: boxes and arrows (Reed, Walton, & Macagno, 2007). Boxes or circles are used to represent the claims, propositions, or statements, and in this way the premises and conclusions, in the diagrammed argument. Arrows or lines joining them are used to represent connections, relationships, or inferences between them, where an arrow indicates the direction of the inference from premise to conclusion. The created (directed) graph provides a visualization of the structure of the argument and displays how the various premises and conclusions are related in a chain of reasoning. Visualizing and unfolding the argument's structure in this manner reveals both the strengths and the limits of a certain argument. An example of an argument diagram can be found in Figure 10.5.

Recently, to aid argument diagramming, ICT-driven approaches emerged. In this field, called *computer-supported argumentation* or *computer-supported argument visualization*, a range of software tools to support and teach argumentation have been developed. Since the task of creating argument diagrams by hand, using pen and paper, is laborious, various researchers have turned to the development of software tools that support the construction and visualization of arguments using diagrams or graphs (Davies, 2011; Kirschner, Buckingham Shum, & Carr, 2003; Okada, Buckingham Shum, & Sherborne, 2008; Scheuer, Loll, Pinkwart, & McLaren, 2010).

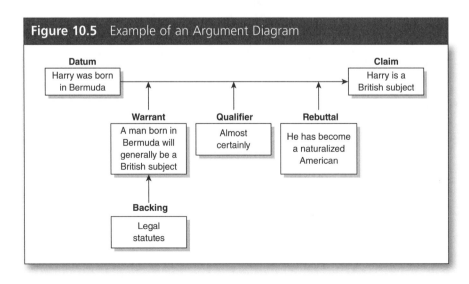

**Figure 10.5** Example of an Argument Diagram

Many different argument diagramming tools, often referred to as sensemaking systems, are currently available. They vary by the type of information that is represented and their expressiveness. Some of these software packages define specific conceptual primitives that are used to construct arguments in a specific target domain. Other packages (e.g., Belvedere, Compendium, Cohere) are more generic, can be used for a wide variety of tasks, and originated partly from the more general concept mapping method for representing knowledge graphically (Novak, 1990). The latter set of tools is particularly attractive because of the interface's user-friendliness and ease of use; it is easier to learn how to use these tools, partly because of their semiformal underlying model, which is tailored to novices or students of critical thinking.

# 5. Practical Applications

- In this chapter we provide an overview of emergent technologies that may be used to facilitate the evaluation of complex programs. These technologies are embedded in contemporary devices and applications, which in turn generate an enormous amount of data. Data warehouses and dataspaces are focused on the integration of data from multiple sources, which is advantageous for the evaluation of complex programs as it may lead to a more comprehensive assessment of multiple components from multiple perspectives.

- However, creating and analyzing such data involves a number of challenges. For instance, data are formatted, organized, and stored on different types of systems. Furthermore, the quality and meaning of the data may differ between datasets. To create a proper set for evaluation purposes, a significant amount of effort is required to ensure compatibility of the data and to enforce consistency between different datasets. We have discussed a number of techniques to clean noisy data, to deal with redundant data, and to link data that allow one to achieve a proper dataset.

- Once useful datasets are created, they have to be analyzed in an effective and efficient way. Depending on the characteristics of the data, one may choose from various techniques. While data mining and big data analytics tools focus on searching for interesting patterns and knowledge in large datasets, whether or not in "real time," argument mapping tools may be used to make the (working) mechanisms behind complex programs (more) explicit. In the light of developments in the field of (advanced) data collection by sensors and analysis of qualitative data, we expect that more and more sources with better quality can be integrated. Therefore, the comprehensiveness of views on phenomena may increase, benefitting complexity-responsive evaluations that seek to include measurements of behavioral changes.

- Today, many of the techniques that have been discussed in this chapter can be found in contemporary tools that support the integration of data sets. However, integrating data may still be a time-consuming task as it often requires domain knowledge. Furthermore, there is also a wide variety of tools, based on data mining techniques, for the analysis of large and complex data sets. These tools are available as commercial products as well as open source products. The latter category of products is free of charge and can be downloaded from the Internet. Although throughout the years these products have evolved as user-friendly tools, it requires some effort to use them properly and effectively. Nonetheless, these tools make it simpler and more affordable to analyze large data sets and to apply data mining.

# References

Alwin, D. (2009). Assessing the validity and reliability of timeline and event history data. In F. Belli, F. Stafford, & D. Alwin (Eds.), *Calendar and time diary methods in life course research* (pp. 277–301). Thousand Oaks, CA: Sage.

Bamberger, M., Rugh, J., & Mabry, L. (2012). *RealWorld evaluation: Working under budget, data, time and political constraints.* Thousand Oaks, CA: Sage.

Belli, F., Stafford, F., & Alwin, D. (Eds.). (2009). *Calendar and time diary methods in life course research.* Thousand Oaks, CA: Sage.

Choenni, S., Bakker, R., Blok, H., & de Laat, R. (2005). Supporting technologies for knowledge management. *Knowledge Management and Management Learning, 9,* 89–112.

Choenni, S., Blanken, H., & Chang, T. (1993). Index selection in relational databases. In *Proceedings of ICCI 1993, Fifth International Conference on Computing and Information* (pp. 491–496). New York, NY: Institute of Electrical and Electronics Engineers.

Choenni, S., & Meijer, R. (2011). From police and judicial databases to an offender-oriented data warehouse. In *Proceedings of the IADIS International Conference on e-Society* (pp. 98–105). IADIS Press.

Choenni, S., Shoae Bargh, M., Roepan, C., & Meijer, R. (in press). Privacy and security in smart data collection by citizens. In G. Garcia, J. Pardo, T., & Nam (Eds.), *Smarter as the new urban agenda: A comprehensive view of the 21st century city.* New York, NY: Springer.

Choenni, S., van Dijk, J., & Leeuw, F. (2010). Preserving privacy whilst integrating data: Applied to criminal justice. *Information Polity, 15*(1–2), 125–138.

Davies, M. (2011). Concept mapping, mind mapping and argument mapping: What are the differences and do they matter? *Higher Education, 62,* 279–301.

Deaton, A., & Grosh, M. (2000). Consumption. In M. Grosh & P. Glewwe (Eds.), *Designing household survey questionnaires for developing countries: Lessons from 15 years of Living Standards Measurement Study* (Vol. 1, pp. 91–134). Washington DC: World Bank.

Elmasri, R., & Navathe, S. (2004). *Fundamentals of database systems* (4th ed.). Boston, MA: Addison-Wesley.

Gibson, J. (2006). Statistical tools and estimation methods for poverty measures based on cross-sectional household surveys. In *Handbook on poverty statistics: Concepts, methods and policy use* (pp. 128–205). New York, NY: United Nations Department of Economic and Social Affairs. Retrieved from http://unstats.un.org/unsd/methods/poverty/chapter51.htm

Hand, D. J. (1998). Data mining: Statistics and more? *American Statistician, 52,* 112–118.

Kalidien, S., Choenni, S., & Meijer, R. (2010). Crime statistics on line: Potentials and challenges. In *Proceedings of the 11th Annual International Digital Government Research Conference on Public Administration Online: Challenges and Opportunities* (pp. 131–137). Digital Government Society.

Kimball, R., & Ross, M. (2002). The data warehouse toolkit: *The complete guide to dimensional modeling* (2nd ed.). New York, NY: John Wiley & Sons.

Kirschner, P. A., Buckingham Shum, S. J., & Carr, C. S. (Eds.). (2003). *Visualizing argumentation: Software tools for collaborative and educational sense-making.* London, UK: Springer-Verlag.

Kumar, S. (2002). *Methods for community participation: A complete guide for practitioners.* London, UK: ITDG.

Netten, N., van den Braak, S., Choenni, S., & Leertouwer, E. (2014). Elapsed times in criminal justice systems. In *Proceedings of the 8th International Conference on Theory and Practice of Electronic Governance.* New York, NY: ACM Press.

Novak, J. D. (1990). Concept maps and Vee diagrams: Two metacognitive tools to facilitate meaningful learning. *Instructional Science, 19*(1), 29–52.

Okada, A., Buckingham Shum, S. J., & Sherborne, T. (Eds.). (2008). *Knowledge cartography: Software tools and mapping techniques.* London, UK: Springer Verlag.

Reed, C. A., Walton, D. N., & Macagno, F. (2007). Argument diagramming in logic, law and artificial intelligence. *Knowledge Engineering Review, 22*(1), 87–109.

Scheuer, O., Loll, F., Pinkwart, N., & McLaren, B. M. (2010). Computer-supported argumentation: A review of the state of the art. *International Journal of Computer-Supported Collaborative Learning, 5*(1), 43–102.

Stembert, N., Conradie, P., Mulder, I., & Choenni, R. (2013). Participatory data gathering for public sector reuse: Lessons learned from traditional initiatives. In *Proceedings of the 5th International Conference on eParticipation* (pp. 87–98). London, UK: Springer Verlag.

Tan, P., Steinbach, M., & Kumar, V. (2005). *Introduction to data mining.* London, UK: Addison-Wesley.

Theis, J., & Grady, H. (1991). *Participatory rapid rural appraisal for community development: A training manual based on experiences in the Middle East and North Africa region.* London, UK: Save the Children, International Institute for Environment and Development.

van den Braak, S., Choenni, S., & Verwer, S. (2013). Combining and analyzing judicial databases. In B. Custers, T. Calders, B. Schermer, & T. Zarsky (Eds.), *Discrimination and privacy in the information society* (pp. 191–206). Berlin, Germany: Springer.

# Notes

1. This section is adapted from Bamberger, Rugh, and Mabry (2012).

2. We assume that prior to the start of the collection of the baseline data it is determined which data should be collected and that this will not change during the collection.

3. This section is adapted from van den Braak, Choenni, and Verwer (2013).

4. This section is adapted from Choenni et al. (2005).

5. See also Chapter 12 of this book.

# CHAPTER 11

# Applying Emergent Technologies to Complex Program Evaluation From the INGO Perspective

Kerry Bruce and Alison E. Koler

*In this chapter we discuss how emergent technologies are being used in complex international development programs and the ways technologies can aid in evaluation. We look at the availability of new types of data, easier access to data, and use of external data to strengthen evaluations. We address the logistical, methodological, and ethical challenges to consider when applying emergent technologies to complex program evaluation. Lastly, we provide practical guidance from the perspective of international nongovernmental organizations to policymakers, program managers, and evaluators.*

Over the past decade there has been massive growth in the volume, types, and quality of evaluations in the international development sector. The emphasis on evaluation has been driven by the Millennium Development Goals initiative (see Chapter 1), by donors' increasing demands and guidance (Department for International Development, 2013; U.S. Department of State, 2012; USAID, 2011), and by the imperative of international nongovernmental organizations (INGOs) to understand what development interventions are working and how.

At the same time, development programs have become increasingly complex, and evaluation practice must continue to evolve to reflect these fundamental shifts. In terms of complexity, the emphasis on sector-wide programs, country programs, and multi-country thematic strategies is now greater, and a given program may have multiple intervention components at different ecological levels while also being closely aligned and interconnected with numerous stakeholders, all working toward the same development goals. Understanding the underlying causal pathways that lead to desired outcomes becomes challenging, especially when considering the realities of nonlinearity, emergence, and feedback loops. Relatedly, practitioners increasingly recognize that development programs do not exist in isolation; rather they are embedded in contexts with specific histories and local economic, political, and social systems. To fully understand nuanced change processes, evaluation of complex programs must reflect how deeply embedded societal practices and systems both influence and are influenced by development activities (see Chapter 1).

Emergent technology may play a role in confronting the challenges related to evaluating complex programs. INGOs are already using emergent technologies in programming as well as for program monitoring and outcome tracking. Thus, the question is: How can these technologies be useful for evaluators of complex programs?

In this chapter we discuss how technology is being used in complex international development programming, the ways it can be used to address challenges related to evaluating complex programs, and the opportunities and challenges of applying emergent technology. We also provide practical guidance from an INGO perspective on using emergent technology to evaluate complex programs.

# 1. Use of Emergent Technologies in Complex INGO Programs

Practitioners have leveraged high mobile phone ownership rates and broadened Internet connectivity to expand program reach and improve outcomes. INGOs are using this backbone to expand programming that uses information and communication technologies for development (ICT4D), specifically for surveillance and reporting, crowdsourced reporting, information dissemination, mHealth, public dialogues, mobile banking, and remote sensing. Some common uses of ICT4D by INGOs are summarized in Table 11.1.

Data generated by emergent technologies can prove important to evaluation efforts; the challenge for evaluators of complexity will be how these data are used. Specifically, it is important to understand how technological interventions logically link to other intervention components and to consider how data demonstrating nonlinearity and feedback loops can be meaningfully analyzed and used for evaluation.

# 2. Using Emergent Technology in Evaluation

In this section we discuss the use of emergent technologies in the evaluation process, looking at each stage of evaluation practice.

## 2.1 Evaluation Design

Designing an evaluation for complex programming must both consider issues around nonlinearity and examine the complex pathways that lead to results—pathways

**Table 11.1**    Technological Applications in INGO Programming and Their Potential for Evaluation

| Type | Description | Common applications | Possible uses in complexity-responsive evaluation |
|------|-------------|---------------------|---------------------------------------------------|
| Surveillance and reporting systems | These databases aggregate reports from various locations/sites to monitor specified indicators; systems are most effective for decision making when reporting is completed in a timely fashion. | • Disease surveillance<br>• Climate change monitoring | • Enable frequent reporting, facilitate better understanding of aspects of delimitation<br>• Provide geographic locations of where reports were submitted or GPS coordinates of cases; allow for geospatial analysis<br>• By tracking changes over time, illuminate activities' short-term effectiveness |
| Crowdsourced reporting systems | Web-based databases aggregate reports submitted by individuals/entities in the broader public and, using GPS coordinates, typically map where reports were generated. | • Conflict reporting<br>• Disaster risk reduction<br>• Disease reporting<br>• Election monitoring | • Provide contextual information and trends about program reach<br>• Enable frequent reporting, facilitate better understanding of aspects of delimitation<br>• Provide geographic locations of where reports were submitted or GPS coordinates of cases, allow for geospatial analysis<br>• Supply information on who reports and how far intervention activities reach (or do not reach)<br>• By tracking changes over time, illuminate activities' short-term effectiveness |
| Information dissemination systems | Short message service (SMS) and Internet technologies are being used to disseminate information and increase access to information among program beneficiaries across the spectrum of development sectors. | • Behavior change communication<br>• Disaster risk reduction<br>• Citizen engagement<br>• Agricultural price information | • Enable dosage/intensity adjustments via changes in messaging frequency<br>• With geographic locations of message recipients, enable mapping interactions with other interventions<br>• In instances of two-way interactions, facilitate capture of potential feedback loops |
| mHealth systems | Wireless technologies and mobile technologies such as phones and tablets support medical and public health services and interventions. | • Patient tracking<br>• Behavior change communication<br>• Point-of-care diagnostics | • Enable mapping interactions with other interventions<br>• Track health service utilization and interactions with mHealth activities, facilitate understanding of potential nonlinearity |

| Type | Description | Common applications | Possible uses in complexity-responsive evaluation |
|---|---|---|---|
| | | • Commodity tracking<br>• Medical algorithms | • In instances of two-way interaction, facilitate capture of potential feedback loops<br>• Track trends over time, illuminate activities' short-term effectiveness |
| Systems for public dialogue | Web-based platforms enhance citizen participation in decision making. | • Citizen engagement<br>• Transparency initiatives among government | • Provide contextual information and trends about program location<br>• Supply information on who engages and how far intervention activities reach (or do not reach)<br>• Track trends over time, illuminate activities' short-term effectiveness<br>• Provide site statistics, facilitate estimates of programming's influence/contribution to short-term outcomes<br>• In instances of two-way interactions, facilitate capture of potential feedback loops |
| Mobile banking systems | Banking solutions via mobile network operators allow for electronic money transfers. | • Social welfare cash transfers<br>• Savings groups | • Track beneficiaries' geographic locations, facilitate mapping of programming's interaction with other interventions<br>• Track trends over time, illuminate activities' short-term effectiveness<br>• Illustrate links to other services and systems that facilitate economic growth and positive change |
| Remote sensing technologies | These technologies facilitate remote recording and observation of objects. | • Climate change<br>• Natural resource management<br>• Medication adherence<br>• Cook stove/ water point use | • Provide unbiased information about use of project resources<br>• By tracking trends over time, illuminate activities' short-term effectiveness |

that, in static programming documents, are often oversimplified and not clearly articulated, even when there has been dynamic learning around the relationships among program pathways or around external, nonprogrammatic factors that are also leading to change.

Ideally, creating the conceptual framework to articulate how a complex program will achieve intended outcomes should begin early in project implementation; such a framework is essential to evaluation design. Open source online software, such as TOCO (www.theoryofchange.org/toco-software), can assist in building, editing, and soliciting feedback on a theory of change. Such tools facilitate easy edits to hypothesized pathways throughout a project and allow stakeholders to participate by providing feedback through the software. Because the tools are online, this software also enables participation by stakeholders in different locations in developing and refining a theory of change.

Designing an evaluation so that it focuses on key program pathways is central to understanding a project's impact. In this design phase, it is also important to consider the types of data that emergent technologies used in the programming will generate as potential data points for evaluation. For example, mobile banking automatically generates accurate, detailed transaction records, data that would require greater resources and time to collect and aggregate without technology. In well-designed programs, consideration is given at the outset to how data will be used, will contribute to the program's broader results framework, and will help answer potential evaluation questions.

As the bar for more rigorous program evaluations continues to rise, practitioners often contemplate quasi-experimental evaluation design, which can be appropriate in complex programming, especially given the greater emphasis on measuring the extent to which a program contributed toward achieving outcomes. Some evaluators are using existing data to construct counterfactual groups, such as luminosity data, as a measure of social transfers and economic growth and development (Villa, 2014). With an increased desire to measure contribution and attribution, counterfactuals that can be drawn from existing data—often drawn from data supplied by emergent technologies—will be sought and used more frequently.

## 2.2 Data Collection

With increased demand for near real-time information from donors, program staff, government, civil society, beneficiaries, and other key stakeholders, applying emergent technologies to monitoring and evaluation processes has become important for INGOs. With mobile technologies presenting the opportunity to minimize delays in data processing—because data are entered directly into the mobile device and uploaded to a Web-based data management system, eliminating the need for a separate and lengthy data entry process (Hoogeveen, Croke, Dabalen, Demombynes, & Giugale, 2014)—there is an increasing expectation in the international development sector that program data should be available in near real time. Previously, the technology to collect data and immediately share the information did not exist. Having near real-time data can facilitate more rapid adjustments to programming based on results and up-to-date reporting to stakeholders so as to engage them in discussions around program adjustments.

Examples of the use of emergent technologies for data collection are numerous; selected technologies are outlined below.

## a. Mobile Data Collection

Over the last decade, mobile phones have become increasingly widespread worldwide. In a survey of 24 non-U.S. and non-European countries, more than half the population owned a phone—up to 75% in most countries surveyed (Pew Research Center, 2014). Mobile providers have invested in expanding and strengthening coverage and networks, and mobile technologies have evolved significantly. Mobile phones can now also run on sophisticated operating systems, allow easy Internet access and Web browsing, and have built-in high-resolution cameras, audio recorders, and GPS capabilities. One of the most common ways that INGOs are applying emergent technologies to evaluation is through the use of mobile phones and tablets to collect survey data that would otherwise have been collected on paper (Bruce et al., 2013; Clear Initiative, 2013; Pact, 2014). Practitioners can use online software to build electronic surveys with skip patterns, question branching, and data validations and launch the surveys on mobile phones or tablets. Data collectors or beneficiaries can enter data directly into the device either while connected to a mobile network or offline. Using mobile technology in this manner can increase data timeliness; transporting of the surveys and a separate data entry process are unnecessary, and data are often cleaner.

Survey data can be collected via short message service (SMS), which can be appealing for programs without the resources to buy smartphones. Surveys administered through SMS can be sent directly to potential participants, who can then respond via SMS technology. End users do not necessarily have to pay for the SMSs required to respond and may be incentivized to participate by an offer of air time credit to be provided upon survey completion. Development programs have used this technique, for example, to collect rapid feedback from a cohort panel of microfinance beneficiaries and responses from a radio advertisement for a public health campaign (Armstrong et al., 2012; Center for Health Market Innovations, 2010). SMS surveys or polls not only can help close the feedback loop and engage beneficiaries throughout a program's lifecycle, but also have the potential to facilitate greater understanding of nonlinearity among posited causal pathways.

Mobile phones can be used to collect routine monitoring data throughout a program. For example, training and community event data (with GPS coordinates) can easily be collected on mobile devices and immediately uploaded. Mobile technology is also providing the opportunity for beneficiaries to become more engaged in data collection. For instance, members of savings groups, community development committees, and health promotion clubs can self-report on activities and outputs, entering data directly into their mobile devices. Similarly, INGOs are providing mobile phones and tablets as job aids to service providers to reinforce training and best practices. How providers use these aids can also become a source of data—for example, showing how many times the algorithm for Integrated Management of Childhood Illness was used and how its use correlated to the final treatment offered.

### b. Web-Based Surveys

With increases in Internet availability and bandwidth in even the poorest developing countries, Web-based survey platforms such as SurveyMonkey, Qualtrics, and Cultureamp are being used increasingly by INGOs for data collection, with challenges similar to those found in the United States and Europe, where these surveys are ubiquitous. Response rates can be low and unevenly distributed, and there can be high rates of incomplete responses, often caused by slow performance of the platform in low-bandwidth contexts (Suarez-Balcazar, Balcazar, & Taylor-Ritzler, 2009).

### c. Audio and Interactive Voice Response

Audio technology, although not new, is being used in evaluations beyond the recording of key informant interviews and focus group discussions. Smartphones and tablets, with their built-in audio recorders, facilitate collection of multiple types of data during a single interaction. Interactive voice response (IVR) technology involves computer audio responses to human voice and keypad inputs. Although more commonly used for telemarketing and in call centers, IVR is quickly becoming integrated into evaluation and research. Prerecorded survey questions can be played over mobile phones to participants, who then respond via keypad inputs. IVR technology can be useful for measurements requiring a large sample and/or questions to be read in multiple languages, yielding results similar to those from written self-administered questionnaires (Lam, Lee, Bright, Korzenik, & Sands, 2009). IVR has also been used in development programs to increase access to information: The Open Institute, with funding from the United States Agency for International Development (USAID), developed an election hotline and used IVR to inform more than 600,000 individuals of how, when, and where to vote during Cambodia's 2013 national elections.[1]

### d. Digital Video and Cameras

As digital video and cameras have advanced and become more affordable, INGOs are utilizing them for monitoring and evaluation. Video is commonly used to document program progress and success stories; footage is typically collected by program staff and shared with donors and other stakeholders to complement quantitative data presented in reports. Used in this way, video is less about data collection than about showcasing success. However, participatory video is a qualitative evaluation method, with beneficiaries collecting footage from interviews, on-site visual monitoring, and most significant change stories, which are then used to systematically capture program information. A citizenship program funded by the Department for International Development trained researchers from Brazil, Bangladesh, Mexico, Jamaica, Nigeria, and Angola on participatory video to document issues relating to citizen empowerment, participation, and accountability (Department for International Development, 2008; Development Research Center, 2008).

Photovoice involves beneficiaries taking photographs to capture their individual perspectives and experiences and mapping what they see as community assets (Catalani & Minkler, 2010). This methodology has been used effectively with marginalized, vulnerable populations such as adolescent immigrants (Streng et al., 2004) and the homeless (Bukowski & Buetow, 2011; Wang, Cash, & Powers, 2000) to give them a voice and influence policy. Both participatory video and photovoice allow inclusion of new (and often underrepresented) individuals and can promote meaningful engagement of beneficiaries in research and monitoring and evaluation.

### e. GPS and GIS

With advancements in geographic information systems (GIS) and increased afford-ability of devices with GPS capabilities, INGOs are increasingly able to integrate geographic data into programming, to map program coverage, and to conduct geospatial analyses. This geographic information allows practitioners to better understand, for example, which communities are in greatest need, the extent of geographic overlap of multiple interventions, and the areas deriving the greatest benefit from programming. GPS units and mobile phones with GPS capabilities make it possible to collect GPS coordinates for health facilities, schools, wells, toilets, and other physical structures as well as for individual residences. Quantitative, qualitative, and even visual data (i.e., images) can be linked to each GPS coordinate to add depth and permit advanced geospatial analyses. Cloud-based information systems, including mobile platforms, can automatically plot GPS coordinates on maps to allow for immediate visualization of geographic program data. GPS technology has been found to be especially powerful for helping to visualize evaluation results (Azzam & Robinson, 2013).

### f. Biometric and Sensor Data

Another emergent technology, biometrics—the measurement of biological characteristics such as fingerprints, faces, ears, or irises—can be used to identify the correct participants in research or evaluations. For example, fingerprints could be used to ensure the proper identity of a participant in a cohort study. Sensor data (e.g., body temperature, motion detectors, water flow sensors), another emergent technology, can be used to measure change or functionality over time. Sensors can be put on prescription medicine bottles, and the times the bottle is opened can be monitored as a proxy for medication adherence. Both of these new types of data can provide precision in measurement that may be useful in an evaluation.

## 2.3 Data Management and Analysis

To understand results with such complex programs, managing, integrating, and making sense of multiple sources and types of data is necessary. Emergent technology can be useful for these functions, although strong data management systems, thorough and well-thought-out analysis plans, and analytical rigor in interpreting results remain essential.

For data management and analysis, perhaps the most useful technology is the Web-based database. With Internet connectivity improving worldwide and advancements in cloud computing, Web-based databases are increasingly common. These systems are hosted "in the cloud" and are sold as "software as a service," with regular upgrades facilitating continuous rollout of new enhancements. Web-based databases allow multiple users in different locations to simultaneously enter data, a feature particularly useful in complex programming that involves multiple implementing agencies. Stakeholders can be granted different levels of access to Web-based databases, enabling wide access to the data without compromising its integrity. Individuals can log in to view program data in near real time, expanding access beyond monitoring and evaluation (M&E) teams to in-country program staff, partner organizations, government officials, headquarters technical advisors, and donors. Although Web-based databases may mainly house data only on reportable performance indicators, it is also possible to integrate with other data systems, including accounting and grants management systems, datasets from implementing agencies and other sources, and government-sponsored national M&E systems, helping practitioners to link relevant data.

Web-based databases can serve as a useful source of data for program evaluation, especially if the data structure is closely linked to the program's theory of change. Although the data in these databases will necessarily reflect the program's own interpretation of its achievement, they offer evaluators a snapshot of program output and sometimes also of outcomes over the life of the project. And given the number and diversity of actors working toward the same development goals, joining data via Web-based databases may facilitate estimation of a particular program's contribution toward shared results.

Another promising emergent technology for evaluators are the new sense-making software applications, which are evolving and changing as fast as the field of big data. Some of these software applications lend themselves to big data applications and as such may not be of much use to an evaluator, unless the project under evaluation involves big data (not a common scenario for INGOs). Other sense-making software applications could be useful because they aim to capture fragmented narratives and help to interpret them, or they allow those providing the data to signify its importance (SenseMaker, http://cognitive-edge.com/sensemaker), or they use fuzzy logic technologies to help derive meaning from inherently complex scenarios (Thicket, http://thisisthicket.net). Still others allow users to link ideas together and to external sources of information and external thinkers (Cohere). This is a rapidly developing field, and a thorough search of the literature is required if sense-making is part of the data management or analysis. Sense-making software and technologies hold the potential to aggregate and visualize large datasets and also to empower respondents to participate more fully in the evaluation process.

## 2.4 Dissemination of Evaluation Results

Most findings from evaluations in the international development sector are disseminated by printing a report and holding a meeting of government officials, NGO representatives, civil society representatives, and other stakeholders. Often notably missing from such dissemination meetings are program beneficiaries and evaluation participants (OECD-DAC, 2001). Although some programs go back to the communities from which they collected data and present the evaluation findings at a town meeting, this is not the norm, given already scant evaluation budgets.

Emergent technology presents the opportunity to disseminate evaluation results more inclusively, to include both participants and program beneficiaries, potentially in an effective manner and at low cost. Social media is used to broadly disseminate results and provide for beneficiary feedback. SMS messages can be sent to beneficiaries with a hyperlink to a Web page featuring a description of results tailored to low-literate populations. For non-literate populations, a toll-free number could be dialed, and results could be explained using IVR technology, with multilingual options. Although the effectiveness of these channels for dissemination would need to be closely examined, new methods that integrate technology are worth exploring, with a goal of reaching beneficiaries, ensuring that findings are comprehensible, engaging beneficiaries, and soliciting their feedback.

# 3. Emergent Technology and Complexity-Responsive Evaluation: Opportunities and Challenges

Emergent technologies present numerous opportunities to evaluate complex development programs. At the same time, there are several methodological, logistical, and ethical challenges related to applying the technology to evaluate complex programs.

## 3.1 Opportunities

Data generated through emergent technologies can be potentially useful for evaluators, and these datasets, often hosted on cloud servers or on Web-based databases, will be increasingly available. The data produced can be used to understand the edges of the interventions—where they start and stop—and the frequency with which beneficiaries engage with intervention activities. Additionally, data generated from information and communication technologies (ICT) can increase the credibility of findings as data from different sources can be compared for consistency and used to triangulate findings. Data generated from emergent technologies can also provide evaluators with important information relating to intervention coverage and, in some cases, an activity's short-term effectiveness.

The application of mobile banking to livelihood projects and mHealth interventions are generating detailed beneficiary data. Data generated from mobile banking help us understand savings and community lending patterns, while data from mHealth can tell us how frequently pregnant women attend antenatal clinics and what services they receive. If models can be developed to link these program-level data to big datasets or even to "data exhaust," the digital footprints left by use of technology—such as mobile phone calls and SMS records, mobile money transactions, and visits to social networking sites (Vaitla, 2014)—we may be able to better predict whether program activities are achieving intended results. Big data can also provide important information about an intervention's context—for example, on social media trends on a particular issue, environmental conditions, or migration patterns (Bamberger & Raftree, 2014).

As we begin to use data generated by ICT-based program activities, evaluators may be less reliant on periodic surveys to capture information and thus less reliant on participant recall as well. Routine monitoring data generated by ICT, such as using an algorithm to support medical decision making, can be used to evaluate programs. Integration of crowdsourcing and social media into development programs adds another layer of beneficiary-generated information that not only provides more data but is increasingly participatory. The voices of vulnerable and underrepresented groups can be heard, their faces seen in photos and videos, and information they produce used to better comprehend how development programs' components are working. More voice and participation in complexity-responsive evaluation should be a positive outcome of emergent technology for the field and should help evaluators move toward greater understanding of nonlinearity and feedback loops from beneficiaries' perspectives.

In addition to more data, technology has produced new types of data: GIS coordinates, audio, photos, videos, biometrics. Data quality is improving because of technology. Collecting data on mobile phones can be more accurate than collecting data on paper, because mobile-based survey apps have built-in skip patterns, question branching, and data validations. Eliminating the need to transfer data from paper increases the timeliness of data and speeds dissemination of results to evaluation stakeholders. In theory, data generated through ICT program activities or collecting data on mobile devices should be cost-effective as they require fewer human resources. The data generated from multiple sources also provide evaluators with sources that can be used to triangulate the validity of findings.

## 3.2 Challenges

Although the opportunities that emergent technologies offer to the practice of complexity-responsive evaluation are clear, challenges and limitations exist. Logistical challenges head the list. In mobile data collection, for example, selecting the right platform and mobile phone from among the many platforms and devices can be difficult and time-consuming (Pact, 2014). It can take time to train practitioners in mobile data collection and building surveys, and using new mobile technology platforms may require technical support to troubleshoot. Logistics around data collection with mobile phones may necessitate developing new policies and procedures to address such issues as how to conduct field supervision when there is no paper to review or how to manage when phones are lost or damaged. How to charge phones in areas without access to power and how to upload surveys in areas with weak network coverage are among other logistical challenges. Although solutions exist, it is essential to anticipate up-front investments in training and piloting any technology in the field.

Methodological issues are also important to consider when using technology that lacks universal accessibility. While SMS surveys may be efficient in collecting data, it is important for evaluation practitioners to recognize how the technological divide may exclude certain populations. Older populations, low-literate populations, and in some contexts women may lack equal access to SMS technology and may therefore be underrepresented (Brännström, 2012; Wesolowski, Eagle, Noor, Snow, & Buckee, 2012). One study that examined 25 datasets from Africa and Latin America found that lower levels of employment, education, and income resulted in lower access to and use of ICT (Hilbert, 2011). The use of ICT both in programs and in evaluation of complex programs may cause selection bias and is important to consider at the design phase.

Another important challenge is that although qualitative data can be collected and generated through emergent technologies, and there are technologies to make that easier, the bias is toward quantitative data collection when using emergent technologies. For example, mobile data collection makes it easier for data collectors to check a box or enter a number than to type a response to an open-ended question. With an increasing demand for near real-time data, the speed at which quantitative data can be collected, aggregated, and visualized compared to intensive, qualitative methods can lead to an overreliance on quantitative data. Truly integrating and triangulating quantitative and qualitative data is a challenge for any mixed methods evaluation, but it is particularly challenging when evaluating complex programs given issues of non-linearity and the need to understand findings within a system of institutions and stakeholders, where a multitude of other factors are also influencing change.

Data generated from emergent technologies can complicate how to understand a program's outcomes, because there can be too much of it. The volume of data INGO programs are generating presents an analysis problem for both program managers and evaluators. Evaluators must be selective about using data that are most essential to the evaluation questions.

There are significant ethical issues related to the use of emergent technologies in complexity-responsive evaluation. Whether data are gathered electronically or on paper, the responsibility to protect respondents' privacy and adhere to ethical research practices is unchanged. While permitting data collection and review with increased precision, data collection built on emergent technologies could potentially harm participants. For example, data collected in a community for an HIV/AIDS program that mapped all homes of HIV-positive individuals who receive medication adherence support could expose participants to stigma if the data were not properly safeguarded. Protections for personally identifiable information are increasingly important for INGOs using ICT4D and for practitioners using emergent technology for evaluation. Although data collected through platforms feature encrypted transmission and data stored on Web-based monitoring sites are password protected, the exported Excel spreadsheets that neatly emerge from these platforms are unprotected—and are easily shared. Clear protocols to protect participant data must be in place, and evaluators must be increasingly cognizant of how data are stored, transmitted, effectively de-identified, and shared. Similarly, it is important to consider and monitor the unintended consequences of the use of technology to collect data, for example, an increase in domestic violence following women being given mobile phones, suspicion from community members in conflict and post-conflict settings, or harassment from police in certain political environments (Institute of Medicine, 2012).

Lastly, it is important to remember that even in this digital, big data era, data systems often remain siloed—with, for example, monitoring and evaluation data in one database and financial program data in another. Similarly, data related to SMS alerts for patient tracking may reside in the platform to implement the technology and need to be joined to a larger program monitoring and evaluation database before analyses can respond to evaluation questions. Issues around resistance to share data among entities external to one another also contributes to siloed data and data systems. There are ever greater sources of data and information outside our organizations that may provide relevant information to our evaluations, but we need to do a better job of understanding what they are, how they are relevant to our program evaluations, and how they can be used alongside our existing datasets.

Table 11.2 summarizes applications of technology to complexity-responsive evaluations, the potential advantages, and the methodological and logistical considerations.

# 4. Practical Applications

Issues for policymakers, program managers, and evaluators who want to use emergent technology for complexity-responsive evaluations programs are discussed in this section.

**Merging and Standardizing Datasets:** In evaluation practice, understanding what other sources of data exist is a key step in evaluation design. Given limited time and budgets for most evaluations, primary and secondary data must be carefully selected. Although the idea of collecting multiple external datasets and merging them with data collected or as a counterfactual for an evaluation may hold appeal, the reality is that without a foundation of larger agreement on common variable definitions and without standardized methods for data collection, this type of merging or constructing a counterfactual will be extremely difficult and time-consuming. Currently, development practitioners rarely reach beyond nationally collected datasets (e.g., Demographic Health Surveys, the Afrobarometer). Policymakers would advance the use and effectiveness of emergent technologies by coordinating the delineation of commonly used codes and numbering systems so that data collected from one source use the same naming conventions as those collected by another. For example, at a basic level, this would result in a common numbering system for regions and districts as well as for schools and health facilities, significantly improving the potential for sharing and using data across organizations and governments. While linking multiple datasets may sound like a better way to understand development outcomes, it is an ambitious task and requires substantial forethought, a systems-thinking approach, and nuanced data architecture.

**Creating a Shared Measurement System at Country or Initiative Level:** If policymakers articulated potentially useful outcomes and coordinated different actors to collect these data, a type of shared measurement system would be

| Table 11.2 | | | Uses of Technology in Evaluation of Complex Programs |
|---|---|---|---|
| **Evaluation stage** | **Relevant technology for use in evaluation** | **Advantages** | **Methodological and logistical considerations** |
| Evaluation design | Online software to build theories of change | • Participatory; can involve stakeholders in different locations <br> • Theory of change may be updated more frequently | • Software limitations cannot always depict causal pathways. <br> • Tracking unintended outcomes in the software can be difficult. |
| | Program data generated by ICT4D (Table 1) | • May provide useful longitudinal data; often detailed at transactional level <br> • No data collection burden (e.g., resources, fatigue from beneficiaries) <br> • Data are already digitized | • Low burden of data collection may generate overreliance on quantitative data. <br> • Higher-level outcomes remain unexamined. <br> • Too many data are available; discernment of what data to use and how is essential. <br> • Selection bias is not always clear (e.g., who got or used technology and who did not). <br> • Data produced may differ from the original expectation of how the technology would be used. <br> • Beneficiary consent to use the data may be required. <br> • De-identification of data and privacy must be ensured. |
| | Datasets from big data to construct counterfactual groups | • Existing data may provide a comparison group; may be low cost <br> • Strengthens evaluation finding (compared with no counterfactual) | • Comparability of counterfactual group with program beneficiaries should be closely examined. <br> • Access to big data may be difficult to obtain and require official requests. |

*(Continued)*

**Table 11.2** (Continued)

| Evaluation stage | Relevant technology for use in evaluation | Advantages | Methodological and logistical considerations |
|---|---|---|---|
| Data collection | Mobile data collection | • More real-time data; data processing/entry not required<br>• Higher-quality data due to skip patterns and validation checks<br>• Photos and GPS coordinates easily collected<br>• Basic data visualizations available in real time through the platform | • Collecting open-ended and complex responses is more difficult; the bias of the technology is toward quantitative data.<br>• Response rates differ by method of administration (e.g., responses are higher with in-person data collectors, lower for surveys via SMS).<br>• If using data collectors, resources are required to train and purchase mobile devices. |
| | Web-based surveys | • Low data collection burden<br>• Basic data visualizations are available in real time through the platform | • Response rates can be low and/or unevenly distributed<br>• Low band width may mean incomplete responses. |
| | Audio and interactive voice response (IVR) | • Audio allows for easy documentation of qualitative data<br>• IVR allows for data collection of large samples<br>• Multilingual questions and responses can help improve response rate | • Informed consent is particularly important when recording participants.<br>• IVR requires up-front investment in the technology. |
| | Digital video and cameras | • Participants' voices better captured<br>• Allows for high levels of participation | • Video and images cannot be repurposed to other uses (i.e., to evaluation from project promotion).<br>• Participants' consent is always needed. |
| | GIS and GPS | • Allows for clear visualization of outcomes by geography | • Sensitive information must be safeguarded when mapped. |
| | Biometric and sensor data | • Allows for nonbiased measurements and verifications | • Personally identifiable information must be safeguarded. |

| Evaluation stage | Relevant technology for use in evaluation | Advantages | Methodological and logistical considerations |
|---|---|---|---|
| Data management and analysis | M&E platforms used to host and visualize program data | • Program data can be entered by multiple partner organizations, government, and other stakeholders<br>• Easy Web-based access to data at different times<br>• Stores longitudinal program data to facilitate review of program progress and trends over time<br>• Allows for near real-time data | • It is more difficult to store and present qualitative data; the technology is biased toward quantitative data.<br>• Merging data from the system with external datasets for evaluation requires specific skills and may be time-consuming. |
| | Sense-making software | • Allows for aggregation and visualization of volumes of data<br>• May allow for greater participant valuation of data | • It requires training an evaluator with prior experience to implement licensing requirements.<br>• Findings still need to be triangulated and cross-referenced against other traditionally collected data. |
| Dissemination of evaluation results | New technologies (e.g., social media, SMS, IVR) for public dialogue and feedback | • Wider reach that includes more beneficiaries and other stakeholders | • New technologies may not be accessible by all beneficiaries.<br>• Findings disseminated via technology must be comprehensible among beneficiaries. |

created, and evaluators would be able to use the data to comprehend how multiple program implementers and development actors are contributing to the same outcomes. We would move closer to understanding the interrelationship among interventions and impacts. But without coordination of research and evaluation at national and regional levels, and without data clearinghouses, evaluation efforts will remain siloed; data from evaluations will remain difficult to access and will have to be recoded to meet the needs of each evaluator. Change is on the horizon for INGOs, especially those funded by USAID, with the advent of its new policy on development data that will require all USAID-funded organizations to share de-identified data.[2] This policy will dramatically increase the amount of data available on development interventions, at least those funded by the U.S. government and other donors requiring open data access. Creating shared measurement systems at a national or initiative level is an attractive solution, but developing these systems can cause huge delays in the bureaucratic process as consensus is sought. Thus, initiating this type of system must be additive rather than restrictive.

**Leadership From Donors:** Leadership is needed at the donor level to direct scarce evaluation resources to add additional value to outcome measurement without duplication of efforts. Donors themselves silo their findings within their organizations across thematic areas (e.g., health, education, governance) to understand the narrow impact of their funding. More could be done to share findings across sectors and create common evaluation agendas. Emergent technology can assist with this, if common systems and shared learning agendas can be established. A shared system for evaluation is increasingly important in evaluating complex programming where multiple actors and stakeholders play roles and may be required to adjust programming to achieve impact. Meta-analysis of evaluation results across donor programs may help understand how outcomes are being achieved in complex programming.

**Examine Existing Data:** Evaluators should begin with the assumption that data on programs and projects being evaluated already exist. Although these data would come from program implementers, they may be increasingly available in different formats and different types of databases. They will also be available from competitors of an organization commissioning an evaluation, from national- or government-level databases, and from research think tanks. How to link disparate (and sometimes not very clean) datasets to evaluations in order to deepen understanding and findings must be considered. Looking at other available data may help save on evaluation expenses, because it may lessen the data collection burden, but it will not completely negate the cost, as external datasets will often need reformatting and cleaning in order to have relevance to an evaluation. Evaluators need to find ways to use existing data and datasets to triangulate their own results. Emergent technology creates the possibility of more data to consider, but evaluators must still assess the value and relevance of those data and consider privacy concerns. The availability of existing data should increase substantially in coming years and should add value to understanding and evaluating complex programs, especially if models can be developed to harness the power in existing knowledge.

**Capacity Development and Training for Evaluators:** Putting staff at ease with technology and having a solution-oriented approach to using emergent technologies for data collection and management are critical to making more data available for evaluators. Training staff on technology and encouraging its use—sooner rather than later—will help institutionalize rigor and quality in the data that are collected. At the same time, program managers should think through their program's existing data architecture and consider how it links (or should link) to other internal and external information sources. If emergent technologies are going to be widely used in monitoring and evaluation practice, basic and more advanced training, system development, and organizational policies on technology use need to be in place to ensure people are comfortable and conversant with technology. Specifically for evaluators, introduction to the different types of technology that can be used in evaluation and the different data sources that can be considered needs to be part of the evaluation design process.

## 4.1 Practicalities: Using Emergent Technologies in the Field

To prevent each organization from going in its own direction, coordination of emergent technologies is a must. For example, in Uganda, because so many mHealth pilots were ongoing, the government put a brief moratorium on these pilots so as to give itself time to develop guidelines and regulations that would better harness innovation and access the potential of mHealth data (McCann, 2012). Using emergent technology systematically can aid complex programming, but creating basic parameters guides the process.

Evaluators should continue using tested methods in evaluation practice and adapting these for emergent technologies in the same way that evaluative methods are being adapted for complexity. This does not mean simply using more data, because more data are generated by emergent technologies, but ensuring the use of the *right data* to answer evaluation questions. This will likely mean using more external data as available and looking for and linking to previously unlinked data systems, such as financial systems for cost-effectiveness analysis.

Program managers should consider all the current constraints of technology (e.g., the need to charge tablets and phones, the need for connectivity, potential respondents' literacy levels and comfort with technology) while understanding that the technology landscape is shifting rapidly. Smartphones and connectivity are likely to be ubiquitous in 5 years, and although the expense of technology use for monitoring and evaluation may be a concern, costs are reduced and cleaner data are available more quickly once the initial investments in purchasing devices and training have been made.

## 4.2 Recommendations for Using Emergent Technology in the Evaluation of Complex Programs

**Clearinghouses for Evaluation Data:** Policymakers need to coordinate and leverage technology to make the best use of data for decision making. In terms of coordination, we recommend creating Web-based organizational or national clearinghouses of evaluation data. For national-level policymakers, this would eliminate instances of overlapping data collection (e.g., mapping of health facilities or schools) and make the data available to others in a downloadable format. This would also allow organizations and evaluators to use existing data and compare them against their data—enriching their data and analysis, introducing another data source for triangulation, and potentially providing counterfactuals at no or low cost.

**The Right Technology:** To evaluators' concern for selecting the right methodology to answer evaluation questions, new technologies have added a new concern: selection of the right technology for the evaluation. Staying abreast of relevant emergent technologies can be difficult as they are constantly evolving, but several websites can help keep evaluators current, providing case studies on how different technologies have been used.[3]

**Disseminating Findings and Adjusting Programming:** How to use evaluation findings is often the caboose in planning an evaluative process. The results may come as anticlimactic to program managers, immersed in day-to-day issues of project implementation and knowing what is working and what is not. Evaluation, whether in complex or simple projects, offers the opportunity to reflect and then, using the data, improve project performance. Emergent technologies can help standardize and disseminate evaluation findings. For example, after a working group decides how evaluation findings can be most effectively used, tasks associated with that improvement can be placed into a Web-based monitoring system that reinforces the timeline and activities to be implemented. Social media can be used to effectively disseminate findings to interested stakeholders and to increase accountability for putting recommendations in place.

**A Better Monitoring System:** Emergent technologies offer an opportunity to build better information systems with data that are better visualized and more timely and that may reduce the need for costly evaluations. Building better monitoring systems that provide wider access to program data and that reduce bottlenecks in data sharing hold the potential to create more adaptive systems. Linking field monitoring information systems with financial and other administrative systems, thus integrating information in a way that mirrors the complex programs these systems are tracking, holds the promise of providing decision makers with better information about what is being achieved—and a brighter promise of solving the intractable problems our programs are trying to address.

# References

Armstrong, K., Liu, F., Seymour, A., Mazhani, L., Littman-Quinn, R., Fontelo, P., & Kovarik, C. (2012). Evaluation of txt2MEDLINE and development of short messaging service-optimized, clinical practice guidelines in Botswana. *Telemedicine Journal and E-Health, 18*(1), 14–17.

Azzam, T., & Robinson, D. (2013). GIS in evaluation: Utilizing the power of geographic information systems to represent evaluation data. *American Journal of Evaluation, 34,* 207–224.

Brännström, I. (2012). Gender and digital divide 2000–2008 in two low-income economies in Sub-Saharan Africa: Kenya and Somalia in official statistics. *Government Information Quarterly, 29*(1), 60–67.

Bruce, K., Kisyombe, D., Ghanai, C., Kindoli, R., Madeleka, L., & Malone, T. (2013, November). *Using mobile phones to collect data for an OVC program in Tanzania.* Paper presented at the American Public Health Association Annual Meeting, Boston, MA.

Bukowski, K., & Buetow, S. (2011). Making the invisible visible: A photovoice exploration of homeless women's health and lives in central Auckland. *Social Science & Medicine, 72,* 739–746.

Catalani, C., & Minkler, M. (2010). Photovoice: A review of the literature in health and public health. *Health Education & Behavior, 37,* 424–451.

Center for Health Market Innovations. (2010). *RapidSMS Malawi.* Retrieved from http://healthmarketinnovations.org/program/rapidsms-malawi

Clear Initiative. (2013). *Mobile based technology: A reference guide for project managers, M&E specialists, researchers, donors.* Retrieved from http://www.theclearinitiative.org/mobile-based-tech.pdf

Department for International Development. (2008). DFID *research: How videos can help to improve research participation.* Retrieved from https://www.gov.uk/government/case-studies/dfid-research-how-videos-can-help-to-improve-research-participation

Department for International Development. (2013). *International development evaluation policy.* Retrieved from https://www.gov.uk/government/uploads/system/uploads/attachment_data/file/204119/DFID-Evaluation-Policy-2013.pdf

Development Research Center. (2008). *Development Research Centre on Citizenship, Participation and Accountability Annual Report 2007–2008.* Retrieved from http://www.drc-citizenship.org/system/assets/1052734665/original/1052734665-cdrc_annual_report_2008.pdf?1398363146

Hilbert, M. (2011). Digital gender divide or technologically empowered women in developing countries? A typical case of lies, damned lies, and statistics. *Women's Studies International Forum, 34,* 479–489.

Hoogeveen, J., Croke, K., Dabalen, A., Demombynes, G., & Giugale, M. (2014). Collecting high frequency panel data in Africa using mobile phone interviews. *Canadian Journal of Development Studies, 35*(1), 186–207.

Institute of Medicine. (2012). *Communications and technology for violence prevention: Workshop summary.* Washington, DC: National Academies Press.

Lam, M. Y., Lee, H., Bright, R., Korzenik, J., & Sands, B. (2009). Validation of interactive voice response system administration of the Short Inflammatory Bowel Disease Questionnaire. *Inflammatory Bowel Diseases, 15,* 599–607.

McCann, D. (2012). *A Ugandan mHealth moratorium is a good thing.* Retrieved from http://www.ictworks.org/2012/02/22/ugandan-mhealth-moratorium-good-thing

OECD-DAC. (2001). *Evaluation feedback for effective learning and accountability.* Paris, France: OECD.

Pact. (2014). *Mobile technology handbook.* Washington, DC: Author. Retrieved from http://pactworld.org/sites/default/files/Mobile%20Technology%20Handbook%202014.pdf

Pew Research Center. (2014). *Emerging nations embrace Internet, mobile technology.* Washington, DC: Pew Charitable Trust.

Raftree, L. & Bamberger, M., (2014). *Emerging opportunities: Monitoring and evaluation in a tech-enabled world.* New York, NY: Rockefeller Foundation.

Streng, J. M., Rhodes, S. D., Ayala, G. X., Eng, E., Arceo, R., & Phipps, S. (2004). Realidad Latina: Latino adolescents, their school, and a university use photovoice to examine and address the influence of immigration. *Journal of Interprofessional Care, 18,* 403–415.

Suarez-Balcazar, Y., Balcazar, F. E., & Taylor-Ritzler, T. (2009). Using the Internet to conduct research with culturally diverse populations: Challenges and opportunities. *Cultural Diversity and Ethnic Minority Psychology, 15*(1), 96.

U.S. Department of State. (2012). *Department of State program evaluation policy.* Retrieved from http://www.state.gov/s/d/rm/rls/evaluation/2012/184556.htm

USAID. (2011). USAID evaluation policy. Retrieved from http://www.usaid.gov/sites/default/files/documents/2151/USAIDEvaluationPolicy.pdf

Vaitla, B. (2014). *The landscape of big data for development.* Retrieved from http://data2x.org/wp-content/uploads/2014/08/Data2X_LandscapeOfBigDataForDevelopment.pdf

Villa, J. M. (2014). *Social transfers and growth: The missing evidence from luminosity data* (WIDER Working Paper). Helsinki, Finland: UNU-WIDER.

Wang, C. C., Cash, J. L., & Powers, L. S. (2000). Who knows the streets as well as the homeless? Promoting personal and community action through photovoice. *Health Promotion Practice, 1*(1), 81–89.

Wesolowski, A., Eagle, N., Noor, A. M., Snow, R. W., & Buckee, C. O. (2012). Heterogeneous mobile phone ownership and usage patterns in Kenya. *PLoS One, 7*(4), e35319.

# Notes

1. For details, see www.usaid.gov/asia-regional/press-releases/jan-7-2014-usaid-recognizes-open-institute-and-8villages.

2. The policy can be found at www.usaid.gov/sites/default/files/documents/1868/579.pdf.

3. Web sites include www.betterevaluation.org and http://mande.co.uk.

# CHAPTER 12

# The Evaluation of Complex Development Interventions in the Age of Big Data[1]

Emmanuel Letouzé,[2] Ana Areias,[3] and Sally Jackson[4]

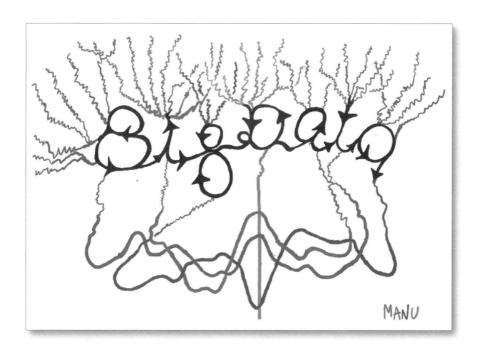

MANU

The advent of big data and its potential applications to monitoring and evaluation (M&E) have stirred a mix of excitement and skepticism in the M&E community. To the external observer, it seems "traditional" M&E methods and actors—with their focus on surveys, pre-post comparison, and administrative data collection—have not evolved sufficiently to leverage the potential of big data to yield insights on complex interventions and systems.

Advances have certainly happened; the term *M&E 2.0* (Docking, 2013), for instance, was coined to describe how advances in technology can help address some of the challenges in M&E with increasingly complex contexts. But it is fair to say that the field of M&E has not fully embraced big data. The question is: Should it? And if so, how?

A voluntarily simplistic description of both ends of a spectrum, ranging from big data enthusiasts to big data critics, would be something like the following. Enthusiasts would argue that big data may provide a fix to the limitations of traditional M&E of increasingly complex interventions in increasingly complex human ecosystems, by providing high-frequency data that can be crunched by data scientists to reveal patterns and trends. On the other end, critics would warn against *hubris*, a term describing "the often implicit assumption that Big Data are a substitute for, rather than a supplement to, traditional data collection and analysis" (Lazer, Kennedy, King, & Vespignani, 2014, p. 1203), and stress that big data faces standard issues of measurement validity and reliability as much as or perhaps even more than small data does.

Although this dichotomy does not really exist—most practitioners realize there is truth in both perspectives—it does surface some of the key parameters of the issue at hand, especially their scientific-technical dimensions. At the same time, these debates often seem too abstract. There is little discussion of the institutional—including legal, organizational, political, ethical—considerations involved; at the end of the day, what matters is whether and how a difference can be made on human populations, and this requires human interventions.

Perhaps above all, conceptual clarity is often lacking, on what is meant by both *big data* and by *complex* (interventions), which we feel is a necessary condition to begin laying out the specific features of their interactions and imagining the future of M&E in the age of big data.

The main objective of this chapter is not to give definitive answers to issues and debates that have emerged only in recent years, but to provide as clear as possible a picture of their main parameters and interactions in order to start crafting the future of evaluation in the age of big data on solid foundations.

Against this background, this chapter is organized as follows: Section 1 presents the genesis and surface of the issue as it initially emerged; Section 2 attempts to paint a clearer, more thorough and up-to-date picture of the debate; Section 3 zooms in on more advanced theoretical considerations; Section 4 discusses institutional aspects and requirements and concludes with a guide to action grounded in desirable principles and possible steps for the future.

# 1. Genesis and Surface of the Issue

## 1.1 The Rise and Applications of Big Data

The broad notion that big data could be relevant to monitoring and evaluating development interventions can probably be traced back to UN Global Pulse's white paper *Big Data for Development: Challenges and Opportunities* (Letouzé, 2012)—written by the main author of this chapter—one of the first contributions in the field. The proposed three-tier taxonomy of the main applications of big data to development challenges consisted of early warning, real-time awareness, and real-time feedback. A subsequent taxonomy developed in a paper on the specific case of conflict prevention distinguished three potential uses as the descriptive, predictive, and diagnostic (and later, prescriptive) functions of big data (Letouzé et al., 2013), with both overlaps with and differences from UN Global Pulse's taxonomy.

The link with and relevance for M&E appears quite clearly too. All M&E initiatives involve and imply some combination of being able to grasp (describe or depict) what is happening on the ground and being able to establish some form of cause-and-effect relationship for their evaluation and learning components.

## 1.2 Big Data's Initial and Superficial Promise for Evaluation

Both taxonomies suggest more or less explicitly that in some near or distant future, big data could help M&E interventions and experts. More data exist than ever before that can be processed by increasingly powerful machines and subjected to ever more complex methods and tools to extract insights from them. Traditionally, M&E has used data such as surveys, pre-post comparison, and administrative data. These data generally are tedious and expensive to collect, and therefore big data may present an alternative.

Examples from the private sector have also contributed to raising these expectations. For years now companies have been drawing heavily on big data to

---

### BOX 12.1 ALTERNATIVE TAXONOMY OF BIG DATA

We propose that big data for conflict prevention be structured around three distinct functions:

1. Descriptive, i.e., how big data can document and convey what is happening;

2. Predictive, i.e., how big data could give us a sense of what is likely to happen, regardless of why;

3. Diagnostic (or prescriptive), i.e., how big data might shed light on why things . . . happen.

SOURCE: Letouzé et al. (2013).

---

**BOX 12.2 UN GLOBAL PULSE'S TAXONOMY OF USES OF BIG DATA**

Properly analyzed, big data offers the opportunity for an improved understanding of human behavior that can support the field of global development in three main ways:

1. *Early warning:* Early detection of anomalies in how populations use digital devices and services can enable faster response in times of crisis.

2. *Real-time awareness:* Big data can paint a fine-grained and current representation of reality, which can inform the design and targeting of programs and policies.

3. *Real-time feedback:* The ability to monitor a population in real time makes it possible to understand where policies and programs are failing and make the necessary adjustments.

SOURCE: Letouzé (2012).

---

better understand their consumers and the impact of their marketing and insights in order to optimize operations and services through customer segmentation, quality monitoring, process delivery, and brand monitoring through sentiment analysis of social media. These are lessons the social sector could learn from.

And so the hope—the argument—is that big data could be used to track and evaluate programs and policies in a roughly similar fashion, whereby consumers would be replaced by beneficiaries or recipients in stakeholder analysis, program satisfaction evaluation, and so on. According to that line of argument, big data

> presents an opportunity. The ubiquity of cell phones and electronic transactions, the increasing use of personal medical probes, and the concept of the electronically wired "smart city" are already providing us with enormous amounts of data. With new computational tools and techniques to digest vast, interrelated databases, researchers and practitioners in science, technology, business and government have begun to bring large-scale simulations and models to bear on questions formerly out of reach of quantitative analysis, such as how cooperation emerges in society, what conditions promote innovation, and how conflicts spread and grow. (West, 2013, para. 4)

Soon, we may know about human populations and the impact of policies and programs through the digital traces left behind, allowing us to establish "what works" versus "what doesn't work"—and to do so in a shorter time span than traditional M&E cycles have historically allowed. The vision is one in which interventions would be monitored and evaluated in real time, with the insights gleaned by

**Table 12.1** Mapping Two Taxonomies of Big Data Uses

| | Applications | Explanation | Examples | Comments and caveats |
|---|---|---|---|---|
| UN Global Pulse Taxonomy (Letouzé, 2012) | Early warning | Early detection of anomalies in how populations use digital devices and services can enable faster response in times of crisis. | Predictive policing, based on the notion that analysis of historical data can reveal certain combinations of factors associated with greater likelihood of increased criminality in a given area, has been used to allocate police forces. Google Flu Trends is another example, whereby searches for some key terms ("runny nose, itchy eyes") are analyzed to detect the onset of the flu season, although its accuracy is debated. | This application assumes that certain regularities in human behaviors can be observed and modeled. Key challenges for policy include the tendency of most malfunction detection systems and forecasting models to overpredict (i.e., to have a higher prevalence of false positives). |
| | Real-time awareness | Big data can paint a fine-grained and current representation of reality, which can inform the design and targeting of programs and policies. | Using data released by Orange, researchers found a high degree of association between mobile phone networks and language distribution in Ivory Coast, suggesting that such data may provide information about language communities in countries where it may be unavailable. | The appeal and underlying argument for this application is the notion that big data may be a substitute for bad or scarce data; however, models that show high correlations between big data–based and traditional indicators often require the availability of the latter to be trained and built. *Real-time* here means using high-frequency digital data to get a picture at time T. |
| | Real-time feedback | The ability to monitor a population in real time makes it possible to understand where policies and programs are failing and make the necessary adjustments. | Private corporations already use big data analytics for development, which includes analyzing the impact of a policy action (e.g., the introduction of new traffic regulations) in real time. | Although appealing, few if any examples of this application exist. A challenge is making sure that any observed change can be attributed to the intervention or treatment. However, high-frequency data can also contain natural experiments (e.g., a sudden drop in online prices of a given good) that can be leveraged to infer causality. |

(Continued)

**Table 12.1** (Continued)

| | Applications | Explanation | Examples | Comments and caveats |
|---|---|---|---|---|
| Alternative taxonomy (Kirkpatrick, 2011) | Descriptive | Big data can document and convey what is happening. | This application is quite similar to the "real-time awareness" application, although it is less ambitious in its objectives. Any infographic, including maps, that renders vast amounts of data legible to the reader is an example of a descriptive application. | Describing data always implies making choices and assumptions—about what and how data are displayed—that need to be made explicit and understood. It is well known that even bar graphs and maps can be misleading. |
| | Predictive | Big data could give a sense of what is likely to happen, regardless of why. | One kind of prediction is predicting what may happen *next*; the predictive policing mentioned above is one example. Another is predicting prevailing conditions through big data, as in the case of socioeconomic levels using call detail records (CDRs) in Latin America and Ivory Coast. | Similar comments as those made for the early-warning and real-time awareness applications apply. |
| | Prescriptive or Diagnostic | Big data might shed light on why things may happen and what could be done about it. | So far there have been almost no clear-cut examples of this application in development contexts. The example of CDR data used to show that bus routes in Abidjan could be optimized comes closest to a case in which the analysis identifies causal links and can shape policy. | Most comments about real-time feedback application apply. Strictly speaking, an example of the diagnostics application would require being able to assign causality. The prescriptive application works best in theory when supported by feedback systems and loops on the effect of policy actions. |

SOURCE: Letouzé (2014).

traveling through short feedback loops to inform adjustments and, ultimately, realize the dream of agile development.

This superficial promise has undergone an important reconceptualization and "complexification" phase, along with the concept of big data itself: Focus has shifted from big data as simply data to being a complex system in its own right.

The next section turns to and attempts to unpack these considerations. It discusses in greater depth the complex nature of each piece of the "big data, complex interventions, and M&E" triptych and their interactions on more solid conceptual and intellectual ground.

# 2. Reconceptualization and Complexification

## 2.1 Big Data as a Complex Ecosystem

### a. The Components

It is useful to clarify what we mean by *big data* so that we can then unpack its potential applications and implications for the evaluation of complex interventions. The term first emerged after the world reportedly entered "The Petabyte Age" (2008). In the years that followed, big data was routinely described with the three Vs of volume (large, complex data sets), velocity (lots of high-frequency data appearing), and variety (from various sources; see Figure 12.1).

Since then, the three Vs framework seems to have clouded our collective thinking about big data's nature and encouraged a flawed focus on big data as being "just" large data streams and sets available for analysis.

In this chapter, we instead approach big data as being the union of three Cs—crumbs, capacities, and community—forming a complex system of its own (see Figure 12.2; for a more detailed discussion, see Letouzé, 2014).

### Crumbs

The concept of *Crumbs* is a reference to Alex "Sandy" Pentland's characterization of the kinds of digital data that humans generate when interacting with digital devices and services, "digital breadcrumbs" that are left behind passively ("Reinventing Society," 2012). These have also been called *exhaust data* in the UN Global Pulse report and elsewhere (e.g., credit card transactions, web cookies, cell phone data know as call detail records). In this chapter, we consider the universe of crumbs to be wider, including two other kinds of data.

The first additional type of crumbs is web-based and social data such as social media posts. They are subject to editorial choices of their emitters ("Reinventing Society," 2012) and typically capture a human action, such as typing a tweet or blog post and pressing send. The second type is sensing data, such as satellite imagery or security cameras, or physical sensors. These require placing or pointing a sensing device.

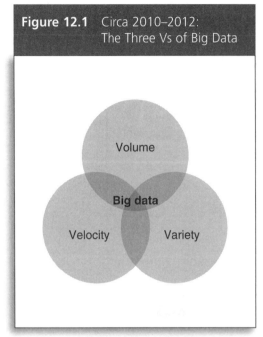

**Figure 12.1**   Circa 2010–2012: The Three Vs of Big Data

Critically, these crumbs are not made available by people with the intent or clear knowledge that they will be analyzed. So as data, big data is not so much "data sets that are impossible to store and process using common software tools, regardless of the computing power or the physical storage at hand" (Scannapieco, Virgillito, & Zardetto, n.d., p. 1), but rather "nonsampled data, characterized by the creation of databases from electronic sources whose primary purpose is something other than statistical inference" (Horrigan, 2013, para. 3).

The term *big data* is largely a misnomer. The difference between big data and "small data," as far as data are concerned, is not principally about size and is well described in Jules Berman's (2013) book, *Principles of Big Data: Preparing, Sharing, and Analyzing Complex Information,* an extract of which is in Table 12.2.

Berman proposes a useful framework for distinguishing between small data and big data along four dimensions. While the distinctions are valid they are often not quite as clear-cut as described in the table.

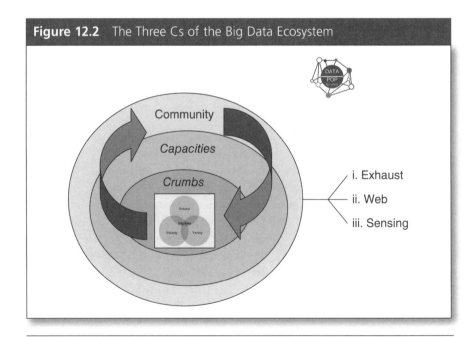

**Figure 12.2**   The Three Cs of the Big Data Ecosystem

SOURCE: Letouzé, E. (2014).

First, the *goal* of small data is usually to address a specific question whereas the goal for the collection of big data is frequently more general. However, the distinction is often not quite so clear as qualitative small data is often collected for exploratory purposes, particularly in emergent evaluation designs, and at least in the initial stages it is often not clear exactly how the data will be used. But even then the goal is more specific than is often the case for big data. Second, the location of small data is usually more restricted, normally being located within one institution and in most cases on a single computer. This contrasts with big data which can be spread through a broad electronic space and distributed across different internet servers. However, again the distinction is often not quite so clear as ethnographic research will often collect data from multiple sources such as video and audio-recordings, interview transcripts, observation and a range of documentary sources. Third, small data is often highly structured and is drawn from a single discipline whereas big data can come from a much wider range of sources many of which are unstructured. Finally, the users of small data usually prepare their own for a specific purpose, whereas big data will often come from many different sources often generated by people who will not use the data. Again the distinction is not so clear-cut as small data is often collected from secondary sources (birth, marriage and death certificates, newspaper articles, graffiti and other gang related insignia) where the generators and users of the data are quite distinct.

| **Table 12.2**   Comparing Small Data and Big Data | | |
|---|---|---|
| | **Small data** | **Big data** |
| Goal | Usually designed to answer a specific question or serve a particular goal | Usually designed with a goal in mind, but the goal is flexible and the questions are protean |
| Location | Typically contained within one institution, often on one computer, sometimes in one file | Typically spread throughout electronic space, typically parceled onto multiple Internet servers, located anywhere on earth |
| Data structure and content | Ordinarily contains highly structured data. The data domain is restricted to a single discipline or subdiscipline. The data often come in the form of uniform records in an ordered spreadsheet. | Must be capable of absorbing unstructured data (e.g., free text documents, images, motion pictures, sound recordings, physical objects). The subject matter of the resource may cross multiple disciplines, and the individual data objects in the resource may link to data contained in other, seemingly unrelated, big data resources. |

SOURCE: Berman, (2013).

## Capacities

This term refers to tools and methods, hardware (parallel computing, more powerful machines), software and skills, and the blending of techniques from the social sciences and the computer sciences, known as statistical machine learning.

The mention of the data use phase (its analysis) above suggests that big data is not about the data, as put by Gary King, and echoes the second part of the definition of big data as

> an umbrella term that refers to these large and ever increasing amounts of digital data that we continually generate as we use digital devices, and to new technology and methods that are now available to analyze large and complex datasets. (*Big Data Monitoring and Evaluation*, n.d., para. 3)

## Community

The third C of big data stands for *community*—the people and institutions, emitters, analysts, and users of big data, who bring out its human dimension. Andreas Weigend even used a psychological lens, defining big data as a mindset that extracts meaning from the mess.

Recognizing the human element in and of big data—*whose* data, *whose* analysis, for *which* purpose, and for *whom*?—is essential to fully understanding its potential applications and implications.

Big data is a complex system of its own, with feedback loops between and within its parts—crumbs, capacities, community. New data generate new methods and ideas that affect the production of data. The ecosystem also overlaps and interacts with others—the interventions and the current M&E data ecosystem.

The divisions between these systems and their components are blurred. The difference between big and small data as two fields of practice isn't always clear-cut. Analyzing each data stream in isolation with traditional methods may be considered small data analysis, while taking diverse and fragmented small data sources then analyzing them as a whole using techniques that could pull new insights from both structured and unstructured information would enter the realm of big data (analytics). A neat small data versus big data dichotomy does not capture well the complexity and interaction of these ecosystems or the full range of potential applications and implications for M&E in the development sector and in a world that is increasingly described and analyzed through the lens of complexity.

## 2.2 Getting Deeper Into Complex Territories

The last few decades have seen complexity theory bring about a revolution in the social sciences. Complex adaptable systems, such as human bodies or public health systems, are made up of many individual parts whose interactions can give rise to systemwide characteristics and processes that cannot be reduced to their constituent parts. A central property of complex systems is *emergent behavior*, describing the fact that collective characteristics of a complex system cannot easily be predicted from underlying components: The whole is greater than, and often very different from, the sum of its parts (West, 2013).

Another key characteristic of complex adaptive systems is feedback loops, which serve as the driver for the evolution of the system. Positive feedback loops amplify initial disturbances to the system; negative feedback loops dampen the effect and drive the system toward equilibrium. Causal relations are not linear, but instead run through various channels and are subject to threshold effects, such that change not only is difficult to anticipate but can result from small disturbances leading to rapid internal shifts.

Complex adaptive systems have the capacity to change and learn from experience. A system that starts in a highly random state can, without outside intervention, become more and more organized through self-organizing behavior, which is related to the concept of robustness of a complex system. Autonomous cooperation and group formation are two processes by which multi-agent systems self-organize. In this way, a system can exhibit purposeful behavior toward a specific function. This all means that the system is prone to unpredictable behavior; it also means that a systemwide approach is necessary since valuable information is lost when studying system components in isolation. Thus complexity theory suggests we adopt a systemic lens and equip ourselves with a theory of systemic change.

How does this relate to evaluation and big data?

Big data has been portrayed as holding the potential to shed light on ever more complex real-world processes.

But big data as a complex system of its own also enhances this evaluability challenge by adding more feedback loops and complexity overall. Indeed, "the digital revolution is driving much of the increasing complexity and pace of life we are now seeing" (West, 2013, para. 4)—and, we shall add, not only because of a multitude of data streams, but also due to the role of all three Cs of the big data ecosystem.

---

**BOX 12.3 RECALLING THE EVALUABILITY CHALLENGES PRESENTED BY COMPLEX SYSTEMS**

- Causal paths can be long and subject to multiple factors.
- Processes of change may take place over long periods of time.
- There may be many different causal paths through which an outcome may be achieved.
- Causality is recursive, with many feedback loops.
- Causality is nonlinear, so small changes may produce large effects while large changes may produce small effects.
- There are often multiple outcomes, each with different causal paths.
- There are many unanticipated outcomes.
- System complexity may make it impossible to predict outcomes.

---

There is also a good deal of frustration or concern regarding the (in)ability of "classic" evaluation methods. Andrew Means (2014) sparked an interesting debate when he argued that "the current framework of traditional, social science driven program evaluation is frankly not embracing the possibilities of today's world. Put simply, program evaluation was not made for the age of big data" (para. 1). His main point is that classic program evaluation is reflective rather than predictive, backward looking rather than forward looking, too focused, in his words, on "proving rather than improving." His main criticism is that the burden of proof about what happened "back then" distracts attention and effort away from trying to change course now, whereas both would be desirable. According to Means,

> once I have my evaluation report I have less of an incentive to innovate or improve because I now have a piece of paper saying that what I do is working. If I were to change my intervention, that piece of paper would become less valid and thus less valuable. (para. 5)

Further, Means rightfully points to a major issue with conventional impact evaluations: the fact that findings are produced too late to be of practical utility. This recognition has led to the development of formative evaluations focusing on program improvement, and summative evaluations, concerned with causality.

The latter is indeed the crux of the issue when dealing with complex systems, even or especially in the age of big data. In other words, it is very hard to prove that a given intervention as part of a system of complex intervention programs is the cause of some outcome.

In order to assess big data's potential and limitations to address all or part of the evaluability challenge(s) requires discussing theoretical considerations in greater depth.

---

### BOX 12.4 WHAT EVALUATION IS AND ISN'T

Evaluation is

- a systematic, intentional, and purposeful process;
- grounded in a set of key questions; the questions provide the boundaries, scope, and direction for evaluation;
- intended to inform decision making; evaluation's ultimate purpose is to inform decisions, be they decisions about process, outcomes, improvements, resource allocation, or even whether to continue a program or initiative or to change a strategy.

Evaluation isn't

- research; the purpose of research is to generate new knowledge, while evaluation is about making evaluative claims and judgments to be used for decision making and action;
- just about measuring impact; evaluation can provide information on a range of things—process, relationships, implementation, changes in systems, and early stage outcomes—not just impact;
- always done by an external third party;
- always expensive.

# 3. Theoretical Considerations, Controversies, and Complementarities

This section clarifies the key theoretical considerations and controversies that arise from the interaction of big data, evaluation, and complex interventions, and discusses possible complementarities between different scientific approaches.

## 3.1 Theoretical Challenges and Possibilities With Big Data

Standard statistical questions pertaining to bias, reliability, stability, and so on need to be applied to the use and analysis of any type of data, including or perhaps even more so with big data.

### a. Comparability Over Time

*Algorithm dynamics:* Studies relying on data gathered from third-party, proprietary, and nontransparent algorithms cannot be sure that their data are comparable over time as they are at risk of what Lazer et al. (2014) term *algorithm dynamics*, as exemplified by Google Flu Trends. Internet services are not static entities but undergo constant change by their in-house engineering teams to improve service provision, and these changes can affect the data-generating process.

*Interaction with users:* Most algorithms now employ machine-learning methods—essentially artificial intelligence programs that change as they collect more user information. In many instances, these generate results that not even their programmers could have foreseen. In addition, the data-generating process can be manipulated to meet personal interests (e.g., marketing campaigns by companies, political outreach through social media).

These arguments echo what is commonly referred to as the "Lucas critique" (2015) and are especially relevant and salient in the case of predictive modeling:

> If the predictive model is used to decide on a policy intervention, the result may not be what the model predicts because the policy change may affect the underlying behavior that is generating the relationships in the data. That is, the models are "predictive" rather than "structural." Of course, this does not render a predictive model useless because the bite of the critique depends a lot on the situation. (Einav & Levin, 2014, p. 7)

In the aforementioned case of Google Flu Trends, the model wrongfully assumed a stable relationship between search terms and the incidence of influenza, with Google's own search algorithms creating a feedback loop, which Google Flu Trends mistakenly interpreted as an outbreak (Chirgwin, 2014). In that case, "the odds of finding search terms that match the propensity of the flu but are structurally unrelated, and so do not predict the future, were quite high" (Lazer et al., 2014, p. 1203).

### b. Nonhuman Internet Traffic

*Bots* are computer programs that are designed to post autonomously and masquerade as humans that will also skew interpretation of results. A recent study estimated that more than 61% of all Internet traffic is now generated by bots, a 21% increase over 2012 (Kerr, 2013).

### c. Representativeness

An additional well-known risk is the belief that with $N$ sufficiently large "$N = All$," that is, that massive data sets covering millions of individuals are somewhat representative of the larger population. This is of course usually not the case because of self-selection effects. Different web and mobile technologies are preferred by different demographic groups, with their uptake and use varying across such population characteristics as education, nationality, religion, and ethnicity. For example, the social media app Twitter is used mostly in cities, and most Pinterest users are upper-middle-class and female (Pfeffer, & Ruths, 2014).

---

**BOX 12.5 HOW TO REDUCE BIASES IN SOCIAL MEDIA STUDIES**

1. Consider how the user base relates to your population of interest, and correct for platform-specific biases in the user base.

2. Consider platform-specific behavior such as data storage policies.

3. Filter nonhuman accounts (bots) in the data.

4. Test robustness of findings on more than one platform or on time-separated datasets for the same platform.

SOURCE: Adapted from Bi (2014).

---

### d. Spatial Autocorrelation

An example suggested by Crawford (2013) is informative: While Twitter and Facebook were used extensively by individuals during and in the days after Hurricane Sandy, most of these posts came from Manhattan. This is not because the area was the worst hit, but because of the high smartphone penetration in the city. In fact, more severely hit locations produced fewer posts since there was no power with which to recharge phones. A similar issue was found after the earthquake that hit Haiti in 2010. If first responders were to guide their action by relying on accounts posted on Twitter, no help would have reached those that were in the worst-hit areas, since those people were what Crawford terms in "the shadow of big data" (para. 6). Most social media studies do not carefully account for platform-specific biases. Ignoring the problem of unrepresentative samples can at best lead to biased estimates. At worst, it can have the political consequence of widening the digital divide.

### e. Attribution and Spurious Correlations

One of the main goals of M&E is to measure impact, that is, to be able to say to what extent an intervention was responsible for the outcome observed, in this way assessing attribution and drawing causal links between phenomena. Identifying causality in big data presents some difficulties, since the more variables one has, the greater the chance of finding spurious but significant correlations between them (i.e., false positives).

The nature of big data means it is easier to be distracted by epiphenomena, that is, effects or variables that are a by-product of a process but are not causally related to it. As a dataset grows larger, falsity grows faster than information (Taleb, 2013; see Figure 12.3).

Big data usually also means higher dimensional data, and with many different variables for each observation, it is possible to compare more and more attributes between two groups, let's say a control group and a treatment group. The more attributes one compares, it becomes more likely that the treatment and control groups will appear to differ on at least one attribute simply by chance alone. This is known as the multiple comparisons problem.

Most successful commercial applications of big data (think Amazon, Netflix, etc.) function on the basis of correlations alone and have no theoretical model of causation behind them. Their success led to early extreme claims that big data meant the end of the need for theory, the demise of the scientific method, and a relegation of causality to a secondary role. This view was based on the idea that the sheer amount of data would allow the numbers to speak for themselves and clue researchers in to relationships between variables without the need to formulate hypotheses and research strategies or to understand how these relationships worked (Anderson, 2013).

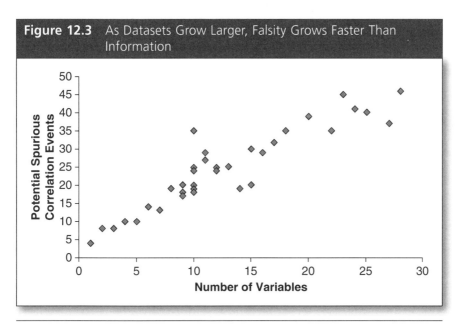

**Figure 12.3**   As Datasets Grow Larger, Falsity Grows Faster Than Information

SOURCE: Taleb (2013).

While a theory-free use of correlations might be enough for some applications, such as predicting user preferences for recommender systems, it is not enough to inform interventions in complex and changing systems, as is the goal of monitoring and evaluation. Correlations identified during a period of stability of a system will break down once the system changes; consequently, a theory of change is necessary if we hope to successfully intervene in a changing environment (Harford, 2014a).

How does one then separate the signal from the noise? Correlations in huge data sets may help us generate new hypotheses, while theories allow us to ask questions of the data in the first place (Bollier, 2010).

This answer could lie in ground-truth, that is, comparing big data measurements or predictions to something we know, such as census data, in order to assess the validity of our models and predictions (NASA, 2012).

---

### BOX 12.6 RESPONSES TO "IS BIG DATA MAKING THE SCIENTIFIC METHOD OBSOLETE?"

Big data does not invalidate the need for theories and models. Jeff Jonas, chief scientist of IBM's Entity Analytics Solutions, believes that huge datasets may help us "find and see dynamically changing ontologies without having to try to prescribe them in advance. Taxonomies and ontologies are things that you might discover by observation, and watch evolve over time."

Patrick W. Gross, chairman of the Lovell Group, challenged the either/or proposition that either scientific models or data correlations will drive future knowledge. "In practice, the theory and the data reinforce each other. It's not a question of data correlations versus theory. The use of data for correlations allows one to test theories and refine them."

SOURCE: Bollier, D. (2010).

---

Another relevant solution is that of data assimilation (Borne, 2014), an ongoing process in which one is constantly updating model predictions with incoming observational data in order to calibrate the model to changing reality.

Experimentation also can be a way to distinguish causation from correlation (Brown, Chui, & Manyika, 2011; Harford, 2014b; McAfee & Brynjolfsson, 2012). Controlled experiments have become a staple in marketing analytics: A/B testing allows a company to provide two versions of its service to randomly chosen groups of users and then measures how the users react. This allows companies to test different e-commerce solutions or web design layouts, all by randomly displaying either a "control" page or a "treatment" page containing the change to users, in order to gauge which is more effective at influencing metrics such as click-through rates. While NGOs have experimented with A/B testing to inform their communications strategy and better reach potential donors and beneficiaries, there has been less done in utilizing testing for service delivery.

## BOX 12.7 ON THE ETHICS OF A/B TESTING: FACEBOOK CONTAGION STUDY

The Facebook experiment (Kramer, Guillory, & Hancock, 2014) is an example of A/B testing that crossed an ethical line. In 2012, for a week Facebook manipulated the content of 689,003 of its users, varying the emotional content of posts that were displayed on each user's Newsfeed to see whether this in turn affected the emotional content of a user's own posts.

The study found evidence of emotional contagion since people who were exposed to content with positive emotional content expressed more emotional content in the days following, whereas those that were exposed to fewer messages of emotion content, either positive or negative, displayed withdrawal and were less emotional themselves in the following days.

Even though the study was effectively legal, since Facebook users sign terms of agreement when they sign up to use the service that allows Facebook to use their data for research, a lot of the media and many academics certainly didn't think it was ethical. Kate Crawford, visiting professor at MIT's Center for Civic Media and principal researcher at Microsoft Research, said, "It's completely unacceptable for the terms of service to force everybody on Facebook to participate in experiments." Slate.com called the experiment "unethical" (Albergotti, 2014).

Natural or quasi-natural experiments, while difficult to find, also can provide an opportunity to use big data to learn about cause-effect relationships (Einav & Levin, 2014; Salganik, 2014). Natural experiments are observational studies that exploit naturally occurring phenomena (e.g., a change in government policy) that expose groups of individuals to experimental and control conditions through a process that arguably resembles random assignment.

Salganik (2014) suggests two ways in which one can combine big data in natural experiments. First, the effects of exogenous variation created offline can be observed with big data sources to compare outcomes between treatment and control groups. It is also possible that natural experiments are created by online changes. The two examples in Box 12.8 show how this is possible:

## BOX 12.8 TWO EXAMPLES OF NATURAL EXPERIMENTS THAT LEVERAGE BIG DATA

An example of using big data to study the effect of an *offline exogenous variation* is Ayers et al. (2011), whose work exploited the fact that in April 2009 the U.S. government nearly tripled the federal tax on cigarettes. The study compared search query volume of smoking-related phrases in the United States and in Canada, which did not have similar policy change. They found that there was

*(Continued)*

(Continued)

a surge in search volume for the phrase "quit smoking" in the United States at the time of the tax increase, but that search volume quickly returned to original levels, suggesting that there was no long-term effect on smoking behavior.

Salganik (2014) points out that this study suffers from the caveat that the outcome in the big data sources (e.g., search volume) was not the same as the real outcome of interest (e.g., change in actual smoking behavior). Therefore, an important consideration in natural experiments is the fit between what is measured and what is actually important.

A *natural experiment created by online changes* was conducte by Brown et al. (2010), who used the fact that eBay changed its policy on price shrouding in October 2004 to study its effect on revenue. Price shrouding is a technique used by sellers that makes it practically impossible for a buyer to ascertain the real economic cost of a product, such as listing shipping and handling fees in very small print.

By comparing similar items sold before and after the policy change, Brown et al. concluded that raising shipping changes increases revenue and the effect is bigger when shipping prices can be shrouded. However, Salganik (2014) notes that the study's conclusions cannot necessarily extend beyond eBay since the effect of shrouding on prices may be heterogeneous across products and platforms.

Finally, big data can also help assess the comparability of the two groups and validate the assumption of "pretreatment equivalence" between the two groups that allows us to treat the assignment as if it is random and underpins the validity of natural experiments.

## 3.2 Theoretical Blending and Complementarities of Diverse Approaches

Big data sources, technologies, and innovative approaches have the potential to provide complementary, actionable information for decision making in the development sector. They do not function as a replacement for different methods; different types of data have different strengths and weaknesses, and one type does not replace the other.

Imagine a scenario in which you want to better understand the mobility of a population—in this particular community, half the population has mobile phones. Here are two possible purist approaches to understanding mobility:

1. The big data purist: Using mobile phone detail records, you would be able to monitor mobility over time for half of the people (those with phones) in the population.

2. The small data purist: Using a survey (with a sample size that was determined as being the best trade-off between information obtained and cost, say, 1% of the population), you were able to find out the mobility patterns of a representative sample of the population over the past month.

In making inferences from these samples, neither method would provide a comprehensive picture of the mobility of the entire population over time.

The mixed methods researcher would be in a win-win situation. Big data methods could be used to understand the movement of half of the population in detail. Small data methods could be used to answer the specific question of how mobility differed between the group of people with phones and the group of people without phones (at a smaller sample size and therefore lower cost than a survey representative of the entire population). Through combining the information, an estimate of the movement of the whole population could be made that would be cheaper and more robust over time than either approach taken in isolation.

Rigorous qualitative methods developed in the social sciences can allow us to collect essential contextual information on big data sources and shine light on where the data under analysis come from, how they were generated and collected, and what biases these choices may imply. In this way, not only do we have big quantities of data, but we also can "add depth to the data we collect" (Crawford, 2013, para. 7). Crawford (2013) suggests joining big data with traditional small data methods, such as complementing analytics with ethnographic studies or combining information retrieval techniques with semistructured interviews.

Large and complex development programs are influenced by many contextual factors such as the local and national (and perhaps international or global) economic, political, ecological, demographic, and sociocultural situation and how these are changing. Most established evaluation approaches are not able to fully capture these broader contextual factors, and this is an area where big data should be able to contribute.

## 3.3 A Complexity-Based Approach to Evaluation

Snyder (2013) argues that the nature of complex adaptive systems should lead us to adopt a feedback-driven adaptive approach for reform. We argue that the same is true for evaluation.

Because no single part of the system directs macro-level behavior and there is no centralized control, effectively intervening in a complex system is difficult. The lack of centralized control means that global standards are less likely to be effective than local solutions that emerge spontaneously from below. The most we can hope for is to seek to maximize the flow of feedback between and across levels in order to allow for self-organization.

Big data could potentially help in this process. New approaches are beginning to appear, such as developmental evaluation, that gather data for ongoing adaptation and experimentation and are keenly aware of unintended consequences and side effects (Patton, 2011).

While M&E should be integrated, monitoring and evaluation have different purposes and information needs, which should be clearly distinguished. The task of integrating big data into monitoring is probably more straightforward (assuming the right kinds of data can be collected and made easily accessible) than integrating into evaluation, which requires addressing issues of attribution.

# 4. Institutional and Cultural Dimensions, Requirements, and Steps

What institutional changes are necessary for big data to become routine in monitoring and evaluation? What challenges and considerations exist that need to be overcome in order to move from isolated cases and proof-of-concept to the integration of big data and analytics into M&E practice?

This chapter details the technical, cultural, and ethical aspects of a big data M&E strategy. How do we ensure data access and acquisition, sharing, standardization, interoperability, and capacity? How do we promote a data culture that is more evidence-based, more innovative and agile—a sort of M&E 3.0? And lastly, how to we close interdisciplinary gaps in practice to ensure that M&E practitioners inform big data norms, standards, and ethics?

## 4.1 Data Access/Stability, Protection, and Privacy

### a. Access

Organizations aiming to utilize big data for M&E face two major hurdles: new types of digital data are held by private corporations, and data are frequently held across different and unlinked spaces and in different formats.

The private sector currently manages enormous datasets that could hold rich insights for the public sector, but few long-term public-private partnerships currently exist. Big data access has, in the majority of cases, come about through ad hoc and limited agreements such as data competitions and data philanthropy, whereby data owners experiment with making proprietary data accessible while preserving their customers' privacy and safeguarding trade secrets. Is this experimental modality of working on the verge of change? Will these experiments in data philanthropy pave the way for more permanent agreements?

---

**BOX 12.9 DATA PHILANTHROPY**

For the *Data for Development (D4D) Challenge,* organized by French telecom operator Orange, relevant ministries defined the priority areas of health, agriculture, urban planning and transport, energy, and national statistics, and a year's worth of anonymous mobile network data was made available for the Ivory Coast. Network data was protected through anonymization and nondisclosure agreements signed by the research teams who submitted entries. Winning submissions included using network data to optimize transport.

*Kaggle* is an online platform through which companies and research institutions will make anonymized datasets available and award prizes for the best prediction algorithm. Kaggle has over 40,000 active participants who compete with each other to solve complex data science problems. An example of a competition with a "social good" component is the National Data Science Bowl, organized by Booz Allen Hamilton and Hatfield Marine Science Center at Oregon State University, which made available nearly 100,000 underwater images and will award $175,000 prizes to the top three algorithms' creators that allow researchers to identify and monitor planktonic organisms.

Twitter gives selected institutions free and easy access to historical Twitter datasets through the *Twitter Data Grants* pilot program. In addition to the data, the company also offers opportunities for the selected institutions to collaborate with Twitter researchers. For this program alone, Twitter says it received more than 1,300 submissions. Selected submissions included a proposal from Harvard Medical School and Boston Children's Hospital to study food poisoning.

### b. Protection

Resources are increasingly being mobilized to establish public-private data partnerships, as is perhaps demonstrated by the European Commission and European data industries' 2014 launch of such a partnership that committed to invest €2.5 billion in strengthening the European data sector (European Commission, 2014).

The current legal and institutional landscape will, however, present challenges to establishing public-private data partnerships and gaining access to data. Serious concerns about liability and risk make companies hesitant to divulge more data and, as is noted in the Preface of the World Economic Forum (2015) *Global Risks Report*, "new technologies, such as the Internet or emerging innovations[,] will not bear fruit if regulatory mechanisms at the international and national levels cannot be agreed upon." Making matters worse, agencies combating the same policy problems often compete with each other for scarce resources, whether it be grants and gifts or recognition from the press and the community. Because of this competition, data sharing between agencies—and even between agencies and the public—is rare (Desouza & Smith, 2014).

It is therefore often difficult for small nonprofits to access the data held by large organizations; they frequently lack the necessary relationships and technical capacity. For small NGOs, other options could include supporting open data in the form of application program interfaces (APIs; a long-term goal) and, in the shorter term, reliance on data philanthropy, crowdsourcing, or web scraping for data acquisition.

Another problem related to how data are held is that data are frequently spread across different and unlinked spaces and in different formats. The value from big data is likely to be most impactful when linking diverse and fragmented datasets with each other to gain new insights from secondary data. Think what might be done if the information were opened to the public and integrated with other data sources, such as economic indicators, transportation routes, and education statistics, among others.

The integration of fragmented data sources is often problematic, as in many cases data are not collected in a consistent format, and when data sources get very large, traditional methods may not have sufficient processing capacity. Information is often held in "silos"—isolated units of information—in different formats and different systems that vary by organization and by the units within them. These silos of information don't just exist on one horizontal layer (e.g., different units within the local government), but they also exist vertically. For example, information from citizens may be held in silos in civil society organizations, but not fed into silos in the local government—and then not linked to silos in the national government. In addition to silos, data are held in a diverse variety of sources (e.g., structured in spreadsheets, written in free text, contained in images). Within each organization, or even subdivisions of an organization, processes for monitoring and evaluation vary.

Only when the data are aggregated with other data, analyzed, visualized, and made accessible to a multitude of stakeholders will the collection be truly valuable.

## c. Privacy

We all agree that data sets should be anonymized and aggregated to ensure full protection of individual privacy, but in the age of big data this is easier said than done. Personally identifiable information is defined as "any information or combination of information that can be used to identify, contact, or locate a discrete individual" (TRUSTe, n.d.). As we increasingly structure data, information, and knowledge through new methods—uniform resource identifier (URI), hypertext transfer protocol (HTTP), resource description framework (RDF), among others—we are increasingly able to link different sources over a network. Combining multiple sources enables us to gain richer insights, but also raises concerns for privacy. When multiple datasets about the same individuals are available, the ability to identify a person increases as anonymized datasets can be linked to other public datasets. Data of high dimensionality presents a fundamental barrier to privacy preservation (Zakerzadeh, Aggarwal, & Barker, 2014). The more variables a single observation has, the more likely that there is a unique combination of variables that uniquely identifies that observation. For example, in the case of users' mobility traces captured by their mobile phones, a team from MIT found that traces were so unique that as few as four spatio-temporal points were enough to uniquely identify 95% of 1.5 million individuals (de Montjoye, Hidalgo, Verleysen, & Blondel, 2013). The same was found to be true of credit card purchase data (de Montjoye, Radaelli, Singh, & Pentland, 2015).

Whereas naïve anonymization processes of removing all direct identifiers such as name, address, and social security number may have been sufficient in the past, it is now clear that this does not adequately preserve anonymity. Privacy researcher Latanya Sweeney found that 87% of the U.S. population—216 million out of 248 million—could be uniquely identified by their date of birth, gender, and ZIP code in the 1990 Census. Stanford University researchers reported similar results using 2000 Census data (Sweeney, 2000).

---

**BOX 12.10 NOTABLE CASES OF ANONYMIZATION GONE WRONG**

*NYC taxis:* In 2013 New York City officials inadvertently revealed driver details for 173 million taxi trips by inadequately anonymizing a dataset of historical trip and fare logs from the city's taxis. Each trip record included the pickup and drop-off locations and times. It also included anonymized taxi license and medallion numbers that had been transformed into cryptographic hashes using the MD5 algorithm. Because MD5 hashes are one-way, they can't be mathematically converted back into their original values. But because taxi license numbers are structured in predictable patterns, it took developers only 2 hours to run all possible iterations through the same MD5 algorithm and then compare the output to the data contained in the 20GB file, easily identifying which driver drove every single trip in this entire dataset.

    *AOL search queries in 2006:* In hope of benefiting academic researchers, AOL released detailed search logs of 20 million Web search queries for over 650,000 users covering a 3-month period. While no name of users where released, personally identifiable information was present in many of the queries, and query records revealed a lot about the users, leading to their identification. Although AOL removed the data, it was too late, and the data can still be downloaded from mirror sites.

---

SOURCE: Pandurangan (2014), Barbaro & Zeller (2006).

---

While ongoing research on privacy preservation techniques (e.g., k-anonymity, splicing, l-diversity, bucketization) advances, it is believed that there will always be a trade-off between privacy and utility, since information loss accrues inevitably due to privacy preservation. Privacy scholar Paul Ohm (2010, p. 1704) concludes there is a "tension . . . [in] data privacy: Data can be either useful or perfectly anonymous but never both."

This does not mean that no data should ever be shared. What we may need is a third party related to data philanthropy that can test and certify datasets as privacy safe to the best known standard.

## 4.2 Capacity, Cultural, and Legal Aspects

### a. Capacities

Due to its sheer size and often complex and unstructured nature, big data presents several analytical challenges that demand continually updated tools and expertise. Required skill sets for big data analysis are diverse, include quantitative and qualitative disciplines, and are likely to be drawn from a team, rather than be possessed by one person.

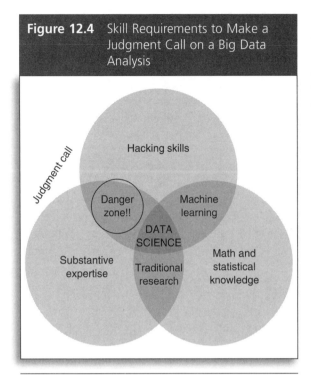

**Figure 12.4** Skill Requirements to Make a Judgment Call on a Big Data Analysis

SOURCE: Drew Conway.

Traditional research moves into the realm of data science with the addition of hacking (computer programming/problem solving) skills. It is key that along with hacking skills, the person leading a big data project has training in the analysis and application of data (discipline-specific) and strong contextual knowledge so that he or she can make appropriate judgment calls. Without this, a project is likely to fall into the "danger zone" (misapplication) or remain only in the digital realm (machine learning in Figure 12.4).

### b. Culture

The model of "build it and they will come" has not worked as a model for open data (Bernholz, Cordelli, & Reich, 2013). The same may prove to be the case for big data. Do we need data ambassadors to drive a cultural change within organizations and societies? And if so, what changes would they need to drive?

To respond to timely data for earlier response to emerging crises, real-time data must be met with real-time institutions. For an agile response, decision makers need to value data, see data as an important factor for consideration among other competing interests (e.g. financial, political), and be in a position to be able to access data as and when needed. To get there, capacity and processes need to be built; data need to be met with sufficient in-house analytical capacity—not just to crunch the numbers, but to interpret the data rapidly and appropriately in context and present them in a balanced way to decision makers. In limited-resource environments the technical expertise to do this is frequently stretched, and improving capacity is usually not simply a matter of hiring, but of building and then retaining capacity. This demands strong and well-managed institutions that can retain capacity, for example, through training and offering competitive employment contracts. This challenge may be difficult to overcome, particularly for developing countries where systems and institutions are likely to be weak. In situations where we struggle to make basic data collection and analysis work for the purposes of M&E, should we really be looking to big data as a solution?

A cultural shift would also be needed for funders. With big data, we are in an experimental phase. Developing tools takes trial and error, so we need to take iterative approaches, which don't fit neatly into funders' existing M&E frameworks. How can we best capture results and lessons learned from iterative innovation experiments and feed them back into the activities' own results management cycle and into the overarching performance monitoring frameworks? More than that, how can we change the culture of "failure"? It is part and parcel of project work, particularly in the development sector where contexts are so varied and issues so complex that much of what we do is, in essence, experimental. How can we create a culture of acceptance to a degree that we can report on and learn from our failures and change the direction of our projects accordingly? The rigidity of current frameworks seems to encourage project managers to succumb to the cultural pressure of reporting results that are skewed to the positive to ensure that they get the next tranche of funding and fit projects to a predetermined track that might not be in the optimal direction.

At this point in time, the concept of big data seems to raise more questions about the limitations in our current way of working than provide immediate solutions to it. To move beyond that—to answer our questions and to realize any potential opportunities that big data may present for M&E—we need to close the gap in understanding between the development sector and big data practitioners. This gap is unsurprising given that big data is a new field of practice and even the basics (e.g., the terms *big data* and *data scientist*) are not well defined, but it presents a huge challenge when we need to increase understanding of the discipline to implement big data projects and move from hype to informed debate. Bridging this gap requires taking a collaborative, interdisciplinary approach. As big data projects use diverse data sources and this requires input from multiple organizations and disciplines (including those in the often-untapped private sector), extensive collaboration is required to pull together information from multiple sources, as is a legal and regulatory environment that supports the sharing of data.

# 5. Practical Applications

The big data field has expanded so quickly that most evaluators have not been able to keep abreast of new developments, and many either feel overwhelmed or believe that big data is a panacea for all of the data collection and analysis problems they face. Big data specialists have a major responsibility for demystifying the subject and providing evaluators with a more realistic understanding of what big data can (and cannot) offer at this point in time.

When embarking on a big data project, determining the best entry point is an essential first step. This will likely be where there is (1) sufficient capacity (data, human resources) to implement big data analytics and (2) sufficient knowledge to interpret and respond to the data appropriately.

When considering the type of analyses to conduct in any given context, thinking about the approach in relation to the fragmentation of the ecosystem and the scale of continuous data may also be helpful. As a data ecosystem becomes more continuous, the focal data "pockets" should merge to become larger fragments of information that have greater utility and facilitate analyses on a larger scale.

## 5.1 Benefits and Improvements

Big data can potentially provide a fix to many of the data constraints faced by conventional monitoring and evaluation systems. It can place the evaluation within the context of the big picture by identifying broader patterns and trends that most conventional M&E systems fail to capture. Local populations tend to generalize based on very local situations that they believe to be unique; however, if these situations are part of broader trends, this can affect the range of options to be considered.

The speed with which data can be generated can be a major benefit in rapidly changing situations such as natural or human-made disasters or rapidly expanding and complex urban systems where programs are affected by multiple factors, all of which interact and many of which are constantly changing. Big data can also help map complex systems, where using data visualization can provide broader insight into the context in which programs are operating and of all the factors affecting program implementation and outcomes.

## 5.2 Risks and Challenges

However, there is a danger of overestimating what big data can achieve, often ignoring the real-world constraints of money, time, technical capacity, and the institutional and political contexts in which most evaluations are conducted. Building capacity for collection and analysis of the radically new kinds of information generated by big data is critical, and a cautious step-by-step approach will usually be required.

There is also a need not only to focus on the supply side of big data, but also to address demand. There is a risk of gaps emerging in available data collected and used as many stakeholders begin with the data and work backward to what problems can be solved. Yet it is equally as important to evaluate the key challenges, even those that cannot be currently addressed through M&E systems, and see what potentially valuable information can be collected and provided to address those problems.

## 5.3 Looking Ahead

An urgent need is to provide guidance to various agencies, with different levels of resources and data management expertise and with disparate information regarding what they realistically can expect from big data—what level of resources will be needed to establish and manage data systems, how long before practical benefits can likely be expected, and what risks and challenges they face. Experience with previous data revolutions, such as computer-generated M&E systems, suggests that it will be essential to adopt a step-by-step approach, testing the new systems, before abandoning the current "old-fashioned" systems, which often work quite well.

Another similar challenge to address is adoption of a mixed methods approach that combines new approaches when they are required with components of the current systems that are working well. Not all projects require sophisticated satellite imagery or real-time data from multiple sources. Mixed methods can be a way to integrate numerical data with a deeper understanding of the local context as well as complex processes of program implementation.

# References

Albergotti, R. (2014, June 30). Furor erupts over Facebook's experiment on users. *Wall Street Journal.*

Anderson, C. (2008, June 23). The end of theory: The data deluge makes the scientific method obsolete. *Wired.* Retrieved from http://www.wired.com

Barbaro, M., & Zeller, T. (2006, August 9). A face is exposed for AOL searcher no. 4417749. *New York Times.* Retrieved from http://www.nytimes.com/

Berman, J. (2013). *Principles of big data: Preparing, sharing, and analyzing complex information.* Waltham, MA: Elsevier. Retrieved from http://www.techgig.com/skill/bigdata/books/Principles-of-Big-Data-Preparing-Sharing-and-Analyzing-Complex-Information/314788

Bernholz, L., Cordelli, C., & Reich, R. (2013). *The emergence of digital civil society.* Stanford, CA: Stanford University, Center on Philanthropy and Civil Society.

Bi, R. (2014). *8 things to check when you analyze Twitter data.* Retrieved from http://www.kdnuggets.com/2014/12/check-when-analyzing-twitter-data.html

*Big data monitoring and evaluation: An overview.* (n.d.) Retrieved from http://bigdatamande.tumblr.com/overview

Bollier, D. (2010). *The promise and peril of big data.* Washington, DC: Aspen Institute. Retrieved from http://www.ilmresource.com/collateral/analyst-reports/10334-ar-promise-peril-of-big-data.pdf

Borne, K. (2014, June 17). 3 ways that big data are used to study climate change: Monitoring, modeling, and assimilation. *MapR.* Retrieved from https://www.mapr.com/blog/3-ways-big-data-are-used-study-climate-change-%E2%80%93-monitoring-modeling-and-assimilation#.VADYyPldU1a

Brown, B., Chui, M., & Manyika, J. (2011, October). Are you ready for the era of "big data"? *McKinsey Quarterly.* Retrieved from http://www.mckinsey.com/insights/mckinsey_quarterly

Chirgwin, R. (2014, March 23). Google flu-finding service diagnosed with "big data hubris." *The Register.* Retrieved from http://www.theregister.co.uk

Crawford, K. (2013, April 1). The hidden biases in big data. *Harvard Business Review.* Retrieved from https://hbr.org

de Montjoye, Y.-A., Hidalgo, C. A., Verleysen, M., & Blondel, V. D. (2013). Unique in the crowd: The privacy bounds of human mobility. *Scientific Reports, 3,* 1376. Retrieved from http://www.nature.com

de Montjoye, Y.-A., Radaelli, L., Singh, V. K., & Pentland, A. S. (2015). Unique in the shopping mall: On the reidentifiability of credit card metadata. *Science, 347,* 536–536.

Desouza, K. C., & Smith, K. L. (2014, Summer). Big data for social innovation. Stanford *Social Innovation Review.* Retrieved from http://www.ssireview.org

Docking, T. (2013). *M&E 2.0: Using big data to kill white elephants.* Retrieved from https://www.devex.com/news/m-e-2-0-using-big-data-to-kill-white-elephants-81737

Einav, L., & Levin, J. (2014). *The data revolution and economic analysis.* Cambridge, MA: National Bureau of Economic Research. Retrieved from http://web.stanford.edu/~jdlevin/Papers/BigData.pdf

European Commission. (2014, October 13). *European Commission and data industry launch €2.5 billion partnership to master big data.* Retrieved from http://europa.eu/rapid/press-release_IP-14-1129_en.htm

Harford, T. (2014a, March 28). Big data: Are we making a big mistake? *Financial Times.* Retrieved from http://www.ft.com/

Harford, T. (2014b, April 18). Seizing the opportunity of big data. *Financial Times.* Retrieved from http://www.ft.com

Horrigan, M. H. (2013, January 1). Big data: A perspective from the BLS. *Amstat News.* Retrieved from http://magazine.amstat.org

Kerr, D. (2013, December 12). Bots now running the Internet with 61 percent of Web traffic. *CNET.* Retrieved from http://www.cnet.com

Kirkpatrick, R. (2011, April 21). Digital smoke signals. *UN Global Pulse Blog.* Retrieved from http://www.unglobalpulse.org/blog/digital-smoke-signals

Kramer, A. D. I., Guillory, J. E., & Hancock, J. T. (2014). Experimental evidence of massive-scale emotional contagion through social networks. *Proceedings of the National Academy of Sciences of the United States of America, 111,* 8788–8790.

Lazer, D., Kennedy, R., King, G., & Vespignani, A. (2014). The parable of the Google flu: Traps in big data analysis. *Science, 343,* 1203–1205. Retrieved from http://gking.harvard .edu/files/gking/files/0314policyforumff.pdf

Letouzé, E. (2012). *Big data for development: Challenges and opportunities.* New York, NY: UN Global Pulse. Retrieved from http://www.unglobalpulse.org/BigDataforDevWhitePaper

Letouzé, E. (2014). *Big data and development: An overview.* New York, NY: Data-Pop Alliance.

Letouzé, E., Meier, P., & Vinck, P. (2013). Big data for conflict prevention: New oil and old fires. In F. Mancini (Ed.), *New technology and the prevention of violence and conflict* (pp. 4–27). New York, NY: International Peace Institute.

Lucas critique. (2015). *Wikipedia.* Retrieved from http://en.wikipedia.org/wiki/Lucas_critique

McAfee, A., & Brynjolfsson, E. (2012, October). Big data: The management revolution. *Harvard Business Review.*

Means, A. (2014, June 25). *The death of evaluation.* Retrieved from http://www.markets forgood.org/the-death-of-evaluation.

NASA. (2012). *Ground truth.* Retrieved from http://science-edu.larc.nasa.gov/SCOOL/ groundtruth.html

Ohm, P. (2010). Broken promises of privacy: Responding to the surprising failure of anony-mization. *UCLA Law Review, 57,* 1701–1777. Retrieved from http://uclalawreview.org

Pandurangan, V. (2014, June 21). On taxis and rainbows: Lessons from NYC's improperly anonymized taxi logs. *Medium.* Retrieved from https://medium.com/@vijayp/of-taxis-and-rainbows-f6bc289679a1

Patton, M. Q. (2011). *Developmental evaluation: Applying complexity concepts to enhance innovation and use.* New York, NY: Guilford Press.

The petabyte age: Because more isn't just more—More is different. (2008, June 23). *Wired.* Retrieved from http://www.wired.com

Pfeffer, J., & Ruths, D. (2014, December 2). *Can we study society via social media?* Retrieved from https://agenda.weforum.org/2014/12/can-we-study-society-via-social-media/

Reinventing society in the wake of big data: A conversation with Alex (Sandy) Pentland. (2012, August, 30). *Edge.* Retrieved from https://edge.org/conversation/reinventing-society-in-the-wake-of-big-data

Salganik, M. (2014, July 25). Natural experiments created by online and offline processes. *Wheels on the Bus.* Retrieved from https://msalganik.wordpress.com/2014/07/25/natural-experiments-created-by-online-and-offline-processes

Scannapieco, M., Virgillito, A., & Zardetto, D. (n.d.). *Placing big data in official statistics: A big challenge?* Retrieved from http://www.cros-portal.eu/sites/default/files/NTTS2013 fullPaper_214.pdf

Snyder, S. (2013). *The simple, the complicated, and the complex: Educational reform through the lens of complexity theory* (OECD Working Paper No. 96). Paris, France: Organisation for Economic Co-operation and Development. Retrieved from http://www.oecd.org/edu/ceri/WP_The%20Simple,%20Complicated,%20and%20the%20Complex.pdf

Sweeney, L. (2000). *Simple demographics often identify people uniquely* (Data Privacy Working Paper 3). Pittsburgh, PA: Carnegie Mellon University. Retrieved from http://dataprivacylab.org/projects/identifiability/paper1.pdf

Taleb, N. N. (2013, February 8). Beware the big errors of "big data." *Wired.* Retrieved from http://www.wired.com

TRUSTe. (n.d.). *TRUSTed cloud certification standards.* Retrieved from http://www.truste.com/privacy-program-requirements/trusted-cloud/

West, G. (2013). Big data needs a big theory to go with it. *Scientific American, 308*(5). Retrieved from http://www.scientificamerican.com

World Economic Forum. (2015). *Global risks report.* Retrieved from http://www.weforum.org/reports/global-risks-report-2015

Zakerzadeh, H., Aggarwal, C. C., & Barker, K. (2014). Towards breaking the curse of dimensionality for high-dimensional privacy. In M. Zaki, Z. Obradovic, P. N. Tan, A. Banerjee, C. Kamath, & S. Parthasarathy (Eds.), *Proceedings of the 2014 SIAM International Conference on Data Mining* (pp. 731–739). Retrieved from http://epubs.siam.org/doi/abs/10.1137/1.9781611973440.84

# Notes

1. The views and positions expressed in this chapter are those of its authors and may not reflect the views and positions of the institutions and organizations the authors are employed by or affiliated with. This chapter also benefitted from inputs and editing support from Natalie Shoup, Program Manager, Data-Pop Alliance. Detailed comments from the editors were received throughout the development of this chapter and are gratefully acknowledged.

2. Lead and corresponding author; Director, Data-Pop Alliance (www.datapopalliance.org).

3. Former Program Manager, Data-Pop Alliance.

4. Former M&E Specialist, UN Global Pulse Lab Jakarta.

# PART IV

## Dealing With Complexity in Development Evaluation: The Institutional Challenges

# CHAPTER 13

# Dealing With Institutional Complexity

## Implications for Evaluation Design, Process, and Use

Estelle Raimondo

*The social and institutional structure of a development intervention is often one of its most challenging features. Complexity emanates from a number of factors, including the multiplicity of stakeholders and their divergent expectations as well as from intricate change processes within organizations. Complexity-responsive evaluations must be aware of these institutional dimensions and how they affect the design, implementation, and use of the evaluation. This chapter starts with a simple framework to map out the evaluation system. It then discusses the implication of institutional complexity for the use of evaluation for learning and for accountability. A number of avenues for making well-established results-based management systems more complexity-responsive are explored.*

In the past decade development evaluation has become increasingly institutionalized in a set of standardized procedures to generate evidence-informed practices. Many international organizations and bilateral development agencies, as well as large NGOs, foundations, and private sector organizations, have both accountability-focused and internal management and learning evaluation functions. The latter is traditionally in charge of quality control, reporting, recommendation follow-up, and, more generally, building evaluation capacity and enhancing evaluation culture. Another dimension of this growing institutionalization of evaluation is the creation of a number of prominent evaluation networks, such as the United Nations Evaluation Group or the Evaluation Cooperation Group, uniting evaluation offices of multilateral development banks. One of the important functions of these interagency groups has been to generate evaluation norms and standards and to provide a forum for sharing good practices. Moreover, there have been two important advances in the institutionalization of evaluation throughout the world: the marked growth in national and regional evaluation societies and the institutionalization of evaluation within national public administrations in developing countries.

In this chapter I use the term *evaluation system*[1] rather broadly to encompass three main dimensions: (1) the multiple stakeholders involved in the evaluation (commissioners, producers, and users) as well as the processes between them in various phases of evaluation exercises; (2) the way the evaluation function is embedded in a larger organizational system; and (3) the culture of evaluation, including its norms, routines, and language.

# 1. Mapping Complex Evaluation Systems

The practice of development evaluation is not taking place in a vacuum, but rather is embedded within organizations and their institutional context. Recall from Chapter 1 that there are many institutional factors that can render the evaluation of a rather straightforward intervention complex. This section proposes a simple framework that unpacks these various institutional dimensions. The first dimension has to do with the multiplicity and diversity of stakeholders and their roles at various points during the evaluation process. The second dimension speaks to the complexity of organizational change processes. The third dimension relates to the notion that, as the field becomes more mature, it generates its own formal and informal norms, roles, and routines. In the sociological sense, we can thus think of evaluation as an institution (Dahler-Larsen, 2012). These three dimensions, taken together, can delineate the boundaries of an evaluation system as defined in Box 13.1 and illustrated in Table 13.1.

## BOX 13.1 DEFINITION OF AN EVALUATION SYSTEM

An evaluation system encompasses permanent and systematic, formal as well as informal evaluation practices. These practices are not ad hoc; rather they take place and are institutionalized in several interdependent organizational entities with the purpose of informing decision making and securing oversight. Within the boundaries of an evaluation system lie the following components:

- multiple actors with a range of roles and processes linking them to the evaluation exercise at different phases (e.g., planning, implementation, use, decision making)
- complex organizational processes and structures
- multiple institutions (formal and informal rules, norms and beliefs about the merit and worth of evaluation)

SOURCE: Adapted from Hojlund (2014), Leeuw & Furubo (2008).

**Table 13.1** Complexity Dimensions of the Evaluation System

| | Dimensions | Sources of complexity | Implications |
|---|---|---|---|
| **Stakeholders** | Multiple stakeholders in planning of evaluation | • Senior management or board of directors<br>• Internal evaluation function<br>• Program managers<br>• Multiple planning and funding agencies | *Competing interests with possible tensions about evaluation agenda, objectives, and budget* |
| | Multiple stakeholders in production of evaluation | • Internal evaluators with multiple roles (change agents, referees, knowledge brokers, etc.)<br>• External evaluators<br>• Multiple planning and funding agencies<br>• Program beneficiaries<br>• Delivery partners | *Competing interests with possible tensions about evaluation method and process, and understanding of the intervention; transaction costs for evaluation teams and evaluand* |
| | Multiple stakeholders in use of evaluation | • Funders<br>• National governments<br>• Networks of evaluators<br>• General public<br>• Program beneficiaries<br>• Delivery partners | *Possible tensions between learning and accountability needs with influence on the evaluation design and process* |
| **Organizations** | Organizational structure and processes | • Complex decision-making processes: negotiations, conflict between competing interests<br>• Multiple nested principal-agent relationships<br>• Organizational change processes are complex: product of chance, choice, and propitious context | *Can trigger nonuse, misuse, symbolic use, or political use of evaluation findings and recommendations* |
| **Institutions** | Norms, routines, incentives, and belief systems | • Multiple layers of evaluation norms and standards competing with other norms and standards in place within or across organizations<br>• Competing belief systems about the worth of evaluation<br>• Ingrained routines that make change difficult<br>• Routinization of evaluation requirements | *Can trigger resistance to evaluation or render the communication between evaluators and other stakeholders complicated* |

## 1.1 Dealing With Multiple Stakeholders

As laid out in Chapter 1, development programs that are carried out in partnerships between a range of organizations are more likely to display some elements of complexity. Yet even evaluations of single-agency programs often present challenges due to conflicting demands of different stakeholders at various stages of the evaluation. During the evaluation process, the main tasks for the evaluators are essentially managing competing expectations and conflicting information, and legitimating and policy needs. At the end of the process, the evaluators also have to deal with competing interpretations of the evaluation's findings and recommendations.

Broadly defined, we can identify three main groups of stakeholders involved at various stages of the evaluation process.[2] First, there are key stakeholders in the planning of the evaluation. These stakeholders may take part in deciding what interventions will be put on the evaluation agenda for a given programming cycle, or they may contribute more directly to delineating the scope and the content of the terms of reference for a given evaluation. Depending on the organization, these stakeholders may include members of the senior management team, representatives of donors (e.g., board of directors, representative of member states), ministers (in the case of bilateral donors or government of developing countries), and members of the operational team (including delivery partners) and the central evaluation unit. It is also often valuable to seek the input of program beneficiaries, through participatory processes, at this early stage of the evaluation design. Parliaments in many developing countries with their own evaluation systems are also taking an increasingly active role in mandating and using evaluation exercises.

The second group of stakeholders who influence the evaluation process are those involved in the production of the evaluation. Again, depending on the organizations, these stakeholders may include external consultants, multiple implementing and funding agencies, multiple program beneficiaries, and internal evaluators. The latter group wear various functional hats, including but not limited to, quality controllers, change agents, referees, knowledge brokers, and special advisors. Each of these roles may in turn lead to competing priorities. These possible tensions are compounded if the evaluation is conducted in the framework of a joint intervention between various development agencies or between organizations with very different mandates and ways of doing business, as is increasingly the case for public-private partnerships.

Finally, the third group of stakeholders who can weigh in on the evaluation design, process, and outcome are those most likely to make use of the evaluation findings and recommendations. To a large extent these stakeholders overlap with those involved in the planning of the evaluation but not always squarely. While funders and evaluators might have a say in the planning of the evaluation, national governments in developing countries and the general public are also potential users of the evaluation findings and recommendations without being directly involved in the planning of the exercise. Additionally, civil society and the mass media are becoming increasingly important players in evaluations, notably through the growth of social media.

To make sense of the various perspectives influencing the evaluation process, it is useful to distinguish between stakeholders (people with common role), stakes (individual values, motivations and incentives), and framing (how the different stakeholders understand an intervention; Williams, 2015). When embarking on an evaluation, it is often beneficial to unpack these multiple and sometimes inconsistent perspectives. As displayed in Box 13.2, Williams (2015) proposes four heuristic questions to help in this meaning-making process.

---

### BOX 13.2 MAKING SENSE OF THE MULTIPLICITY OF PERSPECTIVES

Making sense of the multiplicity of perspectives among stakeholders, and understanding their various stakes and how they frame the intervention, can seem a particularly intricate task, especially when an intervention involves multiple implementing or donor agencies. Williams (2015, p. 12) proposes four main questions to help in this process:

- Who or what are the key stakeholders in the situation?
- What are the key stakes (values, interests, incentives, motivations, etc.)?
- What are the different ways in which the intervention can be framed?
- What plausible intervention objectives do these various framings imply?

SOURCE: Adapted from Bob Williams (2015).

---

The involvement of this intricate net of stakeholders in the evaluation process also affects the cost of the evaluation. Apart from the financial costs associated with the consultation process, there is a range of other transaction and information costs that ought to be accounted for: meeting time, turnover, pressure on field offices and on implementers. These costs are often a function of the degree of participation of the different stakeholders, which move on a continuum from simple information-sharing, to joint deliberation, and joint decision making. Evidently, these costs are also compounded in the case of a multi-donor intervention, in which coordination is often difficult and monitoring and evaluation (M&E) units can be competing and have very different evaluation questions that they would like the evaluation to answer.

## 1.2 Understanding Organizations as Loosely Coupled Systems

A second source of institutional complexity comes from the fact that evaluations are almost exclusively embedded in organizational contexts: solicited and procured by organizations, conducted by organizations, acted upon by organizations (Hojlund, 2014). Organizations do not operate as closed systems, but are in constant interaction with their dynamic environment, constituting instead open and loosely coupled systems (Dahler-Larsen, 2012; Katz & Kahn, 1978; Weaver, 2008). Box 13.3 provides a simple definition of *loosely coupled system*. In this type of system, contradictions between elements assimilated through external pressure and organizations' daily operations may arise and become a permanent feature. For example, the gap between discourse and action in many international organizations is often criticized by NGOs, advocacy groups, and the civil society. This discrepancy can often be explained by the fact that certain parts of the organizations, notably senior management, are more reactive to the diverse demands from the outside, while the day-to-day operation is more secluded from these outside pressures and in turn more influenced by internal dynamics.

---

### BOX 13.3 DEFINITION OF LOOSELY COUPLED SYSTEMS

Loose coupling in an organization means that there are only loose links between what is decided or claimed at the top and what is happening in operation, that inconsistencies between discourse and action can be endemic, and that goal incongruence between various parts of the organizations goes unresolved. On the one hand, loose coupling is a coping mechanism when facing the cacophonic demands from a heterogeneous environment while retaining stability in some values and processes. However, sometimes these inconsistencies may become obvious and rejected from within or outside the organization. The inherent contradictions that allowed the organization to cope with an ever changing environment may be the source of instability, conflict, and change. Evaluation may be called on to resolve these inconsistencies. However, if there is symbolic use of evaluation, it may contribute to loose coupling.

SOURCE: Adapted from Dahler-Larsen (2012), Weaver (2008).

---

Evaluation is often presented as a way to identify and bridge these gaps between discourse and action and an important tool to guide organizational change. Consequently, conceiving organizational change as the product of complex human interrelationships with their environment, deeper structures, institutions, and power dynamics has important implications for understanding the role of evaluation and its use within organizations.

It may be useful to distinguish between two major decision levels that are most likely to be decoupled—policy or strategic decisions and program decisions—keeping in mind that in many organizations there are other mediating levels and a multiplicity of subcultures. These two levels have very different information needs, with key implications for the role and structure of evaluation systems operating in this larger institutional context. Oftentimes, the goal incongruence between these two levels multiplies the external sources of confusion from the many outside stakeholders that have an influence on evaluation design, implementation, and use.

### a. Policy or Strategic Decisions

Decision making at the policy level is often the most unstable because it involves multiple governments (in the case of multilateral development agencies), multiple branches of power (in the case of bilateral agencies), multiple funders (in the case of large NGOs), and multiple board members (in the case of foundations). At this strategic level, decision making is often unordered and nonlinear. This process has come to be characterized as a "garbage can" model (Cohen, March, & Olsen, 1972) or a multiple-streams model (Kingdon, 1995). For an important decision to be adopted at this strategic level, four major elements must come together at a propitious time: an issue must come to the attention of the public, and it must find some resonance among policymakers, and a solution must be identified, and it must satisfy both technical and value feasibility. Managers and evaluators engaged in complexity-responsive evaluation should therefore be cognizant of the intricacies of the decision-making process at each stage of the evaluation. Ignoring these intricacies would run the risk of being irrelevant.

### b. Program Decisions

To a certain extent, program-level decision making is more immune to the relative instability of the organization's outside environment. Internal dynamics are shaped by formal and informal norms, rules, belief systems, values, and ways of interpreting the goals of the organization, which may be quite distinct from those in the external environment (Barnett & Finnemore, 2004; Weaver, 2008). On the one hand, the internal culture can provide a certain degree of stability and efficiency in responding to unpredictable demands from the environment. At the same time, when there are clashes between the external pressure and the internal structures and cultures, the organization can decouple, creating gaps between official goals and actual operations (Lipson, 2007, 2010; Weaver, 2008). These sources of institutional complexity are compounded when the intervention is supported by multiple agencies and evaluators have to deal with several sets of rules, norms, and evaluative culture.

## 1.3 Dealing With Complex Incentive Systems

In light of the existing tensions facing development organizations between outside demands and internal dynamics, evaluation processes are often institutionalized in ways that do not provide incentives to deal seriously with complexity. "In some evaluation contexts, the inherent complexity, conflicts, and dilemmas embedded in an intervention may be too strong" (Hansen & Vedung, 2010, p. 295) and might instead result in prioritizing the lowest common denominator at the expense of a complexity-responsive and deliberative perspective. Consequently, evaluations' terms of reference tend to be overly restrictive and pay insufficient attention to questions such as these: What is the problem? What is the confluence of factors affecting the problem? How does an intervention play a role in a larger system?

Under certain circumstances, advocates of particular issues and programs, among both program managers and decision makers, have an incentive to underinvest in knowledge creation because providing a credible estimate of program effects and their heterogeneity among diverse populations—or delving into unintended consequences—may undermine their ability to mobilize political and financial support for the continuation of their favorite program (Pritchett, 2002; Ravallion, 2008). Other mechanisms can contribute to the knowledge gap about complexity. Asymmetries of information about the quality of the evaluation between the evaluator and the program manager who is not an evaluation expert tend to prevail. Given that less rigorous and less complexity-responsive evaluation designs are often less expensive, they might drive rigorous and complexity-responsive evaluations out of the market. Second, oftentimes project managers or political stakeholders decide how much money should be allocated to evaluation. Yet their incentives are not well aligned with knowledge demands for delving into complexity. Consequently, the overall portfolio of evaluations is biased toward interventions that are, on average, simpler and more successful (Clements, Chianca, & Sasaki, 2008).

Third, decision makers tend to have a rather short political attention span on issues of program effectiveness, and traditional donor countries are putting increasing pressure on development agencies to demonstrate results and to ensure that their taxpayers are getting "good bang for their buck." This produces tensions between the need to understand the complexity of interventions on the one hand and the need to simplify the evaluation to produce measurable outcomes on the other.

## 2. Institutional Complexity and Evaluation Use

The multiplicity of stakeholders, decision levels, and incentive mechanisms accounts for the large array of evaluation usage. Evaluations can, for example, be used for program improvement or for deciding to scale up, replicate, or abandon an intervention (instrumental use); as a new way of thinking about a program or issue (conceptual or enlightenment use); or for ritualistic compliance with an external mandate (symbolic use). These processes of change can come about as a result of the evaluation product or during its process (process use; Alkin & Taut, 2003; Leviton, 2003; Patton, 2008; Weiss, 1998). Figure 13.1 recapitulates this typology.

Overlapping this typology are the broad evaluation purposes of answering accountability demands from donors or enhancing organizational and individual learning. Each of these two overarching goals is associated with various stakeholders (external funders vs. internal staff), evaluation approaches (summative vs. formative), and key evaluation questions.

For evaluations to be used, a number of factors need to come together at the right time. A useful list of such factors was developed early on by Cousins and Leithwood (1986) and forms the basis for a large number of empirical studies on evaluation use (e.g., Balthasar, 2006; Brandon & Singh, 2009; Hojlund, 2014; Johnson et al., 2009; Ledermann, 2012). The framework illustrated in Figure 13.2 refers to 12 specific factors that can influence evaluation use and are divided into two categories: factors pertaining to evaluation implementation and factors pertaining to decision and policy settings. More recently, the focus has been on tracing pathways of evaluation influence that link the factors presented in Figure 13.2 to evaluating intermediate and long-term outcomes on decision makers, be they cognitive (e.g., learning something new), motivational (e.g., change in personal goals), or behavioral (e.g., decision to terminate or expand a program; Henry & Mark, 2003).

However, given the many institutional tensions mentioned and the different information needs at various levels of an organization, the perception is that evaluation use is often symbolic (Carden, 2013; McNulty, 2012; Patton, 2008). In

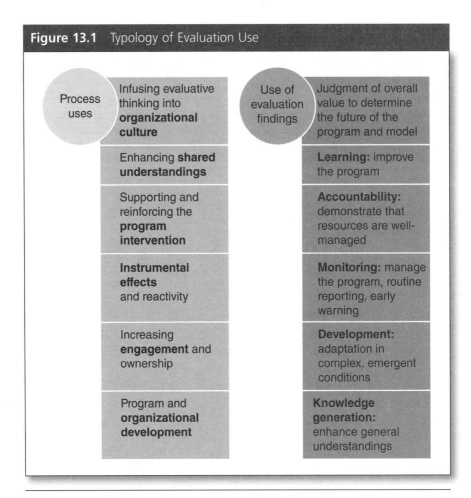

**Figure 13.1**   Typology of Evaluation Use

SOURCE: Adapted from Patton (2008).

his analysis of symbolic use and the ritualization of evaluation, McNulty (2012) identifies a number of factors that can explain the gap between discourse and action in the use of evaluation findings and recommendations: multiple nested principle-agent relationships, misaligned career incentives, the fact that people tend to value instant losses more than future gains, favoring immediate symbolic use with quick returns over more distant and uncertain returns on actual usage of evaluation findings to change the course of action. Chapter 3 discusses a number of reasons why evaluations are often underused or not used the way that the main client and the evaluators had intended.

# 3. Evaluation Use for Learning

Whether they track the implementations of projects, try to assess whether one program works in a particular setting, or try to determine the added value of a corporate strategy or a portfolio of programs, development evaluations are often intended to

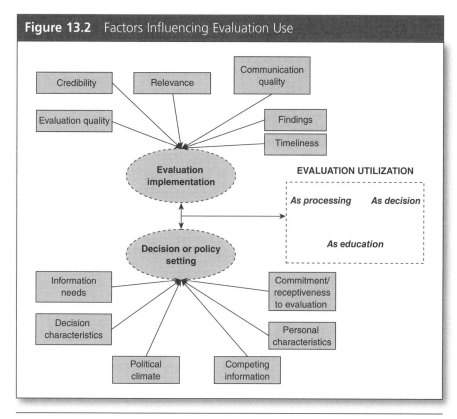

**Figure 13.2**   Factors Influencing Evaluation Use

SOURCE: Cousins & Leithwood (1986).

improve the practice of people in a given organization or ameliorate some processes underlying program planning, design, and implementation. While much learning taking place within organizations is inherently tacit, informal, and peer to peer, the challenge for many organizations is to capture enough of this individual learning to build institutional knowledge (Independent Evaluation Group, 2012; Marra, 2004). There is a diverse range of learning mechanisms that organizations put in place to learn from the findings and recommendations stemming from evaluations. Although overly schematic, this section distinguishes between four models of evaluation learning that often coexist and are likely to be needed in different contexts: a bureaucratic model, a model of learning through experimentation, a participatory learning model, and an experiential learning model. Table 13.2 summarizes the main features of these four models.

## 3.1 The Bureaucratic Learning Model

First, evaluation systems that are currently in place in many bureaucratic development agencies (principally multilateral and bilateral development organizations) tend to rely on a rather top-down model of organizational learning with the general goal of matching the supply of evaluation to the demand for evidence from high-level decision makers (Mayne, 2010; Patton, 2011). The emphasis tends to be less on the evaluation process as a learning moment and more on the evaluation report as a learning repository. In this model, the collaboration between program managers and evaluators can be seen as a threat to the independence of the evaluator and a tempering in the credibility of the findings. Thus, internal evaluation functions are better located in decision-making and accountability jurisdictions (i.e., far from program staff and close to senior management). Evaluators tend to play the role of knowledge brokers to high decision makers. Particular attention is paid to structural elements, also called organizational learning mechanisms, including credible measurement, information dissemination channels, regular review, and formal processes of recommendation follow-up (Barrados & Mayne, 2003; Mayne, 2010). Follow-up mechanisms range from simple encouragement to formal enforcement mechanisms, tantamount to audit procedures.

## 3.2 The Experimentation Learning Model

Learning through experimentation represents a second type of learning model characterizing organizations such as J-Pal, IPA, 3ie, and the World Bank's DIME. In this model, learning comes primarily through evidence stemming from impact evaluations with randomized controlled trials (RCTs) or quasi-experimental designs. RCTs require close collaboration with the implementation team, since the evaluation is part and parcel of the operation. Single studies on a range of development issues are implemented in various contexts, and their results are bundled together either formally through systematic syntheses or more informally in "policy lessons." These studies and syntheses are supposed to feed into a repository of best practices, stocked in "knowledge warehouses," and tapped into by various actors in the organization according to their needs. Many agencies in OECD-DAC countries have built a type of lessons-learned database designed to enable quick access to lessons that can be factored into new projects and programs (Liverani & Lundgren, 2007). In this model, the key learning audiences are both decision makers and the larger research community, and evaluators play the role of researchers.

## 3.3 The Participatory Learning Model

A third model, more likely to be found in foundations or NGOs, relies on participatory learning processes. As noted in Chapter 18, a range of factors can explain why learning is intrinsic to philanthropic giving, including the fact that foundation giving is often quite personal, derived from entrepreneurship; the relationships between beneficiaries and donors is rather tight. In the case of NGOs, other factors come into play to justify the importance placed on learning processes, notably the fact that NGOs are often primarily implementers, rather than only donors. In this type of organization, there is thus a tendency to put in place participatory modes of evaluation. Here, learning starts with participation in the evaluation process as laid out in the theory of evaluative inquiry for learning organizations (EILO; Preskill & Torres, 1999). Fostering evaluation capacity is seen as a key learning mechanism (King, Cousins, & Whitmore, 2007; Preskill & Boyle, 2008). Learning is assumed to occur through dialogue and social interaction, and it is conceived as "a continuous process of growth and improvement that (a) uses evaluation findings to make changes; (b) is integrated with work activities, and within the organization's infrastructure; . . . and (c) invokes the alignment of values, attitudes, and perceptions among organizational members" (Torres & Preskill, 2001, p. 388). The purview of the evaluator is thus no longer restricted to the role of expert, but expands to encompass the role of facilitator, and evaluative inquiry is ideally integrated with other project management practices.

## 3.4 The Experiential Learning Model

Both the bureaucratic learning model and the experimentation model assume that evaluations will feed into a body of evidence that decision makers can draw on when considering a new project, scale-up, or replication. By definition these models require a high level of external validity of findings, an evidence-informed model of policy adoption, and a learning process that is primarily driven by the exogenous supply of information. However, when interventions are complex, when there is no clear solutions to a particular problem, and when organizations are dynamic, these three assumptions tend not to materialize (Pritchett & Sandefur, 2013). A model of evaluation based on the principle of experiential learning has thus emerged as a complement for other forms of learning from evaluation described above. This model attempts to embed rigorous evaluation principles in the project management cycle (Khagram & Thomas, 2010; Ludwig, Kling, & Mullainathan, 2011; Patton, 2011; Pritchett, Samji, & Hammer, 2013).

The primary objective here is to create a space for program designers and implementers to innovate while at the same time providing accountability and an evidence base to funders. Some of the common necessary conditions for continuous adaptation identified in these models include innovations, a learning machinery that allows the system to fail, and a capacity and incentives system to distinguish positive from negative change and to change practice accordingly. There are currently two main versions of this approach: a more qualitative version with Patton's (2011) developmental evaluation and a more experimentalist version with Pritchett and colleagues' (2013) monitoring, experiential learning, and evaluation (MeE) model. In both versions, evaluators play the role of innovators.

In the qualitative version, participatory designs and processes of data collection, analysis, and dissemination are thought to be the most effective ways to learn. The premise of this model is that complexity calls for greater pluralism, with more room for tacit and practitioners' knowledge as well as the knowledge harbored from beneficiaries (Marra, 2004; Patton, 2011).[3]

In the experimentalist version, the focus is on adapting traditional RCTs to the necessity of modifying programs during program cycles. The main idea is to move away from a model of RCT in which the program features are fixed at the beginning of the study and unable to change over time. Instead, evaluations designs try to exploit within-project variations as their own counterfactuals, with short and tight feedback looping right into implementation (Ludwig et al., 2011; Pritchett et al.,

| Learning model | Main features |
|---|---|
| **Table 13.2** Summary of Four Learning Models | |
| Learning model | Main features |
| Bureaucratic learning | • Primary target learning audience: high-level decision makers<br>• Formal reporting and follow-up mechanisms<br>• Focus is more on evaluation report than evaluation process<br>• Emphasis on independence of evaluation function<br>• Evaluators as knowledge brokers |
| Experimentation learning | • Primary target learning audience: research community<br>• Evaluations feed into larger repository of knowledge<br>• Focus is on accuracy of findings rather than learning process<br>• Dissemination channels through journal articles and third-party platforms<br>• Evaluators as researchers |
| Participatory learning | • Primary target learning audience: members of operation team and program beneficiaries<br>• Focus on evaluation process as learning moment<br>• Tacit learning through dialogue and interaction<br>• Capacity-building as part of learning mechanisms<br>• Close integration with operation<br>• Evaluators as facilitators |
| Experiential learning | • Primary target learning audience: members of operation team<br>• Continuous adaptation of program based on tight evaluation feedback during program cycle<br>• Emphasis on learning from failures and allowing an innovation space<br>• Evaluators as innovators |

2013). The general principles underlying these new approaches are closely related to the behavioral economics work on "nudging" and are gaining momentum in some development circles (e.g., Datta & Mullainathan, 2012).

# 4. Institutional Complexity and Evaluation Use for Accountability

Development evaluations have historically been commissioned and used as an oversight mechanism to hold program managers and other agents involved in operations to account for delivering the intended results. In that sense, evaluation has played an important role in increasing transparency and responsibility in the development industry. As long as development interventions were relatively easy to delineate, with observable impacts, delivered by agencies acting alone, and funded by single donors, a fairly straightforward definition of accountability was possible, relying on simple understanding of cause-and-effect relationships. Box 13.4 introduces the widely accepted OECD-DAC definitions of accountability and results-based management.

---

**BOX 13.4 OECD-DAC DEFINITION OF ACCOUNTABILITY AND RESULTS-BASED MANAGEMENT**

OECD defines accountability as "obligation to demonstrate that work has been conducted in compliance with agreed rules and standards or to report fairly and accurately on performance results vis-à-vis mandated roles and/or plans. . . . Accountability in development may refer to the obligations of partners to act according to clearly defined responsibilities, roles and performance expectations." In turn, results-based management is defined as "a management strategy focusing on performance and achievement of outputs, outcomes and impacts."

SOURCE: OECD-DAC (2010).

---

However, the development enterprise is shifting toward interventions that solicit efforts by multiple agencies acting through networks, leveraging multiple financial streams, seeking to reach rather abstract goals. As laid out in Chapter 4, attributing a particular development effect to an identifiable intervention, and responsibility for such intervention to a given actor, is increasingly challenging. As development organizations take on a broader mandate, defining unambiguous goals that are stable over time and can be used for accountability is increasingly challenging. Additionally, translating these goals into meaningful evaluation criteria is an increasingly difficult task. Finally, determining which entity should be held accountable for the non-achievement of targets is also made particularly arduous as decision and implementation processes now frequently involve a network of actors with more diffuse cooperation mechanisms (Dahler-Larsen, 2012, p. 43). Thus simple notions of accountability for results become increasingly hard to fulfill (Williams, 2015). Tensions can therefore emerge between, on the one hand, the need for a stable and socially acceptable oversight system, and, on the other, room for managerial flexibility that complex interventions and contexts demand. Finding a good balance between the two is increasingly necessary. One of the key questions motivating this section is thus: How can results-based management frameworks become complexity-responsive?

## 4.1 Tensions Between Results-Based Management and Complexity

In order to successfully deliver on their oversight mandate, one of the most widely accepted norms in the evaluation institution is the need for evaluators to remain independent from the influence of program managers and to avoid possible conflicts of interest to preserve the credibility of the evaluation process and findings. Although there is ample consensus around the idea that evaluative inquiry must be independent to be credible and usable, the meaning of *independence* and its structural implications are still up for debate (Balthasar, 2006; Gaarder & Briceno, 2010). While there are those who equate independence with a formal and structural detachment of the evaluation function from program management, others consider this interpretation too narrow. Instead they contend that by being too removed from programs, the evaluation function runs the risk of becoming aloof and ultimately irrelevant (Mayne, 2008). Finding a good balance between independence and integration is even more important when dealing with complex interventions. A close connection to the intervention and its context are often critical factors in grasping complex processes of change and institutional environment. Additionally, while a structure that puts evaluation units close to decision makers can foster positive feedback (e.g., reinforce the strategic role that evaluation can play), it can also create negative feedback (e.g., the perception that evaluation is an instrument used to reduce budget; Laubli Laud & Mayne, 2013, pp. 243–244).

Other tensions between the dominant results-based management (RBM) model and complexity may exist. Chief among these are the following:

- Evaluation systems are objectives-based, thereby ignoring unintended outcomes (both positive and negative).
- For accountability purposes, the unit of analysis of most evaluation is a project, a program, or an administratively defined intervention with little linkage to larger systems of interventions (see Chapter 7 for more details on this point).
- The timing of reporting is much shorter than the timing of many effects, which take years to fully materialize.
- There are tensions between breadth and depth of evaluation inquiry. For accountability purposes, the balance often tips in favor of large evaluation coverage. On the other hand, understanding complexity can require in-depth inquiries into intricate processes of change.
- In established RBM frameworks, the commissioning of evaluation is such that the exercise ends up being driven by single clients as opposed to more complexity-responsive lenses such as networks and coalitions of implementers.

## 4.2 Making RBM Complexity-Responsive

While it is still premature to derive specific guidance on how to reform established RBM processes so that they can accommodate the specific needs of complexity-responsive evaluations, some basic principles can be introduced:

- *Building space for "objectives-free" evaluation.* By being objective-based, established evaluation systems can sometimes fall prey to pro-intervention and confirmation biases. Complexity-responsive evaluation systems must break free of the narrow focus on interventions' objectives. Goal-free evaluations have long been seen as necessary for uncovering programs' side effects and adapting to environmental changes (Scriven, 1991; Youker, Ingraham, & Bayer, 2014), but they remain rare.

- *Expanding evaluations' scope.* As highlighted in Chapter 7, complexity-responsive evaluations need to be holistic in their approach. In practice, this means that evaluations should be able to place particular programs into broader systems of intervention. Recently, some bilateral development organizations have started commissioning evaluative studies that are no longer tasked with assessing the role of a particular organization in a particular program, but with studying a type of intervention or a type of implementation mechanism. For example, Chapter 17 presents an example of such a study on coordination against trafficking in persons. Such broad-scope studies tend to trigger distinctive types of learning and accountability.

- *Expanding evaluations' time frame.* As mentioned above, intervention effects sometimes take a long time to materialize, and impact trajectory can vary a lot over time. Some space must be carved out for evaluations that track program effects for a long period of time.

- *Changing the process.* Overall, institutionalizing complexity-responsive evaluation systems within a larger results-based management agenda is a challenging enterprise. However, lessons can be drawn from past attempts to institutionalize new evaluation practices. For example, the Independent Evaluation Group (2009) found that there were three main alternative pathways for the institutionalization of impact evaluation (IE) systems within governments. It is conceivable that complexity-responsive evaluation might follow the same type of processes. Figure 13.3 illustrates the three main pathways: ad hoc, sector-led, whole of government.

An *ad hoc studies* pathway to complexity-responsive evaluation is exemplified by the case of the USAID complexity-aware M&E approach that is being piloted among a number of voluntary interventions that are shepherding a new set of methods (USAID, 2013).

A *whole of government* approach to complexity-responsive evaluation is illustrated by the case of DFID. The agency has started to move toward an evaluation function model privileging closeness and integration through an embedding evaluation approach (Independent Commission for Aid Impact, 2014). The vision driving this reform process was to place evaluation firmly in the program cycle and ultimately drive program design through rigorous evaluations. This process has been supported by a large recruitment, accreditation, and training of staff in evaluation to scale up the evaluative capacity in the organization. At the same time, this approach was made possible by having a separate independent evaluation function with an accountability focus in the Independent Commission on Aid Impact.

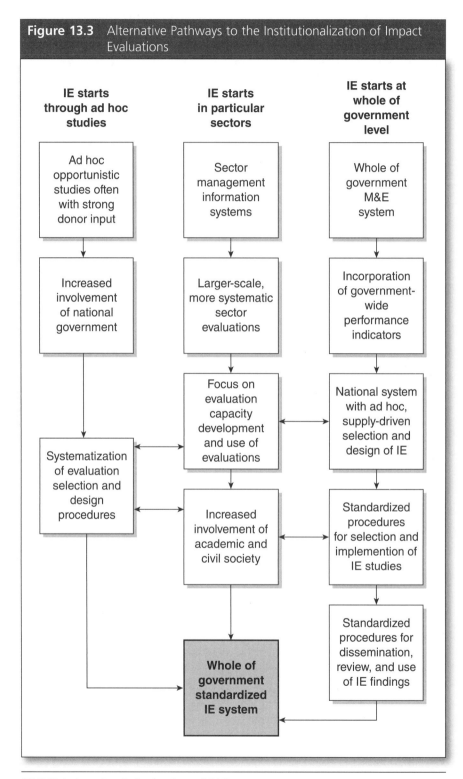

**Figure 13.3**  Alternative Pathways to the Institutionalization of Impact Evaluations

SOURCE: Independent Evaluation Group (2009).

# 5. Practical Applications

- The social and institutional structure of an intervention and its evaluation is one of the most challenging features of an evaluation. Having a good understanding of who the stakeholders are, what their stakes are, and how these stakes evolve during the evaluation process is an important part of a complexity-responsive evaluation.

- Evaluations are embedded within organizations; they are commissioned, implemented, and used by organizations that have their own complex change processes and intricate incentives systems. The level of complexity of an evaluation is often determined by this organizational context, especially if an intervention relies on the collaboration between different organizations, in different sectors, and with different mandates. Navigating these organizational environments is as important for the success of an evaluation as a sound evaluation design.

- Acknowledging that development processes are complex has implications for the way evaluations are used. Learning from evaluations requires accepting a process of trial and error with tight feedback loops into the intervention design and implementation.

- Given the high level of uncertainty attached to complex interventions and that increasingly ambitious programs are more likely to be undertaken through collaborative efforts, established accountability mechanisms must adapt. Building space for collective accountability, for expanding the time frame and the scope of evaluation studies, is a first step toward the long and arduous process of changing organizational and evaluation culture to become more complexity-responsive.

# References

Alkin, M., & Taut S. (2003). Unbundling evaluation use. *Studies in Educational Evaluation, 29*, 1–12.

Balthasar, A. (2006). The effects of institutional design on the utilization of evaluation: Evidenced using qualitative comparative analysis (QCA). *Evaluation 12,* 353–371.

Barnett, M., & Finnemore, M. (2004). *Rules for the world: International organizations in global politics.* Ithaca, NY: Cornell University Press.

Barrados, M., & Mayne, J. (2003). Can public sector organizations learn? *OECD Journal of Budgeting, 3,* 87–103.

Brandon, P. R., & Singh, J. M. (2009). The strength of the methodological warrants for the findings of research on program evaluation use. *American Journal of Evaluation, 30,* 123–157.

Carden, F. (2013). Evaluation, not development evaluation. *American Journal of Evaluation 34,* 576–579.

Chambers, R., Pacey, A., & Thrupp, L. A. (Eds.). (1989). *Farmer first: Farmer innovation and agricultural research.* Rugby, UK: Practical Action.

Clements, P., Chianca, T., & Sasaki, R. (2008). Reducing world poverty by improving evaluation of development aid. *American Journal of Evaluation, 29,* 195–214.

Cohen, D., March, J., & Olsen, J. (1972). A garbage can model of organizational choice. *Administrative Science Quarterly, 17,* 1–25.

Cousins, J. B., & Leithwood, K. A. (1986). Current empirical research on evaluation utilization. *Review of Educational Research, 56,* 331–364.

Dahler-Larsen, P. (2012). *The evaluation society.* Stanford, CA: Stanford University Press.

Datta, S., & Mullainathan, S. (2012). *Behavioral design: A new approach to development policy* (CGD Policy Paper 016). Washington, DC: Center for Global Development. Retrieved from http://www.cgdev.org/files/1426679_file_Datta_Mullainathan_Behavioral_Design.pdf

Gaarder, M., & Briceno, B. (2010). Institutionalisation of government evaluation: Balancing trade-offs. *Journal of Development Effectiveness, 2,* 289–309.

Hansen, M., & Vedung, E. (2010). Theory-based stakeholder evaluation. *American Journal of Evaluation, 31,* 295–313.

Henry, G. T., & Mark, M. M. (2003). Beyond use: Understanding evaluation's influence on attitudes and actions. *American Journal of Evaluation, 24,* 293–314.

Hojlund, S. (2014). Evaluation use in the organizational context: Changing focus to improve theory. *Evaluation, 20,* 26–43.

Independent Commission for Aid Impact. (2014). *How DFID learns* (Report 24). Retrieved from http://icai.independent.gov.uk/wp-content/uploads/2014/04/How-DFID-Learns-FINAL.pdf

Independent Evaluation Group. (2009). *Institutionalizing Impact evaluation within the framework of a monitoring and evaluation system.* Retrieved from http://ieg.worldbank.org/Data/reports/inst_ie_framework_me.pdf

Johnson, K., Geenseid, L. O., Toal, S. A., King, J. A., Lawrenz, F., & Volkov, B. (2009). Research on evaluation use: A review of the empirical literature from 1986 to 2005. *American Journal of Evaluation, 30,* 377–410.

Katz, D., & Kahn, R. (1978). *The social psychology of organizations* (2nd ed.). New York, NY: Wiley.

Khagram, S., & Thomas, C. (2010). Toward a platinum standard for evidence-based assessment by 2020. *Public Administration Review, 70,* S100–S106.

King, J., Cousins, B., & Whitmore, E. (2007). Making sense of participatory evaluation: Framing participatory evaluation. *New Directions for Evaluation, 114,* 83–105.

Kingdon, J. (1995). *Agendas, alternatives, and public policies.* New York, NY: HarperCollins.

Laubli Loud, M., & Mayne, J. (2013). *Enhancing evaluation use: Insights from internal evaluation units.* Thousand Oaks, CA: Sage.

Ledermann, S. (2012). Exploring the necessary conditions for evaluation use in program change. *American Journal of Evaluation, 33,* 159–178.

Leeuw, F., & Furubo, J. (2008). Evaluation system: What are they and why study them? *Evaluation, 14,* 157–169.

Leviton, L. C. (2003). Evaluation use: Advances, challenges and applications. *American Journal of Evaluation, 24,* 525–535.

Lipson, M. (2007). Peacekeeping: Organized hypocrisy? *European Journal of International Relations, 13*(1), 5–34.

Lipson, M. (2010). Performance under ambiguity: International organization performance in UN peacekeeping. *Review of International Organizations, 5,* 249–284.

Liverani, A., & Lundgren, H. (2007). Evaluation systems in development aid agencies: An analysis of DAC peer reviews 1996–2004. *Evaluation, 13,* 241–256.

Ludwig, J., Kling, J., & Mullainathan, S. (2011). *Mechanism experiments and policy evaluations* (NBER Working Paper Series No. 17062). Cambridge, MA: National Bureau of Economic Research.

Marra, M. (2004). The contribution of Evaluation to socialization and externalization of tacit knowledge: The case of the World Bank. *Evaluation, 10,* 263–283.

Mayne, J. (2008). *Building an evaluative culture for effective evaluation and results management* (ILAC Working Paper 8). Rome, Italy: Institutional Learning and Change Initiative.

Mayne, J. (2010). Building an evaluative culture: The key to effective evaluation and results management. *Canadian Journal of Program Evaluation, 24,* 1–30.

McNulty, J. (2012). Symbolic uses of evaluation in the international aid sector: Arguments for critical reflection. *Evidence & Policy, 8,* 495–509.

OECD-DAC. (2010). *Glossary of key terms in evaluation and results based management.* Paris, France: Author.

Patton, M. Q. (2008). *Utilization-focused evaluation* (4th ed.). Thousand Oaks, CA: Sage.

Patton, M. Q. (2011). *Developmental evaluation: Applying complexity concepts to enhance innovation and use.* New York, NY: Guilford Press.

Preskill, H., & Boyle, S. (2008). A multi-disciplinary model of evaluation capacity-building. *American Journal of Evaluation, 29,* 443–459.

Preskill, H., & Torres, R. (1999). Building Capacity for organizational learning through evaluative inquiry. *Evaluation, 5,* 42–60.

Pritchett, L. (2002). It pays to be ignorant: A simple political economy of rigorous program. *Journal of Policy Reform, 5,* 251–269.

Pritchett, L., Samji, S., & Hammer, J. (2013). *It's all about MeE: Using structured experiential learning ("e") to crawl the design space* (Working Paper 406). Washington, DC: Center for Global Development.

Pritchett, L., & Sandefur, J. (2013). *Context matters for size: Why external validity claims and development practice don't mix.* (Working Paper 336). Washington, DC: Center for Global Development.

Ravallion, M. (2008). *Evaluation in the practice of development* (Policy Research Working Paper 4547). Washington, DC: World Bank.

Scoones, I., & Thompson, J. (Eds.). (2009). *Farmer first revisited.* Rugby, UK: Practical Action.

Scriven, M. (1991). *Evaluation thesaurus* (4th ed.). Thousand Oaks, CA: Sage.

Torres, R., & Preskill, H. (2001). Evaluation and organizational learning: Past, present, and future. *American Journal of Evaluation, 22,* 387–395.

USAID. (2013). *Complexity-aware monitoring.* Retrieved from http://usaidlearninglab.org/library/complexity-aware-monitoring-discussion-note-brief

Weaver, C. (2008). *Hypocrisy trap: The World Bank and the poverty of reform.* Princeton, NJ: Princeton University Press.

Weiss, C. H. (1998). Have we learned anything new about the use of evaluation? *American Journal of Evaluation, 19,* 21–33.

Williams, B. (2015). Prosaic or profound? The adoption of systems ideas by impact evaluation. *IDS Bulletin, 46*(1), 7–16.

Youker, B. W., Ingraham, A., Bayer, N. (2014). An assessment of goal-free evaluation: Case studies of four goal-free evaluations. *Evaluation and Program Planning, 46,* 10–16.

# Notes

1. The chapter focuses on evaluation systems in bilateral and multilateral development organizations. See Chapter 18 for a review of evaluation complexity from the perspective of philanthropic organizations and Chapter 15 for an illustration of institutional evaluation dynamics within Oxfam America. NGOs tend to have a somewhat different approach to evaluation, including but not limited to more focus on rights-based approaches as a driving force. While most government agencies make some reference to right, it is rarely a driving force of their evaluation systems.

2. We recognize that there can be very different dynamics between evaluations that are carried out internally, those that are jointly carried out by internal and external evaluators, and those that are carried out entirely through a formal procurement process. While the interaction with stakeholders might change depending on the evaluation configuration, the type of stakeholders remains the same, and all complexity-responsive evaluations should pay careful attention to the dynamics at play among stakeholders.

3. The overreliance on expert knowledge has long been the object of criticism in the development literature, dating back to the pioneering work of Robert Chambers (Chambers, Pacey, & Thrupp, 1989; Scoones & Thompson, 2009).

# CHAPTER 14

# Gender Equality in Development Evaluation

## *The Intersection of Complexities*

Estelle Raimondo and Michael Bamberger

*Development programs that seek to transform gender norms, enhance equality between women and men, and end violence against women are inherently complex. Their evaluations thus need to make sense of this complexity in order to establish whether they contribute to intricate change processes. Moreover, all development projects are laden with gender dimensions, and complexity-responsive evaluations should also be gender-responsive. This chapter begins with a discussion of complexity from a gender equality perspective. It then lays out various methodological developments in gender-responsive evaluations. Section 3 discusses the institutional and operational challenges that such evaluations face and proposes avenues to overcome these challenges. We conclude with practical applications, some of which are illustrated in the following chapter, a rich case study presenting a complexity-responsive evaluation of an initiative to combat gender-based violence in El Salvador.*

The 2012 World Development Report, dedicated to gender and development, called for better evidence on what works to reduce gender inequalities. An area in which there is a knowledge gap that requires increased attention is determining whether there is a differentiated impact between incremental interventions (evolving within established gender norms) and transformative interventions (attempting to change gender norms). The second area is to determine whether a combination of interventions is more effective than individual programs in addressing particularly "sticky" or pervasive gender gaps (World Bank, 2012). This call for better gender-responsive evaluation is made against the backdrop of significant progress in women's rights, education, health, and livelihoods globally, but also of uneven improvements across countries, notably in areas such as gender-based violence, labor market inequalities, and limited control over resources in the household and community.

In this chapter we start by unpacking the various complexity dimensions inherent in development interventions seeking to enhance gender equality. We then examine the various ways in which development evaluation has attempted to make sense of these complexity dimensions. We provide a brief overview of some developments in gender-responsive evaluation frameworks. While these approaches are quite different from one another, they share a number of challenges and follow a number of common principles, which we review in the fourth section. We conclude with practical applications. In the next chapter, a case study on the evaluation of a long-term effort to reduce gender-based violence in El Salvador illustrates some of these challenges and how they can be addressed.

# 1. Inherent Complexities in Gender Equality and Women's Empowerment Strategies

While the past four decades of development work in the area of gender equality[1] have yielded important successes—notably in terms of enhancing girls' enrollment in primary education, improving child and maternal health, and, to a lesser extent, increasing women's participation in the labor force—deeply rooted gender inequities persist despite many policies and development programs targeting them. Evaluation has an important role to play in identifying some of the impediments to equal opportunity between men and women, girls and boys in various aspects of the social, political, and economic lives of people living in both developing and developed countries. Additionally, evaluation is useful in determining what combinations of interventions are successful at triggering a shift in power relationships and what is working to reduce inequality.

The task of the evaluator starts with making sense of a complex social reality laden with gender roles constructed over centuries. These roles interact with many other identity traits and coalesce to create inequity and marginalization. Unearthing these ingrained social structures and challenging prevailing norms and values are not parts of the development evaluator's typical role. However, it should be part and parcel of an approach that seeks to deal with the complexity inherent in gender equality interventions.

While complexity theory can be a valuable tool in making sense of this complex social reality, some evaluation theorists, including feminist evaluators, have highlighted the need to be wary of simply introducing functional abstractions, such as "system," "levels," and "nested models." These concepts might result in covering up, rather than revealing, the complexity of human interrelationships and how development interventions play out in these relationships. In this alternative approach to complexity, one of the key objectives is to map out configurations of power relations expressed in the dynamic relationship of inclusion, exclusion, identity formation, choices that reveal ideology, and the socialization of norms (Mowles, 2014, p. 170).

In this chapter, we thus depart from a complexity science point of view and instead propose an articulation of complexity relations to gender inequality that is more in line with the spirit of feminist theory. That said, we are cognizant that, applied on their own, some feminist approaches may not be able to address other complexity dimensions, particularly when dealing with large, multi-component, multi-level evaluation exercises. We thus propose avenues to integrate a feminist lens into more conventional, possibly quantitative, evaluation frameworks. We begin by highlighting a number of characteristics of gender equality and women's empowerment and strategies that make them complex and difficult to evaluate.

## 1.1 Dealing With the Complexity of Gender Norms

A first dimension that needs to be addressed is the complex nature of the environment in which gender norms and behaviors are formed, enforced, and in which they evolve. All societies have rules governing appropriate forms of behavior for women and men within the household, the tribe, caste, or ethnic group. Economic, religious, political, and cultural organizations also have their own norms governing "correct" behavior for both women and men. Many of these rules are enforced in subtle ways that are difficult to observe. Social networks are also affected by the economic, political, legal, administrative, and physical environments in which they operate, and that can influence the gender equality outcomes of development interventions.

Development interventions that seek to challenge and transform gendered power relations confront a particularly complex challenge. Several decades of research and evaluation of gender interventions has revealed that the transformation of gender roles and women's empowerment requires the realization of economic, political, and social rights that are interlocked. Women and men experience these rights differently in the household or in their community and extended networks. These rights are also mediated by other social characteristics, such as their race, class, and religion (Bishop & Bowman, 2014). Contrary to the prevailing ideas in the 1970s and 1980s, "third-world women" are not a homogenous group, but in fact have very different lived experiences. Evaluations should thus draw on work that examines overlapping social cleavages affecting people's experience with a particular intervention. In some contexts, gender can be the primary factor through which women experience the program. In other contexts, caste, class, or religious identity might be the primary lens. Consequently, evaluations should be based on the understanding that inequality results from complex social processes caused by a range of factors, including but not limited to gender discrimination; ethnic, linguistic, or religious discrimination; structural poverty; natural or human-made disasters; geographic isolation; cultural and social norms; and weak governance (Bamberger & Segone, 2011, p. 4).

Evaluating these interventions requires establishing whether development policies or programs are well attuned to the societal, political, and institutional systems of the countries they seek to affect, given that interventions targeting gender-based inequalities are bound to rub against ingrained societal rules, norms, and beliefs regarding traditional gender roles, including the gendered division of labor, appropriate public behaviors, and participation in various realms of the societal life. Consequently, multiple layers of resistance and push-back will need to be overcome. Managing this resistance and involving men as advocates for women's rights has proven to be a key element of success (World Bank, 2012).

## 1.2 Complex Processes of Change

As stressed in Chapter 1 and studied in depth in Chapter 4, adopting a complexity lens leads the evaluator to challenge the idea of direct and proportional change. The lessons learned from the past decades of development work on gender equality and women's empowerment certainly corroborate the idea that change can at times be achieved through steady small steps, or through large punctuations in a more revolutionary manner, but that it is certainly not immune to reversal. Exogenous changes or shocks can present decision makers with unexpected opportunities to modify the systems of rules and norms underlying gender roles and ultimately improve gender outcomes. Such shocks to a particular gender equilibrium can come from an event that catches the public eye and starts a popular movement, such as the gang rape in Delhi in 2012 that prompted protests in many cities, indignation in the media, and legislative changes. Other shocks can come from climate disasters, such as Hurricane Fifi in Nicaragua in the mid-1970s, because of women's involvement in community preparedness activities. After the disaster, particularly the resulting floods, it was recognized that the community emergency preparedness committees only involved men. At the time of the disaster, no one took responsibility for the rescue of the elderly, people with physical handicaps, or even children. After the hurricane, it was decided that women should also be elected in each community. They were given formal police identification for the first time and paperwork making their role in the community official.

However, as shown by Williamson (1998) and the new economics of institutions more broadly, deeply rooted norms and beliefs, such as gender norms, may take multiple generations to change. Evaluations, which usually take place shortly after the completion of an intervention, are unlikely to capture the full extent of the change process.

The complexity science concept of "path dependency" is particularly useful here to show that incremental reforms in a given gender role system might not be sufficient to overcome institutional rigidities and persistent gender inequalities (Batliwala, 2011, p. 7; World Bank, 2012).

Moreover, change in gender norms stemming from development interventions can sometimes have ambiguous effects concurrently, including enabling, exacerbating, and unintended (often but not always) negative effects. The logic of many widely used evaluation designs makes it difficult to capture these unintended outcomes,[2] particularly when they are the result of multiple causes. Let us take a few examples. The review of microcredit interventions on women's control over household spending, presented in Chapter 16, found evidence that sometimes microcredit enabled women to strengthen their position in decision making in the households, but also found evidence of the opposite. In some programs, microcredit became an element of male domination over women in poor households, exacerbating the power asymmetry between husband and wife. The complexity perspective offers here a particularly useful lens to understand processes of change in gender equality and how multiple factors need to come together in a variety of domains of social life for change to really take place. For instance, economic growth and technological progress can coalesce to reinforce gender inequalities if changes in social norms do not interlock with the two other factors. The continued prejudice against unborn girls in many parts of Asia is a case in point. Because the preference for sons is still unchanged, the use and abuse of new technologies has enabled sex-selective abortions to take place on a wider scale through cheaper techniques like mobile ultrasounds clinics. These practices are responsible for more than a million missing girls in China and India in recent years (World Bank, 2012, p. 78). The challenge for complexity- and gender-responsive evaluation is to identify and make sense of these intricate change processes.

# 2. Main Developments in Gender-Responsive Evaluation Approaches: A Steady Move Toward Embracing Complexity

The practice of gender-responsive evaluation varies dramatically. To a large extent, evaluation practice has paralleled the evolution of gender interventions—initially conceived exclusively in terms of women-centered empowerment and steadily moving toward integrating various dimensions of gender equality and more broadly other dimensions of social equity. Nowadays, many approaches imbued with various traditions coexist. In this section we review key developments in gender-responsive evaluations.

## 2.1 Progress in Gender-Responsive Indicator Frameworks

In the current results-based management paradigm, the saying goes that "only what gets measured gets done." Consequently, over the past decade much effort has been placed in developing gender analysis tools and enriching indicator frameworks that are able to capture the gender dimensions of development interventions. The gender analysis approach is the most commonly used in multilateral and bilateral development agencies, notably those that are not particularly active in the field of gender equality or that are operating under severe resource constraints but have the mandated requirements to look at gender equality issues in their domain of interventions. Early tools such as the Harvard Analytical Framework and the Moser Gender Planning Framework introduced a now commonly used typology for analyzing women's various roles as *productive, reproductive,* and *community.* These evaluation tools have been particularly instrumental in opening the black box of the household that was previously understood as a homogenous unit (Moser, 2007). In general, a gender-responsive indicator measures gender-related changes in a given community or in society—where possible, over time. Two main types of indicators are covered under the umbrella term *gender-responsive*. First, there are sex-disaggregated indicators that provide separate measurement for women and men, boys and girls on a given indicator, such as mortality rate. Second, they may also refer to gender-specific indicators, where change is measured specifically for men or for women, for instance, on male circumcision or women's health programs. Indicators can encompass numbers, factual events, opinions, or perceptions (Moser, 2007). Moreover, no single indicator can capture complex processes such as women's empowerment. Effective measurement strategies instead rely on a combination of multilevel and multidimensional indicators (Moser, 2007).

Two sets of indicators have started to be widely used in the development community: the UNDP composite Gender-related Development Index and the Gender Empowerment Measure. Interestingly, these and other indicator frameworks incorporate both quantitative and qualitative measurement strategies. Large NGOs and foundations have also contributed to developing rich indicator frameworks. For instance, Oxfam GB has built an index of women's empowerment (displayed in Table 14.1) that leaves space for the development of context-relevant gender-responsive indicators (Bishop & Bowman, 2014).

As mentioned in Chapter 7, many agencies resort to indicator frameworks, such as the OECD-DAC criteria, to assess the worth of their intervention portfolio. Nevertheless, until relatively recently, most of the standard rating scales did not shed much light on the gender dimensions of development. Some evaluators have therefore worked to reinterpret generic scales through a gender lens. Box 14.1 provides Espinosa's (2013) reinterpretation of the OECD-DAC main evaluation criteria.

---

### BOX 14.1 REINTERPRETATION OF THE OECD-DAC EVALUATION CRITERIA

- **Effectiveness:** A measure of the extent to which the intervention achieved its objectives, particularly in terms of the benefits achieved by women and men and without reference to the costs incurred to obtain them.
- **Efficiency:** Analysis of the degree to which gender equality results are achieved at a reasonable cost, whether the benefits have an equivalent cost for women and men, and whether these are allocated equitably.
- **Relevance:** A measure of the extent to which the intervention objectives are adjusted to attend to the different problems and needs of women and men. This criterion also focuses on whether the methodology adopted by the intervention helps women to perceive the limitations imposed on them and to overcome them.
- **Impact:** The contribution of the intervention to a broader policy on gender equality, to the sectorial objectives of equality, and to the advancement toward equality on a long-term basis.
- **Sustainability:** The proportion of the achievements in gender equality that are maintained after the funding period. This is linked to the inclusion of strategic gender needs in the intervention and the ownership of it by women and men.

SOURCE: Espinosa (2013, p. 176).

| Table 14.1 | Dimensions Captured in Oxfam GB Women's Empowerment Index |
|---|---|
| **Dimension** | **Characteristics** |
| Ability to make decisions and influence | Involvement in household investment decisions |
| | Involvement in livelihood management decisions |
| | Involvement in income-spending decisions |
| | Involvement in general decisions |
| | Degree of influence in community decision making |
| Self-perception | Opinions on women's property rights |
| | Opinions on women's political rights |
| | Opinions on women's educational equality |
| | Opinions on women's economic and political roles |
| | Opinions on early marriage |
| | Self-confidence |
| | Psycho-social well-being |
| Personal freedom | Literacy |
| | Autonomy in work |
| | Time to pursue personal goals |
| | Support from family in pursuing personal goals |
| | Attitude toward violence against women |
| | Experience of violence |
| Access to and control over resources | Ownership of land and property |
| | Ownership of other productive assets |
| | Independent income |
| | Extent of role in managing/keeping family's cash |
| | Savings |
| | Access to credit |
| Support from social networks | Degree of social connectivity |
| | Participation in community groups |
| | Level of support provided by groups to pursue own initiatives |

SOURCE: Bishop & Bowman (2014).

There are several advantages to introducing a gender analytic framework. First, in many agencies there is concern about increasing the burden of data collection when switching to a sex-disaggregated approach. Therefore, starting with a simple indicator framework can provide a convincing quick win. The introduction of gender indicator frameworks can also be particularly instrumental in turning traditionally gender-blind sectors into recognizing the gender dimensions of their work. For instance, in the 1990s when the World Bank Group launched its gender and transportation program, it was often argued that sectors such as transport or energy were "gender neutral," insofar as in theory everyone would benefit equally from improved transport or energy. The initiative provided small grants to transport sector staff to incorporate gender analysis into the planning or evaluation of their projects. It was successful in demonstrating both the different transport needs of women and men and the many negative consequences for women when they were not involved in the planning of transport projects (e.g., increased women victims of road accidents on previously very slow rural roads, high levels of sexual harassment on public transport, greater risk of sexual assault at night as women's latrines had to be moved farther from the village as the new roads reduced privacy).

## 2.2 Mainstreaming Gender Into the Evaluation Process

The gender and development approach emerged in the 1980s and was institutionalized after the Beijing Fourth World Conference on Gender and Development in 1995 and the resulting Beijing Platform for Action. It introduces a decidedly more structural lens on inequalities between women and men and examines the social construction of gender and gender-specific roles. Moreover, it takes as a starting point the idea that any development intervention has a differential effect on men and women (Espinosa, 2013). The platform thus emphasizes the need to mainstream a gender perspective in all development projects and along the entire programming cycle, from conception to evaluation. Bringing gender into the mainstream relies on the idea that gender inequalities are persistent because they are often invisible and not systematically challenged in development processes. Mainstreaming also means changing the established culture of an organization so that "business as usual" is transformed to incorporate new ideas and new concepts. It can trigger conflicts and resistance to change, often resulting in long periods of dissonance between the official discourse and the reality of practice. While gender mainstreaming has contributed to increasing the demand for gender-responsive evaluation, it has also constituted a particular challenge for the evaluation community and epitomizes the complexity of a process that requires a real transformation of the conventional ways that evaluations look at programs. The evaluators first need to focus on the gender dimensions of manifest inequality by looking, among other things at the unequal access to and control over resources and services between men and women, the degree to which women have control over their bodies, and practical and strategic gender needs (Bamberger & Podems, 2002; Espinosa, 2013; Moser, 2007).

Some of the most common conclusions drawn from evaluation reports of gender equality mainstreaming strategies has been the lack of monitoring and evaluation, the weakness of systems tasked with tracking progress achieved, and the lack of high-level organizational commitment (African Development Bank, 2011). The gender dimension has often been the victim of "policy evaporation" whereby it is included in program design—often to satisfy bureaucratic requirements—and gets dropped during implementation and monitoring due to competing priorities or misaligned incentives. To remedy these trends, the UN system has put in place a number of mechanisms to improve implementation of the UN-System-Wide Action Plan on Gender Equality and the Empowerment of Women (UN-SWAP). One particular mechanism is the inclusion of an evaluation performance indicator. Each agency is supposed to self-assess and report on the extent to which its evaluations are gender-responsive (UNEG, 2014).

## 2.3 Developments in Feminist Evaluation

In recent years, feminist evaluation has become more prominent in evaluation practice. It is an umbrella term that covers a range of practices; nonetheless these practices share some quintessential characteristics that distinguish them from other gender-responsive evaluation approaches (Bamberger & Podems, 2002; Brisarola, Seigart, & SenGupta, 2014; Hesse-Biber & Leavy, 2007; Podems, 2010).

First, evaluations that are deemed gender-responsive without being feminist tend to limit themselves by recording and mapping of the existing inequalities and oppressive relationships at play without attempting to address them (Moser, 1989; Podems, 2010). Conversely, feminist evaluators do not content themselves with assessing the state of gender equality before and after an intervention; they also critically tackle the necessary deep changes and structural factors that are necessary for enhancing gender equality. They tend to promote a transformative and critical analysis of the intervention (Espinosa, 2013) Miller & Haylock, 2014).

Another important marker of feminist evaluation is its self-reflexivity and the necessity for the evaluators themselves to make explicit their particular standpoint. It involves a type of questioning of "what it means to do research, to question authority, to examine gender issues, to examine the lives of women, and to promote social change" (Seigart, 2005, pp. 154–155). Consequently, while in theory feminist evaluation does not prescribe a particular method or framework, in practice the application of the feminist lens and the requirement of reflexivity have been mostly applied through qualitative modes of inquiry. For instance, ethnomethodologies have gained increased traction among evaluators of gender interventions.

Third, in many ways feminist evaluation complicates the evaluator's role by discarding the idea of an independent, neutral, and unengaged observer. Instead, feminist evaluators act as facilitators or even activists for women's rights and gender equality. Feminist frameworks push the evaluator to be creative in designing and using approaches and methods that seek to empower women and girls themselves through their participation in the evaluation process. For instance, the use of participatory evaluation processes often include co-design elements to foster a sense of ownership by the implementing organizations and the beneficiary communities. Co-creation often goes hand in hand with a capacity-building element to strengthen the participants' skills in evaluative inquiry. A particularly useful tool is thus self-assessment techniques. In such processes, what counts as valid evidence is different from established evaluation approaches, as these processes put a high premium on truthfully representing the stakeholder's own point of view and lived experience of the development intervention.

However, evaluating in such an empowering way is a particularly difficult task and is beset by institutional, practical, and ethical challenges (Fetterman & Wandersman, 2002). Moreover, given the strong focus on qualitative methods, there are often issues concerning the ability of feminist approaches to generalize from the findings of in-depth studies. This has implications for the ability of feminist evaluation to contribute to policy issues that often focus on the national level. In the next section we present a number of attempts to integrate the important contribution of feminist theory into the design of evaluations that use a more conventional and often mixed methods framework.

## 2.4 Engendering Evaluation: Using an Integrative Mixed Methods Approach

While feminist approaches propose very powerful research frameworks, when used on their own they have some important limitations, especially in the context of the evaluation of large-scale complex programs. It is thus important to take the significant contributions of feminism and to integrate them into a more mixed methods strategy that permits the incorporation of more quantitative approaches and possibly the use, where appropriate, of experimental and quasi-experimental design (Oakley, 1998). In this section we present two frameworks that have attempted to leverage feminist thoughts into more traditional evaluation strategies: feminist empiricism and equity-focused evaluation.

### a. Feminist Empiricism

This particular strand of feminist theory is premised on the idea that the only source of knowledge humans can access is that which we experience (and measure through our senses; Brisarola et al., 2014). In practice, this approach recommends the use of quantitative survey methods to generate accountability for the increased participation of women in development processes (Espinosa, 2013). Over the past few years, experimental designs such as randomized controlled trials, have been used to evaluate gender-related outcomes of development initiatives, although in many cases the researchers did not claim to be using feminist methodologies.[3]

A number of impact evaluations have notably been conducted to measure the impact of women's political participation in local governance systems. For instance, Duflo and Topalova (2003) examined the impact of the presence of women in Indian village councils on the provision of local public goods. Since the 73rd amendment to the Indian constitution, one-third of the seats on all such councils are randomly selected each term to be reserved for women. Taking advantage of this randomization, the researchers compared the quantity and quality of public goods in two sets of villages. In the same vein, and as further discussed in Chapter 16, an array of impact evaluations has taken place to measure the effect of participating in microfinance schemes on women's empowerment (defined by a range of indicators). The evidence from these multiple impact studies has then been systematized and aggregated in several systematic reviews (e.g., Stewart et al., 2012; Vaessen et al., 2014).

A lively debate is currently taking place in the field about whether RCTs can be gender-responsive.[4] While many of the critiques of RCTs from a feminist point of view are valid, there is also a common misconception that feminism and empiricism are incompatible (Hesse-Biber & Leavy, 2007). In fact, important research has combined the tenets of both. This combination has contributed to a number of advancements in the cause for gender equality, such as "counting women in," with the view of documenting ignored and obscured truths such as sexual harassment and watching for stereotypes. We argue that a strong focus on empiricism, often as part of a mixed methods approach, is a key element in strengthening the feminist contribution to the evaluation of large and complex development interventions that require the combination of rigorous quantitative methods with in-depth qualitative research.

### b. Equity-Focused Evaluation

As mentioned earlier, one of the most precious lessons that feminist theory has to teach to development evaluators is that gender inequality is intrinsically linked to other forms of inequality and that inequality experienced by women differs depending on their class, cultural background, race and ethnicity, and sexual orientation. It is this intersectionality that compounds the complexity of capturing and addressing inequity (Bustelo, 2011; Espinosa, 2013). An equity focus is inevitably more complex as it requires analysis of a range of political, economic, historical, organizational and cultural factors that permit and perpetuate the basis of exclusion of certain groups from access to services. Creative approaches are required to collect data that are often not easily available on the extent of exclusion or inequity, often with political or social pressures not to recognize these issues and consequently not to document them. Social exclusion also involves subtle behavioral processes that are difficult to observe (e.g., how service center staff treat people of high and low status).

The equity-focused evaluation approach builds on this notion and is particularly concerned with the evaluation of programs whose goal is to achieve equitable development results and pay particular attention to the situation of the worst-off groups. An important step in such evaluation is analysis of the gaps that exist between best-off, average, and worst-off groups (Bamberger & Segone, 2011). Instead of predefining the category of beneficiaries that will warrant particular attention prior to the evaluation (e.g., women), this approach is contextual insofar as it identifies the groups who warrant particular attention, those who are particularly difficult to reach and socially marginalized. The worst-off group can be at the intersection of various identity characteristics (e.g., gender, race, religion, class).

One useful model for assessing gender differences in access to services is the Bottleneck Analysis Framework developed by UNICEF (Bamberger & Segone, 2011, pp. 45–50) to identify factors affecting the accessibility of vulnerable populations to program services (see Figure 14.1). Use of services by vulnerable groups is defined in terms of adequacy of utilization, quantitative indicators of use, sustainability of service delivery, and cost-effectiveness of the services (Figure 14.1, box 1). Use is affected by four sets of factors: supply-side factors (box 2), demand-side factors (box 3), how services are delivered (box 4), and contextual factors (box 5).

All of these indicators can be adapted to assess differences in how each of these factors or indicators affect women and men. For example, many factors affect how

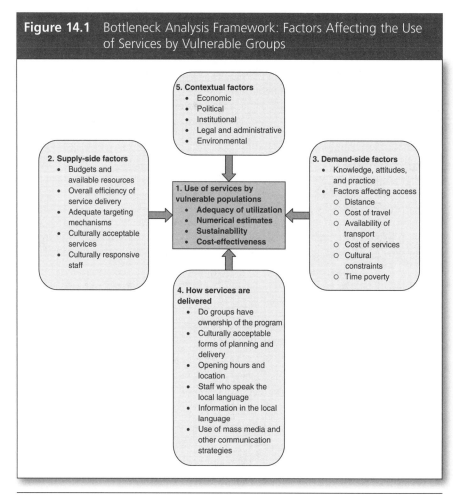

**Figure 14.1** Bottleneck Analysis Framework: Factors Affecting the Use of Services by Vulnerable Groups

SOURCE: Adapted from Bamberger & Segone (2011, p. 48). The published version does not include box 4.

service delivery affects accessibility for women. Are there female staff? Will women feel safe and comfortable in the service center? Will poor women who speak only the local language be treated with respect? Again with respect to demand-side factors, women may face special barriers to access. For instance, it may not be socially acceptable for women to travel to the center (or to do so without a male companion), their husbands may not give them the bus fare, the opening hours may not be convenient, or transport may not be available.

In line with feminist evaluation thought, the equity-focused approach seeks to be transformative by using the evidence gathered during the evaluative exercise to advocate in favor of these evidence-based equity-focused interventions, with the overarching objective to empower the worst-off groups. In the same vein as feminist evaluation, equity-focused evaluation seeks to be culturally sensitive and ethical and to opt for processes of evaluation that "serve to correct, not reinforce, patterns of inequity and exclusion" (Bamberger & Segone, 2011, p. 13).

# 3. Key Challenges

While gender-responsive evaluations can take many forms and span a large array of practices, they share a core set of common challenges. In this section we review both methodological as well as institutional and operational challenges.

## 3.1 Methodological Challenges

- There are many constraints on women's ability to speak freely, making it difficult to capture their perspectives and even to obtain factual information on their situation. Many women also feel constrained to publicly conform to the accepted roles for women[5] and to express agreement with their spouse.
- Gender equality and women's empowerment involves multiple changes at different levels (e.g., family, community, political system, religious organizations, labor market). Women are affected by different combinations of these factors, and both the individual changes and the interactions among levels are difficult to monitor and assess.
- The processes of change, in addition to involving multiple factors, are often nonlinear and nonproportional, and similar outcomes can be produced by different combinations of independent and intervening variables.
- Many of the important changes in the status of women occur over long periods of time (sometimes decades or longer), so they are difficult to observe in the framework of an evaluation that seeks to feed into short-term policymaking processes. Finally, the complexity of gender change means that interventions often produce unintended outcomes (often but not always negative). The logic of many widely used evaluation designs makes it difficult to capture these unintended outcomes, particularly when they are the result of multiple causes.

## 3.2 Institutional and Operational Challenges

### a. Evaporation

While an increasing number of development evaluations attempt to attend to gender issues, the commitment to take gender into account often evaporates during the evaluation process. What is commonly found is that evaluators provide a number of outcome or activity measures in a gender-disaggregated form and leave it at that. Alternatively, some evaluators make a genuine attempt at describing the gender-differentiated effect of an intervention and hint at a number of structural factors, but do not attempt to turn the evaluative exercise into an empowering and transformative experience for the various stakeholders taking part in the process, most notably the beneficiaries.

### b. Lack of Data

Despite the progress made in crafting gender-responsive indicator frameworks, data on this issue remain scarce, which hinders the evaluation process. Consequently, many evaluations tend to focus on women rather than gender and are concentrated on policy domains, such as health and education, where data are more readily available. Many kinds of data on interactions between women and men or measures of behavioral change are inherently difficult to capture. Also, as discussed earlier, agencies may not wish to recognize or document indicators of exclusion or inequitable treatment of certain groups, including some categories of women.

### c. Weak Monitoring Systems

Even in agencies that have a specific gender action plan with dedicated targets and objectives, the weak link lies in the absence of systematic monitoring of progress made. Oftentimes, project or program performance reports that track implementation have no specific section for gender-specific indicators. Progress on gender results is often missing from midterm assessments and still too often sidelined in evaluations. Many evaluations conclude that progress toward achieving gender-specific targets is often not monitored, which leads to the invisibility of gender results and ultimately contributes to lack of interest and awareness (African Development Bank, 2012).

### d. Lack of Integration With Results-Based Management

A related issue identified in evaluations dedicated to assessing gender mainstreaming strategies is that the gender action plan is a parallel document that is not well integrated with other result-based management requirements and is de facto sidelined. This lack of integration is partly responsible for the phenomenon of the "missing middle" (Watkins, 2004, p. 22), a term coined to describe the gap between, on the one hand, changes at the organizational level following the implementation of a gender mainstreaming strategy and, on the other, impacts at the beneficiary level, especially in the lives of women and girls. There are also inherent tensions between the organizational and institutional requirements of aggregating results at the national, regional, or even global level, for reporting use, and the inherent characteristic of gender interventions whose effects are so context-specific. There is also the perception that results-based management's overreliance on short-term and quantifiable indicators significantly hinders the understanding of deeper change processes involving beliefs systems, attitudes, and norms (see chapter 13 for more details on this). Thus striking a good balance between "upward" accountability to donors and agencies and "downward" or "social" accountability to partners in the field and program beneficiaries is a real challenge (Miller & Haylock, 2014).

### e. Lack of Feedback Loops

Weaknesses in monitoring and evaluation systems are particularly detrimental at a time of budget constraints when only programs that can demonstrate results are placed on the policy agenda of donors and governments. Moreover, if results are not fed back into institutional learning processes, the constitution of an evidence base of what works or not is only piecemeal. This is particularly the case for results of policy. Indeed, when results are reported, they remain at the level of the project or program at best and are rarely aggregated at a higher level to allow for a coherent assessment of whether the gender objectives have been attained at the level of the organization. Additionally, while most progress in mainstreaming gender and developing women's empowerment strategy have taken place within conventional project-based modalities, gender is typically absent from newer aid modalities, such as sector-wide approaches or general budget support policy.

### f. Lack of Incentives

There are certainly restrictions in terms of the extent to which institutions want to commission gender-responsive and feminist evaluations. Just as with other transformative evaluation exercises in which empowerment of the target group is a goal, evaluation effectively becomes another intervention, which requires time, staff, and resources. Additionally, some agencies do not wish to recognize inequalities, particularly the related issue of social exclusion. Policymakers often have no desire or incentives to include socially excluded populations. These populations' status is thus not covered in monitoring systems, and there is often resistance to address them in evaluations. Consequently, many governments report only on indicators such as the Human Development Index, which provides an average, and do not wish to examine, for example, widening gaps between the vulnerable and destitute (10%–20% of the population) and the rest.

### g. Broad-Based Strategies

Organizations promoting gender equality may have to adopt a broad-based program strategy to address multiple factors that can promote or inhibit the process of change. Often, in order to address critical contextual factors, an organization may build alliances with other agencies with expertise in areas such as law, political advocacy, finance, or mass media. Consequently, the evaluation may also have to include an organizational assessment of the efficacy of the alliances, how relations with partners are managed, and how alliances affect the objectives of the original program.

# 4. Operational Implications

A gender focus is undoubtedly critical in development evaluation. Given the complexity of addressing gender equality in the evaluation process, it is possible to introduce gender in stages, starting with relatively simple approaches. For instance, a first step could be to introduce sex-specific and sex-disaggregated data that are easy to collect and analyze. A second step would be to focus on "quick wins" such as revealing inequalities between men and women in areas that were perennially considered as gender-neutral. The third step would be to build on these quick wins in order to dig deeper. It would be made easier once the organization comes to recognize the benefits and the case for dedicating resources to gender-responsive evaluation and monitoring.

Chapter 15 presents a rich case study of how some of these principles have been practically applied to the evaluation of gender-based violence prevention. Here we recapitulate some simple ways in which a gender lens can be applied to development evaluation to enhance gender equality and women's empowerment.

## 4.1 Stage 1: Evaluation Questions

- Whose perspective will be captured when answering the evaluation questions?
- Is the design of the intervention in line with what women and men want?
- Are the assumptions that underline the program design and the causal mechanisms that need to be activated for the intervention to reach its intended objective gender-responsive or gender-biased?
- Who is privileged by the design of the intervention?

## 4.2 Stage 2: Evaluation Design

The design of an evaluation can become an important negotiating space to articulate whose vision of success will be reflected in the evaluation.

- How do evaluation design choices influence use?
- What design option will help the evaluator be a transformative agent?
- Who is defining success, and how it is measured?

## 4.3 Stage 3: Practice

- How do the evaluator's background and experiences influence her or his standpoint?
- Is the practice reflexive?
- What criteria are being used to assess the quality of the evidence? Is the conceptualization of rigor used in the evaluation gender-responsive or gender-biased?

## 4.4 Stage 4: Dissemination

- How can the evaluator get traction to present findings that challenge dominant policies and practices?

The United Nations Evaluation Group (UNEG; 2011) has developed a handbook to mainstream concomitantly gender equality and human rights into evaluation. Step by step, the handbook describes how gender equality can be integrated into the evaluation process, from the evaluability stage to the dissemination of findings and recommendations. Table 14.2 reproduces a useful checklist featured in the handbook.

| Table 14.2 | Checklist for Integrating Human Rights and Gender Equality Dimensions Into Evaluation |
|---|---|
| Evaluability assessment | • Was an assessment to determine the evaluability level of human rights and gender equality (HR&GE) intervention performed? |
| Stakeholder analysis | • Was a diverse group of stakeholders identified from the stakeholder analysis, including women and men as well as those who are most affected by rights violations and groups who are not directly involved in the intervention? |
| Criteria | • Were evaluation criteria defined that specifically address HR&GE?<br>• Were additional criteria identified that are specific to the context of the intervention to be evaluated? |
| Questions | • Were evaluation questions that specifically address HR&GE framed? |
| Indicators | • Are there indicators with available disaggregated data?<br>• Were additional specific indicators identified?<br>• Were plans made for how to collect data to inform the additional indicators? |
| Team | • Was an evaluation team with knowledge of and commitment to HR&GE selected?<br>• Is the evaluation team diverse in terms of gender, types of expertise, age, geographical origin, and so on?<br>• Is the team ethically responsible and balanced with equitable power relations? |
| Methodology | • Does the evaluation methodology employ a mixed methods approach appropriate to addressing HR&GE?<br>• Does the methodology favor stakeholders' rights to participation, including the most vulnerable?<br>• Does the evaluation methodology favor triangulation of the information obtained? |
| Data collection and analysis | • Were the various stakeholder groups identified earlier consulted during and after the evaluation to hear their views on the findings and recommendations? |
| Reporting | • Does the report address HR&GE, including in the recommendations?<br>• How will the recommendations affect the various stakeholder groups?<br>• Was the program management response that considers HR&GE issues raised in the report? |

SOURCE: Adapted from UNEG (2011).

# 5. Practical Applications

- Almost all development interventions can have different outcomes for women and men, and consequently almost all development evaluations should be gender-responsive as a standard component. As development programs become larger and more complex, there is a parallel increase in the complexities of understanding gender dynamics. In this chapter we reviewed a range of gender-responsive approaches that can address gender complexity. Many of these are well documented, and a number of organizations have developed easy-to-use gender analysis toolkits.[6]
- One practical strategy is to identify quick wins, whereby findings are presented that are easy to collect but that have immediate practical, operational use.
- While gender analysis and feminist evaluation can, like any other evaluation methodologies, become technically complicated, much of the basic data on differences in project effects on women and men can be incorporated into conventional monitoring and evaluation systems.
- Mixed methods approaches, combining quantitative and qualitative methods, represent a key element of most gender-responsive approaches.[7]

# References

African Development Bank. (2012). *Mainstreaming gender equality: A road to results or a road to nowhere?* Tunis, Tunisia: Author. Retrieved from http://www.afdb.org/fileadmin/uploads/afdb/Documents/Evaluation-Reports-_Shared-With-OPEV_/Evaluation_Mainstreaming%20Gender%20Equality_Synthesis%20Report_www.pdf

Bamberger, M., & Podems, D. (2002). Feminist evaluation in the international development context. *New Directions for Evaluation, 96,* 83–96.

Bamberger, M., & Segone, M. (2011). *How to design and manage equity-focused evaluations.* New York, NY: UNICEF. Retrieved from http://mymande.org/sites/default/files/EWP5_Equity_focused_evaluations.pdf

Batliwala, S. (2011). *Strengthening M&E for women's rights: Thirteen insights for women's organizations.* Toronto, Ontario, Canada: Association for Women's Rights in Development: Retrieved from http://www.awid.org/sites/default/files/atoms/files/strengthening_monitoring_nad_evaluation_-_thirteen_insights.pdf

Bishop, D., & Bowman, K. (2014). Still learning: A critical reflection on three years of measuring women's empowerment in Oxfam. *Gender & Development, 22,* 253–269.

Brisarola, S., Seigart, D., & SenGupta, S. (2014). *Feminist evaluation and research: Theory and practice.* New York, NY: Guilford Press.

Bustelo, M. (2011). Presidential editorial. *Evaluation, 20,* 3–4.

Dodd, S. (2009). LGBTQ: *Protecting vulnerable subjects in all studies.* In D. M. Mertens & P.E. Ginsberg (Eds.), The handbook of social research ethics (pp 474–488). Thousand Oaks, CA: Sage.

Duflo, E., & Topalova, P. (2003). *Unappreciated service: Performance, perceptions, and women leaders in India.* Cambridge MA: Poverty Action Lab. Retrieved from http://www.poverty

actionlab.org/publication/unappreciated-service-performance-perceptions-and-women-leaders-india

Espinosa, J. (2013). Moving towards gender-responsive evaluation? Practices and challenges in international-development evaluation. *Evaluation, 19,* 171–182.

Fetterman, D., & Wandersman, A. (Eds.). (2002). *Empowerment evaluation principles in practice.* New York, NY: Guilford Press.

Hesse-Biber, S., & Leavy, P. (Eds.). (2007). *Feminist research practice: A primer.* Thousand Oaks, CA: Sage.

Karim, N., Picard, M., Gillingham, S., & Berkowitz, L. (2014). Building capacity to measure long-term impact on women's empowerment: CARE's Women's Empowerment Impact Measurement Initiative. *Gender & Development, 22,* 213–232.

Mertens, D. (2014) *Research and Evaluation in Education and Psychology: integrating Diversity with Quantitative, Qualitative and Mixed Methods.* Thousand Oaks, CA: Sage.

Miller, C., & Haylock, L. (2014). Capturing changes in women's lives: The experiences of Oxfam Canada in applying feminist evaluation principles to monitoring and evaluation practice. *Gender & Development, 22,* 291–310.

Moser, A. (2007). *Gender and indicators: Overview report.* Sussex, UK: University of Sussex, Institute of Development Studies. Retrieved from http://www.bridge.ids.ac.uk/reports/indicatorsORfinal.pdf

Moser, C. (1989). Gender planning in the third world: Meeting practical and strategic needs. *World Development, 17,* 1799–1825.

Mowles, C. (2014). Complex, but not quite complex enough: The turn to the complexity sciences in evaluation scholarship. *Evaluation, 20,* 160–175.

Nelson, J. A. (1995). Feminism and Economics. *Journal of Economic Perspectives, 9,* 131–148.

Oakley, A. (1998). Experimentation and social interventions: A forgotten but important history. *BMJ, 317,* 1239–1242.

Podems, D. (2010). Feminist evaluation and gender approaches: There's a difference? *Journal of MultiDiciplinary Evaluation, 6*(14), 1–17.

Power, M. (2004). Social provisioning as a starting point for feminist economics. *Feminist Economics, 10*(3), 3–19.

Seigart, D. (2005). Feminist evaluation. In D. Mathison (Ed.), *Encyclopedia of evaluation* (pp 154–157). Thousand Oaks, CA: Sage.

Stewart, R., van Rooyen, C., Korth, M., Chereni, A., Reelo Da Silva, N., & de Wet, T. (2012). *Do micro-credit, micro-savings and micro-leasing serve as effective financial inclusion interventions enabling poor people, and especially women, to engage in meaningful economic opportunities in low- and middle-income countries? A systematic review of the evidence.* London, UK: University of London, Institute of Education, EPPI-Centre, Social Science Research Unit.

Stryker, S., Whittle, S. (2007). *The Transgender Studies Reader.* New York: Routledge.

UNEG. (2011). *Integrating human rights and gender equality in evaluation: Towards UNEG guidance.* Retrieved from http://www.uneval.org/document/detail/980

UNEG. (2014). *UN SWAP evaluation performance indicator technical note and performance indicator scorecard.* Retrieved from http://www.uneval.org/document/detail/1452

Vaessen, J., Rivas, A., Duvendack, M., Palmer Jones, R., Leeuw, F. L., van Gils, G., . . . Waddington, H. (2014). *The effects of microcredit on women's control over household spending in developing countries.* Campbell Systematic Reviews.

Watkins, F. (2004). *Evaluation of DFID development assistance: Gender equality and women's empowerment. DFID's experience of gender mainstreaming 1995–2004.* Glasgow, Scotland: Department for International Development.

Williamson, O. (1998). Transaction cost economics: How it works; where it is headed. *De Economist, 146*(1), 23–58.

World Bank. (2012). *World development report: Gender equality and development.* Retrieved from https://siteresources.worldbank.org/INTWDR2012/Resources/7778105-1299699 968583/7786210-1315936222006/Complete-Report.pdf

# Notes

1. We recognize that gender is not a binary concept and that there is a spectrum of gender identities. However, this chapter is largely circumscribed to dealing with the complexity of evaluating development programs that seek to bridge the gender gap as commonly understood in development policies and practices, between cisgender (non-transgender) men and women. That said, the equity-focused evaluation approach can equally be used to deal with issues faced by transgender and gender non-conforming populations. For references on queer theory and research and evaluation see, e.g.,Mertens, 2014; Dodd, 2009; Stryker & Whittle, 2007.

2. Many evaluations, such as most experimental and quasi-experimental designs, are designed to assess the extent to which there are statistically significant differences between the treatment and comparison groups but only with respect to intended outcomes. Many of these designs are not intended to, and are not able to, detect unintended outcomes.

3. For example, the Poverty Action Lab has conducted randomized controlled trials on, to name just a few, job networks and gender in Malawi, the effects of gender equity programs on maternal and child health in Uganda, and school-based gender sensitization campaign in India.

4. One of the critiques of RCTs from the feminist lens is that RCTs, along with other techniques imbued with neo-classical microeconomic theories, rely on an understanding of human behavior that tends to absolve the evaluation of the need to know much about the social contexts of the behavior they study (Nelson, 1995; Power, 2004).

5. One of the present authors met with a group of women in rural Angola who reported that all of the men had been absent for more than a year (working elsewhere or serving in the army). However, when asked who made decisions on what to plant each season, they all reported that it was their husbands who made these decisions. Similarly, many women report that their husbands make all major decisions on household purchases, even when it was clear from observation that women were actively involved in these decisions.

6. See, in particular, UNEG Guidance on Integrating Human Rights and Gender Equality in evaluation: http://www.unevaluation.org/document/detail/1616.

7. See Chapter 8 for details on mixed methods.

# PART V

## Complexity of Evaluation in Practice: Case Studies

# CHAPTER 15

# A Case Study in Complexity

*Evaluating a Long-Term Effort to Prevent Gender-Based Violence in El Salvador*

Allison R. Davis and Mélida Guevara

*This chapter explores the evaluation of a complex program by a coalition of actors to combat gender-based violence in El Salvador. The case provides an example of a rights-based approach to evaluation and its corresponding complexity. After presenting the situation of gender violence in the country and the program under evaluation—a new model for creating a culture of prevention shepherded by a broad coalition supported by Oxfam America—the case delves into a rich description of the evaluation as well as its framing and methodological choices. It subsequently engages in a reflective discussion on how to evaluate a complex intervention, within a human rights framework, while understanding the power dynamics around influencing change—for whom and on behalf of whom.*

This chapter explores the evaluation of a complex program by a coalition of actors working to prevent gender-based violence in El Salvador. The case provides an example of a rights-based approach by Oxfam America, a large international nongovernmental organization (INGO), and the corresponding move toward complexity. The field of evaluation has supported this trend with innovations in evaluating policy advocacy, campaigns, networks, coalitions, and private sector collaborations. The rights-based approach has moved large parts of the INGO sector from a "single model, single implementer" approach toward more complex collaborative efforts that can involve multiple donors and actors coordinating over time. As discussed in Chapter 1, the result is sometimes complex interventions (Funnell & Rogers, 2011) as well as an increase in the complexity of the evaluation. This complexity stems in part from the definition of *impact* under a rights-based approach: For organizations such as Oxfam America, positive results for people do not by themselves signal full impact unless they occur in conjunction with empowerment, that is, people better able to claim their rights and an environment that better enacts and upholds people's rights. This means an impact evaluation looks for evidence that people are having more influence on decisions and/or benefit from a more favorable structural (or rights) environment. A rights-based impact evaluation has to accomplish two things at a minimum: It must examine results for people, and it must examine shifts in power dynamics. It requires a more explicit understanding of how people are positioned in relation to other people, processes, markets, institutions, and policies, and an articulation of what needs to shift for more lasting results. A focus on rights also acknowledges that change can be slow to achieve and requires commitment over longer time periods, which calls for evaluative practices geared toward longer term engagement.

The trend has helped to stimulate innovative ideas across the INGO sector. One trend has been to combine different types of grant making, for example, to help to sustain popular movements, seed new private-public partnerships, work with governments toward reform, attempt to shift value chains toward greater justice, or leverage technology for increased accountability (e.g., participatory budgeting). What has been slower to emerge is a parallel process in the field of evaluation on how to study collaborative efforts with changing actors, over a longer term, around more fundamental issues of rights and freedoms.

In this chapter we describe our attempt to frame an evaluation for Oxfam America's Program to Prevent Gender Based Violence in El Salvador. In addition to the complexity of both the intervention and the evaluation framing, there was a great deal of institutional complexity (see Chapter 13). The evaluation needed to cater to various stakeholders—the wide and varied stakeholders involved in the intervention—but also Oxfam management audiences in El Salvador and Boston. There was also pressure to respond to a growing call in the INGO sector for more attention to measuring results while balancing a very strong concern that the evaluation needed to address the learning needs of the stakeholders, which were more focused on process (i.e., what happened in relation to what worked). Finally, there was the institutional complexity of dealing with multiple nested decision-making systems in trying to gather data. For example, each local government in areas where the campaign worked had different standards and methods of data collection on crime, medical, and judicial data.

Oxfam America opened an office in El Salvador in 1996. The office began efforts to prevent gender-based violence in 2005 and continues to work in a coalition on the issue to this day.

# 1. Gender Violence in El Salvador in 2005

El Salvador has been a country with extremely high levels of criminal violence for nearly two decades. There were a minimum of 80 murders on average per 100,000 people in the years following the signing of the peace accords (1994–1997), with a slow but consistent decline from 1998 onward that was reversed in 2003 when murder rates began to steadily rise (Hume, 2008). This trend has continued to the present, and within the overall rise in murder rates, the number of women killed has risen in both absolute and relative terms (Hume, 2008). In 2005, the Inter-American Institute of Human Rights calculated 11.15 femicides per 100,000 women in El Salvador (Hume, 2008). The World Health Organization considers an annual rate above 10 murders per 100,000 inhabitants to constitute an epidemic of violence, and in El Salvador this has been the rate for women alone for over a decade. Female murder is one of the most-used indicators for overall gender violence because it is the most extreme expression of gender violence and because murder is more reliably reported (Hume, 2008).

Historically, public security has been an area of contestation between the two main political parties, and violence against women has been seen as an issue of the left (particularly the *Farabundo Marti National Liberation Front* [FMLN]), further marginalizing it under *Alianza Republicana Nacionalista* [ARENA]-controlled governments (Roper, 2010).[1] Getting violence against women on the agenda was difficult because "women's interests are largely subordinated in the national political agenda. This directly undermines women's citizenship and a certain 'hierarchy of violence' emerges in public discourse in which violence against women is sidelined from both public debate and spending" (Hume, 2008, p. 66).

## 2. A New Model for National Influence

In response, a new vision emerged in 2005 from a coalition convened by Oxfam America. The work was launched as a horizontal coalition across many types of organizations: three major women's rights organizations, an NGO with reach into rural areas, Oxfam America, and the Human Rights Institute of the University of San Salvador.[2] The central objective was to create a culture of prevention around gender violence, positioning the topic in the public agenda, school curricula, public policy, and judiciary reform, always with a view toward prevention. The ultimate goal, of course, was to reduce gender-based violence.

The coalition chose to take a broad and positive approach, having decided against denouncing individual acts of violence or particular cases in pursuing its message (Bird, Delgado, Madrigal, Ochoa, & Tejeda, 2007). It also took an early inclusive approach to involving men in dialogue, awareness training, and generating solutions. It recognized that research was crucial at the beginning to lay the foundation for future advocacy. The coalition commissioned research on the quality of gender violence data, researched municipal budgeting patterns in relation to prevention, researched the legal application of the domestic violence law, and used this research as the backbone for advocacy at a later stage. Another key strategy was to cultivate relationships with key public actors to foster a commitment to the campaign in ways that might transform into political action later.

Another key early strategy was to target seven local municipalities with a grounded presence of trained women leaders who would advocate for improved performance of health service providers, police, and municipal governments in relation to gender violence prevention. They wanted to see mechanisms in which decision makers would have more direct and continuous contact with women's leadership to motivate action toward violence prevention. A key space identified for women's advocacy was *intersectorales* or private-public councils operating at the municipal level in which civil society actors participate in reflection and strategy development with key government actors. Within 2 years of launching, the program also sought to help facilitate women's leadership in navigating the judiciary and public sector services, sponsoring a network for women called Citizen Windows. The women involved developed a specialized knowledge of legal rights and awareness of how to access and navigate the justice system, including working cooperatively with civil servants.

The model of engagement in El Salvador moved beyond earlier models of advocacy on violence against women in the country as well as for Oxfam America. For Oxfam, this effort was perhaps the most comprehensive campaigning and programming model on gender violence attempted across the Oxfam federation, one that worked on public awareness, school curriculum, institutional behaviors, national legislation, and judicial policy all together (or sequenced) over a period of more than 10 years.

Although Oxfam America was the major funding organization, the coalition was self-branded and not solely identified with any one organization, and decision making was joint on the use of funds. The core members also brought in very highly skilled collaborating institutions at key points—a communications firm, a theater group, musicians, school curriculum experts, public opinion pollsters, and a gender justice think tank that created a professional certificate training course in gender violence awareness.

In addition to a shared decision-making model, the coalition worked at multiple levels simultaneously: national, local, and across individual schools. Thus the program was complex not only in the variety of actors involved at different points, but also in levels of intervention.

Oxfam could be considered the backbone organization of the effort, meaning an organization with a set of skills and staff that allowed it to serve as an anchor for the initiative and to coordinate participating organizations and agencies (Turner, Merchant, Kania, & Martin, 2012). Some have argued that the most successful examples of collective impact have such a backbone organization and that evaluation must begin to look more critically at the nature of this role (Turner et al., 2012). One goal of the evaluation in El Salvador was to examine Oxfam's role within the coalition.

# 3. Framing the Evaluation

When the program started in full swing, Oxfam was remodeling its own program and evaluation framework from headquarters. In 2006 Oxfam America outlined wider organizational principles around the importance of longer term funding commitments on specific issues in particular contexts. It asked program officers to move away from thematic grant-making portfolios to more clearly defined efforts at coordinating the use of funds, alliances, and partnerships in contributing to clear goals for social change and to include insights into the potential advocacy role of Oxfam's own policy and campaigning staff. It also asked for more transparency around the *why and how* of activities, through the articulation of a collective theory of change for each program. Core elements included the following guidelines:

- Program coordinators, with support from monitoring and evaluation staff, should facilitate the development of a theory of change with stakeholders, along with a set of long-term impact indicators and short-term (3-year) objectives, with associated outcomes targets and indicators.
- Iterative evaluation with external researchers should be conducted on the program as a whole every 3 to 4 years.
- The program should create ongoing internal data collection and self-commission small periodic studies on select research questions on specific interventions of the program.
- Stakeholders should agree on standards and approaches that ensure participatory inquiry and reflection throughout the life of the program and produce an annual exercise to discuss the program successes and challenges.

By 2007, it was decided to fully try this new evaluation approach with the Program to Prevent Gender Based Violence in El Salvador. That meant commissioning a baseline in 2007, technically 2 years after the coalition had already formed. To avoid confusion, the research product was described as a "reference study" for future comparison, not a pre-intervention baseline.

Some tension should be acknowledged surrounding the new evaluation guidance from Boston. There was an explicit expectation that Oxfam staff would facilitate the articulation of a theory of change, milestones, and impact goals as well as launch an evaluative system. But at the same time, program staff were trying to navigate the complex relationships of a horizontal coalition space in which the emphasis had to be joint processes and learning. In many instances Oxfam needed to be behind the scenes. It was in some ways contradictory, therefore, to have Oxfam take charge of coalition spaces for a reference study and evaluation framework. Evaluation can easily introduce hierarchy into a coalition, especially if understood as something to be done on behalf of the funder's headquarters.

One solution was to involve the core coalition members in vetting the external researcher candidates and to use this external person to help facilitate the development of indicators based on a theory of change. Using outside facilitation allowed Oxfam staff to be actors in the coalition, not the presumed leaders. Another solution was to research what coalition members thought of Oxfam in terms of its position, role, and involvement in the coalition.

# 4. Mapping Outcome Goals and Theory of Change

The coalition had a shared sense of how change would happen and what it was trying to achieve, and it was able to articulate this in the baseline year. Theories of change involve a vision of sequencing of outcome goals, and in this case stakeholders took the long view, attempting to map such change through major milestones over the course of 10 years. The theory of change was summarized in the pathway diagram in Figure 15.1 (Oxfam, 2007b), although the team ultimately preferred a narrative when describing its analysis of how change might happen:

**Figure 15.1**   Theory of Change of the Intervention

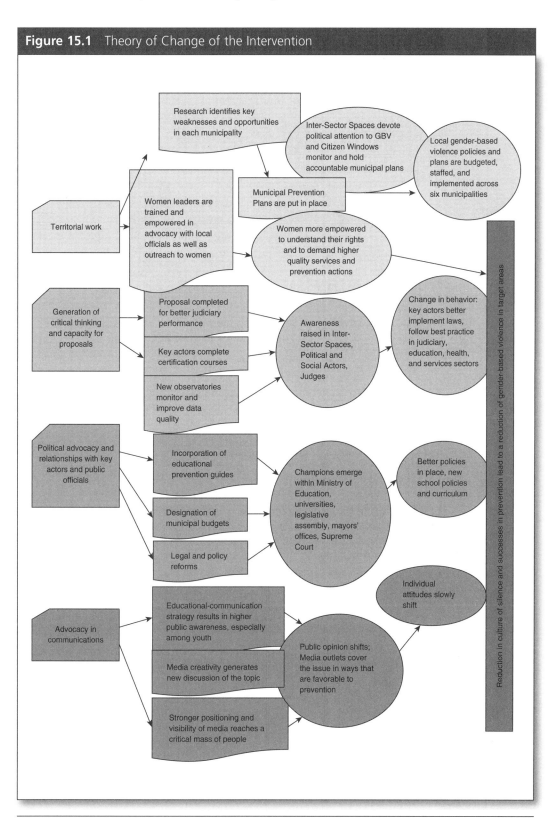

A theory of change was critical to developing an evaluation framework. It surfaced assumptions across the coalition about how the coalition envisioned change might happen and how each actor's work might play a part. From an evaluative perspective, we wanted to test assumptions behind the theory and to anchor an approach to evaluation based on the coalition's own sequence of outcomes. This sequencing was described as a series of benchmark narrative goals, as laid out in Table 15.1. The theory of change included some key assumptions:

- Building more equitable and just relations entails responsibility on the part of state institutions to prevent situations of gender-based violence.
- Coordination between key actors and public institutions contributes to preventing, penalizing, and eradicating gender-based violence.
- When women leaders have direct and frequent opportunities to influence decision makers, there will be more shared understanding, leading to positive change.
- Consciousness and understanding of the problem on the part of political and legal actors ensures the passage and efficient application of public policies and laws focused on preventing gender-based violence.
- As women and girls become more aware of their rights and assemble to share ideas and mobilize, they will better hold decision makers accountable for good prevention actions and policies.
- Critical thinking generated through information sharing, communication, and education contributes to public awareness and generates concrete actions to prevent gender-based violence.
- Engaging youth, men, families, and schools in awareness and critical conversation is needed to change attitudes in the next generation and ultimately reduce a culture of fear and violence.

With outside facilitation, the partners agreed to track the indicators shown in Table 15.2, with differing foci depending on the phase of the work.

# 5. Methodological Considerations

## 5.1 Dealing With a Complex Indicator Framework

Studying any single one of these variables alone is difficult, and in this case the team designing the evaluation was presented with a set of variables for a 10-year period, with different natures, periodicity, and methodological requirements. In complexity theory, a longer time horizon means more complexity. There is a temptation to try to study it all at the beginning; the reference study was a chance to understand the current state for all of these desired outcomes over 10 years. On the other hand, we knew some variables would come in and out of focus depending on the changing emphasis of the program over a 10-year period, and we also knew that trying to study everything would sacrifice quality.

**Table 15.1** Benchmark Narratives

| Short term: Benchmark 2011 | Medium term: Benchmark 2014 | Long term: Benchmark 2017 |
|---|---|---|
| Women and youth benefit from policy initiatives in gender-based violence prevention by 2011, notably at the municipal level. Targeted municipal governments will have new policies and ordinances that are budgeted and implemented in accordance to municipal plans to prevent gender-based violence. At the national level there will be a new law to prevent gender-based violence.<br><br>Sustainable mechanisms exist to bring civil society actors working on gender-based violence together with decision makers at the municipal level (e.g., a network between women and youth that conducts advocacy with decision makers, monitoring bodies of gender violence at the municipal level, women organized into Citizen Windows).<br><br>Women leaders perceive changes resulting from the advocacy with municipalities (e.g., efforts to make key public places safer, new police working groups dedicated to women's concerns, initial gender violence monitoring in schools).<br><br>Women have greater understanding of their rights and know what resources are available to them, and they participate actively with other women in discussing the issues.<br><br>The judiciary makes steps to better apply the Law Against Interfamily Violence in accordance with coalition recommendations. | Women and youth continue to perceive improvements and the effects of prevention measures in their schools and neighborhoods (e.g., areas targeted for safety measures are indeed safer, appointed task forces on gender violence are perceived to be working in good faith). Violence mapping by women's groups since 2006 shows positive geographic change (public sites with high violence have more patrols; more public resources such as places to submit claims to justice; women's shelters, health centers, outreach centers are available). This perception of public responsiveness has been encouraging to women's leadership, and this is evident in changes in the statements and experiences provided by women representing a wide variety of groups across all six municipalities. Evidence suggests that men are beginning to reinforce a culture of accountability with respect to violence against women. This, in combination with initial evidence of stabilizing gender violence statistics, suggests deeper cultural change. Work with the Ministry of Education has resulted in adoption of new educational materials in schools nationwide to discuss gender violence and new codes of conduct for teachers and administrators. | By the end of the program, gender violence prevention programs will have been widely incorporated across El Salvador, including youth prevention educational curriculum and awareness-building workshops, local gender safety initiatives, gender police task forces, and other ideas. There is an active, ongoing public discourse on the issue. The dimensions of social legitimization of violence are changing; domestic violence is increasingly addressed by civil society and communities, rather than ignored or thought of as private. There is a new gender violence prevention law, and the Family Domestic Violence Law is properly enforced relative to the protocol for enforcement. There is an increase in the percentage of actual violent crimes against women that are reported and addressed fairly in accordance with the law through the courts. Women show less fear by being more willing to report abuse. Finally, although very difficult to study, the program and mobilization of many actors across El Salvador has contributed to lowering violence against women. |

SOURCE: Oxfam (2007a).

| **Table 15.2**  Indicators Tracked by the Program | |
|---|---|
| **Indicator category** | **Desired impact** |
| Rates and trends in actual and reported violence against women in El Salvador | • Levels of reporting of violence against women increase at first and then stabilize over the life of the program. (An estimated 80% of gender violence is currently unreported; the program wants to see an increase in reporting.)<br>• Rates of actual gender violence decrease by 2018. |
| Level and quality of women's movement and leadership building with respect to gender violence prevention | • By the end of 2010 the program would like to see marked increase in participation and quality of networking across of a variety of women's organizations and community organizations at all levels: local *(comités de género,* ADESCOS, *cooperativas, comités de mujeres),* municipal *(colectivas de mujeres, comités de desarrollo municipales, grupos de jóvenes, intersectoriales),* and national (Red nacional). This includes the creation of effective monitoring bodies of violence. |
| Civil society participation and level of influence in decision-making processes | • Women and youth leaders participate in gender violence prevention involvement with municipal government forums for decision making in meaningful ways.<br>• There is advocacy evaluation of participants' influence.<br>• Forums for women's participation in decision making are sustainable (funded, respected). (By 2010 the campaign wants to see progress in making these forums more permanent.) |
| Changes in women's "cycle of fear" | • There are changes in women's perceptions of their own options to address and prevent violence and the quality of the social resources available to them.<br>• There is improvement in women leaders' perceptions that public officials will respond with action and resources to the issue of gender violence.<br>• Women are increasingly willing to be involved in finding solutions to violence (reflected in the indicator on women's participation in networks).<br>• Women leaders' increase their knowledge of the law and their civil and political rights. |
| Youth awareness and sense of empowerment | • Youth, especially girls, are increasingly aware of, and confident in, the social resources available to them in the face of violence.<br>• Youth, both adolescent boys and girls, are more aware of the problem of gender violence, its negative effects, and how to protect themselves from it.<br>• Youth use their knowledge from educational campaign messages by transferring knowledge to others, at home to families and other adults. |
| Youth involvement in a movement to prevent gender-based violence | • Youth increase their participation in education and awareness-building campaigns about gender-based violence. |

| Indicator category | Desired impact |
|---|---|
| Youth experiences of gender violence | • The program would like to see a long-term decrease in youth self-reported experiences with, and exposure to gender-based violence at schools. |
| Policy change and government practice change outcomes at the municipal level | • New municipal initiatives are passed and resourced, creating safer spaces for women, new police task forces, etc.<br>• There is greater municipal budget expenditure on gender violence prevention. |

SOURCE: Oxfam (2007a).

For example, the ultimate goal of lowering rates (absolute and relative) of gender violence needed to be studied in some manner over the course of the program. Yet in the first 3 years we knew this indicator was not important for stakeholders. No one expected to see a clear change in gender violence patterns for at least 5 years, and the indicator was ambiguous: An increase might signal more reporting by women or better data collecting practices. Movement of the indicator in either direction could be considered positive or negative. What level of resources should go into evaluating this question?

The team decided to use the baseline to accomplish two main things: (1) summarize program efforts to collect and harmonize baseline statistics on gender violence in seven municipalities and (2) establish two comparative case studies at the municipal level that would cover a suite of variables important to the program around political dynamics and the program's impact on women. In the follow-up evaluation in 2010, these two methods were complemented with a third approach: (3) an advocacy evaluation of the coalition's advocacy for national and municipal policy change.

## 5.2 The Statistics Review: Dealing With Unreliable Data

With limited funds, the team had hoped to use secondary review of the data on gender violence to help compare trends in areas where the campaign did and did not have a local presence, with the premise that the strongest effects of the program would be seen where the program was also doing municipal-level advocacy. In 2006, the program worked with the UN to commission research on gender violence statistics for six of the seven municipalities where it would target advocacy work in order to help establish the role of monitoring centers that would work with state institutions to improve data processing and report figures annually. Unfortunately, there were no observatories planned in municipalities outside of the program areas that would permit matched comparisons.

The hope was that the monitoring bodies (*observatarios*) would help to improve the data gathering and handling of the *Instituto Salvadoreño para el Desarrollo de la Mujer* (Salvadoran Institute for the Development of Women; ISDEMU), the governmental body responsible for compiling information on gendered violence. The quality of information was very low, often dependent on the type of violence under scrutiny.

In 2007, as part of the reference study, the outside researcher examined data collection practices and how they could be improved. She found that local state offices of government bodies that collect violence statistics had weak access to information technology. The local offices of national police did not have computers, and the *Juzgado de Familia* in one municipality recorded all information manually. Initial case information was usually recorded in most institutions (family courts, police offices, health clinics) by a receptionist who had poor training and sometimes disseminated misinformation. The researcher thus recommended the following: (1) police outposts should have computers to enter violent crime information, (2) all incident reporting across agencies should include information on the gender of the victim and suspect, (3) family courts should begin to digitally record information, and (4) when information is transferred from local to national levels, all details should be preserved.

Given this weak data system, the improvement in the data quality itself became an indicator of progress and less emphasis was put on trying to set up a counterfactual. However, by 2011, the reliability of statistical information had not improved (Hume, 2011) and most of the recommendations from 2007 had not been taken up. For example, Hume (2011, p. 9) notes that "the total number of cases of intra-family violence recorded for Ahuachapán in 2009 was zero, although PPGV baseline studies (using data re-analyzed from ISDEMU and other organizations) show 339 cases [of intra-family violence] in total in 2007."

For these reasons the researcher felt that very few conclusions could be drawn from the data on gender violence trends over the 3 years since the baseline. However, when looking at femicides, which are more reliably reported, it was clear that the situation had not improved in most municipalities, and in some had gotten worse.

## 5.3 Comparative Case Studies of the Impact of Municipal-Level Activities on Women's Lives

A central research method was to commission two qualitative case studies that took an in-depth look at the impact of the work in the targeted municipalities and how contrasting cases might test the assumptions of the program strategy. A deeper look at dynamics in particular contexts could also provide a better understanding of the way national changes articulated with local politics and program efforts. For the reference study and subsequent evaluation, two department municipalities were chosen for contrast: the municipality of Ahuachapan in the Department of Ahuachapan and the municipality of San Marcos in the Department of San Salvador. Staff at Oxfam America in El Salvador singled out three key criteria for choosing the case studies: (1) distinct municipal governments (FMLN in San Marcos [politically left] and ARENA in Ahuachapan [politically right]), (2) a record of institutional commitment to the campaign in both, and (3) variance in urban (San Marcos) and rural (Ahuachapan) demographics across the municipality.

For each case study, the research included

- document review of research commissioned and materials generated by the program, research on gender violence trends and statistics for each municipality, general literature and media review on the municipality and the political dynamics in relation to the topic of gender violence;

- key in-depth interviews with national and local decision makers and service providers, women leaders, and program staff in each municipality;
- focus groups with women leaders in each municipality, both involved and not involved in the program, attempting to re-interview the same women 3 years later.

In both case studies women mapped out gender violence hotspots, their perceptions of the quality of local institutions and the quality of services, the mobilization of women, and their own sense of safety. The researcher assessed how well the focus groups understood their rights, the laws, and the resources available to them. All these techniques were then repeated in 2011 to assess change in the two case municipalities. The actions of the coalition in each case were analyzed in relation to the findings.

The analysis showed that while there had been progress in establishing plans and policies, progress was slower in getting work budgeted and implemented. The contrasting cases showed that the political leaning of the municipality was less important to the coalition's progress than the personality, interest, and timing of the election cycle for mayor. The case studies also showed that, in both places, knowledge and activism of women leadership was found to be higher over time and women in leadership positions felt more solidarity and empowerment. Three of the four groups were able to rate various organizations' performance that have a role in gender-based violence prevention. In both places, there had been little to no change in the violence maps or women's overall perception of safety.

## 5.4 Advocacy Evaluation

The advocacy evaluation focused on the advocacy strategy of the campaign as an integrated effort to influence policy and practice at the national and municipal levels, looking at both process and advocacy outcomes to date. The methods used by the evaluator, Laura Roper, included internal document review, in-depth interviews with the program coordinator, in-depth interviews with Oxfam partners, and semistructured, open-ended interviews with key informants, principally policymakers at the national and municipal levels who had engaged with the campaign (20 interviews in total). In addition to one-on-one interviews, two focus groups were conducted, one with field coordinators from member organizations who were responsible for coordinating work at the municipal level and another with community leaders who are part of the Citizen Windows (Roper, 2010). In order to prepare for the study, she conducted extensive document review and interviewed stakeholders in the coalition about the strategic pathways and key moments that marked the progression of their work.

One innovation was using transcribed interviews to analyze how key actors described their knowledge and approach to gender violence. By noting key parallels in terms and framing, the researcher was able to conclude that local and national authorities who had engaged with the program certificate courses had developed and internalized much of the language and critical analysis fostered by the campaign. Roper found, and Hume validated, that there was high congruence in language across respondents who had participated in trainings, whether they operated at the national or local level, regardless of party affiliation, and across governmental organizations (Roper, 2011).

## 5.5 Missteps Along the Way

A major weakness in the evaluation design was the lack of a third comparative case municipality where the program was not present. A third case would have given more information on how other actors did or did not advocate for prevention in these municipalities, and it would challenge the assumption that Oxfam's program was particularly "good" at mobilizing women around advocacy. This also was a serious gap given that separate women's organizations were in fact working in municipalities where the campaign wasn't in place, and it would have been important to clearly understand their approaches and progress in comparison to the Oxfam-funded coalition.

Another weakness was that the research team lacked the time and expertise to do adequate statistical analysis, especially in ways that would compare gender violence reporting, claims, and rates in the seven municipalities to areas without campaign presence. The actual evaluation did not go beyond description of trends from available statistics to one that might attempt to statistically attribute results at the municipal level, albeit tentatively, to program efforts. However, as discussed, the overall validity of such a statistical attempt would have been questionable given the issues surrounding data collection and reporting practices. In fact, improving data collection in the justice, health, and police departments in El Salvador became an advocacy goal of the campaign in and of itself.

Finally, most interviews were with people somehow involved in the program, either as stakeholders or as actors targeted by the program. It would have been ideal to have more interviews from more perspectives outside of the work and networks of the women leaders.

# 6. Which Findings Were and Were Not Useful to Different Audiences

The policy advocacy evaluation was most useful to Oxfam actors in management. It showed the connection between the campaign's strategy and policy achievements, which had been at the core of their theory of change for the initial 3 years. The evaluation also validated the significance of the coalition's successes in establishing formal agreements with institutions such as the Ministry of Education, the human rights ombudsman, the attorney general's office, and the Supreme Judicial Court, and how those agreements reached hundreds of government officials—elected, appointed, and more permanent staff positions—through its training programs and dialogue meant to stimulate critical thinking (Roper, 2010). The training courses were then modified and replicated throughout the seven municipalities. In general, the evaluation showed that "the program has expanded the political spaces where gender-based violence is put on the political agenda, by addressing multiple points of entry" (Roper, 2010, p. 3). The policy wins exceeded all campaign benchmarks.[3] The study was also useful for theorists in policy advocacy or those trying to generalize good practice in campaigning, for example, using multiple points of entry and using critical discourse and certification courses across party lines to transcend political divides.

For the coalition itself, the most interesting parts of the research were Dr. Mo Hume's case study comparisons about the impact of the campaign, which were full of the voices of actual women leaders, and how different local dynamics require flexible, creative, and persistent approaches. There was little evidence of change in popular attitudes or women's perceptions of safety. Although plans in one municipality were passed and budgeted, implementation was not yet perceived by the women leaders interviewed. In the other, competition between circles of political influence made it difficult for the campaign to get traction. However, in both cases women were clearly taking more leadership on the issue in their local spaces, growing their networks, and (hopefully) laying the groundwork for longer term change. The coalition acknowledged that 3 years of advocacy work does not translate into impact and that the next 7 years or so of the campaign needed to be devoted to implementation at the municipal level, interventions in schools, and the endless work of awareness raising and engagement with families, schools, and communities toward changing attitudes and practice. On the other hand, many Oxfam managers did not take the time to read the case studies.

Coalition stakeholders felt the evaluation was missing insights about the processes, techniques, and tools of the Citizens Windows and their work with officials and their interaction in schools. They wanted more information on which processes and techniques in the campaign were working well and which were not, including their engagement in schools, in the *Intersectorales,* and in their advocacy to improve the service delivery of health professionals. Although documentation was fairly robust, it was focused more externally on what needed to be fixed than internally on what processes were working.

Such monitoring is not just for external evaluators, but also internally for the stakeholders involved. A coalition has an internal interest in obtaining data-rich, objective evidence for the advocacy targets it is trying to influence. It needs to be able to identify when it witnesses good practice in a municipality, describe the practice well, try to quantify the results, and then raise examples to the wider coalition as a possible advocacy angle. A central fact of monitoring and evaluation in advocacy coalitions is that often the same data that track progress are actually central to advocacy arguments: Advocates for better practice are constantly trying to identify what works in order to advocate for what works.

The evaluation was used in concrete ways by the coalition, including to adjust the theory of change for the next period, as well as the overall contours of strategy to 2018, along with analysis of new political context. The evaluation helped the coalition understand the importance of linking more closely with other women's organizations in the upcoming years around application of the laws that had successfully passed. The evaluation also allowed for a reflection event in which the people working across different municipalities could come together to support problem solving city by city, using a cross-program lens. Finally, one major change was that the coalition used some of the findings to change the use of the Oxfam logo to be more empowering to the coalition as a whole.

# 7. Lessons Learned

## 7.1 How This Effort Relates to Oxfam Organizational Learning on Gender Evaluation

In 2011, the evaluations were completed at a time when Oxfam International was internally reflecting on different approaches around the world that were working to reduce gender-based violence (Pittman, 2011). It was found that Oxfam America's program was one of the few to have a clear articulation of a theory of change and a strong power analysis, both of which benefitted the evaluation (Pittman, 2011). Oxfam evaluations on programs to end violence against women have not always considered political dynamics to the degree that this evaluation attempted. The cases also explored how individual personalities, like mayors, can have inordinate effects on progress in a particular area or, conversely, create obstruction and fuel competitive dynamics between women's advocates. Reflections on such powerful actors was possible only through in-depth case studies and provided a window on the challenges and opportunities the program faced. This also was the only program across Oxfam that was taking a long-term (10+-year) approach. Therefore, the evaluative frame was unique and interesting for the wider federation of Oxfam.

## 7.2 How This Effort Relates to the Literature in Gender Violence Evaluation

The evaluation, as well as the Oxfam program, sits squarely within a feminist analysis of gender violence. As Pittman (2011) writes, "the feminist models of violence argue that historical dynamics of power and patriarchy are at the heart of any expression of gender violence. The struggle for gender equality is a fundamental struggle to challenge patriarchy and [its historical antecedents]" (p. 12). This contrasts with other frameworks for analyzing violence, as summarized by Pittman:

- The public health model uses an epidemiological approach to describe the incidence and spread of violence. This model focuses primarily on interpersonal relations and on quantifying the frequency of violence. The solutions to violence typically take an anger management approach and do not include a critical analysis of gender.
- The ecological model of violence is based on social learning theory and looks at the different spheres in which violence is socialized, starting from the family, community institutions, the state, and so on. In this model, gender analysis can be neutralized through a focus on social learning.
- The cycle and abuse theory starts with the notion that individuals that are victimized and abused as children will grow up to be perpetrators themselves.

Feminist evaluation takes as axiomatic the centrality of power dynamics. As described in *Capturing Change in Women's Realities* (Batliwala & Pittman, 2010, p. 20), "Our [evaluation] tools of choice will treat gender and social inequalities as systemic and embedded in social structures and will be able to examine the way the interventions being assessed are addressing the structures."

In the case of El Salvador, the evaluation had to match and embrace an understanding of power and political dynamics at the level where the coalition was itself operating, and this was done mainly by hiring researchers with specific competencies in this regard. An analysis of power requires a high degree of competency in qualitative methods and the ability to synthesize a great deal of literature on a place and its dynamics.

According to Pittman (2011), studies on preventing gender-based violence are "often hampered by methodological difficulties surrounding the breadth of sectors and social institutions involved in supporting or deterring gender based violence (Chalk & King, 1998) and measuring the changes in various levels at which gender based violence manifests (Campbell, 2000)" (p. 5). The Oxfam example shows the relevance of comparative case studies in understanding how complex interventions come together and interact through actual experiences. The cases can be compared to the theory of change to look at original assumptions and what may have been unanticipated. Case study methodology can be paired with more quantitative methods that assess progress across efforts or populations.

# 8. Practical Applications

In summary, there were strong points and weak points from this evaluation experience that offer insights to the field in general. Overall the experience offers the following practical lessons:

- It is important to make explicit the theory of change operating across stakeholders, in order to understand program choices and to test the assumptions behind these choices.
- It was helpful to map out long term (10+ year) impact indicators, along with benchmark (3-year) objectives, targets and indicators. It can seem a tedious process up front, but it sets up better reflection, evaluation and adjustment over the whole program period.
- There is a need to balance rigor with the importance of learning. Theoretically, every single evaluation dollar could have been spent in the baseline year coming up with a more rigorous methodology on how to study reporting trends and gender violence statistics. Yet this would have been a terrible choice given the poor data quality, the ambiguity of what the data might reveal in the short term, and the lack of relevance to what the campaign was actually trying to achieve in the first years of the program (with its focus on national and municipal policy).
- In-depth comparative cases are great for dealing with complexity and studying power; they are key to looking at interlinkages across variables in particular places.
- The use of specific participatory methods—such as discourse analysis on the internalization of key concepts from program trainings and neighborhood

violence mapping in the case studies—was very instrumental in deepening the evaluation's understanding of progress (or lack thereof) in specific places over 3 years.

- It is necessary to include a comparison case study from an area where a program is not present.
- It is important to use different researchers with different strengths for the different research questions and to have the patience and resources to hire one of the researchers to summarize across the different results.
- There is still a question as to whether to invest evaluation resources in summative attempts across complex efforts or to invest in really good microstudies of components and high-quality monitoring. Program managers might choose to do summative efforts less often in order to allow an accumulation of more high-quality internal data and interim studies of select components.

Long-term ongoing efforts in rights-based approaches are complex in both intervention and evaluative framing. They often need ongoing data collection and reflective practices that can feed into the advocacy efforts of the work. At the same time, periodic externally conducted evaluations provide a critical check on assumptions and take stock of progress toward impact over time. Power analysis is very important to evaluating rights-based work, and this requires an attempt at a theory of change that can be tested and reconfigured over time.

This case is but one small contribution to a growing field of evaluation of efforts to reduce gender-based violence. Complexity and funding limits require making tough choices, but case studies are a great method for capturing the interplay of many complex variables, especially when paired with other methods that provide more breadth. In El Salvador we used a combination of document review, case studies, and advocacy evaluation as a solution to evaluating a highly complex, rights-based effort.

# References

Batliwala, S., & Pittman, A. (2010). *Capturing change in women's realities.* Toronto, Ontario, Canada: Association for Women's Rights in Development.

Bird, S., Delgado, R., Madrigal, L., Ochoa, J. B., & Tejeda, W. (2007). Constructing an alternative masculine identity: The experience of the Centro Bartolomé de las Casas and Oxfam Americain El Salvador. *Gender & Development, 15*(1), 111–121.

Campbell, J. (2000). Promise and perils of surveillance in addressing violence against women. *Violence Against Women, 6,* 705–727.

Chalk, R., & King, P. (1998). *Violence in families: Assessing prevention and treatment programs.* Washington, DC: National Academy Press.

Funnell, S., & Rogers, P. (2011). *Purposeful program theory: Effective use of theories of change and logic models.* San Francisco, CA: Jossey-Bass.

Hume, M. (2008). *Baseline for the Program to Prevent Gender Based Violence: A comparison of two case municipalities in El Salvador.* Boston, MA: Oxfam America.

Hume, M. (2011). *Salí de esa cueva donde yo estaba, he salido a la claridad y a la realidad: A three-year qualitative evaluation of Oxfam America's Program to Prevent Gender Based Violence (PPGV) in Ahuachapán and San Marcos, El Salvador.* Boston, MA: Oxfam America.

Oxfam. (2007a). *Evaluation framework for the Program to Prevent Gender Based Violence in El Salvador.* Oxford, UK: Author.

Oxfam. (2007b). *Program strategy paper for the Program to Prevent Gender Based Violence in El Salvador.* Oxford, UK: Author.

Pittman, A. (2011). *Making gender based violence programming explicit: An Oxfam review.* Oxford, UK: Oxfam.

Roper, L. (2010). *Advocacy and the campaign for the Prevention of Gender Based Violence in El Salvador: A qualitative evaluation.* Boston, MA: Oxfam America.

Roper, L. (2011). *A summary of two evaluations of the Program to Prevent Gender Based Violence in El Salvador.* Boston, MA: Oxfam America.

Turner, S., Merchant, K., Kania, J., & Martin, E. (2012, July). Understanding the value of backbone organizations in collective impact: An in-depth review of what it takes to be a backbone organization, and how to evaluate and support its work. *Stanford Social Innovation Review.*

# Notes

1. ARENA controlled the presidency from the end of the civil war in 1992 until 2009.

2. The core stakeholders: Movimiento Salvadoreño de Mujeres (MSM), Asociación para la Autodeterminación y Desarrollo de Mujeres Salvadoreñas (AMS), Asociación de Mujeres Tecleñas (AMT), Instituto de Derechos Humanos UCA (IDHUCA), and AGROSAL.

3. The 2010 Special Integrated Law for a Life Free from Violence passed by the parliament was a direct result of the work of female legislators who had taken a certificate course from the program (an early draft of the law was a group project as part of the course). The 2010 Protocol for the Application of the Domestic Violence Law was formulated based on recommendations from the coalition's research. The Ministry of Education adopted prevention curriculum across schools by 2010 that were versions of the curriculum launched and tested in 53 schools by the coalition. Six of the seven municipalities where the program has a presence now have gender or gender-based violence policies. Three of these municipalities now have plans, budgets, or ordinances associated with these polices (Roper, 2010).

# CHAPTER 16

# Microcredit and Women's Empowerment

*Complexity in Systematic Review*

Jos Vaessen, Ana Rivas, and Frans L. Leeuw

*This chapter discusses a systematic review of the evidence on the effects of microcredit on women's empowerment, more particularly, women's control over household spending. The chapter focuses on the following question: What methodological challenges and solutions present themselves when addressing complexity issues (see Chapter 1) in the design and implementation of this particular review and synthesis study? After an introduction we discuss the purpose and methodology of the review, followed by some illustrations of key findings. Finally, we discuss a number of important methodological issues that arise when addressing complexity issues in systematic review.*

Microfinance has spread across the globe, with financial services being provided to tens of millions of poor households in developing and developed countries. Microcredit, the provision of small loans using innovative ways to lower the transaction costs of screening and enforcement of loans, has been the most widespread financial service provided to poor (and non-poor) households, sometimes in combination with microsavings, microinsurance, and other financial services.

Despite the diversity in microcredit schemes across regions and microfinance institutions,[1] many share two characteristics: They target poor women and often rely on some type of group-based lending.[2] Women's empowerment in relation to microcredit has been studied extensively in the context of this type of microcredit scheme. Most of these studies have been carried out in the context of microcredit group schemes in South Asia. Women's empowerment can be broadly defined as an "expansion in the range of potential choices available to women" (Kabeer, 2001, p. 81). It has been argued that access to microcredit can foster changes in individual attitudes of women (e.g., increased self-reliance), power relations within the household (e.g., control over resources), and social status (Malhotra, Schuler, & Boender, 2002).

This chapter discusses a recently published systematic review study on the effects of microcredit on women's control over household spending (Vaessen et al., 2014), which is an aspect of women's empowerment, through a complexity lens. Complexity with respect to this topic manifests itself in different ways. In this chapter, we look at the following question for the concrete example of microcredit and women's empowerment: What methodological challenges and solutions present themselves when addressing complexity issues (see Chapter 1) in the design and implementation of this particular review and synthesis study? Broadly, we distinguish between three main dimensions. The first is the conceptualization and measurement of the construct of women's empowerment. Mayoux (2006) argues that the interlinkages between microcredit and women's empowerment are delineated differently by existing paradigms. More specifically, the financial sustainability paradigm and the feminist empowerment paradigm emphasize women's income-earning activities, whereas the poverty alleviation paradigm emphasizes the effects on household expenditures and particularly the use of loans for consumption purposes. Consequently, one can identify a wide range of measures that try to capture the effect of microcredit on women's empowerment in the literature (Kabeer, 2001).

A closely related distinction is the one between economic outcomes (through empowerment) and empowerment as an outcome of microcredit. The latter includes changes in the sociocultural construct of gender itself. Proxies here are by definition highly context-specific, as gender is a sociocultural construct. For example, in those cases where there are strict gender norms regarding female mobility, which essentially refers to the possibility for women to participate in activities beyond the household, increased female mobility could be a good proxy for empowerment. Second, there may be economic outcomes, in terms of increased spending on education, health, and nutrition, with corresponding developmental effects on household well-being. Regarding the latter, it is important to distinguish between a simple gender division in spending (e.g., the practice in some contexts that a woman tends to spend relatively more on consumption and less on productive activities than the man) and an empowerment effect, in terms of women having a greater say in household spending, resulting in a change in expenditure patterns.

A second dimension of complexity concerns the choice of methodological approach to review and synthesis that has implications for the way empowerment is studied. For example, if one were to employ a meta-ethnography approach to microcredit and empowerment, the reviewers would focus on local meanings of this causal relationship and consequently a set of different context-specific interpretations of pathways toward empowerment induced by microcredit. This would also include mapping and characterizing the construct of empowerment itself through a number of predominant interpretations identified in the review process. A realist synthesis perspective would zoom in on the causal mechanism between microcredit and an assumed behavioral change and would then try to understand under which contextual conditions such a mechanism is likely to be triggered. Finally, a systematic review perspective would focus on one particular outcome variable or set of outcome variables and analyze to what extent microcredit has effectively induced a change in this (set of) variable(s). The main question underlying the latter approach is basically "Does it work?" By contrast, meta-ethnography and realist synthesis would respectively focus on questions such as "What does it mean?" and "How does it work?"

The review and synthesis approach discussed in this chapter was essentially a systematic review in the Campbellian tradition (see Chapter 9).[3] The disadvantage of this type of approach is that an outcome dimension is always analyzed through one or more particular variables, the same (or very similar) across studies. As a result, a complex phenomenon such as empowerment is decontextualized and the fact that, for example, control over resources by a woman can have very different meanings and implications in the context of local gender norms and beliefs is disregarded. On the other hand, the advantage of the approach is that one uses a common lens that is rigorously applied to all contexts. This homogeneous focus also allows for more rigorous and detailed attribution analysis (across contexts) for the particular outcome variable or variables selected for the study. The choice of the outcome variable is crucial. In this case, given the complexity of the phenomenon of empowerment (see Vaessen et al., 2014, for extensive discussion), multiple options were considered.

A commonly studied causal relationship in this context is the potential link between microcredit as a resource and the opportunity space for women receiving loans to act more independently from men. Credit can potentially strengthen the bargaining position of a woman vis-à-vis a man within the household and hence provide the basis for gradual changes in the power balance within the household, the social status of the woman within the household and the community, and ultimately gender relations. Thus, bargaining power or decision-making power, often studied in the context of decisions on household expenditures, is a key intermediate variable that lies at the basis of many manifestations of empowerment (see, e.g., Pitt, Khandker, & Cartwright, 2003). This is one of the main reasons why the systematic review focused on women's control over household spending.

Finally, the third dimension of complexity that we introduce here, the nature of the evidence base, is closely related to the choice of methodology. In the Campbellian tradition, the systematic review focused on studies with a high internal validity of findings.[4] A key threat to the internal validity of findings is selection bias (Cook & Campbell, 1979). Selection bias is likely to arise in microcredit programs targeting the poor, as it may be expected that women who choose to participate in the program are on average more empowered than those who do not (Goldberg, 2005). In practice, the evidence base has often been characterized as weak or contested (e.g., Armendariz de Aghion & Morduch, 2005; Karlan & Goldberg, 2006; Odell, 2010). In fact, the few randomized controlled trials conducted in the context of microcredit interventions that cover aspects of women's empowerment (e.g., Banerjee, Duflo, Glennerster, & Kinnan, 2009; Kim et al., 2007) to a large extent examine different outcomes. Banerjee et al. (2009) look at the effect of microcredit on women's control over household spending, whereas Kim et al. (2007) cover a much larger set of empowerment indicators ranging from changes in self-confidence to changes in gender norms and partner relationships. There is also a substantial number of quasi-experimental and regression-based studies investigating the relationships between microcredit and women's empowerment, including women's control over household spending. Quasi-experiments and, even more so, regression-based analyses have been criticized regarding their limitations in addressing selection bias issues. Apart from the methodological quality of primary studies and the implications for the internal validity of findings, there are other important aspects to consider, especially if the purpose of review is broader than addressing the "Does it work?" question. We will return to this issue later in the chapter.

# 1. Purpose and Methodology

## 1.1 Purpose

The main objective of the systematic review was to assess the effects of microcredit on women's control over household spending in developing countries. More specifically, the review addressed the following questions:

- What does the impact evaluative evidence say about the causal relationship between microcredit and a specific dimension of women's empowerment: women's control over household spending?
- What are the mechanisms that mediate the relationship between microcredit and women's empowerment?

## 1.2 Methodology

Box 16.1 provides a summary perspective for each of the key aspects of the review's methodology, except for the synthesis phase, which is discussed separately in the main text after the box.

---

**BOX 16.1 METHODOLOGICAL BUILDING BLOCKS OF THE SYSTEMATIC REVIEW ON THE EFFECTS OF MICROCREDIT ON WOMEN'S CONTROL OVER HOUSEHOLD SPENDING**

**Inclusion and Exclusion Criteria**

*Types of Studies (Methodological Design)*

The primary focus of the review was on studies with an acceptable level of internal validity of findings with respect to the causal link between microcredit and women's control over

*(Continued)*

(Continued)

household expenditures. The minimum criterion for inclusion was that studies should show evidence of addressing the attribution problem in a systematic manner, through either randomized design or quasi-experimental approaches, for example, statistical matching or regression analysis (see Figure 9.1 in Chapter 9 for methodological guidance).

### Types of Interventions

Microcredit interventions targeting women differ on several characteristics. First, there is a difference between group-based schemes and schemes providing individual loans. Some microcredit institutions use both modalities. Group-based credit schemes usually refer to a system in which credit is provided to women organized in solidarity groups. Within these groups women receive individual loans. Repayment is enforced through mechanisms of group pressure based on principles such as joint liability and contingent renewal. Individual loan schemes directly work with individual female clients. Second, in many cases credit is linked to other services ("credit-plus") such as training or additional financial services such as savings.

### Group Comparisons

Comparisons in primary studies usually concern women with credit versus women without credit. Studies that included comparisons between different types of micro-credit beneficiaries (distinguishing them by specific characteristics, such as young versus older women, recent versus mature clients, male versus female clients) were also eligible for inclusion.[5]

### Types of Outcome Variables

The review included studies estimating the impact of microcredit interventions on women's control over household spending, including women's decision-making power, women's bargaining power, or women's control over expenditures with respect to small or large purchases. These include expenditures relating to any type of consumption good, productive investment, or acquisition of assets (e.g., clothing, education, health, food, house repairs, small livestock, large livestock, land).

## Search for Evidence

The review took into account studies that were published after 1980.[6] Searches included studies published up to December 31, 2011. In terms of types of publication, the review included studies in peer-reviewed and non-peer-reviewed journals, articles in books, gray literature (e.g., policy reports, study documents), and PhD theses.

### The Screening Process

In order to identify studies with the relevant focus in terms of outcome variables, the review applied an appraisal sequence that ultimately led to a selection of a batch of studies to be used for further data extraction and synthesis. This sequence principally relied on two dimensions: assessment of relevance and a risk of bias assessment (see Quality Assessment section in this box).

First titles, abstracts, and, where necessary, the full text of publications were screened to categorize studies into four categories.

Priority 1: Study is on the impact of microcredit on women's empowerment; involves original empirical analysis.

Priority 2: Study is on the impact of microcredit, covering multiple outcome measures that include aspects of women's empowerment; involves original empirical analysis.

Priority 3: Study is on the impact of microcredit and women's empowerment but does not rely on original empirical analysis.

Priority 4: All other studies.

Subsequently, all priority 1 and 2 studies were screened, and purely qualitative studies were discarded. Then all remaining studies were screened for the nature of outcome measures. Studies that did not include causal analysis on microcredit and the effect on one or more aspects of women's control over household expenditures were dropped. The remaining studies were screened for methodological design and quality. Finally, this generated a selection of studies that would be included in the process of data extraction and synthesis work.

### The Search Strategy

The search strategy, as with other methodological aspects, is described in detail in Vaessen et al. (2014). It contained the following elements:

- online searches of published literature using standardized and (where needed) customized key word sequences, covering academic databases (e.g., EBSCO, ISI Web of Knowledge, JSTOR), online portals (e.g., Google Scholar, JOLIS, BLDS), microfinance institutions (e.g., CGAP, Microfinance gateway, SEEP), development institutions (e.g., World Bank, DFID, USAID), and research institutions (e.g., 3ie, JPAL, BRAC Research and Evaluation Division)
- manual searches of journals not covered by any of the above and books in academic libraries of different universities
- use of back-referencing from recent studies (including [systematic] reviews) and (where possible) citation tracking to identify additional relevant studies
- contacting experts on microcredit (and women's empowerment) for (additional) references

## Coding and Data Extraction

The review extracted information on the following aspects:

- Descriptive information:
  - publication data (title, author, year, type of publication)
  - geographical location
  - type of intervention

*(Continued)*

(Continued)

- – credit independent variable (specification)
- – solidarity group mechanism (yes/no)
- – characteristics of clients
- • Information concerning inclusion and exclusion criteria:
  - – study characteristics (see above)
  - – methodological design
  - – quality assessment (see next section)
- • Information for synthesis:
  - – effect size variables relating to women's decision making and control over household expenditures
  - – theoretical mechanisms underlying changes in outcomes
- • Information relevant for the quality assessment (see below)

### Quality Assessment

The review distinguished between assessment of methodological quality (risk of bias assessment) and the quality of the theoretical framework of selected studies. Regarding the former, first studies were categorized according to research design and analytical method (see Chapter 9, Figure 9.1 for guidance; for the detailed assessment, see Vaessen et al., 2014; see also Duvendack et al., 2011). Subsequently, all studies were assessed on the basis of whether the primary study had appropriately addressed the following aspects: selection bias and confounding, spillover effects and contamination, outcome reporting bias, analysis reporting bias, and other risks of bias. The second type of assessment, quality of the theoretical framework, focused on three criteria only: presence of a theoretical framework on women's empowerment and more specifically women's control over household spending, coherence between the theoretical framework and empirical data collection, and whether there was discussion and data collection on control over and use of credit.

SOURCE: Summarized and adapted from Vaessen et al. (2014).

Given the twofold purpose of the systematic review, the review comprised two main lines of synthetic analysis. A quantitative meta-analysis was conducted to develop an overall estimate of the effect of microcredit on women's control over household spending. Yet reviewing and synthesizing quantitative results from studies with a high level of internal validity is only one side of the coin. The other side is to understand what makes them work, or what prevents them from working. This means that the question about what mechanisms are believed to make the program work has to be addressed. The review was inspired by the synthesis approach discussed in Van der Knaap, Leeuw, Bogaerts, and Nijssen (2008; see also Chapter 9), which combines a focus on synthesizing high-internal-validity studies with theory-based evaluation principles of "opening the black box"[7] to examine the mechanisms underlying processes of change.

## a. Meta-analysis

In order to compare and possibly pool the different effect estimates of primary studies, they first needed to be converted to a common scale. Given the diversity of estimation methods found in the selected studies, the review used 12 different effect size formulas, in each case measuring improvements in empowerment-related variables as an increase in the intervention group over the comparison. The meta-analysis consisted of the following steps:

- extraction of parameters to be used in effect size calculation
- selection of effect size formula to be used for each study/variable combination
- effect size calculation
- collation of effect sizes and merging with study characteristics
- description of diversity of studies
- initial calculation of "synthetic" effect size to compute each study's overall effect size
- meta-analysis across studies by subgroups and/or meta-regression

Several challenges needed to be overcome in the above process. Duvendack, Palmer-Jones, and Vaessen (2014) and Vaessen et al. (2014) discuss the multiple technical challenges and how they can be addressed to generate comparable effect size estimates for similar outcome variables. An example of a challenge is the lack of readily available formulas for extracting effect size estimates (e.g., for studies reporting logit, multinomial logit, probit, ordered probit, linear probability, and tobit estimates). Other challenges concern dealing with continuous outcome variables and categorical outcome variables and dealing with within-study dependent effect sizes. Due to the technical nature of these challenges, we do not further discuss them here (see, e.g., Borenstein, Hedges, Higgins, & Rothstein, 2009; Higgins & Green, 2011; Lipsey & Wilson, 2001).

## b. Qualitative Analysis of Mechanisms

A useful way to unpack the construct of empowerment is based on Kabeer (2001), who distinguishes among three interrelated dimensions of empowerment: resources, agency, and achievements. As a basis for uncovering the causality between microcredit and women's control over household spending, the review connected this framework with the concept of behavioral mechanisms. Hedstrom (2005, p. 181) defines a mechanism as "a constellation of entities and activities that are linked to one another in such a way that they regularly bring about a particular type of outcome." Based on Coleman (1990), Hedstrom (2005), and Elster (2007), the review distinguished between three types of mechanisms: situational, action-formation, and transformational.

For microcredit, the meaning of the different types of mechanisms can be summarized through the following example questions:

- Situational mechanism: To what extent and in what ways does the existing opportunity structure of a region/area affect the chances for women to receive microcredit?

- Action-formation mechanism: How do changes in the opportunity structure through microcredit affect the behavior of women vis-à-vis men in the household, and under which conditions? Which social, cultural, and behavioral mechanisms underlie processes of empowerment (e.g., an increase in women's decision-making power within the household) of women receiving microcredit?
- Transformational mechanism: Which mechanisms explain how changes in the behavior of individuals contribute to changes at a macro level (e.g., at community or regional level)?

The following sequence for extracting and synthesizing mechanisms was followed in the review study:

- First, the reviewers analyzed which of the studies in the final batch include a theoretical framework on microcredit and women's control over household spending. The definition of a theoretical framework used here includes not only a set of (deductively structured) propositions on the relationship between microcredit and empowerment, but also the presentation of one or a few hypotheses about this relationship as well as a discussion on theoretical aspects of microcredit and empowerment. Usually, such a discussion is part of a review of the (largely) empirical literature.
- Subsequently, the reviewers searched in the studies for information on mechanisms. Sometimes primary study authors explicitly refer to mechanisms, but more often they do not. By reading between the lines, one is able to detect statements alluding to mechanisms. Using insights from argumentational analysis[8] (Leeuw, 2003; Toulmin, 1958), these statements were identified. The search activity focused on the empirical part of the papers. Statements included both confirmation of hypotheses or assumptions and refutations.
- Finally, the reviewers summarized authors' statements alluding to mechanisms into a narrative overview per type of mechanism.

# 2. Illustrations of Findings

## 2.1 Search Results

Figure 16.1 shows the results of the search. Of 6,000 hits in web-based search engines, targeted searches in journal and books, backward and forward tracking of references and author contact, 310 papers were selected for full-text examination. Of these, 190 studies were found to be of priority 1 and 2, meaning that they focused on the relationship between microcredit and women's empowerment and included original empirical analysis. Of these, 113 studies included quantitative analysis on microcredit and empowerment. Purely qualitative studies (77) were excluded. Of the 113 quantitative studies, 56 were considered to be of relevance to the review's scope, meaning that they focused on the relationship between microcredit and women's empowerment as a dependent variable, as expressed

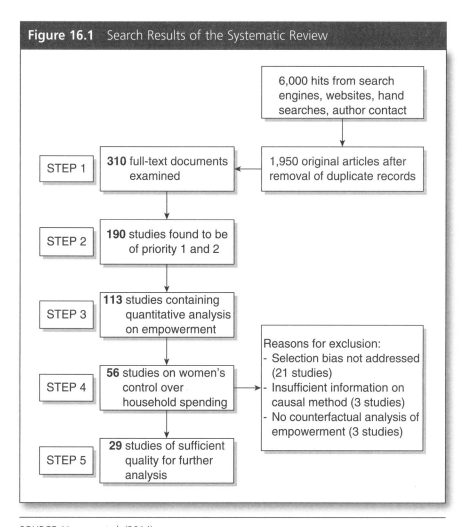

**Figure 16.1**  Search Results of the Systematic Review

6,000 hits from search engines, websites, hand searches, author contact

STEP 1 | **310** full-text documents examined

1,950 original articles after removal of duplicate records

STEP 2 | **190** studies found to be of priority 1 and 2

STEP 3 | **113** studies containing quantitative analysis on empowerment

STEP 4 | **56** studies on women's control over household spending

Reasons for exclusion:
- Selection bias not addressed (21 studies)
- Insufficient information on causal method (3 studies)
- No counterfactual analysis of empowerment (3 studies)

STEP 5 | **29** studies of sufficient quality for further analysis

SOURCE: Vaessen et al. (2014).

NOTE: The 29 identified studies represent 25 independent findings.

through one or more aspects of women's control over household spending. After subsequently applying the final methodological quality inclusion criterion,[9] 29 studies were selected to be included in the review. Of these 29 studies, 25 were found to be independent.[10]

## 2.2 Description of Included Studies

Study designs varied across the studies, with four estimating results from experimental designs (randomized assignment to intervention) and the remaining employing a range of different quasi-experimental and multivariate regression approaches.

A first reading of descriptive results of the selected studies revealed that, in a majority of the included (independent) studies (19 out of 29, or 15 out of 25 independent findings), there is a positive and statistically significant relationship between microcredit and one or more aspects of women's control over household expenditures. At the same time, 10 studies did not find any statistically significant relationship between microcredit and women's control over household spending. Moreover, in most studies that did find some effect, many of the studied relationships between microcredit and aspects of women's control over household resources turned out to be statistically insignificant, depending on the nature of the credit independent variable, the type of outcome measure, and the specific sample of (female) clients covered by particular analyses.

While one might conclude that many studies do find some type of positive effect, this assessment does not take into account the characteristics of methodological design and implementation (risk of bias) of individual studies and the magnitude of effects and study sample size (effect size and statistical precision). A critical appraisal of the evidence base, including assessment of study independence and risk of bias, together with a statistical meta-analysis, weighted by the inverse of study variance, are needed before one can confidently conclude whether this indication truly reflects an overall positive effect of microcredit on women's control over household spending.

## 2.3 Quality Assessment

The assessment of risk of bias assessed the design and implementation of the study methodology according to risks of bias due to confounding, spillovers and contamination, and other biases. A transparent decision rule to reach an overall assessment of risk of bias was used. Overall, none of the (independent) studies included in this systematic review were assessed as having low risk of bias; the majority (16) were judged as having a high risk of bias, while the remaining 9 were assessed as having a medium risk of bias.

In addition, the assessment of the quality of theory in primary studies revealed that 9 (independent) studies, although including empirical analysis on microcredit and women's control over household spending, lacked a theoretical framework on microcredit and empowerment. A further 3 studies used a theoretical framework or theory that discussed causal relationships between microcredit and empowerment (without explicitly addressing women's control over household spending), and 13 presented a theoretical discussion that also dealt with causal relationships between microcredit and (particular aspects of) women's control over household spending.

## 2.4 Quantitative Synthesis of Effect Sizes

Synthesis through meta-analysis is possible only for studies that can be meaningfully compared. In other words, they need to be comparable on a conceptual level, which means that similar constructs and relationships are used and they need to follow similar statistical approaches (Lipsey & Wilson, 2001). The 25 independent findings included in the meta-analysis were selected on the basis of including particular proxies of women's control over household expenditures. However, these still vary by treatment indicator, analytical method, and bias assessment. Moreover, even though the review focuses on one specific dimension of empowerment, there was heterogeneity in outcome variables across studies. The studies reviewed were quite diverse, suggesting that the so-called apples and oranges problem could be an issue.[11]

The review also found heterogeneity of treatment across studies. Treatment indicators can be dichotomous (e.g., membership, participation, receiving a loan) or continuous (e.g., length of membership, number or amount of loans taken). The reviewers pooled studies with membership and participation treatment indicators, in part because these terms are often used interchangeably; however, it is important to bear in mind that microfinance institution (MFI) members may or may not receive microfinance and may or may not receive other dimensions of treatment, such as group discussions, technical assistance, or social support from peers or the MFI. Hence the estimates from these studies are "intention to treat." The reviewers did not include studies with treatment indicators that could not be represented by a dichotomous membership variable, because they were few and could not be put on a comparable basis. The majority of treatment indicators could be treated as dichotomous (92%). In order to address the challenges discussed above, the meta-analysis aimed to address heterogeneity concerns through sensitivity analysis and publication bias assessment (see Vaessen et al., 2014, for detailed analyses).

Figure 16.2 provides an illustration of the types of meta-analytical results that the study generated. The results from randomized controlled trials (see Figure 16.2 and Table 16.1) suggest there is no evidence for impacts of microcredit on empowerment-related variables either in individual studies or when looking at the estimated pooled effect size using inverse-variance weighted random effects meta-analysis (SMD = –0.007; 95% confidence interval: –0.041, 0.027). The studies are largely homogeneous in terms of outcome measure: Banerjee et al. (2009) measured women's decision making with respect to household purchases directly using an index of spending items. Karlan and Zinman (2007) used an index comprising largely spending items but also including a question on fertility. Kim et al. (2007) similarly used an autonomy index regarding decisions over household purchases but also including decisions on child health care and visiting family and friends. Crépon, Devoto, Duflo, and Parienté (2011) used a close proxy of decision making over household spending (share of household activities managed by women).

Analyses with the remaining quasi-experimental studies generated similar results: The results of the meta-analysis suggest that the effect sizes were generally insignificantly different from zero, and when marginally significant were small.

Women's control over household resources constitutes an important intermediary dimension in processes of women's empowerment. Consequently, the review concluded that given the overall lack of effect of microcredit on women's control over household spending, it is very unlikely that microcredit has a meaningful and substantial impact on empowerment processes in a broader sense. While the latter type of impact may have occurred in particular contexts, overall the evidence suggests that this is not the case. As a result, there appears to be a gap between the often optimistic (societal) belief in the capacity of microcredit to ameliorate the position of women in decision-making processes within the household on the one hand and the empirical evidence base on the other hand.

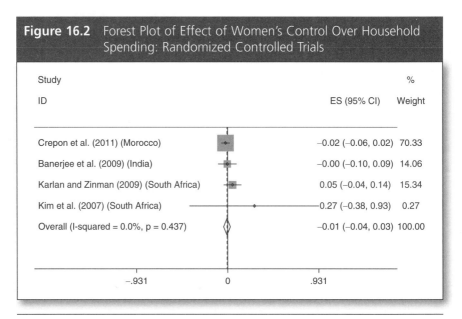

**Figure 16.2** Forest Plot of Effect of Women's Control Over Household Spending: Randomized Controlled Trials

SOURCE: Vaessen et al. (2014).

**Table 16.1** Meta-analysis of Microcredit and Women's Control Over Household Spending: Randomized Controlled Trials

| Panel A | | | | |
|---|---|---|---|---|
| | SMD | 95% Confidence interval | | % Weight |
| Crépon et al. (2011) | −0.021 | −0.062 | 0.020 | 70.33 |
| Banerjee et al. (2009) | −0.003 | −0.095 | 0.088 | 14.06 |
| Karlan and Zinman (2007) | 0.049 | −0.039 | 0.137 | 15.34 |
| Kim et al. (2007) | 0.273 | −0.385 | 0.931 | 0.27 |
| D + L pooled effect size (ES) | −0.007 | −0.041 | 0.027 | 100.00 |
| Panel B | | | | |
| Heterogeneity chi-squared | 2.72 (df = 3), $p$ = 0.437 | | | |
| I-squared (variation in ES attributable to heterogeneity) | 0.0% | | | |
| Estimate of between-study variance Tau-squared | 0.0000 | | | |
| Test of ES = 0 | $z$ = 0.40, $p$ = 0.690 | | | |

SOURCE: Vaessen et al. (2014).

The conclusions on the effects of microcredit on empowerment were also in line with two other systematic review studies on microcredit by Duvendack et al. (2011) and Stewart et al. (2010), who reported to a very limited extent on empowerment effects.[12]

## 2.5 Qualitative Synthesis of Included Studies

Having looked at the possible changes attributable to microcredit interventions, the question now arises of how these causal changes work. How can we explain the nonexistence of effects and heterogeneity in effects found across studies? The most important mechanisms for understanding the effect of microcredit on women's control over household expenditures are situational and action-formation mechanisms.

The systematic review found an interesting array of behavioral mechanisms at work, most importantly eight different action-formation mechanisms, in the context of causal relationships between microcredit and women's control over household spending (see Figure 16.3).

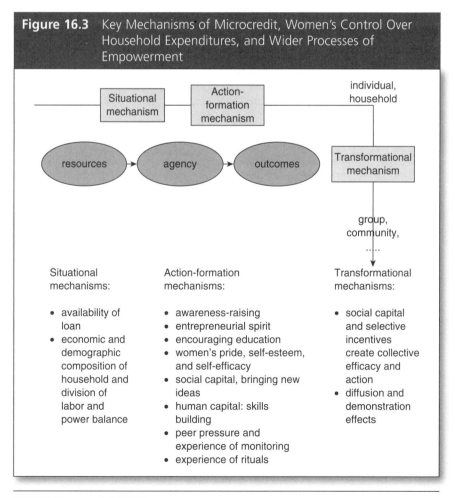

**Figure 16.3** Key Mechanisms of Microcredit, Women's Control Over Household Expenditures, and Wider Processes of Empowerment

SOURCE: Vaessen et al. (2014).

What Figure 16.3 shows is that microcredit, in order to lead to women's empowerment through women's control over household spending, has to trigger behavior through a diversity of mechanisms—not only those that deal with situational factors like the demography and poverty levels of female clients and their households, but also sociological ones like social capital and peer pressure and psychological ones such as self-efficacy and self-esteem.

From the identified mechanisms at work, the review concludes that the way in which microcredit is delivered, in combination with the given gender relations context, seems to determine to a large extent whether microcredit can make a difference for women's decision-making power and control over resources in the household. To address this issue in more detail, and to develop generalizable conclusions about how microcredit affects women's decision-making power across different contexts, a different (complementary) review approach is needed. Some of the aspects that need to be considered in such an approach are discussed below.

# 3. Final Considerations From a Complexity Perspective

The context-specificity of gender relations, and by implication women's empowerment, is a key element that makes learning and generalizing about causal relations between interventions such as microcredit and women's empowerment so complex.

In the literature, several factors have been identified that can explain the different explanatory mechanisms at work regarding microcredit and women's control over household spending (see, e.g., Kabeer, 2001). First of all, primary studies were conducted in different settings, for example, different regions, countries, and rural and urban settings. Empowerment is highly context-specific, and existing gender relations, norms, and beliefs differ widely across regions and countries. Gender relations are shaped by a complex interplay of religious, cultural, and socioeconomic factors. Consequently, what in one case could be called empowering in other cases is not, which has implications for the external validity of findings of individual studies as well as synthesis across studies. For example, it is more likely that microcredit of any type will have an effect on women's participation in household spending in a context where the existing gender norms are not extremely male-biased. In a situation where general gender norms are extremely pro-male, it is less likely that microcredit will be enough to increase women's agency inside the household.

Only a systematic review approach that takes into account context-specific variations in the meaning of women's empowerment, depending on resource conditions and gender relations, for example, is able to generate meaningful patterns of generalization on the causal relationship between microcredit and women's empowerment. Given the substantial variations in gender relations across regions, cultures, ethnic groups, and so on, there is definitely a risk of overgeneralization, where comparisons across the globe on similar variables (as done in the systematic review discussed in this chapter) in some cases lose their meaning given the divergent underlying conditions. For the same reasons, the systematic review did not attempt to articulate an overall theory of change. A related problem is the geographical, cultural, and other types of balance in the group of selected studies for final synthetic analysis. In the discussed review, a high proportion of the studies were from India or Bangladesh.

A second major dimension of complexity concerns the content and quality of the available primary studies. The systematic review study emphasized the internal validity of findings in the selection and analysis of primary studies. Across primary studies, there were differences in the methodologies used to study microfinance impacts, ranging from experimental to quasi-experimental to non-experimental. Moreover, primary studies cover different time spans and lengths of follow-up. Some studies may be based on one data collection moment or a dataset of one particular moment in time only, while other studies may include multiple data collection points with months or years in between these points. In the case of empowerment, a longer time span is warranted for changes to be observed. Changes in some aspects of empowerment may take a long time to materialize; if one implements an impact study after 3 years, it is unlikely that some of the intended changes (e.g., changes in local gender relations) have already taken place.

Also problematic was the lack of other types of information, apart from information on effects, needed to conduct a credible synthetic study. There are substantial differences among microfinance programs and their microcredit activities. As discussed in Chapter 9, systematic review is often confronted with an evidence paradox. Those studies that are strong on the internal validity of findings are often weak on other aspects. In the case of this review, several information gaps affected the potential to explain causal change between microcredit and women's control over household spending. These gaps were partly caused by the general state of the literature but also by the choice of review and synthesis approach. Qualitative studies were not included in the synthetic analysis.[13] Moreover, any other type of documentation relating to the subject[14] (e.g., on the nature of microcredit activities of those interventions that were part of the batch of selected studies) was not included in the synthesis phase.

There were a couple of important information gaps. First, the classical evidence paradox highlighted in Chapter 9 applies here. The fact that more or less half of the studies did not include a proper theoretical discussion on the causal relations studied in the quantitative analysis (with respect to women's control over household spending) reveals an important weakness in the quality of impact studies on this subject. This weakness is particularly problematic given that many also used questionable causal identification strategies. In the exercise of identifying and articulating mechanisms, the reviewers focused only on the information to be found in explicit statements by authors of the selected primary studies on causal relations. An alternative, more accurate approach would have been to reconstruct patterns of regularity by systematically collecting any information from studies that could provide insights into the nature of the intervention, the context, the target group, and so on in order to infer the how and why of proven (absence of) causal relationships. This task would not only have been more cumbersome, it would also likely have proven to be unproductive, especially given the lack of detail on these issues in the selected primary studies.

Second, there is a lot of diversity in microfinance organizations and the exact intervention delivered to microfinance clients (including microcredit and linkages with other interventions). The reviewers were unable to isolate the credit effect from other associated interventions on the independent variable side. In fact, in most studies it was impossible to determine whether credit was the only intervention at work. However, several of the identified mechanisms highlight the importance of membership of a solidarity group in triggering change, as the social interaction among peers can have a significant effect on empowerment processes. These factors are only very partially captured by impact studies.

Third, most microfinance programs, particularly those targeted at women and those studied in relation to the topic of women's empowerment, use group intermediation. While these programs may look very similar at first sight, there are important differences from a gender perspective in the way group intermediation is used, which might explain differential impacts on women's empowerment. Finally, the potential "dark side" of microcredit is under-researched. Impact studies, especially those containing quantitative analysis, underreport (or mostly do not report) on the negative aspects of microcredit, such as the psychological stress of carrying debt or the use of microcredit as a tool for men to strengthen their power over women (see, e.g., Goetz & Sen Gupta, 1996).

# 4. Practical Applications

This particular case has revealed several methodological challenges in systematic review in the context of complexity:

- Systematic reviews have a comparative advantage when looking at the question "Does it work?" Even though there are options for expanding the scope and methodology for looking into questions such as "How does it work and under what circumstances?" other approaches such as realist synthesis are in principle better suited to deal with the latter type of questions. By implication, this makes realist synthesis more appropriate to address complexity issues in review and synthesis (see Chapter 20).

- Empowerment is a highly context-specific phenomenon, and existing gender relations, norms, and beliefs differ widely across regions and countries. Only a systematic review approach that takes into account context-specific variations in the meaning of women's empowerment, depending on resource conditions and gender relations, for example, is able to generate meaningful patterns of generalization on the causal relationship between microcredit and women's empowerment.

- The extent to which systematic reviews can address complexity issues (e.g., patterns of causal change; the interconnectedness between interventions, outcomes, and context) is also highly dependent on the nature and quality of existing evidence. Apart from the evidence paradox (see Chapter 9), there are considerable evidence gaps in individual studies and consequently at the synthetic level in terms of lack of a careful description of the intervention and its context, the time period taken into account to study effects, and the attention to unintended effects.

# References

Armendariz de Aghion, B., & Morduch, J. (2005). *The economics of microfinance*. Cambridge, MA: MIT Press.

Banerjee, A., Duflo, E., Glennerster, R., & Kinnan, C. (2009). *The miracle of microfinance? Evidence from a randomized evaluation* (NBER Working Paper). Cambridge, MA: National Bureau of Economic Research.

Borenstein, M., Hedges, L. V., Higgins, J. P. T., & Rothstein, H. R. (2009). *Introduction to meta-analysis*. Chichester, UK: Wiley.

Coleman, J. S. (1990). *Foundations of social theory*. Cambridge, MA: Belknap Press.

Cook, T. D., & Campbell, D. T. (1979). *Quasi-experimentation: Design and analysis for field settings*. Chicago, IL: Rand McNally.

Crépon, B., Devoto, F., Duflo, E., & Parienté, W. (2011). *Impact of microcredit in rural areas of Morocco: Evidence from a randomized evaluation* (Working Paper). Retrieved from http://www.crest.fr/ckfinder/userfiles/files/pageperso/Impact_of_microcredit_in_rural_areas_of_Morocco_2011_04.pdf

Duvendack, M., Palmer-Jones, R., Copestake, J. G., Hooper, L., Loke, Y., & Rao, N. (2011). *What is the evidence of the impact of microfinance on the well-being of poor people?* London, UK: EPPI-Centre.

Duvendack, M., Palmer-Jones, R., & Vaessen, J. (2014). Meta-analysis of the impact of microcredit on women's control over household spending. *Journal of Development Effectiveness, 6*(2), 73–96.

Elster, J. (2007). *Explaining social behaviour: More nuts and bolts for the social sciences*. Cambridge, UK: Cambridge University Press.

Goetz, A. M., & Sen Gupta, R. (1996). Who takes the credit? Gender, power and control over loan use in rural credit programmes in Bangladesh. *World Development, 24*(1), 45–64.

Goldberg, N. (2005). *Measuring the impact of microfinance: Taking stock of what we know*. Washington, DC: Grameen Foundation USA.

Hedstrom, P. (2005). *Dissecting the social: On the principles of analytical sociology*. Cambridge, UK: Cambridge University Press.

Higgins, J. P. T., & Green, S. (2011). *Cochrane handbook for systematic reviews of interventions*. Retrieved from http://www.cochrane-handbook.org

Kabeer, N. (2001). Conflicts over credit: Re-Evaluating the empowerment potential of loans to women in rural Bangladesh. *World Development, 29*(1), 63–84.

Karlan, D., & Goldberg, N. (2006). *The impact of microfinance: A review of methodological issues*. New Haven, CT: Innovations for Poverty for Action.

Karlan, D., & Zinman, J. (2007). *Expanding credit access: Using randomized supply decisions to estimate the impacts* (CEPR Discussion Papers 6180). London, UK: Centre for Economic Policy Research.

Kim, J. C., Watts, C. H., Hargreaves, J. R., Ndhlovu, L. X., Phetla, G., Morison, L. A., . . . Pronyk, P. (2007). Understanding the impact of a microfinance-based intervention on women's empowerment and the reduction of intimate partner violence in South Africa. *American Journal of Public Health, 97*, 1794–1802.

Leeuw, F. L. (2003). Reconstructing program theories: Methods available and problems to be solved. *American Journal of Evaluation, 24*(1), 5–20.

Lipsey, M. W., & Wilson, D. B. (2001). *Practical meta-analysis*. Thousand Oaks, CA: Sage.

Malhotra, A., Schuler, S. R., & Boender, C. (2002). *Measuring women's empowerment as a variable in international development*. Washington, DC: World Bank, Gender and Development Group.

Mayoux, L. (2006). *Sustainable microfinance for women's empowerment.* San Francisco, CA: Levi Strauss Foundation.

Odell, K. (2010). *Measuring the impact of microfinance: Taking another look.* Washington, DC: Grameen Foundation.

Pitt, M. M., Khandker, S. R., & Cartwright, J. (2003). *Does micro-credit empower women? Evidence from Bangladesh* (Policy Research Working Paper 2998). Washington, DC: World Bank.

Stewart, R., van Rooyen, C., Dickson, K., Majoro, M., & De Wet, T. (2010). *What is the impact of microfinance on poor people? A systematic review of evidence from Sub-Saharan Africa.* London, UK: EPPI-Centre.

Stewart, R., van Rooyen, C., Korth, M., Chereni, A., Rebelo Da Silva, N., & de Wet, T. (2012). *Do micro-credit, micro-savings and micro-leasing serve as effective financial inclusion interventions enabling poor people, and especially women, to engage in meaningful economic opportunities in low- and middle-income countries? A systematic review of the evidence.* London, UK: EPPI-Centre.

Toulmin, S. (1958). *The uses of argument.* Cambridge, UK: Cambridge University Press.

Vaessen, J., Rivas, A., Duvendack, M., Palmer-Jones, R., Leeuw, F. L., van Gils, G., . . . Waddington, H. (2014). *The effects of microcredit on women's control over household spending in developing countries.* Campbell Systematic Reviews.

Van der Knaap, L. M., Leeuw, F. L., Bogaerts, S., & Nijssen, L. T. J. (2008). Combining Campbell standards and the realistic evaluation approach: The best of two worlds? *American Journal of Evaluation, 29,* 48–57.

# Notes

1. The types of institutions providing microfinance services is quite diverse. See, for example, www.mixmarket.org.

2. This term refers to a microcredit modality in which clients are organized in groups. Transaction costs for selection of clients and enforcement of repayment are transferred from the microfinance institution to the group. Regarding the latter, repayment is often based on principles of joint liability (i.e., if one of the group members cannot pay back a loan, other members have to step in) or contingent renewal (i.e., no new loans will be issued to group members if one or more members are in arrears).

3. Some of the principal characteristics of this type of systematic review are peer-reviewed protocol, focus on one or a limited number of (highly similar) outcome variables, hierarchy of evidence (with quantitative experimental approaches featuring at the top), and, where possible, meta-analysis (extracting and pooling effect sizes across studies).

4. In other words, they were supported by a methodological design that enabled the researcher to draw credible conclusions about the attribution of changes to the intervention.

5. In a meta-analysis, one would need to group studies according to the type of comparison or focus on one type of comparison only.

6. Most microfinance institutions were founded in the 1980s or later. A few were founded in the 1970s. The roots of the Grameen Bank, a pioneer institution in the field of microfinance, can be traced back to 1976, but it became an independent microfinance institution in 1983.

7. The black box is a metaphor used in this context to indicate that the causal relationships between an intervention and its effects are all too often hidden and not made explicit.

8. Argumentational analysis can be used for analyzing chains of arguments, and it helps to reconstruct and fill in argumentations. A central concept is the warrant, which is the "because" part of an argument; it says that B follows from A because of a (generally) accepted principle. The "because" part of such an argument is often not made explicit. Consequently, these warrants must be inferred by the person performing the analysis (Leeuw, 2003).

9. Meaning that there is evidence that the study has attempted to address the attribution problem.

10. For a discussion, see Vaessen et al. (2014).

11. Studies that are different in these respects (to an acceptable extent; if not, pooling would not be recommended) should not be pooled without concern for sensitivity analysis (Lipsey & Wilson, 2001).

12. Both systematic review studies had a much broader scope, looking at a range of potential effects of microcredit but with less detailed analysis. A third systematic review (Stewart et al., 2012) did not look at this aspect.

13. Due to time and resource constraints, but also due to challenges in terms of comparability between qualitative and quantitative studies and to some extent the challenges of avoiding bias in selection and achieving comprehensive coverage.

14. Apart from an extensive preparatory study on the general microcredit and empowerment literature.

# CHAPTER 17

# Evaluation of Coordination Against Trafficking in Persons

## *A Case Study of a Complexity-Responsive Evaluation*

Kim Forss

*This case study is an example of a low-budget and quick approach to gathering evidence to support a policy initiative in multilateral cooperation. It shows how a structured approach to gathering data through country- and regional-level case studies and synthesis of evaluations, questionnaires, and interviews could provide a comprehensive analysis that pinpoints short-comings in the global system and identifies organizational reforms that nations can call for in the context of discussing anti-trafficking initiatives.*

Compared to the overarching framework that defines complexity in this volume, this case study might seem to raise the level of complexity even further. The evaluation described here did not target any particular project, program, or policy. There is no specific object of evaluation that might appear more or less complex, and that in itself raises the level of complexity. So what was the starting point? It was a very simple and basic question: What can be done to fight trafficking in persons? Does that sound complex?

The question was formulated at the Swedish Ministry for Foreign Affairs in early 2012, although it was not exactly a question but more an expression of a desire for political action expressed. Sweden wished to show a high profile on working against trafficking. Sweden has a preference for working through the multilateral system to address global issues. The United Nations General Assembly has a rolling program of issues that are brought up for discussions among the member states, and the General Assembly had decided that action against trafficking would be discussed in May 2013. In this meeting, Sweden was keen to contribute and to launch proposals that would lead to better, more effective, and more efficient global action against trafficking.

To have any chance of mobilizing action in the General Assembly, it is necessary to have "done the homework." The issues at hand would need to be well researched, and proposals grounded in a solid understanding, in this case of trafficking as a phenomenon and how to organize efforts to fight it. The Swedish Ministry for Foreign Affairs decided to undertake an evaluation of how the multilateral system addresses trafficking. The Swedish interventions in the General Assembly debate were to be based on evidence of strengths and weaknesses of the multilateral system's response to trafficking. In order to understand the scope of the task it is necessary to acknowledge the following:

- Working against trafficking is part of the mandate of several UN organizations, including funds and programs (e.g., UNODC, UNDP, UNICEF, UNWOMEN, UNFPA) and specialized agencies (e.g., ILO, UNESCO, WHO, FAO) and other international organizations (e.g., UNHCR, OHCHR, IOM).[1]
- Each of these organizations has projects and programs that address different aspects of trafficking. They have country-based programs and projects, regional projects, and some global programs. Some, such as UNESCO, had been active in the past but were not active in 2012. Others were increasing their attention toward trafficking. Many times the agencies work alone on projects and at times they collaborate; competition for funds and for a mandate is also a feature of the scene.
- Working against trafficking takes the form of operational projects in capacity building with, for example, police forces, customs authorities, and social agencies, but also, and importantly, advocacy at global, regional, and national levels and standard setting through multilateral agreements.

It is this "mess" that became the subject of the evaluation, and the challenge was to understand how it works, to what extent it is coordinated, and what could be done—and by whom—to improve it. However, it was not the stark reality of the projects that was to be evaluated. The evaluative focus was on the system of coordination between the agencies that funded and implemented the various projects. That being said, an evaluation of how these agencies coordinate their work must of course also be informed by what they were coordinating. Hence some knowledge of whether the projects and programs were efficient and effective, had a sustainable impact, and were relevant was certainly called for. Without knowing the answer, the hypothesis was that a serious inquiry would indicate room for improvement.

# 1. A Brief Note on the Phenomenon of Trafficking

Trafficking in persons is a huge and growing business. There are many uncertainties about exactly how many people are victims of trafficking, when, and where. It is an illegal industry connected to organized crime, hence many basic facts are hidden. The core of criminal activity is surrounded by practices of uncertain legality, and it is constantly changing in nature. One thing is certain: Trafficking exploits vulnerable persons, in particular women and children, and it is a blatant violation of basic human rights. Trafficking in persons appears in many guises and has been used as an umbrella term for activities that involve one person holding another person in compelled service.

In an increasingly globalized world, the spatial and controlled boundaries of existence are rapidly shrinking. The flows of capital and people are in a constant flux. This means endless opportunities, but also endless new ways of exploiting people. Today, approximately 27 million men, women, and children are victims of human trafficking (State Department, 2012, p. 7), and the International Labor Organization estimates that forced labor claims at least 20 million victims at any time. The real numbers are likely to be higher. Trafficking concerns hidden populations, thus an inherent problem in anti-trafficking work is to assess where, why, and who is being exploited.

*Human trafficking* is a broad and complex term for the many different ways people are exploited. Research, literature, and project work often tend to focus on sexual exploitation, thus concealing the many other forms of trafficking (UNESCO, 2011, p. 141). Particularly, trafficking for purposes of forced labor has been seen as less significant, partly because this group is viewed as less vulnerable, being primarily male and often entering migration work voluntarily to then end up being trafficked. Forced labor is most common in agriculture, mining and construction, and manufacturing industries. Many women and children are exploited as household workers. In countries where dowry is a tradition, many girls are forced to work as housemaids before marriage so as to be able to pay their dowry. Other spheres where trafficking is common include debt bondage, street begging, and recruitment of child soldiers.

This raises the question of how the evaluation could handle the complex issues of gender roles and the norms and cultural factors that shape the practice of all forms of trafficking and forced labor—and the response to curb and eliminate both. As we will see, the evaluation had a low budget and was undertaken quickly to feed into a policy process. The evaluation focused on organizational processes, particularly processes of governance, financing, and coordination. The complexity at "ground level" could be recognized without necessarily affecting the conclusions at the global level. A more in-depth evaluation of projects would have had to take a participatory approach to gain information and understanding from victims of trafficking and those working against trafficking in social services, customs, police, schools, and so on. The approach taken here recognizes the role of gender and the importance of culture, and it builds the understanding of the need for global action on this premise.

# 2. The Evaluation Process

What does it mean to evaluate the multilateral system's activities against trafficking? For one thing, it is clear that none of the organizations mentioned above nor any other international bodies asked for an evaluation. To be sure, most of the agencies have projects and other activities against trafficking, and these are regularly evaluated. But who evaluates the organizations themselves and the agencies as part of a system? Even though it would be hard to imagine a formally commissioned evaluation from the system itself,[2] that does not mean evaluation questions cannot be asked—and answered. Such is the case here: The government of Sweden asked the evaluation question and took the liberty of doing so on its own and for its own purposes.[3]

In such a situation access to data could become problematic. If organizations like UNODC, UNDP, ILO, and the others were not involved in commissioning the evaluation, they would not have any obligation to meet with an evaluation team or provide access to their projects. In this case it helped that Sweden is seen as a strong supporter of the multilateral system and has generously funded all the agencies. Hence, it was unlikely that the agencies would be noncooperative. The Swedish Ministry for Foreign Affairs drafted a brief about the evaluation and circulated this to the agencies. The brief emphasized that Sweden undertook the evaluation to strengthen its engagement in the struggle against trafficking. The brief invited cooperation in the process, outlined a process whereby the agencies would benefit from evaluation findings, and promised a review process whereby the agencies would be able to correct any mistakes in findings.

The overall design of the evaluation was based on the three-level architecture of the multilateral response to trafficking: global, regional, and national. It was decided that a study of anti-trafficking must look at what takes place at a national level and at a global level. Once that was done, it became equally obvious that analyzing some kind of in-between level was also needed given that many multilateral interventions, as well as national interventions, operate through cross-border collaborations.

The multilateral agencies themselves, along with the staff of the Ministry for Foreign Affairs, identified coordination as the weak spot of the system. The conceptual focus of the evaluation was thus set to be the mechanisms of coordination. The first step in the process was to identify possible sources of data that provide information on the strengths and weaknesses of the multilateral response to trafficking and then to identify how one could get access to that information. Three primary sources of information were identified:

- Multilateral agencies themselves, as well as bilateral agencies that provide funding, regularly commission reviews and evaluations. One of the tasks we set ourselves was to retrieve as many as possible and synthesize them to detect common patterns in terms of evaluation criteria: efficiency, effectiveness, impact, sustainability, and relevance.[4] The databases of different donor organizations and the OECD-DAC database contain reviews and evaluations of anti-trafficking efforts by other actors too, such as civil society organizations and bilateral programs, or even the combined activities of organizations. Because there are lessons to be learned from these as well, they were included in the synthesis.[5]

- It would of course be necessary to speak to people in the system, and that took the form of individual interviews with actors in the UN system and their partners at global, regional, and country levels. In the course of the study, visits were made to the headquarters of UNODC in Vienna and to UNICEF, UN Women, and UNDP in New York. Additionally, a country visit to Vietnam and a study of regional coordination in Bangkok were organized. Southeast Asia thus became a case study, first by looking at the multilateral activities in a country (Vietnam) and second by looking at a region. Southeast Asia has long been a hotspot in international trafficking. Consequently, multilateral agencies have a long history of working together, as well as competing, in the region. During the visits the evaluator met with all the agencies, with the national governments in Thailand and Vietnam, with regional organizations in Bangkok, and with the many project partners active at the field level.

- The evaluation had a global scope and could not rely only on a close view of activities in Southeast Asia. Coordination between agencies is a feature in many other regions, such as Southern Africa, Eastern Europe, and Central America. The agencies have projects in several other places too. As the evaluation was done under the auspices of the Swedish Ministry for Foreign Affairs, it was decided to make use of the embassies for information gathering. A survey was designed and sent to the Swedish Embassies in a sample of countries where trafficking is an issue (i.e., countries classified as Tier 2, Tier 2 Watch list, or Tier 3 in the U.S. State Department's *Trafficking in Persons Report* from 2011). The embassies were asked to gather information on what the agencies did to fight trafficking, how they coordinated their activities, and their perception of these intervention effects. Ultimately, the embassy staff got involved in a sort of mini-case study.

These three elements constituted the core of the evaluation task. They were agreed upon between the external evaluator (me) and the Ministry for Foreign Affairs, with a budget and timeline. The work started in March 2012, and the conclusions were written up in a draft report by October 2012. All in all, this contractual part covered 8 weeks of work, but working weeks spread out over 6 months.

Each of these tasks was relatively straightforward, and all relied on rather well-established evaluation methods. They did not address complexity per se, but were designed with an understanding that the phenomenon evaluated was complex. In that sense, they met the first set of requirements of a complexity-responsive evaluation as defined in this book. Given the acknowledged complexity of the topic and its context, the instruments for data collection were open and more geared toward synthesis than analysis, and more on inductive than deductive reasoning. Interview guidelines were brief and gave the respondents ample room to present their views. Similarly, the questionnaires had plenty of space for open feedback. As for the literature review, it focused on context-specific information and explanations while building on a holistic understanding of salient social issues.

The draft report was not the end of the process, though. Sweden intended to use the report to influence and contribute to international efforts against trafficking. The next step was to generate commitment to the cause in the Swedish system, that is, among the different parts of government and its agencies concerned with trafficking. The Ministry for Foreign Affairs organized a workshop to discuss the findings and strategies for influence. The Ministry and the aid agency, Sida, would be key partners in this. This internal/domestic workshop took place in October 2012, which was when the next step in coalition building was developed. In preparation for the General Assembly debate on trafficking, the Ministry organized a 2-day international workshop against trafficking. Six of the most important UN agencies were invited to present their activities and to respond to the evaluation, and a number of countries that were seen as like-minded in the struggle against trafficking were also invited (including Thailand, South Africa, Mexico, Brazil, the Netherlands, and Canada). The United States in particular participated and was invited to present its own annual report on global trafficking—a key intelligence document on the subject. At the time it was emphasized that the evaluation report, and in particular its recommendations, was a living document, and it was modified and developed after the workshop—but to another draft.

When the General Assembly had its discussion on trafficking (May 2013), Sweden organized a side event where the evaluation report was again presented and debated. The event drew participants from all over the world, including most of the NGOs as well as the countries most involved in the global struggle against trafficking. At the same time Sweden announced its own future commitment to strengthen coordination along the lines recommended in the evaluation. At the time of writing this case study, the evaluation is still a public document that could be developed and modified. The Ministry for Foreign Affairs is considering whether to reconvene the group of countries that met in Stockholm in late 2012 to assess developments and consider future action; it is not clear whether coordination has actually improved, and global trafficking continues its grizzly business.

The lesson to be learned from this process is that the gathering and processing of evaluative information was a relatively minor part of the overall effort to fight trafficking that Sweden wished to influence, and to be seen influencing. From the time of the expression of that will in early 2012 to the potential second international workshop, almost 3 years has elapsed. During that time, the diplomatic efforts have been multifaceted. Sweden has, for example, been invited to co-chair the Inter-Agency Coordination Group against Trafficking in Persons (ICAT) and chaired a session during the General Assembly debate. Sweden has indeed been visibly and effectively contributing to the international effort and the evaluation facilitated these diplomatic activities. The complexity of that task—skilled maneuvering, coalition building, and the exercise of horizontal (rather than vertical) leadership—made evaluation a useful tool. But to be useful the evaluation process itself had to have open terms of reference, wide boundaries, and extensive consultations, and it had to be very transparent and communicative.

# 3. Understanding Coordination

Coordination is a difficult subject, and it is often given a narrow interpretation, meaning that coordination takes place through coordination meetings. A common definition is that coordination is

> the synchronization and integration of activities, responsibilities, and command and control structures to ensure that the resources of an organization are used most efficiently in pursuit of the specified objectives. Along with organizing, monitoring, and controlling, coordinating is one of the key functions of management. (WebFinance, 2015)

But this does not reflect the idea of interorganizational coordination, which cannot build on an assumption of hierarchical control as the definition does. Instead, there are a few distinctions to make. First, on the one hand, coordination can be seen as a process that entails a number of activities. On the other hand, coordination could also describe a situation, that is, a state of affairs, in which things are coordinated, meaning that the elements involved are in balance and well ordered in relation to each other.

Second, coordination as a process involves a number of specific tasks that can be summed up as exchanges of information, consultation, and joint decision making.

Third, coordination takes place through a number of organizational instruments with different labels, such as task forces, working groups, technical groups, and others. Coordination can also occur through joint programming in the context of board meetings, steering committees, conferences and meetings, and so on.

Fourth, coordination can be formal as well as informal. When people in organizations pick up the phone and call each other to check progress, compare experiences, engage in other such activities, coordination takes place, just as it does in the formally convened task force with terms of reference, protocol, and membership. But the former is said to be far more cost-effective (Chisholm, 1989).

The evaluation maintained a focus on the process of coordination, but one should not forget that it is the end results that count. Herbert Simon (1959) pointed out that much problem solving that ultimately leads to superior results is very messy in the process, and it is really effective results that are the goal; hence the need to know whether projects were generally efficient and effective. One should also remember that coordination can be quite costly, and it often has declining marginal utility once the first benefits of information sharing have been gained. The evaluation was thus guided by theories on coordination and translated these into the following multilevel approach to data collection:

- A first view of coordination came across via the steering documents on which the organizations relied with respect to trafficking. An important question underlying the evaluation was: Do these documents reflect each other, refer to each other, contain strategic directions in terms of coordination, indicate a division of labor whereby the organizations supplement each other, or point to synergetic effects to be achieved through coordination?

- Second, the evaluation turned to the formal and centralized coordination mechanisms. The discussion in the evaluation report centers on these mechanisms as they were found to be the most significant—and the ones most constraining (rather than facilitating) practical work. While these two coordination instruments are in focus, it is also necessary to remember how they relate to and interact with other means of coordination.

As the choice of words implies, formal and centralized are concepts that suggest three other types of coordination: informal and centralized, informal and decentralized, as well as decentralized and formal. These concepts guided the inquiry into coordination at the global, regional, and national levels, and the evaluation traced where the emphasis lay and which type of mechanisms could be pursued.

# 4. Findings

## 4.1 A Diverse Landscape

Before turning to the management of complexity, the reader might be interested in what the evaluation found. Not surprisingly, the multilateral response that emerges is a complex picture of trafficking that varies significantly across nations and regions. Also not surprising is that the evaluation found that the multilateral system's response to stop the practice also varies. Any other finding would have been conspicuous.

On the one hand, the multilateral response to trafficking appears to be, on the whole, weak and fragmented. The financial and human resources are scarce, and none of the agencies devote a significant share of core resources to anti-trafficking. The overwhelming share of activities is financed through extra-budgetary resources, and the activities do not form part of the organizational priorities. While a number of coordination mechanisms can be found at the national, regional, and global levels, coordination is not strategically undertaken and the existing strategies of individual agencies are partly overlapping and do not articulate any expectation of synergetic effects of working together. Coordination at the global level takes place through ICAT for human trafficking work and the Global Migration Group (GMG) for work related to migration (but anti-trafficking is a subset of activities and the level of attention to this subset seems to be minimal); nevertheless, the roles and division of labor need to be developed and clarified.

On the other hand, there is evidence of impact and many impressive results at the project level. Even if many projects are small and of short duration, they make useful contributions. The contributions are primarily at the national and regional levels and relate particularly to the outcome targets in capacity building and policy development. It is particularly encouraging that important policy processes have been strengthened. Additionally, research and dissemination activities have helped understand how trafficking changes as a result of new developments, including new migration patterns and other socioeconomic changes. In many cases, the agencies work well together on specific activities such as conferences, capacity-building seminars, publications, and development of web resources. The potential to achieve important results is there, but it needs to be more strategically thought through, acted on, and further reinforced. The study suggested the following five areas of action to strengthen the multilateral efforts to eliminate trafficking (discussed in Sections 4.2–4.6).

## 4.2 Addressing the Resource Issue

There must be financial resources to effectively manage a multilateral response to trafficking. A number of design questions need to be further explored and elaborated, notably: Which form should the response take? Many options are on the table: whether at a singular project level or a more consolidated program form, at regional or global levels, within an agency, or partly from the outside (through inter-agency collaboration). One option might be that a core group of donors/funding agencies decide to provide core support for (1) a revitalized ICAT, which works at the global level, with the financial means to properly function as a representative inter-agency expert policy mechanism, and (2) using the resulting ICAT outputs to inform the allocation of funds to the agencies in the system for joint action on the ground.

## 4.3 Providing Directives to the Multilateral System

The multilateral agencies allocate resources and take the initiatives that member states demand. Hence the member states of the multilateral system need to provide clear directives that anti-trafficking is part of the mission and mandate of the organizations, that anti-trafficking actions are clearly stated, and that the organizations are expected to prioritize, coordinate, and deliver results from such activities. Some characteristics of an ideal and well-coordinated system include the following:

- There is alignment between and a clear direction from member states on anti-trafficking action.
- Core agencies in the struggle against trafficking have clearly visible and substantive strategies for their work in this field.
- Such strategies are mutually reinforcing and visibly create synergies between the competencies, capacities, and mandates of the organizations.
- Strategies are bolstered with action plans and budget resources.
- Organizational structures contain visible managerial and professional responsibilities for the activities against trafficking.
- Communication from headquarters to other parts of the organization reinforces the need for inter-agency coordination and creates incentives for that.

The UN agencies have a duty to collaborate to protect and improve the well-being of those at risk and those who have suffered at the hands of traffickers. In line with the principle of "do no harm," the agencies must also take guidance from their core mandate to support the most vulnerable and act preemptively with some flexibility regarding target groups (e.g., potential migrants, children with disabilities) rather than wait for the crime of trafficking or other human rights violations to occur in the first place.

## 4.4 Making Better Use of the Whole System

A core group of agencies are mandated with the responsibility to combat trafficking and are active against the issue almost everywhere. Other agencies still have important contributions to make, but appear to take on the issue not systematically. This leads to wasted effort, failure to capitalize on experiences, and a less than optimal response to the problem from the multilateral system as a whole. On the one hand, it is clear that resources are constrained and there is a limit to how much a small country office might know about what the organization as a whole has achieved elsewhere. This is a problem of internal knowledge management. It became manifest in this study when we saw how UNESCO, UNFPA, and UN Women have been important partners to fight trafficking in some contexts, but are quite absent in other contexts, even though the voice, knowledge, and insight that the agencies have would lend further strength to the voice of the multilateral agencies.

## 4.5 Results and Accountability

Unlike many other fields of global coordination, anti-trafficking work lends itself to effective monitoring and impact evaluation through the use of indicators. However, the performance indicators used to date have not been able to capture the likely impact of specific anti-trafficking activities. The challenge comes partly from the impediments to identifying victims and human trafficking crimes. However, well-crafted indicators could at least measure allocation of resources in terms of, for example, assisting victims or prosecuting and convicting criminals. It is an area where the international community would be able to assess efficiency, effectiveness, and results, provided it truly gives it priority.

The data collected should be harmonized globally, based on key datasets that can be used to develop indicators of progress. Such indicators should be based on consistent application of the trafficking definition from the Protocol to Prevent, Suppress and Punish Trafficking in Persons, especially women and children. Funding to do this should be an integral part of any counter-trafficking project to ensure that data are comparable while maintaining the personal integrity of trafficked persons. Donor nations must also agree on this as the UN system, like others, is dependent on the priorities set by the donors.

## 4.6 Reinforce Global Coordination

The roles and responsibilities of ICAT and GMG need to be developed and articulated, and the difference between the two groups made clear. ICAT appears to be gaining some momentum, moving from the more passive role of the past to new initiatives and a more active role as a global forum, and it would be important to keep the momentum of those changes. Following the evaluation of the UN Global Initiative to Fight Trafficking, there are suggestions on how to reform and bolster ICAT, which are articulated in UNODC's strategy for anti-trafficking activities. There is strong interest and commitment to this from several of the agencies concerned, especially those that are current members of ICAT, but there are other agencies that are not sufficiently involved in the process. Global coordination needs to be an inclusive process, and all the agencies that have mandates that somehow relate to trafficking need to be engaged and, in turn, commit to that engagement.

The roles and responsibilities of the Office of the Special Rapporteur on Trafficking in Persons has so far not been extended to organizational issues, but in theory it should be possible to view this office as an additional attentive eye on the response of the multilateral system—not least in support of coordination. This would probably require a review of the directives of that office and of its technical and financial resources.

This was the strategic thrust of the first draft evaluation report that was presented in October 2012, and even though some recommendations have since changed as other actors have brought ideas to the process, the thrust remains the same. An interesting feature of the evaluation follow-up process is that although the evaluation has been presented on at least three occasions, it was never officially closed as a document; it continues to be discussed and is considered by the Ministry for Foreign Affairs to be a living document.

# 5. Managing Complexity

How did this evaluation differ from other, simpler evaluation processes, and what specific features here could be said to emanate from the complexity of the undertaking? I structure the analysis according to the four elements of managing complexity that are presented in *Evaluating the Complex: Attribution, Contribution and Beyond* (Forss, Marra, & Schwartz, 2011):

1. Understanding the level of complexity and designing the appropriate response (be concrete)

2. Dealing with causality through methodological innovation (be inventive)

3. Assessing worth and merit through many perspectives (be flexible)

4. Varying and tailoring responses to the evaluation task (be specific)

Even so, we editors of *Evaluating the Complex* emphasized that the four bullet points would not provide concrete advice on how to do good evaluations of complex policies. Our edited volume showed that there were fairly general lessons to learn, and these lessons rather emphasize the loneliness of the complexity-responsive policy evaluator. The main lessons found in the book were negative: "do not use the most common approach," "do not apply standardized tools and methods," and so on. An evaluator might find some inspiration in the past, but by and large each complexity-responsive evaluation assignment is unique and needs to be treated as such.

## 5.1 Be Concrete

One could easily be overwhelmed by the fragmented, shifting, and evolving nature of the multilateral response to trafficking. The first step in being concrete was to separate the national, regional, and global levels and single them out for separate treatment.[6] That may seem obvious in retrospect, but it was not a distinction found in the system. The very simple, geographically based analytical distinction made it possible to deal with three levels of coordination rather than an undefined global mess. The use of models is another key feature of managing complexity. Models can be used to illustrate complexity, such as feedback loops, nonlinear relations, multiple causality, and boundary conditions. The most helpful modeling in this case was the models being used to understand coordination. These came from organization theory, and by distinguishing formal and informal, centralized and decentralized coordination mechanisms and processes, the evaluation could tease out what seemed to be efficient and effective coordination—and also show where the current weaknesses were in very practical terms. The evaluation also used the more common distinctions between roles in development coordination and based this on previous analyses of the UN system. Finally, the distinctions between the categories of responses to trafficking (prevention, protection, prosecution) were used for portfolio analysis and the discussion of roles and coordination.

## 5.2 Be Inventive

If a standard evaluability assessment had been done, this evaluation might never have taken place. An evaluation normally starts by looking at objectives, but in this case there were no objectives for the system as a whole. The different agencies had aims and objectives, but there was no such thing as a stated purpose for the multilateral response to trafficking as a whole. Hence the notion of a causal linkage (as causality is defined in classical texts on scientific method: cause must be proven *necessary and sufficient* for the effect to be produced) between unique components (programs and projects) also becomes problematic. This and other evaluations of complex policy initiatives face a major challenge of attribution.[7]

Evaluation is sometimes defined as the systematic inquiry into the worth or merit of an object. Although that is a contested definition, and many think it is too vague and open. But it allows the multilateral response to trafficking to be perceived as an object, and worth and merit are values that can be analyzed. The conclusion that the multilateral response to trafficking is weak and fragmented thus pronounces an evaluative conclusion on something that does not necessarily have a specific object, nor was it purposefully constructed to be strong and cohesive. But if one wishes to strengthen the system, it is useful to know that it is actually weak and fragmented, which can serve as a starting point for improvement.

The message of this case study, in line with the message of this volume, is that despite boundary uncertainty and fluidity, a real-world evaluation can address and come to terms with such complexity. The combination of global-level interviews among agencies; country and regional case studies; a synthesis evaluation of other studies, reviews, and evaluations; and a survey with accompanying field work at the Swedish embassies provided sufficiently rich empirical evidence to substantiate the overall findings.

Understanding cause-and-effect relationships was not the main complexity dimension nor a major hurdle in this evaluation. While the literature on complexity and evaluation often digresses on the challenges to understanding causality in nonlinear, multi-causal change processes, it was possible to find shortcuts. First, the synthesis evaluation gathered evidence from other evaluations and hence presented conclusions on causality and impact to the extent that other publicly available studies had arrived at any such conclusions (of course, with a critical and reflective eye on whether these findings could be trusted). Second, the merit of coordination efforts/practices was directly assessed based on an understanding of management, organizational structures, and processes. It was, for example, not necessary to look for an effect in order to conclude that, due to the differences in responsibilities (at different organizational levels) between agencies, harmonization of efforts was difficult.

## 5.3 Be Flexible

The challenge entailed in the guiding principle to be flexible is to assess worth and merit through many perspectives. The evaluation process outlined here could accommodate several perspectives: those of the different actors in Sweden, the many UN agencies, the international civil society organizations, and others that came to be partners. Each of the follow-up meetings was centered on dialogue, and other partners were invited to present analytical work, policy papers, evaluations, or any other material that could be found useful. None of the occasions had this evaluation as the only item on the agenda.

In addition, the evaluation itself holds many perspectives. The three building blocks of synthesis evaluation, survey addressed to embassies, and the global/regional/national case studies conducted during the evaluation all provided different perspectives on the subject. Furthermore, within each of these, there were differences. When a large number of evaluation reports are put together, it is obvious that some will have found successful projects and others failures, and the experiences between agencies and projects will obviously differ. Similarly, the realities reported by the embassies differed. The Swedish embassy in Cairo had other experiences to show than the embassy in Bogotá, and the embassy in Pretoria others than the embassy in Belgrade. The case studies also point to differences between agencies and contexts. The problem is not that diversity exists, but that it becomes cumbersome to describe in an evaluation report and also to see the pattern of the whole and not get lost in details. The evaluation report is not short and does require an interested reader. In a world where evaluation reports are often prescribed to hold a maximum of 20–30 pages, it becomes very difficult to handle multiple perspectives in a methodologically diverse process of inquiry. Fortunately, this evaluation was not required to have a maximum number of pages, and while it is relatively long at 60 pages, it portrays a diversity of perspectives on the global struggle against trafficking.

## 5.4 Be Specific

It is a truism that evaluators need to understand the issues that they evaluate. In practice, those who commission evaluations and those who evaluate usually strike a balance between, on the one hand, the need for independent expertise and general knowledge of methods and evaluation process and, on the other hand, the need for expertise on a specific subject matter. Quite often that balance is maintained in such a way that the independent stance and general methodological knowledge weigh more heavily than the specific and substantive competence.

In the previously quoted book by Forss et al. (2011), the authors argued that when the subject matter being evaluated is complex, the balance between the general methodological competence and specific subject matter insights needs to be reconsidered. What, then, was the subject matter of this evaluation? It was certainly a weakness that I, the evaluator, had no background in working with trafficking. This had to be mitigated, and this was done by working closely with Ministry for Foreign Affairs staff who had worked with UNICEF, UNODC, and the other agencies over the years. Some had direct operational experience from project management before joining the Ministry. During the process, there were also meetings with representatives of the Swedish Police Force who worked on anti-trafficking internationally. Knowledge of the subject matter of anti-trafficking was brought into the evaluation. But the real subject matter of the evaluation was the system of coordination, the network of agencies, and the links that kept the network together. I brought to the evaluation the knowledge of organization theory and, in particular, a theoretically based understanding of coordination as well as of finance and governance in the multilateral system. The evaluation therefore went much deeper into the practice of coordination than is commonly found. It looked at the design of coordination mechanisms, the processes of coordination, and the outcomes.

External expertise would often be expected to bring methodological competence, and as I have a long background as an evaluator, one could say that I brought methodological competence to the task. That was also being said (at least by me), but frankly speaking, the methods employed here were not that technically challenging. Most people with a social science degree would be able to plan and conduct interviews, undertake the synthesis evaluation, organize the national and regional case studies, and conduct the survey to embassies. The skill lies rather in seeing the whole, combining approaches, and dovetailing the basic methods to a deep pursuit of the subject matter of coordination.

# 6. Practical Applications

- This case study illustrates a real-world effort to seek and develop an evidence base for policy decisions. It is not difficult for a skilled evaluator to point to shortcomings in the analysis and to call for other and more data, more sophisticated methods, and so on. The point is that even in the context of complex policy issues (e.g., human trafficking), a relatively simple methodological approach combined with a thorough understanding of the subject matter (coordination issues) can lead to very useful evaluation outcomes.

- Sometimes it might be better to dare to search for insights and results even with modest means; a "quick and dirty" approach could be better than no approach at all. Without any limitations on resources, time, and data, it would be possible to construct a far more elaborate and methodologically sophisticated evaluation. At the same time, it is telling that the conclusions presented in the evaluation were considered to add evidence and insights at the time and were not disputed by people with more knowledge of the field. The message to evaluators is that even highly complex subjects can be grasped with an evaluator's structured approach to assessing worth and merit.

# References

Chisholm, D. W. (1989). *Coordination without hierarchy: Informal structures in multiorganizational systems*. Berkeley: University of California Press.

Forss, K., Marra, M., & Schwartz, R. (Eds.). (2011). *Evaluating the complex: Attribution, contribution and beyond*. New Brunswick, NJ: Transaction.

Simon, H. (1959). Theories of decision making in economics and behavioral science. *American Economic Review, 49*, 253–281.

UNESCO. (2011). *Trafficking in human beings*. Paris, France: Author.

U.S. State Department. (2012). *Trafficking in persons report*. Washington, DC: Author.

WebFinance. (2015). *Coordination*. Retrieved from http://www.businessdictionary.com/definition/coordination.html

# Notes

1. UNODC provides a succinct presentation of what the main organizations do: www.unodc.org/unodc/human-trafficking.

2. As there is no central authority, an evaluation terms of reference would have to be initiated and managed by the agencies to be evaluated themselves, and as the text shows, the boundary issues, authority issues, and resource allocation decisions would make such decisions practically difficult.

3. The Ministry for Foreign Affairs approached me and initiated an open discussion of whether such an evaluation could be done, and that led to the process of data collection and analysis described below.

4. As explained in detail in Chapter 7, the evaluation criteria of the OECD-DAC are widely used as a way to unpack programs and policies' performance.

5. Any synthesis implies that the quality of reports has to be taken into account, so the process was a nuanced and critical reading of the secondary data, treating the reports more as aspects to be assessed and judged and possibly used, rather than undisputed evidence.

6. Chapter 7 proposes various ways of unpacking complex interventions into discrete parts.

7. For a general discussion on attribution in the context of complexity, see Chapter 2, and for more detailed methodological guidance on how to deal with attribution issues, see Chapter 4.

# CHAPTER 18

# Complexity From the Perspective of Philanthropic Foundations and Their Evaluation Practices

Leny van Oijen

*This chapter starts with an overview of the increasingly complex aid landscape and zooms in on philanthropic foundations. As their engagement in development is increasing, there is growing interest in how they operate and how they deal with evaluation. Not much is written about their evaluation practices, so the analysis includes a brief review of evaluation approaches in philanthropic foundations in general. This is followed by an exploratory discussion on what complexity means in the development work of foundations, guided by the complexity framework described in Chapter 1.*

# 1. Background

## 1.1 The Increasingly Complex Development Cooperation Landscape

The vast aid literature has tended to focus on traditional donors (official development assistance [ODA]). In 2013, ODA reached its highest level ever, totaling nearly US$135 billion per estimates of OECD's Development Assistance Committee (DAC). ODA has been on the rise during the past two decades, notwithstanding cuts in aid budgets in several DAC member countries in recent years, particularly as a result of the global economic crisis. About three quarters of these traditional aid flows consist of bilateral aid, with multilateral aid covering around one quarter. In addition to flows from DAC donors, support from other countries (non-DAC donors) has been increasing.

Yet other inflows of aid to developing countries are growing also, in particular diaspora remittances and the resources emanating from philanthropic actors. According to estimates of the Hudson Institute (2013), remittances in fact largely exceed total ODA (US$211 billion in 2011). Estimated at US$59 billion in 2011, private philanthropy constitutes the smallest category of aid sources, yet is increasing and already amounts to almost half of ODA.[1] In fact, it is actually reported to grow faster than ODA (Development Initiatives, 2013).

With more and different players, diverse implementation modes and delivery channels, the aid landscape has become increasingly complex and fragmented. Efficiency and effectiveness concerns explain why the call for better aid has become as important as the call for more aid. It is illustrated by numerous events and declarations pertaining to aid effectiveness, starting with the Monterrey Consensus (2002) and subsequent declarations (Paris, Accra, Busan), and is reflected in ongoing discussions on the post-2015 framework. Another feature of the development cooperation landscape is the relative decline of its overall importance in a growing number of developing countries, notwithstanding the increase in aid flows and in the number of players. This "paradox of aid" puts further pressure on all aid players to rethink their strategies and practices (Fengler & Kharas, 2010).

The aid effectiveness debate has so far primarily taken place among ODA donors. Yet there is a growing recognition of the need to also involve non-ODA players, including private donors. In line with the "new reality of aid" (Kharas, 2007), private aid is gradually gaining more attention in the aid literature. Debates on development cooperation and aid effectiveness increasingly refer to and involve the private sector. It can also be observed that more and more ODA donors are seeking to develop partnerships with private aid players.

## 1.2 Growing Engagement of Philanthropic Foundations in International Development

Private donors comprise a vast and heterogeneous group of players, whose activities vary from one-to-one remittances and private micro-initiatives to more structured forms of giving, such as through foundations or trusts established by high-net-worth individuals, corporate foundations, social purpose activities of companies, social investors, and private voluntary organizations. Also, new forms of private giving are emerging, in particular e-philanthropy and crowd funding.

This chapter focuses the complexity lens on a subset of private players: *endowed philanthropic foundations*. These are defined here as nongovernmental nonprofit organizations that possess a principal fund of their own and are self-managed by a board of trustees.[2] This subgroup is heterogeneous in terms of endowment size, annual expenditures, longevity, and delivery modes. And the regulatory context in which foundations operate varies across countries and regions, among other factors, in terms of reporting requirements.

The ones best known are very large yet rather atypical for the foundation sector, as most foundations are relatively small in terms of the size of their assets and funding levels. There has been an increase in the number of newly created foundations in the past two decades (not only in the United States and Europe but also in emerging and developing economies). Some are set up as temporary entities ("spend-out organizations"), meaning that they will be closed after a predefined number of years of operation, once the allocated funds have been spent. Finally, there is a growing diversity in models (e.g., the emergence of venture philanthropy) and differences in approaches or schools of thought (e.g., strategic philanthropy, effective philanthropy).

With respect to international development, some foundations work exclusively in developing countries, whereas for others development cooperation constitutes a minor aspect of their work. Given gaps in aggregate data on foundation giving and relying on survey findings, it is estimated that the average proportion of international giving by foundations ranges anywhere from around 10% to 25% of their total funding, with major outliers at both ends (European Foundation Centre, 2008; Foundation Centre, 2011; World Bank, 2007).

Development-related priorities vary, with some foundations being highly focused on a specific sector or thematic area, whereas others spread their support over a wider range of fields. Health, education, other social services, environment, agriculture, and food security are the main focus areas. With respect to geographic focus, emphasis is mainly on Africa and Asia (Pharoah & Bryant, 2012; World Bank, 2007).

Foundations use various delivery channels. Some foundations engage purely in grant making through intermediaries, whereas others are operating foundations (directly engaging in project implementation). There are also hybrid variants, such as channeling funding to third-party organizations or through vertical funds that also include ODA sources. Relatively few foundations have offices in the recipient developing countries. This is not surprising, as many foundations are relatively small in terms of funding for development purposes.

## 1.3 Diverging Perceptions on the Work of Philanthropic Foundations in Development

General perceptions on the work of philanthropic foundations differ widely. Some stakeholders primarily perceive foundations as a source of new resources, approaches, and even solutions, bringing in expertise and know-how, while others are more critical and raise concerns about such issues as transparency and accountability, the degree of ownership of operations, and effectiveness. One could distinguish, in essence, two general types of claims, as shown in Table 18.1.[3]

| **Table 18.1**  Two Types of Claims: Supportive and Skeptical Views | |
|---|---|
| **The supportive view** | **The skeptical view** |
| • Sense of social responsibility<br>• Problem-solving drive<br>• Search for making a difference (high expectations on results)<br>• Readiness and ability to take risks<br>• Flexibility<br>• Longer term view | • Accountability only to boards<br>• Self-interest<br>• Single-issue and isolated interventions<br>• Focus on technical approaches underestimating social concerns<br>• Weak reporting and no systematic evaluation (need to go beyond "success stories")<br>• Depth of innovation and potential impact oversold |

# 2. Evaluation Approaches of Philanthropic Foundations in General

## 2.1 Why to Expect Differences From Traditional Aid Players in Dealing With Evaluation

It remains an open question why philanthropists decide to set up their own foundations and run their own projects rather than channeling the majority of their resources through organizations that traditionally have the mandate and also the experience to design and implement development cooperation. Could it be because this allows them to decide what their resources are used for and to monitor more closely their actual use? Or because they think they can be more efficient and more effective in aid delivery, with lower transaction costs as compared to channeling the funding through ODA? Or to engage in "flag planting" and enhance their visibility?

Focusing on the dimension of evaluation, the following interrelated arguments try to explain why one would expect differences in approaches compared to traditional donors.

- **Foundation giving is often personalized.**

Even though it is recognized that foundations are often managed by professionals who are not the principals (funders), foundation giving is highly influenced by the motivations and priorities of its funders—an individual, family, or corporation—that are, per definition, diverse. There can be many determinants for their philanthropic behavior. According to the "warm glow giving" theory (Andreoni, 1990), givers are motivated not only by the welfare of the recipients of their donation (pure altruism), but also by the positive emotion (warm glow) they derive from giving or simply by (enlightened) self-interest. The literature review conducted by Bekkers and Wiepking (2011) identified various motives for giving: awareness of need, solicitation, costs and benefits, altruism, reputation, psychological benefits, values, and efficacy. In practice, the decision to establish a foundation is most likely based on a combination of reasons.

Committing one's own resources in development cooperation is expected to go hand in hand with a desire to maintain control over the use of these resources, the aim being a priori to spend them efficiently and effectively. This drive is expected to be less strong when dealing with "other people's money." Compared to endowed foundations, motivations and incentives in public aid agencies are more complex (institutional, political, individual), thus covering not only developmental issues but also organizational survival and growth.

- **An entrepreneurial mindset influences approaches.**

In cases where the assets of philanthropic foundations are derived from entrepreneurial activities, it is assumed that foundations have a strong interest in the efficiency of the delivery of support and in results as a key feature of their giving. As "social entrepreneurs" they look for opportunities to create social value and engage in a process of continuous innovation, adaptation, and learning—borrowing from what Dees (1998) called an idealized definition of social entrepreneurs or special breed of leaders.

This would imply that they put weight on rigorous knowledge management (i.e., monitoring and learning from interventions) and on the need for flexibility to adjust objectives and implementation approaches as required. Compared to public aid agencies, they are expected to face fewer institutional and administrative obstacles to maintain such rigor and flexibility. This being said, the rival theory is that compared to other organizations engaged in development, there is less pressure on foundations to conduct rigorous evaluations and cost-effectiveness analyses, which could result in the opposite: a weaker accountability system than in the case of traditional donors.

- **The reporting lines between the foundation (donor) and the recipient are relatively short.**

Endowed foundations commit their own resources and are expected to have a strong results focus. They often keep a close eye on implementation, especially since the reporting lines are short. The high degree of involvement in the causes selected for support implies that philanthropic actors are rarely passive donors (Micklewright & Wright, 2013). Several studies point to foundations being keen to be directly engaged with funded organizations, wanting to "be in touch," and combining funding and advice (e.g., De Las Casas & Fiennes, 2007; Moran, 2012). The latter is also in line with World Bank's observation that foundations want to be approached for their technical expertise (and thus their expected contribution to generate results) and not just for their funding (UK House of Commons, 2012).

In the case of traditional donors, the chain of interactions from taxpayers to aid beneficiaries via implementers (public aid agencies/their subcontractors) is more complex in that it is long and more bureaucratic. This has given rise to increased emphasis on accountability, sometimes referred to as an "audit explosion" in public management, with adverse consequences (Power, 1994). The evaluation approaches followed by foundations are expected to be different: less formalistic, more practical and focused on their actual use. The latter is often reported as a challenge with respect to evaluations conducted by traditional donors/aid agencies.

In this context it is relevant to refer to observations pertaining to evaluations and their use in the aid sector at large. Based on the literature, McNulty (2012) drew attention to the prevalence of the symbolic use of evaluations in the international aid sector, highlighting, among other factors, the gap between rhetoric (the demand for more evaluative evidence) and practice (the often limited use of evaluative evidence), a tendency toward accountability-driven evaluation, and the resistance to and underinvestment in knowledge generation. While not making an explicit distinction between ODA and non-ODA players, McNulty's argument is focused on traditional donors (as can be deduced from the examples and references to aid agencies). Why would one expect less non-use, under-use, and mis-use of evaluations by philanthropic foundations? In line with the initial theory on evaluation practices in foundations (presented above), in most cases one would expect more efficient learning cycles and less resistance to change.

## 2.2 Seeking Focus and Evidence of Results

A flagship publication and contribution to the early debate on aid effectiveness (Centre for Global Development, 2006) drew attention to the weak evidence on the effects of development support at large. This publication was the outcome of a process of extensive consultations with different stakeholders of the Evaluation Gap Working Group put together in 2004, with support from the Gates Foundation and the Hewlett Foundation. Other initiatives aimed at contributing to development effectiveness through better use of evidence (e.g., International Initiative for Impact Evaluation/3IE, Poverty Action Lab) benefited from foundation funding. This suggests that at least some of the large foundations are an integral part of the growing emphasis on results and measurement. It goes beyond the scope of this chapter to assess the extent to which the foundations that actively promote rigorous evaluation through these wider initiatives actually apply such an approach (including in the requirements for monitoring and evaluation systems of their grantees).

In their field-based study on foundations that operate in Tanzania, Lundsgaarde, Funk, Kopyra, Richter, and Steinfeldt (2012) observed that for foundations the search for impact was pivotal, as shown in their emphasis on measurable indicators of success, return on investment, financial sustainability, and calculated risk taking. They also mentioned the tendency toward a more narrow focus of interventions with a view to increasing the likelihood of impact. Along the same line, Martin and Witte (2008) reported that foundations tend to concentrate on few sectors and focus on projects in which reasonably quickly results can be generated (health, education).

One can observe a tendency of increased targeting of aid from foundations. According to a review of UK trusts and foundations (De Las Casas & Fiennes, 2007), most foundations were considered generalist funders, with few focusing their assistance geographically and/or thematically. An update of this review (Pharoah & Bryant, 2012), however, reported a tendency toward more targeted support and longer term funding commitments.

Analyzing the cooperation of the German Agency for International Cooperation (GIZ) with the Gates Foundation in the context of the African Cashew Initiative, Kramer and Sattler (2011) noted the Gates Foundation's emphasis on the evaluation of investees through due diligence, on measuring and tracking investments, and, in general, on the use of business metrics. In a case study of the interventions in the context of this Cashew Initiative in one country (Ghana), Heinrich (2012) found that implementing partners perceived the reporting requirements of the Gates Foundation to be quite demanding. Still, partners were found to appreciate the foundation's business mentality, which was seen as a positive force for the project, notwithstanding the high pressure to rapidly show results, going to scale, and an early attention in the project cycle to exit strategies.

## 2.3 Foundation Interest in Evaluation

From a historical perspective, evaluation in foundations is certainly not a new phenomenon and has gotten attention since the 1960s, particularly in the United States. Public skepticism as regards the value of the growing number of foundations and the motives of their founders and executives (e.g., suspicions related to tax exemptions) resulted in regulations, including reporting requirements for foundations. In fact, interest in evaluation in general has grown particularly since the 1990s, including in the nonprofit sector. This is particularly the case for NGOs that have been under pressure (much more than foundations) to develop accountability systems and assess the effectiveness (including cost-effectiveness) of their programs. The results orientation of donors and trustees and the professionalization of nonprofit management are some of the factors that contributed to this growing attention to evaluation (Hall, 2004).

Findings from secondary sources provide some indications of how philanthropic foundations actually deal with results and measurement. A survey of 31 foundations conducted in 2012 focused on evaluation staffing, investments, practices, and use in foundations (Coffman, Beer, Patrizi, & Heid Thompson, 2013), comparing these elements with a study conducted in 2009. The findings revealed the following:

- Foundation commitment to evaluation is rising (as in 2009, the majority of foundations had increased expenditures related to evaluation).
- The average number of staff dedicated to evaluation increased (from 3.0 in 2009 to, on average, 4.2 full-time staff in 2012); not surprisingly, smaller foundations had fewer evaluation staff members.
- Evaluation responsibilities are expanding: "Evaluation unit responsibilities now go well beyond managing evaluation contracts or assessing individual grantee results. Many are now leading a range of evaluation practices that include performance management, knowledge management, organizational learning and strategic learning" (Coffman et al., 2013, p. 40).
- This expansion is related to complexity issues: "As foundations grapple with generating meaningful data for difficult decisions associated with increasingly

complex strategies, they are experimenting with the role and scope of their evaluation functions" (Coffman et al., 2013, p. 40).

- Expansion of responsibilities is not without challenges, especially if the number of staff involved is limited and expectations on evaluation related activities are high. Responses indicated that "going deeper on fewer evaluation activities and identifying where they can be applied most appropriately might deliver more useable evaluation information than multiplying the types of evaluative activities foundations perform" (Coffman et al., 2013, p. 41).

- Evaluation staff of foundations of all sizes felt that the growth in evaluation activities resulted in more and more data, yet they felt constrained in facilitating learning based on the data: "Better balancing their activities between producing high-quality information and working with foundation staff to use it—e.g., by helping them to ask better questions at the right time—might be a more productive use of their time" (Coffman et al., 2013, p. 42).

- Whereas evaluation staff increasingly participate in strategy-related discussions and decisions (implying that evaluation data need to be timely and useful), "evaluation use and learning continues to be a challenge" (Coffman et al., 2013, p. 46).

- There is more attention to broad-scope evaluations of initiatives/programs and of foundation performance and aggregate impact in general, which is recognized to be more complex than assessing individual grants or projects.

In short, the study found a trend toward serious commitment to evaluation in foundations and a growing link between evaluation and programming/strategy. This being said, as in the case of traditional development assistance, the use of evaluations was found to remain a challenge, a finding confirmed by a study conducted for the Evaluation Roundtable[4] (Patrizi, Heid Thompson, Coffman, & Beer, 2013). Also, as shown in the findings of earlier work of the Evaluation Roundtable, leadership matters. Having a foundation CEO interested in and committed to performance measurement and learning, and with evaluation units reporting directly to the CEO, more resources (financial, staffing) tend to be dedicated to the evaluation function (Heid Thompson & Patrizi, 2011).

Similar to evaluation networks such as the DAC on development evaluation (a network of bilateral and multilateral donors) and the United Nations Evaluation Group (UNEG, covering UN agencies, funds, and programs), the foundation sector is also engaged in reflection about evaluation. More than in the case of traditional donors/aid agencies, alliances among private donors are often thematic or sector-focused. The absence of a certain sense of competition often observed between traditional donors/aid agencies could explain why, for philanthropic foundations (which are not competing for resources), collaboration with those engaged in the same intervention areas is a commonsense approach.

## 2.4 Going Beyond Traditional Evaluation Approaches

As most foundations are small, they lack dedicated staff and other resources to commission formal evaluations. Also, the scale of the interventions matters. For small projects, reporting tends to be limited to concise progress and financial (sometimes audited) reporting. In such cases it is simply too costly to engage in formal evaluations. Based on the notion that evaluation approaches need to be commensurate with the scope and scale of interventions, there are indications that foundations—from large to small—are thinking beyond traditional evaluation methods.

This point is illustrated by Symonds, Carrington, and Weisblatt's (2012) study on the practice of evaluation and learning for a cross-section of 26 (both recently established/older and larger/smaller) foundations in Europe. The following findings show a shift in thinking by the foundations surveyed:

- They use a mix of different assessments to examine the outputs, outcomes, and impact of the interventions they fund: periodic external reviews, internal reviews, and (increasingly) client perception studies.
- There is a growing emphasis by foundations on the how of the support and on seeking improvements during the project life through continuous (real-time) monitoring and evaluation rather than retrospective project evaluation at the end of the cycle.
- Foundations want "to shift away from external so-called objective evaluation, which is seldom owned by the participants—either funders or those funded—towards creating space within organizations for reflection and better sharing of experience" (i.e., more emphasis on internal learning and stimulating a self-critical culture than on external evaluations; Symonds et al., 2012, p. 7).
- They recognize the need for deepening collaboration (peer learning and benchmarking of foundation practice as well as guidelines for different evaluation approaches).

Despite the specificities of the study's sample (not claiming to be representative of the foundation sector as such), the findings are considered to be of broader relevance, as they illustrate the search for different tailor-made performance assessments rather than the use of standard evaluation approaches. In particular, newer foundations were found to question established evaluation approaches and explore new avenues for learning (moving toward an internally driven process, tailor-made to each project or program).

Earlier research by Kramer, Graves, Hirschhorn, and Fiske (2007) resulted in comparable conclusions based on the analysis of evaluation practices by some 25 foundations of different sizes. Findings show emphasis on the adaptation of approaches to circumstances and a focus on the search for pragmatic evaluation processes aimed at the timely collection of information on the performance of interventions with a view to enhancing their overall effectiveness.

# 3. How Philanthropic Foundations Deal With Complexity in Development Evaluation

## 3.1 Complexity in Development Interventions of Foundations

The above general review of the increasing engagement of philanthropic foundations in evaluation sets the stage for discussing the core theme of this book applied to the work of foundations: How do philanthropic foundations deal with complexity in development evaluation?

In general, research findings indicate that, notwithstanding their search for focus of interventions, foundations look at the bigger picture, recognizing the importance of systemic issues and the need for holistic development approaches (Pharoah & Bryant, 2012). Moreover, being less restricted by budget cycles than ODA players, foundations are often described as having a more long-term vision on development support. Also, it can be observed that foundations (especially larger ones) can be more flexible than many of the traditional donors/aid agencies in terms of combining different and complementary support instruments in one support package (or intervention), such as research, technical assistance, investment in infrastructure, and advocacy. However, it is difficult to generalize, and the degree of complexity of the work funded or implemented by foundations varies from case to case and among foundations.

More specifically, applying the complexity framework of Chapter 1 to the situation of philanthropic foundations, the following four interrelated complexity dimensions can be characterized as follows.

- **The nature of the intervention**

Foundation support can cover a simple project or more complex programs. It is understood that complexity increases with, among other factors, the number, range, and scope of activities and the levels of intervention (local, national, regional, global). In this regard, particularly large foundations are involved in sector-wide or multi-country thematic support programs, corresponding to more complex programs.

Whereas smaller foundations tend to deal with smaller projects, it would be an overly simplified picture of reality to consider their interventions as simple. Even small funding can cover different levels of interventions and seek to influence wider processes of change. Thus, size of funding is an imperfect indicator of complexity.

- **The institutional context and stakeholders**

The number and range of stakeholders/partners concerns another dimension of complexity. It refers to foundation clients, beneficiaries (grantees), implementation agencies such as international and local NGOs, and other donors/development partners. Factors that can influence the degree of complexity in this respect include the absorption capacity of the beneficiary and the need for cooperation with different stakeholders at the program or project level.

In the case of multi-stakeholder initiatives, the partners do not necessarily "speak the same language," as they come from different backgrounds and do not always constitute a homogeneous group of actors. Such initiatives require flexibility and openness to new ways of working, including the understanding that such partnerships bring together different perspectives, experiences, and expertise. For example, when foundations (many of which have their roots in the business sector) partner with traditional development actors, the differences in expectations, viewpoints, and interests may significantly affect the speed of decision making.

- **Causality and change**

Depending on the degree of complexity of an intervention, the causal change process can be relatively straightforward and direct or more diffuse and complex. According to the skeptical view on foundations (see above), the latter are considered to favor a short-term perspective and focus on the "low hanging fruit." However, this is not in line with previously mentioned research findings (Pharoah & Bryant, 2012) that indicate that contributing to systemic change is among the objectives of many foundations. Also, their readiness to test approaches and involve other partners in replication and scaling-up processes is an example of foundations looking at the bigger picture.

- **Embeddedness**

The economic, social, and political context of an intervention matters. Contextual factors explain, for example, why support can be successful in one context, but does not necessarily generate the same results in another. On the side of the donor, foundations are less constrained than traditional donors to determine which countries, beneficiaries, or themes they support. This implies that a foundation (to some extent) can avoid working in particularly complex environments, such as countries in a crisis or post-crisis situation. Often (small) foundations refrain from working with government entities and focus instead on working with nongovernmental intermediaries (whereas large foundations can be observed to work with governments). Another example concerns the fact that not all countries have a regulatory framework that enables the work of foreign or homegrown foundations. In some (albeit more rare) cases, private sector organizations such as foundations may even be looked at with some degree of suspicion.

- **The evaluation process**

It is recognized that the relative importance of complexity dimensions varied across evaluation contexts. Some evaluation settings may be labeled as complex particularly because of the multitude of stakeholders and interrelated intervention levels, others mainly because of the complexity of the operating environment. This being said and considering the above four dimensions of complexity, what are the implications for the fifth dimension of complexity: the evaluation process itself?

Here are the main questions in this regard:

- To what extent and how do philanthropic foundations address the different dimensions of complexity when evaluating their interventions (programs and projects)?
- Are there any innovative approaches being developed and used by philanthropic foundations to address complexity in evaluation?
- To what extent are foundations engaged in "upstream" work in this regard (research, training, publications on complexity)?

To some extent these questions are explored below.

## 3.2 Debate on Approaches

The recent growing attention to complexity issues in development cooperation can also be observed in the foundation sector. This is illustrated by the questioning of practices and approaches assessed by some as traditional, rigid, or mechanistic and suggesting new, more flexible approaches claimed to be better aligned to dealing with complex problems. In this respect there have been some lively debates that reflect different schools of thought that can be characterized by terms such as *effective, strategic,* or *emergent* philanthropy.[5]

It is not the aim of this chapter to cover the different arguments and viewpoints of this debate. However, it is of interest to briefly present the guidelines developed in line with the *emergent* approach aimed at addressing complexity that are targeted to evaluators, philanthropic leaders and staff, nonprofit leaders, and others (Preskill, Gopal, Mack, & Cook, 2014). As the actual "newness" of this approach has been questioned in the debate among foundation practitioners, it is assumed here that the propositions (and related data collection methods) for evaluation practice are not truly new for many of the sector stakeholders. The propositions for complexity-responsive evaluation are the following (Preskill et al., 2014, p. 5):

1. Design and implement evaluations to be adaptive, flexible, and iterative.
2. Seek to understand and describe the whole system, including components and connections.
3. Support the learning capacity of the system by strengthening feedback loops and improving access to information.
4. Pay particular attention to context and be responsive to changes as they occur.
5. Look for effective principles of practice in action, rather than assessing adherence to a predetermined set of activities.
6. Identify points of energy and influence, as well as ways in which momentum and power flow within the system.
7. Focus on the nature of relationships and interdependencies within the system.
8. Explain the non-linear and multi-directional relationships between the initiative and its intended and unintended outcomes.
9. Watch for patterns, both one-off and repeating, at different levels of the system.

## 3.3 Why Complexity-Responsive Evaluations Are Expected to Matter to Foundations

There is no indication of studies on the actual evaluation strategies used by foundations to deal with complexity in development evaluation. This is not surprising, as the subject is relatively new and the same is expected to be the case for ODA players. However, based on secondary sources used for the discussion of evaluation approaches of foundations in general (Section 2), there are a few indications of attention to complexity in foundation evaluation practices:

- expanding the scope of evaluations, going beyond individual projects/grants by engaging in broader scope evaluations
- engaging in joint initiatives (peer learning that is often thematic or sector focused) aimed at extracting and exchanging lessons
- adapting evaluation approaches to circumstances using a mix of assessment approaches, such as the involvement of beneficiaries to track progress, client perception studies, internal reviews, and continuous adjustment, in addition to (or instead of) traditional external evaluations

Obviously, the foundation sector being so heterogeneous, it ultimately varies from foundation to foundation how evaluations (and thus attention to complexity in evaluation approaches) are dealt with. Preliminary thoughts on what one could expect in this regard (that would need to be tested empirically) include the following arguments:

- There would be an a priori incentive for foundations to incorporate complexity dimensions in their evaluation approaches. If the aim of evaluation is indeed learning and program improvement, ignoring complexity would mean ignoring problems and opportunities and possibly compromising the chances for successful implementation and impact. Underperformance in terms of output delivery and achievement of outcomes because of neglect of complexity issues is directly felt by the principal (the donor), and there seems no point in oversimplifying evaluations in cases where complexity dimensions may significantly affect performance.
- Dealing with complexity issues in evaluation does not necessarily require complex monitoring, evaluation, and reporting systems from grantees. It involves (1) a focus on the main indicators that realistically measure progress in work as well as the potential risks to performance and sustainability, keeping in mind complexity issues, and (2) the rigorous pursuit of monitoring outputs, outcomes, and risks on the basis of these indicators. Evaluations build on these data to assess the relevance, efficiency, and effectiveness of interventions. Finally, addressing complexity issues in evaluation is expected to go hand in hand with a certain sense of pragmatism and flexibility in evaluation design.

However, as argued by the Evaluation Roundtable, while foundations in practice engage in complex environments and complex policy and societal issues (e.g., poverty, global warming, food security in Africa), at the same time they have created "traps that hamper (them) in advancing the kind of robust learning needed to guide strategy in these complex environments" (Patrizi et al., 2013, p. 52).[6] The traps faced by foundations as identified by Patrizi et al. (2013, p. 52) are the following:

- linearity and certainty bias: framing the strategies as a set of linear, causal, and certain actions and failing to address the complexity surrounding the issues and systems they hope to change
- autopilot effect: taking distance from strategy as it unfolds, thereby failing to learn from implementation
- indicator blindness: tracking and monitoring their strategies through performance indicators that reinforce the linear, causal, and often unchecked assumptions built into the work

Whereas these constraints are identified based on observations of how foundations deal with complexity and complexity-related learning, such traps are certainly not alien to the work of traditional donors/aid agencies. In general, and again using the wording of Patrizi et al. (2013), it is an illusion that development work is simple and certain in complex settings.

# 4. Practical Applications

- As the amount of funding for development purposes in the case of many philanthropic foundations is relatively modest, traditional independent evaluations are often too costly to implement, calling for flexibility in evaluation approaches. In practice, a combination of different approaches is warranted:
  - reporting guidelines for grantees to cover key performance indicators on which they are expected to periodically report to the donor (foundation)
  - putting emphasis on rigorous monitoring by foundation/project staff (in case of foundations directly engaging in project implementation)
  - periodic client perception surveys to assess output delivery and outcomes and to identify possible constraints
- The above implicitly questions the ability of (especially) smaller foundations to address complexity issues in evaluation (see Chapter 3). Apart from capacity issues and issues relating to methodological and conceptual approaches (see Parts I and II of this book), a number of pragmatic strategies can be employed to enhance the opportunity space for foundations to deal with complexity:
  - adopting/building on monitoring and evaluation systems already developed by large players in the international development community
  - participating in learning networks among peers (other foundations)
  - developing communities of practice that bring together traditional donors and philanthropic foundations

# References

Andreoni, J. (1990). Impure altruism and donations to public goods: A theory of warm-glow giving. *Economic Journal, 100,* 464–477.

Bekkers, R., & Wiepking, P. (2011). A literature review of empirical studies of philanthropy: Eight mechanisms that drive charitable giving. *Nonprofit and Voluntary Sector Quarterly, 40,* 924–973.

Centre for Global Development. (2006). *When will we ever learn? Improving lives through impact evaluation.* Washington, DC: Author.

Coffman, J., Beer, T., Patrizi, P., & Heid Thompson, E. (2013). Benchmarking evaluation in foundations: Do we know what we are doing? *Foundation Review, 5*(2), 5.

De Las Casas, L., & Fiennes, C. (2007). *Going global: A review of international development funding by UK trusts and foundations.* London, UK: New Philanthropy Capital.

Dees, J. G. (1998). *The meaning of social entrepreneurship.* Stanford, CA: Stanford University, Graduate School of Business.

Development Initiatives. (2013). *Investments to end poverty.* Bristol, UK: Author.

European Foundation Centre. (2008). *Foundations in the European Union: Facts and figures.* Brussels, Belgium: Author.

Fengler, W., & Kharas, H. (2010). Delivering aid differently: Lessons from the field. Washington, DC: Brookings Institution.

Foundation Centre. (2011). *Foundation growth and giving estimates.* New York, NY: Author.

Hall, P. D. (2004). A historical perspective on evaluation in foundations. In M. T. Braverman, N.A. Constantine, & J. K. Slater (Eds.), *Foundations and evaluation: Contexts and practices for effective philanthropy* (pp. 27–50). San Francisco, CA: Jossey-Bass.

Heid Thompson, E., & Patrizi, P. (2011). *Necessary and not sufficient: The state of evaluation use in foundations.* Retrieved from http://www.evaluationroundtable.org/documents/ Necessary-and-Not-Sufficient-Final.pdf

Heinrich, M. (2012). *Case study of the African Cashew Initiative: Lessons from working with new and multiple partners—Emerging results.* Donor Committee for Enterprise Development.

Hudson Institute, Center for Global Prosperity. (2013). *The index of global philanthropy and remittances.* Washington, DC: Author.

Kania, J., Kramer, M., & Russell, P. (2014, Summer). Strategic philanthropy for a complex world. *Stanford Social Innovation Review,* pp. 26–33.

Kharas, H. (2007). *The new reality of aid.* Washington, DC: Brookings Institution.

Kramer, A., & Sattler, A. (2011, September). *New private actors in development: Is a "privatisation" of development cooperation under way?* Presented at the Rethinking Development in an Age of Scarcity and Uncertainty conference, York, UK.

Kramer, M., Graves, R., Hirschhorn, J., & Fiske, L. (2007). *From insight to action: New directions in foundation evaluations.* Retrieved from http://www.fsg.org/tabid/191/ArticleId/177/ Default.aspx?srpush=true

Lundsgaarde, E., Funk, E., Kopyra, A., Richter, J., & Steinfeldt, A. (2012). *Private foundations and development cooperation: Insights from Tanzania.* Bonn: German Development Institute.

Martin, R., & Witte, J. M. (2008). *Transforming development? The role of philanthropic foundations in international development cooperation* (Research Paper No. 10). Berlin, Germany: Global Public Policy Institute.

McNulty, J. (2012). Symbolic uses of evaluation in the international aid sector: Arguments for critical reflection. *Evidence & Policy, 8,* 495–509.

Micklewright, J., & Wright, A. (2013). *Private donations for international development* (Working Paper A03/12). Southampton, UK: University of Southampton, Social Statistics Research Centre.

Moran, M. (2012). *The philanthrocapitalist turn: Implications for the aid architecture.* Melbourne, Australia: Swinburne University of Technology, Asia-Pacific Centre for Social Investment and Philanthropy.

Patrizi, P., Heid Thompson, E., Coffman, J., & Beer, T. (2013). Eyes wide open: Learning as strategy under conditions of complexity and uncertainty. *Foundation Review, 5*(3), 50–65.

Pharoah, C., & Bryant, L. (2012). *Global grant-making: A review of UK foundations' funding for international development.* London, UK: Nuffield Foundation.

Power, M. (1994). *The audit explosion.* London, UK: Demos.

Preskill, H., Gopal, S., Mack, K., & Cook, J. (2014). *Evaluating complexity: Propositions for improving practices.* Retrieved from http://www.fsg.org/tabid/191/ArticleId/1204/Default.aspx?srpush=true

Symonds, J., Carrington, D., & Weisblatt, K. (2012). *Shedding light on our own practice: Lessons about the impact and effect of our own behaviour.* Report prepared for the European Philanthropy Learning Initiative.

UK House of Commons, International Development Committee. (2012). Private foundations, Thirteenth Report of Session 2010-12. HC 1557.

World Bank. (2007). *Philanthropic foundations and their role in development assistance.* Washington, DC: Author.

# Notes

1. Both in the case of ODA and other aid flows, the accuracy of the numbers is often questioned. Given factors such as gaps between commitments and actual spending, ODA is likely overestimated, whereas private aid is likely underestimated as reporting is less systematic (voluntary). It is also to be noted that, notwithstanding its importance for development, the largest flow (private investment) is not discussed here as it is distinct from development cooperation.

2. In line with the definition of Martin and Witte (2008) and of the UK House of Commons (2012).

3. A synopsis of different views on foundations is given in a 2012 UK House of Commons report on private foundations. Its International Development Committee looked into the role of foundations, covering hearings as well as the collection of written evidence from different stakeholders (also outside the United Kingdom).

4. A network of foundation evaluation leaders (United States, Canada, United Kingdom) that seeks to improve how foundations learn about their results and increase their impact.

5. Reference is made in particular to the recent debate around the article "Strategic Philanthropy for a Complex World" (Kania, Kramer, & Russell, 2014).

6. The article also includes questions that are seen as the starting point for reflection to avoid "trap-like thinking."

# CHAPTER 19

# Evaluating General Budget Support

Antonie de Kemp and Geske Dijkstra

*This chapter seeks to unravel the complexities of budget support and to explore ways of analyzing the instrument in a rigorous way.[1] We start with a brief introduction to the subject, followed by an analysis of methodological challenges for an evaluation, caused by the complexity of the modality. Taking these challenges into account, we review the virtues and vices of the main approaches for evaluating budget support. We then introduce an eclectic approach that allows researchers to deal with the complexity of the instrument. In the final sections we draw lessons and discuss practical implications.*

The first decade of this millennium saw development cooperation blaze a new trail. Donors were moving from isolated projects toward sector-wide approaches. Harmonization and ownership became central tenets of the development architecture. With the Paris Declaration of 2005, donors committed themselves to deploy at least 66% of their aid through program-based approaches and at least 50% of bilateral aid through the partner countries' systems. The provision of budget support fit into this mold. Several parallel developments contributed to its rising prominence (De Kemp, Leiderer, & Ruben, 2011; IOB, 2012). One of these was a growing dissatisfaction with project aid. As a result of the fragmentation of aid efforts, poor coordination, and a lack of ownership, the modality was not always efficient or effective. Results were not sustainable since the projects were not necessarily a priority of the recipient country. Recipient governments and donors alike realized that local ownership and partnership around country-owned development programs were prerequisites for enhancing aid effectiveness with a higher likelihood of achieving sustainable results (Koeberle, Stavreski, & Walliser, 2006). Moreover, it was felt that the Millennium Development Goals (MDGs) could be achieved only by dovetailing development assistance with government structures in the recipient countries.

In addition, research in the late 1990s revealed that conditionalities, focusing on (promises of) policy reforms, were ineffective in forcing governments to change their policies in return for aid (P. Collier, Guillaumont, Guillaumont, & Gunning, 1997; Dijkstra, 2002; Dollar & Svensson, 2000; Killick, Gunatilaka, & Marr, 1998; Temple, 2010). According to the influential World Bank (1998) publication *Assessing Aid*, aid would have beneficial impacts only if countries pursue sound economic policies. This conclusion was instrumental in promoting greater reliance on budget support. It provided the arguments for stronger country ownership and greater selectivity, that is, only "good performers" were to be eligible for budget support (Faust & Leiderer, 2008; Koeberle et al., 2006).

In spite of the euphoria, within 10 years budget support became one of the most contested modalities. According to critics, the modality is a blank check that disappears into the pockets of corrupt officials and impairs domestic taxation and accountability. It is therefore more likely to undermine than to reinforce socioeconomic development. Corruption scandals in a number of recipient countries contributed to this image, even if there was not a direct link with the instrument. Countries such as Germany, Sweden, and Finland became more reserved on the provision of budget support. They tightened their rules or even discontinued its use (as in the Netherlands). Forced by a number of countries, the European Commission became more selective in the provision of budget support, linking the instrument more to the quality of governance and moving away from general budget support to sector budget support.

The dwindling popularity of budget support is related to its complexity, involving multiple instruments, many actors with diverging interests, and multiple and broad objectives. Much more so than with project aid, it is difficult to determine how much general budget support has contributed to the realization of the objectives. The "donor dollar" is impossible to monitor, and it is also not easy to gauge how much influence donors have had on partner countries' policies. The complexity also creates challenges for a rigorous evaluation (Bamberger, Rugh, & Mabry, 2012; Rogers, 2008).

# 1. Complexity of Budget Support

Chapter 1 distinguished between five interrelated dimensions of complexity: the nature of the intervention, institutions and stakeholders, embeddedness and the nature of the system, causality and change, and the evaluation process. The complexity of budget support relates to all five dimensions:

## 1.1 The Nature of the Intervention

*Changes in design and purpose:* Originally, budget support was introduced to enhance donor harmonization and coordination and predictability of funds as well as to further ownership and accountability of partner countries through the insistence on using recipient government systems and improved public finance management (PFM), to reduce transaction costs, and to strengthen local systems. This would positively impact the implementation and effectiveness of poverty reduction policies, with more sustainable results, provided that the recipient country had the right socioeconomic policies in place and the capacity to implement them. (See Table 19.1.)

In practice, donors not only required sound macroeconomic policies, a commitment to reduce poverty (as witnessed by a Poverty Reduction Strategy Paper [PRSP]), and a minimum level of transparency and quality of PFM, but they also introduced new selection criteria such as good governance, with characteristics such as rule of law, respect for democracy and human rights, and absence of corruption. Moreover, they did not stick to the entry conditions, but rather demanded that recipient countries commit themselves to improvements on these principles. Increasingly, the provision of budget support became a way of encouraging macroeconomic, socioeconomic, and political reforms (Dijkstra, 2013a; Hayman, 2011; Molenaers, Cepinskas, & Jacobs, 2010). This meant a return to the conditionality that had accompanied earlier forms of program aid. In addition, changed policies and institutions not only were considered a means toward an end, but also became an end in itself. This also implied a change in emphasis on the instruments. Budget support became an instrument for "buying a seat at the table," with the policy dialogue as the main vehicle for enforcing government reform. Ownership became commitment to the donors' reform agenda (Whitfield, 2009).

**Table 19.1** Original and Changed Policy Theory for Budget Support

|  | **Original theory** | | **Practice** | |
|---|---|---|---|---|
| Inputs | Selectivity | Resources | Selectivity and preferences for the policy dialogue | Resources |
| Implementation | Respect for ownership | Alignment  Harmonization  Predictability | Attempts to influence policies | Alignment  Harmonization  Predictability |
| Outputs | Better policy implementation | Strengthening local systems  Reduced transaction costs  More resources for social sectors  Increased local accountability | Implementation of changes desired by donors | Strengthening of local systems  Reduced transaction costs  More resources for social sectors  Increased local accountability |
| Outcomes | Enhanced government effectiveness | | Enhanced government effectiveness | |
| Impact | Greater poverty reduction | | Better policy and improved governance  Greater poverty reduction | |

SOURCE: Adapted from Dijkstra & De Kemp (2015, pp. 85–86).

*Multiple objectives*: As a result of the changed application of the instrument, budget support was supposed to be a vehicle for realizing multiple (potentially conflicting) objectives. With budget support, donors aim to realize many different objectives at the same time, including institutional change (improvement of public financial management, enhanced transparency and accountability, macroeconomic stability, further liberalization of the economy, and effectiveness of public administration) and impacts at the beneficiary level (poverty reduction, improvement in delivery of and access to social services). Multilateral donors (banks) focused on government actions and bilateral donors on outcome indicators that were not necessarily "smart" (specific, measurable, attainable, relevant, and time-bound). The diverging set of objectives culminated in overloaded performance assessment frameworks (PAFs) with different triggers and variable tranches. The result was a fragmentary and technocratic approach, which did not necessarily reflect country ownership (Tilley, 2014).

*Many instruments*: Budget support may be defined as the financing of a partner country's budget through a transfer of resources to the government's national treasury (Organisation for Economic Co-operation and Development, 2006). In practice it involves a lot more than just that. It rather comprises a mix of instruments including the funding, accompanying conditionalities (underlying principles and an agreed set of performance indicators with different triggers and incentive tranches), an intense policy dialogue, and capacity-building measures (technical assistance) that are aimed at strengthening the recipients' policies and implementing capacities (Hammond, 2006). All these instruments are applied in a heterogeneous mix, depending on the donors involved, acceptance by recipient countries, and political and institutional context. Conditionalities, policy dialogue, and involvement in the PRSP process contributed to an institutionalization of donors in the planning process, leading to micro-management and involvement in daily practices (De Kemp, Faust, & Leiderer, 2011; Lawson, 2014).

## 1.2 Institutions and Stakeholders

*Multiple actors with diverging interests*: While budget support was supposed to contribute to a more coordinated, harmonized, and aligned approach, in practice donors, especially at headquarters level, continued to push for their own interests and priorities (Tilley, 2014). Conversely, governments in recipient countries had learned to incorporate donor demands in their poverty strategies and development plans, but these documents often lacked concrete proposals and realistic time frames. Patrimonial politics and clientelism in recipient countries conflicted with donor assumptions about the feasibility and impact of reforms. In addition, differences between the ministry of finance vis-à-vis sector ministries negatively impacted the position of the former. Sector ministries are more interested in receiving sector support than general budget support (De Kemp, Faust, & Leiderer, 2011).

## 1.3 Embeddedness and the Nature of the System

*Diverging country contexts:* According to the original policy theory, budget support would be effective only in specific circumstances. Recipient countries should satisfy minimum entry conditions of ownership of poverty reduction policies as well as the capacity to address development issues. In practice, donors did not hold on to this point of departure. The modality was provided to countries that differed enormously in income levels, socioeconomic policies, and government effectiveness. Least developed countries, post-conflict states, as well as upper-middle-income countries were among the recipients.

*Contagion:* A further complication for an evaluation of budget support is that it is not an isolated intervention, but an element in a much wider set of programs, interventions, incentives, and political, social, and cultural value systems. In practice, it may be difficult to distinguish between budget support programs and other aid modalities. Changes in outcome and impact indicators may be partly (or even predominantly) effected by other causes, including other aid modalities, direct government actions, and other exogenous factors. The heterogeneity of interventions makes it difficult to isolate budget support from other interventions. Intermediate effects may not be straightforward to measure, let alone to attribute proportionately to multiple causes, particularly in a dynamic context where budget support is only one of the influencing factors in a continuously changing environment.

## 1.4 Causality and Change

*No detailed theory of causality and change:* The rationale for budget support was more detailed than the theory of change. There is no accepted theory of change how the budget support instruments are supposed to result in realizing stated objectives. The assumed chain of causality is long, both conceptually and temporally. The further the outputs and outcomes are logically away from the inputs, the more difficult it is to make hard statements on attribution. Economic growth, good governance, and investments in social sectors were expected to be the main vehicles for realizing poverty reduction, without much elaboration on the specific context and the assumed behavioral reactions along the causal chain. Donors assumed that political will and financial incentives were sufficient to achieve results, and they hardly paid attention to institutional constraints (Tilley, 2014). This has an impact on the effectiveness of the modality. In addition, it was assumed that institutional reforms were imperative for generating economic growth and combating poverty (Acemoglu & Robinson, 2012; North, 2005; North, Wallis, & Weingast, 2009). Empirical evidence about a causal relation is weak, however (Chang, 2011; Dijkstra, 2013b; Khan, 2012).

## 1.5 The Evaluation Process

The complexity of the instrument of budget support, combining multiple instruments and objectives in a context where the modality is just one of the many interventions contributing to these objectives, creates serious challenges for its evaluation.

*Delineation:* A project has a clear-cut start, but budget support often contributes to existing programs, making it more difficult to determine the before and after situation. The intervention is not discrete and not necessarily targeted at a specific group. This complicates an assessment of the effectiveness of the instrument.

*Data challenges:* The PAFs contributed to a high monitoring burden and increased data requirements, thereby creating challenges for existing monitoring and evaluation systems. In general, these indicators do not reflect a clear priority framework of donors and recipient countries on the expected progress. There is little evidence of an overall strategy, trying to link the main objectives to results indicators and actions. The measurement of indicators is often problematic. Sectors are not able to provide the basic data, and it may even be difficult to get the right reliable information about budget support flows. Various indicators try to assess elements of a recipient country's policies and governance, but these indicators may be based on perceptions and not necessarily reflect objective values. Moreover, it may be difficult to compare indicators between countries, and the importance of a specific indicator may differ from country to country.

*Attribution and endogeneity:* In addition, the complexity makes it difficult to attribute realized objectives to the budget support instruments. Almost always, budget support is just one of the instruments helping to realize the agreed objectives, and in many cases it may take some time (even years) to establish effects. It may seem appealing to follow the logical sequence from inputs (budget support) to outputs (government behavior) to outcomes (service delivery) to impact (health outcomes, for example). However, this procedure also involves some risks. Elbers, Gunning, and de Hoop (2009) point to possible endogeneity in all steps of this analysis: One or more other (unobserved) variables may be correlated with both cause and effect in every step of the causal chain. This problem of endogeneity is not new and not limited to program support, but it is often ignored. This may easily lead to erroneous conclusions, as has been shown in the aid-growth literature (Clemens & Bazzi 2009; Dalgaard, 2010; Roodman, 2008). The endogeneity problem may even be more prominent with general budget support, due to the correlation between budget support and other aid modalities and reverse causality in the relation between budget support, governance, and income. Countries may be eligible for budget support *because* they already have good macroeconomic policies in place. Neglecting this relationship may potentially result in the impact of budget support on economic development being overestimated.

# 2. Practice: Evaluation of Budget Support

A range of country case studies have been conducted to assess general budget support: Tanzania (Booth, Lawson, Williamson, Wangwe, & Msuya, 2005); Burkina Faso, Malawi, Mozambique, Nicaragua, Rwanda, Uganda, and Vietnam (IDD and Associates, 2006); Ghana (Lawson et al., 2007); Nicaragua (Dijkstra & Grigsby, 2010); Tunisia (Caputo, Valmarana, Mouley, & Corm, 2011); Mali

(Lawson et al., 2011); Zambia (De Kemp, Faust, & Leiderer, 2011); and again, Tanzania and Mozambique (ITAD, 2013, 2014). The first evaluations mainly focus on inputs, processes, donor practices, and implementation issues such as the extent of alignment, harmonization, the resources, conditionalities, and predictability. They use a political economy analysis to assess the donor influence on government policies and institutions via the policy dialogue. They also examine intermediate outcomes in terms of changes in policies and institutions, improved government systems, improved domestic accountability, and changes in resources for defined priority sectors. The studies attempt to assess the impact on access to public services, usually education and health, usually by analyzing trends at the macro level, supplemented with interviews.

---

### BOX 19.1 POLITICAL ECONOMY ANALYSIS

Political economy analysis investigates how political and economic processes interact in a society. It focuses on the distribution of power and wealth, interests and behavior of groups and individuals to explain how politics works, how wealth is created, and how developmental change happens, and the processes that create, sustain, and transform these relationships over time. The analysis includes the following elements:

- Political processes: contestation and negotiation of power, wealth, and goods
- Economic and financial processes and their link with politics
- Formal and informal institutions
- Relations, incentives, and interests of actors "under the surface"

SOURCE: Adapted from DEVCO (2012) and Bossuyt (2007).

---

A challenge for these country evaluations is to attribute changes to the instrument of budget support. The studies analyze the relationship between different inputs, implementation issues, and induced outputs, but they do not include rigorous methods that allow for more definitive statements about attribution at outcome and impact level. Moreover, external validity is a challenge. Country case studies may be able to explain why the instrument worked in specific circumstances, but it is impossible to generalize the findings from one specific case.[2]

Several more recent evaluations of budget support tried to provide more rigor by analyzing the impact of government interventions to which budget support has contributed, using quasi-experimental designs (De Kemp, Faust, & Leiderer, 2011; Lawson et al., 2011; Lawson et al., 2013, 2014). These studies combine a qualitative political economy analysis for assessing the impact of budget support on government interventions with a quasi-experimental design for evaluating the impact of these interventions on beneficiaries (households). They use the variation in the provision and use of (public) services to analyze how changes in

**Table 19.2**  A Typology of Approaches for the Evaluation of Budget Support

|  | **Qualitative** | **Quantitative** |
|---|---|---|
| Country case study | Empirical analysis of the policy theory for one country (Lawson et al., 2007; Dijkstra & Grigsby, 2010) | Analysis of the impact of government interventions using regression-based approaches (De Kemp, Faust, & Leiderer, 2011; ITAD, 2013, 2014) |
| Cross-country | Comparison of country case studies (IDD and Associates, 2006) | Cross-country regressions (Bigsten. Platteau, & Tengstam, 2011; Cordella & Dell'Ariccia, 2003) |

SOURCE: Typology adapted from Dijkstra & De Kemp (2015, p. 87). The mentioned publications are examples of each approach.

the provision of public services (health facilities, classrooms) lead to changes in the use of these services (vaccination, school attendance) and their impact (reduction of diseases, test and examination results).[3]

An alternative approach for assessing the impact of budget support is using econometric techniques to explain differences between countries (See Table 19.2.). A counterfactual is introduced by comparing results in countries with more and less or no budget support. Econometric techniques also enable dealing with endogeneity problems.[4] This approach has been used, for instance, to determine the drivers of economic growth (see Barro & Sala-i-Martin, 2004) as well as to evaluate the impact of aid (for an overview and recent results, see Arndt, Jones, & Tarp, 2010). For program aid and budget support, the results are mixed (Cordella & Dell'Ariccia, 2003; Ouattara & Strobl, 2008). More recently, Bigsten, Platteau, and Tengstam (2011) concluded that budget support has a stronger positive impact on economic growth than other aid modalities, especially after a number of years.

# 3. Dealing With Complexity

The different approaches are not competitors or mutually exclusive, but rather complementary and mutually reinforcing: Qualitative techniques focus more on identifying causal mechanisms, while quantitative techniques aim at establishing causal effects. This chapter therefore advocates an eclectic theory-based approach that allows for applying different methods to test different assumptions along the causal chain (Leeuw, 2012; Leeuw & Vaessen, 2009), combining qualitative approaches such as political economy analysis, process tracing, contribution analysis, and qualitative comparative analysis with the application of quantitative econometric techniques to test the policy theory at different levels of the causal chain.

Dijkstra and De Kemp (2015; IOB, 2012) provide an example of such an approach for a policy review of budget support. The analysis includes the following steps:

1. Literature review, which helps to provide the theoretical underpinning of specific topics (e.g., the heavily debated relation between institutions and economic growth)

2. The construction of an intervention theory for understanding how budget support is supposed to work and whether it worked in practice

3. Formulation of hypotheses on the impact of budget support

4. Selection of country case studies for in-depth analysis

5. Testing of hypotheses using qualitative and quantitative techniques

Like the technique of *process tracing*, the approach follows the causal chain of the intervention theory and the formulation of hypotheses about the connection between output, outcome, and impact, relying on social science literature, past evaluations, and other documents on budget support. The use of a number of different case studies would also allow applying the technique of qualitative comparative analysis (QCA), by examining different cases with different permutations of conditions and outcomes (White & Phillips, 2012). However, the reliance on past evaluations and other documentation in combination with the complexity of the instrument and the heterogeneity of countries also limits the possibility to apply the testing procedures of process tracing in and developing the truth table as prescribed in QCA in a strict way. Nevertheless, the approach discussed here follows the causal chain, tries to establish recurring empirical patterns (D. Collier, 2011), and tests hypotheses about the connections and the relation between the instrument and outcomes and impact (as advised by Elbers et al., 2009). While combining elements of process tracing and QCA, the qualitative approach mainly used contribution analysis for establishing the causal relations.

In line with basic steps outlined by Mayne (2011), the study

- set out the cause-effect relations, acknowledging attribution issues and determining other influencing factors;
- developed the postulated theory of change;
- gathered existing evidence and assessed the strengths of the links;
- set out the contribution story;
- sought out additional evidence;
- revised the contribution story; and
- developed the contribution story for each additional sub-theory of change.

An example may help to explain the approach. The study examines not only final outcomes such as poverty reduction or the secondary objective of improving governance, but also the transmission mechanisms that are important for an understanding and assessment of the impact of budget support.

The budget support flows may be used for investments, to increase spending in social sectors, or to reduce budget deficits, but governments in recipient countries may also use them to reduce debts or simply enlarge the foreign exchange at the central bank. Through a more qualitative assessment for the seven case studies, as well as through cross-country regressions, the approach analyzes how budget support has an impact on government expenditure, the budget deficit, and taxation. Next follows an evaluation of the actual spending of the resources and the impact of this additional spending. If budget support leads to more efficient, effective, and sustainable poverty reduction policies, this should be visible in pro-poor expenditures and in the results of these expenditures. The study traces the process for individual case studies, focusing on the contribution story and additional evidence and competing hypotheses (such as the impact of governance and economic growth on expenditure) combined with a comparative analysis of the country case studies.

In the same way, the approach analyzes the impact of budget support and the policy dialogue on governance issues, though here the case study approach is more instructive than the cross-country comparison. The analysis includes an assessment in a standardized way of context; motivations, expectations, and conditionalities; implementation; ownership and (donor) influence; intermediary effects; and impact. The econometric approach helps to test hypotheses on the impact of budget support on governance.

For the case studies the country selection is determined by trying to generate heterogeneity along two axes that were supposed to have an impact on the implementation of budget support and the outcomes for the objectives of poverty reduction and improving governance: the size of the support in relation to government expenditure and differences in scores on the Worldwide Governance Indicators (WGI) for 2004–2010. Differences in governance scores are an indicator of agreement of preferences between donors and recipients. The more agreement exists, the less need there will be for governance conditions and the more one can expect from the results of general budget support (GBS). This section includes seven case studies: Ghana, Mali, Mozambique, Nicaragua, Tanzania, Vietnam, and Zambia. Between 2004 and 2010, in Tanzania and Mozambique, budget support contributed about 15% of the funding of government expenditure; for Zambia, Mali, and Ghana this was about 6%–7% and for Vietnam and Nicaragua is was about 2%–3%.

The cross-country analyses control for differences in country context by including income levels, economic growth, and the quality of governance as control variables.[5] The indicators for good governance are also used to assess the impact of budget support on reform. In addition the analyses control for time-invariant differences using fixed effects and a trend variable to control for omitted variables common to all countries but that vary over time.[6] In order to deal with potential reverse causality, the approach instrumented for budget support (and other aid modalities), essentially following Rajan and Subramanian (2005) and Arndt, Jones, and Tarp (2010).[7] In these studies, aid per capita (aid/population) is the dependent variable and it is a function of colonial relations, a common language, the relation between the donor's population and the recipient country's population, interaction effects, and fixed donor effects. For the econometric analyses, OECD-CRS data on budget support disbursements, available for the years 2002–2010, have been used. These data have been supplemented with the Poverty Reduction Support Credits (PRSC) from the World Bank. For the influence objective, the study examined changes in WGI.

# 4. Results

The results show that donors did not apply selectivity in a strict way. The seven countries only partially met the selection criteria. They had an agreement with the IMF as well as a PRSP, but in several countries there were doubts about the quality and/or government commitment to these strategies. The quality of public financial management also varied, with Nicaragua doing best and Vietnam worst. Scores on other governance indicators were low, with relatively higher figures for Ghana and Tanzania.

Most case studies report a positive impact of budget support on PFM. By providing funding through the government budget and because of fiduciary risks, donors had reasons to insist on improvements in this area, while a better functioning PFM also did not conflict with interests of the political elite. The impact of budget support on reform, especially on governance reform, including control of corruption, rule of law, and democracy, is limited. Donors did not succeed in producing fundamental reforms in recipient countries, such as establishing an independent judiciary, greater involvement of civil society, or ending clientelism in the public sector. Cross-country analyses support this conclusion: The study did not find an impact of budget support on governance indicators. In a way, donors have contributed to this result. They often failed to realize the agreed coordination and harmonization, thereby jeopardizing some of the main advantages of the modality. At the same time, there is also no proof of worsening governance indicators as a result of budget support. Several authors have suggested that aid, and especially budget support, to governments in neo-patrimonial states undermines local accountability and may contribute to increased corruption (Moyo, 2009; Sogge, 2002). Individual country evaluations and cross-country analyses do not support this assumption (IOB, 2012). In general, it appears that countries that have received budget support had improving scores on the (perception of) control of corruption, while for other countries these scores tended to deteriorate.

In contrast with the results on governance indicators, most country case studies as well as the cross-country regressions point to a strong impact of budget support on government expenditure (Appendix, Table 1) and especially expenditure on health and education. Table 1 in the Appendix shows that when budget support is increased by one percentage point of GDP, this goes hand in hand with increased expenditure of more than 0.6 percentage point. This would mean that 60% of each euro of budget support is spent directly. Separate estimates for health and education are together even higher, suggesting that there is a stronger focus on social expenditure and that budget support induces government investments in these sectors. This conclusion is in line with findings from case studies. In Zambia, Mali, and Tanzania, budget support proved to have a leverage effect in the sense that the

**Table 19.3** Results of Country Case Studies and Cross-Country Analyses

| | Ghana | Mali | Mozambique | Nicaragua | Tanzania | Vietnam | Zambia | Cross-country |
|---|---|---|---|---|---|---|---|---|
| *Entry conditions:* | | | | | | | | |
| Stable macro-economy | Yes | Yes | Moderate, but improving | Yes | Yes | Yes | Yes | |
| PFM | Not met | Not met, but improving | Weak | Yes and improving | Not met, but improving | Not met, but improving | Not met, but improving | |
| PRSP | Yes, but donor driven | Doubts about commitment | Yes | Doubts about commitment | Yes | Yes | Yes | |
| Institutional capacity | Reasonable | Moderate | Weak | Reasonable | Reasonable | Good | Moderate | |
| Good governance | Fairly well | Doubts about control of corruption | Moderate | No, but confidence in improvements | Positive assessment by donors | Weak | Positive assessment by donors | Not significant |
| *Impact on donor behavior:* | | | | | | | | |
| Predictability | Not good, but improved | Good | Improved | Varied | Improved | Fair | Good | |
| *Impact of policy dialogue:* | | | | | | | | |
| PFM | Yes | Yes | Yes | Yes | Yes, stagnated later | Yes | Yes | |

| | Ghana | Mali | Mozambique | Nicaragua | Tanzania | Vietnam | Zambia | Cross-country |
|---|---|---|---|---|---|---|---|---|
| Macroeconomic stability | Not a subject in the dialogue | No, influence by IMF | Weak | No, not necessary | No, not necessary | No, not necessary | No, not necessary | Positive on growth |
| Good governance | Very limited | Very limited | Weak | Very limited | Very limited | Very limited | Very limited | Not significant |
| Business climate | Yes | Yes | No | No | No | Somewhat | No | |
| *Positive impact on:* | | | | | | | | |
| Tax revenue | No | Light/no | No | No | No | No | No | Not significant |
| Government expenditure | Yes | Yes | Positive | No | Yes | Limited | Yes | Positive |
| Poverty expenditure | Yes | Yes | Positive | Yes | Yes | Some | Yes | Positive |
| Education indicators | Positive | Positive | Positive | No | Positive | Positive | Positive | Positive |
| Health indicators | Limited | Positive | No | No | Positive | Improved, but not as a result of budget support | Positive | Mixed |
| Poverty | Decreased | Decreased | Slightly decreased | Stable | Stable | Decreased | Moderate reduction | Small positive effect |

SOURCE: Compiled from IOB (2012) and ITAD (2014).

increase in social expenditure was much larger than the GBS resources. Nicaragua is an exception. An explanation is that disbursements came late in the budget year and were often not predictable (Dijkstra & Grigsby, 2010). There is no evidence of a negative impact of budget support on taxation.

Countries that received budget support spent (relatively) more on social sectors and were able to realize larger impacts in these sectors. They also made more progress on a number of MDGs than other countries (Beynon & Dusu, 2010). The seven country case studies find strong impacts on education and, to a certain extent, on health. The results of the cross-country regressions support these findings. (See Table 19.3.)

It is more difficult to discern impacts on economic growth and poverty reduction, as this may take time. Nevertheless, there is some positive evidence (see Bigsten et al., 2011; Cordella & Dell'Ariccia, 2003). Countries with a PRSC (the budget support instrument of the World Bank) had higher growth rates than comparable countries without (IEG, 2010). On average, growth was almost one percentage point higher. PRSC countries also witnessed a stronger decline in poverty than non-PRSC countries. IOB (2012) noted that on average, in countries receiving budget support, economic growth coincided with a larger reduction of poverty (see also Alvi & Senbeta, 2012). This does not mean that economic growth is a sufficient condition for poverty reduction. In several countries (e.g., Tanzania, Zambia) a high population growth limited the impact on growth per capita. Governments, as well as donors, expected too much from a more or less automatic trickle down. However, economic growth often took place in sectors where few people work, such as mining, construction, telecommunications, and banking (e.g., in Mozambique, Tanzania, Zambia, and Ghana).

On average, poverty decreased more in countries receiving budget support than in other low- and lower-middle-income countries. Differences are not very large, but point in the same direction: In countries receiving budget support, the income share of the poorest 20% was higher and increased more than in other countries, poverty decreased more, and the Human Development Index (HDI) improved more (see Appendix, Table 2). Overall, budget support helped to generate improvements on the UN Human Development Index, which is based on income, education, and health indicators. About 15% of the increase in HDI between 2000 and 2010 can be ascribed to the modality. This completely explains the difference with other countries.

The results lead to the following conclusion: Ownership and congruence of interests and strategies between recipient countries and donors are conditions for effective budget support. A next condition is that support is predictable and disbursed on time, allowing the recipient government to spend the resources as envisaged. Budget support is much less effective for enforcing governance reform.

# 5. Lessons Learned

The analysis points to a number of lessons for an evaluation of budget support or comparable complex programs:

1. Individual country case studies help to understand the functioning and challenges in a specific context, but external validity is low. Moreover, in the absence of an explicit counterfactual, it is difficult to establish impact.

2. Quantitative cross-country studies, on the other hand, may deal with the potential endogeneity of the instrument and have higher external validity, but they are not suitable for dealing with the complexity of the modality.

3. The results show that an eclectic approach, combining a qualitative comparison of a larger number of case studies with cross-country evidence, is useful for evaluation of complex programs such as budget support.

4. With the publication of a larger number of evaluations (country case studies), it becomes interesting to further refine the methodology with the application of qualitative approaches such as qualitative comparative analysis.[8] This may help to simplify the evaluation approach.

5. Future research may focus on the (even more complex) interaction between budget support and other aid modalities.

# 6. Practical Applications

The instrument of budget support is a good example of a complex intervention. The analyses point to some guidelines for policymakers intending to evaluate budget support:

- Budget support usually involves many stakeholders (donors as well as recipient countries). Therefore, the modality should be evaluated preferably as a joint effort among major stakeholders.
- Evaluation should be an integral part of the budget support process and therefore should be part of the memorandum of understanding. Otherwise there is a risk that the evaluation has to be negotiated with donors and partner countries, and this may be a lengthy process.
- An evaluation should include:
  a. a political economy and budget analysis, including the role of the donors, and an assessment of the direct impact of budget support on government behavior using approaches such as contribution analysis and/or process tracing; and
  b. a more rigorous analysis of the impact of government actions to which budget support has contributed, using quasi-experimental designs and a combination of administrative data and household surveys.
- A budget support evaluation requires careful planning. It may be helpful, for instance, to align the evaluation with the availability of new survey results (e.g., living conditions, monitoring surveys) so that these may be used for analyzing impacts.

A rigorous evaluation of budget support may be time-consuming (more than a year) and expensive (about US$300,000–500,000), depending on the availability of recent sector studies. The evaluation demands, first of all, expertise on the macro-economy and political economy of the country, institutional constraints, budget support processes, donor and partner country relations, public finance management, fiduciary risks, as well as sector expertise. As a rule of thumb, one could say that one sector evaluation costs about US$100,000. It involves sector specialists as well as statistical and econometric experts for assessing data availability, the quality of data, and the analyses.

What are the benefits of such an investment?

• The evaluation may help to redefine relations between donors and recipient countries. There is a risk that over time donors include additional demands, conditions, and variable tranches that tend to undermine the consistency of the budget support framework and resort to micro-management, thereby undermining ownership. On the other hand, budget support is a contract and involves more than just collecting money under the flag of ownership. Ownership also involves responsibilities and obligations. Over time unrealistic expectations may develop on both sides, leading to tensions in the relationship.

• There is a tendency among donors and partner countries to focus on progress on indicators of the performance assessment framework, without questioning their value in the context of the overall budget support objectives, their validity, and their reliability. More important, while some of these indicators may be useful for monitoring purposes, this should not be confused with an analysis of the impact of budget support or actions by the recipient government. For a complex process such as budget support, annual reviews are not a substitute for a rigorous evaluation. Practice shows that the instrument was more effective than judged by several donors. In addition, donors and partner countries have not always addressed the major constraints. Evaluations conclude that the instrument could have been more effective.

• For new country evaluations it may be useful to compare expectations and findings with Table 19.3 in this chapter.

The findings of individual country evaluations as well as of our more synthetic approach suggest that budget support works best if the original policy theory is respected, meaning country ownership, sound socioeconomic policies, and institutional capacity. Conditionalities are not effective.

It may be interesting to apply the presented approach to other areas as well, especially areas where complexity and heterogeneity coincide. Objects for evaluation could be, for instance, global public goods or trade relations.

# References

Acemoglu, D., & Robinson, J. (2012). *Why nations fail*. New York, NY: Crown Business.

Alvi, E., & Senbeta, A. (2012). Does foreign aid reduce poverty? *Journal of International Development, 24*, 955–976.

Arndt, C., Jones, S., & Tarp, F. (2010). Aid and growth: Have we come full circle? *Journal of Globalization and Development, 1*(2), 1–26.

Bamberger, M., Rugh, J., & Mabry, L. (2012). *RealWorld evaluation: Working under budget, time, data, and political constraints.* Thousand Oaks, CA: Sage.

Barro, R. J., & Sala-i-Martin, X. (2004). *Economic growth.* Cambridge, MA: MIT Press.

Beynon, J., & Dusu, A. (2010). *Budget support and MDG performance* (Development Paper No. 2010/01). Brussels, Belgium: European Commission.

Bigsten, A., Platteau, J., & Tengstam, S. (2011). *The aid effectiveness agenda: The benefits of going ahead.* Gothenburg, Sweden: SOGES.

Booth, D., Lawson, A., Williamson, T., Wangwe, S., & Msuya, M. (2005). *Joint evaluation of general budget support Tanzania 1995–2004.* Dar es Salaam, Tanzania: Daima Associates/ODI.

Bossuyt, J. (2007). *Some key policy issues in supporting domestic accountability: Implications for evaluating PILA.* Presentation at the Expert Meeting on Evaluating Policy Influence, Lobbying and Advocacy, The Hague, Netherlands.

Caputo, E., Valmarana, C., Mouley, S., & Corm, G. (2011). *Evaluation des opérations d'aide budgétaire de la Commission Européenne à la Tunisie entre 1996 et 2008* [Evaluation of budget support operations of the European Commission in Tunisia between 1966 and 2008]. Brussels, Belgium: DRN.

Chang, H. (2011). Institutions and economic development: Theory, policy and history. *Journal of Institutional Economics, 7,* 473–498.

Clemens, M., & Bazzi, S. (2009). *Blunt instruments: On establishing the causes of economic growth* (Working Paper 171). Washington, DC: Center for Global Development.

Collier, D. (2011). Understanding process tracing. *Political Science and Politics, 44,* 823–830.

Collier, P., Guillaumont, P., Guillaumont, S., & Gunning, J. W. (1997). Redesigning conditionality. *World Development, 25,* 1399–1407.

Cordella, T., & Dell'Ariccia, G. (2003). *Budget support versus project aid* (IMF Working Paper No. WP/03/88). Washington, DC: International Monetary Fund.

Dalgaard, C. (2010). *Evaluating aid effectiveness in the aggregate: A critical assessment of the evidence.* Copenhagen, Denmark: Danida.

De Kemp, A., Faust, J., & Leiderer, S. (2011). *Between high expectations and reality: An evaluation of budget support in Zambia* (IOB Evaluation No. 356). Bonn, Germany: BMZ/IOB/Sida.

De Kemp, A., Leiderer, S., & Ruben, R. (2011). Too much, too quickly, the woes of budget support. *The Broker, 26,* 16–19.

DEVCO. (2012). *Using political economy analysis to improve EU development effectiveness* (draft). Brussels, Belgium: European Commission.

Dijkstra, G. (2002). The effectiveness of policy conditionality: Eight country experiences. *Development and Change, 33,* 307–334.

Dijkstra, G. (2013a). Governance or poverty reduction? Assessing budget support in Nicaragua. *Journal of Development Studies, 49*(1), 110–124.

Dijkstra, G. (2013b). *Paradoxes around good governance* (Inaugural lecture). Rotterdam, Netherlands: Erasmus University.

Dijkstra, G., & De Kemp, A. (2015). Challenges in evaluating budget support and how to solve them. *Evaluation, 21,* 83–98.

Dijkstra, G., & Grigsby, A. (2010). *Evaluation of general budget support to Nicaragua* (IOB Evaluation No. 329). The Hague, Netherlands: IOB, Ministry of Foreign Affairs.

Dollar, D., & Svensson, J. (2000). What explains the success or failure of structural adjustment programs? *Economic Journal, 110,* 894–917.

Elbers, C., Gunning, J. W., & de Hoop, K. (2009). Assessing sector-wide programs with statistical impact evaluation: A methodological proposal. *World Development, 37,* 513–520.

Faust, J., & Leiderer, S. (2008). Zur effektivität und politischen ökonomie der entwicklungszusammenarbeit [The effectiveness and political economy of development cooperation]. *Politische Vierteljahresschrift, 49*(1), 129–152.

Hammond, M. A. (2006). A framework for evaluating general budget support. In S. Koeberle, Z. Stavreski, & J. Walliser (Eds.), *Budget support as more effective aid?* (pp. 91–104). Washington, DC: World Bank.

Hayman, R. (2011). Budget support and democracy: A twist in the conditionality tale. *Third World Quarterly, 32,* 673–688.

IDD and Associates. (2006). *Evaluation of general budget support: Synthesis report.* Birmingham, UK: University of Birmingham, International Development Department, School of Public Policy.

IEG, Committee on Development Effectiveness (2010). *Poverty reduction support credits: An evaluation of World Bank support* (Report No. CODE2009-0091). Washington, DC: World Bank.

IOB. (2012). *Budget support: Conditional results.* The Hague, Netherlands: Ministry of Foreign Affairs.

ITAD. (2013). *Joint evaluation of budget support to Tanzania.* Hove, UK: ITAD.

ITAD. (2014). *Joint evaluation of budget support to Mozambique.* Hove, UK: ITAD.

Khan, M. H. (2012). Governance and growth: History, ideology and methods of proof. In A. Noman, K. Botchwey, H. Stein, & J. E. Stiglitz (Eds.), *Good growth and governance in Africa: Rethinking development strategies* (pp. 51–82). Oxford, UK: Oxford University Press.

Killick, T., Gunatilaka, R., & Marr, A. (1998). *Aid and the political economy of policy change.* London, UK: Routledge.

Koeberle, S., Stavreski, Z., & Walliser, J. (2006). *Budget support as more effective aid? Recent Experiences and Emerging Lessons.* Washington, DC: World Bank.

Lawson, A. (2014). *Meta-evaluation of budget support: Synthesis analysis of the findings, conclusions and recommendations of seven country evaluations of budget support.* London, UK: Fiscus.

Lawson, A., Boadi, G., Ghartey, A., Ghartey, A., Killick, T., Kizilbash Agha, A., & Williamson, T. (2007). *Joint evaluation of multi-donor budget support to Ghana.* London, UK: ODI/CDD.

Lawson, A., Habas, J., Keita, M., Paul, E., Versailles B., & Murray-Zmijewski A. (2011). *Evaluation conjointe des opérations d'aide budgétaire au Mali 2003–3009* [Joint evaluation of budget support operations in Mali 2003–2009]. Brussels, Belgium: ECO Consult.

Leeuw, F. L. (2012). Linking theory-based evaluation and contribution analysis: Three problems and a few solutions. *Evaluation, 18,* 348–363.

Leeuw, F. L., & Vaessen, J. (2009). *Impact evaluation and development.* Washington, DC: NONIE & World Bank.

Mayne, J. (2011). Contribution analysis: Addressing the cause and effect. In K. Forss, M. Marra, & R. Schwartz (Eds.), *Evaluating the complex: Attribution, contribution, and beyond* (pp. 53–95). New Brunswick, NJ: Transaction.

Molenaers, N., Cepinskas, L., & Jacobs, B. (2010). *Budget support and policy/political dialogue: Donor practices in handling (political) crises* (Discussion Paper No. 2010-06). Antwerp, Belgium: University of Antwerp/IOB.

Moyo, D. (2009). *Dead aid: Why aid is not working and how there is another way for Africa.* London, UK: Allan Lane/Penguin Books.

Nordtveit, I. (2014). *Partner country ownership: Does better governance and commitment to development attract general budget support?* (Working Paper 02/14). Bergen, Norway: University of Bergen.

North D. (2005). *Understanding the process of economic change.* Princeton, NJ: Princeton University Press.

North, D., Wallis, J., & Weingast, B. (2009). *Violence and social orders.* Cambridge, UK: Cambridge University Press.

Organisation for Economic Co-operation and Development. (2006). *Harmonising donor practices for effective aid delivery, Volume 2: Budget support, sector wide approaches and capacity development for public finance management.* Paris, France: Author.

Ouattara, B., & Strobl, E. (2008). Aid, policy and growth: Does aid modality matter? *Review of World Economics, 144,* 347–365.

Rajan, R., & Subramanian, A. (2005). *Aid and growth: What does the cross-country evidence really show?* Washington, DC: International Monetary Fund.

Rogers, P. (2008). Using programme theory to evaluate complicated and complex aspects of interventions. *Evaluation, 14,* 29–48.

Roodman, D. (2008). *Through the looking-glass, and what OLS found there: On growth, foreign aid, and reverse causality* (Working Paper 137). Washington, DC: Center for Global Development.

Sogge, D. (2002). *Give and take: What's the matter with foreign aid?* London, UK: Zed Books.

Temple, J. R. W (2010). Aid and conditionality. In D. Rodrik & M. R. Rosenzweig (Eds.), *Handbook of development economics* (Vol. 5, pp. 4415–4523). Amsterdam, Netherlands: Elsevier.

Tilley, H. (2014). *The political economy of aid and accountability: The rise and fall of budget support in Tanzania.* Farnham, UK: Ashgate.

White, H., & Phillips, D. (2012). *Addressing attribution of cause and effect in small n impact evaluations: Towards an integrated framework.* New Delhi, India: 3IE.

Whitfield, L. (Ed.). (2009). *The politics of aid: African strategies for dealing with donors.* Oxford, UK: Oxford University Press.

World Bank. (1998). *Assessing aid: What works, what doesn't and why?* Washington, DC: Author.

# Appendix

| Table 1 Relationship Between Budget Support and Government Expenditure, 2002–2010 | | | | | | |
|---|---|---|---|---|---|---|
| | **Fixed effects** | | **Fixed effects with zero stage estimate** | | **IV fixed effects** | |
| GBS/GDP | 0.59 | ** | 0.62 | *** | 1.65 | *** |
| | (0.26) | | (0.23) | | (0.50) | |
| Ln (GDP per capita) | −1.23 | | −2.45 | | −1.65 | |
| | (2.07) | | (1.93) | | (1.36) | |
| GDP growth | −0.08 | * | −0.08 | | -0.08 | |
| | (0.05) | | (0.05) | | (0.03) | |
| Expenditure t-1 | 0.61 | *** | 0.60 | *** | 0.60 | *** |
| | (0.04) | | (0.04) | | (0.03) | |
| WGI | 1.77 | ** | 1.83 | ** | 1.41 | ** |
| | (0.73) | | (0.72) | | (0.61) | |
| Trend | 0.27 | ** | 0.29 | *** | 0.27 | |
| | (0.10) | | (0.10) | | (0.06) | |
| Constant | 18.72 | | 26.92 | ** | 20.95 | ** |
| | (13.83) | | (13.17) | | (9.19) | |
| | | | | | | |
| N | 866 | | 848 | | 848 | |
| Groups | 100 | | 99 | | 99 | |
| $R^2$ | 0.79 | | 0.71 | | 0.71 | |

NOTE: Robust standard errors in parentheses; for the IV fixed effects, regression standard errors in parentheses.

* $P < 10\%$; ** $P < 5\%$; *** $P < 1\%$.

**Table 2** Relationship Between Budget Support and Changes in the Human Development Index

| | OLS (1) | | OLS (2) | | 2SLS (3) | | 2SLS (4) | |
|---|---|---|---|---|---|---|---|---|
| GDP per capita growth | 0.0059 | *** | 0.0057 | *** | 0.0059 | *** | 0.0058 | *** |
| | (0.0006) | | (0.0007) | | (0.0007) | | (0.0007) | |
| WGI 2000 | −0.0041 | * | −0.0050 | ** | −0.0052 | ** | −0.0060 | ** |
| | (0.0022) | | (0.0024) | | (0.0021) | | (0.024) | |
| ΔWGI | −0.0031 | | −0.0032 | | −0.0041 | | −0.0048 | |
| | (0.0048) | | (0.0045) | | (0.0047) | | (0.0044) | |
| Average GBS 2002–2010 | 0.0061 | *** | 0.0084 | *** | 0.0057 | *** | 0.0086 | ** |
| | (0.0018) | | (0.0025) | | (0.0021) | | (0.0038) | |
| Average other aid | | | −0.0006 | | | | −0.0006 | |
| | | | (0.0005) | | | | (0.0007) | |
| Constant | 0.0349 | *** | 0.0367 | *** | 0.0347 | *** | 0.0358 | *** |
| | (0.0029) | | (0.0033) | | (0.0029) | | (0.0034) | |
| $R^2$ | 0.48 | | 0.49 | | 0.48 | | 0.49 | |
| N | 101 | | 101 | | 97 | | 97 | |

SOURCE: Dijkstra & De Kemp (2015, p. 93).

NOTE: Robust standard errors in parentheses.

* $P < 10\%$; ** $P < 5\%$; *** $P < 1\%$.

# Notes

1. The chapter is based on research for the Policy Review Budget Support: Conditional Results, conducted by the authors for the Policy and Operations Evaluation Department (IOB) of the Netherlands Ministry of Foreign Affairs, and also uses information from Dijkstra and De Kemp (2015).

2. The synthesis report of the Joint Evaluation of Budget Support (IDD and Associates, 2006) has tried to overcome this limitation by analyzing seven case studies, though the sample remained small for generalizing findings.

3. The quasi-experimental approaches such as difference in difference techniques and fixed effects regressions deal with (time-invariant) unobservables (see, e.g., Elbers et al., 2009; Leeuw & Vaessen, 2009).

4. A limitation of most cross-country studies, however, is an almost exclusive focus on economic growth.

5. Measured as a factor score of the six Worldwide Governance Indicators of the World Bank. It has been suggested that other indicators should be used, such as the CPIA scores and/or the Freedom House indicators. In practice, these indicators are highly correlated (IOB, 2012; Nordtveit, 2014).

6. The method of fixed effects controls for country-specific differences by including country fixed effects. As a result, the computation of the coefficients is based only on changes within countries and not on differences between countries. This procedure eliminates time-invariant unobservables.

7. The instrumental variable technique solves endogeneity problems (due to unobservables or reverse causality) by finding an exogenous variable that is correlated with the endogenous regressor, but not with the dependent variable (or more precisely, with the error term). This way, the analysis consists of two stages: (a) regressing the endogenous regressor on the exogenous instrument and (b) regressing the dependent variable on the newly created variable. This study used an additional zero stage regression because the instrumentation was done at a lower level of analysis, the individual donor-recipient relationship. The main analyses have been done at the more aggregated recipient level using the newly created (aggregated) variable as instrument. For a more extensive explanation of the instrumentation approach, see IOB (2012).

8. It must be noted, nevertheless, that the potential for a successful application of these techniques is larger in a more homogenous context.

# CHAPTER 20

# Dealing With Complexity in a Realist Synthesis

*Community Accountability and Empowerment Initiatives*

Gill Westhorp, Bill Walker, and Patricia Rogers

Community accountability and empowerment interventions, like many interventions in international development, are complex in nature. They are inserted into diverse contexts; they attempt to achieve different goals; they work in different ways; they are affected by a wide variety of factors at national, subnational, and local levels; and effective interventions are responsive and adaptive. This chapter presents the methodology and findings of a review study on this topic using a realist synthesis approach, which is particularly suited to address complexity issues. The chapter begins with an overview of the review in terms of its scope, processes, and findings. It then analyzes the review in terms of Pawson's VICTORE framework to demonstrate the complexity of the review topic, how complexity was reflected in the findings, and how the methodology of realist synthesis helped us manage and deal with complexity. We then discuss how the findings from a realist synthesis can assist in dealing with the complexities of policy and program management in the real world.

Realist evaluation (Pawson & Tilley, 1997) and realist synthesis (Pawson, 2006) were developed to assist policymakers and program staff to find pathways through complexity—specifically, to develop and test usable theories about complex and varied interventions applied across multiple contexts. One of the central ideas is that understanding how and why something works, or does not, in particular contexts can assist with practical decision making: whether to use a particular kind of program in a particular situation, how to adapt a program to a particular context, and so on. But if complication and complexity are the norm in social programs (Rogers, 2008; Westhorp, 2012, 2013), how exactly does realist synthesis address this? Can it in fact deal with the complication and complexity of real programs and real decisions? And how might practitioners and policymakers actually use the results? This chapter explores these questions through the lens of a recently completed realist review[1] of community accountability and empowerment initiatives.

# 1. Overview of the Review

## 1.1 Review Methodology

Realist review (or realist synthesis) is a type of systematic review of existing evidence, grounded in a realist philosophy of science (Pawson, 2006). It is theory-based and seeks to infuse every step of the review process with theory. The RAMESES standards for realist reviews (Wong, Greenhalgh, Westhorp, Buckingham, & Pawson, 2013) make it clear, for example, that a realist review

- examines not a program but an aspect of program theory;
- seeks to answer realist questions—not whether a program works overall, but for whom, to what extent, in which respects, in what contexts, and through what mechanisms;
- uses iterative search strategies that relate to program theory, rather than a single front-end, search terms–based strategy;
- uses inclusion and exclusion criteria of relevance (i.e., relevance to program theory) and rigor (i.e., the aspects of the primary text that will be used in the review are of sufficient quality to support the conclusions that will be drawn from them in the review); realist reviews do not include or exclude texts on the basis of research design (e.g., randomized controlled trial [RCT], quasi-experimental);
- involves a synthesis which refines elements of theory, rather than aggregating outcome data; and
- produces an improved program theory.

For reasons that are explained below, this was more a theory-building review than a theory-testing review.[2]

## 1.2 Background to the Review

Since the 1990s, community accountability and empowerment interventions (CAEIs) have been advocated as a way to improve educational outcomes by improving the quality of educational services and participation by students and families. CAEIs seek to increase the ability of communities to hold governments, funders, bureaucracies, and service providers accountable to them for the provision of services and opportunities that meet basic rights. Community accountability can also involve questioning the standards to which public organizations are held and the extent to which these are responsive to community needs. Voice is therefore important—processes for the community to express their preferences, opinions, and views. Changing accountability structures involves changing power relationships, so power is also critical (Walker, 2009). Key elements of accountability include transparency of decision making, answerability, enforceability, and the ability to sanction (Rocha Menocal & Sharma, 2008, pp. 5–6).

The review identified four different types of initiatives related to community accountability in education. *Specific accountability interventions*, including community scorecards, citizen report cards, textbook monitoring, and monitoring of teacher attendance, have been designed to address specific problems and operate, at least in part, at the local level. *Decentralization* may be relevant to community accountability and empowerment because it empowers local communities directly or because it establishes a context in which it is easier for local communities to hold (closer) levels of government to account. *School-based management* is a particular form of decentralization in which various decision-making powers and forms of budgetary control are devolved to school level. Types of school-based management in which parents hold control, or share control with school staff, may strengthen accountability of staff to communities. *Community schools* are a relatively common response to shortages of education provision, often involve significant control by community members, and are sometimes integrated into government strategies for expanding education access and improving accountability.

While there have been examples of positive results from some of these initiatives, overall research and evaluation of community accountability and empowerment initiatives has found mixed results (Joshi, 2013; Ringold, Holla, Koziol, & Srinivasan, 2012). This review therefore sought to understand more about how and why various strategies work differently in different contexts. It focused on the primary education sector and on accountability at the local level.

It has been argued that community accountability and empowerment interventions improve educational outcomes by improving the quality of educational services and the participation of students and families in education. However, there has been no agreement about what is meant by "community accountability" or "community empowerment" in relation to education. The range of interventions that might affect accountability and empowerment was broad and evidence of impacts was mixed. This set of circumstances—contested understandings and mixed evidence—is by no means uncommon in international development. It provided part of the rationale for undertaking a realist review.

## 1.3 Negotiating the Boundaries of the Review

The review was contracted by the Department for International Development (DFID) as part of a joint call with the Australian aid agency (AusAID, now part of the Department of Foreign Affairs and Trade) and the International Initiative for Impact Evaluation (3IE). The initial call for proposals framed the research question in terms of a dichotomous question: "Do community accountability and empowerment initiatives improve education outcomes, especially for the poor, in low and middle income countries?" Given the state of knowledge in the area, we proposed a revised research question and a realist review methodology to answer it: Under what circumstances does enhancing community accountability and empowerment improve education outcomes, particularly for the poor?

Following consultation with the funding body, the foci for the review were agreed on: low- and middle-income countries (LMIC); primary school education, because one of the Millennium Development Goals is to achieve universal primary education; a focus on girls and on marginalized populations, because they are frequently disadvantaged in relation to education; public (i.e., government-provided) education, because that is most directly within the capacity of governments to affect; interventions whose primary intention is to improve accountability of governments and education service providers to communities, because these were the primary mechanisms of interest in the review question; and interventions that entail local-level participation or implementation, because the focus of the question was on community-level accountability and empowerment.

These agreements, along with the key terms *community accountability* and *empowerment*, set the conceptual boundaries for the review. Setting conceptual boundaries is important, not just from a pragmatic point of view but also from a complexity theory perspective. Complexity theory is a member of the family of open systems theories, and open systems theories recognize that in reality, systems do not have neat edges. It is therefore necessary for the analyst to draw conceptual boundaries around the system under consideration and to determine what is considered to be "in" and what is "out" in each case (Cabrera, Colosi, & Lobdell, 2008; Midgley, 2000). This same principle is reflected in the RAMESES standards for realist review:

> Because a realist synthesis may generate a large number of avenues that might be explored and explained, and because resources and timescale are invariably finite, the expectation is that the review must be "contained" by progressively focusing both its breadth (how wide an area?) and depth (how much detail?). (Wong et al., 2013, p. 6)

Even with these parameters established, the scope remained broad and the potential for complexity remained high. Just as one indicator: There were over 100 low- and middle-income countries in scope for the review, each with different histories, cultures, sources of disadvantage, education systems, education reforms, existing accountability relationships, and so on.

Program theory, at least in principle, provides a way through such complexities. It provides a focus for what questions to ask, what data to extract, how to analyze and interpret the data, and how to explain the different patterns of outcomes. Realist program theory, with its particular focus on causal processes and the features of context necessary for their operation, provides a lens for doing so.

## 1.4 Logistics of the Review

An initial literature review informed the development of the initial proposal. After acceptance of the research proposal, a protocol for the review was developed, describing its aims and rationale, definitional and conceptual issues, and the policy and practice background as well as outlining the proposed methods to be used to search for and review studies and to extract and synthesize evidence. The protocol was revised in response to peer review and feedback from the funding agency and then formally published (Westhorp, Walker, & Rogers, 2012).

Search strategies involved a combination of keyword searches in numerous databases, document searches of relevant websites, keyword and targeted searches using Google Scholar, snowballing of references of included documents, and consultation with end user group members.[3] Checking reference lists identified many additional sources that had not been captured through the database and website searches. In fact, of the 268 documents included after initial screening, only 46 (17.2%) were identified through the original Boolean search strategy; of those, only 28 were eventually included in the review. This is consistent with previous studies, which found traditional searches to be a relatively poor basis for theory-based reviews (Greenhalgh & Peacock, 2005). The search process continued throughout the review.

We initially identified 21,000 documents. These were reduced to 140 documents using inclusion and exclusion criteria. Inclusion criteria related to the agreed foci for the review: education sector interventions that sought to improve accountability of governments and education service providers to communities; in low- and middle-income countries; including a focus on girls and on marginalized populations; and entailing local-level participation or implementation. Studies could be included for addressing any of these elements.[4] Texts in English and published after 1995 were included. Exclusion criteria were being outside the agreed foci for the review or insufficient quality. Quality assessment did not refer to a hierarchy of designs, and all types of empirical studies were eligible for inclusion. Coded studies included formal research and evaluations, various types of case studies, RCTs, comparative analyses, and quasi-experimental studies.

Studies outside the agreed foci for the review or of insufficient quality were excluded. In keeping with the RAMESES standards for realist review, the quality assessment was done at the level of specific claims rather than entire studies. Material was reviewed by two team members, who conferred as required to make judgments about the trustworthiness of data in reports, referring documents to one of the lead investigators for discussion when they had doubts.

Included documents fell into two groups. The first comprised 30 core studies, which met inclusion criteria and provided interim or education outcomes data. Of these, 16 studies provided evidence of impacts on student learning itself, in India, Indonesia, Uganda, Kenya, El Salvador, Guatemala, and Nicaragua. Many of these studies also reported intermediate outcomes. Another 14 studies provided evidence of intermediate education outcomes such as enrollment, attendance, or reduced corruption. The second group of around 110 documents provided evidence in relation to particular mechanisms or features of context.

Originally, we had intended to use NVivo to code materials and we had developed a detailed coding framework to provide consistency across the review team. In practice, given the diversity of material and the theory-building nature of the task, this proved simply too cumbersome to use. Instead we developed a set of data extraction templates tailored to the particular review.

The final version of the report, after revisions in response to peer review and feedback from the funding agency, summarized the evidence for intermediate outcomes and student-learning outcomes from the included studies and presented significant theory development in terms of the causal mechanisms by which these interventions worked, the contexts in which they worked, and the relationships between accountability and empowerment (Westhorp et al., 2014).

## 1.5 Theory Development

It became apparent very early in the review process that programs in the area of community accountability and empowerment were generally under-theorized. Many programs referred to accountability, but most were vague about exactly how or why they expected to generate it, who would become accountable to whom, or how it would improve education outcomes if they did. Some reports referred to a model of accountability as requiring transparency of decision making, answerability (the requirement to justify decisions), enforceability, and the ability to sanction (Rocha Menocal & Sharma, 2008, pp. 5–6). However, few were clear about exactly which of these aspects would be affected by their interventions. Many more referred to empowerment but were unclear whether this was individual or collective, psychological or political, or what the relationships between these might be. In some cases, it appeared that programs assumed that the provision of information was sufficient to both motivate and empower communities to hold schools, teachers, and education departments accountable. None of the reports or research reviewed clearly theorized the relationship between accountability and empowerment.

This was problematic because realist reviews are by their nature theory-based. Our response was to accept that the review would be more theory-building than theory-testing and, as befits a broad question in an under-theorized area, to aim for breadth more than depth of understanding. The review moved through six iterative components of theory development:

1. Development of the initial program theory, later revised to a hierarchy of outcomes

2. Operationalization of key terms: *community accountability* and *empowerment*

3. Development of a typology of CAEIs

4. Identification of 11 causal mechanisms involved in producing outcomes of interest

5. Identification of 13 contexts affecting mechanisms and 30 specific propositions

6. Theoretical model for the relationship between empowerment and accountability

The first piece of theory development was undertaken during the development of the research protocol. A workshop involving the research team, practitioners in accountability interventions, and academics was conducted. Results from the workshop were used to develop an initial program theory for the overall class of community accountability and empowerment interventions, using an expanded hierarchy-of-outcomes format. This framework informed the development of search terms and strategies. It was then revised during the review process. The revised hierarchy of outcomes is shown in Figure 20.1.

**Figure 20.1**  Hierarchy of Outcomes for Community Accountability and Empowerment Initiatives

| Activities | Immediate | Short term | Intermediate | Intermediate education | Final education |
|---|---|---|---|---|---|
| Engagement strategy<br><br>Information provision<br><br>Capacity building<br><br>Deliberation and planning processes<br><br>Implementation processes | Involvement of necessary stakeholders<br><br>Increased awareness relevant to project<br><br>Increased knowledge and skills for project roles<br><br>Plans tailored to local contexts<br><br>Plans implemented | Application of sanctions and incentives<br><br>Stronger relationships between stakeholders<br><br>Community structures established or strengthened<br><br>Stronger voice in advocacy or decision making<br><br>Participation in planned activities | Reduced corruption<br><br>Improved teacher attendance<br><br>Improved pedagogy<br><br>Improved teaching and learning resources<br><br>Improved buildings and facilities<br><br>Stronger parent support for education | Increased student enrollment<br><br>Increased student attendance<br><br>Increased student engagement<br><br>Improved student retention<br><br>Decreased grade repetition | Improved student learning outcomes |

SOURCE: Westhorp et al. (2014).

The second component of theory development involved operationalizing the two key terms of *community accountability* and *empowerment*. During development of the research protocol, we defined these terms. *Community accountability* was understood to refer to the ability of communities (primarily local communities) to hold governments, funders, bureaucracies, and service providers accountable to them for the provision of services and opportunities that meet basic rights. *Empowerment* has many definitions and is surrounded by some confusion. Underlying these multiple meanings are long-running theoretical controversies over the nature of power. To reflect at least some of these meanings, *empowerment* was initially operationalized by slightly adapting Friedmann's (1992) model of empowerment. This resulted in a model of eight bases of social power: spaces, surplus time over subsistence requirements, appropriate information, knowledge and skills, financial resources, productive assets, social networks, and social organizations. These various kinds of resources either are required for communities to be able to hold authorities and service providers to account (in realist terms, are necessary features of context) or may be developed as a result of community accountability and empowerment interventions (in realist terms, are outcomes of interventions that then create a new context in which accountability interventions may operate).

During the early phases of the review, the third component of theory development was undertaken—the development of the typology of four types of interventions relevant to community accountability and empowerment in education that was outlined earlier.

A basic program theory for each of these types of programs was developed. This later helped in understanding the kinds of mechanisms that might be expected to fire in particular kinds of initiatives. There was, of course, a dilemma in trying to relate program mechanisms to the four categories of intervention. On the one hand, programs' purposes and activities affect the kinds of mechanism that might be triggered; mechanisms involve an interaction between what the program provides and how targets respond. On the other hand, some mechanisms fire in multiple kinds of interventions. We addressed this dilemma in two ways: first, by listing the mechanisms we believed, on the basis of the review, were most likely to be triggered by interventions in different categories, and second, by identifying the features of interventions we believed were most likely to be necessary for specific mechanisms to fire.

Our project then moved on to the meat of a realist review, identifying program mechanisms and the features of context that affect whether and how they work. After months of detailed reading, extracting, analyzing, and discussing, the fourth component of theory development was complete: 11 proposed mechanisms, described in some detail, and with examples of each provided from the literature. These mechanisms are briefly summarized in Table 20.1.

The ninth mechanism, Mind the Gap, is possibly the most common intended mechanism in information for accountability interventions. However, we found extremely limited evidence that this mechanism fires as anticipated. Rather, we theorize that information is a necessary but not sufficient condition for changed behaviors.

In realist terms, mechanisms are causal forces or processes that generate a particular outcome. The outcome generated by a particular mechanism can lie at any stage along an implementation chain or at any level on a hierarchy of outcomes. It is worth noting that none of these mechanisms (when they work) generate education outcomes per se. Rather, they generate outcomes at intermediate levels, which then create contexts in which education outcomes are more likely to be achieved or in which other actions can be taken. In order for the final intended outcome (in this case, improved student learning outcomes) to be achieved, sequences of activity— necessarily involving participation by different stakeholders—and sequences of mechanisms, each generating its own outcome, may be required.

| Table 20.1 | Mechanisms Identified in the Review |
|---|---|
| **Label** | **Description** |
| Eyes and ears | Community members act as local data collectors for monitoring purposes, forwarding information to another party, which has the authority to act. The outcome of this mechanism is the action taken by the party that receives the information. |
| Carrots and sticks | Actors respond to actual application of rewards or sanctions. |
| Big brother is watching | Actors respond in anticipation of the application of rewards or sanctions. |
| The power to hire and fire | A direct, employment-based accountability relationship is established between a school management committee and school staff. |
| Increasing community capacity | Provision of training and "learning by doing" support communities to develop knowledge, skills, and self and collective efficacy required for other actions. |
| Elder/council authority | Strengthened relationships between school committees and other local authorities lend credibility and authority to the school committees to take specific actions to support education. |
| Increasing the capacity of local politicians | Local representatives develop an understanding of local issues and needs and increased confidence and skill to advocate for them. |
| Mutual accountability | All parties to an agreed action plan monitor the performance of all others, building mutual accountability. |
| Mind the gap | Discrepancies between rights or entitlements and actual provision surprise or concern local citizens, who demand change in response. |
| Our children's future | Increased understanding of and support for education motivates individual or collective action by parents to support children and schools. |
| It's working! | Seeing positive outcomes from an action operates as a positive feedback loop, motivating further action. |

SOURCE: Westhorp et al. (2014).

The next stage of theory development was therefore the fifth component of theory development: to organize a map of some causal pathways (sequences of activity and mechanisms) that appeared to generate particular intermediate outcomes. Complexity theory focuses attention on interactions and relationships between elements of systems and on the local rules that guide those interactions. Pawson and Tilley's (1997) construct of a mechanism (reasoning and resources) has interaction between the program and the decision makers built into its very core. Unsurprisingly, every mechanism identified in our review involves interactions between different elements of systems. Equally unsurprisingly, local culture constructs the local rules that guide those interactions. There were numerous examples of parents being unwilling to monitor or supervise teachers because they perceived teachers to be more knowledgeable or because they felt teachers were more power-ful than themselves. As Fitriah (2010, pp. 87–88) noted, in Indonesia, when pri-mary schooling was made free, parent participation in schooling and complaints about schooling decreased. No longer making a financial contribution, they per-ceived that they had lost the right and authority to do so.

Features of context that appeared to affect the operations and outcomes of interven-tions were identified through close reading of texts and sorted into 13 categories: the broader political and social environment, the education system, information systems, de jure (legal), and de facto (actual) powers of local management committees, attitudes and roles of school management committees and school staff, the capacities of local communities, school facilities, gender, sustainability, engaging communities and enabling voice, engaging service providers and officials, and the roles of facilitators. Thirty specific propositions about the circumstances in which community account-ability and empowerment interventions are more likely to generate improved educa-tion outcomes were developed. For example, one of the propositions focused on social norms, drawing on evidence including the quote above parents' perceptions the proposition was that: "Community-accountability and empowerment interventions are most likely to engage parents where they take into account social norms, parent resources and parents' intrinsic motivations" (Westhorp et al., 2014, p. 123).

Another example focused on education assessment systems: "Community accountability and empowerment interventions are more likely to generate improved learning outcomes when there is a high-quality national system for assessment of student learning and when assessment systems are constructed to support collective action" (Westhorp et al., 2014, p. 113).

Each of the propositions was explained and supported with evidence, usually from multiple programs and countries.

These 30 propositions might be considered the direct answer to the overarching question for the review ("In what circumstances do community accountability and empowerment improve education outcomes . . ."). However, taken in isolation, they do not constitute a realist understanding, because a realist view seeks to understand how context affects mechanisms (i.e., affects whether and which mechanisms fire). While there was evidence to support the influence of each of these propositions, at least in some contexts, there was not clear evidence to support linkages with par-ticular mechanisms. Consequently, the next stage of theory-building was the con-struction of a provisional context-mechanism-outcome configuration (CMOC) table (Westhorp et al., 2014, Table 4). This was developed by aligning significant features of context against mechanisms on the basis of evidence where it was avail-able or on the basis of logic where it was not.

The sixth and final component of theory development was a theoretical model for the relationship between empowerment and accountability, proposed on the basis of the findings. Each element of the empowerment model was re-described in relation to the specific sections of the evidence that had been reviewed. The ways in which those elements interact with elements of the accountability model were also described. The ability to use formal theories and program theory to inform each other is part of the rationale for realist reviews.

The CMOC table and the empowerment and accountability model constitute the revised theory that is the intended product of a realist review. That theory remains to be tested and further refined through future research and evaluation.

# 2. Applying the VICTORE Framework to an Analysis of the Review

Pawson's (2013) VICTORE framework is a useful way of understanding the many ways in which programs are complex (or, some might argue, ways in which they are complicated). The VICTORE model refers to Volitions, Implementation, Contexts, Time, Outcomes, Rivalry, and Emergence (see Chapter 5).

## 2.1 Volitions

The term *volitions* refers to participants' motivations and reasoning. It relates closely to Pawson and Tilley's (1997) construct of program mechanisms as constituting some interweaving between the resources and opportunities provided by the program and the reasoning of participants in response.

A number of the mechanisms identified in our review operated at this level, although not all referred to program participants per se. One example is the Our Children's Future mechanism. As parents participate in program activities (the resource), they develop greater understanding of the value of education for their children and of their own potential roles in contributing to education outcomes (intermediate outcome and mechanism). Because (most) parents want the best for their children, this increased understanding generates action to support education. Actions might be private, such as monitoring their children's attendance, providing school lunch, or supervising homework, or they might be public, such as contributing to building facilities or monitoring teacher attendance. The Carrots and Sticks and Big Brother Is Watching mechanisms both describe staff reasoning (i.e., volitions) in response to incentives, either positive or negative (i.e., resources).

The implication for program evaluation and review methodology is clear and in fact lies at the heart of realist methodologies. Understanding the reasoning of stakeholders and participants enables evaluators and researchers, and the stakeholders on whose behalf we work, to understand how outcomes are or are not generated and why they vary across contexts. We noted, as have many before us, that traditional RCTs were, generally speaking, poor sources of data about stakeholder reasoning, that qualitative data can be a rich source of understanding, and that the few theory-based evaluations we found were particularly strong.

For example, Lieberman, Posner, and Tsai (2012) reported on the first phase of the Uwezo initiative in Kenya, a two-phase project to provide information to communities about how much their children are learning and how parents might support learning. A second phase of the project will involve broad dissemination of student assessment results and "stimulation of a multi-faceted national discussion about children's learning" (p. 1). The program theory is that "these measures will empower citizens to hold their governments accountable for improving the quality of their children's education, and also equip them with the knowledge necessary to contribute themselves to improving their children's learning" (p. 8).

Lieberman et al. (2012) systematically assessed the assumptions implicit in the theory of change for the first phase in order to identify "the ways in which the treatment may have influenced outcomes—the mechanisms" (p. 16). They found no evidence of impact on any of the outcomes of interest from the first phase (p. 28) but note that outcomes are not expected until the second phase. They were able to discount implementation failure as the cause of the early lack of outcomes, but discovered through careful testing that almost all the assumptions underpinning the program design were incorrect.

*Implications for community empowerment and social accountability practitioners.* How parents, children, teachers, and other key actors are or can be motivated to participate and to exact accountability and how they reason and make choices—and who makes those choices—are important for program outcomes. Practitioners might consider whether the mechanisms identified in this review are likely to fire in their programs. Alternatively, they might consider their own program designs and ask practical questions: Who does this program intend to do what to? What would motivate them to do so? What does the program provide that is intended to motivate them to do so? These questions can be used as a guide to theorize mechanisms.

## 2.2 Implementation

Most programs have long implementation chains and involve many processes, which implies that there are many decision-making points. This was certainly true for most of the programs included in our study. Constructing our hierarchy of outcomes highlighted the chain, even though the diagram starts at the local implementation level (because of the focus of our review) and ignores earlier stages. Three of the categories of context we identified related specifically to implementation strategies: approaches to engaging communities and enabling voice, strategies for engaging service providers and officials, and the roles of facilitators.

Processes of implementation were generally well described in formal research studies but relatively poorly described in most evaluation studies. Differences in implementation in different sites were rarely addressed in any depth. From a realist perspective, differences in implementation can affect the resources available to stakeholders and thus their capacity to enact change. Similarly, they can affect the reasoning of stakeholders and thus their motivations to participate or to sustain changed behaviors. Without good data about implementation, it becomes significantly harder to ascertain what matters about implementation and thus to use this to inform future policy and programs.

*Implications for community empowerment and social accountability practitioners.* The details of implementation—who does what, at what stage along an implementation chain, with whom—are likely to make a significant difference to the nature of the outcomes achieved. This is not because the activities themselves actually cause the outcomes, but because the activities provide resources and opportunities to which decision makers along the implementation chain respond. Policymakers and practitioners need a clear sense of both the what and the why of implementation strategies to monitor whether implementation processes are generating intended outcomes. Further, recent evidence in relation to social accountability indicates that multiple accountability and empowerment strategies are much more successful than those involving single tactics (Fox, 2014). This increases the "complicatedness" of implementation, which in turn may increase complexity (as more parts may interact, or different elements are affected by different aspects of context, this may generate more differentiated patterns of outcomes). Long implementation chains can also mean that more attention needs to be paid to sequencing of program elements. The challenge therefore is to remain clear and focused in planning, without expecting outcomes to follow in a linear manner.

## 2.3 Contexts

Contexts are a linchpin of realist analysis. The term refers to the fact that programs are by definition implemented in existing systems and communities. More specifically, a realist approach acknowledges that programs are implemented in multiple, open, interacting systems and draws attention to the fact that particular aspects of the context will have particular implications for whether and how programs work. Pawson draws attention to some of these: program stakeholders, relationships, institutional settings, norms, values, culture, and history among them. In formal complexity theory terms, context is reflected in the ideas of sensitivity to initial conditions and controlling parameters—features that influence whether and how systems move between different ways of operating.

As discussed above, investigation of context was a major feature of our review. Effects of context were rarely investigated directly in the original studies. However, the process of realist synthesis enabled us to draw "nuggets" of evidence from multiple studies to examine how and why particular features mattered. One clear example was that of adult literacy, which appeared to have multiple impacts on community accountability and empowerment interventions.

> Where members of SMCs [school management committees] are not literate, it is more difficult for them to administer schools effectively or exert influence on schools (Fuller and Rivarola, 1998, p. 39). Low parent literacy levels also appear to impede the ability of parents to assess their children's progress at school and, therefore, to judge whether or not the school is operating effectively (Banerjee et al., 2008, re: India; Blimpo and Evans, 2011, re: Gambia). Parents who can make those assessments may be more likely to make complaints (Blimpo and Evans, 2011, p. 27) or to intervene in school management (Gunnarsson et al. 2004, re: ten Latin American countries). (Westhorp et al., 2014, p. 122)

*Implications for community empowerment and social accountability practitioners.* The diversity of contextual factors that can affect whether and how programs work has two implications for practice. First, practitioners need to think carefully about the assumptions built into their program designs and consider whether those assumptions are in fact met in the local context. Second, practitioners may need to undertake an analysis of the context, identifying the factors that are most likely to affect the ways in which their programs will work, and add or tailor strategies to suit the local conditions. Some contextual factors are given (relatively fixed), while others are more amenable to change, especially at the community level. For example, existing community social capital (one of the contextual factors we identified) is not a fixture but may be built before an intervention is implemented. Some programs deliberately use a developmental phase to help build contextual features that will support the program or limit those that may undermine it.

## 2.4 Time

Pawson notes that the term *time* has many implications for programs: the idea of historicity (the idea that actual history creates the specific situation in which the program operates and the program then contributes to the history of the place or organization), already familiar through complexity theory, but also the idea of program duration and the various effects of sequences of programs. Historicity was evident in some features of context in our review, including the broader historical context in particular countries and the evolving nature of their education systems. Sequences of interventions were also apparent in some countries. For example, in India the Janshala (Community Schools) program was succeeded by the Sarva Shiksha Abhiyan (the Education for All Movement), the Indian government's primary policy for universal primary education. Other projects and programs took place in the context of these broader policy initiatives, both past and present.

The issue of program duration was also significant, particularly in relation to sustainability. Previous research had demonstrated that it can take a number of years for programs to generate changes that improve student learning outcomes (Patrinos et al., 2007). Successful interventions were often those that had been sustained over a significant period, including the oft-cited Philippines Textbook Watch program. There was also evidence that programs that are not sustained are not effective. Turnover of personnel means that the impacts of training are lost; unless new personnel are also trained, momentum and enthusiasm are lost (Evans et al., 2012, p. xii). As our review noted, different kinds of sustainability had different contextual implications:

> For some initiatives, being sustained means that policies and funding systems are sustained (political and economic context). For others, sustainability means that capacities are developed at the local level (local community context). This may require support and training by external organisations over a period of time, until sufficient members of the community are trained (implementation context). (Westhorp et al., 2014, p. 124)

*Implications for community empowerment and social accountability practitioners.* Pawson (2013) suggests that policymakers and practitioners should map the major programs or initiatives that have preceded a new initiative and give careful consideration to the effects those earlier programs may have on responses to the new offering. Policymakers and funders may need to allow time (i.e., provide funds over sufficient time) for development and "bedding down" of programs. In some sectors, including education, it may be many years before impacts on final outcomes become evident, and sustained effort may be required to achieve intended goals. However, longer durations for programs also means that there is an increased chance that other contextual factors will change, so careful monitoring and revisions of planning to adapt to changes in context will be required.

## 2.5 Outcomes

In his discussion of outcomes, Pawson notes that they may be short, medium, and long term; that there may be multiple indicators for any indicator; and that outcomes do not speak for themselves but must be interpreted.

Because it does not require aggregation of outcomes or an average effect, the selection and analysis of evidence about outcomes is one of the areas in which realist synthesis is strikingly different from other forms of systematic review. Our use of a hierarchy of outcomes enabled us to include, arrange, and make logical sense of evidence in relation to a wide range of outcomes as successive stages in long processes leading to improved learning outcomes.

For realists, outcomes are generated by mechanisms operating in specific contexts. A single intervention could involve multiple mechanisms, each affected by specific aspects of context, to produce outcomes at different levels. We demonstrated this point by developing a detailed CMOC table for a single study: the Vidya Chaitanyam project in Andhra Pradesh, India. The project promoted collective action by a large network of mothers already in self-help groups (SHGs), using a simple traffic-light scorecard process to track several dimensions of school quality (Galab, Jones, Latham, & Churches, 2013). The table demonstrates many things: how earlier stages of work generate intermediate outcomes that create new contexts in which later stages can work, how the same mechanisms can fire for different stakeholders, and how different features of context relate to different mechanisms.

Note that CMOC tables are read across and as a sentence. Using the first line of Table 20.2 as an example: Where education quality is known to be poor, existing self-help groups have high levels of social capital and there is appropriate local infrastructure, participation by local officials triggers the authority mechanism (described elsewhere in the report), resulting in self-help groups agreeing to address education. While each CMO configuration is shown in a separate row, they can be linked; for example, the outcome from one CMO configuration can produce a changed context for another CMO configuration.

*Implications for community empowerment and social accountability practitioners.* Practitioners in the education domain may be able to use the hierarchy of outcomes from this review to position the outcomes they expect to generate, to consider the relationships between earlier and later outcomes, and potentially to refine plans or consider timelines for their projects. Practitioners in other domains could consider constructing a similar hierarchy, using domain-specific content, to make sense of outcomes that are likely to be causally related over time.

| Table 20.2 | Context-Mechanism-Outcome Configuration for a Single Intervention | |
|---|---|---|
| **Context** | **Mechanism** | **Outcome** |
| Education quality in Andhra Pradesh is known to be poor (p. 14)<br><br>Existing self-help groups (SHGs) have built up social capital over many years (pp. 16, 17)<br><br>Existing infrastructure of school management committees (SMCs), village organizations, district/mandal officials | **Authority**<br><br>(A variant of council/elder authority) Clear state-sanctioned authority for role of SHGs (p. 17)<br><br>Legitimation of state authority by officials regularly attending higher level meetings (pp. 16, 18) | SHGs agree to add education to their agenda (implicit in subsequent actions)<br><br>State-sanctioned authority structure exists (p. 17) |
| Vidya Chaitanyam (VC) project is designed for low-literacy self-help-groups, using scorecards developed in conjunction with district-level officials (p. 18)<br><br>Information campaigns regarding rights[5] | **Capacity building**<br><br>SHGs trained to use scorecards (pp. 15, 18)<br><br>Increased awareness of rights (pp. 15, 22, 25) | Parents understand school quality and how to use scorecards (pp. 18, 24)<br><br>Parents develop capacity to question both SMC and teachers |
| Parents understand school quality and use data to ask questions of SMC and teachers (pp. 25, 35)<br><br>SMCs meet regularly | **Eyes and ears**<br><br>Parents monitor and report data to SMC (pp. 23, 25, 26) | SMCs discuss issues raised by parents using scorecards showing gaps in school quality (pp. 22, 23, 24) |
| Scorecards reveal gaps in school quality (pp. 28–30)<br><br>Parents aware of their rights (pp. 15, 25) | **Mind the gap**<br><br>Parents/SMCs concerned about gaps shown by scorecards (pp. 28–31) | Parents report the gaps to SHGs, SMCs, and district/mandal officials and ask questions after SMC meetings (pp. 18, 25) |
| SMCs discuss issues monitored and raised by parents (pp. 23, 24) | **It's working!**<br><br>Positive feedback loops between parents and both SMCs and teachers | SMCs respond regularly to parents and SHGs (pp. 21–24)<br><br>Parents gain increased capacity and confidence to monitor, measure, and report performance (pp. 24–26, 35) |
| Parents have increased capacity and confidence to monitor, measure, and report school performance (pp. 24–26, 35) | **Capacity building**<br><br>Parents learning by doing in asking questions of teachers and SMCs (pp. 25, 35) | Parents question school performance, directly to teachers and via SMCs (pp. 25, 26) |

| Parents question teacher performance<br><br>Parents report on teacher performance to district and mandal<br><br>Parents report on school quality regularly to SHGs, SMCs, and district/mandal authorities (pp. 18, 23, 24, 27) | **Big Brother is watching**<br><br>Teachers are aware that authority structures of SHGs, SMCs, and districts and mandals are "watching" | Improved teacher effort: Teachers attend more regularly/on time (pp. 25, 26, 28, 29, 31, 32) |
| Parents' belief in value of schooling (pp. 22, 24)<br><br>Increased parent capacity and confidence (pp. 24–26, 35) | **Capacity building**<br><br>Parents trained with regard to quality of pedagogy and testing of students (p. 18) | Parents and students observe improved teacher pedagogy (pp. 32, 33) |
| Parents and students observe improved teacher pedagogy (pp. 32, 33) | **Big Brother is watching**<br><br>Parents backed by authority system and students backed by parents (pp. 32, 33) | Teachers adopt more inclusive/engaging teaching methods, techniques, and materials (pp. 32, 33) |
| Teachers adopt more inclusive/engaging teaching methods, techniques, and materials (pp. 32, 33) | **It's working!**<br><br>Teachers, parents, and students see this is working (pp. 32, 33) | Teachers sustain and increase use of inclusive/engaging teaching methods, techniques, and materials (pp. 32, 33)<br><br>Improved student learning outcomes (A grades) (pp. 29, 35)<br><br>Increased learning reported by students and parents (pp. 22, 32, 33) |
| Educational authorities report SMCs meeting regularly, scorecards enhance parental questioning, teacher effort in response (p. 26) | **It's working!**<br><br>Education authorities see positive results | Authorities support and sanction ongoing use of approaches (p. 26) |

SOURCE: Adapted from Westhorp et al. (2014, pp. 59–60).

NOTE: Page numbers refer to Galab et al. (2013).

Similarly, the CMOC tables in the review may assist practitioners to identify which aspects of context are likely to affect which mechanisms do and do not fire and therefore which outcomes are or are not generated. This information can be used to refine program design, to design evaluations, and/or to explain patterns of findings in an evaluation.

## 2.6 Rivalry

The term *rivalry* in the VICTORE model refers to the fact that multiple policies and programs are likely to operate concurrently in any policy area, some of which will be mutually reinforcing but others of which may be competing or undermining each other. While this is undoubtedly true, we found no evaluation studies that overtly took account of the effects of other programs in their analysis. Few even described the wider policy context in which they operated.

*Implications for community empowerment and social accountability practitioners.* Program outcomes are likely to be strengthened if policy and program personnel take account of rivalry when designing, implementing, and evaluating programs. Pawson (2013) suggests mapping surrounding policies and programs to understand the context for the program under consideration (the evaluand). In evaluation terms, this helps to deal with problems of attribution, either to avoid falsely attributing positive outcomes to the evaluand or to understand why programs do not achieve their intended effects. We suggest that such mapping be undertaken during program planning. If it is done then, planning can seek to build synergies between programs and/or take account of the potential negative consequences of other policies for the evaluand.

## 2.7 Emergence

Pawson's construct of *emergence* is that program elements interact with each other, and with existing elements of systems, to create new elements of systems, or (in more familiar terms for those familiar with realist evaluation) that successful programs change the contexts in which they worked and therefore should not necessarily be expected to continue to work. In systems theory terms, programs might create a positive feedback loop (in which change breeds more of the same change: success breeds success) or a negative feedback loop (in which change damps the intended change). We saw many examples of programs making some change to systems at the local level, and a handful of long-term program evaluations, but no rigorous studies of long-term systemic change. This might in part be a product of the kinds of studies that are funded.

The Galab et al. (2013) study referred to earlier provided a good example of feedback loops generating changes to local systems, which we summarized as follows:

> Parental action in monitoring schools appears to have been sustained by a series of positive feedback loops in which parents saw that their collective actions were yielding increasingly effective outcomes as measured by their own score cards. They saw that their increased efforts as parents in encouraging their children to attend school and learn resulted in increased school attendance and learning; their attempts to engage SMCs and teachers garnered increasing responsiveness and, over time, generated the school-quality reforms they sought; and their own observations, recorded in score cards verified that

measures of school quality were indeed improving over time. Further, the study claims and provides some evidence that, over the 18 months, this project was studied, a sense of joint ownership of school issues developed, which embraced collective problem solving and action by parents and the school—that is, both parents, SMCs and schools believed that their efforts were effective over the period studied (pp. 28–31, 36). (Westhorp et al., 2014, pp. 48–49)

*Implications for community empowerment and social accountability practitioners.* Some current development practices create rigid expectations about the rates at which programs are expected to progress and tie funding disbursements to those expectations. However, the emergent nature of these programs and the operations of positive and negative feedback loops within them suggests that more adaptive and responsive planning and funding models might be more effective. This in turn implies that monitoring practices should be adapted to capture emerging outcomes—expected and unexpected, positive and negative, and including any restructuring of systems and relationships in response to change.

So far, this chapter has considered how features of complexity, as described in Pawson's VICTORE model, were manifest in our review. In the final sections we identify the contributions to knowledge from the review and then consider the ways in which a realist review helps policymakers and practitioners deal with complexity.

# 3. Summary

Despite its challenges and limitations, we believe that the review contributes to existing knowledge in a number of important ways. It identifies the categories of intervention within which community accountability and empowerment interventions fit. It collates the evidence for intermediate outcomes and student learning outcomes from the included studies. It proposes and provides examples of 11 mechanisms through which community accountability and empowerment interventions may work and identifies 13 categories of contextual features (representing a total of 30 elements of context, or circumstances) that affect whether and where community accountability and empowerment interventions work. It proposes relationships between mechanisms and the elements of context most likely to affect them. Finally, it presents a new conceptual model for the relationship between accountability and empowerment.

Community accountability and empowerment interventions, like many interventions in international development, are complex in nature. They are inserted into diverse contexts; they attempt to achieve different goals; they work in different ways; they are affected by a wide variety of factors at national, subnational, and local levels; and effective interventions are responsive and adaptive. Theories of change, methods of evaluation, and methods of systematic review all need to be complexity-responsive. By focusing on the how and why in addition to the what, realist methods are among those that can.

# 4. Practical Applications

Realist syntheses, like realist evaluations, are intended to be useful for policy and practice. Our review provided both brief main messages for policymakers and much more detailed advice about using the various products that the review produced. Here we both summarize the specific guidance from this review and extract some main messages about the value of realist synthesis for policy and practice.

- There is credible evidence that community accountability and empowerment interventions can contribute to improved education outcomes—in some circumstances. The programs that had best demonstrated effectiveness seemed to have fired multiple mechanisms, sometimes concurrently and sometimes in sequence. This often required multiple program strategies.
  - Reviews that identify multiple mechanisms and the program strategies to which they relate, as well as the other contextual factors necessary for the mechanisms to fire, are likely to be useful for both policy and practice.
- Planning of community accountability and empowerment interventions (CAEIs) should begin with assessment of the broader social and political context to determine whether CAEIs are feasible, followed by an assessment of the education system to see whether CAEIs are the most appropriate response to local issues, and finally assessment of community capacities to determine the most appropriate type or design features for the intervention.
  - This broad sequence may be applicable to many other sorts of interventions. "Portable" findings such as these are a feature of realist reviews.
  - Realist reviews can thus frame the sorts of questions that need to be answered in preparation for new policy or program initiatives.
- The planning process should articulate the program's theory of change and identify the different elements that are required for the multiple mechanisms that are needed for outcomes to be achieved and sustained. Programs should be designed in such a way that they can be adapted to local contexts. Focusing on what it takes for the main mechanisms to operate in a given context shifts planning from a step-by-step guide to action, in which fidelity of implementation is valued, to a more principles-based and complexity-consistent approach, in which the fit of the intervention to the local context is valued.
  - This is a strength of realist methodology.
- The theory of change needs to be specific about the different types of accountability involved: who is to be held accountable, to whom, and for what. Accountability arrangements necessarily involve power, and careful attention must therefore be paid to the nature of existing power relationships, the perceived problems in the power relationship, and how those problems contribute to poor education outcomes before design can be attempted.

We also provided more detailed advice about the way the various theory products of the review might be used. For example, we proposed particular questions about mechanisms that could be used for program planning, formative evaluation, and summative evaluation. Mechanisms, however, do not stand alone. In realist analysis, context, mechanism, and outcome are inextricably linked. CMO statements are intended to be read as a sentence: "In this context, that mechanism generates these outcomes for those groups." CMO statements provide meaningful interpretation of otherwise inexplicable patterns of data. Our table of CMOs might be used as a starting point for planning particular interventions, as a basis for developing more detailed or specific CMOs for particular interventions in particular contexts, and as a basis for evaluation design.

The new theoretical model for empowerment and accountability could be used to analyze relevant features of the context and to design community accountability and empowerment interventions.

There were, of course, challenges in undertaking a synthesis of this size. Not surprisingly, we found that many studies failed to collect or report data about important aspects of the interventions we wished to examine (see also Chapter 16). We therefore recommended that future studies should take account of and test the theory of change for the intervention, including variations in responses and outcomes across contexts; identify the different mechanisms expected to operate in and explicitly gather and make available data to better understand them and the contexts in which they work; seek to identify and understand barriers to engagement in CAEIs and how these might be overcome; and ensure that detailed information from studies, including access to detailed reports and datasets, is available to later researchers to enable secondary analysis. These recommendations are likely to be relevant in almost any field of study. The better the quality of the evaluations, the more useful the syntheses based on them are likely to be.

# References

Banerjee, A. V., Banerji, R., Duflo, E., Glennerster, R., & Khemani, S. (2008). *Pitfalls of participatory programs: Evidence from a randomized evaluation in education in India* (Policy Research Paper 4584). Washington, DC: World Bank.

Blimpo, M. P., & Evans, D. K. (2011). *School-based management and educational outcomes: Lessons from a randomized field experiment.* Stanford, CA: Stanford University.

Cabrera, D., Colosi, L., & Lobdell, C. (2008). Systems thinking. *Evaluation and Program Planning, 31,* 299–310.

Evans, D., Purwadi, A., Setiadi, A., Losert, L., Wello, M., Bimo, N., . . . Amd Savitri, T. (2012). *Indonesia: Decentralized basic education project final evaluation volume I: Main report.* Washington, DC: USAID. Retrieved from http://muir.massey.ac.nz/bitstream/handle/10179/1370/02_whole.pdf

Fitriah, A. (2010). *Community participation in education: Does decentralisation matter? An Indonesian case study of parental participation in school* (Unpublished master's thesis). Massey University, Palmerston North, New Zealand.

Fox, J. (2014). *Social accountability: What does the evidence really show?* Washington, DC: World Bank/GPSA.

Friedmann, J. (1992). *Empowerment: The politics of alternative development.* Cambridge, MA: Blackwell.

Fuller, B., & Rivarola, M. (1998). *Nicaragua's experiment to decentralize schools: Views of parents, teachers, and directors* (Working Paper No. 5). Washington, DC: World Bank, Development Economics Research Group.

Galab, S., Jones, C., Latham, M., & Churches, R. (2013). *Community-based accountability for school improvement: A case study from rural India.* Reading, UK: CfBT Education Trust.

Greenhalgh, T., & Peacock, R. (2005). Effectiveness and efficiency of search methods in systematic reviews of complex evidence: Audit of primary sources. *BMJ, 331,* 1064–1065.

Gunnarsson, L., Orazem, P., Sanchez, M., & Verdisco, A. (2004). *Does school decentralization raise student outcomes? Theories and evidence on the roles of school autonomy and community participation* (Working Paper 04005). Ames: Iowa State University, Department of Economics.

Joshi, A. (2013). Do they work? Assessing the Impact of transparency and accountability initiatives in service delivery. *Development Policy Review, 31,* s29–s48.

Lieberman, E., Posner, D., & Tsai, L. (2012). *Does information lead to more active citizenship? An evaluation of the impact of the Uwezo initiative in Kenya* (Draft paper). Dar es Salaam, Tanzania: Twaweza.

Midgley, G. (2000). *Systemic intervention: Philosophy, methodology and practice.* New York, NY: Kluwer Academic/Plenum.

Patrinos, H., Fasih, T., Barrera, F., Garcia-Moreno, V., Bentaouet-Kattan, R., Baksh, S., & Wickramesekera, I. (2007). *What do we know about school-based management?* Washington, DC: World Bank.

Pawson, R. (2006). *Evidence-based policy: A realist perspective.* London, UK: Sage.

Pawson, R. (2013). *The science of evaluation: A realist manifesto.* Thousand Oaks, CA: Sage.

Pawson, R., & Tilley, N. (1997). *Realistic evaluation.* London, UK: Sage.

Ringold, D., Holla, A., Koziol, M., & Srinivasan, S. (2012). *Citizens and service delivery: Assessing the use of social accountability approaches in the human development sectors.* Washington, DC: World Bank.

Rocha Menocal, A., & Sharma, B. (2008). *Joint evaluation of citizens' voice and accountability: Synthesis report* (No. EV692). London, UK: DFID.

Rogers, P. J. (2008). Using programme theory to evaluate complicated and complex aspects of interventions. *Evaluation, 14,* 29–48.

Walker, D. W. (2009). Citizen-driven reform of local-level basic services: Community-based performance monitoring. *Development in Practice, 19,* 1035–1051.

Westhorp, G. (2012). Using complexity-consistent theory for evaluating complex systems. *Evaluation, 18,* 405–420.

Westhorp, G. (2013). Developing complexity-consistent theory in a realist investigation. *Evaluation, 19,* 364–382.

Westhorp, G., Walker, B., & Rogers, P. (2012). *Under what circumstances does enhancing community accountability and empowerment improve education outcomes, particularly for the poor? A realist synthesis.* London: University of London, Institute of Education, Social Science Research Unit, EPPI-Centre.

Westhorp, G., Walker, D. W., Rogers, P., Overbeeke, N., Ball, D., & Brice, G. (2014). *Enhancing community accountability, empowerment and education outcomes in low and middle-income countries: A realist review* (No. 2207). London: University of London, Institute of Education, Social Science Research Unit, EPPI-Centre. Retrieved from http://r4d.dfid.gov.uk/pdf/outputs/SystematicReviews/Community-accountability-2014-Westhorp-report.pdf

Wong, G., Greenhalgh, T., Westhorp, G., Buckingham, J., & Pawson, R. (2013). RAMESES publication standards: Realist syntheses. *BMC Medicine, 11*(1), 21.

# Notes

1. *Realist review* is another label for a realist synthesis.

2. See Chapter 9 for a discussion on different review and synthesis approaches.

3. End user groups comprise people who may use the end product of a funded review, for example, policy and program personnel, not necessarily from the funding agency.

4. Realist reviews do not have to be constricted to studies in particular program areas, but there was more material in the education domain than could be managed in the available resources. It was not feasible to include material from other domains.

5. Community accountability interventions usually provide communities with information about their rights and entitlements in the issue area (here, education), under law and under international treaties.

# Glossary

**Attribution** The extent to which a particular change is caused by an intervention, taking into account (or controlling for) other factors.

**Big data** A term used to refer to datasets that are large, complex, and often difficult to process using standard tools. The analysis of big data opens up new avenues for real-time evaluation among other things.

**Case-based design** A methodological approach that encompasses a wide range of methods that use the case as the principal unit of analysis. A case can be a household, community, country, and so on. Particular methods can look within and/or across cases. Examples are process tracing and qualitative comparative analysis.

**Complex intervention** In the conceptual framework on complexity used in this book, one of the five dimensions of complexity concerns the nature of the intervention. A complex intervention refers to an intervention with multiple (different) activities at different levels bringing together multiple stakeholder groups and influencing reality through multiple causal pathways.

**Complexity** In this book complexity is defined by five interrelated dimensions. More specifically, complexity in evaluations is shaped by different dimensions residing in the nature of the intervention, the institutional context of interventions, and finally the nature of causal change. In turn, these three dimensions are embedded in and shaped by underlying political, social, cultural, and other contextual factors affecting the norms, beliefs, and opinions of different stakeholder groups connected to an intervention. In all, this determines the opportunity space for evaluators (and other evaluation stakeholders) for developing creative solutions to improve their understanding and delimitation of intervention contexts and the design, implementation, and use of evaluations.

**Complexity, general** A school of thought in complexity theory that perceives complexity not only in terms of human agency but also as resulting from the properties of (interconnected) systems and focuses on the epistemological and philosophical underpinnings of complexity.

**Complexity-responsive evaluation** An evaluation that explicitly addresses complexity issues. It usually builds on (a combination of) established evaluation approaches, methods from complexity science, and principles such as unpacking.

**Complexity, restricted** A school of thought in complexity theory that perceives complexity essentially as the product of human agency and focuses on a scientific and methodological approach to complexity.

**Complexity science** Umbrella term referring to a field of academic inquiry that focuses on complexity and complex systems with specific concepts and methods.

**Contribution** The idea that a particular change is brought about by a confluence of factors (including the intervention).

**Contribution analysis** A widely used evaluation approach designed to identify the contribution that a particular intervention is making to an observed outcome. It relies on a step-by-step approach to incrementally test the plausibility of the intervention's theory of change. By mobilizing all available evidence, the contribution narrative is revised and strengthened.

**Counterfactual** A term that refers to the situation that would have occurred if the intervention had not taken place. Some methodological approaches (e.g., experimental designs, particular varieties of theory-based evaluation) rely on counterfactual analysis as a principle for looking at causal change and attribution.

**Emergence** A characteristic of systems whereby a number of interconnected elements form a new and more complex collective behavior. Emergence is not the property of any single element of the system but rather the product of complex interactions between the elements of a system.

**Established evaluation approach** Term used to refer to a well-known and widely used evaluation approach in development evaluation that does not (explicitly) address complexity issues.

**Experimental design** A methodological approach that relies on the principle of random assignment of program benefits to assess the attribution of change to an intervention. In its simplest form it relies on the comparison over time (ex ante and ex post) of a randomly selected group of program beneficiaries with a (random) control group. Examples are randomized controlled trials and cluster randomized controlled trials.

**Mixed methods design** A methodological approach that combines quantitative and qualitative methods in one or more stages of an evaluation.

**Participatory design** A methodological approach that relies on different degrees of stakeholder involvement in different phases of the evaluation. Participatory evaluations are often employed to understand (divergent) stakeholder views. In addition, they can strengthen stakeholder ownership over the evaluation (and the intervention). Examples are participatory rural appraisal, deliberative democratic evaluation, and empowerment evaluation.

**Quasi-experimental design** A methodological approach that relies on a variety of statistical techniques to compare (ex post or over time) program beneficiaries with a (nonrandom) comparison group. Examples are propensity score matching, regression discontinuity, and pipeline designs.

**Reassembling** The process of synthesizing or aggregating the findings of an assessment of particular aspects or components of an intervention into an overall picture.

**Results-based management** A management strategy that focuses on the performance of an organization and the achievements of results in terms of outputs, outcomes, and impacts.

**Review and synthesis** A methodological approach that aggregates and synthesizes information from (selected) primary empirical studies into an overall picture. Examples are systematic review, narrative review, and realist synthesis.

**Selection bias** (in impact evaluation) A bias resulting from a situation in which (some of) the factors that determine the selection (or decision to participate) of program beneficiaries are correlated with the program outcome variables.

**Simple intervention** In the conceptual framework on complexity used in this book, one of the five dimensions of complexity concerns the nature of the intervention. A simple intervention refers to an intervention with a limited number of activities targeting a clearly delineated target group in a particular time frame.

**Statistics, descriptive** The analysis of data (expressed in variables) for a particular set of observations (e.g., a sample).

**Statistics, inferential** The analysis of data (expressed in variables) for a (random) sample of observations that, under particular conditions, can be used to make generalizations about the population from which the sample was drawn.

**Systems thinking** Analytical perspective and approach that consists in understanding reality as made up of whole systems and interrelated parts within these systems. Systems thinking usually describes the world in terms of interconnection, processes, perspectives, and boundaries. A distinct set of analytical tools are associated with systems thinking, such as causal loop diagrams, stock and flow diagrams, and critical systems heuristics.

**Theory-based evaluation** A methodological approach that relies on the principle of reconstructing and making explicit the assumptions underlying an intervention. This intervention theory, or theory of change, constitutes the framework for empirical data collection to further refine and test the theory.

**Unpacking** The process of deconstructing an intervention into evaluable parts.

**Validity** A term that refers to the quality or underlying rigor of a finding. Different frameworks of validity are used in evaluation. A well-known framework distinguishes between internal validity, external validity, construct validity, and statistical conclusion validity.

# Index

# About the Editors

**Michael Bamberger** has been involved in development evaluation for fifty years. Beginning in Latin America where he worked in urban community development and evaluation for over a decade, he became interested in the coping strategies of low-income communities, how they were affected by and how they influenced development efforts. Most evaluation research fails to capture these survival strategies, frequently underestimating the resilience of these communities—particularly women and female-headed households. During 20 years with the World Bank he worked as monitoring and evaluation advisor for the Urban Development Department, evaluation training coordinator with the Economic Development Department and Senior Sociologist in the Gender and Development Department. Since retiring from the Bank in 2001 he has worked as a development evaluation consultant with more than 10 UN agencies as well as development banks, bilateral development agencies, NGOs, and foundations. Since 2001 he has been on the faculty of the International Program for Development Evaluation Training (IPDET). Recent publications include (with Jim Rugh and Linda Mabry) *RealWorld Evaluation: Working under budget, time, data and political constraints* (2012, second edition); (with Marco Segone) *How to design and manage equity focused evaluations* (2011); *Engendering Monitoring and Evaluation* (2013); (with Linda Raftree) *Emerging opportunities: Monitoring and evaluation in a tech-enabled world* (2014); (with Marco Segone and Shravanti Reddy) *How to integrate gender equality and social equity in national evaluation policies and systems* (2014).

**Jos Vaessen** is Principal Evaluation Specialist at the Internal Oversight Service of UNESCO in Paris and lecturer at Maastricht University, The Netherlands. After completing his M.Sc. in 1997 (Wageningen University) and prior to starting his current position at UNESCO in 2011, he has been involved in research, teaching, and evaluation activities in the field of international development at Antwerp University and, more recently, Maastricht University. Over the last fifteen years or so, he has worked for several multilateral and bilateral international organizations mostly on evaluation-related assignments. His fields of interest include theory and practice of evaluation, impact evaluation, rural development and environment. In addition to managing and conducting evaluations, Jos regularly serves on refernce groups of evaluations of different organizations. He has been (co-) author of more than 30 publications, including three books. Recent publications include: *Impact evaluations and development—NONIE guidance on impact evaluation* (2009, co-author, with F. Leeuw), *Mind the gap: perspectives on policy evaluation and the social sciences* (2009, co-editor, with F. Leeuw), and *The effects of microcredit on women's control over household spending in developing countries* (2014, coordinator and first author, with A. Rivas, M. Duvendack, R. Palmer Jones, F. Leeuw, G. van Gils, R. Lukach, N. Holvoet and J. Bastiaensen, J. G. Hombrados, and H. Waddington).

**Estelle Raimondo** is an evaluation researcher and a Ph.D. candidate at the George Washington University's Trachtenberg School of Public Policy and Public Administration, where she specializes in development evaluation. Prior to joining GWU, she served as an Associate Evaluation Specialist for the United Nations Educational, Scientific and Cultural Organization (UNESCO). In this capacity, she conducted numerous evaluations and policy reviews, especially in Africa, and worked closely with the United Nations Evaluation Group on integrating gender into evaluation practice. Over the last five years, Estelle has worked on evaluation and research assignments for a range of organizations (e.g., the World Bank, the Independent Evaluation Group, UNEG, the Polish government, the NSF, The GW Regulatory Center). Her current research focuses on how monitoring and evaluation can contribute to organizational change in international development agencies. She is notably exploring issues of evaluation culture, knowledge brokering and result-based management's adequacy for organizational learning. She also teaches evaluation and research methods. She graduated summa cum laude from Sciences Po Paris with an M.A. in International Economic Policy and holds a master's in International Affairs in Economic and Political Development from Columbia University's School of International and Public Affairs (SIPA), where she studied as a Fulbright scholar.

# About the Contributors

**Ana Areias** is a development economist working at the intersection of data science and public policy. Most recently, Ana coordinated research for Data-Pop Alliance, a Harvard-MIT-ODI collaboration exploring how to use Big Data for public good. She also does statistical consulting for international organizations such as the World Bank and pro-bono data science work for NGOs such as DataKind. She holds an MPA in International Development from the John F. Kennedy School of Government at Harvard University.

**Kerry Bruce** is the Chief Measurement and Impact Evaluation Officer at the Global Fund to End Slavery. She drafted the chapter that appears in this book while working as Pact's Senior Director for Global Health and Measurement. She has worked for nonprofit organizations in the public health sector for more than 20 years and specifically in measurement and evaluation for 12 years. She has a passion for using technology to improve the efficiency of development programming. Kerry holds a DrPH from the University of North Carolina, an MPH from Johns Hopkins University, and a Master of Arts degree in Geography from the University of British Columbia.

**Sunil Choenni** heads the Statistical Information Management and Policy Analysis Division at WODC, which is the Research and Documentation Centre of the Dutch Ministry of Security and Justice. He is also a professor of human centered ICT at Rotterdam University of Applied Sciences in Rotterdam. He holds a PhD in database technology from the University of Twente and a MSc in theoretical computer science from Delft University of Technology. Prior to joining WODC, he held several teaching and research positions at different universities and research centres. His research interests include big data, data mining, databases, e-government, cyber security, and human centered design. He has published several papers in these fields and acts as PC member for several conferences.

**Allison R. Davis** is currently Deputy Director of Programs at Global Greengrants Fund and previously the Senior Global Evaluation Advisor at Oxfam America. She is a sociocultural anthropologist by training with degrees from the University of Arizona. The past ten years she has studied the relationship between outside aide flows and the efforts of local communities to transform their own lives, and under what circumstances the two articulate well. She has taught courses on West African history, as well as mixed methods research.

**Antonie de Kemp** is coordinating evaluator for development cooperation and impact evaluation at the Policy and Operations Evaluation Department (IOB) of the Netherlands Ministry of Foreign Affairs. He has been working in several research institutes in the Netherlands, combining statistical and econometric techniques with qualitative approaches. His areas of research include basic education, sector support, budget support, private sector development and the impact of ending aid. Together with Geske Dijkstra he published for IOB *Budget support: Conditional results* (2012).

**Geske Dijkstra** is Professor of Governance and Global Development in the Programme of Public Administration of Erasmus University, Rotterdam, and senior evaluator with the Policy and Operations Evaluation Department (IOB) of the Dutch Ministry of Foreign Affairs. Her research interests evolve around issues of economic development, focusing in particular on the role of aid, institutions, and governance. She is associate editor of *Feminist Economics*. She published extensively in international journals such as *Development and Change, Feminist Economics*, and *World Development* and is the (co-)author or (co-)editor of eight books, among which *The Impact of International Debt Relief* (2008) and *Programme Aid and Development: Beyond Conditionality* (2003, co-authored with Howard White).

**Kim Forss** works out of his company Andante—tools for thinking AB, specializing in evaluation policy, design of inquiring systems, organisational learning, and scientific method. He is the author of publications and commisisoned studies in these fields, internationally as well as in the domestic environment—Sweden. He has recently co-edited *Evaluating the Complex: Attribution, Contribution and Beyond* and *Speaking Justice to Power—Ethical and Methodological Challenges for Evaluators* both with Transaction Publishers.

**Mélida Guevara** is a qualified nurse and has a bachelors in economics. She has extensive experience working with national and international agencies in the fields of human rights of women, children, and adolescents; health; social development; and gender violence prevention. She has worked with Oxfam America since 2001 as Program Coordinator on Justice, Gender, and Gender Violence Prevention in El Salvador and Guatemala. Her contribution to this book draws on her experience in gender violence prevention working with civil society, women's networks, youth, and public officials.

**Sally Jackson** is an independent epidemiologist and life scientist with several years of international research experience in Africa, Asia, and Europe. She has worked in multidisciplinary teams on a variety of research studies, including investigating the feasibility and potential applications of big data in the development sector in Indonesia with UN Global Pulse.

**Alison E. Koler** is a Results and Measurement Advisor at Pact, where she provides technical assistance in the areas of monitoring, evaluation, research, and learning to health, livelihoods, and governance projects across Africa and Asia. She has managed HIV research in Africa and has experience in Latin America, having consulted on locally implemented health programs in Peru. She earned her Master's degree from Columbia University's Mailman School of Public Health and her Bachelor's degree from Wesleyan University in Middletown, Connecticut. Alison has over eight years of experience as an international development practitioner and currently resides in Dar es Salaam, Tanzania.

**Frans L. Leeuw** is Professor of Law, Public Policy and Social Science Research at Maastricht University, the Netherlands, where he teaches evaluation studies and empirical legal research. He is also the director of the Research and Documentation Centre of the Netherlands Ministry of Security and Justice, The Hague, the Netherlands, which is the National Institute of Applied Research in this field. His fields of specialty are theory-driven evaluation, performance auditing, empirical legal research, and development aid evaluation. Earlier he was director at the Netherlands National Audit Office, faculty member at IPDET, President of the European and the Netherlands Evaluation Society, Chief Inspector of Higher Education, and Dean at the Netherlands Open University.

**Emmanuel Letouzé** is the Director and co-Founder of Data-Pop Alliance co-created by the Harvard Humanitarian Initiative, the MIT Media Lab, and the Overseas Development Institute, where he is respectively a Fellow, a Visiting Scholar, and a Research Associate. Emmanuel is the author of UN Global Pulse's White Paper "Big Data for Development" (2012) and a regular contributor on big data and development. He worked for UNDP in New York (2006-2009) and in Hanoi for the French Ministry of Finance on public finance and official statistics (2000-2004). He holds a BA in Political Science and an MA in Economic Demography from Sciences Po Paris, and an MA from Columbia University, where he was a Fulbright fellow, and he is a PhD candidate at UC Berkeley. He is also a political cartoonist for various media outlets.

**Leny van Oijen** MA and MSc, began her career in the U.N. System and worked from 1985 to 2002 for the United Nations Industrial Development Organization (UNIDO), holding both field and headquarters positions. At the end of 2002 she started her own consulting business and works for different clients. She has some 30 years of professional experience, in particular in the field of private sector development related programme/project design, management, monitoring, and evaluation. Her research interests include private aid and, being a part-time PhD student at the Maastricht Graduate School of Governance, she expects to defend early 2016 her thesis on philanthropic engagement in development.

**Ana Rivas** is an associate researcher at the Institute of Development Policy and Management, University of Antwerp. Her research in the field of applied economics covers different dimensions of globalization (trade, migration) and their relation to poverty alleviation (wage inequality, working conditions, women empowerment). The author of several articles and book chapters, she is also the co-author of a systematic review on The Effect of Microcredit on Women's Control Over Household Spending in Developing Countries, Campbell Collaboration (2014).

**Patricia Rogers** is Professor of Public Sector Evaluation at RMIT University, Australia, and Director of BetterEvaluation, an international platform for generating and sharing information about better ways to choose and use evaluation methods and processes. Co-author of *Purposeful Program Theory: Effective Use of Theories of Change and Logic Models*, she has contributed to international discussions about ways of generating and using evidence to inform policy and practice in situations of complication and complexity. She has received the Myrdal Award for Evaluation Practice from the American Evaluation Association and awards for evaluation theory and practice from the Australasian Evaluation Society.

**Susan van den Braak** is a researcher at the Statistical Information Management and Policy Analysis Division of the Research and Documentation Centre (WODC) of the Ministry of Security and Justice in the Netherlands. She holds a PhD in Computer Science from Utrecht University and an MSc in Artificial Intelligence from Radboud University Nijmegen. Her doctoral dissertation focused on argument mapping software for crime analysis. For the Ministry of Security and Justice, she is currently working on various projects that involve combining and analyzing various large databases. Her research interests include e-government, law enforcement, argumentation and visualization, databases, and data science. She has published several papers in these fields.

**Bill Walker** is Senior Research and Evaluation Advisor for Social Accountability at World Vision Australia. He designs, evaluates, and researches interventions in and strategies for social accountability and participatory governance, at community level and beyond. Over the last decade, he helped develop Citizen Voice and Action (CV&A) which is designed to empower active citizens who can increase government accountability for public service delivery. He is studying for an action research PhD on power in governance at Monash University.

**Gill Westhorp** is a specialist in realist research and evaluation methodologies, with an interest in the relationship between realist and complexity theories. She is director of a small research and evaluation consultancy company specializing in realist approaches; a Principal Research Fellow at Charles Darwin University, Darwin, Australia; an Associate at RMIT University, Melbourne, Australia; a member of the core team for the RAMESES I (standards for realist synthesis) and RAMESES II (standards for realist evaluation) projects based in Oxford, UK; and a member of the Advisory Committee for the Centre for the Advancement of Realist Evaluation and Synthesis (CARES) at Liverpool University, UK.